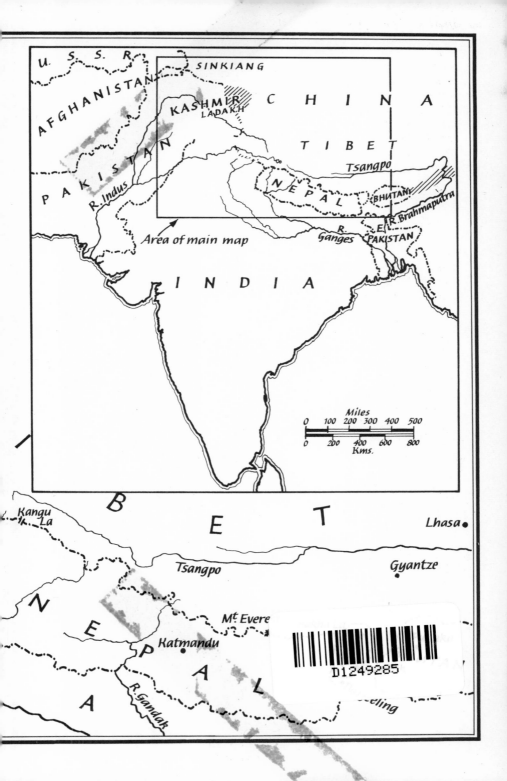

INDIA'S CHINA WAR

NEVILLE MAXWELL

INDIA'S
CHINA WAR

Now, it is a question of fact whether this village or that village or this little strip of territory is on their side or on our side. Normally, wherever these are relatively petty disputes, well, it does seem rather absurd for two great countries . . . immediately to rush at each other's throats to decide whether two miles of territory are on this side or on that side, and especially two miles of territory in the high mountains, where nobody lives.

But where national prestige and dignity is involved, it is not the two miles of territory, it is the nation's dignity and self–respect that becomes involved. And therefore this happens.

Jawaharlal Nehru, Lok Sabha, September 4th, 1959

JONATHAN CAPE
THIRTY BEDFORD SQUARE LONDON

FIRST PUBLISHED 1970
REPRINTED 1971
© 1970 BY NEVILLE MAXWELL

JONATHAN CAPE LIMITED
30 BEDFORD SQUARE, LONDON WCI

ISBN 0 224 61887 3

PRINTED IN GREAT BRITAIN
BY EBENEZER BAYLIS & SON LIMITED
THE TRINITY PRESS, WORCESTER, AND LONDON
BOUND BY G. & J. KITCAT LIMITED, LONDON

Contents

List of Maps

General maps of the western and middle sectors and the eastern sector of the Sino-Indian borders are in the front and back endpapers, respectively.

TO EVELYN

Preface

The Sino-Indian boundary dispute was one of the most dramatic passages of international relations in the mid-twentieth century. It saw the world's two most populous states, Asia's great new republics, which had seemed to be set on a path of amicable co-operation in spite of their opposed political characters, fall out over tracts of desolate, difficult and useless territory, and ultimately fight a short, fierce border war. It sharply reduced the role and status of India in world affairs. Friendship with China had been the keystone of the foreign policy Jawaharlal Nehru had set for India: non-alignment, the refusal of India to throw in her lot with either of the blocks, Communist and anti-Communist, into which the world seemed then so neatly divided; self-reliance in defence, independence in foreign policy; concentration upon economic development, at the risk of allowing the armed forces to run down — all of these depended upon friendship with China, and a peaceful northern border. Hostility with China, a live border in the north demanding huge defence outlays — these would bring down the whole arch of Nehru's policies. With them would go Nehru's political dominance.

The dispute, and the border war which was its climax, confirmed the general view of China as a bellicose, chauvinist and expansionist power. When, at the end of the decade, the Sino–Soviet boundary dispute became acute and those giants began to move towards war, recollection of China's quarrel with India predisposed world opinion to accept the Russian version of the new dispute, and even encouraged the thought that China might now be getting what she deserved for her general intransigence over border questions. Of all recent quarrels between nations, none has been so fully documented as that between China and India: both sides explained their positions at great length and repeatedly, to each other and for anyone else who would listen. And yet the facts beneath the dispute seemed so obscure — and so few were ready to inquire into them objectively — that no recent international incident has been so widely and totally misunderstood as this.

My interest in the subject began with my arrival in New Delhi to take up the assignment there as correspondent of *The Times* at the end of August 1959, when I immediately became engaged as a reporter in the events which this book recounts. The Longju incident, the first armed clash on the Sino-Indian border, had occurred a few days before I arrived; and for the next three years, until after the climax of the border war, India's dispute with China, with all its ramifications, was a staple of my work.

I first came to rewrite the story of the Sino-Indian dispute as a section of a book I had planned on India in the 1960s, hingeing on the death of Nehru in 1964. Initially I saw this as a matter of recasting and elaborating the tens of thousands of words I had written on the dispute as it developed, in my dispatches; but as I read again through the evidence in the diplomatic argument between the two Governments, set out in the long series of Indian White Papers, I realized that something much more full, fundamental and searching was required. This book is the product of my subsequent reappraisal. Its basic inspiration remains, however, my personal knowledge of the dispute as it was handled and felt in New Delhi. Personalities, in action and interaction, attitudes, even moods, played an important part in the dispute, and in the related political developments in India—and it is here, perhaps, that the journalist who watched the events has an advantage over the scholar coming later to the trail, when the evidence lies on paper only, and the smiles and frowns, the tones of injury or pride, the unregistered asides, have been forgotten.

Until I left India in mid-1967 I pursued my re-inquiry in long and repeated interviews with the politicians and officials who had been responsible for India's handling of the dispute, and with the soldiers who had tried to give military expression to their Government's policy. When I came as a senior fellow to the School of Oriental and African Studies in London to complete this study and write the book, I tried first to put the subject into historical context: to see it not only as the collision of the two greatest Asian powers of the mid-twentieth century, but also as the continuation of one hundred and fifty years of political, military and diplomatic manœuvring across and around the Himalayas. During the 1960s historians and other scholars had done much to elucidate the history of the Himalayan zone and of the borders that lie within it, and I have drawn on their work for the first section of the book. This traces the history of the disputed boundaries, and is essential, I think, for the understanding of what follows.

The scheme of the book is roughly chronological, but there are frequent overlaps in the different sections. An incident touched upon in one may be fully developed in another; or an event told from one point of view in one section may in the next be retold from the opposite side. The section, 'The View from Peking', is an attempt to see the dispute through Chinese eyes, and touches again on many of the developments described in the two previous sections. This attempt was required, I believe, because the whole dispute has so consistently been seen from the Indian point of view: and, as one Englishman observed of another early in the century, 'it is no doubt difficult to convince anyone from India that there is a Chinese point of view which deserves consideration.'*

Wherever possible, I have given references for statements or quotations; but it will be seen that the density of such notes falls off sharply in the sections dealing with the border war and its preliminaries. In those (and at some other points in the book) I have drawn on material from unpublished files and reports of the Government of India and the Indian Army: I was given access to these by officials and officers who believed that it was time a full account was put together, and who trusted me to write it fairly. I cannot, of course, name them, nor cite the documents or files from which I have drawn the material; I can only thank them, and hope they will not be disappointed.

D. R. Mankekar, in his research for a history of the post-independence Indian Army, was similarly given access to unpublished files, and I am grateful to him for allowing me to quote from his original transcription of a crucial memorandum.

I have tried to understand what motivated both parties in the dispute —and believe I have succeeded to the extent, at least, that it can be seen that sometimes misunderstanding of the other's position played its part in accentuating the differences between New Delhi and Peking. My intention has been only to narrate and clarify a historical incident which I believe has been widely misunderstood, and which I myself misunderstood while it was happening. I have not meant to indict either side and indeed believe it can be seen that both often acted from motives of injured rectitude—which of course served only to sharpen the conflict.

One unavoidable imbalance in the book derives from the fact that my access to information has been immensely freer on one side of the

* See p. 53 below.

dispute than on the other. India must be one of the most open societies in the world so far as its political processes are concerned, and in my research for this book I have greatly benefited from that virtue. But in this instance the Indian Government, in the short run at least, has perhaps suffered by its openness. A close scrutiny of the relationship between public words and private—indeed secret—attitudes rarely puts any government in anything but an invidious light; and Nehru, whose on-the-record utterances were so prolific, must be particularly vulnerable to the count of inconsistency, and transparent in his deliberate ambiguities. In contrast, no government is more secretive as to its inner processes than that of the People's Republic of China, and in tracing Chinese policy formulation I have had nothing to go on beyond what is on the public record. That is unusually full, but of course it must wholly omit the evidence of hesitation, inconsistency and division—and even dissimulation—which sometimes emerges from the record of the inner deliberations of the Indian Government and military. China's policy therefore probably looks far more monolithic, perhaps even more pragmatic, than it would if one had in Peking the sort of access I have had to Indian records. Perhaps future students of these events will be able to repair this imbalance, and, with fuller documentation at their disposal, will reveal inadequacies in the narrative and errors in interpretation.

I owe the opportunity to devote nearly two years to writing this book to the School of Oriental and African Studies of London University, and especially to its director, Professor C. H. Philips, whose interest, encouragement and advice were invaluable to me.

Among others whom I especially thank are: Ronald Segal, who has encouraged and counselled me in many matters concerning this book; Dr S. Gopal, whose encouragement to write the book has never been weakened by his certainty that he will totally disagree with it; Professor Michael Brecher, for a rigorous reading of the MS.; Professor Alastair Lamb, who also helpfully read the MS., and let me cite an unpublished paper of his on Aksai Chin; and Professor John Kenneth Galbraith, who from his own immediate knowledge of these events pointed out some errors of detail and emphasis. Miss Dorothy Woodman allowed me to draw on some new material in her *Himalayan Frontiers*; Kuldip Nayar gave me an advance reading of his book, *Between the Lines*; Professor Robert Huttenback read and commented upon my historical introduction; David Wilson, editor of *China*

Quarterly, and Richard Harris, Far East specialist of *The Times*, read and commented upon my section on the Chinese view of the dispute; John Addis permitted me to quote from his unpublished Harvard paper on the Sino-Indian dispute. The maps are by D. R. Baker. Graham C. Greene's interest in my writing, long sustained, has been a steady prop. Dr A. P. Rubin helpfully read my final draft. I am grateful to all these.

Responsibility for errors or misjudgments remains, of course, my own.

Historical Introduction

THE LIMITS OF EMPIRE

(i) The Western Sector

Following the logic of power, empires in their expansive phases push out their frontiers until they meet the resistance of a strong neighbour, or reach a physical barrier which makes a natural point of rest, or until the driving force is exhausted. Thus, through the eighteenth and nineteenth centuries, British power in India expanded, filling out its control of the peninsular sub-continent until it reached the great retaining arc of the Himalayas. There it came into contact with another empire, that of China. In the central sector of the frontier zone, where lay petty states and feudatories, there began a contest for dominance over these marcher lands that continues to the present day. In the north-west and the north-east, where no minor, independent polities existed to act as buffers, the British sought secure and settled boundaries with China: these they failed to achieve, and the failure was to lead in the middle of the twentieth century to the border war between India and China.

* * * * * * * * * * *

As the advancing British frontier approached the great knot of the Hindu Kush and the Karakoram mountains in the north-west, so Imperial Russia advanced towards the same point from the other side. The same process made for the advance of both powers, conquest entailing the need for further conquest. The Russians explained the compulsion behind their advance:

> . . . Russia had found herself brought into contact with a number of semi-savage tribes, who proved a constant menace to the security and well-being of the empire. Under these circumstances, the only possible means of maintaining order on the Russian frontier was to bring these tribes into subjection; but as soon as this had been accomplished it was found that the new converts to civilisation had in turn become exposed to the attacks of the more distant tribes. And so it became necessary to establish fortified

19

posts among the outlying peoples, and by a display of force to bring them into submission.[1]

More pithily and less apologetically, an Englishman later described the imperial drive for expansion as 'the natural impulse of the civilised to overrun the uncivilised on their borders.[2] But although these approaching empires were both in fact subject to the same compulsion to expansion, each concluded that the other was advancing in deliberate menace. The expectation of collision informed frontier policy in both St Petersburg and London.

A constant and basic British aim developed: to keep the Russians as far as possible from the plains of India and their politically volatile cities; but the tactics varied in accordance with the attitudes of those setting policy in London and in India, and with the significance these attached to the role of the third factor in all their calculations—China. There were two principal schools of frontier policy: first, the forward school, which wished to see Britain advance to meet the Russian threat directly and as far away from the plains as possible; second, the moderate school, which pointed to the cost and risk of trying to establish boundaries in remote and immensely difficult country, suggested that the limits of British power should be set where they could more easily be supported, and proposed that the aim of keeping Russia back could best be served by interposing a third power between the lion and the bear. There were various possible players for that role: Afghanistan was one; sometimes small states such as Hunza looked likely; but, throughout, it was recognized that China, established in the area a century before British or Russian power reached there, would best be fitted for the part—if the Chinese were capable of it, and if they could be persuaded to play. But there, the British were to discover, was the rub. Perhaps it was because experience with Russia had taught China that, in the hands of her imperial neighbours, boundary treaties were blades with which Chinese territory could be pared away; but in any event, the Chinese shied away from most British attempts to settle common boundaries with them.

The history of British boundary policy in the north-west is an alternation of the forward and moderate schools in influence in London and India. These shared, however, a common purpose, the creation of a linear boundary. This was something required by modern states, but unfamiliar and even alien to their predecessors; to those, a sovereignty that shaded off into no-man's-land, giving a frontier of separation rather than contact, was both more familiar and more natural. 'The idea of a demarcated frontier is itself an essentially modern conception, and finds little or no place in the ancient world', Lord Curzon observed at the beginning of this century, pointing out that, until then, 'it would be true to say that demarcation has never taken place in Asiatic countries except under European pressure and by the intervention of European agents.'[3] But a distrustful China was, for the most part, able to resist or evade British pressure, and so, at both ends of the Himalayas, no-man's-lands still separated China and India when these became independent in the mid-twentieth century; their quarrel arose from the need to translate those zones into lines, and from the failure to agree on a method.

In the nineteenth century the border with China in the north-west did not much concern the British. Their attention was focused on the border with Afghanistan, and on the Russian threat that was believed to lie beyond it, and the pendulum of official favour swung between forward and moderate policy in that regard for decades. To the moderates, 'the natural and impregnable boundary of our Empire' was the Indus River.[4] But with the annexation of the Punjab in 1849 the British, inheriting the domains of the conquered Sikh kingdom, advanced their power to the mouth of the Khyber pass, where they felt imperial logic beckoning them on to Kabul, and from there, perhaps, to Herat. The strategic argument of the forward school could hardly be better put than it was by Lord Curzon:

> India is like a fortress, with the vast moat of the sea on two of her faces and with mountains for her walls on the remainder; but beyond these walls, which are sometimes of by no means insuperable height, and admit of being easily penetrated, extends a glacis of varying breadth and dimension. We do not want to occupy it, but we also cannot afford to see it occupied by our foes. We are quite content to let it remain in the hands of our allies and friends, but if rivals creep up to it and lodge themselves right under our walls, we are compelled to intervene because a danger would thereby grow up which might one day menace our security. . . . He would be a short-sighted commander who merely manned his ramparts in India and did not look beyond.[5]

By 1880, however, the attempt to occupy the Afghan glacis of empire had led, as London complained, to two wars, 'the employment of an enormous force and the expenditure of large sums of money [while] all that has yet been accomplished has been the disintegration of the state which it was desired to see strong, friendly and independent.'[6] The forward school suffered eclipse, the moderates, with their prescription that Afghanistan should be a buffer state, held sway in Whitehall; and the British, relinquishing Kandahar, withdrew again behind their mountain ramparts. The problem became one of stabilizing Afghanistan, settling boundaries for it with Russia and Persia,* and then of agreeing with the Afghans on a boundary between themselves and the British; and that was not so easy.

The limits of British administration lay along the foot-hills, beyond which the turbulent and martial Pathan tribes made any British incursion costly and ineffective. But the Afghans claimed sovereignty over those tribes, and exerted at least influence over them; thus, to apply Curzon's phrasing, creeping over the wall and lodging themselves inside it, where they could threaten Peshawar and the trans-Indus territories. British policy was therefore directed to excluding Afghan claims from as much of the tribal territory as possible. The outcome was an agreement in 1893 in which the Amir of Afghanistan accepted a boundary drawn by the British along the crest of the mountains: the Durand Line, named after the Englishman who negotiated it.

The Afghans seem to have regarded the Line as something of a one-way-traffic sign, with the NO ENTRY side facing the British, since they continued to deal with the tribes across it. The British had no intention at the time of advancing their administration to the Durand Line; they saw that as a means of excluding the overt presence of the Afghans, not as a step towards expanding British territory. As boundaries go, the Durand Line was not a good one, being 'illogical from the point of view of ethnography, of strategy and of geography';[7] but it served the British purpose. The Afghans were treaty-bound to keep well back from the practical limits of British administration, and the Durand Line gave Britain a purchase from which to protest if Afghan

---

* Afghanistan had good reason to be pleased with the boundaries which the British and Russians gave her — for their own purposes, of course. The British helped the Afghans keep the Persians back from Herat; agreement between London and St Petersburg gave the Afghans a northern boundary along the Oxus, over territories which, had it not been for the desire shared between Russia and Britain to preserve Afghanistan as a buffer, would almost certainly have gravitated towards the Russian sphere. Only the Durand Line left the Afghans dissatisfied. For a discussion of Afghanistan's boundaries see Lamb, *Asian Frontiers* (Pall Mall Press, London, 1968), pp. 86 ff.

influence in the tribal territory became too assertive; the Russians were, by and large, respecting Afghanistan's buffer status; and although the Pathan tribes remained a problem for the British to the very end of their rule in India, the Durand Line survived. It was demarcated* along a good deal of its fifteen-hundred-mile length, that extremely arduous task being ably performed by a Captain Henry McMahon, who had been a member of Durand's 1893 mission to Kabul—and of whom this account will later have more to tell.

If the problem of the light-triggered Pathan tribes made the Afghan sector of the north-west frontier the most troublesome for Britain in the nineteenth century, the Kashmir sector, where the frontier marched with Sinkiang and Tibet, also from time to time attracted the attention of the strategists and statesmen in London and India.

Kashmir fell to Britain in 1846 as one of the fruits of the first Sikh war; but, rather than try to occupy it themselves, the British opted to set up Kashmir as the 'guardian of the northern frontier, without the hostility, expense and added responsibilities which its annexation would involve'.[8] (The Governor-General of the time thought that an attempt at annexation would merit 'a straitwaistcoat and not a peerage'.[9]) Accordingly, they made over Kashmir to Gulab Singh, a local Dogra ruler whom the Sikhs had made Governor of the hill state of Jammu, but who had turned his coat to the service of the British. Thus they created the state of Jammu and Kashmir—setting Hindu rulers over a Muslim people and planting the seed of the bitter quarrel between the heirs to their power on the sub-continent—and thus, as that border-conscious proconsul Lord Curzon put it, they 'carried the strategical frontier into the heart of the Himalayas'.[10] That happened because the Treaty of Amritsar left Gulab Singh under the suzerainty of Britain and because Gulab Singh, himself no mean empire-builder in a small way, had, several years before, conquered the little kingdom of Ladakh.

Ladakh, lying in the valley of the upper Indus at an altitude of twelve thousand feet and more, was part of Tibet up to the tenth

* Although even recent dictionaries give the words 'demarcate' and 'delimit' as synonyms, they have taken on distinct meanings; the distinction, crucial to clarity in any discussion of boundaries, was drawn by Henry McMahon in 1897. As he spelled it out later: ' "De-limitation" I have taken to comprise the determination of a boundary line by treaty or otherwise, and its definition in written, verbal terms; "Demarcation", to comprise the actual laying down of a boundary line on the ground, and its definition by boundary pillars or other physical means.'[11] In this book the words will always be used in these distinct meanings.

century, when it broke off as an independent kingdom. In the four-teenth century the conquering tide of Islam reached Ladakh, to retreat, then return in the sixteenth century when the kingdom became a tributary state of the Moghul empire.[12] With the decline of the Moghuls, the Ladakhis again asserted their independence; but, being Buddhist and within Lhasa's cultural and political pull, Ladakh tended to gravitate back to Tibetan overlordship in the absence of conquerors strong enough to pull it away. So, in the nineteenth century,

> Ladakh was probably best regarded as part of Tibet, and much on the same footing as other petty polities located in the valleys of the Tibetan plateau; all owed some sort of obedience to the Lhasa government, which derived its authority from the transcendental position of the Dalai Lama and enforced it by the theocratic net-work of surveillance administered by the Lamaist monastery organization. Tibet was at this time unquestionably under the control of China.[13]

But in 1834 Gulab Singh's Dogras invaded Ladakh, to make it tribu-tary, through himself, to the Sikh rulers of the Punjab. They did not stop there, but embarked on what they intended as the conquest of Tibet, turning Lhasa's fealty towards Lahore rather than Peking.[14] The Dogras marched in the spring of 1841 and, crushing Tibetan forces sent against them, by the end of the summer were in possession of all the territory up to and including the sacred lakes of Rakas Tal and Manasarowar—territory which, not incidentally, gave the Sikh king-dom control of the areas from which came most of the wool for the rich cashmere shawl trade. Indian historians have acclaimed this cam-paign as a brilliant feat of arms, and with gratification noted that it was carried out beyond the natural mountain barriers of Hindustan;[15] but the Dogra general rashly decided to winter in Tibet, was besieged and —'marooned at a height of twelve thousand feet in the midst of a vast sea of drifting ice and snow'[16]—was in due course killed with all his force. The Tibetans then advanced to liberate Ladakh, but themselves suffered a reverse just short of Leh at the hands of Gulab Singh's rein-forced army. With the honours of war even, the leaders of the two forces in October 1842 signed what was in effect a non-aggression pact. This bound each to respect the territory of the other—but it did not specify a boundary between them, referring only to 'the old, established frontiers'.[17] That this imprecise formulation was acceptable to the

Tibetans and the Dogras seems to reflect that fact that their domains, although neighbouring, were not clearly contiguous; either would have had to dispatch an expeditionary force to attack the other, first crossing mountainous no-man's-land. Each side would have had a general idea of where its own frontier lay; but, as the two frontiers were separated, there was no need to specify them—nor, in all probability, could they have been specified, so rudimentary were the parties' ideas of geography.*

The British had watched Gulab Singh's abortive foray with concern, alive to the danger that China would 'impute the invasion of its territories by the Sikhs [whom Gulab Singh served] to the instigation of the British Government',[18] and react accordingly against Britain. They had those recent misgivings in mind when, in 1846, they recognized Gulab Singh as Maharajah of Jammu and Kashmir, and were apprehensive that 'the hope of plunder and the desire of revenge'[19] might tempt him to try another attack on Tibet, with an increased likelihood that Britain would be embroiled. Accordingly, the Treaty of Amritsar forbade Gulab Singh from adding to his territory without British consent; and, to make sure that he did not do so by clandestine expansion, it provided for the demarcation of the boundary between Tibet and Ladakh—and thus, the British hoped, removal of 'the most common cause of all disputes in the east—an unsettled boundary'.[20]

The British informed the Chinese Government of the proposed boundary demarcation and invited it to participate, writing both to Lhasa and to the viceroy in Canton of the Chinese Central Government. There was no British mission in Peking at this time, and it was very difficult even to contact the Chinese Government, let alone to elicit any reply. The nearest to a reply the British received on this occasion was the evasive observation by the Canton viceroy that 'the borders of these territories [i.e. Tibet and Ladakh] have been sufficiently and distinctly fixed, so that it will be best to adhere to this ancient

* That the 1842 agreement had any treaty force at all was vigorously denied by an English official who looked into it on the instructions of the Governor-General six years later. He pointed out that the Tibetan signatories had been 'commissioned to exterminate the Dogra invaders of Tibet and not to make treaties with them', and that the agreement, 'extorted from [the Tibetans] under the pressure of a reverse', had not been ratified by either Government. Even before that report was made, Lord Hardinge had unilaterally cancelled sections of the 1842 agreement which he judged injurious to Britain's interest—an action that could, it seems, be considered tantamount to abrogation of the whole agreement.[21]

arrangement, and it will prove far more convenient to abstain from any additional measures for fixing them.'[22] Later this Chinese official intimated that, after all, his Government would send a delegation to join in marking the boundary; yet when the British boundary commissioners reached the frontier, not only were there no Chinese officials awaiting them, but they were met with active hostility by the Tibetans.[23]

Demarcation of a boundary can only follow delimitation (i.e. agreement on where it should run by the Governments concerned) and is invariably a joint process; since neither the Chinese nor the Tibetans would co-operate, there could be no demarcation of the Tibet-Ladakh boundary in 1846.* But the first purpose of the British was to draw a line beyond which they would not allow Gulab Singh to expand, and that they could achieve unilaterally. Accordingly, the British officials were instructed to survey the frontier and draw a map boundary. They were told to 'bear in mind that it is not a strip more or less of barren or even productive territory that we want, but a clear and well-defined boundary'.[24] In other words, they were to take into consideration not only the assumptions and practice of the local population —very scanty indeed—but also use their own judgment over where a practical boundary *should* lie.

Working in 1846 and 1847, the commissioners drew a boundary from a little north of the Pangong Lake to the Spiti River; but they stopped there, and of the terrain to the north, between the Pangong Lake and the Karakoram Pass, one of the commissioners observed that it 'must be viewed as *terra incognita*, so that in the direction of the north-east the boundaries of Tibet cannot be correctly defined'[25]; but his conclusion that, as the area was totally uninhabited, the alignment of the boundary there was not of much consequence was to be belied. It was to be at the heart of the Sino-Indian boundary dispute just over a hundred years later.

A boundary alignment that filled the gap between the Pangong Lake and the Karakoram Pass was provided by an officer of the Survey of India, W. H. Johnson, who visited Khotan in 1865 and then trekked back across Aksai Chin—the name means 'desert of white stones'. This high and desolate plateau, 17,000 feet above sea level, where nothing grows and no one lives, lying between the towering ranges of the Karakoram and the Kuen Lun—this desolation was to be the bone of

---

* See p.30 n below.

contention between the Republic of India and the People's Republic of China in the middle of the twentieth century. But, desolate and forbidding as the region is, for all its total absence of fodder or shelter and its killing winds, it has not been without its human importance. An ancient trade route lay across it; and in its brief summer, when for a few hours around noon the ice melted in the streams to give water for beasts, caravans of yaks crossed it from what is now Sinkiang to Tibet, carrying silk, jade, hemp, salt or wool.

Aksai Chin, together with a broad slice of territory to the north of the Karakoram Pass, W. H. Johnson showed as within Kashmir in a map he drew on the strength of his adventurous journey to Khotan and back. It has been suggested that Johnson's version of the boundary reflected the expansionist hankerings of the ruler of Kashmir[26]—an inference that finds some circumstantial corroboration in Johnson's appointment soon after this as Kashmir's commissioner in Ladakh. The claim Johnson made for Kashmir was treated with scepticism by other Englishmen at the time. 'The Maharaja [of Kashmir] has no more rights in Shahidulla [north of the Karakoram Pass] than I have,' one of them wrote. 'He has never had any rights [there, and] it is the more astonishing that our recent maps have given effect to his now abandoned claim, and have included within his frontier a tract where he does not possess a square yard of ground and whose only inhabitants are the subjects of another state.'[27] Another traveller in these regions stated that the line along the east of the Karakoram range, from the Karakoram Pass to the Changchenmo River 'may be definitely fixed in its geographical and political bearing as constituting the limit of the Maharajah of Kashmir's dominions to the north'.[28] Nevertheless, the Johnson line was shown as the boundary of Kashmir in an atlas published in 1868, and thence found its way on to numerous other maps which drew upon that. British frontier policy in this sector in the 1860s was marked by 'avowed conciliation and scrupulous forbearance' towards the ruler of Kashmir (by then it was Gulab Singh's son), as the Governor-General prescribed it;[29] and perhaps this accounted for the cartographic currency given to Johnson's version of the boundary.

The chimerical hope of greatly expanding the flow of trade between India and central Asia informed British frontier policy in this period, and this was stimulated by a rebellion in China's westernmost territories. By 1866 an independent state, Kashgaria, had come into existence there under the redoubtable Yaqub Beg. Unlike the Chinese

whom he had thrown off, he showed every desire to establish cordial
relations with the British; in London and India hopes blossomed of a
new and almost boundless market for Indian tea and British manu-
factures. (At the same time the Russians, who had already taken
Tashkent and were considering seizing Kokand, saw equally inviting
commercial prospects in Yaqub Beg's domain, and were confident
that the barriers of the Karakoram and Kuen Lun ranges would
exclude the British; events proved them right.[30]) British hopes of
trade and influence in Kashgaria and fears that the Russians might steal
a march there waxed and waned for the next fifteen years, with high
hopes in the early 1870s of developing a new caravan route up the
Changchenmo valley. But the British confidence that Yaqub Beg's
kingdom was to be a permanent factor in the central Asian balance
was dashed by the victorious return of the Chinese. They marched
back into Kashgaria in 1877, reclaiming the territory that the British
had believed Peking had lost for good, and renaming it Sinkiang, the
New Dominion.

During this period, trade and rivalry with Russia for influence in
Kashgaria had dominated British frontier policy, virtually excluding
any consideration of the actual boundary. The British, however,
accepted that the natural alignment for such a boundary, when it came
to be drawn, would be along the Karakoram mountains from the
Changchenmo valley to the Karakoram Pass: in 1873 the India Office
in London prepared a map for the Foreign Office showing that alignment.[31] But the proximity and steady advance of Russian power, the
alarming prospect that the Karakoram mountains might soon 'form
the first common boundary the world may ever see between the
dominions of Old England and Holy Russia',[32] encouraged the perennial forward school of frontier strategists. In the same year, 1873, one
of these urged that the Kashmir boundary should be pushed up from
the Karakoram to the Kuen Lun mountains—which Yaqub Beg
regarded as the southern limit of his territory—so as to absorb the
no-man's-land of Aksai Chin.[33] On this occasion the moderates pre-
vailed, pointing to the immense difficulties of the terrain, to the
rashness of claiming a boundary where it was impossible to uphold it,
and to the unreality of the Russian threat to India.

It remained British policy, however, to prevent contact between
their territory and Russia's in central Asia—an objective which Russia
in fact shared. While the British soldiers were warning their civilian

masters of the danger of a Russian invasion of India, their opposites in the Tsar's army were apprehensive of a British attack upon them, across the Pamirs, highlands of nearly twenty thousand feet![34] Both Governments might have profited from the advice given a decade earlier by London to the Governor-General in India: 'You listen too much to the soldiers .... you should never trust experts. If you believe the doctors, nothing is wholesome: if you believe the theologians, nothing is innocent: if you believe the soldiers, nothing is safe.'[35]

The common interest of Britain and Russia in keeping a buffer between their dominions was demonstrated in the Pamirs settlement of 1895, by which they drew out a thin promontory of territory (the Wakhan strip), which they agreed to regard as part of Afghanistan. This was meant to meet the western boundary of China (who had declined to participate in the Pamirs settlement); and it became British policy to induce China to fill out and thus complete the buffer, leaving no vacuums into which Russian or even British power could be drawn. In 1889 the then Viceroy, Lord Lansdowne, noted:

> The country between the Karakoram and Kuen Lun ranges is, I understand, of no value, very inaccessible, and not likely to be coveted by Russia. We might, I should think, encourage the Chinese to take it, if they showed any inclination to do so. This would be better than leaving a no-man's-land between our frontier and that of China. Moreover, the stronger we can make China at this point, and the more we can induce her to hold her own over the whole Kashgar-Yarkand region, the more useful will she be to us as an obstacle to Russian advance along this line.[36]

For some years after their reconquest of Kashgaria/Sinkiang, the Chinese followed the practice of Yaqub Beg in treating the Kuen Lun mountains as the southern limit of their territory.[37] They had their hands full not only with reasserting and consolidating their hold on their regained provinces, but in resisting and, where possible, pushing back the eastward-thrusting Russians. By treaties in the 1860s, China had lost a great tract of territory in Central Asia to Russia; and the Russians exploited the rebellion of Yaqub Beg to take more. They explained that they were advancing only to put down dangerous disturbances on their border, and assured China that when she reasserted

her own authority in Central Asia they would restore the territory—
but they attempted to renegue the pledge when it came to the point.
Russia's greatest annexations of Chinese territory were taking place at
this time in the Far East, however. There the Russians had renewed
their southward thrust in the middle of the century, taking advantage
of China's weakness as other European powers were doing, and had
taken all the territory north of the Amur River and east of its tributary,
the Ussuri, founding the port of Vladivostock and cutting off China
from the Sea of Japan. China was forced to accept the loss of these
huge tracts in the Treaties of Aigun (1858) and Peking (1860). From
this experience the lesson must have been painfully obvious: never
negotiate boundary settlements from a position of weakness. This goes
far to explain China's approach to boundary questions until the middle
of the 1950s.*

In the early 1880s China began to turn her attention to her southern
frontier, where the British as well as the Russians were probing. In 1890
Captain Younghusband (who fourteen years later led the military
expedition to Lhasa) was sent to the Pamirs with the objectives of
tracing the theoretical limits of China's claim there and encouraging
the Chinese to fill out to them.[38] The Chinese told Younghusband that
their boundary ran along the Karakoram range and the watershed
between the Indus and the Tarim basin;[39] and in 1892 they gave
physical expression to that claim by erecting a boundary marker in the
Karakoram Pass with an inscription proclaiming that Chinese territory
began there. This move was welcomed by the British, who 'expressed
themselves in favour of the Chinese filling up the no-man's-land
beyond the Karakoram'.[40]†

The Karakoram Pass thus became a fixed and mutually accepted
point on the Sino-Indian boundary, but on both sides of that pass the
alignment continued indefinite. (The stretch to the west, between the
pass and Afghanistan, does not concern this narrative, except in so far
as it later deals briefly with the 1963 settlement between China and
Pakistan.)‡ Further expressing their claim to a Karakoram boundary,
the Chinese in 1891–2 dispatched an official, Li Yuan-ping, to explore
the whole stretch of their southern border. He travelled up the

---

* See Part III below.
† They noted, however, that since there had been no joint demarcation, the Chinese
boundary marker could not be regarded as having any value in international law, making
the point that it takes two to make a boundary agreement.
‡ See pp. 215–17 below.

Karakash River to Haji Langar* and thence turned south across Aksai Chin, crossing what seems to have been the Lingzi Tang salt pan and reaching the Changchenmo River.[41] Li was a hardy and determined traveller but he was not a surveyor, and his description of his journey[42] was vague; but George Macartney, an Englishman by then established as Britain's representative in Kashgar, learned of Li Yuan-ping's journey and did not doubt the authenticity of his report.[43]

By the mid-1890s, then, the Chinese authorities had some knowledge of the border sector from the Karakoram Pass to the Changchenmo River; and they claimed Aksai Chin as their territory. They voiced that claim to Macartney in 1896. He had presented the leading Chinese official in Kashgar with a copy of an atlas which showed the boundary as W. H. Johnson had drawn it, putting Aksai Chin within British territory. The Chinese objected to this version of the boundary (it appears that its adverse implications to China had been pointed out by Russian officials in Kashgar, to whom the Chinese had shown their new atlas)[44] and told Macartney that Aksai Chin was theirs.[45] Reporting this to his principals in India, Macartney commented that 'probably part [of Aksai Chin] was in Chinese and part in British territory'.[46] A British intelligence report of the same year noted Macartney's observation, and agreed with it.[47]

Meanwhile in London, however, an influential strategist of the forward school was urging that in order to anticipate a Russian advance on India, the British should include within their boundaries not only the whole of Aksai Chin, but almost all the territory that Johnson's alignment of 1865 had given to Kashmir. This proposal was made in a paper written by Major-General Sir John Ardagh, an old India hand who was by then Director of Military Intelligence on the British General Staff, and submitted to the Foreign Office and India Office on January 1st, 1897. It exemplified the reasoning and apprehensions of the forward school; and, although it was not accepted at the time, it continued for years to exercise influence in the perennial debate on frontier policy.

Ardagh's premise was that China's weakness made her 'useless as a buffer between Russia and the Northern Frontier of India'. Citing the 'eagerness with which [Russia] has advanced her borders towards India',

---

* A stone shelter (langar) built by W. H. Johnson on his traverse of Aksai Chin and named by him after the then ruler of Khotan, Haji Habibullah Khan.[48] The road the Chinese constructed in the 1950s passes this spot.

he predicted that she would eventually annex at least the eastern areas
of Sinkiang and would then 'endeavour to push her boundary as far
south as she can'. He noted that the British Government had been
accustomed to regard the Karakoram mountains as the natural frontier
of India in the north-east, and conceded that 'in a general sense they
form an acceptable defensive boundary, easy to define, difficult to pass,
and fairly dividing the peoples on either side'. But, he went on,

> the physical conditions of these mountains, their great extent,
> high altitude, general inaccessibility and sparse population, render
> it impossible to watch the actual watershed; and the measures
> requisite for security, and for information as to the movements of
> an enemy, cannot be adequately carried out unless we can circulate
> freely at the foot of the glacis formed by the northern slope, along
> those longitudinal valleys which nature has provided on the
> northern side at a comparatively short distance from the crest.

British policy should be directed to 'keeping our enemy from any
possibility of . . . occupying these longitudinal valleys and there preparing to surprise the passes', he concluded; and therefore should aim
at a boundary which would leave the northern approaches to the passes
in British possession.

Ardagh's memorandum then specified such a boundary, following
not the line of the Karakoram watershed but the crests of a series of
ranges to the north of the Karakoram, among them the Kuen Lun.
By following the Kuen Lun range, Ardagh's proposed boundary
would have included Aksai Chin in India, and the upper courses of the
Yarkand and Karakash river systems as well.[49]

In London the tendency would naturally have been to give full
weight to the strategic prescriptions of the Director of Military
Intelligence, but comments by officials in India suggest that they saw
Ardagh's proposal as no more than the impractical theorizing of an
armchair general. The Viceroy, Lord Elgin, warned London that, since
the Chinese claimed Aksai Chin, any attempt to implement Ardagh's
line would entail a real risk of strained relations with China, and
furthermore might precipitate the very Russian advance which Ardagh
wished to forestall. Ardagh might be right in his view that the crests
of a mountain range did not ordinarily make a good boundary in
military terms, Elgin observed; but in the particular instance of the
Karakoram frontier, 'we see no strategic advantage in going beyond

mountains over which no hostile advance is ever likely to be attempted.'
He rubbed in the point that his own strategic thinking, unlike Ardagh's,
was based on the reports and opinions of officers who had actually
visited the region in question:

> They unanimously represent the present mountain frontier as
> perhaps the most difficult and inaccessible country in the world.
> The country beyond is barren, rugged and sparsely populated. An
> advance would interpose between ourselves and our outposts a
> belt of the most difficult and impracticable country; it would
> unduly extend and weaken our military position without, in our
> opinion, securing any corresponding advantage. No invader has
> ever approached India from this direction, where nature has placed
> such formidable barriers.[50]

While thus rejecting Ardagh's forward solution to the problem
posed by Russia's advance, the Viceroy and his advisers were as alive
to that problem as anyone in London. In 1895, two years before he
thus rejected Ardagh's proposal, Elgin had, indeed, put forward his
own for putting 'a definite limit' to Russia's advance: that Britain
should settle the China-Kashmir boundary by a direct approach to
Peking.[51] Before any approach could be made to the Chinese, however,
it was necessary for the British to make up their own minds about the
boundary they wanted, and this they did in 1898. Elgin adopted
Macartney's suggestion that Aksai Chin should be divided between
Britain and China along a boundary following the Lak Tsang (or
Loqzung) range, a line of hills running roughly east–west, and dividing
the Aksai Chin proper, on the northern side, from the Lingzi Tang
salt plains, to the south. London approved this boundary alignment,
and it was proposed to China on March 14th, 1899, by Sir Claude
MacDonald, the British Minister in Peking.

Of the various conceptions held at different times in London and
India about just where the north-west boundary with China should lie,
this was the only one that was ever actually proposed to the Chinese
Government, and it has therefore a particular significance. This 1899
(or Macartney-MacDonald) line was a compromise between Britain's
strategic hankering for a boundary forward of the Karakoram range,
and the recognition that—since it takes two to settle on a boundary—a
practical proposal must also take China's interests into account. Thus
it left to China the whole of the Karakash valley, a trade route and an

2

ancient source of jade, and almost all of Aksai Chin proper; but, by following the Lak Tsang range, it left on the Indian side the Lingzi Tang salt plains and the whole Changchenmo valley, as well as the Chip Chap River farther north.* This proposal was put to China in a note couched to sound as magnanimous as possible, and to take account of the known Chinese disinclination to engage in boundary demarcation. None such would be necessary, it suggested; since the boundary would follow the crest of inaccessible mountains, it would be sufficient if this were agreed verbally. But, although the British learned unofficially that the local Chinese authorities in Sinkiang had intimated that they had no objection to the proposed alignment,[52] China never replied to the 1899 proposal. Elgin's successor as Viceroy, Lord Curzon, urged that as China had not rejected the 1899 proposal, she should be told that Britain intended henceforth to treat the line there described as the boundary. But the proposal was not followed up, and the fluctuations of British frontier policy were resumed, in reaction to the two variables: Russian pressure and Chinese weakness.

Through the first decade of the twentieth century, British policy adhered to the 1899 proposal, and aimed at establishing Aksai Chin as part of Tibet, not Sinkiang.† The point of this was that in 1907 the British negotiated with St Petersburg a convention by which the Russians as well as themselves engaged to keep out of Tibet; ergo, if Aksai Chin were Tibetan, they would have to keep out of that too. The overriding British interest in Aksai Chin was to exclude the Russians from it, and the simplest way of doing that seemed to be to confirm that the region was Tibetan/Chinese.

But what appeared to be the collapse of Chinese power in central Asia, in consequence of the revolution in China at the end of 1911, brought about another sharp change in the tactics of frontier policy in

---

* This is the crux of the proposal, so far as it concerned the sector east of the Karakoram Pass:

From the Karakoram Pass [the boundary would follow] the crests of the range east for about half a degree (100 *li* [33 miles]), and then turn south to a little below the thirty-fifth parallel of north latitude. Rounding then what on our maps is shown as the source of the Karakash, the line of the hills to be followed runs north-east to a point east of Kizil Jilga, and from there in a south-easterly direction follows the Lak Tsang range until that meets a spur running south from the Kuen Lun, which has hitherto been shown on our maps as the eastern boundary of Ladakh. This is a little east of 80° east longitude.'[53]

† Although the forward school was still very much alive; Sir Louis Dane, Foreign Secretary of the Indian Government, was described in 1904 as being 'mad keen to extend the Indian frontier to the Kuen Lun mountains, thus annexing Western Tibet'.[54]

India. The objective remained the same—to keep Russia as far from the plains of India as possible—but the disappearance of China as a significant power in central Asia meant that the means had to be revised. Russian annexation of Sinkiang had long been expected by the British; now it appeared imminent and ineluctable, and to anticipate it Lord Hardinge, by then Viceroy, seized upon the forward prescription of Ardagh. He urged London that, to forestall Russian annexation of Sinkiang, Britain should demand recognition of a boundary that placed Aksai Chin not only outside Russia but within *British* territory.[55] The London Government did not act on that recommendation, however, and no intimation that the British were reconsidering the boundary alignment proposed in 1899 was ever given to China. That the British Government in fact held to the 1899 proposal was indicated in the map accompanying the Simla Convention two years later, in 1914; this showed Aksai Chin as part of Tibet.*

During the period with which this account has been dealing, the sector of the frontier from Afghanistan to Nepal was considered by the British as a whole; but the 1947 partition of the Indian sub-continent, confirmed by the first Indo-Pakistan war in Kashmir, divided it at the Karakoram Pass. To the west, the frontier became Pakistan's responsibility; to the east, India's.† So far the narrative has not dealt with that portion of the frontier which was to fall to Pakistan, but it is necessary to do so in tracing what appears to have been the final pulsation of British boundary policy in this sector.

It appears that in 1927 the Government of India again looked into the north-west frontier with China, and decided that the boundary from Afghanistan to the Karakoram Pass (where the Chinese had erected a boundary pillar thirty-five years before) should run along the crest of the main Karakoram range—rather than far to the north, where the Johnson-Ardagh line had placed it.[56] What was decided then about the sector to the east of the pass—which was to be the crux of the Sino-Indian dispute—is not known. But at all events, the 1927 decision did not find its way on to British maps; and when India became independent, in 1947, and for several years thereafter, most official Indian maps still showed the boundary in accordance with the extreme forward formulations of Johnson and Ardagh.

* See p.53 n below.
† India, however, claimed legal responsibility for the western, Pakistani-held sector, too. See below, p. 216.

After 1899, however, there was, as far as the historical record shows, no further attempt by Britain to get China to agree to a boundary alignment in the north-west. The sector from Afghanistan to Nepal remained undelimited, a problem in the mid-twentieth century for the two inheritors of Britain's power on the sub-continent, India and Pakistan, and for the People's Republic of China.

For all the discussion in London and India about the boundary between Kashmir and China and the variations in conception of where, in Britain's interest, it should lie, there were no matching moves of troops or administrators. The frontier territory continued as it had always been, bleak, hostile and empty. From the British side came only a few explorer-travellers and political agents, and then huntsmen, trekking into the Changchenmo valley to shoot yak or antelope — to such effect that long before the British left the sub-continent both animals, previously plentiful, had almost vanished from the valley. Such travellers had, by the 1940s, arguably established a prescriptive right at least to the lower reaches of the Changchenmo, up to the Kongka Pass, and perhaps as far as the Lanak Pass, some thirty miles east. But Britain had never attempted to exert authority on Aksai Chin, or to establish outposts in it — far less, to set up posts or exercise authority up to a boundary on the Kuen Lun range on the other side, which would have cut off the headwaters of the Karakash River and the Sinkiang–Tibet caravan route that crossed Aksai Chin. The boundary alignment which would have entailed such an expansion had remained a strategist's theoretical formulation.

The threat that nourished British desire for a boundary which would leave Aksai Chin within India continued almost to the end of their rule, however. In 1940–41 the Government of Sinkiang, then under the warlord Sheng Shih-tsai, and leaning towards the Soviet Union, conducted a survey of Aksai Chin with the help of Russian experts.[57] British intelligence must surely have learned of this, and the presence of Russians in Aksai Chin might well have been enough to swing official favour in New Delhi back towards a forward claim line.

★ ★ ★ ★ ★ ★ ★ ★ ★ ★ ★

In the middle of the great arching gable of the Indian sub-continent along which the British and Chinese empires impinged, a string of small states provided both a buffer and a natural arena of imperial competition. When the British reached the area, these states, Nepal, Sikkim and Bhutan, were all in varying degrees in dependence upon or allegiance to China. Nepal had been created in the eighteenth century when the Gorkhas, a Hindu hill-people, invaded the Tibetan polities which had hitherto existed there and unified them under their own rule. Then they invaded Tibet proper, to be defeated in 1792 by Chinese-led troops who in counter-attack penetrated almost to Katmandu and imposed a treaty which left Nepal a tributary of China. Lhasa looked upon Sikkim as a Tibetan dependency,[58] and made periodic assertions of suzerainty over Bhutan.[59] Inevitably, the British saw such Tibetan – and hence indirectly Chinese – hegemony over these cis-Himalayan states as a challenge, potentially a menace, to their own position. The achievement of British policy through the nineteenth century was the reversal of the allegiance of the Himalayan states, in reality so far as Nepal was concerned, and in form as well in the cases of Bhutan and Sikkim.

The British considered annexing Nepal after they had defeated her in the Gorkha War (1814–16)[60] but decided that the move would be too likely to incur Chinese reaction. They were content thereafter with a situation in which Nepal continued in form under China's suzerainty, but in fact accepted British control of her internal and external affairs. In 1890 China signed with Britain a convention recognizing Sikkim as a British protectorate and delimiting the Sikkim-Tibet boundary; in 1910, over the protests of China, the British signed a treaty with Bhutan in which that kingdom bound herself to be guided by Britain in her foreign relations.

Again the logic of empire beckoned British power forward, and the first decade of the twentieth century saw Britain attempting to establish exclusive influence over Tibet. Curzon believed that the Russians' 'passion for a pan-Asiatic dominion'[61] was now focused on Tibet, and meant to thwart them by making Tibet a buffer. This policy succeeded in so far as Russian influence was kept out of Tibet (though the seriousness of Russian designs in that direction is questionable); Curzon failed, however, in his objective of bringing Tibet under some measure of protection from India, and so the reassertion of Chinese authority there was inevitable once a strong central Government established itself in Peking.

In the narrow sub-sector of frontier between the Aksai Chin region and Nepal,* British policy was more categorical. After the Gorkha War Britain annexed one of the small hill states there, Kumaon, and attempted to bring others into exclusive political relations with herself. But the British found that these small states continued in practice in dual allegiance, and that while their own authority was nominal, the Tibetans exercised *de facto* control. This situation continued unresolved throughout the British years, and when, after 1947, the new Indian Government consolidated their administration, to the exclusion of Tibetan authority, Tibet, and later China, protested. As a scholar noted in 1960, 'any assertion of exclusive rights by either side would necessarily involve the denial of rights in the other party which have been more or less regularly and openly exercised for a great many years.'[62] So far as the boundary in this sub-sector was concerned, the British appear to have regarded the main passes as the boundary features, indicating a watershed boundary; but the Tibetans continued to exercise authority in territory on the Indian side of the passes.[63]

With Nepal, Sikkim and Bhutan converted into what Curzon in 1907 described as a chain of protectorates,[64] the British were content to rest their boundary there comfortably beneath the foot-hills. So long as Britain was confident that her influence over those states was sufficient to exclude that of rival powers, a boundary on the plains was satisfactory; the approaches to India could be guarded by obedient feudatories as securely as by British power itself, and far more cheaply.

---

* In the terminology of the Sino-Indian dispute this became the 'middle sector'.

(ii) *The McMahon Line*

To the east of Bhutan, too, the boundary of British India lay, at the beginning of the twentieth century, beneath the foot-hills; but in this sector of the frontier the situation was very different. To the north lay not coherent states, amenable to British pressure or diplomacy, but a scattering of separate tribes, thinly populating a sixty-mile-broad belt of mountainous, densely jungled country. Here was another no-man's-land, acceptable as a frontier only so long as no other strong power approached it from the north; otherwise, a standing source of worry—or temptation—to those responsible for the defence of India.

Assam, which the British added to their Indian empire in 1826, consisted at first essentially of the Brahmaputra valley; the hills which pressed upon it from north and south were long left outside the pale of British administration. The terrain there was forbidding, the tribal people inhospitable when not actively hostile. But in the second half of the nineteenth century, the tide of development began to lap into the foot-hills bordering the Brahmaputra valley to the north; the tea planters visualized wide new gardens on the slopes above the plains, while timber companies saw in the thick forests not a barrier but a rich resource waiting to be exploited. That uncontrolled commercial penetration into the foot-hills would quickly breed trouble with the tribes there was appreciated by the administration, and in 1873 the British drew a line, short of the foot of the hills, which no one could cross without a pass or licence. This 'Inner Line' created a protected zone beneath the hills, a *cordon sanitaire* to control the spread of commercial and other potentially disturbing interests. The Inner Line was laid down in detail and demarcated for some of its length; and, as well as a barrier to prevent unlicensed travel into the hills, it served as an administrative boundary (taxes were not collected beyond it).[65] It was not, however, regarded as the international boundary. That was the Outer Line, coextensive with the southern border of Bhutan and running along the foot of the hills where they rise abruptly from the plains for their steep climb to the Tibetan tableland.

During the nineteenth century there were occasional short pene-
trations into the hills by British officials;[66] but the only deep exploration
of the hill country was up the Lohit valley, which from the first had
been seen by many Englishmen as a potential trade route to China.
In 1886 a British official trekked right up the Lohit to Rima, in Tibet,
and returned to recommend that a road be built along his route to the
Tibetan border as a trade outlet for British goods.[67] The Government
in India was unenthusiastic. From long experience it knew that the flag
followed trade in such circumstances, and that traffic through such wild
country, with a potentially hostile population, would almost inevitably
entail escorts and punitive expeditions. To move anywhere into the
hills, indeed, was seen to be setting foot on an endless path: annexation
of tribal territory in the lower hills 'would only bring us into contact
with tribes still wilder and less known', an Englishman wrote in the
1880s; 'nor should we find a resting place for the foot of annexation
till we had planted it on the plateau of High Asia; perhaps not even
then.'[68]

The prickly hedge of tribal country was not an all-embracing barrier
around British territory in the north-east, however; there was one
salient gap. Immediately to the east of Bhutan, a wedge of Tibetan
territory ran right down to the plains; here, a British official noted in
1844, 'the two great Governments of Britain and China . . . are coter-
minous, and this is the nearest route by which the produce of the
north-western provinces of China and of the eastern provinces of Tibet
and Tartary could be brought into the British dominions.'[69] This
wedge of territory was known as the Tawang Tract, from the great
monastery of Tawang in the north through which it was administered,
and it was populated by tribes deeply influenced by Tibetan culture,
and for the most part Buddhist. There was an important trade route
through this territory, and the British encouraged it by establishing an
annual fair at Udalguri, near its southern extremity. That this whole
tract, sixty miles deep, was Tibetan was never doubted or challenged
by the British, who indeed sometimes found the fact of Tibetan administration a convenience. For example, in 1872–3, when demarcating a
boundary with Bhutan, they were able to extend this into a demarcated
stretch of boundary with Tibet, running along the foot of the hills,
because Tibetan officials instructed local tribal chiefs to co-operate.[70]

The British preoccupation with what was seen as the menacing
Russian advance towards India dominated policy towards Tibet in the

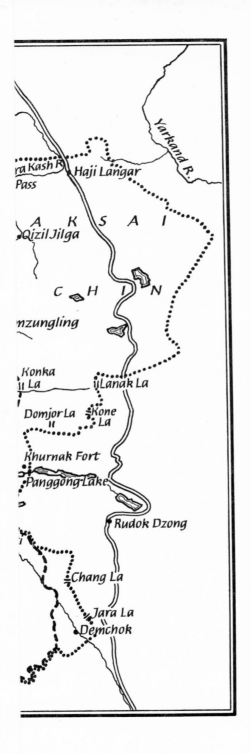

A great Empire, the future military strength of which no man can foresee, has suddenly appeared on the North-East Frontier of India. The problem of the North-West Frontier thus bids fair to be duplicated in the long run, and a double pressure placed on the defensive resources of the Indian Empire. . . . China, in a word, has come to the gates of India, and the fact has to be reckoned with.[73]*

The authorities in India, of course, needed no such warnings. Always sensitive to developments beyond the frontiers, they had watched the rapid reassertion of Chinese power in Tibet with mounting misgivings, and reacted with alarm when in May 1910 the Chinese occupied Rima, demanded taxes from the inhabitants, and gave orders for the cutting of a road through the tribal belt to Assam.[74] By moving into the tribal belt the Chinese would raise an immediate strategic threat to Assam, and here were no wastelands such as lay on the north-west frontier, but the spreading gardens of a rich British-owned tea industry, coalfields and other British economic interests: 'Think of the howl the planters would let out' if menaced by China, an official wrote at this time, 'and the rise in the price of tea.'[75]

A forward school promptly formed, and arguments began to be urged both in India and in London for an advance of British administration in the north-east to anticipate further Chinese moves. The Lieutenant-Governor of East Bengal and Assam (then a single province), noting that 'we only now claim suzerainty up to the *foot* of the hills', recommended a more active patrolling policy, with officials touring in the hills beyond the frontier, and improvement of the trade routes to the principal villages 'so far as they lie within our recognized frontiers and further, if unopposed'.[76] The retiring Viceroy, Lord Minto, was less tentative, proposing that the Outer Line should be extended to include all of the tribal territory. (At this time, it should be noted, all such forward proposals left the Tawang Tract aside, accepting that it was unchallengeably Tibetan/Chinese and had to be lived with since it could not be changed.)

As a general rule, enthusiasm for a forward policy seems to be felt in indirect proportion to the distance from the frontier concerned:

* Before long, similar anxiety was being expressed by newspapers in China about British intentions on this frontier! The *Szechuan Kung-pao* in 1912 noted that the British were 'taking advantage of our troubles to peer and pry' across the border.[77]

those on the frontier are all for pushing it forward, while those at a cool distance see the difficulties more clearly than the advantages.* So it certainly was in 1910. The Government of India, under the new Viceroy, Lord Hardinge, rejected the advice of the forward school, declaring that it 'saw no necessity at present for incurring the risks and responsibilities entailed by a forward movement into tribal territory now beyond our control'.[78] If the Chinese ever attacked India, Hardinge pointed out, Britain would surely react with an attack on China herself from the sea; 'he was therefore opposed to running risks or spending money on endeavours to create a strategic frontier in advance of the administrative border', and his conclusion was that 'any forward move of the administrative frontier was strongly to be deprecated'.[79] The Government in Calcutta (which was then the capital) could, of course, take a broader view than did the officials on the frontier, or those directly responsible for it. Calcutta felt more sharply, too, London's aversion to the sort of administrative advances that, experience had taught, always led to the expenditure of money, sometimes of blood, and consequently to awkward questions in Parliament, or even political storms. A very explicit section of the Act under which India was governed laid down that, except under 'sudden and urgent necessity', the revenues of India must not be used to finance military operations 'beyond the external frontiers',[80] and the Government of India was accordingly inhibited from embarking on any policy which promised to entail such military ventures.

But if the Government in Calcutta had the final say on policy, questions of implementation had to be decided lower down the administrative scale, and it was there that the forward school often came into its own. Interpretation of a directive, phrasing of an order for an officer setting out on patrol, even sometimes the timing of a departure to make sure that negative instructions were not received[81] — the cumulative room for latitude was wide. Thus it happened that in 1911, despite the Government's refusal to approve patrolling across the Outer Line, a British official, Noel Williamson, was murdered by tribesmen well to the north of it, having crossed to investigate the extent of Tibetan influence beyond. Although Williamson had disobeyed orders to reach the place at which he was killed, his murder could not go unpunished, and London authorized a punitive expedi-

---

* For a signal exception to this rule of thumb, see Part II below.

tion. But the objectives of the expedition were not purely punitive.*
It was also ordered to explore and survey as much of the country as
possible, thus providing the 'knowledge requisite for a suitable
boundary between India and China . . . keeping her as far as possible
removed from our present administered area'.[82] Explaining the reversal
of frontier policy to London, Lord Hardinge said that 'during the past
few months there have been further developments in the Chinese
policy of expansion which it is impossible to ignore', citing Chinese
moves in the tribal territory. These circumstances, he went on, had
forced the Government to revert to his predecessor's proposal that
'endeavour should be made to secure, as soon as possible, a sound
strategical boundary between China-cum-Tibet and the tribal territory', and to make this 'the main object of our policy'.[83]

Spelling out the forward policy which had now been adopted,
Hardinge took up Minto's proposal that the Outer Line should be
pushed north so as to take in all the tribal territory—not including, of
course, the Tawang Tract.† There would be no need to demarcate it,
he suggested, and the Inner Line, marking the limit of British administration, would not be affected. He considered 'that our future policy
should be one of loose political control, having as its object the minimum of interference compatible with the necessity of protecting the
tribesmen from unprovoked aggression . . . and of preventing them
from violating either our own or Chinese territory'.[84] Once the new
boundary had been determined to British satisfaction, formal intimation of its alignment should be given to China.

In 1911 and 1912 several expeditions, in addition to the punitive
foray to avenge Williamson's death, were sent into the tribal area, and
in September 1911 the General Staff of the Indian Army prepared a
memorandum for the surveyors attached to the expeditions, to guide
them in their quest for a strategic boundary. This noted wistfully that a
'scientific frontier' for the north-east, which (like the Ardagh line in the
north-west) would give Britain control of the forward slopes as well

---

* A Chinese newspaper in Szechuan noted of this and other expeditions that 'the British
pretend that they are avenging the murder of Englishmen by savages', but wondered
with some percipience 'whether this is not a pretext to pick a quarrel'.[85]

† Minto's proposal was that 'the external boundary should run, approximately, from the
east of the wedgeshaped portion of Tibetan territory known as the Tawang district,
which runs down to the British frontier north of Udalguri, in a north-easterly direction to
latitude 29°, longitude 94°, thence along latitude 29° to longitude 96°; thence in a south-
easterly direction to the Zayul Chu [River] as far east and as near as possible to Rima;
thence across the Zayul Chu valley to the Zayul Chu-Irrawaddy watershed'.[86]

as the passes, was unobtainable, since the Chinese had already established themselves in effective occupation of the Tsangpo valley and at the headwaters of several of the rivers which flow down into Assam. Asking the surveyors to keep the military aspect 'prominently in view', the memorandum proposed a boundary following mountain crests eastward from a point on the Bhutan border a few miles south of Tawang.[87] This proposal looked to annexing the lower portion of the Tawang Tract, but leaving Tawang itself to Tibet. A few months later, however, the soldiers had second thoughts, and proposed more radical surgery to 'rectify' that sector of the north-east boundary to Britain's advantage. The Chief of the General Staff warned that the Chinese would be able to exert pressure or influence through the 'dangerous wedge' of the Tawang Tract. 'Rectification of the boundary here is therefore imperative,' he concluded, and recommended as the ideal line one which would bring into India not only Tawang but a sizeable slice of Tibet above the Tawang Tract, including Tsona Dzong, another Tibetan administrative centre.[88] The Government did not accept the full forward proposal of the C.G.S., but two years later did adopt his recommendation in so far as that looked to bringing Tawang itself within the limits of India.

From 1911, then, the Government in India was embarked on a deliberate advance of the north-eastern boundary, which looked not only to bringing the tribal territory under 'loose political control' but also to annexing a salient of territory which the British had recognized to be China's ever since they reached Assam nearly ninety years before. To let that intention be known, however, would not only invite vigorous Chinese protests about the Tawang Tract, but also a formal expression of the claim, hitherto made only in Chinese maps, to China's suzerainty over the tribal belt. It would also open the Government in London to charges that it was deliberately infringing the provision of the India Act which required the permission of Parliament before military operations were launched 'beyond the external frontiers'. In consequence, not only were the expeditions into the tribal belt and beyond, into Tibet, kept as quiet as possible, but when the Government's critics in Parliament did get wind of what was afoot they were deliberately put off the scent. Thus an M.P. who challenged the Government's right to undertake the operations in the tribal belt without Parliament's permission was told that the area in question was not beyond the external frontiers; when he produced official British maps showing that it was, the Government retorted that the maps were not accurate in their depiction of the frontier. At last he was fobbed off with the statement that 'it is not intended . . . to increase the area administered by the Government of India'.[89] This was literally true, in so far that the Inner Line was not to be advanced; but of course it burked the crucial point—which was that the Outer Line *was* to be advanced.

The sudden collapse of Chinese power in Tibet in 1911–12 which, as has been seen, converted Lord Hardinge to the forward school of thinking over the north-west frontier with Tibet and Sinkiang, seemed to open an opportunity to take steps to avert future threats along India's north-eastern boundary. Moreover, having been made uncomfortably aware of the dangers in an active Chinese presence on the frontier of India, the British decided that their interests, political as well as strategic, would best be served by an arrangement that excluded effective Chinese power from Tibet. The Anglo-Russian Convention of 1907 had set up Tibet as a buffer between the Russian and British empires; what was needed now was a parallel arrangement which made Tibet serve too the second purpose of being a buffer between the Chinese and British. To further this objective, Britain convoked a conference at Simla in October 1913 — China attending under constraint, the Tibetans, of course, with alacrity. Definition of India's north-eastern boundary was not among the functions of the conference — at least not so far as London was concerned.

The aim of the British was that 'Tibet, while nominally retaining her position as an autonomous state under the suzerainty of China, should in reality be placed in a position of absolute dependence on the Indian Government, and that there should be set up an effective machinery for keeping the Chinese out on one hand and the Russians on the other.'[90] But by this time central Asian relations between the great powers had become intricately complex; the rival interests of Russia and Britain in and around Afghanistan, Mongolia and Tibet were balanced into a delicate and wary *détente*. The Anglo-Russian Convention of 1907 was the pivot of that balance, and this precluded Britain from having any dealings with Tibet except through the Chinese, and from annexing Tibetan territory. Any attempt to gain Tibetan territory in a direct deal with the Tibetan Government was a double infringement of Britain's treaty with Russia and had therefore to be embarked upon with the greatest care and secrecy.

The British presented the Simla Conference as an attempt to mend relations between China and Tibet, between whom fighting was going on at the time: Britain would be 'the honest broker', the Government explained in Parliament.[91] In fact the British delegation worked throughout in close co-operation, not far short of collusion, with the Tibetans, and it was later to be conceded by the London Government that the Simla negotiations failed 'simply and solely because the Government of India attempted to secure for Tibet greater advantages than the Chinese Government were prepared to concede'.[92]

The Simla Conference is a story in itself, an intricate exercise in diplomacy, power politics, and espionage, played out in the queen of the hill stations at her very prime, on the eve of the First World War.* The British delegation was led by Henry McMahon, the same who as a young captain, twenty years before, had accompanied Durand on his mission to Kabul and then spent two hard years demarcating the Durand Line—and dealing with such hazards as attacks by rabid wolves. McMahon, by now Sir Henry and Foreign Secretary of the Indian Government, was a man of marked moral force, of the kind that Curzon must have had in mind when he spoke of the 'frontier school of character', where men were moulded 'in the furnace of responsibility and on the anvil of self-reliance'.[93] Perhaps McMahon, like Curzon, relished the creation and laying down of boundaries, holding it to be not a science but an art, 'so plastic and so malleable are its forms and manifestations'.[94]

The main thrust of the open British effort at the conference was to get China to accept a division of Tibet into two zones, Inner and Outer Tibet, such as had recently been agreed between China and Russia in the case of Mongolia. China's suzerainty over the whole of Tibet was to be recognized, but she was to enjoy no administrative rights in Outer Tibet—and would thus be kept back from the borders of India. The Chinese were not prepared to accept the British proposal, but neither did they reject it out of hand: weakness had brought an unwilling China to the conference, weakness and the coercive diplomatic methods of Britain—and of McMahon himself—kept her there. The Chinese representative and intelligence agent in Calcutta, Lu Hsing-chi, put it succinctly: 'Our country is at present in an enfeebled condition; our external relations are involved and difficult and our

---

* For full accounts see Alastair Lamb's two-volume study, *The McMahon Line*, and Dorothy Woodman, *Himalayan Frontiers*.

finances embarrassed. Nevertheless, Tibet is of paramount importance to both [Szechuan and Yunnan] and we must exert ourselves to the utmost during this conference.'[95] The Chinese delegate at Simla was Chen I-fan (or Ivan Chen), a polished and experienced diplomat who had served for years in London; but Lu Hsing-chi, who described himself both as Chinese Consul in Calcutta and Chinese Amban (viceroy) in Lhasa (the British recognizing him in neither capacity) was the key man from China's point of view. Lu's intelligence network was excellent, he had an astute political mind, and his advice to Peking was consistent throughout: yield nothing. His drawback as an intelligence operative was that all his messages to China, and those to him from Simla, were being monitored by the British, who therefore knew for most of the Simla Conference not only what was in their opponent's hand, but what he knew of what was in theirs.

The Chinese were deeply resistant to the proposal for the zonal division of Tibet, no doubt seeing plainly the purpose it was designed to serve, which in their eyes was simply the separation of Tibet or a great part of it from China.* Their opposition to the proposal was oblique, however, focusing not on the essence, the question of division, but on where the proposed line of division should run. This was the issue upon which the conference finally broke down. McMahon was able in early April 1914 to induce Ivan Chen to *initial* the draft treaty which had been under discussion, and its illustrative map; but Chen did so only 'on the clear understanding that to initial and to sign them were two separate actions'[96]—and his Government repudiated even this action the moment it learned of it, severely rebuking Chen for his unauthorized compliance. McMahon noted that thereafter Chen's confidence appeared much shaken. After all this, however, the draft convention which Chen had been pressured into initialling was amended by the British (after they had referred it to Russia), which plainly cancelled what validity—if any—had been given it by Chen's repudiated initials.

Even McMahon must have recognized that after this it would be useless to press Ivan Chen to exceed his instructions again. In July therefore he accepted that China would not sign the convention, and brought the conference to a close. McMahon had all along been under instructions from London not to sign bilaterally with the Tibetans if

---

* Just this happened in the case of Mongolia, when in 1950 China recognized as the Mongolian People's Republic what had been Outer Mongolia.

the Chinese refused; but he chose to interpret London's bluffing warning to China of just such an Anglo-Tibetan agreement as indicating a change of line. London's confirmation that he was not to sign bilaterally with Tibet did not reach him in time (because no one of the requisite seniority was in the Foreign Office in London before lunch on the day the telegram was dispatched!).[97] McMahon therefore proceeded to sign with the Tibetan representative a joint declaration that the re-drafted convention, as now again initialled by themselves alone, would be binding on both their Governments. The signing took place with the knowledge of Ivan Chen—although he was sent into the next room while it took place—but he was not told what it was that was being signed, and the declaration was not published for many years.

The Simla Conference thus ended in diplomatic hugger-mugger, with two participants in what was meant to be a tripartite conference openly signing a secret declaration; with one text of a draft convention initialled by all three parties, another initialled by two, and a map initialled by all three. All this provided much fertile ground for international lawyers, and was to be sieved over again and again in the Sino-Indian argument half a century later. But the central conclusion remains wholly clear, and was accepted as such by the British Government at the time: *the Simla Conference produced no agreement to which the Government of China was a party*. McMahon admitted this himself: 'It is with great regret that I leave India without having secured the formal adherence of the Chinese Government to a Tripartite Agreement', he wrote in his final report to London. ('The fact [is] that the negotiations convened in Simla last year broke down', the British admitted in 1915, and went on to explain why—because the Government of India had been 'unduly anxious to secure the best terms they could for Tibet').[98] Secondly, China, who denied that Tibet enjoyed sovereign identity or the treaty-making powers that go with it, stated formally, emphatically and repeatedly at the time that she would not recognize any bilateral agreement between Tibet and Britain.*

There had in fact been such an agreement, as a secret by-product of the Simla Conference. In February and March 1914 there were discussions in Delhi between the British and the Tibetans about the Tibet-Assam boundary, and as a result an alignment was agreed upon—

---

* Ivan Chen, the Chinese representative, made this statement at the conference on July 3rd, 1914, and the Chinese Minister in London made the same declaration to the Government there.

the McMahon Line. The Chinese were not invited to participate, nor were they informed of the discussions. In fact every effort was made, then and for twenty years after, to keep these exchanges secret—they were, after all, in breach not only of the Anglo-Chinese Convention of 1906 in which Britain had 'engage[d] not to annex Tibetan territory', but also of the Anglo-Russian Convention of 1907, in which she had engaged 'not to enter into negotiations with Tibet except through the intermediary of the Chinese Government'.[99] That, in spite of British precautions, the Chinese delegation or the well-informed Lu Hsing-chi in Calcutta got wind of the secret Delhi discussions with the Tibetans is more likely than not; but, if they did, they gave no other intimation of their knowledge than can be inferred from China's repeated declarations that she would not recognize any treaty or agreement that might then or thereafter be signed between Britain and Tibet.

The British conception of the boundary alignment that would best serve their interests changed during the period of the Simla Conference, with the line being moved progressively northwards.[100] In a memorandum of October 1913 McMahon indicated that Britain would have to abide by Tibetan possession of the entire Tawang Tract; then in November it was decided that the boundary should run through Se La, a pass just under twenty miles south-east of Tawang, thus amputating most of the Tibetan salient but leaving the Tawang monastery itself to Tibet; finally in February the British advanced their demand again, so that the line ran, on McMahon's maps, about twelve miles north of Tawang. This was still short of the alignment proposed by the Chief of the General Staff but, by annexing some two thousand square miles of Tibetan territory, it cut off the 'dangerous wedge' of the Tawang Tract which had so worried the soldiers. McMahon explained to London that his objectives had been to secure a strategic watershed boundary and with it access to the shortest trade route into Tibet, together with the control of the Tawang monastery necessary to free that route from the undue exactions and oppressions which the Tibetan authorities there had been imposing. The details of the border negotiations are not on the record (it appears that McMahon did not report them fully to London) so just how the Tibetans were persuaded to cede the Tawang Tract is not known; but from later events it appears that they saw this as the price for the desired boundary with and status vis à vis China that they believed the British were obtaining for them—and that they understood that if the British failed in that regard, the deal would be off. At all events, the Tibetan delegate was 'much blamed' by his Government for 'surrendering the Tawang Tract'.[101]

McMahon was able to draw his line with a reasonable degree of precision thanks to the surveying and mapping done in the tribal territories during the preceding two years. He was filling out detail on his maps up to the last moment. After the Simla Conference opened Captain F. M. Bailey completed an adventurous trek which had taken him up into Tibet, westward along the valley of the Tsangpo, and then south again into the tribal areas to Tawang, following a difficult but direct trail which was to play a significant role in the Sino-Indian border war half a century later; when Bailey got back to Calcutta he found a telegram from McMahon summoning him to Simla,[102] and the details he was there able to supply of the topography in the Tawang sector presumably enabled McMahon to draw the western extremity of his line with more confidence.

The line was drawn on two map sheets at a scale of eight miles to an inch,[103] and was accepted by Tibet in an exchange of letters between McMahon and the Tibetan plenipotentiary on March 24th and 25th, 1914.[104] The letters included no verbal description of the new boundary, and made no mention of any principle upon which it had been drawn, so that the only authority for the McMahon alignment lies in the original maps, of which copies were kept in Lhasa as well as by the British.

Essentially what the McMahon alignment did was to push the boundary northward about sixty miles, lifting it from the strategically exposed foot of the hills to the crest line of the Assam Himalayas. It did not create a real watershed boundary line, as was later to be argued, since it cut several rivers, including the Tsangpo-Brahmaputra, flowing south. As the maps on which it was drawn plainly show, the alignment followed for most of its length the edge of the great Tibetan plateau where that abruptly gives way to the broken, sharply ridged country which shelves down to the Brahmaputra valley. By following that topographical feature, it became also to a very large extent an ethnic boundary, since the Tibetans had generally found the damp valleys beneath their high plateau uninviting, and had not settled them. The outstanding exception to that characteristic was at the western end of the line where that cut off the Tawang Tract, an area which had been heavily influenced by Tibetan culture—which was, indeed, Tibetan in every sense.

With this alignment, McMahon sought to do for British India in the north-east what Durand had attempted twenty years before on the Afghan frontier, bringing what was for most of its extent a tribal no-man's-land under nominal British sovereignty. The Tibetans, like the Afghans in the case of the Durand Line, seem to have regarded the McMahon Line as something which was to affect the British more than it did themselves. McMahon gave them to understand that they would continue to have the right to collect taxes (or 'dues') in the Tawang Tract; and, judging by what he reported to London, he assured the Tibetans that the Line would be open to modification in their interest 'in the light of more detailed knowledge which [may be acquired] in future'.[105] The most recent historian of the Simla Conference concludes that the McMahon Line was 'to some extent provisional and experimental'.[106]

The Tibetans were later to say that they regarded the McMahon boundary as part of a package deal, in which they were to be recompensed for the cession of some territory to the British by gaining, with Britain's help, a satisfactory boundary with and a large degree of independence from China. Since the British had failed to produce those compensatory concessions, the Tibetans argued that they could not be held to their agreement on the McMahon Line.[107] At all events, it was to be many years before the line that McMahon drew as the boundary made any practical difference to the Tibetans.

Before seeing what happened to the McMahon Line after 1914, it is necessary to glance back at the aborted Simla Convention. While the subject of the boundary between Tibet and India was never included in the tripartite discussions and not mentioned to the Chinese, it was at the last and indirectly introduced into the proceedings by what might be called a piece of cartographic legerdemain. The map accompanying the draft convention showed the proposed division of Tibet into two zones, Inner and Outer Tibet—marking the frontier of Tibet in red and the proposed boundary between the two Tibetan zones in blue. But the red line, which for the greater part of its length showed a boundary between Tibet and China, curved round in its southern extension to show what would have been the boundary between Tibet *and India*— and in that sector it followed the alignment which McMahon had agreed with the Tibetans. Thus, if China had accepted the proposed zonal division of Tibet and signed the convention, a case could have been made that she had also accepted the McMahon alignment. As, in fact, China did neither, but forcefully repudiated the convention and the map with it, the point is an academic one; but Sir Henry McMahon's diplomatic sleight-of-hand was later to be the rather frail basis for arguing that China *did* accept the McMahon Line.*

The First World War broke out a few weeks after the closing session of the Simla Conference, and north-east frontier policy became a matter of remote concern to the Governments in London and Delhi. A British officer who visited Tawang at the beginning of 1914 recommended that permanent British posts should be established there and at places in the tribal belt, pointing out that 'as soon as China settles down this Tibetan Frontier will become of great importance'.[108] But his proposals were not even forwarded to Delhi, since his superiors knew that the Government of India was 'averse from anything in the shape of a forward move upon the frontier at the present moment'.[109] McMahon himself had gone on home leave, and was then appointed British Commissioner in Egypt. He seems to have felt that the home Government had not properly backed up his efforts in what he later described as 'one and a quarter years of polyglot negotiation';[110] on meeting McMahon in London at this time, a colleague noted that 'it is no doubt difficult to convince anyone from India that there is a Chinese point of view which deserves consideration'.[111]†

In 1919 the British tried to induce China to resume the tripartite negotiations, under the threat that, if the Chinese refused, Britain would recognize Tibet as 'an autonomous state under the suzerainty of China and . . . deal with Tibet in future on that basis[112]. The Chinese avoided an outright refusal, but would not agree. The British began to give the Tibetans what would now be called military aid—arms and ammunition, and training in their use.[113] They did not, however,

---

* Professor Alastair Lamb has pointed out that the red line on the Simla Convention map at its north-western extremity curves precisely round where Aksai Chin would be if it were marked, and infers from this that the British were still at this time hoping to make Aksai Chin part of Tibet, in the hope of excluding the Chinese from it as well as the Russians. He makes the point that, if it is argued that the Simla map gives legal strength to the Indian claim for a McMahon Line boundary, it would give just as much weight *against* their claim to a boundary in the north-west which left Aksai Chin in India.[114]

† Dr A. P. Rubin said of the Simla Conference that the records showed 'responsible officials of British India to have acted to the injury of China in conscious violation of their instructions; deliberately misinforming their superiors in London of their actions; altering documents whose publication had been ordered by Parliament; lying at an international conference table; and deliberately breaking a treaty between the United Kingdom and Russia'. McMahon and other 'strong and honourable men', he concluded, 'were corrupted by provincial power into misleading their political superiors and bullying the foreign representatives with whom they came in contact'.[115]

challenge the Chinese suzerainty in Tibet which they had explicitly
recognized in treaties with Russia, China, and the Tibetans. Neither
did they publish any of the diplomatic products of the Simla Conference: not the draft convention, nor the secret Anglo-Tibetan declaration accepting the draft as binding, nor the secret exchange of letters
between the British and the Tibetans on the Assam-Tibet border. The
original 1929 edition of Aitchison's *Treaties*, the authoritative record,
said of the Simla Conference only this:

> In 1913 a conference of Tibetan, Chinese and British pleni-
> potentiaries met in India to try and bring about a settlement with
> regard to matters on the Sino-Tibetan frontier, and a Tripartite
> Convention was drawn up and initialled in 1914. The Chinese
> Government, however, refused to permit their plenipotentiary to
> proceed to full signature.[116]

The Foreign Secretary of the Indian Government in 1928 had explained
the omission from the forthcoming edition of Aitchison's *Treaties* of
the Simla documents and the trade agreement which Britain had gone
on to sign with Tibet, again secretly; if the documents were published,
he wrote, 'a short account of the Tripartite Convention and of its
secret history would have to be given. In view of the possibility that
publication now of the facts of the Declaration (though it seems unlikely that China is still unaware of its existence) may force her to take
overt notice of it and so afford a fresh handle for anti-British propaganda', it seemed 'on the whole most prudent' to leave the documents
out.[117]

As for the McMahon Line, that seemed a dead letter. The British
authorities in Burma were informed of the existence of the Anglo-
Tibetan boundary agreement (which concerned them, too), but not
those in Assam, and the state Government there was left in the belief
that its boundary was beneath the foot-hills. The Tawang Tract continued part of Tibet. In the twenty years after the Simla Conference
occasional British forays, usually punitive expeditions, were made
into the tribal belt, but there was no attempt to make McMahon's
map line the effective boundary. The McMahon Line was, in effect,
forgotten.

It was remembered only in 1935, 'almost by chance'; a deputy secretary in New Delhi, Mr Olaf Caroe, noted that the question of the

north-east frontier arose only 'on a side issue',* and said that it was 'only with considerable difficulty and almost by chance that we were able to unearth the true position'.[118] Caroe immediately began to urge a forward policy, at least on paper. He proposed that the Anglo-Tibetan agreements should be published without further delay, as their omission from Aitchison's *Treaties*, if noticed by the Chinese Government, 'might well be used by them in support of the argument that no ratified agreement between India and Tibet [was] in existence'. He also suggested that steps should at once be taken to show the McMahon Line as the boundary on official maps, pointing out that authoritative atlases such as those of *The Times*, following the official Survey of India, were still showing the boundary along the foot of the hills—as did Chinese atlases.[119] The London Government agreed that the Simla documents should be published in a new edition of Aitchison:[120] 'the reason for this new edition is that we want to publish unobtrusively the 1914 Tibetan Convention (never ratified by China)',[121] it was explained. So that the record might be changed 'unobtrusively'—indeed 'with the minimum publicity'—the new edition of volume XIV of Aitchison, published in fact in 1937, was passed off as the 1929 edition; and all copies of the original edition were ordered recalled and destroyed.[122] The only copy known to have escaped this suppression is in the Harvard Library. This falsification of evidence by the British Government looked to its arguing one day that it had regarded the Simla Convention as valid ever since 1914, and had therefore published the documents in the normal way in the first edition of Aitchison's *Treaties* after the conference. (Just this claim was in fact made in 1960, by independent India.)[123]

Also at this time, 1937, the Survey of India began to show the McMahon Line as the north-east boundary, qualifying it only as 'Undemarcated'. (Apparently not all departments were advised of the change, however, and a map of Tibet published by the Survey in 1938 showed the Tawang Tract as Tibetan, with its southern tip—where the boundary had been demarcated in 1872-3†—marked as a full international boundary.)[124] Commercial atlases followed suit, the first to

---

* This was the row caused by the unauthorized visit to Tibet of a British botanist and renowned traveller, F. Kingdon Ward. The Tibetans, who had admitted Ward on several previous occasions, were most annoyed when he entered their country in 1935 without seeking their permission, and complained to the British. That Ward's interests went beyond flora is suggested by his urging the British occupation of Tawang in the journal of the Royal Central Asian Society of October 1938.

† See p. 40 above.

reflect the change apparently being *The Times Handy Atlas* of 1940; but not all cartographers were as alert or responsive, and for years afterwards atlases sometimes showed India's north-eastern boundary at the foot of the hills. (The first edition of Jawaharlal Nehru's *Discovery of India*, published in 1946, had a map showing the boundary thus, and even in 1969 a new biography of Gandhi by Robert Payne was published with a map showing India's boundary beneath the foot-hills.)

The substituted new edition of Aitchison and the changed depiction of the north-east boundary in official maps signalled that the Indian Government had now taken the step which in 1914 it had not been prepared to take, and decided that the McMahon Line should be treated as the legal boundary. 'The continued exercise of jurisdiction by Tibet in Tawang might enable China or, still worse, might enable any other power which may in future be in the position to assert authority over Tibet, to claim prescriptive rights over a part of the territory recognized as within India by the 1914 Convention,' the Assam Government suggested[125] (the Russian bogey died hard). It was realized that maps and the covert publication of documents would not outweigh the fact of effective, long-established and indeed unchallenged Tibetan administration in Tawang, and New Delhi instructed the Assam Government to 'emphasize the interest of British India in the Tawang area either by *actual tours* or by *collecting the revenue* ourselves'.[126] The Governor of Assam replied that 'more impressive and permanent action is required if Tawang is to be effectively occupied and possible intrusion by China into that area forestalled'; and he proposed that a British officer with a substantial military escort be sent to reside in Tawang every summer. The Government in India was chary, however, and agreed only to a preliminary reconnaissance by a small expedition which would go to Tawang to 'examine the country, get in touch with the inhabitants, and form some estimate of its revenue possibilities' before a final decision was made.[127] True to rule, the Delhi Government balked when the local authorities urged a forward policy.

This expedition, under a Captain Lightfoot of the Indian Army, reached Tawang in April 1938. He had been told by the Government of Assam that there could be 'no possible doubt that the Indo-Tibetan boundary was definitely determined [by the McMahon Line]', and instructed to be 'scrupulously careful to give no impression that the matter can be reopened'. His presence in Tawang with an escort would itself be an assertion of British authority, he was assured; 'but your conduct in all things should be such as may be calculated to cause least shock to Tibetan susceptibilities'.[128] No sooner had Lightfoot reached Tawang than the Tibetan Government lodged a formal protest and asked for the withdrawal of the British party. In Tawang the Tibetan officials flaunted their authority by collecting taxes under his nose. He asked for permission to demand a Tibetan withdrawal from Tawang; that was refused, but he was told that he could 'inform all concerned that Tawang is by treaty Indian and not Tibetan territory, and should impress this on Tibetan officials if he meets them'. He was warned, however, to give no assurances to the local inhabitants, but simply to tell them that he was on a mission of inquiry and that 'Government will decide after he returns whether to take any further interest in them or not'. The Government had the grace to admit that those instructions might 'create difficulties for Lightfoot', but concluded that they were the only possible procedure until future policy had been decided. They were, at all events, averse to 'any action which would commit them to permanent occupation and further expenditure'.[129]

On his return Lightfoot, strongly backed by the Assam Governor, urged that the Tibetan officials be asked to withdraw from Tawang, and the head lamas of the monastery as well: 'so inextricably are State and Religion intermingled in Tibet that till the Tibetan monastic officials are withdrawn Tibetan influence and intrigue must persist in the surrounding country', he wrote. The local tribe, Monpas, who are Buddhist, should be encouraged to take over the monastery themselves, he thought; and as they disliked the Tibetans that should not be difficult to accomplish. Two agents of the British administration, 'Tibetan-speaking persons of good social position', should be appointed for the Tawang area to replace the ousted Tibetans; and the Assam Government hopefully put the low price-tag of Rs. 41,617 non-recurring and Rs. 37,896 recurring on the policy they were trying to sell.[130]

The argument for a forward policy was cogently urged by Sir Robert Reid, the Governor of Assam,* but, as always in these discussions of frontier policy, the moderates also had their say. At the beginning of 1939 H. J. Twynam, by then acting-Governor of Assam,

---

* Whose *History of the Frontier Areas Bordering on Assam* (Government of Assam Press, Shillong, 1942) is definitive. Reid wrote his book for the use of administrators concerned with border policy, and quotes fully from official files. It appears that the Government of China — like most people — was unaware of the existence of Reid's book when it argued its case from 1959 on.

challenged the proposal to complete the annexation of Tawang, on both practical and legal grounds. He reminded the Viceroy (Lord Linlithgow) that the Government itself had come to the view that the danger from China in the north-east had materially decreased. Then he asked: 'Are we on absolutely firm ground juridically as regards our rights under the Convention of 1914? . . . If one of three parties to a tripartite convention does not ratify, can another party to the convention claim that it is binding between itself and the third party?' He pointed out that the letters exchanged in 1914 between McMahon and the Tibetans were 'lacking in the formalities associated with a treaty'; and suggested that the fact that the Government had taken no steps to implement the McMahon Line from 1914 to 1938 must adversely affect its position, both in equity and in international law. Since it was part of British policy to remain on good terms with Tibet, he advised that alternatives should be considered before the Government occupied 'an area which has always been oriented towards Tibet ethnographically, politically and in religion', and which was under Tibetan administration. Among the alternatives Twynam proposed was that the McMahon Line should be modified to run through Se La, a towering pass a few miles to the south-east of Tawang, so that that monastery would be left to Tibet.*

Whether by force of argument or because the shadow of war in Europe put strategy on the north-east frontier in a different light—or simply for reasons of financial stringency— the moderates won the day on this occasion. New Delhi not only rejected the proposal for permanent occupation of Tawang, but also refused to authorize Lightfoot to repeat his visit lest that make permanent occupation necessary 'in order to fulfil obligations to the Monpas'.[131] They noted that all attempts in the previous two years to get Lhasa to acknowledge British rights in the Tawang area had failed, and concluded that for them to occupy it 'would be strongly resented by the Tibetan Government and endanger the friendly relations we have been at pains to cultivate. . . .' And anyway the Indian Government, discarding the theories of the armchair strategists, had now come to the conclusion that the 'McMahon Line would not be at all satisfactory [as a] defensive line owing to difficulty of access during the greater part of the year'. Accordingly London was

* The writer is indebted to Dr Karunakar Gupta for bringing this correspondence to his attention. It is in the India Office Library, under the reference Political (External) Department, Collection No. 36, File 23, and this letter is dated March 17th, 1939.

informed that it had been 'decided not to pursue the scheme for establishing control over Tawang'.[132]

The Tibetan Government had made it quite clear in 1936 that it was not prepared to accept any change in the status of Tawang. In the autumn of that year the British political officer in Sikkim, on a visit to Lhasa, discussed Tawang with officials there. He reported their attitude to be:

> That (1) up to 1914 Tawang had undoubtedly been Tibetan; (2) They regarded the adjustment of the Tibet-Indian boundary as part and parcel of the general adjustment and determination of boundaries contemplated in the 1914 [Simla] Convention. If they could, with our help, secure a definite Sino-Tibetan boundary they would of course be glad to observe the Indo-Tibetan border as defined in 1914; (3) They had been encouraged in thinking that His Majesty's Government sympathised with this way of regarding the matter owing to the fact that at no time since the Convention and Declaration of 1914 had the Indian Government taken steps to question Tibetan, or assert British authority in the Tawang area.[133]

In other words, the Tibetans held that their agreement to the McMahon alignment was dependent upon the *quid pro quo* of Britain's securing for them the status *vis à vis* China which they had sought in 1914.

The Second World War initially distracted the British from the problems of the north-east, as the First had done; but the entry of Japan and the consequent threat to India revived the forward policy and spurred a purposeful attempt to make the McMahon Line the effective boundary. As one of the officials concerned put it: 'The sudden realization that India's eastern borders were vulnerable had convinced the Government of the need to fill the political and administrative vacuum which had been allowed to persist between Assam and Tibet ever since the establishment of British rule.'[134] The task of making good the McMahon Line was given to J. P. Mills, the Government's adviser on tribal affairs, who saw it in these terms:

> The tribes to be incorporated [in India] belong naturally more to Tibet than to India. In race and in language they are Mongoloid. They all speak Tibeto-Burmese languages which have nothing in common with the Assamese of the Aryans of the plains. It follows

therefore that what one might call the cultural and social pull is
towards Tibet. . . . The [McMahon Line] therefore suffers from
the disability that though it may look well on the map . . . it is in
fact not the natural boundary, whereas the frontier along the plains
is the natural one.

Mills went on to point out that the tribal areas were commercially as
well as culturally tied to Tibet rather than to India, exporting grain and
madder (for dyeing monks' robes) to Tibet, and importing salt. He
concluded that 'the attachment [of the tribal areas] to India is an
unnatural one and therefore all the more difficult to maintain'.[135]*

Mills nevertheless took up his task energetically; he strongly believed
that, natural boundary or not, the extension of British administration
was in the interest of the tribal people. Taking a force up the Lohit, he
visited Rima and, over the protests of the Tibetans, established a post
at Walong; the Chinese had put up boundary markers just below
Walong in 1910, and the Tibetans maintained that the boundary lay
there and not some twenty miles upstream where the McMahon Line
put it. Moving up the valleys, 'penetrating slowly by gaining the
goodwill of the inhabitants by giving them much-needed medical
assistance' and pacifying their incessant feuds, and turning back
Tibetan tax-collectors, the British extended their hold. In 1944 Mills
moved into the Tawang Tract and reached Dirang Dzong. Here he was
in country very different from the tribal areas proper, to the east, with
their primitive, warring tribes; 'here one finds Buddhist monks, prayer
wheels, Buddhist temples and the rest,' Mills wrote. 'The population is
a settled one, with fixed cultivation, living in stone houses and using
plough cattle, which means they have excellent cantilever bridges to
enable them to take their cattle across the rivers. . . . The whole impression is that of a settled, civilised land.'[136] In fact Mills had moved
from the tribal areas into a part of Tibet, and he noted without surprise
that 'our claim to this country was strenuously opposed by both
Tibetan secular frontier officials and by monastic tax collectors.' Ignoring the protests of the Tibetan officials, he prevented them from collecting taxes ('they said that if they did not they would be executed when

---

* Sir Robert Reid said that the tribes 'are not Indian in any sense of the word, neither in
origin, nor in language, nor in appearance, nor in habits, nor in outlook, and it is only by
historical accident that they have been tacked on to an Indian province'.[137] After independence the tribes began trying to undo that accident, and strong separatist movements
developed in the 1960s.

they returned home—I said I could not help that') and set up an Assam Rifles post at Dirang Dzong. The Tibetans there reported to their superiors at Tsona Dzong:

> British officers and men came to Dirang. Like the little devils who trespassed on the land of the Buddha, they have defied the laws of the state, forcibly occupying the land and inciting my subjects by saying that it is forbidden to abide by the law and render services to Tibetan personnel such as rendering official services and paying taxes. Armed sentinels have been assigned with the special task of guarding all important passage ways. They have resorted to threats of armed force to prevent us from exercising authority on our own land. . . . Having reached the end of our patience we, your humble servants, cannot [but] appeal and report to our superiors and request that in the future we may be ensured of the exercise of authority over such properties as the estates on which our living depends. . . . If the present state of affairs should continue for long it will inevitably lead to a situation in which the guest would have usurped the place of the master of the house.[138]

The Lhasa authorities replied that 'the land in Monyul [the Tibetan name for the Tawang Tract] has always belonged to us beyond the shadow of a doubt' and ordered the local officials to continue collecting taxes and exacting corvée, while they protested to the British representative in the Tibetan capital, H. E. Richardson, and the political officer for the area, Basil Gould. They were told that the British would not withdraw from Dirang Dzong, since Britain regarded that territory as legally her own, and they were asked 'to give up minor considerations for broader interests, be far-sighted' and instruct their local officials not to try to levy taxes or corvée. But Gould made a significant and material concession, telling the Tibetans that his Government 'was willing to change the boundary, namely that starting from Se La it should run not to the north but to the south of Tawang'.[139]* McMahon had drawn his line to annex Tawang only at the last moment, it will be remembered, and he himself suggested that the boundary should be open to modification, 'should it be found desirable in the light of more detailed knowledge' acquired later.[140] Se La would in fact make a much better boundary alignment than the

* He confirmed this in an aide-mémoire which the Chinese side introduced in the 1960 officials' talks.[141]

one which McMahon arbitrarily drew north of Tawang, where there
is no salient topographical feature to which the boundary can readily
be related. Se La is on a towering ridge; the pass itself is at an altitude
of nearly 16,000 feet, and the ridge is a watershed, dividing streams
running north-west into the Tawang River from those running south-
east. The great monastery at Tawang was, for the Tibetans, the heart
of the matter, and if that had been left to them their attempts to retain
Dirang Dzong and the rest of the Tawang Tract might well have been
dropped. At all events, the concession offered to the Tibetans by Gould
in 1944 indicates that the Government in India had accepted Twynam's
suggestion that Tawang should be left to Tibet, by modifying the
McMahon Line to run through Se La.

By 1947, when they relinquished their Indian empire, the British
had thus made a start in translating the McMahon Line from the maps
—upon which it had begun to appear only ten years before—to the
ground as the effective north-east boundary of India. Posts had been
established at Dirang Dzong, Walong, and several other places in the
tribal territory, manned by the Assam Rifles (a para-military border
force), and Tibetan administration had been extruded from those areas.
Expeditions up other valleys had made the tribesmen aware of Britain
as the administering power. The departing British were assured by
their successors in New Delhi that the new Indian Government would
complete their work in the tribal belt: 'If anything, they intended to
pursue an even more forward policy than had the British.'[142]

* * * * * * * * * * *

The position along the northern borders which the British bequeathed to independent India was thus of mixed value: there were
some sound assets, but there were also unsolved problems.

The Chinese had been unable since 1911 to assert themselves in
Tibet, which had enjoyed *de facto* independence for more than thirty
years. British influence reached across the Himalayas, and was expressed in Tibet in the presence of a permanent British official in Lhasa,
through whom Tibet could be said to be in quasi-diplomatic relations
with Britain. The British also enjoyed the right to maintain small
military escorts for their trade officers at Yatung and Gyantse, and had
set up postal, telegraph and even telephone services linking the main
trading centres in southern Tibet. A dozen rest-houses had been built

to accommodate officials on the move between the trade agencies, or touring the various markets for the trans-Himalayan trade. All of these rights and facilities were inherited by independent India in 1947; but they derived formally from agreements Britain had with *with China,** and the Chinese had throughout made it plain that, as far as they were concerned, Tibet was part of China. Tibet had no international identity, her independence was shadowy and tenuous—a reflection, indeed, only of the weakness of the Chinese Central Government. Up to the last the British sustained their attempt to nourish and confirm Tibet's *de facto* independence, beneath 'formal Chinese suzerainty', and in 1943 proposed to the United States that Tibet's right to exchange diplomatic representatives with other powers should be recognized. But the Americans rejected the proposal:

> The Government of the United States has borne in mind the fact that the Chinese Government has long claimed suzerainty over Tibet and that the Chinese constitution lists Tibet among areas constituting the territory of the Republic of China. This Government has at no time raised a question regarding either of those claims.[143]

If the always rather high-flown hope of making Tibet a buffer state by formally and permanently excluding Chinese power had thus eluded the British, they had been far more successful in the cis-Himalayan states, Nepal, Sikkim and Bhutan. Nepal, though not in formal subservience to Britain, had relations with no other government and was plainly and exclusively within Britain's sphere of interest. Sikkim was a British protectorate by treaty; Bhutan was treaty-bound to be guided by Britain in the conduct of her foreign relations. The 'chain of protectorates', as Curzon had called it, was secure. But the British had failed to anchor it with boundary agreements with China.

In the north-west, the British had made no further formal move about the boundary alignment after their abortive approach to Peking in 1899, and there had been no boundary delimitation whatever; that task was left to the successor powers, India and Pakistan. In the north-east, the McMahon Line had secretly been agreed with the Tibetans; but from the beginning it had been repudiated by China, and was in practice being ignored by Tibet.

---

* The Anglo-Tibetan trade agreement signed in 1914 in pursuance of the Simla Conference had been published in 1937, but had of course never been recognized by China.

Britain had enjoyed great advantages which her heirs would lack: first, power of a reach and magnitude that could be brought to bear far beyond the confines of the Himalayas; secondly, the fact that the boundaries of her Indian empire were not the object of popular political pressures, either in England or in India. The territorial imperative was never engaged. British statesmen and officials, therefore, did not have to concern themselves with the emotional connotations of soil and sovereignty, they could 'bear in mind that it is not a strip more or less of barren or even productive territory that we want, but a clear and well-defined boundary'.[144] That, in spite of those advantages, Britain left unresolved boundary problems to the inheritors of her authority on the sub-continent must be counted a considerable failure, and it was one which would cost India dear.

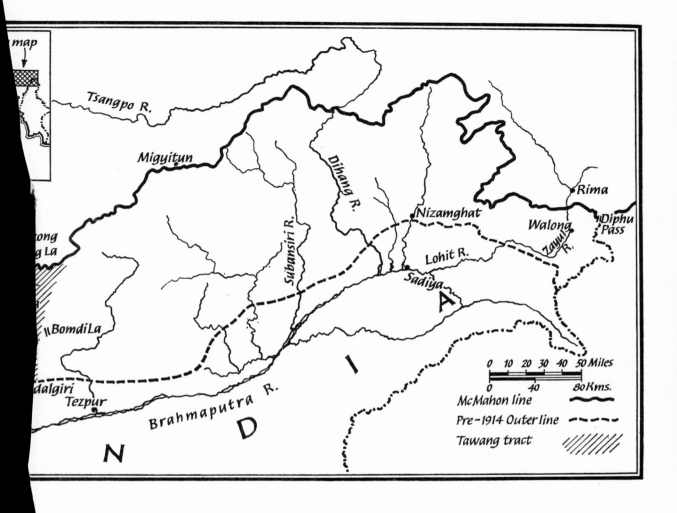

map

Tsangpo R.

Migyitun

Dihang R.

Subansiri R.

Nizamghat

Rima

Walong

Diphu
Pass

Lohit R.

Zayul R.

Sadiya

ong
g La

A

Bomdi La

I

dalgiri

Tezpur

N

Brahmaputra R.

D

0 10 20 30 40 50 Miles

0   40   80 Kms.

McMahon line

Pre-1914 Outer line

Tawang tract

Area of main

Tsona Dz
Khinzemane
Tulung
Tawang
Tawang R.
Jang R.
De L
BHUTAN

Part I

COLLISION COURSE

Our maps show that the McMahon Line is our boundary and that is our boundary, map or no map. That fact remains and we stand by that boundary, and we will not let anybody come across that boundary.

Jawaharlal Nehru, Lok Sabha, 1950.[1]

Whoever by words written or spoken, or by signs, or by visible representations or otherwise, questions the territorial integrity of India in a manner which is, or is likely to be, prejudicial to the interests or safety or security of India, shall be punishable with imprisonment for a term which may extend to three years, or with a fine or both.

Indian Criminal Law Amendment Act (1961) Section 2

It is queer that lines drawn by British officials should have been consecrated as precious national assets of the British Indian Empire's non-British successor states. At the time when those lines were drawn the transaction produced no stir among the . . . Indian . . . subjects, as they then were, of the British crown. If any of them paid any attention to what Durand and McMahon were doing, they will have written it off as just another move in the immoral game of power politics that the British Imperialists were playing at the Indian tax–payers' expense. The present consecration of these British–made lines as heirlooms in the successor states' national heritages is an unexpected and unfortunate turn of History's wheel.

Arnold Toynbee[2]

The first and almost instinctive reaction of every new government was to hold fast to the territory bequeathed to it. What the colonial power had ruled, the new state must rule.

Gunnar Myrdal[3]

(i) *The Course is Set*

At midnight on August 14th, 1947, when India, in Jawaharlal Nehru's words, kept her tryst with destiny and became an independent nation, an invisible but profound change came over her boundaries. Until that moment they had been the concern of Englishmen: strategists and statesmen seeing the interest of the sub-continent in terms of Britain's stake there, concerned with the repercussions of the threat from Russia or China on British investments, or on Parliament in London. The national interests of Indians were not a factor in British calculations, except in so far as it occurred to Englishmen that it would not do for the people they ruled to come into unsettling contact with either Russians or Chinese across the borders. 'The prestige indispensable to the rule of the British over India demanded that their subjects should not be allowed to see on any horizon the rise of a power even remotely comparable to that of the British empire.'[4] As for the Indians, they saw in Britain's attempts to consolidate India's borders nothing but measures to confirm their own subjection, and deplored the Government's frontier policy—when they noticed it at all.*

With independence, all that changed. The boundaries of India ceased to be the pawns of the British in their Great Games with their imperial rivals, and became the cell walls of a new national identity. No longer could boundaries be conceived or shifted by men whose concern was not territory but strategic advantage; henceforth they enclosed the sacred soil of the motherland, and politicians could tamper with them only at their peril.

So far as the northern borders were concerned, the policy of the new Indian Government diverged not at all from that of the departed British. In the case of Sikkim, India in 1949 seized the opportunity of a local uprising against the ruler to send in troops, and bring the state

---

* In 1921 the Congress Party resolved that the Government's policy had 'been traditionally guided by considerations more of holding India in subjection than of protecting her borders . . . that India as a self-governing country can have nothing to fear from her neighbouring states . . .' and therefore urged those states 'having no illwill against the people of India . . . to refrain from entering into any treaty with the Imperial Power'.[5]

into closer dependence as a protectorate than it had formally been under
the British; in the same year India signed a treaty with Bhutan, in
which she took over Britain's right to guide Bhutan in foreign affairs.
New Delhi's influence in Nepal continued to be paramount, and was
increased in 1950 when the Indian Government helped the King of
Nepal to break the century-old rule of the Rana clan. The new Government thus took over and consolidated the 'chain of protectorates', as
Curzon had described the Himalayan states.

Independent India also at first continued British policy towards
Tibet. This continuity was symbolized — and no doubt reinforced —
by the retention of the last British representative in Lhasa, H. E.
Richardson, to represent India. The British mission in Lhasa formally
became the Indian mission on August 15th, 1947. 'The transition was
almost imperceptible,' Richardson was to write; 'the existing staff was
retained in its entirety and the only obvious change was the change in
the flag.'[6]

The Tibetan Government was at this time seeking to give legal
status and international recognition to the *de facto* independence it had
enjoyed since 1911, and the Nationalist Government in China, by then
on its last legs, could do little to head off this attempt. In mid-1949 the
Tibetans expelled the Chinese mission from Lhasa, with the explanation that they feared the Chinese might be, or become, Communist;
the Chinese Nationalists suspected the hand of Richardson and the
Indians in this act.[7] The Tibetans, alarmed by such portents as the drip
of water from the mouth of a gilded wooden dragon in Lhasa[8] — as
well, perhaps, as by the prospect of a new and strong Government in
Peking — began to build up their army. A request to India for arms and
ammunition was favourably received, and high-ranking officers of the
Indian Army were sent to Tibet to get this programme of military aid
under way.[9]

This continuance of British encouragement of Tibetan separatism
was only reasonable, from the Indian point of view. It was not only
that their strategic and geopolitical thinking was conditioned by the
long British precedent, policy formulation in the new Government
continued often in the same official care as it had been just before independence. Senior Indian officers of the Indian Civil Service of course
continued in the ministries, moving up to replace their British colleagues; Richardson's reports and advice from Lhasa must have carried
much weight, and his commitment to the cause of an independent

Tibet shows clearly in his book, *Tibet and its History*. But by almost any considerations, continued exclusion of China's authority from Tibet was plainly in India's interest, and therefore the new Government, like the old, directed its policy to that end, and to the increase of Indian influence in Tibet. It was equally natural, however, for the Chinese to see such policy as hostile to their own interests, and even before they came to power the Chinese Communists were denouncing India, and especially Nehru, for cherishing 'imperialist designs for the annexation of Tibet'.[10]

The Indian Government was soon shown that unresolved territorial problems along the northern borders were among its inheritance. The Chinese Nationalist Government had been complaining in a series of notes since 1945 about British inroads into the tribal territory beneath the McMahon Line; at the earliest opportunity, in February 1947, they lodged this complaint with the Indian mission which was by then established in China. The complaint was rejected with the retort that the tribal belt in the north-east was Indian territory. One of the last acts of the Chinese Nationalists' Ambassador in New Delhi was to remind the Indian Government that China did not recognize the McMahon Line, and held the Simla Convention invalid.[11]

The Tibetans, for their part, seem to have hoped that the transfer of British power to the Indians offered an opportunity for them to regain all the territory that the British had taken from them over the previous century or so. In October 1947 they formally asked India to return to Tibet a wide swathe of territory from Ladakh to Assam, and including Sikkim and the Darjeeling district.[12]* In reply, the Indians merely asked for an assurance that Tibet would agree to the continuance of relations on the basis previously existing with the British Government.

If the Indians' attempt to continue British policy in the Himalayas and beyond was understandable, it was almost most unlikely to succeed. For the previous hundred years and longer, the dominant influence in the Himalayan belt had been that of the British Raj. Not only did Britain have a great local preponderance of power, she could also bring vast economic and military resources to bear outside the

---

* The British had noted the charms of the hill village of Dorji-ling, in Sikkim, in the 1820s, and concluded that it would make a splendid resort from the blazing heat of the plains. There were political considerations, too: it occurred to the British that 'an island of well-governed British territory in the prevailing sea of Sikkim misrule' must benefit their interest in the cis-Himalayan areas. In 1835 the ruler of Sikkim reluctantly agreed to cede the tract, now spelled Darjeeling, to Britain.[13]

sub-continent when necessary, and these had in fact repeatedly been deployed against China. The withdrawal of British power from the sub-continent in 1947 prepared the way for a reversal of the balance that had existed across the Himalayas; the emergence in China of a strong central authority, with the establishment of the People's Republic in 1949, confirmed the shift. Henceforth the advantage would lie north of the Himalayas, not south. This change was demonstrated and confirmed by China's reassertion of her authority in Tibet.

The reassertion of central authority in Tibet at the earliest possible moment had been the repeatedly affirmed intention of the Chinese Communists, as it had been of the Nationalists; and almost as soon as the People's Republic of China was established (October 1st, 1949) it was announced in Peking that the army would shortly be marching into Tibet. India reacted sharply. In a diplomatic note New Delhi warned the new Government in Peking that Chinese military action in Tibet would jeopardize the efforts that were being made — with India in the leading role — to have the People's Republic rather than the Nationalist rump on Formosa represent China in the United Nations. But a few days after that was delivered in Peking it was announced that the army had been ordered to move into Tibet; and New Delhi followed up with an angrily worded protest, deploring the 'invasion' of Tibet and China's use of force to settle the question of her relationship with the Tibetans. China's reply was just as sharp: 'Tibet is an integral part of China, and the problem of Tibet is entirely a domestic problem of China. The Chinese People's Liberation Army must enter Tibet, liberate the Tibetan people, and defend the frontiers of China.' China said she wished to continue peacefully negotiating with the Tibetans — and blamed India for detaining a Tibetan delegation bound for Peking — but warned that no foreign interference would be tolerated. As for India's point that military action in Tibet would injure China's reputation in the world, Peking replied that if unfriendly governments used the exercise of China's sovereign rights in Tibet as a pretext for further obstruction of her U.N. membership, that would only be another demonstration of their hostility. The two problems, the Chinese said, were unrelated.[14]

It appears that up to this time, while recognizing that in the past the *de jure* relationship between Tibet and China had been closer, the Indian Government hoped that Peking would be content with a position in Tibet parallel with India's in Bhutan; that is, one that would

leave the Tibetans to run their own domestic affairs, with China insisting only that they have no relations with any government other
than China's. This suggestion derives from the Indian use in these
notes of the term 'suzerainty' to describe China's position in Tibet.*

In the view from Peking, however, the apparent Indian desire to see
Tibet enjoying semi-independent status was seen as a preliminary to an
attempt to draw Tibet out of China and bring it under Indian influence. 'Since the Indian Government has announced its suzerainty
over Bhutan and declared that Tibet has never recognized Chinese
suzerainty,' a writer in the *People's Daily* asked in September 1949,
'will it not declare suzerainty over Tibet?'[15] The inference was neither
far-fetched nor unfair. The Himalayan marches of China and India are
naturally and inevitably an area of competition between them, with
both using whatever inducements or pressures may serve the purpose
of extending or confirming their own influence there and, if possible,
excluding the other's. But, and again perhaps inevitably, each side is
ready to regard the other's actions as sinister or malign; hence China's
angry and suspicious reaction to India's *démarche* over the Chinese
move into Tibet; hence the anger and apprehension in India when the
Chinese did return to Tibet, and the dismay later when China opened
diplomatic relations with Nepal, thus becoming an open competitor
in what had previously been an Indian diplomatic preserve.

Faced with the accomplished return of Chinese power to Tibet in
1950, the Indian Government reacted pragmatically. The attempt to
foster at least a degree of Tibetan independence, to maintain some
element of buffer status for Tibet, had failed. Physically, there was
nothing India could do about it: military intervention, braving immense logistical difficulties as well as war with China, was beyond
practical consideration.† The choice was between commitment to the

---

* A curious feature of the 1950 Indian notes about China's intentions in Tibet was that in
the text of the notes released in New Delhi the word 'suzerainty' is used; while in the text
released by the Chinese Government the word 'sovereignty' appears instead. Did the
Indian Government modify the term for consumption at home, where its Tibet policy
was already under attack? Or, as later widely suspected in India, did the Indian Ambassador, K. M. Panikkar, substitute 'sovereignty' for 'suzerainty' before delivering the note
in Peking? Or did the Chinese change the word before releasing the text of the Indian
note? The last explanation would seem to justify a strenuous Indian objection, which was
not forthcoming; the puzzle remains unsolved.
† Or was the Indian Government tempted to intervene militarily in Tibet in 1950? The
last British officer in command of India's eastern defences, Lieutenant-General Sir Francis
Tuker, had recommended only three years before that 'rather than see a Chinese occupation of Tibet, India should be prepared to occupy the plateau herself',[16] and according to
one writer President Truman offered transport aircraft to help India defend Tibet; 'The

lost cause of Tibetan independence, or of pursuing a policy of friendly relations with China. Friendship with China had always been central to Nehru's thinking about India's foreign policy, and the choice cannot have been difficult. India did not support Tibet's appeal to the United Nations, and as the Chinese confirmed their authority in Tibet so Indian ambivalence about China's right to be there faded, and with it the Tibet question as a cause of ill-will between Peking and New Delhi. The Chinese did not make a public issue of India's protest at their actions in Tibet. They published the diplomatic exchanges, but then soft-pedalled the whole affair.[17]

The arrival of Chinese power on the northern borders in 1950 alarmed political opinion in India, just as the reassertion of Manchu power forty years before had alarmed the British. The alarm was greatest on the political right, where the Communist nature of Chinese power was most feared, and Nehru and the Government were attacked for acquiescing in China's move into Tibet. This meant that the sharpest critics of Nehru's China policy were also his opponents in every other aspect of policy, domestic and foreign; this seems to have made him stronger to resist them at first, and, later, more reluctant to affront them.

The Government's Tibet policy was strongly attacked in Parliament, and Vallabhbhai Patel, deputy Prime Minister and Nehru's great rival, wrote him a long, critical letter in November 1950. Patel implied that Panikkar, the Indian Ambassador in Peking, had had the wool pulled over his eyes by the Chinese, whom he accused of perfidy and malevolence and described as a potential enemy. He warned that China's move into Tibet 'throws into the melting pot all frontier and commercial settlements with Tibet, on which we have been functioning and acting during the last half a century'. Implicitly accusing Nehru of complacency and vacillation, Patel proposed a fundamental reappraisal of China policy, including redeployment of India's forces to guard areas likely to be the subject of dispute.* Nehru's reply to this

---

estimate was that India had only to send a brigade of troops to Tibet and China would have held off. Truman is reported to have concurred and expressed his willingness to make the required air transport available.' (A. B. Shah, in *India's Defence and Foreign Policies*, Manaktala, Bombay, 1966; p. 87.)

To entangle China in a second front against India during the Korean war might have suited Washington; but, if the offer was made, New Delhi must have seen the risks and sterility of such an expedition in the steps of Younghusband, and declined.

* This letter was published for the first time in 1968, in a Bombay weekly. It is published as an appendix in Dalvi, *Himalayan Blunder* (Thacker & Co., Bombay, 1969) and Kuldip Nayar, *Between the Lines* (Allied Publishers, Bombay, 1969).

letter has not been published, but its gist might be inferred from what
he did: he maintained his policy of friendship to China, continuing to
champion her cause in the United Nations; but he had already ordered
Indian administration to be extended through the North-East Frontier
Agency (NEFA), as the tribal belt beneath the McMahon Line had now
been named.

At the end of 1949 the situation in NEFA was much as the British had
left it, with a post at Walong, near the McMahon Line's eastern extremity, but Indian positions still well back from the Line in other
sectors. Penetration of the Tawang Tract was still halted at Dirang
Dzong; Tibetan administration in Tawang was still unchallenged.
Within another year, however, twenty additional posts were set up in
NEFA, and in February 1951 an Indian official with an escort and several
hundred porters moved into Tawang. The Indian Government had
apparently decided against the modification of the McMahon Line
that (by the evidence of Gould's 1944 proposal to the Tibetans) their
predecessors had favoured at the last, and meant to push their boundary
up from Se La to the alignment McMahon had drawn. The Tibetan
authorities in Lhasa protested, but were simply told by the Indian
political officer that India was taking over Tawang. The Tibetans protested again, accusing the Indian Government of 'seizing as its own
what did not belong to it'. This 'we deeply regret and absolutely cannot accept', the Tibetans went on, and asked New Delhi to withdraw
their force from Tawang immediately.[18] The protests were ignored; the
Indians stayed on in Tawang and forced out the Tibetan administration, as the British had forced it out of Dirang Dzong in 1944. With
this, the 'dangerous wedge' of Tibetan/Chinese territory that had so
worried the British General Staff was at last physically removed, and
the McMahon Line was in general transposed from the maps to the
ground as the *de facto* north-east boundary of India.

That the Indian Government should have directed notice of their
intention to take over Tawang to the Tibetan Government at Lhasa —
rather than to Peking — is understandable. Although New Delhi now
accepted China's sovereignty in Tibet it made diplomatic sense to treat
the matter of Tawang as a local question, leaving it to Peking to protest. In the event, the Chinese Government made no comment at all
on the Indian move, so far as the record shows. This otherwise puzzling
silence can be construed only as China's acquiescence in India's filling
out to the McMahon Line.

3*

The move into Tawang met with only verbal resistance from the Tibetans, but the tribal people took a toll in blood for the extension of Indian administration elsewhere in NEFA. A strong Assam Rifles patrol, moving up the Subansiri River in the early 1950s, was warmly welcomed by one of the tribes, feasted and given shelter—and then massacred almost to a man. Seventy-three riflemen and civilians died. The Government dispatched a punitive expedition but seems, under Nehru's orders, to have been content with an overwhelming show of force and did not burn villages and take prisoners as the British would certainly have done.[19]

That the Indian Government would continue its predecessor's policy towards the McMahon Line was more than natural, it was axiomatic.

The strategic and geopolitical considerations that had formed Britain's approach to the north-east border applied with equal force for the new Government. Strategically, a boundary which put the Chinese on the verge of the Brahmaputra valley was as intolerable to the Indian General Staff as it had been to their British predecessors; a boundary on the crest-line, where McMahon had drawn it, had every advantage over a line at the foot of the hills. It was recognized that the population along the north-east frontier was ethnically and culturally closer to Tibet than to India, but this was seen as the more reason to bring it under Indian administration.[20] Beneath such practical considerations, the territorial imperative in its political expression was now, no doubt, engaged; as Gunnar Myrdal puts it, 'the first and almost instinctive reaction of every new government was to hold fast to the territory bequeathed to it. What the colonial power had ruled, the new state must rule'.[21]

The only question for the Indian Government, then, was how should it deal with the fact that China had repudiated the McMahon Line? Again, the British precedent provided part of the answer; India would simply treat the McMahon Line as the boundary, leaving it to China to protest if she liked at the *fait accompli* of Indian administration of the tribal areas. But, furthermore, it was decided that *India would refuse to open the question to negotiation when or if the Chinese did raise it*. To the Indians this latter decision may have seemed a corollary of the policy of making the McMahon Line the *de facto* boundary; but, as later developments will show, the decision to refuse to submit the McMahon Line to the process of negotiation was itself a major step, pregnant with momentous consequences. It was, indeed, to make the Sino-Indian boundary problem insoluble.

The step from insistence on a particular boundary alignment to refusal to open boundary negotiations is in fact a leap from diplomacy to an absolutist approach. However unyielding the position taken at negotiations, the context allows the parties to evolve at the least face-saving formulations, at the best, through concessions in some other area or dimension, a mutually satisfactory compromise. But an un-yielding position coupled with a refusal to negotiate leaves no way out except acquiescence by one side in a resolution unilaterally imposed by the other. When such an approach is applied to boundary questions it points the way to armed contention for disputed territory.

The adoption of this approach to the McMahon Line as Indian policy was signalled in November 1950, under the device of a parliamentary question. The Prime Minister (and Nehru was also Minister for External Affairs) was asked to state whether India had a well-defined boundary with Tibet, and replied:

Tibet is contiguous to India from the region of Ladakh to the boundary of Nepal, and from Bhutan to the Irrawaddy/Salween divide in Assam. The frontier from Bhutan eastwards has been clearly defined by the McMahon Line which was fixed by the Simla Convention of 1914. The frontier from Ladakh to Nepal is defined chiefly by long usage and custom.

A member asked whether the boundary was recognized by Tibet: 'I think parts of it have been recognized,' Nehru replied; 'it depends on what part the honourable member is considering.' He was then asked about reports that a new Chinese map showed a boundary on the Brahmaputra valley. 'No, sir. There is no new map of China so far as we know. But all the maps of China for the last thirty years have shown a certain portion of that north-east frontier which is now part of India as not part of India.' Pressed further on the subject of Chinese maps, Nehru closed the exchange with this statement: 'Our maps show that the McMahon Line is our boundary and that is our boundary—map or no map. That fact remains and we stand by that boundary, and we will not allow anybody to come across that boundary.'[22]

This approach—making it clear, on the ground and in official statements, that India regarded the McMahon Line as the boundary, *while making no direct communication to China on that score* — was challenged within the Indian Government in 1952.

By this time India had already let pass one opportunity to formalize the status of the McMahon Line. In September 1951 Chou En-lai, Prime Minister of China, suggested to the Indian Ambassador in Peking that the question of stabilization of the Tibetan frontier should be taken up as early as possible, and proposed that it should be done through discussions between India, China and Nepal. Chou also stated, according to the Indian record of the conversation, that 'there was no territorial dispute or controversy between India and China'[23] — further confirmation that China had decided to accept the McMahon align-ment as India's north-east boundary.

The Indian Government replied that it would welcome negotiations such as Chou En-lai had proposed. But the Chinese did not follow up their own suggestion, nor did the Indians: 'It was our belief that since our frontier was clear, there was no question of raising this issue by us,' Nehru explained later.[24] Instead, the two Governments took up the question of adapting India's imperial inheritance of rights in Tibet to contemporary conditions. In July 1952 China formally proposed settling 'pending specific problems' arising from India's inherited rights and assets in Tibet, citing such heads for discussion as commercial inter-course, trade, and the treatment of Indian nationals. India, having previously intimated to China that she was prepared to come to a mutually satisfactory settlement over India's existing rights in Tibet, agreed. Neither side referred again to the boundary question.

It was at this point that the decision not to raise the question of the McMahon Line was challenged in India, at a high level. Sir G. S. Bajpai, one of the most distinguished members of the Indian Civil Service with which the British had ruled the country, had been inde-pendent India's first Secretary-General.* By 1952 Bajpai had retired, and was now Governor of Bombay. From that position he wrote to his old ministry, urging that India should take the initiative in raising the question of the McMahon Line with the Chinese Government. He warned that to China the McMahon Line might be one of those 'scars left by Britain in the course of her aggression against China, [who] may seek to heal or erase this scar on the basis of frontier rectifications that may not be either to our liking or our interest'.

---

* The Secretary-General was the senior official in the Ministry of External Affairs; next came the Foreign Secretary, and then the Commonwealth Secretary.

Nehru discussed this suggestion with K. M. Panikkar, the Ambassador to China, who was in New Delhi for consultations, and Panikkar replied to Bajpai. He told him that the Prime Minister had decided that it was not in India's interest to raise the question of the McMahon Line. Nehru, he explained, had taken the view that, since India had unequivocally and publicly stated that she regarded the McMahon Line as the boundary, it should be left to China to raise the subject. If India were to do so, 'we would force [the Chinese] to one of two attitudes: either the acceptance of a treaty signed by us with Tibet, or a refusal of it [coupled] with an offer to negotiate. The first is not altogether easy to imagine, considering that every previous Chinese Government has refused in terms to accept an Indo-Tibetan treaty as binding on them. The second would not be advantageous to us.'

If, on the other hand, 'China raised the issue', Panikkar went on, 'we can plainly refuse to reopen the question and take our stand that the Prime Minister took [in his public statement], that the territory on this side of the McMahon Line is ours, and there is nothing to discuss about it.'

Bajpai was not persuaded. He pointed out that China had asked for a settlement of all 'pending problems', and that the Chinese, 'never having accepted the McMahon Line as the frontier between Tibet and us, can hardly regard this frontier as settled. Naturally, they have no intention of raising it until it suits their convenience.' He argued that India should simply take the opportunity to inform China that she regarded the McMahon Line as the boundary, and intended to treat it as such. The Chinese could then either agree, ignore the statement (allowing silence to be interpreted as acquiescence), or disagree. In any case, India would know where she stood. But the decision had already been taken, and Bajpai's last comments were a footnote to a closed issue.[25]

So the Indian delegation in the 1954 negotiations for a new agreement on trade and intercourse in Tibet made no mention of the boundary question, and indeed went out of their way to avoid the subject. Not only that, the Indians made no allusion to the trade agreement the British had signed with the Tibetans in 1914, in pursuance of the Simla Convention, but treated the negotiations as if their only antecedent lay in a 1908 trade agreement which *China* had signed with Britain. This expressed the reversal in Indian policy towards Tibet which had taken place when the Chinese reimposed their authority there. In 1948 the Nationalist Chinese Government had pointed out to India that the 1908 agreement, valid for thirty years, was due for re-negotiation. The Indian Government replied that it recognized the validity only of the 1914 agreement with Tibet; it was this reply that drew from the Chinese Nationalists the reaffirmation that China held the Simla Convention and all its products invalid.[26]

By waiving the 1914 antecedent, the Indians may have appeared to the Chinese to be moderating their earlier stand, and tacitly conceding that the Simla Convention and its related agreements were not legally valid. The Chinese at this time can have been in no doubt that India meant to keep the McMahon alignment as her north-eastern boundary, and, as has been seen, they had already indicated their acquiescence in this; but the Indian position at the 1954 negotiations could have suggested that India would be prepared in due course to submit the *de facto* north-east boundary to ratification by diplomatic process.

The 1954 negotiations were thus concerned only with the Indian mission at Lhasa; the trade agencies at Gyantse, Yatung and Gartok, and general trade questions; postal and telegraphic installations; the military escorts which, by right inherited from Britain, India maintained in Tibet; and pilgrimages. The boundary question came up indirectly, however, in discussion of the use of passes in the middle sector* of the borders. The Chinese draft said, '[China] agrees to open the following passes . . . for entry and exit by traders and pilgrims'; the wording reflected the claim that Tibetan (and therefore Chinese) jurisdiction extended beyond the main passes in this sector. The Indians — like the British before them — maintained that the boundary followed the watershed and that consequently the main passes were themselves boundary features. Therefore they rejected the Chinese formulation; but, rather than bringing the issue into the open, they accepted a wording which avoided the question of ownership of the actual passes: 'Traders . . . may travel by the following passes. . . .'[27] The two delegations agreed, at least tacitly, that the boundary question should not be introduced into these negotiations.

Later, when the dispute had emerged, the Indians were to maintain

---

* For the sake of clarity, the discussion between New Delhi and Peking in the 1960s divided the boundary into three sectors: the western sector, running from the Karakoram Pass to Demchok on the Indus; the middle sector, running from there to the Nepal boundary and covering, on the Indian side, Uttar Pradesh and Himachal Pradesh; and the eastern sector, running from Bhutan to Burma — i.e. the McMahon Line. Those terms will be used here throughout.

that they had not raised the boundary question on this occasion 'because, so far as the Government of India were concerned, the boundary was well known and beyond dispute, and there could be no question regarding it'.[28] They went on to say: 'The Indian delegation throughout took the line that all questions at issue between the two countries were being considered and, once the settlement was concluded, no question remained.'[29] But it can be seen from the Bajpai/Panikkar correspondence that in fact the Indian Government was fully aware that China did not regard the McMahon Line as formally settled. Moreover, the Chinese draft which the Indians rejected showed that the two sides disagreed over the boundary alignment in the middle sector. The later Indian argument that the negotiations on trade in Tibet foreclosed the boundary question appears therefore to have been disingenuous. It suggests that the Indians' intention in 1954 was to put China in a position which would make it possible to argue that, because the Chinese had not raised the boundary question, they had tacitly agreed that it was already settled.

Confirmation that in effect the Indians were at this time attempting to foreclose the boundary question, on their own terms, is to be found in a memorandum dictated by Nehru in July 1954, three months after the Tibetan agreement had been concluded. But before considering that memorandum something must be noted of the substance of the 1954 agreement on trade in Tibet.*

This unequivocally recognized China's sovereignty in Tibet — referring to the latter as 'the Tibet region of China' — and thus formally buried the attempt, started by the British and carried on tentatively by India immediately after independence, to deal with Lhasa as if Tibet were independent. Then, the agreement stated in its preamble the famous 'Five Principles of Peaceful Co-existence', or 'Panch Sheel', as the Indians called them:

Mutual respect for each other's territorial integrity and sovereignty.
Mutual non-aggression.
Mutual non-interference in each other's internal affairs.
Equality and mutual benefit.
Peaceful co-existence.

* Agreement between the Republic of India and the People's Republic of China on Trade and Intercourse between the Tibet Region of China and India, signed at Peking on April 29th, 1954. The text of the agreement and the related notes is given in White Paper I, pp. 98–107.

There was nothing new in the five principles themselves—indeed the first and fourth of them had been articulated as principles of China's foreign policy in just those words by Mao Tse-tung, in a speech in 1949.[30] According to one account, this application of the term 'Panch Sheel' can be credited to Nehru, who said that he had heard the 'happy phrase' in Indonesia but claimed that it had its roots deep in Indian moral tradition. 'Panch Sheel' has aptly been described as 'a catchword, suggestive of ancient concepts but without any real links with the past other than a spirit which can be found in the heritage of all known religions';[31] but it became the slogan for the moral aspirations behind India's foreign policy at this time, and especially it signalled and symbolized the opening of a period of demonstrative friendship between India and China. Opposition to and criticism of Nehru's China policy continued in India, but only as an undercurrent. The vision of the two great new republics of Asia marching in friendship towards a reformed future had a powerful appeal to Indian nationalism, and Panch Sheel was felt to be not only the guide for India's relations with China, but a beacon for all nations.

Nehru's memorandum tied the agreement on Tibet to the question of the boundaries. Circulated to the ministries concerned, this memorandum described the agreement as 'a new starting point of our relations with China and Tibet'. The Prime Minister then wrote: 'Both as flowing from our policy and as a consequence of our agreement with China, this [northern] frontier should be considered a firm and definite one, which is not open to discussion with anybody. A system of checkposts should be spread along this entire frontier. More especially, we should have checkposts in such places as might be considered disputed areas.'[32]

The intention behind this crucial policy directive is clear: India should fill out to what she considered her proper boundaries, and then decline to discuss them with China. Having agreed in the Panch Sheel preamble to respect India's territorial integrity and sovereignty, China would have no course but to accept the *fait accompli*.

So far as Nehru and his advisers were concerned, this may have seemed no more than the application to the whole northern border of the policy previously applied to the McMahon Line: that India would make clear the alignment she regarded as her boundary, treat it as such, leaving it to China to protest, and then 'refuse to reopen the question'. In the four years since Nehru had publicly declared the McMahon Line to be India's north-eastern boundary there had been no demurral from Peking; indeed Chinese acquiescence in the 1951 Indian take-over of Tawang showed that Peking was not going to make an issue out of the McMahon Line. To extend this approach to the other sectors of the boundary must have appeared to the Indians to be a logical and necessary step. But, in fact, by ruling that the remaining stretch of the northern borders should be regarded as a 'firm and definite' alignment, 'not open to discussion', Nehru had taken the step which was to transmute a boundary problem into a dispute, and the dispute ultimately into a border war.

The decision not to submit the McMahon Line to re-negotiation had closed off the possibility of formal agreement between India and China on that alignment. But at least the McMahon Line was a known alignment, marked clearly—though not precisely—on maps, and known to both the Indians and the Chinese. In the western sector, to which Nehru now applied the same approach, the situation was fundamentally different. There, there had never been any proposed alignment as clear as the McMahon Line, nor indeed had the area been sufficiently surveyed to make it possible to draw such a line. Furthermore, there had, over the years, been wide variations in the alignments favoured by the British—by one count, eleven different variations, reflecting three basic alignments.[33] Nehru's directive meant that one of these was now to be selected unilaterally by India, put into effect as the *de facto* boundary, and then treated as a subject 'not to be discussed' with China. If India selected an alignment acceptable to China, no real harm would be done. Formal delimitation of the boundary would probably be impossible if the subject were really 'not to be discussed'; but a mutually acceptable *de facto* boundary in such remote and desolate terrain would serve quite satisfactorily. There was plainly the risk, however, that the Indians would choose an alignment in the western sector that was not acceptable to China.

Before seeing what alignment the Indians did select for the western sector of the boundary an attempt must be made to answer the question: why did the Chinese not bring up the boundary question for negotiation at this time? Chou En-lai's later explanation that 'the time was not ripe' lends itself to sinister interpretation, and may have reflected the Chinese belief, well-founded in their experience, that boundary negotiations are best left until they can be conducted from

positions of strength.* But in 1951, Chou himself had proposed early
negotiations on the border, so his later phrase might simply have
meant that China saw no reason to propose opening border negotiations when the neighbour concerned showed no interest in doing so,
and when there was no pressing boundary problem to be attended to.
Certainly Indian and Chinese maps gave widely divergent versions of
their common borders, but in the Chinese view, as stated later, it was
'natural that the two countries should hold different opinions regarding
the boundary' since that had never been delimited.[34] China was already
accepting the McMahon Line as the *de facto* boundary, so no urgent
problem was to be anticipated there. A year after the conclusion of the
Panch Sheel agreement Chou En-lai, speaking at the Bandung conference, explained China's approach to the question of boundaries
with her neighbours:

> With some of these countries we have not yet finally fixed our
> border-line and we are ready to do so. . . . But before doing so, we
> are willing to maintain the present situation by acknowledging
> that those parts of our border are parts which are undetermined.
> We are ready to restrain our Government and people from cross-
> ing even one step across our border. If such things do happen, we
> should like to admit our mistake. As to the determination of com-
> mon borders which we are going to undertake with our neigh-
> bouring countries, we shall use only peaceful means and we shall
> not permit any other kinds of method. In no case shall we change
> this.[35]

Comparison of the Chinese approach, as expressed there, with
India's approach, as expressed in the Bajpai/Panikkar letters and in
Nehru's memorandum, shows fundamental differences. The Chinese
intend to determine their boundaries in discussion with their neighbours—the Indians have decided that boundary questions should not
be open to discussion; the Chinese acknowledge that parts of their
borders are undetermined, and intend to maintain the *status quo* pending such determination—the Indians intend to argue that their boundaries are already determined, and have decided to establish checkposts

---

* In the Rajya Sabha on December 9th, 1959, Nehru explained India's silence about the
borders in the early 1950s in almost such terms: 'We felt we should hold by our
position and that the lapse of time and events would confirm it and by the time, perhaps,
when the challenge to it came we could be in a much stronger position to face it.'

all along them, 'more especially . . . in such places as might be considered disputed areas'. Plainly, the ingredients for an explosive situation are there already, and it needs only a conflict in territorial claims to
light the fuse.

Implementation of Nehru's 1954 directive required that India
decide precisely where her boundaries lay, and that the desired alignments be shown on her maps. Until 1954 the maps issued by the
official Indian survey office (the Survey of India) were still depicting
the northern boundaries as the British had been doing since 1936. The
McMahon Line was shown as the boundary in the north-east, marked
with a broken line to indicate that it was undemarcated.* From Nepal
westward to Afghanistan the maps showed no boundary line at all;
there was, however, a colour wash, its edge marked 'Boundary Undefined', and this showed the old Johnson/Ardagh claim to a trans-
Karakoram border in its fullest expression—that is, with Aksai Chin,
and much more beside, marked tentatively as within India.[36] In 1954
the depiction of the northern boundaries in official Indian maps was
sharply changed. The variation was least in the eastern sector, where
the McMahon Line was now simply marked as a full international
boundary, with no reference to the fact that it was undemarcated.†
Similarly in the west, between Nepal and Afghanistan a full international boundary now replaced the undefined colour wash—but this
showed a substantially different claim. From Afghanistan to the Karakoram Pass the new maps pulled the boundary back to run it more or
less along the main Karakoram chain, thus giving up the forward
claim of the Johnson/Ardagh school in that sector. But to the east of
the Karakoram Pass the boundary on the new maps swung north
again, reverting to an approximation of the Johnson/Ardagh line so
as to loop up to the Kuen Lun mountains for a stretch—and thus included Aksai Chin in India.

The Aksai Chin claim had been, in British days, a strategist's formulation, conceived to anticipate a Russian advance and keep the Russian

---

* i.e. not marked out on the ground. The British maps were showing the McMahon Line
as delimited, i.e. formally agreed upon between the parties concerned. See p. 23 n.
† The change in boundary-marking for Bhutan and Sikkim was radical, however. In pre-
1954 maps both these states were shown as outside India, but in the 1954 editions both
were included in India. The change did not reflect the treaty relationships. Bhutan is a
fully sovereign country; Sikkim's independence is more theoretical, but the Indian Constitution does not list Sikkim as part of India, and in 1967 the Minister of External Affairs,
M. C. Chagla, confirmed in the Lok Sabha that Sikkim was not part of India. Indian maps
continue to show both states within India, however, in spite of protests from Sikkim and
Bhutan.

presence as far as possible from Tibet and India. It had been favoured in Delhi and London at various times, discarded at others; but it had never been expressed as a formal boundary proposal; and it had never been reflected on the ground in extension of administration — a measure that was as far from the desires of the British as it was beyond their capacity. The claim had had long currency on some British maps but, as has been seen, this did not always reflect even British boundary policy; and there was nothing to prevent the British from making tentative boundary claims on their maps; such could always be modified without awkward questions. But when the Government of independent India put a categorical claim to Aksai Chin on their official maps the consequences were quite different. By claiming the territory as Indian soil they had so far as their own political opinion was concerned, and indeed even to some extent constitutionally,* made it such. It would be very difficult, perhaps even impossible, to retract the claim.

Why did the Indian Government claim Aksai Chin when they marked a definitive boundary on their maps in 1954? According to their own account, they relinquished the claim to a trans-Karakoram boundary to the west of the Karakoram Pass† because the British had done so in 1927, accepting then that the claim had no relation to the facts of administration, but failing to transcribe that decision to their maps.[37] But then why did the Indians claim a trans-Karakoram alignment in the Aksai Chin sector? That is the crucial question, and it is one to which a definite answer cannot be given as the 1927 British decision has not been published by the Indian Government (whose files for the period are still closed) or traced in the British archives. A possible answer can, however, be inferred. As has been seen, British frontier policy in this sector fluctuated between a forward and a moderate alignment. It is quite possible that in 1927, when the British accepted that the long-established Chinese presence on the Karakoram Pass itself made a claim to a boundary north of it nugatory, they decided on the other hand that a claim to Aksai Chin should be maintained on their maps. The Russian threat was alive again at the time, since Sinkiang was falling under Soviet influence, and if the British had no effective administration on Aksai Chin, neither, it might

* See p. 153 below.
† By 1954 the Indian claim to the whole of Kashmir had hardened and she therefore assumed a Sino-Indian boundary between the Karakoram Pass and Afghanistan, territory which was *de facto* Pakistani.

have been argued, had the Chinese. Why not, then, maintain a claim to Aksai Chin? If the worst came to the worst, this might be used to deter Russian expansion; or, alternatively, when the time came to negotiate a boundary in this sector with China, it could be bargained away against the fullest Chinese claim to produce such a compromise line as that proposed to China in 1899.

If this was the drift of the British decision in 1927 the rest would follow. When in 1954 the Indian Government came to check the British precedents to see where the boundary in the western sector should lie, they would have found a proposal for an Aksai Chin claim. In the hands of the British that might have been a tentative claim, for use as a diplomatic counter in future dealing with Moscow or Peking; but in the context of Indian attitudes of 1954, it would have been metamorphosed into a categorical statement. Nehru had ruled that 'the northern border should be considered a firm and definite one which was not open to discussion with anybody.'

In that reading, the heart of the Sino-Indian boundary dispute lay in a historical accident. If the Englishmen who in 1927 reconsidered the north-west boundary with China had suggested that in the Aksai Chin sector the boundary should follow the alignment proposed to China in 1899,* the territory crossed by the Sinkiang–Tibet road to be built by China in the 1950s would have been left outside India on Indian maps. Thus the intractable nub of the dispute would have been avoided.

The 1954 map changes made Aksai Chin part of India on paper, but were not reflected in the situation on the ground. The most advanced Indian post in Ladakh was at Chushul, far short of Aksai Chin. An Indian patrol had been sent up to the Lanak Pass in 1952, and this patrol was repeated in 1954, setting up an Indian flag at the pass,[38] but no patrol went as far as Aksai Chin.[39] In pursuance of Nehru's memorandum, the Ministries of External Affairs, Home Affairs and Defence conferred in September 1954, and identified the border areas in the western and middle sectors which were disputed; it was proposed that these should be made the responsibility of the Defence Ministry (policing the borders was normally the Home Ministry's job) but the Army demurred[40]—presumably they had enough on their plate. It was decided, however, that where possible, border posts should be advanced

* See p. 34 n above.

into disputed territory, and both in the middle and eastern sectors posts were thus moved forward.[41]

The Indian move forward in the middle sector occasioned a prompt complaint from China, who protested in July that Indian troops had intruded into Chinese territory, and thought the move 'not in conformity with the principles of non-aggression and friendly co-existence between China and India' which had just been codified in the Panch Sheel agreement.[42] The Indian Government replied that the territory in question belonged to India, threw back Peking's point about the Panch Sheel agreement, and asked the Chinese to keep their personnel out. In this middle sector of the Sino-Indian border, where Uttar Pradesh and Himachal Pradesh meet Tibet, there was a long-standing dispute over the alignment of the boundary;[43] there the Tibetans controlled not only the passes but patches of pasture beneath them, and it was into those areas that the Indians now moved in an attempt to make the passes themselves the boundary features. Both sides pulled back in the winter, so it became an annual race to get to the high pasture before the other side. Diplomatic exchanges about the middle sector sputtered on through the middle 1950s, and there was an infructuous meeting on the subject in New Delhi in 1958; it was a tuning up or rehearsal in microcosm for the main boundary dispute, and need not be traced in detail. It can be noted, however, that the Indian Government accused China of aggression because Chinese parties crossed the passes,[44] although in fact the border forces of the two sides had come into contact in consequence of a forward move by the Indians — which Nehru himself confirmed in Parliament some years later.[45] In the diplomatic argument the Indian Government maintained that in the 1954 agreement on trade in Tibet the Chinese had acknowledged that the boundary ran through the passes,[46] whereas, as has been seen, the Chinese had made plain that they regarded the passes as being wholly within their own territory. Finally, the accusation, reversing the actuality, that it was China who began to 'probe forward' before the ink was dry on the Panch Sheel agreement became one of the charges in India's indictment of China's good faith — and was almost universally believed. Another charge in that indictment was that China furtively and treacherously built a road across Aksai Chin, knowing it to be Indian territory, and that touched the heart of the dispute.

Aksai Chin is bleak and difficult terrain for any traveller, but it

presents a rather different face to those on the Chinese side of the Karakorams than it does to those on the Indian side. To the Chinese, Aksai
Chin is, first of all, far more accessible than it is to the Indians, an
ancient trade route lying from Khotan up the Kara Kash on to Aksai
Chin and wending on across the plateau to Tibet. It is thus a stage,
albeit a difficult one, on a natural route. From the Indian side, on the
other hand, Aksai Chin is much more difficult to reach, through the
Karakorams or the Ladakh mountains; and, more important, it leads
nowhere. The British attempts in the nineteenth century to develop
caravan routes up the Changchenmo valley and across Aksai Chin to
the Kara Kash foundered because they turned out to be even more
difficult than the traditional route across the 18,000-foot Karakoram
Pass.

So, when the Chinese reasserted the central Government's authority
in Sinkiang and turned in 1950 to Tibet, it was natural for their forces
to take the Aksai Chin route into western Tibet—indeed this was the
sole practicable way, because to the north lay the great Sinkiang *gobi*
(desert). On November 17th, 1950, the *Statesman* reported that the
Indian Government had been informed of the movement of Chinese
troops from Sinkiang to western Tibet by its agent then at Gartok, in
western Tibet itself.

The Chinese used the Aksai Chin route to supply western Tibet
through the first half of the 1950s,[47] and claimed that during this time
they patrolled and surveyed the whole Aksai Chin area—'the footsteps of
this survey team covered every place in Aksai Chin and Lingzitang',
the Chinese said later.[48] In March 1956 they began laying a motorable
road, striking up into the hills near Yarkand and reaching Gartok after
crossing Aksai Chin. The work took nineteen months, and the Chinese
said later that it had been done by their frontier guards 'together with
more than three thousand civilian builders, working under extremely
difficult natural conditions . . . cutting across high mountains, throwing
bridges and building culverts'. Of the total length of some seven hundred and fifty miles, about one hundred and twelve lay across territory
that was to be claimed by India.

Did the Chinese Government know about the Indian claim when
they surveyed and built the road? Their own maps, of course, showed
Aksai Chin as Chinese territory, with the boundary following the Karakoram range to the west of it, and they had regarded it as theirs at least
since Li Yuan-ping's exploration in 1890 and probably, more vaguely,

even before that. If officials in Peking had looked into the boundary question in the western sector in the early 1950s they would have noted that Indian maps showed an indeterminate claim which included Aksai Chin. But these maps—in which the boundary was shown only by an undefined colour wash, marked 'undetermined'—also embraced territory which had been under demonstrated Chinese control since they set up their marker in the Karakoram Pass in 1892: the maps might therefore have been dismissed as expressing an unreal claim of the imperialist era which the Indians were merely keeping on their maps until a boundary could be delimited with China—just as the Chinese were doing with their own maps. The Indian Government had made clear in domestic statements that it regarded the McMahon Line as the boundary in the eastern sector, and since 1951 had treated it as such on the ground; but it had not specified any boundary in the western sector, and until 1958 the Indian presence there fell well short of what the Chinese regarded as the proper boundary.

The modification to the western boundary as shown on the Indian maps put out in 1954 must, if the Chinese embassy in New Delhi was doing its job, have alerted Peking to the possibility of a dispute over Aksai Chin; but, again, the Indians made no attempt to raise the boundary question, and it was left to China to bring up the subject. Chou En-lai did that in his talks with Nehru in New Delhi in 1956, but he referred only to the McMahon Line.[49] It was not until 1958 that India made a formal claim to Aksai Chin. Before that, if the Chinese had consulted their Foreign Ministry's archives to see what the British ideas about an Aksai Chin boundary had been they would have found only the Macartney-MacDonald proposal of 1899, and that alignment would have left the entire Aksai Chin road in Chinese territory.[*]

The Chinese activity on Aksai Chin in the 1950s did not arouse the Indian Government for the good reason that they knew nothing about it.[†] The few Indian patrols sent out from Leh to the north-east did not

---

[*] It has been argued that the 1899 line would cut the Chinese road for some ten miles in the south-east corner of Aksai Chin; but if the 1899 line is transposed on to a modern map it can be seen that the whole road lies on the Chinese side.

[†] It has been suggested that the Indian Government did know about the Chinese road-building, and that the information was kept from Nehru 'by persons in high position more strongly, or more recklessly, committed than he was to winning the favour of China'. This inference seems to have sprung from a failure to trace on a map the routes of the patrols which the Indians claimed to have made: that step would have shown that, as the Indians admitted, 'no Indian reconnaissance party was sent to the area in Aksai Chin where the Chinese . . . had built a new road.'[50] (See G. F. Hudson in *St Anthony's Papers* No. 14, Chatto & Windus, London, 1963.)

cross Aksai Chin—two of these might have reached its westernmost edge but they went nowhere near the road. The first the Indian Government learned about that was from gratified notices in the Chinese press about the completion of this major road-building feat. These the Indian Ambassador in Peking reported to New Delhi in September 1957. The Ambassador's reference was to a small-scale sketch map in a Chinese magazine, and from that the Government in New Delhi could not be sure just where the road did run. A direct inquiry to the Chinese would not have sat with the Indian approach, and so it was decided that two patrols should be sent to investigate the lie of the road.* They could not be sent during the winter because the cold was too extreme, so it was not until July 1958 that they left Leh, the Indian base. One of the patrols reported in October from the southern sector of the road that this did indeed cross territory claimed by India; the other patrol, which had been ordered to the northern end of the road, disappeared.

★ ★ ★ ★ ★ ★ ★ ★ ★ ★ ★

By 1958 the two no-man's-lands which the imperial era had left at opposite ends of the Sino-Indian frontier had thus been occupied, each side pre-empting the area which was important to it on strategic and practical considerations. In the east the Indians had completed the work left unfinished by the British and made good the McMahon Line, not only asserting administration over the tribal territory but extruding Tibetan—potentially Chinese—administration from Tawang. The area had been renamed the North-East Frontier Agency, listed as Indian territory in the 1950 constitution. and was being administered by members of the newly formed Indian Frontier Service. Work had begun on roads into the tribal territory, notably one that was ultimately to reach Tawang.

In the west, unknown to India, a parallel process had been going on simultaneously, with the Chinese using and then developing the old caravan route across Aksai Chin and turning it into a road which the administration required for what they were to describe as the main traffic artery between Sinkiang and Tibet.

Each side in extending administration into these new areas knew that the other had map claims to it (in the case of India, it is known

---

* Why aerial reconnaissance was not used is hard to say; perhaps because it might have induced a Chinese protest, while a ground patrol might not be detected?

that the Government had this knowledge, in the case of China it can be assumed); but each, for its own reasons, preferred not to raise the issue. Looking back, it might be said that both Governments were misguided in not putting an understanding on their boundaries at the top of the agenda when they opened relations at the beginning of the 1950s. As U Nu of Burma put it: 'It is of the utmost importance that even the best of neighbours . . . should know where the territory of one ends and the other begins, so as to apply faithfully the principle of respect for each other's sovereignty and territorial integrity.'[51] But, on the other hand, it might also be said that by 1958 their boundary problem had gone a long way towards solving itself. The two Governments were on the best of terms, each country had filled out into the no-man's-land of importance to itself, and all that was needed was an agreement to give binding diplomatic expression to what by all appearances was a mutually satisfactory *status quo*. If both sides were in fact satisfied there would be no Sino-Indian boundary problem at all; if on the other hand both — or either — stood by map claims to territory occupied by the other, the problem would be insoluble.

* * * * * * * * * * *

After the death of Sardar Patel in 1950 Nehru had no peers in India, and for the rest of the decade he bestrode the political scene. As well as Prime Minister he was at various times Defence Minister, he sometimes took on the presidency of the Congress Party, he was chairman of the Planning Commission and the Atomic Energy Commission, and until his death he retained the portfolio of External Affairs. During the long years of the independence movement he had insisted that his colleagues in Congress should give thought to the foreign policy to be followed by the free India for which they were striving, and he himself had been almost exclusively responsible for the shaping of that policy. That he should be Minister for External Affairs as well as Prime Minister went without saying in 1947, and was never challenged even when it appeared that the range of India's internal problems which he made his personal responsibility was already too much for one man. His colleagues in the Government were content to leave foreign policy to Nehru; their own interests or ambitions directed them towards the patronage and power that sprang more plentifully from the domestic portfolios.

The Cabinet system has never worked in India except in name, and in the 1950s Nehru rarely bothered even to pretend that the Cabinet was the centre of the system. Once in a long while there were complaints about the Prime Minister's 'cavalier and unconstitutional' methods, as a Finance Minister who resigned over them put it in 1956,[52] but generally his colleagues preferred to go along with them and adopt the same procedures themselves. 'There have been numerous cases . . . of Ministers who have quite simply and deliberately gone their own way and announced publicly policy decisions without securing the prior approval of Cabinet,' a senior civil servant observed.[53] Nehru's highly personal style was, if anything, more marked in his handling of foreign policy than of domestic affairs. There was a Cabinet committee for foreign affairs but that, too, he ignored more often than not, and time and again crucial foreign policy decisions were taken and announced — even acted upon — without either the committee or the Cabinet being aware of them.[54] This was true of the handling of the boundary question with China, which was kept not only from the Cabinet and its foreign affairs and defence committees, but also from Parliament until armed clashes made it impossible to suppress.

India's foreign policy in the 1950s was thus the conception of Nehru himself, and its implementation the concern of Nehru and the senior officials of the External Affairs Ministry. Even there, in the early years Nehru tried to run the ministry as if that were his only charge, often drafting even simple telegrams himself and not consulting his officials. Of the Indian Foreign Service in Nehru's day one perceptive observer wrote that 'it was not a good service — nothing like good enough for a country of India's importance. There was not enough training or professional competence, not enough *esprit de corps*, and too much eagerness to please the boss. Nehru was too busy and too preoccupied to get to know the necessary detail, or to get to know the officers except for a handful of very senior ones or a few favourites. This encouraged sycophancy, personal *ad hoc* approaches, and a mixture of amateurishness and subjectivity.'[55]

Nehru's personal approach towards China was at the beginning positive and warm, even fraternal, springing from a long-held belief that the future of Asia, and even of the world, would be marked by the friendship of what he conceived to be two kindred and equal giants. In 1942 he wrote: 'The future of which I dream is inextricably interwoven with close friendship and something almost approaching union with China.'[56] He first visited China in 1939, spending twelve days in Chungking, the Nationalists' seat of government, and returned convinced that 'a new China is rising, rooted in her culture but shedding the lethargy and weakness of ages, strong and united.'[57] He went again in 1954 and returned to India much impressed by the energy and discipline which the Chinese were showing in the task of nation-building, which he thought gave China 'a terrifying strength'.[58] On that visit he met Mao Tse-tung and is said to have come away from the encounter feeling as if he had been 'ushered into a presence, as someone coming from a tributary or vassal state of the Chinese empire'[59] — neither the first nor the last indication of a clash of assumptions between the Chinese and the Indians about who should show more respect to whom.

While Nehru was anti-Communist in Indian domestic terms, he tried always to separate that from his approach to Communist governments. He saw the establishment of the People's Republic of China as the triumph of nationalism and as a manifestation of Asia's political renaissance rather than as a victory for Communism, believing that in the long run Chinese civilization would digest Marxist dogma and the Communist structure to produce perhaps a new synthesis. He was aware of the political dimension in which China and India, with their opposing systems, must be rivals in Asia and the world, but believed that this rivalry need not sour the relations between the two countries. His policy of friendship towards Peking and his support for the People's Republic's claim for recognition in the United Nations brought him a good deal of opprobrium in the domestic as well as the international sphere. From 1950 onward Nehru's domestic critics attacked his China policy as one of appeasement and argued that India should never have acquiesced in what they saw as China's invasion of Tibet. They warned him that China's presence on the northern borders must inevitably expose the country to a threat from Chinese expansionism — and were later, of course, to believe that all their prophecies had been fulfilled. But in the middle 1950s, when resentment and alarm at the assertion of Chinese authority in Tibet had died down, the policy and slogan of *Hindee Chinee bhai-bhai*, or India-China brotherhood, became popular in India. Chou En-lai, when he returned Nehru's visit in 1956, was cheered by large crowds wherever he went.

Chou took the opportunity on this occasion to raise the subject of the McMahon Line.* At their meeting two years before in China, Nehru had made a passing reference to Chinese maps which showed 'a wrong border-line', and according to his own account was told that such were reproductions of old maps which the Chinese had not had time to revise.†[60] Later Nehru, presuming, he said, 'on our friendly relations with China', had written to Chou En-lai about the Sino-Burmese boundary negotiations, which then appeared to be deadlocked. He had warned Chou that the Burmese were apprehensive about both their big neighbours, and suggested that the Chinese should take steps to remove Burma's misgivings. He proposed that U Nu might be invited to Peking to discuss the borders — as was later done.[61] The 1956 meeting of Nehru and Chou En-lai took place a few months after Nehru's letter about Burma, and it was in reference to the Sino-Burmese boundary negotiations that Chou raised the subject of the McMahon Line. In Nehru's account of this conversation, Chou En-lai told him that China had accepted the McMahon Line as the boundary with Burma because, although 'this line, established by the British imperialists, was not fair . . . it was an accomplished fact and because of the friendly relations which existed between China and the countries concerned, India and Burma, the Chinese Government were of the opinion that they should give recognition to this McMahon Line.'[62]

Chou En-lai here applied to the McMahon Line what was to be the Chinese Government's approach wherever an alignment established by her former imperialist neighbours had become the effective boundary. In some instances, such as the Sino-Russian boundary on the Ussuri and Amur Rivers, the effective line had been established for nearly a century. The Indians had made the McMahon Line the *de facto* boundary only five years before, but the Chinese approach remained the same: accept the 'accomplished fact' and go on from there. This was really the only practical course for the Chinese Government to follow. To refuse to accept 'accomplished facts' and lay irredentist claims to lost territories would have been to create intractable and poisonous disputes with every one of her neighbours.

* The belief that it was Nehru who brought up the McMahon Line in his discussions with Chou En-lai in 1956 is now central to the Indian understanding of the development of the boundary dispute, but it is erroneous. Nehru himself made clear that the initiative was Chou's.[63]

† 'It did not occur to the Indian prime minister that the Chinese could with equal justice have asked him about *his* maps, which also reproduced the previous imperialist government's claims without prior consultation with the neighbour concerned.' (Dick Wilson, *Asia Awakes*, Weidenfeld and Nicolson, London, 1970; p. 83.)

There was a corollary to Chou En-lai's assurance to Nehru, however, which it appears he did not make clear. While prepared to accept
the McMahon *alignment*, China would not simply confirm the
McMahon Line. Peking has been consistent in this regard. Where
there is a boundary treaty China observes it; but will insist that, if
further negotiations are required to define the alignment and settle
disputes, they should issue in a new treaty. That would in general
confirm the old alignment but, negotiated between equals, would, in
the Chinese view, erase the stain of the old 'unequal treaties'. This was
to be China's approach to the Sino-Soviet boundaries. But the
McMahon Line, as the Chinese saw it, had no treaty basis. Therefore
the basis for delimitation could only be the *status quo*. For practical as
well as political reasons, however, even the ratification of a known—
though not precisely defined—boundary such as the McMahon Line
would need negotiations. Chou might have assumed this to be self-
evident. He was speaking in the context of the Sino-Burmese negotiations and, he said later, he believed that India would no more wish to
endorse old imperialist treaties than did China.[64] Moreover, he had
just assured Nehru that China would not use negotiations to try to
change the boundary.

The question remains: why did Chou En-lai not raise the subject of
the *western sector* of the Sino-Indian border at this time? Nehru, it
seems, had no inkling then that since 1954 Indian maps had been claiming in Aksai Chin an area which China regarded and used as her own.
But the Chinese Government must have been aware of the recently
confirmed Indian map claim to Aksai Chin. They were already dealing
with the boundary dispute in the adjoining middle sector, so it can be
assumed that Chou En-lai had been briefed about the potential for a
dispute in the west too. It has been seen that Nehru and his advisers
had taken the view that India's interests would best be served if it were
left to China to bring up her map claims to territory occupied by India
(the area beneath the McMahon Line); perhaps the Chinese took the
same approach to the Indian map claim to what they regarded as their
Aksai Chin territory.

Whatever the reason for it, Chou En-lai's failure to bring up the
western sector when he was discussing the eastern border with Nehru
in 1956 had far-reaching and malign consequences. If, in the context of
what Chou certainly saw, and Nehru probably accepted, as a Chinese
concession on the McMahon Line, he had gone on to point out that

Indian maps were showing an incorrect boundary in the western sector, it is highly probable that the dispute would have been avoided. The glow, almost euphoria, of *Hindee Chinee bhai-bhai* was then at its zenith and Nehru would surely have seen a marginal modification of Indian maps, bringing them into accordance with actuality on the ground, as a negligible price for its continuance—indeed, he might have welcomed the opportunity to match Chou's pragmatism about the McMahon Line. But the opportunity passed unseen, and two years later the situation was wholly changed. To have it civilly pointed out that your maps do not accord with actuality is one thing; to discover that a neighbour, without a by-your-leave, has built a road across territory your maps show as your own is quite another. The objective reality may be the same but the perception is not, and in this case the perception was everything.

The Indian Government reacted to the discovery of the Aksai Chin road in a note to Peking on October 18th, 1958. This claimed that the territory traversed by the road had been 'part of the Ladakh region of India for centuries', and said that it was a 'matter of surprise and regret that the Chinese Government should have constructed a road through indisputably Indian territory without first obtaining the permission of the Government of India', or even informing it. The note asked if China had any information about the missing patrol.[65] The reply came as a brusque counter-complaint, stating that Indian armed personnel had unlawfully intruded into Chinese territory and been detained. 'In the spirit of Sino-Indian friendship' the Indians had already been deported,* but Peking described their intrusion as inconsistent with the five principles of peaceful coexistence and asked for a guarantee that there would be no repetition.[66] With this exchange the conflict of claims over Aksai Chin at last came into the open, and in a prompt reply the Indian Government said that the question of whether the area was Indiag or Chinese was 'a matter in dispute'. This was the only time India conceded the existence of a dispute, and a few weeks later this position was reversed.

While awaiting reports from the patrols about the lie of the Aksai Chin road, the Indian Government had formally broached the subject of China's maps, pointing out in a note to Peking that a sketch map in a recent Chinese magazine showed as Chinese various areas which

* By putting them across the 18,000-foot-high Karakoram Pass. The Indians had no post near by at the time, and the little Indian party was lucky to be discovered and rescued.

the Indians held to be their own. In the eastern sector, Chinese maps continued to ignore the McMahon Line and showed the Sino-Indian boundary along the foot of the hills; Nehru had alluded to this in 1950, when he said that 'all the maps of China for the last thirty years have shown a certain portion of that north-east frontier which is now part of India as not part of India'.[67] In the western sector, Chinese maps showed the boundary lying south-east from the Karakoram Pass to the Changchenmo River valley. As has been seen, this alignment coincided with the view of the boundary taken by the British authorities in the nineteenth century before they became alarmed by the advance of Russian power towards India and began to modify their boundary thinking accordingly.* It put the whole of Aksai Chin in China.

The Indian note recalled that Nehru had mentioned maps to Chou En-lai in 1954 and gave as the latter's reply that 'current Chinese maps were based on old maps and that the Chinese Government had had no time to correct them.'[68] It was now high time, the Indians suggested, that corrections should be made. Again, the Chinese reply was disconcerting to the Indians. It confirmed that Chou En-lai had said in 1954 that current Chinese maps were based on old, pre-liberation maps, but said that he had explained that this was because the Government had 'not yet undertaken a survey of China's boundary, nor consulted with the countries concerned'. In due course, a new way of drawing the boundary of China would emerge from those consultations, and in the meantime China would make no changes in the boundaries on her own.[69] This note was delivered on the same day as China's complaint about the patrols, and disclosed that as well as a conflict of claims there was a fundamental difference of approach to the whole question of boundaries. Since at least 1950 the Indian policy towards the northern borders had been that they must not be opened to negotiation. In its original formulation that policy had referred primarily to the McMahon Line, but in 1954 it had been applied to the whole reach of the Sino-Indian border. Now it was clear that Peking's approach to the question was quite contrary, and that the Chinese expected to discuss the boundary alignments before confirming them.

Objectively, the Chinese approach sounded rational, but in New Delhi it was read as an alarming intimation that China intended to advance territorial claims at a time of her own choice. The *bhai-bhai* mood vanished; that had been at bottom a rhetorical and emotional

* See p. 28 above.

expression of Indian-cum-Asian nationalism, and perhaps the deeper and more genuine Indian feeling towards China had always been touched with distrust. As the Chinese approach to the boundary question became clearer that distrust burgeoned into outright suspicion, and soon became resentful hostility.

Nehru opened the prime ministerial exchanges which were to be a connecting thread for the whole diplomatic debate with a letter to Chou En-lai in December 1958. The letter was friendly in tone, beginning with praise for China's progress before turning to the question of the boundaries. Nehru recalled their discussion of the McMahon Line in 1956, when, he said, Chou En-lai had told him China would recognize it; India had been 'under the impression that there were no border disputes between our respective countries'. The latest statement of the Chinese Government, with its reference for the need of surveys and consultations, had therefore puzzled him. Nehru then stated the Indian position, which he was thereafter to hold unyieldingly: 'There can be no question of these large parts of India [shown as Chinese in China's maps] being anything but India and there is no dispute about them.'[70]

Chou En-lai replied with equal cordiality, thanking Nehru for the congratulations he had sent on China's achievements, returning the compliment, and thanking him for India's efforts to 'restore China to its rightful place in the United Nations'. Turning to the boundary question, Chou then stated the basic position from which China was not to budge from then on. 'First of all,' he wrote, 'I wish to point out that the Sino-Indian boundary has never been formally delimited. Historically no treaty or agreement on the Sino-Indian boundary has ever been concluded between the Chinese central Government and the Indian Government.' Consequently there were discrepancies between the maps published in India and China, and there were border disputes. Chinese maps showed the boundaries as they had consistently done for several decades, if not longer, and while 'we do not hold that every portion of this boundary line is drawn on sufficient grounds,' it would not be right to make changes in it without having surveyed the ground in consultation with the neighbours concerned. In order that minor border incidents of the kind that had already occurred could be avoided, Chou En-lai proposed that 'as a provisional measure the two sides temporarily maintain the *status quo*'.

The Chinese position, then, was that the boundary had never been

4

delimited, that there were disputes, and that these could only be settled by mutual consultation and joint survey. But 'the existence of the border question absolutely should not affect the development of Sino-Indian friendly relations', Chou said. After proper preparations and with friendly talks, the question, which had been carried over from the past, could certainly be settled reasonably on the basis of the five principles of peaceful coexistence.

So far as the specific disputes were concerned, Chou was as categorical about Aksai Chin as Nehru had been about the entire boundary. This area in the southern part of Sinkiang 'has always been under Chinese jurisdiction', he said; it had been continually under patrol by Chinese border guards, and the Sinkiang–Tibet highway ran through it. He was far less definite about the eastern sector of the boundary, explaining his Government's position at some length.

As you are aware, the 'McMahon Line' was a product of the British policy of aggression against the Tibet Region of China and aroused the great indignation of the Chinese people. Juridically, too, it cannot be considered legal. I have told you that it has never been recognized by the Chinese central Government. Although related documents were signed by a representative of the local authorities of the Tibet Region of China, the Tibet local authorities were in fact dissatisfied with this unilaterally drawn line. And I have also told you formally about their dissatisfaction. On the other hand one cannot, of course, fail to take cognizance of the great and encouraging changes: India and Burma, which are concerned in this line, have attained independence successively and become states friendly with China. In view of the various complex factors mentioned above, the Chinese Government on the one hand finds it necessary to take a more or less realistic attitude towards the McMahon Line and, on the other hand, cannot but act with prudence and needs time to deal with this matter. All this I have mentioned to you on more than one occasion. However, we believe that, on account of the friendly relations between China and India, a friendly settlement can eventually be found for this section of the boundary line.[71]

This passage and later restatements of it in the course of the continuing diplomatic exchanges about the boundaries are crucial. The Indians read it as a circumlocutory rejection of the McMahon Line, a reading that was taken to be confirmed when, later, China equated the area in dispute in Aksai Chin with the area below the McMahon Line. But is that what the passage sought to convey?

Chou En-lai was replying to Nehru's reminder that he had said in 1956 that he would recognize the McMahon Line as the border with India; he may have intended tacitly to confirm that he stood by that with the phrase: 'All this I have mentioned to you on more than one occasion.' He drew a distinction between the legality of the agreement which produced the line, which he repudiated, and the line itself, of which he said that 'the Chinese Government . . . finds it necessary to take a more or less realistic attitude', in the light of the friendly relations it had with India, as with Burma. In the context, it would be tenable to assume that Chou was intimating that when China and India sat down to settle their boundaries, China would accept the McMahon *alignment* as the boundary in that section. This distinction between the legality of the agreement which produced the line and the alignment itself is understandable: to accept the legality of the Anglo-Tibetan agreement, reversing the position taken by every Chinese Government since 1914, would have been to admit that Tibet had then been sovereign, and thus to concede that the 1950 Chinese move into Tibet was more an invasion than the reassertion of temporarily lapsed central power. The Dalai Lama, after his flight to India, made this point himself, in its converse formulation: 'If you deny sovereign status to Tibet, you deny the validity of the Simla Convention and therefore deny the validity of the McMahon Line,' he told an audience in New Delhi.[72]

If, however, China was prepared to accept the McMahon alignment as the boundary, why did Chou not say so explicitly? The Chinese Government expected negotiations on the entire length of boundary with India, and no doubt counted their intimated acceptance of the McMahon alignment as one of their 'gives' in a process of give-and-take. That hard bargaining would be involved had already been made clear by India's categorical claim to an area through which ran a section of the important Sinkiang–Tibet road. In these circumstances, no government could have been expected to discard one of its prime bargaining counters by formally committing itself to acceptance of the McMahon Line before negotiations had begun — in fact before the other side had agreed to negotiate at all. Chou had gone as far in reassuring Nehru on that score as he could have been expected to do in writing; and only two years before he had orally made the assurance quite explicit.

The reading that Chou En-lai was confirming his Government's readiness to make the McMahon Line the boundary in the eastern sector is substantiated by Peking's later handling of the whole dispute. Why, then, did Nehru and his advisers not take it in that sense? First, perhaps, because a hitherto submerged distrust of China had now hardened into the suspicion that for territorial aggrandisement or simply to assert predominance over India the Chinese meant to take or claim territory which India regarded as her own. More tangibly, the Sino-Burmese negotiations were just then more or less deadlocked, and the Burmese seem to have told the Indians that China was being unreasonable or intransigent.[73] If that was a factor, it should have been removed two years later when China signed a boundary agreement with Burma accepting the McMahon Line and, with minor modifications, the other alignments claimed by Burma;* but in 1959 the Indians would not have found it easy to read assurances from between the lines of Chou En-lai's letter. Finally, and perhaps most important, China was asking the Indian Government to reverse the central premise of the border policy it had been following since its very inception, the stand that the McMahon Line should not be opened to re-negotiation. Why the Indian Government saw re-negotiation as tantamount to giving up the McMahon boundary is not clear; the *sine qua non* of all negotiations is that both sides go into them without prejudice to their positions, and there seems no reason why the Indians could not have been as adamant in negotiation with China over their northeastern boundary as they have been, for example, in negotiations with Pakistan over Kashmir. Perhaps the very fact that China insisted on negotiating the boundaries made it impossible for the Indians, in their own view, to reconsider their basic position.

That position had its own logic:

(1) No territory south of the McMahon Line can be ceded in any circumstances.

(2) Therefore there can be no negotiation over the McMahon Line.

(3) Therefore there can be no negotiation over any section of the border (because China would be unlikely to agree to negotiations over part of it, and anyway for India to agree to that would weaken her refusal to negotiate the McMahon Line).

* See p. 212 n below.

(4) Therefore the Indian claim in the western and middle sectors must be made as categorical as the insistence on the McMahon Line.

This chain of reasoning entailed further positions:

(5) The only acceptable ground for refusal to negotiate a boundary with a neighbour is the contention that a boundary is *already in existence*. So far as the McMahon Line was concerned this argument could be based on the 1914 agreement as well as on the *de facto* situation—it had been the effective north-eastern boundary of India since 1951. But the same claim had to be elaborated for the western sector.

(6) Even when thus argued, a sustained refusal to negotiate could be invidious for any government, more especially for India because of Nehru's consistent advocacy of negotiation to resolve all disputes; therefore the essential and unvarying refusal had to be blurred.

It is not suggested that Nehru and his advisers saw their course of action in those terms, but it will be seen that they were drawn step by step along that course from the initial decision that the McMahon Line must not be opened to re-negotiation.

Nehru's reply[74] to Chou En-lai elaborated and extended the essential position he had taken up in his first letter: that the boundaries were already clearly and firmly set and there could be no question about them. He argued that in all of its three sectors the boundary claimed by India was based on geography and tradition as well as, in most parts, 'the sanction of specific international agreements between the then Government of India and the Central Government of China'. As examples of the latter he cited the 1842 treaty between Gulab Singh and the Tibetans,* and he maintained that the McMahon Line derived normally and legally from the Simla Convention. Those factors, he suggested, should convince Chou that the delineation of the boundary on Indian maps was 'based on natural and geographical features [and] also coincide[d] with tradition, and over a large part [was] confirmed by international agreements'. Independent India, he pointed out, 'would be the last country to make any encroachments beyond its well-established frontiers'.

Turning to Chou's proposal that, pending agreement on the boundary, the two sides should maintain the *status quo*, Nehru said: 'I agree that the position as it was before the recent disputes arose

* See pp. 24, 25 above.

should be respected by both sides and that neither side should try to take unilateral action in exercise of what it conceives to be its right. Further, if any possession has been secured recently, the position should be rectified.' This was the first use of a debating technique that was often to be employed by the Indian side as the dispute developed — couching rejection so as to make it sound like agreement. The question of the *status quo* was to be crucial to the whole dispute, and already here it had been fundamentally confused. Chou En-lai had proposed joint maintenance of the *status quo*; 'I agree,' Nehru replied — but he then went on to suggest *the restoration of previous positions, not the retention of the present ones* ('the position as it was before the recent disputes arose should be respected [and] . . . if any possession has been secured recently, the position should be rectified'). Nehru thus did not agree with Chou's proposal of maintenance of the *status quo*, but in effect suggested restoration of what India held to be the *status quo ante*. He foreshadowed here the Indian demand for China's evacuation of Aksai Chin, which was later to be hardened into an absolute pre-condition for discussion of the borders.

In those first letters to Chou En-lai, written some twelve months before the boundary dispute became a matter of public knowledge or political agitation in India, Nehru took up the position which he was to hold throughout: there was no boundary dispute with China, that is, there could be no question about the alignment of India's boundaries. These were where the Indian Government said they were — therefore there could be no negotiation. Secondly, the *status quo ante* (always called by India 'the *status quo*') must be restored, that is, where the Chinese were on territory claimed by India, they must withdraw.

This was a collision course, and it was set by Nehru and his advisers on their own judgment, not under the pressure of an aroused public opinion. Political pressure later made it extremely difficult for Nehru to change course, but it cannot be blamed or credited for having formed the Indian approach. For that Nehru must take responsibility.

* * * * * * * * * * *

The Prime Ministers' exchanges were not to be continued for another six months, and by the time Chou En-lai answered Nehru's second letter, in September 1959, the context of relations between the two countries had changed radically. The rebellion of the Khampa tribes-

men, which began in the north-eastern areas of Tibet in the spring of
1956, spread by early 1959 into central and southern Tibet and became
a much wider insurrection. Refugees in thousands crossed the border
into India. In March fighting broke out in Lhasa, and the Dalai Lama
and his Government threw in their lot with the rebels, proclaiming
Tibet independent. Peking informed India that the local Government
in Tibet was in armed rebellion, assuring Indian citizens in Tibet of
protection.[75] The Dalai Lama fled Lhasa and made his way to India,
following the old trade route across the McMahon Line to Tawang,
where he was taken under the wing of the Indian Government. These
events attracted world-wide attention and had an immediate and
damaging effect on Sino-Indian relations. In India the latent suspicion
of China was revived, and all the misgivings expressed in 1950 when
the Chinese marched into Tibet were sharpened. There was a renewed
outcry against the Government's policy, which had from the beginning
been much criticized for its acquiescence in China's moves in Tibet.
There were demonstrations in Indian cities against China and in sympathy with the Tibetan rebels, culminating in Bombay in April with
a crowd organized by the Socialist Party pasting a portrait of Mao
Tse-tung on the wall of the Chinese consulate and throwing eggs and
tomatoes at it—'a huge insult to the head of state', the Chinese called it
in an angry protest.[76]

Nehru was in a quandary. For years his Government had played
down and, when possible, suppressed reports from Tibet about resistance to the Chinese, and so he was open now to charges of wilful
blindness. Among the Indian political class there was general sympathy
for the Tibetans and especially for the Dalai Lama. Nehru shared these
feelings but, having recognized China's sovereignty in Tibet at least
since that was reasserted in 1950, he also accepted that, however sympathetic he and his compatriots might feel towards the Tibetans, what
happened in Tibet was China's business—certainly it could be of no
official concern to India. He tried therefore to balance actions of hos-
pitality towards the Dalai Lama with gestures of correctness towards
the Chinese; and expressions of sympathy for the Tibetans with re-
bukes for those Indians who, by their street demonstrations and angry
speeches, were putting a strain on the good relations with China which
he still hoped to maintain. Not surprisingly, he pleased no one. His
Indian critics accused him of appeasement when he refused to be
drawn into denunciations of China—while in China he was attacked

for meddling in China's domestic affairs, to the point of suborning rebellion.

Peking had for years been complaining that Kalimpong (the terminus of the trade route to India through the Chumbi Valley) was being used as a base to instigate resistance in Tibet—and with good reason. As early as 1953 Nehru had admitted that Kalimpong was 'a nest of spies': there were spies of every country there, he said, 'and sometimes I begin to doubt if the greater part of the population of Kalimpong does not consist of foreign spies'.[77] Chou En-lai brought up this complaint in his talks with Nehru in 1956, saying that Kalimpong was being used by American and other agents to undermine Chinese influence in Tibet.[78] At the beginning of 1958 Peking complained again, Chou bringing up the subject in a discussion with the Indian Ambassador, and the Chinese Government following up in a diplomatic note with a detailed and circumstantial description of the 'stepped-up' activities of émigrés and American and Kuomintang agents in Kalimpong.[79] The Chinese said these were preparing an armed revolt in Tibet with the objective of separating it from China. The Indian Government replied that Peking must have been misinformed: there was no evidence of foreign activities in Kalimpong.[80] At the beginning of August, however, 'every Tibetan official of note in India, including the Dalai Lama's brother and their cabinet ministers, together with guerrilla leaders as delegates from the fighting rebels, met in Kalimpong to draw up a final appeal to India and the United Nations.'[81] Peking complained again. In March 1959 the Chinese declared that the rebellion which had just broken out in Lhasa had been engineered from the 'commanding centre' in Kalimpong.[82]

It is evident that support and direction for the Tibetan rebels came through Kalimpong, and that the Government of India connived at this. There is some evidence that the Indian role was more active. George Patterson, an Englishman then living in Kalimpong and with close Tibetan contacts, wrote later that in 1954 he was approached by an Indian official to bring a rebel leader to Kalimpong 'to work for Tibetan independence'.[83]

On the outbreak of the rebellion and flight of the Dalai Lama the Indian Government informed Peking that the latter had asked for political asylum, which was being granted. New Delhi offered assurances, however, that the Dalai Lama would not be allowed to carry on political activities in India.[84] Chou En-lai was later to describe the granting of asylum to the Dalai Lama as 'normal international practice' and to say that China had no objection to it.[85] From immediately after his arrival in India, however, the Dalai Lama began to make statements giving his side of events in Tibet, and attacking China; these statements were initially released through the publicity media of the Indian Government, and later distributed by Indian missions abroad – and that China did object to, strongly.* (The Chinese suspected that the Indians in fact wrote the Dalai Lama's first statement, on his arrival in India, and there is internal evidence to justify the suspicion.)† The Chinese National People's Congress was in session in Peking at this time, and there were angry references there to 'Indian reactionaries', who were accused of giving aid and comfort to the rebellious feudal forces, and of 'working in the footsteps of the British imperialists, and harbouring expansionist ambitions towards Tibet'.[86] Old suspicions had been revived on both sides.

That the Chinese Government was, like Nehru, torn between indignation and recognition that good relations with a big neighbour were in its long-term interests is suggested by a remarkable statement made at this time to the Indian Foreign Secretary by the Chinese Ambassador.[87] A rejoinder to and rejection of New Delhi's complaints about the attacks on India made in the National People's Congress, the statement traced the recent 'deplorable abnormalities' in the relations between China and India to the 'serious interference in China's internal affairs and sabotage of Sino-Indian friendship' involved in the outcry in India about the Tibetan rebellion, and to the demonstrative welcome given to the Dalai Lama by the Indian Government. After reciting China's grounds for resentment and stating her hope, notwithstanding, that 'the dark clouds overcasting Sino-Indian relations for a time will speedily disperse', the Ambassador reached the nub of his message. This was a reminder that China's enemy lay in the east, where 'vicious and aggressive American imperialism' had many military bases directed against China. India, he went on, had not joined SEATO;

---

* It occurred to one Indian M.P., Joachim Alva, that Indian reaction would have been much the same if Sheikh Abdullah, the Kashmiri leader then in prison, had escaped to China and been treated there as the Dalai Lama had been in India. He drew this parallel in the Lok Sabha on September 12th, 1959.

† For example, the statement carefully specified the point at which the Dalai Lama crossed the McMahon Line into India, which he said was Khinzemane (for the significance of this see pp. 292–3 below). The Tibetan attitude to the line was ambivalent, to say the least, and that the Dalai Lama would himself have been at pains to specify its exact alignment – and in the Indian version at that – in a statement made immediately after his flight from Lhasa seems more than improbable.[88]

4*

is not an opponent but a friend to our country. China will not be so foolish as to antagonize the United States in the east and again to antagonize India in the west. The putting down of the rebellion and the carrying out of democratic reforms in Tibet will not in the least endanger India. . . . We cannot have two centres of attention, nor can we take friend for foe. This is our state policy. The quarrel between our two countries in the past few years, particularly in the last three months, is but an interlude in the course of thousands upon thousands of years of friendship between the two countries, and does not warrant a big fuss on the part of the broad masses and the Governments of our countries. . . . Our Indian friends! What is in your mind? Will you be agreeing to our thinking regarding the view that China can only concentrate its main attention eastward of China, but not south-westward of China, nor is it necessary for us to do so? . . . Friends! It seems to us that you too cannot have two fronts. Is it not so? If it is, here then lies the meeting point of our two sides. Will you please think it over?[89]

The Ambassador concluded by sending his best regards to Nehru.

In the whole correspondence between the two countries in the dispute that statement is unique in the urgency and directness, even familiarity, of its phrasing. It was certainly undiplomatic, in the sense that it discarded the customary observances of diplomatic wording, and it could be read as concluding on the hint of a threat. But it can also be read as an attempt to reassure the Indian Government by laying China's own cards on the table.* If that was the intention, the gesture failed. A week later the Chinese Ambassador was called back to the Ministry to hear an indignant reply, and rebuked for having used 'discourteous and unbecoming language'. It was pointed out to him that India treated all countries as friends, 'in consonance with India's past background and culture and Mahatma Gandhi's teachings'.[90]

While the diplomatic exchanges in the summer of 1959 reflected and perhaps intensified the embittering of relations engendered by the uprising in Tibet, movements along the borders brought the two countries towards physical collision. In the eastern sector the concen-

---

* One student of China's policies, Harold C. Hinton, had no doubt about the meaning of this statement. 'Despite its quaint English, the drift is clear enough . . .,'he wrote; 'What was evidently worrying [the Chinese Government] was the possibility that it might be faced with a more or less co-ordinated set of pressures on the Tibetan frontier and in the Taiwan Strait, and it was pleading with India to withdraw or not to take part.' (*Communist China in World Politics*, Macmillan, London 1966, p. 288.)

tration of Khampa rebels in southern Tibet, between the Tsangpo and the McMahon Line, brought Chinese troops into that area in strength, and they moved right up to the boundary to prevent the rebels from crossing for sanctuary and to cut off the flow of refugees. On the other side of the border the Indians were also pushing their outposts right up to the McMahon line—and in places over it.

The McMahon Line, of course, has never been demarcated (whether the Anglo-Tibetan notes exchanged in 1914 amount to legal *delimitation* is disputed between India and China; but that the Line has never been demarcated—i.e. marked out on the ground—is agreed by both parties). For a good deal of its length it follows an unmistakable and inaccessible crest-line, but elsewhere it is drawn over indeterminate topographical features and there the only way to determine the lie of the boundary is to trace out on the ground the co-ordinates of McMahon's original map. Often that process would create an inconvenient or nonsensical boundary, and since the line marked thickly on the original, eight-miles-to-the-inch map covers about a quarter of a mile, even this could produce no precise delineation on the ground. But, short of a joint Sino-Indian demarcation, there is no other way to fix the McMahon Line on the ground.

One of the places in which McMahon made his line diverge from what his map showed as the highest ridge was near a village called Migyitun, on a pilgrimage route of importance to the Tibetans. In order to leave Migyitun in Tibet the line cut a corner and for about twenty miles, until it met the main ridge again, followed no feature at all.* As the Indians reconnoitred this area in 1959 they discovered that the topography made a boundary alignment immediately south of Migyitun, rather than about two miles south as shown on the map, more practical from their point of view, and they set up a border picquet accordingly. The reasons for the Indian adjustment of the line here have not been stated clearly, but it seems probable that it was decided that a river, the Tsari, running roughly west–east just south of Migyitun, should be the boundary feature. Advancing the boundary to the river put a hamlet called Longju, on the opposite side of the valley from Migyitun, within India, while providing a more practical site for the Indian border picquet.

* The original maps on which McMahon drew his line have been published in the Indian Government's 1960 *Atlas of the Northern Frontiers of India*, in *The Sino-Indian Boundary Question* (Enlarged Edition), (Peking, 1963,) and in Dorothy Woodman's *Himalayan Frontiers*. The Migyitun corner is between 93° 15′ and 93° 30′ east.

The reasoning was unexceptionable; minor variations from a map line are almost invariably found necessary in boundary demarcation. But demarcation must be a joint process, and the Indians on this occasion were acting unilaterally, establishing their border post on what their own maps showed as Chinese territory without seeking China's approval, or even intimating their intention. Later the Indians made no secret of their action. In September 1959 Nehru told the Lok Sabha* that, while by and large the McMahon Line was fixed, 'in 'some parts, in the Subansiri area† or somewhere there, it was not considered a good line and it was varied afterwards by us, by the Government of India'.[91] In a letter to Chou En-lai in the same month Nehru rejected the Chinese complaint that the Indians were over-stepping the McMahon Line; but in the same breath he admitted that the Indian claim in the Migyitun area 'differs slightly from the boundary shown in the treaty map'. He justified this with the explanation that the Indian modification 'merely gave effect to the treaty map in the area, based on definitive topography', and argued that it was in accordance with established international principles.[92] So it would have been, if done in consultation with China.

While the Indian Government refused to submit the McMahon Line as a whole to negotiation, it was at this time offering to discuss the exact alignment of the line at specific points, including Longju.[93] Nehru even declared his willingness to submit such questions to arbitration; but these offers were in the context of India's insistence not only that China should first formally recognize the McMahon Line, but that she *should also accept the boundary India claimed in the western sector.* Later, China was to agree to interim discussions on particular points in dispute; but she required that such discussions be preliminary to comprehensive negotiations on the boundaries. The way even to interim discussions on marginal questions of alignment was thus blocked on both sides.

At the same time as the Indians adjusted the McMahon Line to suit their requirements at Migyitun, they similarly crossed the map-marked line at other points: at a place east of Migyitun called Tamaden, and, notably, at the western extremity of the line at Khinzemane, in an area that three years later was to be the flint for the border war. But it

---

* The House of the People, the lower house of the Indian Parliament. The upper house is the Rajya Sabha, or House of the States.
† Migyitun adjoins the Subansiri division of the North-East Frontier Agency.

was Longju which produced the sparks now. Peking protested at these forward moves by India, and then complained that, on August 25th, Indian troops had intruded south of Migyitun and fired on Chinese border guards, who had fired back.[94] Next day New Delhi protested, saying that it was the Chinese who had moved into Indian territory and opened fire, forcing the Indians out of Longju. The note accused China of 'deliberate aggression' in an attempt to implement border claims by force, and warned that the Indian frontier posts had been ordered to 'use force on the trespassers if necessary'.[95] This threat was in fact bluff—the Indians were soon after ordered not to fire unless fired upon—but it seemed to be challenging China to a showdown at Longju. Peking pointed out that as the two Governments differed over where exactly the boundary lay, Chinese personnel stationed on what they regarded as their own territory could be called trespassers by the Indians, and fired on more or less at will.

The Indian threat to use force in these circumstances does not seem to be well founded in international law. As one authority puts it, while every state has the inherent right to defend its borders against violation and to protect its territorial integrity, 'where the sovereignty over the territory a state claims to protect is disputed, as will surely be the position in a boundary dispute, it can no longer afford a basis upon which to rest the right of self-defence.'[96] The issue here is: when is a boundary dispute not a boundary dispute? A factitious or spurious boundary claim is a familiar cloak for aggression, and the Indians acted as if that is what they faced on the McMahon Line and, later, in the western sector. But denial of the existence of a genuine dispute can equally be a cloak for intransigence, and that is what the Chinese had now begun to feel they faced.[97]

China's account of the Longju incident was wholly contrary to India's. The Chinese denied that they had launched any counter-attack to what they described as the unprovoked attack of the Indians, maintaining that the Chinese border guards had done no more than return the Indians' fire, and that the latter withdrew from Longju of their own accord.[98] There is no way of telling which account was nearer the truth, and it is quite likely that one of the two Governments was being misled by the reports of its border forces. The fact that China did not attack the other Indian posts set up across the McMahon Line at Khinzemane and Tamaden does, however, militate against the Indian charge that the Longju incident was a deliberate attack (and the Indians soon after this withdrew the Tamaden post, admitting that it had been on Chinese territory).[99] The safest interpretation must be that the Longju incident was an accidental clash of the kind to be expected when armed troops of opposing sides press close to an undemarcated boundary.

In India, however, there was no doubt about the origin of the incident in Chinese aggression. The *Times of India* speculated that among the motives behind the Chinese 'border offensive' was the wish to 'lower the morale of the border people and, by a provocative display of apparently superior military might, create a wider impression in Sikkim, Bhutan, Nepal and Burma that India is really in no position to defend them'.[100] The Praja Socialist Party denounced Chinese 'expansionism' and the 'cynical contempt with which it treats the noble concepts of friendship, toleration and co-existence'. The resolution concluded that 'a new danger and a new challenge face the Indian people—but only by facing such dangers and meeting such challenges does a nation develop its manhood and its personality'.[101] A newspaper columnist suggested that the Chinese were testing the defences of NEFA.[102]

While the first shooting affray of the boundary dispute thus took place on August 25th, 1959, on the McMahon Line (the Indians said they had one killed and one wounded),[103] the point of collision was simultaneously being approached in the western sector. The Indian Government had decided during the summer that border posts should be set up at three points north-east of Leh. These were well short of the boundary shown on Chinese maps, even that being then for most of its length beyond the logistical reach of the Indians. At the same time it was decided, however, that a patrol should go up the Changchenmo valley to the Lanak Pass, which India regarded as the boundary feature, to establish a post there.[104] Moving up the Changchenmo valley after having set up the other posts, this patrol of about seventy men of the special border police* came into contact with the Chinese at the Kongka Pass—the Chinese regard that as the boundary feature and, getting there first, had established a post. An Indian scouting party of three was detained by the Chinese on October 20th; next day in a sharp affray nine of the main Indian force were killed and seven taken prisoner. The Chinese also suffered casualties, but probably of only one killed. Once again the accounts of the incidents were contradictory.

---

* A para-military force like the Assam Rifles.

The Indians reported that they had been ambushed from a hill-top; the Chinese said that the Indians, meeting a small Chinese patrol, had attempted to capture it and then opened fire, but had been beaten off. Statements confirming the Chinese account were made by the captured Indians, including the patrol commander, but were retracted after the men had been released, with the charge that they had been extorted after prolonged interrogation in conditions amounting to coercion. As in the Longju incident, there is no corroborating evidence that would show which side's account was nearer the truth.

But in India, naturally enough, there was no doubt. What one newspaper called 'the brutal massacre of an Indian policy party',[105] coming so soon after what was seen as an unprovoked and calculated Chinese attack at Longju, turned the political public's attitude towards China from one of distrust into open bellicosity.

* * * * * * * * * * *

India's border policy was evolved in Nehru's discussions with his officials in the Ministry of External Affairs; it was implemented in the movement of patrols and troop formations in the high wastes of the western sector and the jungle beneath the McMahon Line; it was argued in the diplomatic exchanges with Peking; and it was expounded, debated and confirmed in Parliament. There, and especially in the Lok Sabha, the drama of action that was played out on the frontiers to its crashing finale in the border war, and the diplomatic drama of the lapse into enmity of Asia's two greatest powers, were reflected in words. In the three years after the Longju and Kongka Pass clashes in the autumn of 1959 Parliament devoted perhaps hundreds of hours to the dispute with China. Parliament was the scene, too, of another, subtler drama in which the dominating moral authority of Jawaharlal Nehru was eroded and at last crumbled with the debacle of the Indian Army. In a parallel development, the legislature began to assert its control over the executive.

In 1959, between the second and third general elections, the Congress Party held seventy-four per cent of the five hundred seats in the Lok Sabha. The chamber of the lower house in the huge, circular Parliament building, in its colonnaded smoothness the happiest product of Britain's imperial architecture, is semicircular, the members' benches arranged in wedge-like segments like the slices of a halved cake, and the Congress Party's giant share left only the last two slices for the Opposition. There technically sat no such thing as an Opposition party (the Lok Sabha's criterion for party status being a membership of at least fifty) but a collection of sub-groups. Largest of these at the time was the Communist Party of India, with thirty-one members. Next, with nineteen seats, came the Praja Socialist Party, the main splinter of the Congress Socialists who had quit the mother party some years before and then broken up. After that no party had as many as ten seats, although a few had cobbled together groups for the sake of convenience in obtaining speaking time and other privileges. The new-born Swatantra Party, conceived as the voice of a secular and demo-cratic Right alternative to Congress; the Jan Sangh, the voice and vehicle of Hindu orthodoxy and reaction; the Socialist Party, another of the Left's splinters; the Republicans, representing the Untouch-ables: these and even smaller parties together with numerous Inde-pendents filled the rest of the Opposition benches. Considering their small numbers, these Opposition members put up a stout verbal resis-tance to the mass weight of the Congress, and most of the Lok Sabha's best debaters were on the Opposition side. These included Acharya Kripalani, formerly president of the Congress Party, now leader of the Praja Socialists, who would rise in his front seat, like the Ancient Mariner with his persistence and his long grey locks, to assail the Government, making Krishna Menon, the Defence Minister, his special target; Asoka Mehta, also then with the Praja Socialists, the anti-Communist, liberal intellectual to a T; Professor Ranga from Andhra Pradesh in the south, heading the Swatantra delegation, with Minoo Masani, ex-socialist turned Rightist with all the fervour of the apostate; Professor Hiren Mukerjee, the model of the Communist in Parliamentary clothing, suave, strong and precise in debate, an alert upholder of his Party's civil liberties and Parliamentary rights. Among the Independents Frank Anthony, the leader and nominated member for the Anglo-Indian community, was outstanding, his contributions to debate always cogent, at times as cutting and glittering as ground glass, standing out in the chamber as much for his invariable and imma-culate Western attire as for his oratory. At this time the great bulk of Parliament's business was conducted in English, the occasional passage of Hindi coming only when a member used it because his English was inadequate, or — more rarely — on principle.

It was a characteristic of the Lok Sabha that almost all the leading members on the Opposition side had once been in the Congress Party, comrades-in-arms with their opponents across the floor when politics were sublimated, or at least blurred, in the independence movement. The associations of past fraternity sometimes added bitterness to the exchanges in the House, but they also provided an underlay of familiarity and remembered friendship.

On the Government side Nehru towered. He was then seventy, but carried his years lightly, still with a two-stairs-at-a-time springiness in his walk, the stoop of age showing in his neck and shoulders only when he was tired. Much as he went his own way in decisions—or their avoidance—Nehru paid regular and punctilious observance to the primacy of Parliament, rarely missing a question hour, usually present for major debates, and always there for discussions of foreign affairs. A poor debater, his speeches too long and more like soliloquies than communications, he was a parliamentarian by commitment rather than by temperament. Enjoying his dominance in the House, his sallies were often touched with contempt for his opponents—'infantile', 'childish' were favourite words of rebuke for them. His authority was accepted, and in fact Nehru rather than the Speaker held the reins of the House; when, as not infrequently even in those days, it was bolting into noisy disorder with the Speaker's calls ignored, it would be Nehru's cutting voice which overrode the tumult and restored contrite decorum.

But Nehru's dominance was by no means absolute; it was tempered by his basic amenability to the will of the House and particularly to the submerged but powerful opposition to him within the Congress Party itself. That was represented even on the front bench: by Pant, the Home Minister at this time, a dotardly bearing disguising a still astringent mind; Morarji Desai, the demonstratively Gandhian Finance Minister; S. K. Patil, the party boss of Bombay whose contribution as Food Minister was to tap the supposedly inexhaustible supply of America's grain surpluses; the burly Jagjivan Ram, the Congress Party's leader of Hinduism's submerged caste of Untouchables, who was using the Railways portfolio to advance the interests of his caste. Colleagues like this were often deeply opposed to Nehru's approach; but they never fought him, being content merely to thwart—just as Nehru himself, it often seemed, was content merely to exhort. In the massed back benches of the party disapproval of Nehru's policies was widespread too, although latent and usually muted. But the border question gave such Congress critics of Nehru occasion and courage to attack him directly, confident that so long as they spoke for the nation's security and territorial integrity they could reply upon almost universal support in the House.

Krishna Menon, Defence Minister since 1957, in a seat directly behind the Prime Minister, served as a substitute target for those who preferred not to attack Nehru directly. Closer to Nehru personally than anyone else in the Government, Menon added to that cause of jealousy an undisguised contempt for the bulk of his colleagues. His backing in the party was very limited; he had no state base (he came from Kerala but had spent most of his political life in London), and the Congress Left, which counted him their leader, was a weak reed indeed. Menon's real roots of influence and power lay in his friendship with Nehru, and so long as the Prime Minister backed him he was safe against his many enemies in Congress. But Menon had long been besieged in Parliament, and the first disclosure of the existence of the Chinese road in Aksai Chin and the Longju incident coincided with the aborted resignation of the Chief of Army Staff, General Thimayya, and brought on a clamour for his resignation.*

Nirad Chaudhuri, a perceptive but unsparing anatomist of Indian society, saw in Nehru

one fatal weakness, his incapacity to stand up to more determined colleagues. ... Therefore he yields ... to popular feeling whenever he thinks, and as a rule wrongly, that it is too strong for him. Moreover, this ill-judged yielding in him has an extraordinary feature: he then becomes a whole-hearted and even passionate advocate of the very courses he condemned before. For instance, from time to time he lost his patience with the Hindu bluster against China, and employed strong language about it, but when at last he gave in he showed an exuberance which was not less than that of his critics.[106]

That 'bluster against China' began to pick up volume in the monsoon session of Parliament in August 1959, and as criticism of the Government's China policy developed, so it broadened its scope. The attack, which came as strongly from the non-Communist Left as from the Right, took in non-alignment as well as 'doctrinaire' economic policies, and hit as hard at the Government's domestic policies as at its handling of foreign affairs. The dispute over the boundaries and the Government's

* This incident is described in the following section.

China policy acted as a lens for a whole spectrum of Opposition criticisms; all manner of policies, attitudes and personalities were called into question, and perhaps Gunnar Myrdal is right when he says that 'at bottom [the critics'] real target was the social and economic revolution [Nehru] stood for, and which they had already done so much to obstruct or emasculate'.[107] The boundary dispute gave them a handle, and the use Nehru's domestic critics made of it must have fed his resentment against the Chinese—who were in his view solely responsible for the dispute.

In August 1959 public feeling against China was already strong in India—but what exactly did that mean? Myrdal makes the essential point, in commenting on the feeling in India against China:

> It must be remembered that these shifting currents of attitude and opinion took place mainly within a small upper-class group, though in India, as in all South Asia, they are referred to as 'middle-class', and their views as 'public opinion'. The masses do not participate much in the political process except as mobs to be roused to riot and demonstrations, or as voters to be cajoled by appeals that had little to do with national issues.[108]

The 'public opinion' which formed around the boundary question in India was not deep. It found expression primarily in Parliament, and in newspapers—especially those in the English language—in the capital and some of the major provincial cities. As the quarrel with China sharpened, so the public interest in it in India quickened and spread, but only when fighting broke out on the border did it become more than the concern of the middle class, in Myrdal's formulation.*

So August saw the political public's apprehension and excitement about the northern borders mounting. The newspapers carried numerous reports of Chinese troop concentrations just across the McMahon Line; questions were raised in Parliament when the short monsoon session opened about the problems Indian traders were facing in Tibet, and then in mid-August about a report that the Chinese had been talking about 'liberating' Sikkim, Bhutan, Ladakh and NEFA. That brought Nehru to say that it was India's responsibility to go to the aid of Bhutan—a statement which was promptly contradicted by the Prime Minister of Bhutan, who pointed out that his country was not

---

* Where this narrative refers to 'Indian reaction' or 'Indian opinion' it should be taken as shorthand allusion to the narrow political class.

an Indian protectorate, and that there was no reference at all to defence in the India–Bhutan treaty.[109] On August 24th an adjournment motion was tabled in the Lok Sabha on 'the grave situation arising out of the hostile attitude of the Chinese Communists towards India. . . .'[110]

Nehru's attitude to Sino-Indian relations at this time was still positive and measured. He sympathized with many of the expressions of disapproval of Chinese actions in Tibet that were being voiced in India, and perhaps also with some of the expressions of anxiety about China's intentions towards India. But he had told the Lok Sabha in May:

> Looking at the subject from any long perspective, or even in the short perspective, it is a matter of considerable consequence that China and India should be friends, should be co-operative. It does not mean that they should go the same path, but they should not come in each other's way; they should not be hostile to each other; it is neither good for India nor for China. . . . It is in the interest of both these countries, even though they function in different ways, not to be hostile to each other.[111]

Up to almost the end of August 1959 he had told Parliament nothing at all about the boundary dispute with China, about the road that crossed Aksai Chin, or about Peking's opposed approach to the whole question of boundary settlement — and for once the secret had been very well kept. It was not only a matter of secrecy; Nehru did not hesitate to mislead Parliament when members picked up the scent of the boundary dispute. In mid-August an Opposition member from Assam asked whether China had of late communicated to India the view that 'the McMahon Line no longer describes the international boundary as it was not ratified by the Chinese Government, and as it was only a British creation there should be some sort of redrawing of the line'. This can be recognized as a fair summary of Chou En-lai's first letter, received in January; but Nehru replied: 'No, sir; we have received no such communication now or at any earlier stage.'[112] On August 28th the chickens thus hatched came home to roost.

The Longju incident of three days before was reported in the newspapers that morning. Word had also at last got out of the existence of the Chinese road across Aksai Chin, and members came to the House demanding information on both subjects. Nehru coolly confirmed the existence of the road 'through a corner of our north-eastern Ladakhi territory' and told the House how the Government had learned of it.

He pointed out that in the western sector 'nobody had marked [the boundary], but after some kind of broad surveys the then Government had laid down that border which we have been accepting and acknowledging'; but while generally playing down the dispute so far as it applied to the western sector he concluded that 'there have been cases and there are continuing cases in one or two places, of Chinese aggression.' Turning to the McMahon Line, he described the Longju incident, noting that the Chinese had been given a different account by their own men, but that he naturally preferred to believe that of the Indian border force. He then summed up his approach to the whole border problem. Minor border incidents and differences should be settled by negotiations, he said, they were long-standing, matters of 'a mile of grazing ground here or there', and although 'we think we are right let us sit around a conference table and settle them'. But when it came to 'the broad approach of the Chinese maps which have brush-coloured [as Chinese] hundreds of miles of Indian territory', that was 'totally and manifestly unacceptable' and could not be 'a matter for discussion'.[113]

A few days later in the Lok Sabha Nehru gave a fuller statement of his approach. The Chinese, he said, were saying that it was India who had committed aggression at Longju:

Now, it is a question of fact, whether this village or that village or this little strip of territory is on their side or on our side. Normally, wherever these are relatively petty disputes, well, it does seem to me rather absurd for two great countries — or two small countries — to rush at each other's throats to decide whether two miles of territory are on this side or on that side, and especially two miles of territory in the high mountains, where nobody lives. But where national prestige and dignity is involved it is not the two miles of territory, it is the nation's dignity and self-respect that become involved in it. And therefore this happens. But I do not wish, in so far as I can, to press the issue so far that there is no escape for either country, because their national dignities are involved, except a recourse to arms. . . .

It is highly objectionable, highly improper for the Chinese Government to go on issuing maps colouring half of the North-East Frontier Agency, one-third of Assam and one-third of Bhutan as if they belong to China. That is really an affront. . . . But

[China] having accepted broadly the McMahon Line, I am prepared to discuss any interpretation of the McMahon Line; minor
interpretation here or there – that is a different matter – not these
big chunks but the minor interpretation, whether this hill is there,
or this little bit is on this side or on that side, on the facts, on the
maps, on the evidence available. That I am prepared to discuss
with the Chinese Government. I am prepared to have any kind of
conciliatory, mediatory process to consider this. I am prepared to
have arbitration of any authority agreed to by the two parties
about these minor rectifications, where they are challenged by
them or by us, whichever the case may be. That is a different
matter. . . . I do not take up that kind of narrow attitude that
whatever I say is right and whatever the other person says is
wrong. But the broad McMahon Line has to be accepted and so
far as we are concerned it is there and we accept it.[114]

Nehru then turned to the western sector, saying 'the position about
Ladakh is somewhat different.' He explained that the McMahon Line
did not extend there (a lot of M.P.s were at this time hazy in their
border geography) and that the border was governed by the 1842
treaty between Gulab Singh and the Tibetans – stating, erroneously,
that the Emperor of China had also been party to that treaty.* 'Nobody
has challenged that,' he said. 'Nobody challenges it now.'

But the actual boundary of Ladakh with Tibet was not very carefully
defined. It was defined to some extent by British officers who went
there, but I rather doubt if they did any careful survey. They
marked the line. It has been marked all along in our maps. They
did it. As people do not live there, by and large, it does not make
any difference. At that time, nobody cared about it.[115]

In his statements in Parliament about the western sector at this time
Nehru was not only vague, he was tentative:

It is a complicated thing, but we have always looked upon the
Ladakh area as a different area, as, if I may say so, some vaguer
area so far as the frontier is concerned because the exact line of the
frontier is not at all clear as in the case of the McMahon Line. . . .[116]
This place, Aksai Chin area, is [Indian] in our maps undoubtedly,

* See pages 24 and 25 n in Part I for the 1842 treaty. Not only was China not a party to
it, but neither, according to the British officer who investigated the matter for the Viceroy
a few years after it was concluded, was the Tibetan Government.[117]

but I distinguish it completely from other areas. It is a matter for argument as to what part of it belongs to us and what part of it belongs to somebody else. It is not at all a dead clear matter. I have to be frank to the House. It is not clear. I cannot go about doing things in a matter which has been challenged, not [only] today but for a hundred years. It has been challenged to the ownership of this strip of territory. . . . It has been in challenge all the time. . . . I cannot say what part of it may not belong to us, and what parts may. The point is, there has never been any delimitation there in that area and it has been a challenged area.[118]

But while Nehru was thus fending off demands in Parliament that the Chinese road on Aksai Chin be 'bombed out of existence'[119] by pointing out that there was real doubt about the ownership of the territory the road crossed, no hint of such open-mindedness appeared in his communications to Peking. There he was maintaining that Aksai Chin was and always had been Indian territory, that the boundary claimed by India in the western sector, and the McMahon Line, had 'always been the historic frontiers' of India.[120]

Nehru's tentativeness about the western sector did not last long even in his domestic utterances, and its disappearance can be traced to the return from London of Dr S. Gopal, director of the Historical Division of the Ministry of External Affairs. Gopal, not a senior official but respected by Nehru (and son of Dr Radhakrishnan, then Vice-President), had been sent to London to go through the material on India's northern borders in the India Office and Foreign Office archives. He was given no brief, in fact Nehru told him explicitly that his job was to disregard all contemporary political considerations, make an objective appraisal of the historical evidence, and report back. In November 1959 Gopal told Nehru that India's claim to the Aksai Chin area was clearly stronger than China's.[121] He took the Prime Minister over the historical evidence which had led him to that conclusion, and Nehru concurred. As has been seen, it had long been the Indian Government's policy that the McMahon Line must not be submitted to re-negotiation, and in 1954 Nehru had extended that principle to the rest of the northern borders, saying they were 'not open to discussion with anybody'. Now Gopal's report confirmed Nehru in that approach, and apparently removed the reservations he had until then expressed about the certainty of India's claim in the western sector.

There appears to have been some uneasiness among Nehru's Cabinet colleagues and other advisers at the conclusions for India's policy towards China that he had drawn from Gopal's report. By this time Nehru was keeping the Cabinet's Foreign Affairs Committee* closely informed about the handling of the dispute with China, and Gopal gave the committee an oral account of the result of his investigations. Krishna Menon afterwards demurred to Gopal, saying that this historical approach to questions of boundary agreement was not the way to go about it, that what was needed was a political decision. Others in the Cabinet also apparently felt that between them Nehru, the amateur historian, and Gopal, the professional, were taking the Government on a wrong course, and expressed such misgivings to Gopal.[122] But the latter was the wrong man to complain to, he could take no policy decisions; and no one was prepared to stand up to Nehru in Cabinet and squarely disagree with him.

If Nehru had decided that India's interests lay in a settlement with China and instructed Gopal accordingly, the latter could have produced a historical justification for a compromise boundary line in the western sector — indeed, in the MacDonald–Macartney line of 1899 one was ready made. But, as a marked change in Nehru's public comments on China at this time make clear, he was by then resentful and suspicious of China, angered by what he had begun to see as Peking's cavalier and overbearing approach to the boundary question.

As Nehru saw it, equality of regard was fundamental to good relations between governments. 'Natural friendship does not exist if you are weak and if you are looked down upon as a weak country,' he told Parliament at the beginning of September. 'Friendship cannot exist between the weak and the strong, between a country that is trying to bully and the other who accepts to be bullied. . . . It is only when people are more or less equal, when people respect each other, that they are friends. So also [with] nations.'[123] In Nehru's reading of events on the borders and of the diplomatic correspondence, China was not fulfilling that prescription for friendship, but was on the contrary using the boundary question to assert superiority, even perhaps dominance, over India. As he expressed it apropos the Longju incident, the Chinese might have intended that 'just to show us our place . . . so that we may not get uppish'.[124] A few days later he confirmed the charge. 'Now,

* This consisted of Nehru, Pant (Home Affairs), Morarji Desai (Finance), Krishna Menon, Lal Bahadur Shastri (Commerce and Industry), and A. K. Sen (Law).

what is happening in China today?' he asked, '. . . I do not wish to use strong words, but it is the pride and arrogance of might that is show-ing, in their language, in their behaviour to us and in so many things that they have done.'[125] China was trying to bully India:

> Nothing can be a more amazing folly than for two great countries like India and China to go into a major conflict and war for the possession of a few mountain peaks, however beautiful the moun-tain peaks might be, or some area which is more or less uninhabited. [But] it is not that, as every member of this House knows. When such conflicts occur, something happens which stirs our innermost convictions, something which hurts our pride, our national pride, self-respect and all that. So, it is not a question of a mile or two, or ten or even a hundred miles. It is something more precious than a hundred or a thousand miles and it is that which brings up people's passions to a high level, and it is that which, to some extent, is happening in India today. It is not because of a patch of territory but because they feel that they have not got a fair treatment in this matter, that they have been treated rather casually by the Chinese Government and an attempt is made, if I may use the word, to bully them.[126]

Nehru was here speaking as if of others, but it is plain that he was also speaking for himself. He had tacitly renounced his earlier attitude — in which he had maintained that the boundary question was not one in which national pride was at stake — and was speaking now as if that pride were fully and properly engaged. This led him to the sort of hyperbole that, in the mouths of other politicians, he would no doubt have denounced as demagogy. He said China was asking for the Himalayas to be handed over to her as a gift, the Himalayas which he described as 'the crown of India', part of her 'culture, blood and veins';[127] and could naturally conclude from such formulations that it was 'a claim which it is quite impossible for India or almost any Indian ever to admit, whatever the consequences.'[128] He accused China of acting from 'the pride and arrogance of might', confessed himself puzzled by 'the Chinese mind', and suggested that China might be suffering from paranoia.[129] That all this was delivered in Nehru's customary periods, rambling, reflective and calm, and coupled with exhortations to his compatriots to remember Gandhi and abjure anger, did not make it less inflammatory.

Nehru was plainly speaking from a strong sense of injury and resentment. He felt that the Chinese had failed to give due weight to India's importance in the world—they forgot, he said, that 'India is not a country which can be ignored, even though she may speak in a gentler language.'[130] An element of Nehru's reaction was undoubtedly personal, and perhaps it was a strong one. All of India's foreign policy was an extension of Nehru's political personality; but no part of it was more markedly associated with him personally than India's friendship with China. He had long been under attack for it from his domestic critics; now they were gleefully reminding him of their past warnings. To this humiliation, weakening to his own political position, must have been added the sense of betrayal by the Chinese, and particularly by Chou En-lai.

How strong Nehru's sense of injury was can be assessed by its consequence, which was nothing less than the reversal of what had until then been a key element in India's foreign policy: the policy of friendly co-operation with China. That this had always been close to Nehru's own heart has been seen; but it was also a policy that, from every consideration of India's interest, was not only sound, but imperative. That it could now be dropped, in anger and resentment at China's approach to the question of the boundaries, suggests that India's foreign policy in Nehru's day could be largely subjective, and was closely tied to Nehru's own pride, and perhaps prestige.

The change in Nehru's attitude towards China was sudden, and can be related to two events; the Longju clash (Nehru ignored the fact that this was a consequence of India's admitted unilateral modification of the McMahon Line) and, secondly, the receipt of a long letter from Chou En-lai.

This letter, dated September 8th, 1959, and a belated reply to Nehru's of six months before, confirmed all the Indian misgivings and resentment about the Chinese approach to the boundary question. In a tone markedly less cordial than in his previous letter, Chou reaffirmed the basic point: that the Sino-Indian boundary had never been delimited. He rebutted Nehru's argument that the 1842 treaty for the western sector, and the Simla Conference for the eastern, had amounted to delimitation; he pointed out that China had not participated in the former—which anyway made no specific provision for the boundary—and that the McMahon Line was not even a product of the Simla Conference proper, and had never been recognized by any Chinese

Government.* Arguing then that all the territory between the McMahon Line and the foot-hills had been Chinese, an area he put at 56,000 square miles, he asked: 'How could China agree to accept under coercion such an illegal line which would have it relinquish its rights and disgrace itself by selling out its territory – and such a large piece of territory at that?' As for the western sector, where China's maps showed Aksai Chin as Chinese territory, that, he said, was the customary boundary alignment.

Chou En-lai restated his Government's approach. A settlement of the boundary question, fair and reasonable to both sides and taking into consideration both the historical background and existing actualities should be sought through friendly negotiations. In the meantime the *status quo* should be observed by both sides and provisional agreements could be negotiated on specific isolated places in dispute.

China, he said, had expected that because India, like herself, had been subjected to imperialist aggression, she would take the same approach to the boundary question, adopting 'an attitude of mutual sympathy, mutual understanding and fairness and reasonableness'. But instead, 'the Indian Government demanded that the Chinese Government give formal recognition to the situation created by the application of the British policy of aggression against China's Tibet region as the foundation for the settlement of the Sino-Indian boundary question'; and, more serious, had applied 'all sorts of pressures . . . not even scrupling the use of force'. The fact that India would not recognize the undelimited state of the boundary and was trying to bring pressure on China, 'militarily, diplomatically and through public opinion, cannot but make one suspect that it is the attempt of India to impose upon China its one-sided claims on the boundary question'. That attempt would never succeed, but would only impair the friendship between the two countries, thus complicating the boundary question and making it more difficult to settle. Chou concluded by asking that 'trespassing Indian troops and administrative personnel' be withdrawn,

---

* 'Contrary to what you wrote in your letter [Chou En-lai wrote] the so-called McMahon Line was never discussed at the Simla Conference, but was determined by the British representative and the representative of the Tibet local authorities behind the back of the representative of the Chinese Central Government through an exchange of secret notes at Delhi on March 24th, 1914, that is, prior to the signing of the Simla treaty. This line was later marked on the map attached to the Simla treaty as part of the boundary between Tibet and the rest of China. . . . The Simla treaty was not formally signed by the representative of the then Chinese Central Government.'[131]

As has been seen, this was an accurate summary of the origins of the McMahon Line.

a measure by which he said 'the dark clouds hanging over Sino-Indian relations would be speedily dispelled'.[132]

This letter was read in New Delhi as a barely veiled claim for the whole of NEFA north of the Brahmaputra—a claim, as Nehru described it, 'which it is quite impossible for India or almost any Indian ever to admit whatever the consequences'.[133] If this was a misreading—and the evidence suggests that it was—the Chinese must bear some of the blame. Chou En-lai's former assurance that when it came to negotiations China would accept the McMahon alignment had here almost disappeared, dwindling into the reference to 'existing actualities' as one of the factors upon which a boundary settlement should be based. He had also greatly exaggerated the extent of Tibetan/Chinese penetration into the tribal belt enclosed by the McMahon Line; *apart from the Tawang Tract*, that, as has been seen, had not in fact reached more than a few miles down some of the bigger valleys, but Chou now suggested that Chinese administration had extended throughout the tribal belt. This was as tendentious as the Indian claim that the McMahon Line simply formalized the previous 'natural, traditional, ethnic and administrative boundary'.[134] Each side, it can be seen, was by now maintaining that what had in fact been a no-man's-land had always been under its own administration.

Chou En-lai's letter was taken in New Delhi as amounting to what Nehru a little later called 'a definite breach of faith [by the Chinese] with a country which tried to be friendly to them'.[135] But analysis of the letter, putting it into the context of Chinese statements before and after, and of the moment in Sino-Indian relations in which it was written, seen from Peking, suggests that Chou may have meant to express no alteration in China's basic approach to the boundary question. When the letter was written relations had been severely strained by the rebellion in Tibet and the reaction to this in India, vociferously sympathetic to the rebels. Peking suspected that India's sympathy extended to covert assistance to the rebels, allowing them to raid back into Tibet from sanctuary below the McMahon Line, and letting agents of the Kuomintang regime in Formosa operate freely in Kalimpong, smuggling saboteurs, weapons and ammunition into Tibet.[136] There had been an outburst of violently anti-Chinese feeling in India, going as far as calls for war, and, while Nehru had until then by and large maintained his friendly and calm tone, he too had publicly sympathized with the Tibetan rebels, giving that sympathy demonstrative expression by a much publicized visit to the Dalai Lama as soon as the latter was settled in his exile in an Indian hill-station. It was already clear that India's assurance that the Dalai Lama would not be expected to engage in political activity was not going to be kept; at a press conference in June he had, to all intents and purposes, declared the formation of an émigré Government.[137] As for the boundary question, Nehru had not only ruled out a settlement by negotiation, but had advanced a categorical claim to a segment of territory which would sever the only land route from Sinkiang to Tibet. Furthermore, in both the McMahon Line and the western sectors Indian forces had been pushing forward: over the map-marked McMahon Line at Khinzemane, Longju and Tamaden, and around the Pangong Lake in the western sector, where another Indian patrol had been apprehended by the Chinese in July[138] (the clash at the Kongka Pass had not yet occurred.) If all that is put together, and looked at from Peking's viewpoint, it seems enough to account for Chou's cold and accusatory tone. His inference that India was trying 'to impose upon China its one-sided claims on the boundary question' was not amiss—unfair and even grotesque as the accusation must have seemed to Nehru, that was in fact what India was doing, and would continue to do.

But Chou also restated the essential Chinese position; that a boundary settlement could be reached, 'fair and reasonable to both sides', in accordance with 'existing actualities' as well as the historical background. There was, too, a substantive qualification implicit in his repudiation of the McMahon Line: how could China agree to accept such an illegal line 'under coercion'? he asked—with the connotation, there for the reading, that perhaps if there were no attempt at coercion it could be accepted, illegal or not. And at their previous meeting Chou of course had personally assured Nehru that, in such circumstances, it would be accepted. But in September 1959 the Indian Government was in no mood to try to read between the lines of Chou's letter, and found in it instead proof that, as Nehru put it, what they had to face was 'a great and powerful nation which is aggressive'.[139]

Nehru replied accordingly, expressing 'great surprise and distress'. He argued at length that the boundaries India claimed had 'always been the historical frontier' and were in every sector settled by 'history, geography, custom and tradition'. 'It is true that the Sino-Indian boundary has not been formally delimited along its entire length,' he continued, apparently confirming his admission in Parliament a few days before that there had been no delimitation in the western sector; but then he went on to say: 'Indeed the terrain of the Sino-Indian border in many places makes such physical demarcation on the ground impossible.' Thus, by suggesting that when he said 'delimitation' he meant 'demarcation' Nehru in effect cancelled his admission about the indeterminate nature of the border in the western sector, and resumed his earlier stand — that the boundary was already settled everywhere, and that it lay just where India said it did. (At home Nehru retracted his admission by simply saying that he had been 'quoted out of context', and declared that 'neither in the eastern nor the western sector [is] the Indian border indeterminate'.)[140]

The Indian arguments, as they had by then been set out in a series of diplomatic notes to Peking and in Nehru's letters to Chou En-lai, were different in character as they applied to the two main sectors in dispute, the eastern and the western. So far as the McMahon Line was concerned, the first line of defence was the argument that the Anglo-Tibetan exchanges which produced it 'must, in accordance with accepted international practice, be regarded as binding on both China and Tibet'.[141] This argument was sustained by burking the central issue — which was that the Chinese had not participated in the secret Anglo-Tibetan exchanges — and by ignoring the fact that China in 1914 and later had explicitly repudiated any and all such agreements between the Tibetans and the British. The officials and historians of the Indian Ministry of External Affairs, and no doubt Nehru, knew as well as the Chinese that this was a misrepresentation of what took place at the Simla Conference. But the Indian Government had decided that it would be dangerously against the country's interest to negotiate a boundary settlement with China. This was not only because of the expectation that, whatever hints the Chinese might drop beforehand, at such negotiations they would introduce sweeping irredentist claims; the Indians had also come to see any compromise boundary settlement with China as unacceptable, because it would signal that India had had to back down, and thus relegate her to secondary status in Asia. The only reasonable ground for refusing to negotiate a boundary settlement is the argument that the boundary is already in fact delimited, and the Indians argued accordingly, not, of course, for the benefit of the Chinese, but for the international community at large, which was by now trying to follow the Sino-Indian debate.

The second line of India's verbal defence was the claim that the

McMahon Line was never a new boundary, but did no more than 'formalize the natural, traditional, ethnic and administrative boundary in the area'.[142] This pre-existing boundary, in the Indian account, was ancient indeed; they claimed that it had lain 'approximately where it now runs for nearly three thousand years'.[143] To substantiate this claim, the Indians drew on the Upanishads, the Mahabharata, the Ramayana, the corpus of Hindu literature; for centuries, they told the Chinese, 'the striving of the Indian spirit was directed towards these Himalayan fastnesses'.[144] This line of argument found a receptive resonance among Indians, and Nehru referred frequently to the place of the Himalayas in Indian thought as a factor in the boundary dispute; but the Chinese were not impressed, saying that 'myths and legends could not be cited as basis for the alignment claimed by India'.*[145]

This accumulation of argument, to the point that the boundaries stood 'defined without the necessity of further or formal delimitation',[146] was presented with sustained forensic skill. The purpose was not, of course, to convince the Chinese, any more than a lawyer arguing a case in court is concerned with convincing his opponents, who presumably know the facts of the case as well as he does. By this time, September 1959, the Indian Government was publishing its communications to Peking almost as soon as they were delivered, and in this process of open diplomacy, publicly pursued, diplomatic notes inevitably became propaganda devices. As Nehru was to put it later: 'What I am aiming at is either winning over the other party or weakening the other party in its own opinion and in the world's opinion and in my own.' That, he said, 'is the normal practice.'[147] In a sense it was, and any culpability here attaches not to the Indians but to the jury, as it were, of the informed world public who took the Indian argumentation as the work not of lawyers making a case, but of scholars concerned only with truth.

The Indian argument so far as the western sector was concerned was

---

* The Indian argument from Hindu literature presents a forbiddingly dense textual surface, sufficient to deter any explorers except those equipped with their own detailed knowledge of the sources. In a close analysis of this aspect of the Indian case, Professor A. R. Field of the University of Calgary concluded that the Indian Government was 'in serious error' when it maintained that 'the ancient evidence [was] supported by the continuity of tradition and custom as the basis for the boundary'.[148]

This Indian argument seems to be related to what Curzon called the 'class of so-called natural frontiers . . . namely those which are claimed by nations as natural on grounds of ambition, or expediency, or more often sentiment'. The attempt to realize such frontiers 'has been responsible for many of the wars, and some of the most tragical vicissitudes in history', Curzon concluded.[149]

essentially different. In the east, the Indian position was really that the McMahon Line was the *de facto* boundary and by every consideration of national interest must remain so, and the arguments were shaped to that purpose. But in the case of the Aksai Chin area, the Indians were convinced that their claim had a stronger historical foundation than that of the Chinese. This conviction rested basically on the report of Dr Gopal, who was responsible for the elaboration and presentation of the Indian historical argument throughout.

The Indian argument was most effective in countering the Chinese version of the 'traditional and customary boundary line'. In detail, the Chinese case for the line shown on their maps was weak, and the Indians were able to cite much evidence to indicate that the Chinese claim was too far to the west. The Chinese counter was that because no boundary had been delimited, any 'traditional and customary' alignment had to be vague, by its nature; precision was to be expected only after delimitation and demarcation, processes which the Indians were maintaining were not required. If the Chinese case for their version of the traditional and customary boundary was not strong, however, the Indian evidence to substantiate their own claim that a fully determined international boundary existed along their claim line was also weak. They could adduce evidence that at various times the Kuen Lun mountains had marked the southern limit of Chinese territory in this area; but they could adduce none to show that effective Indian or British administration had ever been exercised up to the Kuen Lun. Aksai Chin had in practice been a no-man's-land, and no linear boundary had ever run across or around it. The creation of such a boundary had been left to independent India and China.

One curious element of the Indian presentation of their case was the treatment of the 1899 Macartney-MacDonald line. This, as has been seen, was the only boundary alignment ever proposed to China by the British; and it would have left the territory crossed by the road built by the Chinese in the 1950s on their own side. But the Indians persistently inverted the implication of the 1899 line;* for example, Nehru claimed in his letter to Chou in September 1959 that the 1899 line 'signified beyond doubt that the whole of Aksai Chin area lay in Indian territory' — the reverse of the truth. This error can only be

---

* For the Indian side's mis-statements of the 1899 proposal see: *Officials' Report*, p. 55; Note of November 24th, 1959 (W.P. II, p. 25); Note of February 12th, 1960 (W.P. II, p. 87); Note of November 4th, 1959 (W.P. II, p. 22); and this letter of Nehru's (W.P. II, p. 36).

explained, it seems, as a mistake of transliteration from the original British note in the archives.* It could have been a small slip, but it had very large implications.

Having argued in detail against the basic Chinese position – that the boundary had never been delimited – and ruled out negotiations to perform that task, Nehru in his reply to Chou En-lai turned to the Chinese proposal of maintenance of the *status quo* pending a settlement. 'We agree,' he wrote, but then again blurred the point. 'In the meantime both sides should respect the traditional frontier and neither side should seek to alter the *status quo* in any manner. Further, if any party has trespassed into the other's territory across the international frontier, it should immediately withdraw to its side of the frontier.'[150] Thus (with a 'further', when the context called for 'but') Nehru again introduced the Indian demand for restoration of the *status quo ante*, which was in fact a veiled demand for unilateral Chinese withdrawal: 'There can be no question of withdrawing any Indian personnel,' he stated. Nehru then articulated a new Indian requirement: 'No discussions can be fruitful unless the posts on the Indian side of the traditional frontier now held by the Chinese forces are first evacuated by them and further threats and intimidations immediately cease.' Krishna Menon made the same point in the United Nations at this time, insisting that 'Chinese troops must withdraw from areas now controlled by China before any negotiations [can] take place.'[151] This became another essential part of the Indian position.

Nehru thus added another layer to the wall he had constructed between himself and any possibility of reaching a settlement, short of China's reversing her approach and surrendering to the Indian demands. But at this time he was, in fact, following a more cautious course than the tone of the Indian diplomatic communications suggested – and the warnings to Peking that Indian border forces had been authorized to use force against 'trespassers' were bluff. On September 13th, 1959, Nehru recorded this directive:

(a) We must avoid actual conflict until it is actually forced down upon us. That is to say, we must avoid armed conflict not only in a big way, but even in a small way. On no account should our forces fire unless they are actually fired at.

---

* The 1899 proposal was for a boundary that 'follows the Lak Tsang range until that meets a spur running south from the Kuen Lun' (see p. 34 n); but in the Indian version the proposal became for an alignment 'along the Kuen Lun range'.[152]

(b) In the event of any Chinese armed detachment coming over to our side, they should be told to go back. Only if they fire should our people fire at them.

(c) [This gave detailed instructions for the Chushul area.]

(d) The Aksai Chin area has to be left more or less as it is as we have no check-posts there and practically little of access. Any questions in relation to it can only be considered, when the time arises, in the context of the larger question of the entire border. For the present, we have to put up with the Chinese occupation of this north-eastern sector [of Ladakh] and their road across it.

(e) Our general instructions to our people on the border should be that they should avoid any provocative action, but should remain firmly on our side of the line and not allow themselves to be pushed away easily.

(f) I think it is unlikely that the Chinese forces will take up any aggressive line on this frontier, that is, try to enter into our territory any further. If they should do so, they will have to be stopped and the matter reported to us immediately for instructions.*

When this minute was dictated, the large Indian patrol detailed to set up a post at the Lanak Pass was already setting out and, as has been seen, on October 21st it clashed with the Chinese at the Kongka Pass and suffered fatal casualties. In its protest note of November 4th New Delhi compared China's actions on the borders with 'the activities of the old imperialist powers against whom both India and China struggled in the past', and warned that India would resist aggression by all means available. This same note carried a detailed and complete description — the first — of the boundary which India claimed existed in the western sector. In Parliament in August and September Nehru had made repeated statements to the effect that no clear boundary had ever been defined in the western sector: now a boundary putting the whole of Aksai Chin in India was described with exactitude, and the Chinese were told that 'any person with a knowledge of history . . . would appreciate that this traditional and historical frontier of India has been associated with India's culture and tradition for the last two

---

* This minute, a document of the Government of India, is still unpublished. As with much material quoted later in this book, the writer is not free to state where or how he obtained it. This should be taken to be the case where documents are cited without reference to source.

thousand years or so, and has been an intimate part of India's life and thought.'[153]

After the Longju incident the Government had announced that the NEFA border was being made the responsibility of the Army; now the same measure was applied to the western sector of the border too.*

Coming only two months after the Longju incident, the clash at the Kongka Pass — seen as another treacherous Chinese attack — had a convulsive effect on Indian political opinion. Parliament was no longer in session and Nehru's first comments on the incident were made in the public speeches which always occupied a good deal of his time, and in these he attempted to pacify, or at least control, the outburst of anger which the Indian dead at Kongka Pass had aroused. Speaking at Meerut, not far from New Delhi, a few days after the clash, he tried to put the incident into the perspective of long Sino-Indian friendship, and cautioned against impulsive action. 'Whatever step we take, we will have to ponder over it and not take it in anger or passion, but in a far-seeing way so that no bad effect is felt in Asia or the world,' he said. His references to the Chinese expressed sorrow rather than anger, were chiding rather than denunciatory, and he even admitted again that there could be two views about ownership of the place in which the clash occurred.

This speech brought upon his own head a storm of criticism fiercer than he had faced before. 'Irrelevant', 'hypocritical', 'fatuous', 'dishonest' were some of the adjectives applied to his speech by one newspaper, which accused him of having shown 'an over-scrupulous regard for Chinese susceptibilities and comparative indifference towards the anger and dismay with which the Indian people have reacted'.[154] The trouble is, another commented, 'that Mr Nehru generally treats the nation as so many grown-up children. He thinks that, like the upset juvenile, the nation can be calmed by soothing words. He is wrong.'[155] One critic blamed the Kongka Pass incident on Nehru's 'weak and appeasing leadership', which was losing India more and more territory,[156] and the Jan Sangh passed a resolution calling on the Government to take immediate action to 'throw out' the Chinese. There were demands that India should drop non-alignment, join military pacts against China, and rearm. Nehru dismissed such talk as 'utterly wrong

---

* Normally the policing of the Indian borders was the responsibility of the Home Ministry The NEFA border was covered by the Assam Rifles, responsible to the central Government through the Governor of Assam.

and useless', the utterances of those with 'cold feet and warm heads', and offered repeated assurances that the country was militarily strong enough. 'I can tell this House', he said in the Lok Sabha, 'that at no time since our independence, and of course before it, were our defence forces in better condition, in finer fettle, and with the background of our far greater industrial production . . . to help them, than they are today. I am not boasting about them or comparing them with any other country's, but I am quite confident that our defence forces are well capable of looking after our security.'[157] The same claims, even more measured, were made by respected commentators in the press. A columnist in the *Times of India*, reflecting high-level briefings, wrote of the Prime Minister's 'full confidence in the ability of our defence forces to maintain the integrity of our northern border should the Chinese be so foolish as to challenge it. This confidence is not mere bravado but is based on a careful and studied appreciation of the military and logistical situation along the Sino-Indian border.'[158] How wide of the mark such views were will be seen later.

Nehru had a public meeting called in New Delhi so that he could answer these attacks. He explained that in his Meerut speech he had been speaking to a rustic audience, and that therefore he had used simpler language and ideas; and now he began to take a tougher approach. 'We will defend our country with all our might,' he said; 'there is no fear in my mind that somebody will attack us and sit on our chest. . . . We are strong enough to meet any challenge.'[159]

That the Kongka Pass incident came to have a drastic effect on Nehru's thinking as well as on public opinion was revealed in a memorandum sent by Nehru to key ambassadors abroad and leaked to the *New York Times*, which published its gist on November 12th:

According to this secret memorandum, Mr Nehru is believed to be of the opinion that India may have to use armed force to push Chinese troops out of the Indian territory they have occupied.

Mr Nehru is reported to have pointed out that China throughout her history has never willingly surrendered any territory or abandoned any territorial claims. He is said to be convinced now that China in the present dispute is only after territorial gains from India and not interested in a settlement based on traditional frontiers: therefore he does not see much chance of a reasonable negotiated settlement of the dispute. He is further reported to have noted that China's territorial claims have been growing rather than diminishing, and there have been veiled threats that unless India made a territorial concession in the Ladakh sector, China would start trouble on the North Eastern Frontier.[160]

When Parliament met later in November Nehru began to talk of war, always disapprovingly, indeed with expressions of horror, and coupling his allusions to reflections on the pacific traditions of India. But he was in a dilemma. He could rebuke the most bellicose of his critics for their blood-and-thunder battle cries; but to go too far and rule out all possibility of war over the borders would have been to open himself to new criticism that he was tying the country's hands, supinely letting China get away with what he himself had called aggression. His repeated allusions to the possibility of war, coupled with his steady assurances that the defence forces were ready for any-thing, inevitably nourished the impression that war with China over the border was a possibility, and that it could be won if it came.

Nehru had been on the defensive even before the Kongka Pass in-cident, blamed not only for having let his commitment to *Hindee Chinee bhai-bhai* blind him to the threat to the borders, but also for having kept the beginnings of the dispute with China from Parliament and the public. 'We thought at that time that it might be easier for us to deal with the Chinese Government without too much publicity,' he explained to the House, but he admitted that this had been an error.[161] On September 7th he laid before Parliament the first White Paper on Sino-Indian exchanges, covering the period from 1954 and including the first letters exchanged between himself and Chou En-lai. 'If I have erred in the past in some delay in placing the papers [on the boundary dispute] before the House, I shall not err again,' Nehru promised; '. . . the situation is such that we have to keep the country and especially Parliament in full touch with developments.'[162]

Thereafter all the diplomatic exchanges with China were promptly put before Parliament or, if Parliament was not in session, released to the press, and brought together from time to time in further White Papers. Thus Nehru, citing the Government's obligation to take Parlia-ment into its confidence, effectively surrendered to the legislature the executive's power and responsibility to conduct the country's foreign relations. This was probably partly calculated, as Nehru's approach to the boundary question required that the arguments India was advancing

in the diplomatic correspondence with China should be publicized.*
But it brought about that derangement of the governing power which
Walter Lippmann has described, when 'the power of the executive has
become enfeebled, often to the verge of impotence, by the pressures of
the representative assembly and of mass opinions.'[163]

Lippmann went on to observe that this 'has forced the democratic
states to commit disastrous and, it could be, fatal mistakes'; but before
applying this to the Indian Government's handling of its dispute with
China it must be remembered that the collision course was set by Nehru
and his advisers long before this, when they were under no significant
public pressure. Furthermore, that while Nehru's surrender to legis-
lative supervision of policy was almost complete, that worked only
to push him on *in directions he had chosen himself*. Public and Parliamentary pressures did not make him do anything he was not himself
inclined to do; nor did they prevent him from doing anything he
really wished to do. Political opinion in India was aroused by the end
of 1959, and it was plain that any attempt to compromise with China
would be denounced as appeasement, or cowardice, or worse. So the
controls were locked—but in the positions in which Nehru had set
them, and from which he was never seriously to attempt to move
them.

---

* Why did Nehru publish the White Papers? Walter Crocker asks in his study of the late
Prime Minister: 'They were bound to unleash nationalist passion in India, probably to a
degree which could deprive him of any leeway for negotiating. Pique? Nationalist
passion in himself? or calculation, for instance to exert pressure on China as well as to
anticipate criticisms of his border policy in India? Perhaps all three were part of the moti-
vation; but probably the biggest factor was that after ... the exposures made in Parliament in 1959, the safest course was to make a clean breast of it.'[164]

(ii) *Evasive Action*

At the end of 1959 China attempted to switch the focus of the dispute from historical argument to discussion of ways to resolve it, and meanwhile to de-fuse the situation on the borders. Chou En-lai wrote again to Nehru on November 7th, 1959, after the Kongka Pass incident. He described this as unfortunate and unexpected and said that, unless the two Governments quickly worked out a solution, border clashes which neither wanted to see might occur again. Noting with gratification that Nehru had accepted the principle that pending a settlement the *status quo* should be maintained (which in fact, as has been seen, was not the case) he proposed that the armed forces of both sides should each be withdrawn twenty kilometres from the McMahon Line and from 'the line up to which each side exercises actual control' in the western sector. He asserted that China had 'never had the intention of straining the border situation and the relations between the two countries', and then proposed that he and Nehru should meet in the immediate future to discuss the boundary question and Sino-Indian relations generally.[165]

The proposal of a summit meeting and interim measures of demilitarization appeared to be in consonance with the general approach to the settlement of international disputes with which India, and particularly Nehru, were associated. The expectation outside India was, therefore, that Chou En-lai's proposals would be accepted; but in fact the Chinese approach had been ruled out by India even before it was articulated. The gap was already unbridgable, but it was obscured by the careful wording of India's diplomatic communications.

When Chou En-lai proposed that 'the two sides should maintain the long-existing *status quo* of the border' he meant that they should both stay in the frontier areas into which they had extended administration in the preceding decade or so, and make no attempt to disturb the other's occupation. The McMahon Line would thus continue to be observed by China as the *de facto* boundary; while in the western sector stabilization of the position would leave the two sides for the most part widely separated, with China in occupation of Aksai Chin. As the Chinese

135

used the phrase, *status quo* meant 'the situation obtaining at present', i.e. on November 7th, 1959, when Chou made his proposal. As the Indians used the phrase, however, it meant 'the situation as it was before China moved into Aksai Chin'. Thus, when China proposed maintenance of the *status quo*, she meant that everyone should stay where they then were; when India seemed to adopt the proposal, she meant in fact that the Chinese should evacuate the areas India claimed, while India remained in possession of the territory China claimed. This word-juggling created a situation where India could call it 'maintaining the *status quo*' when her patrols moved into Chinese-held territory. It also made it impossible to reach any standstill agreement pending settlement.

By the end of 1959 the general Indian perception of the situation on the borders was that China had by stealth seized a large area of incontrovertibly Indian territory in the west and, when challenged, had brazenly advanced a factitious claim to an even bigger area below the McMahon Line. After the Kongka Pass incident the Chinese Defence Ministry had coupled the two areas in a statement, saying that if the Indians insisted on a right to patrol in Aksai Chin because they claimed that territory, the Chinese could similarly claim a right to patrol into the area south of the McMahon Line.[166] This was read in India as a threat, but also as the hint of a bargain in which China would give up her claim to the territory below the McMahon Line if India gave up hers to Aksai Chin. In the Indian reading, the Chinese were saying: 'You forget about what we have stolen, and we will not try to steal any more'; and backing that up with the implied threat that, if India persisted in trying to regain the stolen western territory, China would swallow NEFA too.

The Indian approach to the border question becomes intelligible if it is seen in this light: suppose one morning it is discovered that in a surprise and secret move the Chinese army has irrupted through an unguarded border pass and swarmed into the Punjab, occupying several thousand square miles and beginning to run traffic across it. Chinese troops set up road blocks on the Grand Trunk Road and turn back Indian travellers; in an ambush, they kill several of a police patrol. New Delhi challenges Peking, charging her with clandestine invasion and aggression. China blandly replies that the area now occupied has always been under Chinese control. She expresses willingness, even eagerness, to settle the boundary question as a whole through peaceful negotiations; but suggests that first both sides undertake to observe the *status quo*. New Delhi would of course instantly reject the idea of negotiations; repudiate the suggestion that the *status quo* could be made the basis of even a temporary arrangement; and commit India to throwing back the Chinese by force if they did not withdraw voluntarily. In the circumstances of this far-fetched scenario, such an Indian reaction would not only have been wholly understandable, it would have been mandatory. In fact, as has been seen, this was exactly how the Indians did react; and they did so because they had convinced themselves that China had in Aksai Chin seized territory that *morally* was as much a part of India as was the Punjab.

Judging by Nehru's admission in Parliament that the boundary in the west was undelimited, that the Aksai Chin area was something vaguer than the McMahon Line, he did not at first hold that view himself. But he had been brought to it, by his responsiveness to the public anger in India; by his own indignation at what he saw as China's bullying betrayal; and perhaps by Gopal's report. As the Indian argument that the boundaries had always been just where she claimed they were was elaborated, so it seems that Nehru, like many others in India and elsewhere, came to believe it. From this it followed that China's presence in Aksai Chin must be a standing act of aggression, and the Indian Government was therefore bound to reject any arrangement which appeared to acquiesce in its continuance.

Nehru had also ruled out discussions such as Chou proposed with his observation that 'no Government could possibly discuss the future of such large areas which are an integral part of their territory.'[167] He had gone even further, and made discussions on the precise alignment of the boundary (distinguishing those from general boundary negotiations) conditional upon unilateral Chinese withdrawals.[168] That Chou En-lai, in spite of the stated Indian position, now proposed a summit meeting suggests either that the Chinese had not yet appreciated how adamant the Indian stand was, or that Peking wished to put New Delhi in the position of openly refusing to negotiate.

That India would refuse both of Chou En-lai's proposals was, then, a foregone conclusion; but the rejection of the idea of a demilitarized zone all along the borders was coupled with a counter-proposal. In his reply, Nehru first distinguished the eastern and middle sectors from the western sector, saying that the danger of clashes would be avoided in the first two if both sides simply stopped sending out forward patrols —

5*

which, he said, India had in fact already done. Turning to the western sector, he reiterated the claim that India had exercised jurisdiction over Aksai Chin by sending regular patrols there, and ruled out an agreement to maintain the *status quo* because, he said, 'the facts concerning the *status quo* are themselves in dispute'. He then advanced his own proposal:

> I suggest, therefore, that in the Ladakh area both our Governments should agree on the following as an interim measure. The Government of India should withdraw all personnel to the west of the line which the Chinese Government have shown as the international boundary in their 1956 maps which, so far as we are aware, are their latest maps. Similarly, the Chinese Government should withdraw their personnel to the east of the international boundary which has been described by the Government of India in their earlier notes and correspondence and shown in their official maps. Since the two lines are separated by long distances, there should not be the slightest risk of border clashes between the forces on either side. The area is almost entirely uninhabited. It is thus not necessary to maintain administrative personnel in this area bounded by the two lines on the east and west.[169]

In its conception this was a diplomatic ploy, not a proposal made with any expectation that it would be accepted. The Chinese proposal for joint military withdrawals had put India on the diplomatic defensive. Now Nehru riposted by ingeniously using the language of mutual withdrawal to advance what was in fact the same Indian demand for total and practically unilateral Chinese withdrawal from the disputed territory in the western sector. Implementation of Nehru's proposal would have involved Indian evacuation of one post, Demchok, in the extreme south-east of the disputed area, and perhaps fifty square miles around it. For China, on the other hand, it would have meant evacuating about twenty thousand square miles, an evacuation that would have left no land route from Sinkiang to Tibet — except in so far as India might have been prepared to allow the Chinese to use the Aksai Chin road for civilian traffic. (That modification to the original proposal was suggested at the time by Nehru in a press conference in New Delhi.)[170]

Nehru's counter-proposal was widely welcomed by Indian political commentators, who saw it as 'eminently reasonable and practicable' and offering China an 'opportunity of vacating its aggression without undue loss of prestige'.[171] The politicians were by no means so approving. In the lobbies of Parliament members complained that a principle had been surrendered and aggression condoned. Acharya Kripalani expressed what many of his colleagues felt, on both sides of the House, when he said that 'in their eagerness for a negotiated settlement Government have suggested that India would withdraw from what has always been India in return for the Chinese withdrawing from areas which are also ours.'[172] Asoka Mehta charged that the Government had weakened India's case in its eagerness to negotiate; a Jan Sangh speaker said that offering to make a no-man's-land out of a corner of India amounted to 'putting a premium on aggression'.[173] Through the press and directly, Government spokesmen and officials tried to assuage these misgivings, emphasizing the smallness of the area which India would have to vacate and that the Prime Minister's proposal would, if accepted, achieve India's main objective of getting the Chinese out of the Aksai Chin area. It was also pointed out that even full Chinese compliance would not mean that India's boundary claims became negotiable. The negotiations that might follow Chinese withdrawals in implementation of the Nehru proposal would still only be about marginal boundary adjustment, not about 'great chunks' of India.[174]

Nehru's rejection of Chou En-lai's suggestion of an immediate meeting of the two Prime Ministers, on the other hand, was almost universally welcomed in India. Opinion there was solid that there should be no discussions with Peking until the Chinese had withdrawn from Aksai Chin. Newspapers hammered at this point editorially. 'We must make it clear that there can be no discussions of any kind while Chinese provocation lasts.'[175] 'The Indian Government and the Indian people are determined that there shall be no appeasement of any expansionist neighbour. They will not countenance any compromise which will eat into Indian national territory. . . . There can be no negotiations on the boundary question so long as the Chinese remain on Indian soil.'[176] 'New Delhi's willingness to negotiate is not unconditional and cannot be until China vacates its aggression and thereby acknowledges supremacy of peaceful and friendly negotiations. [New Delhi must not] deviate an inch from its position of insisting in the first place on the total withdrawal of Chinese forces as the price for negotiations.'[177] Opposition M.P.s urged, with Kripalani, that 'negotiations can take place only on the basis of prior acceptance by China of our frontiers and the immediate vacation of territories forcibly occupied by them.'[178] Congressmen felt the same way. Atulya Ghosh, the Congress boss of West Bengal, put it in moral terms: 'With China continuing her aggressive activities no man of self-respect would entertain the proposal of a meeting between the Prime Ministers of India and China.'

Nehru took no bows to the applause for his refusal to meet Chou En-lai; indeed with spirit and persistence he maintained in his domestic utterances that he was not only ready but eager to meet the Chinese, and was determined to go on seeking to negotiate! 'So far as I am concerned, and so far as this Government is concerned,' he said at the end of 1959, 'we will negotiate and negotiate and negotiate to the bitter end. I absolutely reject the approach of stopping negotiations at any stage. That, I think, is not only a fundamentally wrong approach but . . . it is also a fundamentally anti-Gandhian approach. . . . Negotiations will go on as long as this Government functions, to the end'.[179] He would argue to the Opposition that the only alternative to negotiations was war, and, while never ruling out the possibility of war over the boundaries, he would again insist on the need to talk — 'though that does not mean that any action which is necessitated will not be taken'.[180] Nehru would override suggestions that he should not meet Chou En-lai: 'As far as I am concerned, I am prepared to meet anybody in the wide world,' he told correspondents at his regular monthly press conference in January 1960. 'There is nobody whom I am not prepared to meet . . . [but] one does not rush to a meeting because a meeting is talked about, [it] may be mistimed, misjudged and therefore produce bad results.'

Since these reaffirmations of his resolute personal commitment to negotiations were coupled with reiterations that India's boundaries were not negotiable, Nehru's position began to cause a certain amount of puzzlement in New Delhi. At the same press conference, when Nehru in his letter to Chou En-lai had seemed to rule out a summit meeting, a journalist followed up the Prime Minister's remarks about his willingness to negotiate with the question: 'Is it still the Indian stand that our frontiers are not negotiable?' 'That is our stand,' Nehru replied; 'at the same time there is nothing that is not negotiable.' He caught himself up on this paradox, and explained: 'It seems to be contradictory. But there is no question of negotiation or bargaining about the matter [of the boundaries]. But it is a somewhat different matter in dealing with them in letters and talks. One cannot refuse to talk to another country.'[181]

The apparent contradictions in Nehru's utterances on 'negotiations' are resolved when it is seen that for him the word had two distinct meanings. When he seemed to be saying: 'We are ready to negotiate the boundaries, but we will never negotiate the boundaries,' he meant: 'We will never compromise on our boundaries, but we are prepared to consider minor adjustments to them and to *talk* to the other side about them.' He later made the essential distinction explicit:

> There is a difference between negotiations and talks, there is a world of difference. . . . Talking must always be encouraged wherever possible. Negotiation is a very formal thing; it requires a very suitable background; it should not be taken up unless a suitable background comes. . . . Talking is an entirely different matter. Talking may not yield any result; maybe; at any rate it helps in understanding, in probing other's minds.[182]

The distinction between 'negotiate' in its dictionary meaning of 'confer with a view to finding terms of agreement' and in Nehru's sense of 'discuss with a view to persuading the other side of the validity of the Indian position' has since become a staple device of Indian foreign policy articulation, understood and accepted in India,* but at the turn of 1959–60 its subtleties were not yet appreciated in New Delhi. The strong impression there was that Nehru would refuse to meet Chou En-lai until the Chinese had signalled their acceptance of the Indian version of the boundaries by withdrawing behind the Indian claim line, or 'vacating their aggression'. The wider, international failure to appreciate the ambiguity of Nehru's words when he pledged himself and his Government to negotiations must explain the almost universal belief that it was China, rather than India, who refused to negotiate a settlement of the boundary problem.

The confidence in India that Nehru would not agree to a summit meeting hardened after Chou En-lai pressed his proposal and received a curt refusal. Writing again in December, Chou reiterated his proposal for joint military withdrawal all along the border, pointing out that this measure would not prejudice the claims of either side. He

---

* For example, the Indian Government even after the 1965 war with Pakistan frequently reiterated its willingness to talk with Pakistan over Kashmir, while at the same time reassuring domestic opinion that Kashmir was and would remain 'not negotiable'.

welcomed Nehru's proposal that to avoid clashes each Government should order its outposts to stop forward patrolling, saying that China had in fact taken that precaution after the Kongka Pass incident; but he asked for clarification of India's intentions in this regard; did Nehru's proposal apply to the whole border? (Nehru's letter had been ambiguous on that point but the context indicated—and the fact was—that his suggestion that forward patrolling should be stopped applied only to the McMahon Line. Freedom to patrol into the disputed area in the west was central to the Indian Government's approach to the boundary dispute, then and later.)

Turning to Nehru's proposal for joint withdrawal behind the other's claim line, Chou made a detailed rebuttal. Firstly, there was no reason to treat the western sector as a special case, the line up to which each side exercised control was as clear there as it was in the other sectors; secondly, the Nehru proposal worked against the principle of maintaining the *status quo* 'agreed upon earlier by the two countries' (as has been seen, India had not in fact agreed to that, and had no intention of doing so); thirdly, while the proposal 'might appear "equitable" to those ignorant of the truth' it was in fact unfair. By its terms the Indian withdrawal would be theoretical, while China would have to withdraw from an area of 33,000 square kilometres which 'has long been under Chinese jurisdiction and is of great importance to China . . . as the traffic artery linking up the vast regions of Sinkiang and western Tibet'. If the Indian Government still stood by the Nehru proposal, Chou asked, was it ready to apply the same principle to the eastern sector of the border? In that case, the Chinese would make the same sort of theoretical withdrawal behind the McMahon Line (which they were in fact already behind) while the Indians on the other hand would have to evacuate the great bulk of NEFA in order to withdraw behind the boundary as China's maps showed it.

Chou En-lai's tone in this letter, as in the previous one, was no longer minatory, but persuasive and friendly. Nehru had explained his rejection of a meeting by saying that without preliminary agreement 'we would lose ourselves in a forest of data'. Chou replied that a summit meeting was essential so that agreements on principles could be reached; 'without such guidance, there is the danger that concrete discussions of the boundary question by the two sides may bog down in endless and fruitless debates.' He then proposed that he and Nehru should meet on December 26th, that is, nine days after the letter was delivered. Any place in China would serve as venue, he said, 'because there are in China no activities hostile to Sino-Indian friendship' (a reference to the anti-China demonstrations in Indian cities); or if that were not convenient for Nehru, and Burma agreed, Rangoon.[183]

By proposing the time and place for a meeting, Chou may have hoped to cut short the debate on the merits into which the Prime Ministers' correspondence had fallen, so that it was no more than paralleling the continuing and copious exchange of diplomatic notes and memoranda. Nine days was hardly enough notice for a summit meeting, but Chou asked Nehru to suggest another date if that were not acceptable, so that convenience or practicability could not serve to justify refusal. Nehru's reply was prompt, brusque and cold. He expressed deep regret that his 'very reasonable proposals' for joint withdrawals in the western sector had not been accepted. He said again that no agreement could be reached upon principles when there was such complete disagreement about facts; and he added that anyway it was entirely impossible for him to go to Rangoon or any other place within the next few days.[184]

* * * * * * * * * * *

With India's refusal of China's summit gambit the diplomatic game was stalemated. The borders were quiet too. The Chinese continued to observe the McMahon Line as the *de facto* boundary in the eastern sector, and, in spite of a series of 'final serious warnings' to evacuate which had been delivered to the post commander at Khinzemane,[185] that outpost in Indian-claimed territory north of the line was not under any but verbal pressure. The other post the Indians had attempted to maintain across the map-marked line, Longju, was under Chinese control, but Nehru had suggested that it be demilitarized, and the Chinese before long withdrew from it. Both sides had stopped patrolling near the McMahon Line. The western sector had also been quiet since the Kongka Pass clash. The Chinese had suspended patrolling there too, and winter had stopped Indian patrols – winter and the extreme logistical difficulties the Indians faced there.

Quiet borders and diplomatic stalemate left China unchallenged in possession of the territory India claimed in the west. In the Indian perception of the situation, this amounted to acquiescence in China's aggression, to accepting by default a *de facto* settlement of the borders, on China's terms. The Chinese, it was believed, would use the opportunity to consolidate their occupation of Aksai Chin and perhaps extend it, preparatory to the next step in what the Indians were now convinced was a long-term programme of expansion at the cost of India. From the moment they began to describe China's presence in Indian-claimed territory as 'aggression' the Indian Government had assumed an obligation to do something about it, and Nehru, pressed for a commitment to launch military operations against the Chinese, had invariably left the implication that if or when the time came for that step, the Government would be ready to take it. 'We do not intend to start military operations against any of these places [held by China] at a time when we are dealing with them on a political level,' he told a press conference in October.[186] With the diplomatic exchanges stalemated it could hardly be said that the Government was still dealing with the problem on a political level, and with the summit unscaled it could not be said that all diplomatic approaches had been exhausted. Accordingly, at the beginning of 1960 the Indian Government began to reconsider Chou En-lai's urging of an early meeting with Nehru.

Other factors were conducive to reconsideration. The chill had come off the cold war, Krushchev's visit to the United States had generated 'the Camp David spirit' and, although that was soon to be dashed by the fiasco of the Paris summit, the setback was only temporary. For the general thaw, New Delhi and Nehru personally claimed some credit. For years Nehru's India had been the persistent advocate of a rational and civilized approach to the world's quarrels, of the use of the negotiating table as a lightning conductor for international storm-clouds. Now the shaping *détente* between Moscow and Washington was taken to show that the great powers had at last accepted and begun to put into practice the Indian prescription. When his foreign policy was assailed, Nehru at this time would cite the fact that the great powers seemed to be emulating India as evidence of the correctness of his approach, and remind his critics of the high regard in which India was generally held. The esteem of the world at large had long been taken for granted in India. 'The high position of prestige in the comity of nations that we have come to occupy is obviously the result of our disinterested approach to international problems and the special viewpoint of tolerance and peaceful co-existence, stemming from our cultural inheritance, which has characterized the stands that our leadership has always taken on international issues,' an Indian official report noted in 1956.[187] At the end of 1959 Nehru told the Lok Sabha that 'whether it is in the United Nations or whether it is elsewhere, we are respected all over the world,' and wondered why that was so.

> It has been an amazing thing . . . that India's voice has counted for so much in the councils of the world in the last several years, since independence. . . . We may have become conceited about it – there was some room for conceit, I admit – but the fact is that a country which in the modern world is in terms of physical might not to be compared with the great powers or with many of the armed nations . . . which is poor and is struggling hard to get rid of its poverty . . . has counted for so much in the world for the last few years.

It might have been partly clever diplomacy, partly the world's remembrance of the radiance of Gandhi, Nehru suggested, but more it was

> that we have spoken with conviction and earnestness and sincerity about peace and our desire for peace and . . . for tolerance and when we have talked about co-existence and all that it was not a phrase in our mouths and lips – it was a deep feeling from inside our hearts and a deep understanding of the world as it is today.[188]

This self-congratulation did partly, no doubt, reflect that claim to special wisdom and moral status which has been a part of Asian and perhaps especially Indian nationalism (as it once was of European and especially British nationalism) but there was a solid truth beneath it. At the end of the 1950s India did occupy a unique position in the world's affairs, called on as referee, peacemaker or arbitrator from Gaza to the Congo and Korea, listened to with respect and courted for understanding. As the prime articulator of the concept of non-alignment as a dynamic in international relations, and as accepted spokesman for the non-aligned countries, India, personified in Nehru, had done much to blunt the conflicts of the cold war. The success of India's foreign policy in terms of acceptance by both Washington and Moscow was demonstrated just at this time by the successive visits to New Delhi of the Presidents of the U.S.A. and the U.S.S.R. and then of Krushchev.

President Eisenhower's visit in December 1959 put the seal on a marked change in American policy towards non-aligned countries, and India in particular. The old disapproval of 'immoral neutralism' was dead with John Foster Dulles and replaced by cordial sympathy, verging at times on a suitor's ardour—Eisenhower told the Indian Parliament that their country 'speaks to the other nations of the world with greatness of conviction, and is heard with greatness of respect. India is a triumph that offsets the world failures of the past decade, a triumph that . . . a century from now may offset them all.'[189] More material expression of America's backing was given in a sudden multiplication of economic aid: in the twelve years to mid-1959 the U.S.A. had given India about $1·7 billion worth; in the next four years American economic aid to India amounted to about four billion dollars' worth. One factor in the changed American attitude to India was India's falling out with China, of which the Americans had been apprised before it became public knowledge. In May 1959 Senator Wiley Smith, after visiting India, told the Senate Foreign Relations Committee that Nehru and his close advisers had expressed concern about China. 'From the standpoint of the United States', he said, 'it is a hopeful sign that the Indian Government is becoming somewhat alarmed over Red Chinese operations on the border' and China's speedier pace of industrialization.[190]

At the beginning of 1960 the seriousness of the rift between China and the Soviet Union was not appreciated in the outside world. The Indians feared that their mounting quarrel with China would estrange them from Moscow, as the Russians stood by their great Communist partner, with consequent damage to India's non-alignment. Material interests would have suffered too; Russian economic aid to India, though relatively small, had begun to make itself felt with the Bhilai steel plant. But, in the event, these fears were belied. From the beginning, Moscow took a dispassionate view of the Sino-Indian dispute, not allowing the hostility between China and India to affect the relations between Moscow and New Delhi. The Longju incident occurred on the eve of Krushchev's visit to the United States and the Russians appeared to have been carefully neutral about it, deploring only the use to which they said the incident was being put to 'discredit the idea of peaceful co-existence'.[191] Russian neutrality over the Sino-Indian dispute was all that the Indian Government could have hoped for and more than it expected. Nehru drew attention to the Russian statement: 'The issue of that statement itself shows that the Soviet Government is taking a calm and more or less dispassionate view of the situation,' he told the Lok Sabha.[192] In fact, for the Soviet Union to be explicitly neutral over a serious dispute between a Communist and a non-Communist power was in the international and ideological context to shift away from the obligations of fraternal solidarity. As Peking was to observe later, by making no distinction between the two states and expressing dispassionate regret over the Longju incident Moscow, for those who could read between the lines, 'in reality condemned China's stand'.[193]

This tacit Russian support was of high importance to India. Western countries could be expected to accept the Indian version of the dispute without question and to condemn China with, or even before, New Delhi; but the sympathy and support of the non-aligned and especially of other Asian countries might not be so readily forthcoming, since by no means all of those countries were prepared to accept uncritically the proposition that China was wholly in the wrong. Continued Russian endorsement of India's *bona fides* was thus a strong card in New Delhi's hand, and therefore Russian reaction had to be taken into consideration as the Indian Government formulated its moves.

An invitation to Krushchev to make a return visit to India had been outstanding for some time (his tour of India with Bulganin in 1956 had opened the chapter of active Indo-Russian friendship) and at the end of December 1959 the Indians were informed that he would like to combine a visit to them with his forthcoming trip to Indonesia. The prospect of a meeting with Krushchev opened the possibility that, in a private dialogue with Nehru, he could be made to see even more clearly the validity of the Indian approach to the boundary dispute; and that Moscow's influence, which the Indians believed to be very strong in Peking, could be enlisted to make the Chinese accept it. But the Russians had already made plain that they believed negotiations were the only way in which the border dispute could be resolved;* the fact that India had twice rejected China's proposal for a meeting of the Prime Ministers, thus walling off the only visible way to a negotiated settlement, could not be expected to sit well with Moscow's friendly counsels.

That was one good reason for reappraising Nehru's refusal to meet Chou En-lai. Another was found in a long Chinese note received in New Delhi at the end of December. This appears to have been the brief

---

* Although when it came to their own boundary question with China the Russians, like the Indians, were to refuse to enter into general negotiations. (See Part III.) Similarly, the Indians had advised the Burmese Government to negotiate a boundary settlement with China, although they had no intention of doing so themselves.

which the Chinese Foreign Ministry had prepared for the early meeting
of the Prime Ministers that had been expected in Peking. Basically, the
note consisted of a detailed and measured refutation of the Indian
argument that the boundaries were already delimited in accordance
with the Indian claim lines; and a restatement of the Chinese position –
that the dispute was a bequest of the British which could be settled
through friendly negotiations, 'taking into account the historical background and the present actual situation'. There was nothing in the note
to indicate that the Chinese approach had shifted, but the tone was
sustainedly reassuring. Instead of brusquely dismissing the Indian
charge of 'aggression' as Peking had done in previous notes, here the
charge was calmly analysed, reassurances reasonably advanced. China
was still very backward economically and culturally and would need
decades to overcome this backwardness; she had a vast territory, more
than half of it sparsely populated, was rich in natural resources and had
a huge domestic market – why should she wish to expand? Peking
apologized for the length of the note and explained that its intention
was 'not to argue but to bring arguing to an end'; that rather than
'answer attack with attack' they assumed that the Indian Government
'really has some misunderstanding about China's intentions'. The note
closed with an expression of China's 'ardent desire that the two countries stop quarrelling, quickly bring about a reasonable settlement of
the boundary question, and on this basis consolidate and develop the
great friendship of the two peoples in their common cause'.[194]

When the note was studied in New Delhi the avowals of desire to
end the dispute were felt to be sincere, and this strengthened the view
that there might be something to be gained by talking to Chou En-lai.
There was nothing to indicate that a meeting of the Prime Ministers
could have tangible results; the Indians had no intention of changing
their approach, and there was no hint that China would accede to
that. Nevertheless, it began to appear that India's interests would be
served by agreeing to summit talks. That would reassure the watching
world that India was being consistent to its own prescription, that
Nehru, the advocate of negotiations in every dispute, would not
shrink from adopting the same approach to India's problems. Accordingly, at the end of January 1960 the Indian Government decided that
Chou En-lai should after all be invited to New Delhi to explore with
Nehru 'avenues which might lead to a peaceful settlement'.[195]

It was obvious, however, that this reversal of policy, dropping the insistence on Chinese withdrawals as a pre-condition for a summit meeting, would intensify the persisting domestic criticism of the Government. Nehru had been on the defensive since August. The relatively cautious tone with which he reacted against the jingoism of his critics, his reproofs to those who demanded ultimatums to China and swift military action to 'evict the aggressors', and his reiterated commitment to 'negotiations', had engendered the strong suspicion that he intended to compromise with China. The retreat from insistence on Chinese withdrawals before the opening of any discussions would inevitably nourish that suspicion, and invite charges of appeasement. Faced with the necessity of a change of course under fire, the Government began to lay a semantic smoke-screen.

The smoke was Nehru's distinction between 'talks' and 'negotiations'. Since, by his own definition, the intended summit meeting would not be negotiations, Nehru felt able to go on saying there was no prospect of negotiations with China even while his letter inviting Chou En-lai to New Delhi was being delivered. The letter was delivered in Peking on February 12th.* Krushchev had arrived in New Delhi the previous day and Nehru went straight from a morning's discussions with him to Parliament, where he again ruled out any possibility of negotiations with China. 'I see no ground whatever at the present moment, no bridge between the Chinese position and ours,' he said. 'That is, the present positions are such that there is no room for negotiations on that basis, and therefore there is nothing to negotiate at present.'[196] As the general expectation had been that Krushchev's persuasions would be exerted to bringing about negotiations between India and China, the timing of Nehru's reiteration that there was no ground for them seemed to make it even more categorical. Certainly it occurred to no one that Nehru had already invited Chou En-lai to New Delhi—as was in fact the case.† Nehru's statement confirmed the impression in Parliament and at large that he had no intention of meeting Chou. The smoke-screen was thus at its densest

---

* The decision to invite Chou En-lai to India was taken at the end of January; the invitation was drafted about February 3rd but was held over so that it could be delivered personally by the Indian Ambassador to China, then G. Parthasarathi.[197]
† In dispatches to *The Times* the writer had been reflecting the Government's changed approach and saying that a summit meeting was now in the offing, but accepted Nehru's statement as a contradiction: 'With this emphatic statement the Prime Minister appeared to stultify those who had confidently been expecting a meeting between himself and Mr Chou En-lai in the near future; and simultaneously he shattered the hopes of those who had looked to Krushchev to act as a go-between.'[198]

and most baffling when the critical manœuvre it was being laid to cover was being executed in Peking, with delivery of the invitation.

Not surprisingly, there was anger as well as astonishment in India when, only four days later, it was disclosed that Chou En-lai had been invited to New Delhi. Nehru's letter of invitation was cordial, even warm, in marked contrast to the coldness of his previous one six weeks before—he even returned to the salutation 'My dear Prime Minister' instead of the cooler 'Dear Prime Minister', for the first time since his opening letter of August 1958. 'It has pained me deeply', he wrote, 'that the relations between India and China, which have in the past been so friendly and which we have endeavoured so much to strengthen, should have deteriorated rapidly and led to bitterness and resentment.' He again rejected the Chinese premise that the Sino-Indian boundary had never been delimited, and said: 'On that basis there can be no negotiations.' He repeated that there could be no negotiations (his letter was, of course, to be published) but went on: 'Still I think it might be helpful for us to meet.' It would not be possible for him to leave India for the next few months, he said, and he asked Chou En-lai to come to New Delhi, anticipating any demurrals about the mood of the public there with the assurance that 'you will be our honoured guest when you come here.'[199] With this short and friendly letter was delivered a long note rebutting the previous Chinese argument and restating the Indian position.

Members of Parliament learned of the invitation from the newspapers on February 16th, and the Opposition came to the House fuming and tabled an adjournment motion on the Government's 'sudden and unwarranted reversal' of policy. A few days later it was fully debated. Minoo Masani described the invitation as a 'national humiliation' and was strongly supported from the Opposition benches. Nehru and the Government were charged with breach of faith, Kripalani going so far as to say that India had been 'betrayed by the leaders of the present Government . . . our honour is not safe in the hands of dishonourable people'.[200] The press was also critical of 'Mr Nehru's somersault' or 'climbdown' as it was called. Nehru, of course, had his defence ready and maintained that no change of policy was involved in his invitation to Chou En-lai, emphasizing again that the meeting would not be *negotiation*, and citing the numerous occasions on which he had said he would always be prepared to *talk* to the other side.[201] His critics gagged on the distinction. 'It is quite clear that this meeting is negotiations and

nothing else,' as Masani put it;[202] the *Times of India* observed that the
Prime Minister was 'making a distinction that is not entirely honest,
since a meeting between [himself] and Mr Chou En-lai cannot but be
in every sense of the word negotiations of the greatest importance'. A
wrangle over whether Nehru had reversed himself, whether there was
a substantive difference between 'talks' and 'negotiations', occupied a
good deal of Parliament's time in the succeeding weeks. The Opposition leaders made the running with their criticism of the Prime Minister; but on this occasion he had the support of Congress and of a good
number on the Opposition back benches too for his argument that it
would do no harm and might do some good to talk to Chou. Rajago-
palachari, the former Congressman and Governor-General turned
Swatantra leader, spoke for that school when he said there was
nothing wrong in inviting Chou En-lai to India; 'as long as one is firm
in mind it is good to make every attempt to meet the other party.'
There were cheers from the Congress benches when, on March 1st,
Nehru rose in the House to confirm that Chou had accepted his
invitation.

Chou En-lai accepted with 'deep gratitude'. It was arranged in further correspondence that he would come on April 19th and stay seven
days—the Indian Government would have been happier with two.[203]
With the date set, the politicians who suspected that Nehru intended to
use the meeting to compromise with China began to concentrate on
preventing him from doing so. Opposition parties declared that 'no-
surrender week', a programme of demonstrations in New Delhi and
other cities, would be arranged to coincide with Chou En-lai's visit,
and there was talk of 'making things hot' for the Chinese party. Nehru
and his colleagues in the Government succeeded in dissuading the
Opposition leaders from organizing demonstrations while the Chinese
were in New Delhi; in a nice compromise it was agreed that 'no-
surrender week' would end the day before Chou arrived. In return,
the Government undertook that none of the customary public recep-
tions would be held in Chou En-lai's honour. Claiming in a letter to
the Prime Minister that they expressed popular feeling, the non-
Communist Opposition leaders reiterated their view that there should
have been no talks without 'Chinese vacation of aggression', and urged
that there should be 'no dilution of the boundaries, and that nothing
will be done which may be construed as a surrender of any part of
Indian territory'.[204] The same point was made more clamantly by the

Jan Sangh two days before Chou's arrival, with a demonstration in which several thousand people went to the Prime Minister's residence, led by motor cyclists, the column forested with saffron banners and waving placards: INVADERS, QUIT INDIA; NO SURRENDER OF INDIAN TERRITORY; DOWN WITH CHINESE IMPERIALISM and the like. The crowd massed at the gates, held back by a large force of police, and one of its leaders was allowed in to deliver a memorandum. This asked for Nehru's personal assurance that 'there will be no abdication of our claim over any part of Indian territory, whether in our possession or presently under China's illegal occupation,' and further that 'nothing will be done to limit our right to take all necessary measures to liberate Chinese-occupied areas.' In the official account of what passed between Nehru and the Jan Sangh delegate, the Prime Minister said only that he had nothing to add to what he had already said in Parliament. But when the Jan Sangh leader came back from his talk with the Prime Minister he stilled the turbulent crowd to announce that Nehru had promised that 'India will not cede even an inch of her territory to China.'

Indian political opinion had by this time found an additional, international reason for refusing to negotiate with Peking. Seeing India as the leader, and indeed the bulwark of non-Communist states, opponents of settlement with China pointed to the ill-effects such compromise would have in the rest of Asia, 'shatter[ing] the morale of all those countries . . . who are aspiring to build themselves up independently and in a democratic way', as the Jan Sangh memorandum put it. Settlement had come to be seen in India as humiliating defeat at China's hands, and so the failure of the approaching talks came to be desired as victory for India. If the talks succeeded, 'China's prestige and power will be enhanced in the eyes of the smaller Asian countries, for India's action will be construed as acquiescence in and compliance with China's attitude', as one editorial put it on the eve of Chou En-lai's arrival;* if the talks broke down, 'India will be held up as unreasonable, [but better] to be held up temporarily as unreasonable than to be dismissed as weak and pusillanimous'.[205] There were very few exceptions to the unanimity of political utterances in India urging

---

* The same point was made in the U.S.A. The Washington *Evening Star* said: 'Firm resistance on the part of India would shore up the spirit of all its neighbours. It is essential to Mr Nehru's leadership in his own country and to India's future position in Asia that there should be no appeasement of the Peiping visitor in New Delhi.'[206]

the Government not to settle. The Communist Party advocated peaceful settlement; the *National Herald*, a respected provincial paper, pointed out that Kripalani and his vociferous colleages on the Opposition benches had no right to claim to speak for India; reacting against the battle-cries of their communal enemies in the Jan Sangh and the Hindu Mahasabha—who were taking the most extreme jingoist line—some of the smaller Muslim journals suggested meaningful negotiations. But these latter were minor and exceptional voices.

A month before Chou En-lai's arrival a ruling of the Indian Supreme Court reinforced the Government's inflexible approach to the question of the northern boundaries. In 1958 Nehru had compromised over minor but intractable boundary disputes with Pakistan, agreeing among other things to divide a small patch of disputed territory, called Berubari Union, between West Bengal and East Pakistan. This involved the transfer of several square miles, including a number of villages, to Pakistan, and the Government's right thus to cede Indian territory was challenged in the courts. The Supreme Court upheld the challenge. On March 14th, 1960, it ruled that the Government's attempt to 'reach an amicable settlement of the boundary dispute [over Berubari] on an *ad hoc* basis' involved cession of territory, and that therefore before it could be implemented the agreement Nehru had reached with the Pakistani Prime Minister would have to be ratified by amendment of the Indian Constitution.*[207] The Government took a legal opinion on the implication of this for its handling of the border dispute with China, and was told that in the light of the ruling a constitutional amendment would be required if it sought to cede territory or even to modify any of its boundary claims. In other words, if Nehru reached agreement with Chou on a compromise boundary for the western sector, for example, he would have to have the agreement approved by a two-thirds majority of Parliament, and by more than half of the then fourteen state legislatures.

This would certainly have been difficult. But Nehru's dominance of the Congress Party was still unchallenged, and the party controlled the state assemblies as well as Parliament with big majorities. The Berubari amendment was passed that year,† and it is possible that if

---

* The Indian Constitution lacks any provision giving the executive power to cede or acquire territory. Since the territorial extent of the Indian Union is defined in the Constitution any alteration requires amendment.

† At the time of writing (1970), however, the Indian Government has still not been able to implement the 1958 agreement in so far as that concerned the Berubari tract.

Nehru had thrown all his weight behind a compromise settlement with China at this stage, he could have carried it constitutionally. But in fact, as has been seen, he was determined not to come to any such compromise, and the Berubari ruling served to underline that determination.

Constitutional factors, added to political pressures, thus worked to cement Nehru into the position he had taken up. He had moved into an absolutist position on all of India's boundary claims, giving up the uncommitted, even tentative tone which at first informed his comments on the western sector. By speaking of India's honour and dignity and accusing China of arrogance and aggression, he had himself helped to infuse the boundary question with the passions which a few months before he had urged his compatriots to avoid. With word-splitting not far short of casuistry he had aroused misgivings about his approach to the dispute even among his supporters, and confirmed the distrust of his critics. Thus by his own words and actions he had helped deprive himself and his Government of all room for manœuvre: only unconditional Chinese acquiescence in India's claim to Aksai Chin, coupled with formal acceptance of the McMahon Line—in other words, China's surrender to India's demands—could free him. Unless Chou was prepared to make his visit to New Delhi a journey to Canossa, the mission had failed before the Chinese party set foot on New Delhi airport. That is what it amounted to when Nehru assured his public that his meeting with Chou En-lai would not be negotiations.

The Indian Government's position was affirmed once again before the summit meeting, in an equally long rejoinder to the full statement of the Chinese approach Peking had made in December. New Delhi argued again that the Sino-Indian boundaries had long been fixed by custom and tradition, and for the major part of their length confirmed by treaty and agreement; therefore 'an amicable settlement cannot be reached on the basis that a new agreement has to be negotiated to determine afresh the entire Sino-Indian boundary.' But India would be prepared to discuss 'specific disputes in regard to the location of particular places on the boundary, and to make minor frontier rectifications by agreement where they may be considered necessary'.[208]

The Chinese rounded off this rally in the diplomatic exchanges with another note explaining that its purpose was not argument, but 'in the hopes of promoting the understanding of the Indian Government and narrowing down the differences between the two sides so as to facilitate the forthcoming meeting between the two Premiers'. The note reiterated that the boundaries had never been delimited and that therefore 'over-all negotiations' should be conducted. But Peking then introduced a significant new proposal: 'As for the question of the undelimited boundary between the two countries, so long as both sides are willing to maintain the *status quo* of the border pending a settlement, it need not prevent the establishment of normal relations between them.'[209] In other words, if India was not prepared to negotiate a general settlement on the boundaries they could be left undelimited, with both sides observing the lines of present actual control as *de facto* boundaries. Seeing that Nehru was explicitly and publicly committed not to negotiate a settlement, Peking seems here to have been indicating a way out: leave well alone, until, in due course, when the heat and tension had drained out of the question and the usual friendly relations resumed between the two Governments, they could coolly reconsider the matter.

* * * * * * * * * * *

By the beginning of 1960 New Delhi had been long and well established on the itineraries of travelling statesmen, and the protocol and programme of their visits were familiar. Winter was the season for them, when warm sun and brisk nights, a profusion of flowers and just enough rain to lay the dust made visitors listen askance to complaints about the climate from residents still haunted by recollections of summer. At the beginning of every winter the capital would be dressed for these occasions, flag posts erected on the roads used by the visitors in their official drives, pot-holes filled in, bright orange gravel re-laid on verges and walks—it would fade and blow away with the hot winds of summer. The municipal authorities would bestir themselves in response to the Government's indication of the importance of the visitor. Trucks would be supplied to bring people to wave on the routes, inducement in cash or kind provided to draw the near-by villagers to the environs of the airport in their bullock carts or on their camels, paper flags distributed. The winter of 1959–60 had been a vintage year for official visits, so the capital still looked spick and span for Chou En-lai though he came at the season's end, with intimations of the weight of summer in the sun and the winds already dust-laden. The forms were observed for him, Chinese flags alternating with

Indian along the route from the airport. But the only requirement of crowd control for the police was to see that some demonstrators bearing black flags were kept off the route.

Chou En-lai, accompanied by Marshal Chen Yi, the Foreign Minister, and a large party, travelling in three aircraft, arrived in New Delhi from Rangoon late on the afternoon of April 19th, 1960. Under the marquee at the airport the greeting gathering consisted of little more than the diplomatic corps, reinforced by a doughty remnant of the hosts who only a year before would have turned out to cheer the Chinese visitors. One of these did raise the cry of yesteryear with a reedy 'Hindee Chinee bhai-bhai' as Chou En-lai descended from his aircraft, but otherwise there was only a polite patter of applause from the diplomats. Speeches of greeting were exchanged; Nehru's, most unusually for him, and emphasizing the cold formality of the Indian welcome, had been prepared in advance, and in Hindi.* He recalled the good will that had existed between India and China on Chou En-lai's previous visits (this was his fourth); but, he went on, 'unfortunately other events have taken place since then which have put a great strain on the bond of friendship and given a great shock to all our people. Our relations have been imperilled in the present and for the future and the very basis upon which they stood has been shaken.' It would be a hard task to recover that feeling of good faith and friendship, but their efforts must be directed to undoing much that had happened. Chou in his reply referred to the common interests of their countries: 'Both of us need peace, both of us need friends,' and, recalling *panch sheel*, said: 'There is no reason why any question between us cannot be settled reasonably through friendly consultations in accordance with those principles.' He concluded: 'I have come with the sincere desire to settle questions.' Then into a car with Nehru for the direct and speedy drive to the President's palace (formerly the Viceroy's), where the Chinese party was to stay. The route was empty except where rush-hour traffic had been bottled up, and there the crowds stood silent.

Next morning, the Chinese party made the customary gesture of laying flowers on the place where Gandhi was cremated, and then the Prime Ministers had their first formal exchanges — at the insistence of the Indians these were all held at Nehru's residence. The colloquies between the Prime Ministers were to take up more than twenty hours

---

* Nehru almost invariably used English on such occasions, and spoke extempore.

during the six days of the visit, lengthy exchanges even when time is allowed for translation, and the summit dialogue was echoed lower down the slopes.

It had been planned that the Chinese should meet as many of the Indian Cabinet as possible, the idea being that they should encounter a preconcerted solid front. The Indians wished to leave their visitors no room for doubt about the force of their resentment over the boundary dispute, and it was arranged that as far as possible everyone the Chinese met should speak forcefully to the same point. (Nehru had been criticized for keeping the initial development of the boundary dispute to himself; it is probable that he now had the secondary motive of involving as many of his colleagues as practicable in his discussions with Chou, and so sharing responsibility for whatever emerged from them.) Accordingly, Chou En-lai and Chen Yi made a round of the ministers' houses. Pant, the Home Minister, and the most influential man in the Government after Nehru, had prepared himself to argue the Indian case in detail; the Vice-President, Dr Radhakrishnan, lectured Chou on the philosophical basis of the Indian position; Morarji Desai, the Finance Minister, was blunt to the point of rudeness; and others, in their various styles, reiterated the Indian position.

There was one signal omission from the list of calls the Chinese were to make — there was no provision in the initial arrangements for them to see anything in private of Krishna Menon. Political opinion in India was still suspicious that, in spite of his protestations to the contrary, Nehru meant to do a deal with Chou En-lai. The suspicion had been nourished by his reiterated commitment to peaceful settlements, expressions of moral aversion from war and declarations of his ever-readiness to negotiate. Many in New Delhi half expected to see Nehru emerging from his meeting with Chou En-lai waving a scrap of paper and proclaiming 'peace in our time' — the parallel with Munich was frequently drawn, and any compromise would certainly have been denounced as blind appeasement. But if Nehru was suspected of hankering for settlement at any price, Krishna Menon had already been tried and convicted, so to speak, on that charge. Menon's public utterances had in fact generally been as strong in denunciation of China as Nehru's or stronger, but it was known that he regarded Pakistan, not China, as the main military threat to India, and the Right generally held him to be a crypto-Communist. He was close to Nehru personally and was believed to be a malign influence on him, urging him to settle with China. So that he could not sway Nehru during the Chou En-lai visit, efforts were made in the Cabinet and the Ministry of External Affairs to keep Menon as far as possible from the discussions, and Nehru appeared to acquiesce in his exclusion.

But Menon himself did not. Acting on a remark Chou made to him at the airport, looking forward to opportunities to talk further, Menon simply called at the latter's suite in the President's palace and had a private talk with him on the first full day of the conference. There was an immediate outcry. The Secretary-General, N. R. Pillai, protested to the Prime Minister at Menon's unscripted intervention,[210] and there was irate comment in the newspapers next day at what one called Menon's 'inexplicable and inexcusable irruption . . . into the centre of the stage'.[211] The fuss was irrational, the Defence Minister could hardly make concessions that the Government would not, but it demonstrated not only the rancorous distrust of Krishna Menon but also the fear that the Chinese would out-manoeuvre the Government if any weak spot offered itself.

The fear was groundless; the Indian Government was as adamant as its hottest critic could have wished. Nehru and his officials stood four-square and immovable on the position that there could be no general boundary negotiations. They maintained that the boundaries were already delimited and ran just where India said they did, and that the Chinese must withdraw before there could be any of the discussions on 'minor rectifications' which were all they would agree to. They rejected the Chinese proposals for settlement, they refused to accept the Chinese proposals for freezing the boundaries until some indefinite future when the subject could be discussed more calmly. They were absolute. Members of the Chinese delegation told East European diplomats that they had been shocked at Nehru's inflexibility, at his refusal, as they saw it, to try to understand their point of view.

What was the Chinese point of view? It was quite clear at the time (although since then it has been suggested that the Chinese put forward no specific proposals). China's general approach had been repeatedly stated in the diplomatic correspondence, and Chou En-lai reiterated it at a state banquet on his second night in New Delhi. The Sino-Indian boundary question, he said, had been left over from history, it had not been created by either of the two Governments; it was 'only an issue of a limited and temporary nature' and, while it was complicated and had its difficult aspects, it was 'entirely possible to achieve a fair and reasonable overall settlement'. In that, both the historical background and the present actualities should be taken into account.

China's specific proposals for settlement were reported in the press within a few days of the opening of the talks (these were meant to be secret, of course, but New Delhi is an excellent capital for journalists). The Chinese were proposing 'reciprocal acceptance of present actualities in both sectors and constitution of a boundary commission'.[212] This would have meant that the Chinese accepted the McMahon alignment in the eastern sector, while the Indians accepted the positions then obtaining in the west — where the forward posts on the two sides were still well apart. No physical withdrawals would have been involved, but India would have dropped the claim to Aksai Chin, and China would have negotiated a boundary along the McMahon alignment. The boundary commission would then have marked out on the ground with pillars, cairns or other markers the lines agreed to in the New Delhi talks, or in later, more detailed, negotiations. Such a commission, made up of both Indian and Chinese officials and surveyors, would have been competent to settle the marginal disputes over such places as Longju and Khinzemane. This was the normal procedure for the delimitation and demarcation of boundaries, and it was the procedure China was to follow with her other neighbours and had already agreed on with Burma.

There was no departure or reversal for Peking in that proposal, it had been inherent in the Chinese approach to the boundary question from the first time it was discussed between Nehru and Chou En-lai. The latter then said that although the McMahon Line was not fair, nevertheless it would be accepted by the Chinese Government because of its friendly relations with Burma and India. That position was tacitly reaffirmed in Chou's first letter to Nehru on the border question. After the Indian claim to Aksai Chin was first verbally expressed in the note of October 18th, 1958, China consistently equated the Indian presence in the territory south of the McMahon Line with her own in Aksai Chin. Sometimes this was done in riposte, as in Peking's comment on the Kongka Pass incident when the Chinese pointed out that, if the Indians insisted on the right to patrol in Chinese-held territory in the west, China might claim reciprocal rights in the east; sometimes it was done in Peking's suggestion for settlement of the dispute in accordance with 'the present actual situation'. The references in Chinese diplomatic communications carried the same implication; for example in the full

Chinese note of December 26th, 1959, Indian maps are described as *'cutting deep into Chinese territory'* in the western sector, while of the eastern sector it is said only that 'the whole boundary line is pushed northward, including an area of about 90,000 square kilometres *which originally belonged to China'*[213] — a crucial change of tense.*

For the conclusion that in the summit talks the Chinese made clear that they were prepared to accept the McMahon alignment provided the Indians accepted the Chinese control line in the west, confirmation comes from the participants. After the talks Chou En-lai told the press in New Delhi:

> We have asked the Indian Government to adopt an attitude towards this western area similar to the attitude of the Chinese Government towards the area of the eastern sector; that is, it may keep its own stand, while agreeing to conduct negotiations and not to cross the line of China's administrative jurisdiction as shown on Chinese maps.[214]

At an impromptu press conference by Nehru at the airport just after Chou left, a journalist pointed out that in saying that as far as the eastern sector was concerned there were 'only some individual areas to discuss', Chou had accepted the Indian position: 'Yes,' Nehru replied, 'but now they tie it up with the west.'[215] An hour later Nehru told the Lok Sabha that 'the attempt was made to equate the eastern sector with the western sector. That is, according to the Chinese, although in the eastern sector we have no right to be there, we had nevertheless advanced gradually in the course of the last few years . . . to the . . . McMahon Line.'[216] Chou En-lai, talking to Pandit Sunder Lal, founder-president of the India-China Friendship Association and one of the very few non-official Indians to meet the Chinese delegation, is said to have summed up what he called his 'give and take' approach like this: 'You keep what you hold, you take too anything that is in dispute and occupied by neither, and we keep what we hold.'[217]

That China was prepared to accept the McMahon alignment has stronger evidence than anything said at or reported from the summit talks, or during the previous or subsequent diplomatic exchanges. Chou En-lai and his party came to New Delhi direct from Rangoon

---

* Emphasis added by the writer.

where they had signed with the Government of Burma a boundary agreement *in which China accepted the McMahon alignment.** After that, it would have been diplomatically impossible and geographically impracticable for China to have refused to accept it in delimiting her boundaries with India.

The Chinese may have believed that the conclusion of the Sino-Burmese boundary agreement so clearly demonstrated their good faith and intention to confirm the boundary which the Indians wanted in the eastern sector that the Indian Government's apparent obduracy would evaporate; certainly all the signs were that they arrived in New Delhi expecting to come to terms with India, as they had with Burma —and would immediately after with Nepal. But they found that the McMahon Line was not the crux of the question so far as India was concerned. The *sine qua non* of a boundary settlement in the Indian view was that China must concede that Aksai Chin was Indian territory *as well as* accepting the McMahon Line. In India it had been recognized from the end of 1959 that China proposed to exchange recognition of the McMahon alignment for India's waiver of her Aksai Chin claim, and this was seen as China's attempt to 'barter' what she held illegally against what she claimed unreasonably — 'You condone my last theft and I won't steal any more.' No sooner was the Chinese approach understood than Indian opinion had set solidly against any such settlement. 'Nothing could be more thoroughly unacceptable to this country than the suggestion that the *status quo*, which is a product of Chinese aggression, should be one of the guiding principles of a final solution,' as the *Times of India* put it at the beginning of 1960.[218] As usual Nehru gave full—and probably excessive—weight to public attitudes. At a meeting at the turn of 1959-60 attended by himself, Pant, N. R. Pillai (the Secretary-General), and one other, the Chinese 'barter' proposal was discussed; Nehru is reported to have closed the discussion with the observation: 'If I give them that I shall no longer be Prime Minister of India—I will not do it.'[219]

So it was a foregone conclusion that Chou En-lai's attempt to reach a settlement on that basis would meet with a point-blank Indian refusal. As Indian officials explained that refusal at the time, the Chinese proposal of 'reciprocal acceptance of present actualities in both sectors' was unacceptable to India because it would be 'a derogation of the

---

* The Sino-Burmese boundary settlement is dealt with on pp. 210-12 below.

6

juridical validity of the northern border and would also compromise the territorial integrity of the country'.[220]

Finding India adamant that recognition of 'present actualities' could not be the basis of settlement, the Chinese then tried to give effect to the proposal they had made just before the conference: that, failing a settlement, the two sides should simply agree to maintain the *status quo*. Such an agreement could be achieved in the apparently more limited — and for Nehru less invidious — formulation that both sides would suspend patrolling along the borders; and in the latter part of the conference the Chinese tried to get the Indians to agree to that. Again they failed, although in this regard the Indian refusal was somewhat muffled. Ever since the boundary dispute became a political issue in India the Government had been under pressure to throw the Chinese out of Aksai Chin, or at least to move into the area itself to assert Indian claims there. Parliament was on the alert for any concession by Nehru that would foreclose such moves by India — hence the demand the Jan Sangh delivered to him on the eve of the meeting that 'nothing will be done to limit our right to take all necessary measures to liberate Chinese-occupied areas.' That India's hand would be kept free in this regard was a prime concern of the Indian side in the talks.

The position about patrolling was slightly blurred at this time. China had suspended forward patrolling in all sectors of the frontier,[221] while India had suspended it in the eastern sector only.[222] The Indian position on patrolling in the western sector had been left ambiguous in the diplomatic correspondence. For the record at least, Peking was assuming that New Delhi had suspended patrolling there too,[223] but wanted to have this point clarified and formalized. In fact the Indians had not *suspended* patrolling in the western sector; they were not sending out any patrols because they were not logistically able to support them. The Indian Government's position, however, was that nothing must derogate from India's right to send patrols into her own territory in the west (i.e. the disputed, Chinese-held territory), and that this right would be exercised in due course unless the Chinese voluntarily evacuated the area.

To have said as much to Chou En-lai, however, could have been taken as an open threat and would certainly have invited the rejoinder, already made in Peking's statements, that China would in that case have to reserve the right to give similar expression to her claims south of the McMahon Line. The Indian refusal to accept the suspension of patrolling had, therefore, to be oblique and imprecise—as Nehru told Parliament after the conference. 'We found that it is very difficult and partly undesirable to be precise about [patrolling],' he said.[224] The Chinese proposal was that 'in order to ensure tranquillity on the border so as to facilitate the discussions both sides should continue to refrain from patrolling along all sectors of the boundary';[225] Indian resistance transmuted that point into the following in the communiqué: 'During the period of further examination of the factual material, every effort should be made by the parties to avoid friction and clashes in the border areas.' In the Indian interpretation this meant no more than that when their forces began to move into Chinese-claimed territory in the western sector they would not *attack* Chinese positions or patrols. As Nehru explained to Parliament, so far as the Indian Government was concerned 'our people will be completely free to move about these areas without coming into conflict.'[226]

That the summit conference had failed was plain from the outset, but neither side wished it to break down. It continued, therefore, for its full five days, but the joint communiqué released at the end of the talks stated that the differences had not been resolved. The Indian side were prepared to leave it at that;[227] but the Chinese wished to keep the diplomatic ball in play, and it was agreed that officials of the Governments should meet to collate all the historical evidence and prepare a report listing the points of agreement and disagreement. At the Indians' insistence a deadline of four months was put on the officials' work. No further step was agreed; the communiqué simply said that the officials' report 'should prove helpful towards further consideration of these problems by the two Governments'.

During the visit the Indian Government not only honoured their undertaking to the Opposition parties that there would be no public functions in the visitors' honour but also did what they could to see that the Chinese delegation was isolated from private or press contacts. On the last day of the conference foreign correspondents asked the Ministry of External Affairs if a press conference could be arranged for Chou En-lai, who usually met the press at the conclusion of such visits. The request was refused—but that evening the Chinese themselves announced that Chou would give a press conference at ten-thirty p.m.

The New Delhi press corps rather prided itself on the sharpness with which it treated Indian and visiting politicians. Even Nehru, who in those days held a formal press conference every month, was treated with cavalier familiarity by the Indian correspondents, who were just as ready to harangue, instruct, or admonish as to question him.* The Indian journalists, to a man committed to their Government's position in the boundary dispute, were accordingly expecting to put Chou En-lai through a mincer of questions that would expose what they believed to be China's naked aggression against India; but from the moment he entered the room, one of the pillared halls of the President's palace, its walls hung with life-size portraits of the last of the Viceroys and his Vicereine,† Chou dominated the press conference.

The Chinese began by distributing a statement by Chou En-lai in which he concisely reiterated the Chinese position: that the boundary had never been delimited, that the question could be settled through friendly consultations, and that, pending settlement, 'both sides should maintain the present state of the boundary and not change it by unilateral action, let alone by force'. In the meantime the friendship between China and India should not, and could not, be jeopardized by the boundary question. The nub of the statement lay in six points which he described as 'common points, or points of proximity' between the two sides:

I. There exist disputes with regard to the boundary between the two sides.

II. There exists between the two countries a line of actual control up to which each side exercises administrative jurisdiction.

III. In determining the boundary between the two countries certain geographical principles such as watersheds, river valleys and mountain passes should be equally applicable to all sectors of the boundary.

IV. A settlement of the boundary question between the two countries should take into account the national feelings of the two peoples towards the Himalayas and the Karakoram Mountains.

V. Pending a settlement of the boundary question between the two

* Except for occasional explosions of irritation Nehru tolerated this treatment, thus setting a precedent that was to be uncomfortable for his successors. Lal Bahadur Shastri gave one formal press conference in New Delhi and was treated so offensively that he never gave another, and Mrs Indira Gandhi at first held them very rarely.
† There could hardly have been a more telling symbol of the vast political and psychological distance that separated the two Governments than these two paintings. For the Chinese, it must have been incomprehensible that proud and patriotic Indians could allow such reminders of past servitude to decorate important rooms in their President's palace.

countries through discussions, both sides should keep to the line of actual control and should not put forward territorial claims as pre-conditions, but individual adjustments may be made.

VI. In order to ensure tranquillity on the border so as to facilitate the discussions, both sides should continue to refrain from patrolling along all sectors of the boundary.[228]

There was still a certain distance between the two sides on these points, Chou said, but continued consultations could narrow and then eliminate it. He then declared himself ready to answer all questions, requesting only that his answers be reported in full.

The press conference went on for two and a half hours,* but did not greatly extend the public knowledge of the positions taken during the talks. Asked which sector occupied most of the Prime Minister's time, Chou En-lai said the western sector, over which 'there exists a relatively bigger dispute'. He reiterated that his Government, like those before it, could never recognize the McMahon Line because it was 'illegally delineated through an exchange of secret notes by British imperialism with the Tibetan local authorities'. Nevertheless, he said, China was observing the Line as the boundary, and had not put forward territorial claims as pre-conditions in the negotiations. He then summarized the Chinese position on the western sector, and said he had asked the Indians to adopt towards that an attitude similar to China's towards the eastern sector: 'the Indian Government has not entirely agreed to this,' he said.

A Western correspondent asked whether the Indian side in the talks had taken the position that China had committed aggression against India. Chou replied that no such suggestion had been made, adding that if the Indians had made such a point 'it would not only [have been] out of keeping with objective reality, but would also [have been] extremely unfriendly'.[229]

The Indians were displeased by the fact as well as by the content of Chou's press conference, and Nehru waited only until the Chinese were

---

* It ended only after the writer had asked Chou En-lai to put a term to it for the sake of newspaper deadlines. The interpreter was slow and only twenty-five questions were put in the one hundred and fifty minutes of the conference. They included two by an American woman reporter, who wanted to know whether Chou would consider inviting President Eisenhower to Peking 'provided it does not involve recognizing Red China'; and as she thought Chou looked exceptionally fit for his sixty-two years, how he cared for his health—by diet or regular exercise? 'Thank you,' Chou replied, 'I am an Oriental and I follow an Oriental way of life.'

airborne and dwindling in the eastern sky on their way to Katmandu before having his own say to correspondents at the airport. Referring to Chou's proposal of mutual accommodation on the basis of 'present actualities', he said: 'There could be no question of barter in this matter.' He confirmed that the Chinese had been prepared to accept the Indian position so far as the eastern sector was concerned, but said they had 'tied it up with the west'.[230]

The disclosure in the morning's papers that, according to Chou En-lai, the Indian side in the talks had not accused China of having committed aggression confirmed Indian suspicions that Nehru had not been sufficiently blunt to the Chinese. The journalists at the airport challenged him on this score, and M.P.s raised the same point in Parliament; Nehru there duly pronounced the shibboleth of loyalty and outrage that the charge of aggression had become in India. He explained that he was 'not quite sure . . . whether [he] used that word or not', but said that the whole context of the talks had been one of China's aggression; Chou En-lai 'came here because something important had happened, the important thing being that according to us they had entered our territory . . . which we considered aggression'.[231] Chou was not amused when his erstwhile host's words were reported to him in Katmandu. 'He did not say it to our face but as soon as we had left he attacked the Chinese Government as aggressors,' he said. 'That is not an attitude to take towards guests. We were very much distressed by such an attitude, particularly as we respect Prime Minister Nehru.'[232]

Nehru went straight from the airport to the Lok Sabha to give an account of the conference. He quoted Chou En-lai's six points, saying that the Indian Government did not agree with them, and then subjected them to a cursory and misleading analysis:

I. There exist disputes with regard to the boundary . . .
Nehru: 'Of course there exist disputes.'
(This was the crux of the whole question. The Indian position was that there was no dispute about the overall alignment of the boundaries and that China had concocted factitious disputes to camouflage territorial demands.)

II. There exists . . . a line of actual control up to which each side exercises administrative jurisdiction.
Nehru: 'It is obvious, I do not know where the importance of it lies.'

(Nehru's refusal to agree to Chinese proposals for the maintenance of the *status quo* had been based on the argument that the actual situation was unclear; 'An agreement about observance of the *status quo* would be meaningless as the facts concerning the *status quo* are themselves disputed,' he had told Chou En-lai earlier.)[233]

III. In determining the boundary . . . geographical principles such as watersheds [etc.] should be equally applicable to all sectors . . .
Nehru: 'It is a principle laid down that watersheds are applicable, and we naturally agree that watersheds are very important factors; it is the most important factor in mountainous regions, river valleys, etc. It does not carry us anywhere.'
(The Indians described the McMahon Line as a watershed boundary, maintaining that as such it was the proper alignment in the eastern sector. If the watershed principle were applied to the western sector it would point to a boundary along the Karakoram Mountains which form the watershed between the Central Asian drainage and the streams flowing into the Indian Ocean.)

IV. A settlement of the boundary question . . . should take into account the national feelings of the two peoples towards the Himalayas and the Karakoram Mountains.
Nehru: 'I take it as a response to the fact that the Himalayas are an intimate part of India and Indian culture and all that. . . . If the Chinese feel strongly about the Karakoram [Mountains] they are welcome to do so, I have no objection to it.'
(The dispute in the western sector was essentially about whether the boundary should follow the Karakoram range or, as the Indians maintained, jump at the Karakoram Pass to the next range north, the Kuen Lun. Taking up the claim to India's mystical affinity with the Himalayas which as an argument for the McMahon Line had repeatedly been advanced by Nehru, Chou En-lai was here claiming the same sort of Chinese ties to the Karakoram Mountains. The implication was that in return for China's acceptance of the McMahon Line India should give up her claim to a trans-Karakoram boundary in the western sector.)

V. Pending a settlement . . . both sides should keep to the line of actual control and should not put forward territorial claims as pre-conditions. . . .
Nehru: 'Presumably it means that they will not discuss anything

unless the territorial claim is accepted, maybe that . . . it is not quite clear.'

(India had a territorial claim to Aksai Chin and was insisting that before there could be substantive discussion on the actual align-ment of the boundaries China must accede to that claim and evacuate the territory. Nehru here reversed the Chinese point to suggest that China was insisting on Indian acceptance of the Chinese claim before there could be negotiations!

In the Indian perception, this is what it would have amounted to if substantive negotiations had been started while the Chinese were in occupation of Aksai Chin.)

VI. . . . both sides should continue to refrain from patrolling along all sectors of the boundary.

Nehru: 'This is not something that I agreed to.'

(As has been seen, this was China's attempt to de-fuse the boundary situation so that its settlement could safely be left to some later date; and the Indians had rejected it. Nehru was not yet ready to declare that his Government intended to patrol forward into the Aksai Chin territory—he was speaking in public with the Chinese, so to speak, in the audience. Therefore he could not reassure his critics in Parliament, and was in a quandary when he was pressed on this point:

Question: . . . as our Prime Minister has said that we agreed to avoid clashes, does it mean that our patrol personnel cannot go to patrol our territory?

Nehru: . . . in this communiqué it is said that every effort should be made by the parties to avoid friction and clashes in the border areas. That is a general directive which we take and which we give. We found it is very difficult and partly undesirable to be precise about it. I think we cannot immobilize people so that they can go and sit and not go to the right or left. I think it was right anyhow to tell them that they should not take any step which obviously brings them into conflict.

Question: . . . what will be the situation if our patrol personnel are not allowed to go to patrol the territory because whenever they went to patrol our territory they were arrested by the Chinese?

Nehru: Our people will be completely free to move about these areas without coming into conflict.

Question: Does it mean that Government has committed itself
that pending factual investigation, no steps will be taken to eject
the Chinese from Indian soil?
Nehru: I should think that was absolutely clear. . . . You either
have war or you have some kind of, call it talks or steps; you
cannot have something in between the two. We cannot declare
war on the frontier and at the same time talk about discussions or
sending official teams. The two cannot go together.)[234]

Comment in Parliament and the press on the talks and their outcome
was generally negative, and focused on two related charges. First, that
by agreeing to the officials' consultations Nehru was simply giving the
Chinese time to consolidate their positions, pursuing futile discussions
while China was 'in occupation of thousands and thousands of square
miles of our sacred motherland', as Ranga, the Swatantra leader, said
in the Lok Sabha—'soiling our motherland with their cancerous
fingers'.[235] And, secondly, that the Government had made no statement of intention to force China to 'vacate her aggression'. Those who
approved the Government's handling of the summit talks did so because Nehru had stood 'firm as a rock', as Congress M.P.s put it, and
one newspaper suggested that 'the fact that India has not been over-
awed by China will not be lost on Asian opinion.'[236]

* * * * * * * * * * *

The summit meeting, on which apparently the Chinese had set great
store, failed; broken, Nehru said, on the 'rock of an entirely different
set of facts',[237] but really on the unyielding refusal of India to give up,
modify or hold over her claim to the Aksai Chin territory. For his
swing around south Asia, Chou En-lai had two successes to show, one
failure. In Burma and then in Nepal he had been able to sign treaties of
friendship and boundary agreements, leaving neither of those small
neighbours feeling that they had been bullied or even pressured by
their huge neighbour. In the case of Burma, the Chinese had accepted
the McMahon alignment as the basis of the boundary; in the case of
Nepal they had agreed that, where there were disputes, 'adjustments
be made in accordance with the principles of equality, mutual benefit,
friendship and mutual accommodation'.[238] There had been the makings
of a dispute over Mount Everest, which Chinese maps showed within

6*

China, but the Chinese accepted the Nepali (and general) view that the peak itself marked the boundary. China and Nepal agreed to keep their armed personnel out of a forty-kilometre zone along the boundary.

So far as the Sino-Indian dispute was concerned, although Chou En-lai maintained that the talks had not failed, that 'further understanding has been achieved anyway', all that the summit meeting had done was to clear the way for a worsening of the situation on the borders. The officials' consultations, as Nehru foresaw,[239] would do no more than produce two contradictory reports. The dispute could not be resolved by what Nehru called 'facts', it required political compromise. The Indians had refused to come to any agreement to suspend patrolling in the western sector so as to keep their hands free for the move forward into Chinese-controlled territory in Aksai Chin to which Nehru and his Government were already implicitly committed.

The Chinese approach hardened after the summit failure. No more was heard of the suggestion Peking had made before the talks, that perhaps the Indians genuinely misunderstood China's intentions.[240] Chen Yi expressed the strain of indignation that was henceforth to mark Chinese comments on the boundary dispute when, after listening to Chou En-lai being questioned by American and Indian correspondents at the Katmandu press conference, he broke in with: 'I want to call your attention to the fact that China is a country which is being wronged. I want to stress, China is a country which is being wronged.'[241]

Part II

THE FORWARD POLICY

We thought it was a sort of game. They would stick up a post and we would stick up a post and we did not think it would come to much more.

An Indian Army officer[1]

It was a game of Russian roulette, but the highest authorities of India seemed to feel that the one shot in the cylinder was a blank. Unfortunately for them and for the country it was not so. The cylinder was fully loaded.

General J. N. Chaudhuri[2]

When you shut the door, what remains? Either sitting sullenly and doing nothing, like an old woman—or going out, sword in hand or whatever weapon you have, and fighting. There is nothing else left.

Jawaharlal Nehru[3]

It was not the failure of the New Delhi summit that closed the door to a negotiated settlement of the boundary dispute. India had closed that long before; indeed, had walled it up when border policy was first considered by the new Indian Government in the first years after independence. But with Chou En-lai's departure, the Government was squarely faced with the question: 'What next?' There was never any doubt about the answer, it had been inherent in the Indian position from the beginning of the dispute.

That was that Aksai Chin had always and incontrovertibly been Indian territory and that the Chinese claim to it was factitious, concocted to camouflage illegal and clandestine seizure. If, caught and denounced, China refused to withdraw from the area, India would have to turn to measures other than argument to recover it, lest the situation set into permanence—a *de facto* settlement by default. Therefore India had parried or rejected China's attempts to obtain an agreement on maintenance of the *status quo* of 1959, from the proposal in Chou En-lai's first letter to his attempts in the summit talks to get Nehru to accept a joint suspension of patrolling.

The Government, by describing the Chinese presence in Indian-claimed territory as an act of aggression, had brought upon itself the obligation to do something about this, by force if diplomatic methods failed. While resisting the Opposition's clamour for the use of bombs, paratroops or infantry to hurl the Chinese off Indian soil, Nehru habitually coupled his rejection of war with a commitment that, if diplomacy and talks failed, the Government would not supinely accept the situation. If ejection of the Chinese by the direct use of military force was ruled out because it would lead to war, and acquiescence in the *status quo* on the boundaries was ruled out because it would amount to defeat, a third way early suggested itself to the Indians. As the *Times of India* put it in an editorial in October 1959:

New Delhi must assert its rights by dispatching properly equipped

patrols into the areas currently occupied by the Chinese, since any
prolonged failure to do so will imply a tacit acceptance of Chinese
occupation, and a surrender to Peking's threat to cross the
McMahon Line in force should Indian patrols penetrate into the
disputed areas of Ladakh.[4]

The Government had reached the same conclusion by the time that
Chou En-lai left New Delhi. The day he left, the writer was told by a
key official not to expect the borders to relapse into quiet, as Indian
patrols would have to begin probing the Chinese-occupied area.
There would be no attacks on Chinese positions (the summit communiqué committed the parties to 'every effort . . . to avoid friction
and clashes'); but the Indian patrols would penetrate the spaces between
them.

This forward policy, as it came to be called, was not formulated in
the normal processes of government; it emerged in a kind of virgin
birth out of the situation in which the Indian Government found itself
at the beginning of 1960. Various—and varying—claims about the
paternity of the policy were put forward later: proud boasts of father-
hood before it brought disaster, disavowals when events had bas-
tardized it. As late as October 1962, General Kaul, then Chief of the
General Staff, told the writer that the forward policy had been his own
conception, 'sold to Nehru over the head of Krishna Menon'; but
in that officer's later accounts responsibility for the policy is shifted
away from himself and towards Nehru, Menon and his own military
superiors.[5] Krishna Menon has been more consistent and more honest,
conceding that the policy derived from the situation and maintaining
that if it had been continued 'as a game of chess', it need not have
failed.[6]

The objectives of the forward policy were, first, to block potential
lines of further Chinese advance; secondly, to establish an Indian
presence in Aksai Chin which would make Indian participation in the
joint withdrawals proposed by Nehru more than theoretical, and thus
give strength to that diplomatic lever for getting the Chinese out of the
area. Beyond that, implicit at the outset, was the intention to undermine Chinese control of the disputed areas by the interposition of
Indian posts and patrols between Chinese positions, thus cutting their
supply lines and ultimately forcing them to withdraw. But the objectives emerged after the policy was formulated, and were more a

rationale; the forward policy really sprang from the conclusion that there was nothing else India could do.

At no time were the implications thought through in New Delhi. The policy was legalistic, assuming that as possession is nine-tenths of the law India had only to go and stand on as many parts of Aksai Chin as possible to turn the tables on China, or at least attain a position of equality with her. It was reckless, ignoring the often repeated Chinese warning that assertion of Indian claims in the western sector courted retaliation across the McMahon Line. And at bottom it was irrational, because its fundamental premise was that no matter how many posts and patrols India sent into Chinese-claimed and -occupied territory the Chinese would not physically interfere with them—provided only that the Indians did not attack any Chinese positions. From the very beginning of the dispute in 1954, after the advance of Indian boundary posts in the middle sector brought them into contact with the Chinese, India had been ready to threaten force against Chinese who tried to maintain positions across the Indian claim lines;* but Nehru and his colleagues were absolute in their faith that the Chinese would not do likewise. When it is remembered that India accused China of trigger-happy aggressiveness in the Longju and Kongka Pass incidents, the faith that China would not use force against Indian troops who penetrated into Aksai Chin becomes more curious—unless it is taken to suggest that New Delhi suspected that the Chinese version of those incidents, in which it was alleged that the Indians attacked, was true.

The forward policy smacked of *satyagraha*, the passive civil disobedience movement which Indians employed against the British. In this case the *satyagrahis* would be armed troops, able to fight back if attacked; but the confidence in a kind of moral unassailability which would dissuade the Chinese from attacking recalled the belief that the British would be reluctant to use force, and that if they did it would redound against them. It seems to have reflected Nehru's perception of

---

* For example in a note of September 26th, 1956, India informed Peking that the presence of Chinese armed personnel in territory India claimed would be regarded as aggression and resisted as such. Again on August 28th, 1959, India warned China that Indian border forces would 'use force on trespassers'. Peking commented that as there were divergences between the two countries' conceptions of the boundary and their maps, with India regarding large tracts of what Peking considered Chinese territory as Indian, the Indians would call Chinese troops or civilians there 'trespassers'. New Delhi had thus given its border forces authority 'to use force more or less freely', and Peking suggested that the Longju and Kongka Pass incidents were a consequence of that *carte blanche*.[7] See p. 109 above.

his country as one unique in the world's experience for the depth of its pacific instincts, and his belief that the world—including China— shared that view. India's reputation in the world would go with the patrols into Aksai Chin like a moral armour.

If these assumptions were unreal, there was a deeper illogicality about the forward policy, because with its other objectives it looked ultimately to changing the military balance in Aksai Chin to the point at which India could use force to eject the Chinese. 'My whole soul reacts against the idea of war anywhere,' Nehru often said;[8] but, when not in his apocalyptic vein, he could be quite pragmatic about the prospect of war. 'A certain aggression has taken place on our territory,' he told the Lok Sabha in 1961, when the forward policy had begun to be put into effect. 'How do we deal with it? First of all, what is the objective? Obviously, our objective can only be to get that aggression vacated. How do we get that aggression vacated? By diplomatic means, by various measures, and ultimately if you like by war. . . . We go on strengthening our position to deal with the situation whenever we think it is strong enough to be dealt with by us, and not from a weak position.'[9] How it could be believed that the Chinese would stand idly by while India gradually and laboriously built up positions of strength from which to attack them is difficult to understand; but that Nehru and his colleagues did believe it was to be demonstrated not only in the western sector, but below Thag La ridge in the east—until they were brutally disabused in October 1962.

Nehru's utterances on war in this period were usually set off by the bellicose rhetoric of Opposition speakers. With the sole party exception of the Communists, the Opposition benches were solid in their calls on the Government to use force to evict the Chinese if they did not evacuate the areas that India claimed, and there was strong—if largely silent—sympathy for that view on the Congress side. It was denied that such action would amount to war. 'To defend your own territory is not to wage war,' Masani said;[10] 'I have never known this suggestion before, that if you throw out bandits from your territory you are engaged in an act of war. It is just police action on your own territory.' The phrase 'police action' was consistently used by the Government's critics to describe what they had in mind for the Chinese. It had first been used in India to describe military operations in 1948, when the vacillation of the Nizam of Hyderabad over the future of his state was cut short by India's marching the Army in, and it was soon to be applied to the seizure of Goa. It implied an assumption of moral authority on the part of the attacking or 'police' force as well as their overwhelming strength, and so was doubly comforting to Indian sensibilities — as it is, of course, in other countries proposing to use force to attain their ends. 'We as a peaceful nation who are members of the U.N. do not believe in war as any remedy,' an Independent M.P. summed it up in the Lok Sabha at the end of 1959; 'therefore . . . the only way is to have a police action whereby we can push the Chinese out of our territory, create the *status quo ante*, vacate aggression, and after that have a basis for negotiation.'[11] This nominalist fallacy—that the nature of an act could be changed by calling it something different —was always impatiently rejected by Nehru, and then the Opposition would change tack and claim that, in any event, war was not the ultimate catastrophe or even an unmixed evil. Small, local wars could not always be avoided, Kripalani argued. 'When such wars are fought, thanks to the wisdom of the world, they are localised and after some time a workable solution is found. . . . So we need not scare ourselves that any resistance to Chinese aggression will lead to a world war and a destruction of humanity. The world will see to it that this does not happen.'[12]

Opposition members liked to point to the silver linings on the clouds of war, suggesting that the experience of war would unite and temper the Indian people—'It is conflict that brings out the best in a country, that brings about unity,' as Kripalani put it—and that even the danger of it could be turned to good effect. 'The threat [to our borders] can and must be used to achieve national cohesion and spur national endeavour,' Asoka Mehta counselled the Government: 'Confronted by aggressive footsteps along our traditional ramparts the nation will be willing to bear additional sacrifices.'[13] This vision of a nation girded for combat was not without its Faustian attraction for Nehru, who saw India, if at last faced with war, becoming 'a nation of armies', with 'every single activity, every single thing that we do, planning et cetera, conditioned by one major fact—because that will be a struggle for life and death'.[14] But more consistently he emphasized the dangers of war, not only for India and Indians but for the world as a whole. 'War between India and China would be one of the major disasters of the world,' he said in the upper House at the end of 1961, ' . . . for it will mean world war. It will mean war which will be indefinite. We would not be able to limit it in time, because it will not be possible for China to defeat us and it will be impossible for us to march up to Peking across Tibet.'[15] This warning that war in the Himalayas would inevitably set the world alight was testily rejected by those who wanted to see the Indian Army launch operations to evict the Chinese. 'One of the fantasies with which New Delhi hypnotizes itself into inactivity is the supposition that a Sino-Indian conflict on the border issue would plunge the entire world into a nuclear holocaust,' one editorial put it at the end of 1961.[16]

The tone of Nehru's utterances on war oscillated. First, reacting against the wild trumpet calls from the Opposition benches, he would speak of Armageddon, the horrors of war; then, backing away lest he be taken to be damping down the patriotic ardour which the boundary dispute was arousing, and of which he confessed he was proud (though he said that he wished the young men who sent him pledges signed in their blood would find more constructive outlets),[17] he would reaffirm India's readiness to fight if war did come. Drum-beating and strong language were wrong and dangerous, he said; 'war is a dangerous policy; but if war is thrust upon us we shall fight and fight with all our strength. But I shall avoid war, try to prevent it with every means in our power, because it is a bad thing, it is a dangerous thing. . . .' On the other hand, 'there are some things which no nation can tolerate. Any attack on its honour, on its integrity, on the integrity of its territory, no nation tolerates, and it takes risks, grave risks even, to protect all that.'[18]

Varying as his utterances on war were in their tone, they did in sum tend to give currency, even respectability, to the idea that India would go to war with China for Aksai Chin unless that territory was surrendered. Led on by the hot cries of the Opposition even while rejecting them, Nehru from very soon after the boundary dispute became a political issue in India began to speak of war with China as a possibility. (He even went so far as to allude to it in a speech at the state banquet in New Delhi for Chou En-lai.) But in those rhetorical allusions to the ultimate possibility of war, the conceived context was always that of India, patience at last exhausted and a position of strength achieved, going to war for the territory she claimed. That war might arise from Chinese reaction to or anticipation of Indian moves never crossed civilian minds in New Delhi. From beginning to end, Nehru and his colleagues were unwavering in their faith that, whatever India herself did along the borders, China would not attack. That was the basic assumption of the forward policy, a military challenge to a militarily far superior neighbour.

* * * * * * * * * * *

The 1950s had been a decade of neglect for the Indian armed forces. The Army especially suffered from the stepmotherly attitude of the new Congress Government after independence. That may have derived partly from the resentment of the Congressmen against those who had served the foreign rule while they themselves suffered gaol or worse trying to oust it, but the attitude was confirmed by two major policy conclusions of the new Government. The first of these was that there was no danger of any attack on India.

This belief can be traced back in the pre-independence utterances of Nehru as far as 1928 when, in a speech to Congress, he enumerated the countries which might be considered to present possible threats to India and one by one ruled them out, to the conclusion that 'no danger threatens India from any direction, and even if there is any danger we shall be able to cope with it.'[19] British defence strategy had focused on the north-west approaches to the sub-continent, and been informed by apprehension of a challenge from Moscow ever since the Russians absorbed the khanates and reached the frontier of Afghanistan in the 1880s; and this obsession persisted even in the 1920s, although soon afterwards it was put aside in favour of the more limited contingency of a war with Afghanistan. Nehru dismissed the Russian bogey as 'largely imaginary' and saw the danger from Afghanistan as, at most, that of a few raids. As for China, the Himalayas made 'an effective barrier and not even air fleets could come that way'.[20] India's size, its geo-strategic position and the interest of the great powers in seeing that it did not fall under foreign dominion again would, in Nehru's view, keep his country immune from any significant external attacks: 'No country will tolerate the idea of another acquiring the commanding position which England occupied for so long. If any power was covetous enough to make the attempt, all the others would combine to trounce the intruder. This mutual rivalry would in itself be the surest guarantee against an attack on India.'[21] Nehru continued to hold this rational and pragmatic view of external threats to India after independence and indeed until the main Chinese assault in November 1962.

In the first years of independence, there was no apprehension in India of any military threat from Pakistan—the boot was very much on the other foot. Pakistan's share of the pre-partition Indian Army was, naturally, smaller than India's, and the rudimentary resources and sketchy organization of the new state of Pakistan magnified India's military superiority. In India, Hindu nationalist feeling against Pakistan was intense, the desire to 'avenge the wrong' of 1947 and undo partition openly expressed. Nehru stood squarely against such sentiments, but only time could suppress them. War between India and Pakistan was close during the Kashmir fighting in 1947–8; again in 1950 when communal massacres broke out afresh in the two Bengals; again in 1951 when the Kashmir dispute came to a head once more. On all these occasions the Indian Army concentrated on the Punjab border, threatening Lahore. In 1951 Pakistan informed the Security Council of the threat from the Indian Army; the passing of this crisis seems to have owed something to American diplomatic intervention.[22]

It became clear to the Pakistanis that they would have to live under the recurrent threat of Indian attack until they built up their own forces to at least a deterrent level. John Foster Dulles's pactmanship made that possible in 1954,* and as the United States equipped and trained Pakistan's armed forces it appeared that it would no longer be easy for India to knock out Pakistan—and there could be no more one-sided military confrontations. The possibility that India might launch an attack on Pakistan faded, to be replaced with the possibility that Pakistan, emboldened by the strength of her American-armed forces, might try conclusions with India again over Kashmir. (The reversal was signalled in the changed attitudes to the question of a 'no-war pact'. That was originally urged by Liaquat Ali Khan, Prime Minister of Pakistan, and turned down by Nehru;[23] after the middle 1950s it began to be urged by India, and rejected by Pakistan.)

So, through the 1950s, in the strategic context first of attack, then of defence, the exclusive possibility of war with Pakistan informed the strategy and training of the Indian services. The Army, cautious by profession, proposed that some thought be given to the defence of the northern borders against China, but met with a political ruling that no military preparations against China were called for.[24] A suggestion in the early 1950s that an infantry manual on Chinese battle tactics be

---

* American military assistance became available to Pakistan after she had joined the Baghdad (later CENTO) and SEATO pacts, and was meant to be used against Communist aggression. It seems probable, however, that Washington appreciated that it would serve to stabilize South Asia if India's military predominance over Pakistan were diminished.

prepared, drawing on American and British experience in Korea, was rejected.[25] As late as 1958, 'to the utter amazement and consternation of the Indian Army', according to one officer,[26] a high-ranking Chinese military mission was taken on a tour of major military establishments.* Ironically, in Punjab the Chinese watched a demonstration of fire support for an infantry assault mounted by 4 Division, then under command of Major-General B. M. Kaul; both the division and its then commander were to play central parts in the border war with China four years later.

The second policy consideration, deriving from the first (that there was no danger of India being engaged in hostilities except with Pakistan), was that expenditure on the defence forces must be kept to the barest practicable minimum, so that the resources available for development would not be spent unproductively and unnecessarily.

India's share of the old Indian Army that was sundered in the creation of Pakistan was about 280,000 men. The new Government's first intention was to reduce the size of the Army—Nehru explained that a highly mechanized and relatively small force was preferable to a large but ill-equipped 'foot' force[27]—but this plan was not put into effect, and the Army instead slowly grew. By 1953 it numbered just under 350,000, organized into seven divisions, six infantry—of varying standards of completeness, training and equipment—and one armoured.† The Army's peacetime deployment reflected a balance between the possibility of war with Pakistan and the requirements of internal security, almost as much a consideration with Indian military planners as it had been with their British predecessors. Three infantry divisions were in Kashmir, with one of their battalions at Leh in Ladakh— where, too, it was at that time facing south, against the Pakistanis, rather than north. The Pakistanis had nearly taken Leh in the Kashmir war, and it was in reaction to that northward move that the Indian Army had moved into Ladakh. The Indians had decided that in the

---

* The leader of the Chinese delegation, Marshal Yeh Chiang-ying, visited the Staff College at Wellington in South India, and to commemorate the occasion was presented with a silver replica of the college emblem—an owl. A shadow was seen to pass over his face as he examined the gift, and when he thanked his hosts he explained that in China the owl was a bird of ill omen, and could hardly be regarded as an auspicious gift between friends!

For that matter, the owl is not auspicious in India either—and is commonly a term of abuse, connoting stupidity—but for the Englishman who chose the Western bird of wisdom for the staff college, the classical associations were stronger than the local attitudes.

† The 4th, 5th, 10th, 19th, 26th and 27th Infantry Divisions, and the 1st Armoured Division. There was also an Independent Armoured Brigade at Patiala in Punjab, and the Paratroop Brigade at Agra.

event of another Pakistani attempt to take Kashmir by force, they would have to react by attacking towards Lahore, and a two-division counter-strike force for that purpose was kept in Punjab. The armoured division was based at Jhansi in central India.

These dispositions continued until 1956, and the Army was more or less static in size as well as equipment. The rebellion of the Naga tribes in 1956 necessitated a progressive build-up of forces in the north-east, and by the end of the 1950s a division was tied down in guerrilla fighting in the Naga hills. East Pakistan presented no strategic threat; the great bulk of Pakistan's forces were kept in that country's west wing, most of it in Punjab facing India, some on the north-west frontier to deal with tribal turbulence and possible trouble from Afghanistan—the old threat from the north-west from which partition had relieved India. As the demands of the Naga campaign increased, so more units of the Indian Army were siphoned across from Punjab to the north-east. New units were formed to sustain the Punjab force's strength, and consequently the Army began slowly to grow again.

After the Longju and Kongka Pass incidents of late 1959, with the realization that an intractable dispute might develop over the boundary question, the expansion of the Army became more purposeful, and faster. In November–December 1959, 4 Division was hurriedly trans-ferred from Punjab to the north-east, and a new division, the 17th, created. In the north-east, 4 Division was placed under a new forma-tion, XXXIII Corps, which, with its H.Q. at Shillong, was responsible for Sikkim; the boundary with Bhutan; NEFA and the McMahon Line; East Pakistan; and Nagaland. 4 Division's responsibility was the McMahon Line, from Bhutan to Burma, about 360 miles; but one of the division's brigades was promptly detached for service in Nagaland.

The transfer of 4 Division made little immediate difference to India's defence posture in the north-east. At this time no roads reached more than a few miles from the plains into the foothills, and there were no lateral roads in NEFA at all—the north–south lie of the great ridges running down from the Himalayas made lateral movement almost impossible, and access to the different sectors of the McMahon Line was from the Brahmaputra valley. The division's move into NEFA was painfully slow. In January 1960 one infantry company established itself at Bomdi La; in March another reached Tawang; and it was not until August 1960 that Tawang became a battalion H.Q. By this time, two other battalions were in NEFA, and the headquarters of 7 Infantry

Brigade was at Bomdi La. Such was the slow reality behind Nehru's declaration in August 1959 that the McMahon Line had been made the direct responsibility of the Army.

Vocal political opinion in India was, until late in the 1950s, against any increase in defence expenditure. Kripalani expressed it in the Lok Sabha in 1958:

> We had believed that in a non-violent India the last thing the Government would contemplate would be an increase in the military budget, but I am sorry to say, and I think it would disturb the soul of the father of the nation [Gandhi], that in recent years there has been an increase of about [Rs. 1,000 million] more than in the previous year, and then in the supplementary demands there was an increase of [Rs. 140 million]. . . . May I ask why we are increasing our military establishment?[28]

While the Gandhians were thus criticizing the Government from one side, the services were complaining that the budgetary restrictions under which they operated were preventing proper upkeep of their establishments, let alone allowing modernization. The services' difficulties were exacerbated by the political rivalry and personal hostility between Krishna Menon and Morarji Desai, which informed the interworking of their respective ministries. Writing in 1961 an American journalist in New Delhi observed that 'if India had anything approaching cabinet government, the conflict between Menon and Desai and their respective ministerial advisers would long ago have become unmanageable.'[29]

The complaints from the Army became more pressing in the early 1960s, and in 1961-2 a series of letters went from Army H.Q. to the Defence Minister enumerating deficiencies in equipment and supplies, and warning that these could be crippling in the event of war. The letters were drafted by General Kaul, by now Chief of the General Staff, and in the last and most urgent of them he described the quandary in which Government policy had placed the Army: 'On the one hand we are required to raise additional forces as soon as possible, failing which we run the risk of our territory being occupied by foreign aggressors; on the other hand, the weapons, equipment and ammunition available to us are so meagre that we are finding it impossible to equip the new raisings.'[30] This particular letter included the request that it be placed before the Defence Committee of the Cabinet, reflecting the soldiers' belief that Krishna Menon was not passing on their urgent warnings. But, like its predecessors, it had no effect in increasing the Army's budget allocations. Kaul made use of the personal access to Nehru that he enjoyed to carry the Army's case farther, and, by his own account, met this answer:

If we imported the weapons and equipment needed by the armed forces we would have to spend foreign exchange, of which we were already very short; so much expenditure on defence would result in a major economic setback to the country, which he could not accept. In view of these and some political considerations, he said we must mainly rely upon indigenous production of weapons and equipment, which was really the answer in the long run. He finally said that we must stand on our own feet as foreign countries might withdraw or modify their support to us at any time.[31]

This was a cogent sketch of the Government's policy. Development must come first; military aid from abroad was unacceptable since it would impair India's non-alignment and be unreliable; and the only answer to the predicament of the services lay in the long-term plan of steadily building up defence production inside India. Thus the needs of the services would be filled while at the same time the country's industrial resources were augmented. Nehru repeated the argument again and again at this time to meet the complaints and warnings advanced by, and on behalf of, the services.

The thinking was unexceptionable, but it did not sit well with the risks of the forward policy. For all the political compulsions that produced it or, in the Indian view, its justification, such a policy meant physically challenging a militarily far more powerful neighbour. No settlement of the quarrel with Pakistan was in sight—or indeed being sought—and the Government's policies set the Army an onerous new task, inviting confrontation with one of the world's strongest infantry powers, without having either trimmed its obligations elsewhere or materially increased its budget. In the spring of 1961 India contributed a brigade group for action with the United Nations in suppressing the Katanga secession in the Congo, and a battalion had been in U.N. service in the Gaza strip since 1956.

By the beginning of the 1960s, then, the Indian Army's limited resources were coming under considerable strain; but it was in a very poor position to register its disquiet. Since independence, relations between the Army and the civilian leadership had tilted to the disadvantage of the soldiers, with the Government's positively pacific, almost pacifist approach to international relations, the emphasis on development, the insistence on non-alignment, all reinforcing the Gandhian disapproval of men of war which was part of the Congress attitude. Krishna Menon's appointment as Defence Minister in 1957 was at first warmly welcomed in the services, where it was felt that for the first time they had been given an energetic and politically relevant minister; but the honeymoon was short, and soon distrust and resentment on both sides began to inform the daily contacts between the senior soldiers and their civilian superiors. Menon was never an easy man to work with: he was sharp-tongued and quick-tempered, veering between angry impatience and remorseful cordiality with associates and subordinates; open in his contempt for those he regarded as fools, and given to an intellectual superiority which inclined him to judge most people as fools at one time or another. These characteristics did not make for smooth relations with the senior soldiers and soon soured the general welcome to Menon's appointment. To personal friction between Menon and General Thimayya, who had become Chief of Army Staff (C.O.A.S.)* at the same time as Menon became Defence Minister, was added growing concern in the military at what they saw as their minister's improper, sustained and, by inference, purposeful interference in matters which traditionally had been left to the soldiers. Thimayya and some of his colleagues suspected that Menon was not conveying their complaints and proposals to the Prime Minister or the Defence Committee of the Cabinet; but they knew that Menon was overriding their recommendations in the crucial matter of promotions to high rank, and it was that which underlay the rumpus in September 1959 when it emerged that General Thimayya had submitted his resignation.

The military's misgivings about Menon's interference in promotions had been felt for some time, and focused, then and later, on the steady ascent of Brij Mohan Kaul, an officer who was to play a central and disastrous role in the border war and its preludes.

* In 1955 the title of Commander-in-Chief had been changed to that of Chief of Army Staff, bringing the Army into parity with the other two services. In his thorough study of this phase of the Army's history L. J. Kavics suggests that replacing the C.-in-C. with 'three autonomous services, each formulating its own policy, competing with each other for budgetary allocations from an economy-minded and remarkably apathetic political executive, and maintaining parallel bodies with the most scrupulous canons of parity' vitiated the advisory function of the military leadership.[32]

Kaul's was an ambiguous and complex character, and the ups and downs of his career reflect it. Before independence, he was unmistakably marked for something less than success in the Army; after, he aspired to and nearly reached the topmost military office, only to be brought down in failure and disgrace. From a middle-class background in a Kashmiri Brahmin family, and after an adolescent flirtation with the nationalist movement, Kaul won one of the places reserved for Indians at Sandhurst, graduating from there in 1933. After the customary year's service in a British unit he was accepted into the Rajputana Rifles, serving on the N.W. Frontier; but only two years later he transferred to the Army Service Corps. This branch offered higher pay, more postings in stations where an officer could have his family with him, and generally an easier life; but for a young Sandhurst officer to transfer to the Service Corps was to turn away from the rewards the combat arms offered to ambition, as well as from the risks. According to his own account,[33] Kaul made several attempts to get back to his original regiment or to another infantry unit but failed to do so. This suggests that the Rajputana Rifles did not want him back, and that he had failed to measure up to the standards of the fighting arm. But Kaul was an energetic, intelligent and personable officer, and lack of success with the infantry did not close the door to advancement—though, in the normal course of events, it would have been a barrier to high rank as a general officer. In 1942 he was promoted acting lieutenant-colonel, with a public relations job in south India. In the following year he was transferred to the war theatre and commanded a motor transport unit in the Kohima area, where, he later wrote, he 'went through hazards, hardships and other unpleasant situations which normally go with an operational theatre'.[34] After a few months he was posted back to base duties, and at the end of the war was in public relations again, this time in New Delhi. That in nearly six years of war, while the Indian Army was enormously expanded and fought in so many theatres, Kaul, a regular officer Sandhurst-trained for infantry, never served with a combat arm, can suggest only that he was judged not suitable for combat command—or that he did not seek it.

The period between the end of the war and independence must have been one of strain for Indian officers of the Army and other services, caught more sharply than ever in the contradiction that to be true to their salt was, in the eyes of many of their compatriots, to be false to their country. For about twenty-five thousand men of the Indian Army who had been captured by Britain's enemies, the contradiction had been resolved by their joining the Indian National Army to fight alongside the Japanese. Kaul had not been given that choice, but showed that he was with the I.N.A. in spirit by filching a document from Army files to give the lawyers defending I.N.A. officers on trial in Delhi at the end of 1945; he recounts the incident, with apparent pride, in his autobiography.[35] By then political mishandling by the British had done much to swing Congress sympathy, at first ambivalent towards the I.N.A., wholeheartedly behind it, and Nehru himself was one of the defending lawyers.[36]

Kaul had made himself known to Nehru before this, and had called on him when the future Prime Minister went to Simla, on his last release from gaol in 1945, to see the Viceroy. Thereafter, until the debacle of 1962, Kaul enjoyed ready access to Nehru and a warm personal relationship with him, and his career flourished in the steady sunshine of the Prime Minister's favour. Hindsight might suggest that Nehru here again showed the blind spot in his appreciation of men's qualities that often led him to mistake glitter for gold, and consequently to make appointments that turned out disastrously. But there was much about Kaul to commend him powerfully to Nehru. Dapper, handsome and articulate, he was not only, like Nehru, a Kashmiri Brahmin, but also of distant kin to the Prime Minister; Nehru's family name was Kaul, and his wife was a Kaul.* Furthermore, he was a nationalist in a way that set him quite apart from his Indian fellow-officers of similar Sandhurst background, who were only patriots. Kaul was energetic and imaginative, a get-things-done man with little respect for what could be presented as the more hidebound military traditions. A fellow-officer with no reason to like Kaul still noted in him 'many admirable qualities. . . . He was dynamic and a go-getter. He had a clear brain and was dedicated to his work. His personal conduct was above criticism. He had a warm heart and was generous.'[37] These qualities might have led Nehru to assume that Kaul was a brilliant all-round soldier, while affection perhaps blinded him to Kaul's limitations. Nehru was blind,

---

* An official (non-Kashmiri, non-Brahmin) who worked closely with Nehru for a time wrote that 'enemies of the Prime Minister used to say that his search for talent and gift for talent-spotting was limited to those around him and particularly to Kashmiris, and amongst them, those who were in one way or another connected with the Nehru family'.[38] Certainly the record does substantiate the suspicion that Nehru was drawn to Kashmiris, and he never found in close family ties reasons *not* to appoint people to high office. But it can be said that often such appointees had—or appeared to have—high qualities, and probably Nehru's favouritism was unconscious.

too, to the corrosive effect that his direct and open dealings with a junior officer had on discipline and morale in the officer corps. The damage this did only increased, of course, as Kaul's rank advanced.

After independence, Kaul's climb was steady and rapid, political preferment coming first and being complemented by military appointments. At the end of 1946 he was made secretary of a committee responsible for Indianizing the Army (until then, of course, overwhelmingly British-officered); then he was sent to Washington as military attaché, and subsequently to Lake Success as military adviser to the Indian mission. In 1948 he returned to India. He hoped to be given command of an infantry battalion in the Kashmir war but this again eluded him, and instead he was put in charge of the Kashmiri militia. He fell out with Sheikh Abdullah, then Prime Minister of the state; Nehru had Kaul transferred away and, having been promoted, he was given command of an infantry brigade—at last the return to infantry which was essential if Kaul were to continue to advance in the service. The alternation of political with military appointments continued with Kaul's attachment to the Neutral Nations' Repatriation Commission in Korea; then his promotion to major-general, and appointment to command of 4 Infantry Division. Command of a division was traditionally a requirement for promotion above the rank of major-general, and was thus another essential step in Kaul's career.

By this time Kaul had been taken up by Krishna Menon, too. Again, there was much to commend Kaul to the Defence Minister: first, probably, the obvious and indeed demonstrative favour in which Nehru held him, with the help of which Kaul had risen in a decade from lowly P.R. officer to commander of a crack division; then, the disapproval in which Kaul was held by the very senior officers with whom by then Menon was at loggerheads; and, last but not least, Kaul's administrative drive. This was most clamantly demonstrated in 'Project Amar', the building of a township of some fifteen hundred houses for soldiers' families which Kaul put through with 4 Division while he commanded it in 1958–9. The use of an operational infantry division for such engineer corps or civilian tasks had been opposed by Army H.Q., but the project was authorized by Krishna Menon. At all events, the accommodation was badly needed and the job was done in about six months—Kaul having been given special powers and independence to that end. Whatever the merit of the project, however, it is clear that Kaul also used it for self-advertisement. Menon laid the foundation stone, and when the township was completed Nehru and half the Cabinet, with other politicians and the service chiefs, came to the inauguration. Kaul had had a patriotic ditty written for the occasion and taught to the division; 'when Nehru heard this stirring song [sung by twenty thousand men] he was thrilled,' he wrote later.[39]

The next step up for Kaul came in May 1939, when, against the resistance of General Thimayya, he was promoted to lieutenant-general and brought into Army H.Q. in a key post. A vacancy in the office of quartermaster-general (Q.M.G.)—one of the principal staff posts, carrying the rank of lieutenant-general—provided the opportunity for Kaul's advancement; but there was an impediment in the fact that two other major-generals, P. S. Gyani and P. P. Kumara-mangalam, were senior to him. Thimayya recommended that Gyani be made Q.M.G. But although Gyani's record was distinguished he had not commanded an infantry division, and by the Army's own practice in promotions that had come to be regarded as a prerequisite for the rank of lieutenant-general; on that ground Krishna Menon overruled Thimayya's recommendation. That left Kumaramangalam still in Kaul's way, however, and to supersede him would have been invidious; not only was Kumaramangalam's record distinguished, including a D.S.O. from the Second World War, he came from a family of some political importance.* The solution was to create another vacancy entailing promotion. This was done, Kumaraman-galam being made adjutant-general. The way thus cleared, Thimayya was unable—without making an issue of it—to block Kaul's appointment as Q.M.G., although he was sharply averse to it—not only was the Q.M.G.'s a key post, it carried membership of the Army's Selections Board,† whence Kaul would henceforth be able to exert considerable influence on the promotion of others.

Kaul had by this time become a bitterly divisive figure in the officer corps. The question 'Are you pro-K. or anti-K.?' needed no spelling

---

* Kumaramangalam's father was Dr Subharayan, a Congress leader from Madras, who after independence became an ambassador. Of Dr Subharayan's three sons one was a member of the Indian Civil Service; one was the soldier; and the third, Mohan Kumara-mangalam, was a member of the Communist Party. Dr Subharayan used to say that through his sons he had ensured against all the possible courses of Indian political development.

† The Selections Board consists of the C.O.A.S., the Army commanders (i.e. the G.O.C.s-in-C. of Western Command, Eastern Command, etc.) and the principal staff officers in Army H.Q.

out in most messes. Kaul flaunted his access to Nehru. 'He used to boast about it,' a senior officer complained. 'He openly used to boast about it, and we used to see him; he used to go in to the Prime Minister, and he would go in the evening when the Prime Minister was most relaxed.'[40] In the way of courts and courtiers, of course, that access was both proof and source of Kaul's influence. 'Everyone in the Army was petrified of the Prime Minister,' a less senior officer recalled, and went on to make the point that this was no ordinary Prime Minister: 'Few men in history have been given such voluntary, pleni-potentiary powers. Anyone who had his ear and confidence wielded immense power.'[41]

As a rising star, Kaul inevitably attracted followers—his critics dubbed them 'the Kaul-boys'. The resentment that always attaches to the recipient of open favouritism was all the more intense because Kaul had never been a combat soldier. He had long been held in cordial contempt by his peers; now that contempt was no longer cordial.

The promotion of Kaul to lieutenant-general over his own recom-mendation might have been in itself occasion enough for Thimayya to force a showdown with Menon; but, while in many ways an out-standing soldier and held in high respect and affection in the Army, Thimayya was averse to battles of this kind, and it took a good deal more to screw him to action. But then he acted impulsively, going off half-cocked, so to speak, and was made to look irresponsible, even pusillanimous. All three service chiefs had had enough of Krishna Menon. Their minister had often berated or ridiculed them in front of their subordinates, and treated them cavalierly, summoning them at any hour of the day or night for conferences that were frequently inconsequential or even cancelled at the last moment. More seriously, they had found their own technical recommendations often overruled on what to them seemed subjective or irrelevant grounds; accordingly, they agreed, it is believed, to go jointly to the Prime Minister with their complaints about Menon. But then, on August 31st, Thimayya, acting, he was later to tell friends, on the spur of the moment and because he was 'fed up'[42] wrote out his resignation and sent it to the Prime Minister.

The resignation of the Chief of Army Staff made an acute dilemma for Nehru. Krishna Menon was already under attack from the Opposi-tion benches and in the press for mishandling the services and inter-fering with promotions. The Longju incident had occurred only a few days before and the Government, Menon particularly, was being criticized for neglecting the defence of the borders. Thimayya's resignation would be seized upon by Menon's enemies as confirmation that he was not a suitable Defence Minister, and it was clear that the pressure might be such that Nehru would have to drop him from the Cabinet— Menon's enemies were, if anything, more numerous in Congress than in the Opposition. He was close to Nehru both personally and politically and, as Nehru knew, many of the attacks on the Defence Minister were really indirect attacks on the Prime Minister. To let Menon go would mean a surrender to such criticism and, moreover, would unbalance the Cabinet in favour of the more orthodox and conservative members of the Congress Party.

Nehru handled this awkward situation with his usual political finesse. He called Thimayya to his house and persuaded him to withdraw his resignation. Having acted on a shallow impulse, Thimayya was amenable; and he later told colleagues that Nehru had assured him that he would personally look into Thimayya's complaints and intervene with Menon to remove their cause. Submission and retraction of Thimayya's resignation took place on the same day, but word of it leaked to the press, which bannered the news next morning. With this, the rumours of conflict between Krishna Menon and the military leadership, which had long been circulating in political circles, were dramatically confirmed. The storm Nehru had hoped to avoid began to blow up; but, Thimayya's resignation having in fact been withdrawn, Nehru was in a much stronger position to handle it. He presented the whole affair as a storm in a teacup, and put responsibility for it squarely on Thimayya. The latter's resignation, Nehru told Parliament, had been 'peculiarly unwise', and 'not the right thing at all'—indeed, 'a most extraordinary thing to do'. The difficulties between the Defence Minister and the Chief of Army Staff had been at bottom 'temperamental' differences, which were 'trivial and of no consequence', he said. Playing upon the Indian politicians' latent mistrust of the military, he suggested that this was a case in which the supremacy of the civil order must be upheld, and gave Krishna Menon's stewardship of the Defence Ministry a glowing tribute. When an Opposition M.P. asked whether he might not have a kind word too for a soldier as distinguished as Thimayya, Nehru obliged with a bow to a 'very gallant officer', but insisted: 'I will not congratulate him on his letter of resignation.'

Nehru thus turned the tables, using the aborted resignation as the occasion to commend Menon and give Thimayya a humiliating public dressing-down. Menon came out of the incident with all flags flying, and Kaul's position was resoundingly strengthened. Thimayya's prestige in the Army suffered because he was seen to have backed down and accepted humiliation. Perhaps if Thimayya, on learning how Nehru had gone back on his assurance to look into the Army's difficulties with Menon, and instead had publicly rebuked him, had resigned again, and stuck to it, the history of the next few years in India would have been very different. As it was, the Thimayya affair tended to confirm Nehru's reliance for military advice upon Menon and the coterie of officers the latter was encouraging. For the soldiers, it carried the lesson that it did not pay to raise professional objections to the civilian handling of military matters.

Nehru's reliance upon Kaul, and the way in which Kaul stepped outside the normal Army procedures to serve it, are well illustrated in an incident soon after the Thimayya affair. On the Prime Minister's asking him about the situation on the ground at Longju, Kaul promptly volunteered to go there himself. The trek took him nearly three weeks, and as he did not get quite within sight of Longju it is difficult to believe that this personal mission by a lieutenant-general and Quartermaster-General achieved anything that another and more junior officer could not have done; but Nehru got his eye-witness account and Kaul confirmed his reputation as a man who would brave hazards and privation in, or beyond, the line of duty. His severest critics had to admit that the trek nearly to Longju and back was a good effort for a man just short of fifty. In similar style some time later Kaul went on a risky test flight over some of the highest terrain in Ladakh in a Russian helicopter, a flight which he ordered—against Menon's instructions— because he believed that Menon was committing the Air Force to purchases of Russian machines without adequate trials.

Kaul seems to have been under a compulsion continually to test or demonstrate his courage. Perhaps this can be understood in the light of his never having commanded troops in combat, and the taunts about this that paralleled his rise in the service; but courage of this kind is not the same as nerve, and a compulsion to go and get within range of shot and shell does not sit well with high command, as later events showed.

Kaul's next step up came when Thimayya reached retirement age early in 1961. The choice for his successor lay between Lieutenant-

General Thapar, then G.O.C.-in-C. Western Command, and Lieutenant-General Thorat, Eastern Command, two officers of very nearly equal seniority. Thapar had a narrow advantage in that regard (two months, to be precise) but Thorat's record was more distinguished and accordingly Thimayya recommended him. Again Thimayya's recommendation was overruled, and not only was Thapar made Chief of Army Staff but, over the active objections of Thimayya, Kaul was appointed Chief of the General Staff, a position second in importance in the military hierarchy at the time only to that of the C.O.A.S. himself.* Thapar was a competent but undistinguished officer, inclined to take the easier course, and furthermore the circumstances of his appointment left him indebted to Kaul, whose powerful influence had been exerted on his behalf. Thapar repaid the obligation by making Kaul C.G.S. although the latter possessed none of the qualifications or experience necessary for that key post.

These appointments made the whole question of Army promotions a live issue again. A letter signed 'Demoralized Army Officers' appeared in the Bombay political journal *Current* on April 5th, 1961, accusing Menon, 'the evil genius of independent India', of manipulating promotions to create a clique personally loyal to himself. The letter, showing familiarity with records and the basis of recent promotions that only senior soldiers could be expected to have, warned that appointments were being managed to clear the way for Kaul's early succession to the post of C.O.A.S. In Parliament, Kripalani pointed out that this was the first time an officer with a predominantly Army Service Corps background had headed the General Staff. He saw in Kaul's appointment evidence of the 'hanky-panky' that he said had recently 'led to heart-burning among officers and discontent among the ranks', and closed with a philippic against Krishna Menon: 'I charge him with having created cliques in the Army. I charge him with having lowered the morale of our armed services. I charge him with having wasted the money of a poor and starving nation. I charge him with the neglect of the defence of the country against the aggression of

* The Indian organization followed the British pattern. Beneath the Chief of Army Staff were four Principal Staff Officers (P.S.O.s): the Chief of the General Staff, the Adjutant-General, the Quartermaster-General, and the Master-General of Ordinance. Of these the key post was that of C.G.S. He was responsible for co-ordination, plans, operations, training, intelligence, the purchase of weapons and related equipment, and the issue of equipment in short supply. Beneath him were other key officers, such as the Director of Military Intelligence (D.M.I.) and Director of Military Operations (D.M.O.). The post of C.G.S. has since been abolished in India.

Communist China.'[43] But Menon coolly denied any interference in promotions, Nehru backed him up, and the protests died down.

With Thapar as C.O.A.S. and himself as C.G.S., Kaul could feel that he held the reins himself, and he soon began to make others feel it too. Officers of his choice were moved into the key posts at Army H.Q., and senior soldiers of what by that time could plainly be identified as the anti-Kaul camp were victimized. Just before Thimayya's retirement, rumours circulated in Government circles and Army H.Q. that he was planning a *coup d'état*. Even a date was given (January 30th, 1961) and Krishna Menon told the Chiefs of Navy and Air Staff about his suspicions and warned civilian officials to keep an eye on Thimayya. Kaul, already officiating as C.G.S., asked the latter for explanation of troop movements that were thought to have been suspicious.[44] The conditions which could have made a coup feasible were wholly absent in India at that time, and the rumours were groundless if they were not mischievous. They were followed by formal inquiries into remarks alleged to have been made by Thimayya on the eve of his retirement, and others on similar charges against Lieutenant-General Thorat and another officer, Lieutenant-General S. D. Verma. These investigations were directed not by the Adjutant General, as would normally have been the case, but by Kaul himself as Chief of the General Staff. Thapar acquiesced.

The atmosphere of witch-hunt found its sharpest expression, however, in the Manekshaw case. Major-General Sam Manekshaw, then Commandant of the Staff College at Wellington, was only a year junior to Kaul but was in every way his antithesis. A graduate of the Indian Military Academy at Dehru Dun, he was in attitude and record far nearer to the Sandhurst norms than Kaul had ever been; a fighting soldier who had won the Military Cross in Burma, he had little time for politicians and less for soldiers who courted them. Outspoken and with a sharp wit (he was credited with the pun 'Kaul-boys') he did not hide his contempt for Kaul.

These two officers were representative, almost symbolic, of two divergent and, indeed, antipathetic strains in the officer corps of the Indian Army. Manekshaw (the name is Parsee) personified the British-rooted tradition of the Army. At its best, this expresses itself in the highest professionalism and a zest for soldiering, complemented by an impatience for intrigue and politics—often treated as synonymous—and a marked preference for regimental rather than staff duties. But it sometimes carries with it an emphasis on the manners and *mores* of British regimental mess life which in independent India could often be abrasive. Before the Second World War little that was Indian in bearing, except the servants, intruded into most Army messes; the Indian officers of the Indian Army, to the last a minority, tended to be as British as the British. Curry was for Sunday lunch, when it would be eaten with spoon and fork; dinner-jackets were mandatory when mess uniform was not worn; to be teetotal was a suspect oddity, vegetarianism was for the men, not the officers; Indian music was an irritating caterwauling; and to talk in an Indian language, a gaffe. But with the great expansion of the Army during the war, officers of a new generation and class of Indians were commissioned; from a less affluent and more urban background, bourgeois rather than aristocratic, politically aware and even engaged, where their seniors saw politics as dirty when not actually seditious. The majority of this generation, too, adapted to the traditional ways of the mess, but some resisted or resented them. For these, curry was the normal food, and to be eaten with the fingers at that; any one of the myriad forms of Indian dress was more acceptable and far more comfortable than dinner-jackets; to shun alcohol and meat was to do no more than follow the ways of their own people and their own inclinations. After independence such apparent trivialities could become the battleground of a deeper division, between those nationalist officers who blamed their seniors for having served the British and even looked down on them for aping the former rulers, and those, like Sam Manekshaw, who tended to see any Indianization of mess ritual as a slackening of standards. For the Manekshaws, the traditions were sacrosanct not because they were British in origin, but because they *were* the traditions of the Army. For their critics, however, they were the servile affectations of officers who had not come to terms with all the implications of India's independence.

Kaul was in spirit with the more nationalistic of the younger officers, though of older generation himself, and his autobiography suggests that he early formed a dislike for the British and those of his compatriots who, in his view, tried 'to please their masters and earn cheap popularity [and] rose later to occupy the highest military posts'.[45] There was fertile ground for antipathy towards the very British Manekshaw, and reports of the latter's acid and public mockery of Kaul, along with highly disrespectful references to Menon, provided an occasion to strike back at him and others like him in the latter part of 1961. As Kaul tells it:

> Some of our senior Army officers were in the habit of making tendentious and indiscreet remarks openly against our national leaders and extolled the erstwhile British rulers of India. They suggested at times that some sort of dictatorial rule was the only way to get our affairs out of the mess in which they were. . . . I came to know of specific cases of anti-national and indiscreet utterances—some made in the presence of foreigners—on the part of a few senior officers. I, accordingly, brought them to the notice of . . . General Thapar in writing, who put this matter up to the Defence Minister who in turn reported it to the Prime Minister.[46]

A board of inquiry was set up to investigate the charges against Manekshaw, which were that he had been insubordinately critical of his superiors and of the civilian leadership and, by implication, disloyal. Manekshaw fought the charges, and the military board, while noting that he might have kept a better guard on his tongue, not only exonerated him but recommended that action be taken against his accusers—not Kaul, of course, but those junior officers who had reported Manekshaw's remarks. Yet the result of the charges was that Manekshaw's promotion was held up, and if it had not been for the debacle of 1962 he would have had to retire as a major-general.

The lesson of the Manekshaw case was clear, and destructive to the already strained morale and cohesion of the officer corps. Officers began to speak guardedly even when with friends, as it became plain that the path to preferment lay only through the favour of Kaul and his supporters. From watching one's words out of fear of informers it is only a step to choosing one's words to please superiors, military or civilian; the cost of having senior officers who had become either courtiers or cowed was to be painfully demonstrated in the border war.

The motives behind all this are not as clear as the consequences. That Kaul aimed to become C.O.A.S. is certain, and it is almost as certain that, but for the border war, he would have succeeded General Thapar. Did his ambition reach further? By the end of 1961 some political observers in India had come to believe that it did. 'Kaul is the man to watch,' *Current*, the Bombay political weekly, said at this time. 'He will not only become Chief of Army Staff, he may one day even become Prime Minister of India.' The thinking behind the prediction was muddled. 'Nehru has learned to have confidence in General Kaul and regards him as an insurance against any possible breaches of Army discipline and disruption of democracy. . . .' But, apparently without perceiving the contradiction, *Current* continued: 'If Nehru ever felt inclined to name a successor to himself it is even possible that discarding all the old and known Congress types, he would not be averse to making so unorthodox a choice as General Kaul.' That Kaul could come to political power in a constitutional context, as the chosen leader of the Congress Party, was always out of the question, the suggestion was grotesque; but the speculation at the time about his future looked more often to his achieving power as the result of an Army coup, engineered by himself or brought on by the general failure of civil authority. This prospect was pictured by an American writer, Welles Hangen:

> Military rule could be imposed on India while Kaul stayed discreetly in the background. He could be a Nasser to Thapar's Naguib or some other venerable façade. . . . Moreover, Kaul would not be an unattractive military ruler. He could rationalize the demise of Indian democracy as skilfully as he does his relationship with Menon. His performance would certainly have more drive and polish than does the faltering Indian democracy in the second half of a cyclonic century of change. . . . He could be the idol of all lovers of order.[47]

That, too, was far-fetched, not only because the possibility of military intervention was remote (in the early 1960s, when the passage was written, it was) but because Kaul, whose roots of power lay in the civilian order, specifically in the favour of Nehru and Menon, was the last man who could ever have led it. But if the thought of his extending his power beyond the Army was unreal it still seems likely that it was one that occurred to Kaul; in a long and admiring profile of the latter, taking him very much at his own high estimation, the writer quoted above notes that Kaul 'has an Indian's respect for horoscopes, and his foretells that he will one day rule India'.[48]*

---

* Apart from Welles Hangen's sympathetic study there are two other prose portraits of Kaul. In a perceptive novel about the Indian Army during and immediately after the war by Manohar Malgonkar (*Distant Drum*, Asia Publishing House, 1960), Kaul may be discerned in the character Kamala Kant, an intriguing, politically ambitious officer who, having spent the war in staff jobs, rejoins the infantry to advance his career and then goes off to be military attaché in Washington. It is a satirical picture, drawn from the viewpoint of an Indian officer of the Manekshaw school. Then there is Kaul's self-portrait, *The*

Menon's motives at this time are also open to doubt. He was suspected of building up a clique of creatures in the Army to give himself a base from which, after Nehru's death, he could make a bid for power; the *Hindustan Times*, at the time of the Thimayya resignation affair, referred to 'cabalistic meetings of Mr Menon's chosen officers, who fancied themselves as the men who had to prepare for the political mission that the [armed] forces would some day be called upon to play'. But the supposition that Menon was attempting to create a military base of power for his own ultimate benefit probably reflected nothing but the degree of suspicion and antipathy in which he was held; there was no evidence that he harboured extra-constitutional ambitions, and he was probably too much of a realist to have bothered with such dreams. Menon appears to have been as committed a democrat as Nehru, and moreover deeply loyal to the Prime Minister and his ideals.

Rather than that Menon was paving the way for a coup in his own favour, it is possible that he thought he was taking steps to prevent the senior soldiers staging one of their own. Distrust of the soldiers and even fear of a coup has never been far from the minds of the politicians in India—perhaps they never really shared the confidence many Western political scientists have in the invulnerability and vitality of the civilian order in India. By interfering in promotions, putting his own men into key positions and seeing that those he particularly distrusted were passed over, Menon may have been working to divide the Army high command so as to make plotting impossible. Certainly, unless the charges made against Thimayya and S. D. Verma were wholly cynical, Menon and his civilian colleagues did have some apprehension that the senior soldiers were developing political ambitions.

By the time he became C.G.S. Kaul's influence was pre-eminent in internal army matters—but it did not reach to questions of military expenditure or the deficiencies of army equipment. Kaul used his relationship with Nehru to take the Army's complaints and warnings directly to him again, but on that score got no farther than had his colleagues with their approaches through the customary channels.

Untold Story, anything but frank but very revealing. Written in self-exculpation and indictment of his critics after his downfall, the book suggests that one of Kaul's faults may have been a romantic perception of his own role and personality—there is something in it of Walter Mitty.

Such matters had to be put into a political context, and Nehru, naturally enough, preferred to rely on his own judgment when it came to
foreign policy. So, after hearing Kaul out, Nehru, in the former's
account, said that he and the other generals 'did not quite understand
the situation. . . . Apart from creating tension, neither China nor
Pakistan was in a position to provoke a war with [India] as they had
their own problems.'[49] There again was the fundamental premise of
the forward policy—that the Chinese would not react forcefully to it.
To the related assumption, that in any small-scale clashes the Indian
Army would worst the Chinese, Kaul strongly subscribed until
October 10th, 1962.

* * * * * * * * * * *

The conception of the forward policy, that moment when the
thought that India might one day have to move patrols and posts into
Chinese-held territory became an intention to do so, can be traced
back to the beginning of 1960; but it was not really put into effect until
the end of 1961. The long delay between the adoption of the forward
policy and the first attempts to implement it reflected the Army's
unwillingness to undertake a course for which the military means were
wholly lacking.

The Government's policy at the end of 1959, as set out in Nehru's
September memorandum, was to maintain the *status quo* on the
boundaries and carefully avoid any provocation, 'not only in a big
way but even in a small way'.* Military expression was given to that
policy in instructions from Army H.Q. to the regional commands
concerned; in November Eastern Command was told to make clear
to all ranks that 'we must avoid actual conflict with the Chinese unless
actually forced upon us,' and that no patrols should approach closer
than two miles to the McMahon Line except in those places (such as
Khinzemane) where posts had been set up practically on the line itself.
In February 1960 Western Command was ordered to take up positions
along a line roughly between Murgo, Tsogstsalu, Phobrang, Chushul
and Demchok and given as its task the prevention of any *further*
Chinese incursions. The westernmost positions of the Chinese at that
time were believed to be at Qizil Jilga, Dehra La, Samzungling (on
the Galwan River), Kongka Pass and Khurnak Fort; so distances of

* See p. 129 above.

between twenty and fifty miles would accordingly separate the two sides (except at Demchok, which was less than twenty miles from the southern extremity of the main Chinese road) even when the Indians had set up these posts.

Even for this limited and defensive task, however, the Army's resources were deficient. There were only two battalions of the Jammu and Kashmir Militia* in Ladakh—no regular troops, no supporting arms. There were no roads to, or within, the western boundary sector. Construction of the road from Srinagar to Leh had been begun in 1954 but suspended four years later, pending an inquiry into corruption in its financing, and Leh could still only be reached by mule track or by air. There were landing-strips at Leh and Chushul, but other places had to be supplied by air-drop. At this time Western Command's estimation of its needs was for a brigade group (i.e. five infantry battalions plus supporting arms) in addition to the militia battalions already in the sector.

This requirement was based on intelligence suggesting that the Chinese already had more than a regiment in the area (equivalent to an Indian brigade) with supporting arms, including some armour; and on recognition that the network of Chinese roads, which was already well advanced, gave them immense advantages of supply and manœuvrability. Western Command wanted four infantry battalions to be inducted during 1960, the fifth in 1961.

In May 1960, at a meeting under Krishna Menon in the Defence Ministry, it was decided that the Army should establish itself on the old trade route running north from Shyok, and set up a post as near the Karakoram Pass as possible. When this had been done the possibility of patrolling eastward up the Chip Chap valley would be explored. In the meantime, unoccupied areas were to be patrolled; but the troops were to avoid clashes and, if they encountered Chinese, to report their position without attempting to dislodge them. This decision might be said to have cast a tentative glance towards implementation of the forward policy, but was still well short of any explicit and immediate instructions.

The first evidence of these appears in a minute signed by the Foreign Secretary, S. Dutt, on May 29th, 1960. This pointed out that there were no restrictions on India's sending out forward patrols (at Nehru's

---

* A lightly armed, locally recruited force. This militia fought so well in the 1962 hostilities that they were made into regular units, and renamed the Ladakh Scouts.

meeting with Chou En-lai any such commitment had been avoided, of course); the only commitment was to *avoid border clashes*. The minute therefore proposed a more active patrolling policy, in the western sector, with the troops steering clear of Chinese posts but not hesitating to probe into, and set up posts in, areas across the Chinese claim line where, as far as was known, the Chinese were not established. The troops should, however, still be ordered not to use force against Chinese posts or patrols.[50]

This minute was passed to the Defence Ministry and on to Army H.Q., but it was not reflected in orders to the troops for three months. A signal from Army H.Q. to Western Command only four days after Dutt's minute was signed in fact confirmed the earlier orders. It stated that the Government's policy was to maintain the *status quo* on the boundary, 'maintaining our positions firmly on our side of the inter-national border under our control at present. So far as the disputed areas are concerned the *status quo* that has existed for some time is to be maintained.' In the context of that policy, it was necessary for the army to 'exercise effective control over the areas which are undisputed/ unoccupied [and] also to prevent any further infiltration into our territory', the signal went on; 'these requirements in some cases necessi-tate probing forward and establishing additional . . . posts ahead of our present defensive positions.' The operative part of the signal concluded with the order that troops must avoid any clashes with the Chinese, and fire only in self-defence. While reflecting the wording of Dutt's minute in calling for more active patrolling in the western sector, Army H.Q. had thus carefully omitted its nub, which required Indian troops to move into Chinese-claimed territory. Army H.Q.'s instruc-tions referred only to such areas as were 'undisputed/unoccupied' — that is, areas *outside the Chinese claim line* where the Indians had not yet been able to set up posts or dispatch patrols.

That the Government's requirement for forward patrolling in the western sector was pressed can be inferred from new instructions issued by Army H.Q. at the turn of August–September 1960. In these, Western Command was advised that patrols could be sent into areas *claimed but not occupied* by China, 'to determine the extent of the Chinese ingress [and] to ensure that no further advance is made by Chinese troops in the area where no static posts have been established by them so far'. This signal provided for the implementation of the forward policy; but it was permissive, not mandatory. The dispatch of

7*

patrols into Chinese-claimed territory was left to the discretion of
Western Command, the decision to be taken in the light of tactical and
logistical factors. Army H.Q. was quite plainly stalling on the implementation of instructions that the Government had issued without
proper consideration of the military factors.

At the same time as it sent the new instructions down to Western
Command, Army H.Q. warned the civilian arm of the serious military
risks entailed in the forward patrolling for which the Government was
pressing. In a minute from the General Staff to the Ministry of Defence,
the Army pointed out that forward patrolling as called for by the
Government would invite a sharp Chinese reaction, with 'the possibility of the international border, which is dormant at the moment,
becoming active'. The acute difficulties of transport and supply in the
western sector had prevented the induction of additional troops, it
went on, and with the limited strength available the Army would not
be in a position to counter effectively any large-scale incursion by the
Chinese. (General Thimayya was still C.O.A.S., his C.G.S. was
Lieutenant-General L. P. Sen, who wrote this minute.)

The Defence Ministry passed this warning on to the Foreign
Secretary, whose comment was: 'It is surprising that the decisions
reached in May have not yet been implemented.'[51] Army H.Q. was
asked to explain what was considered to have been the military's
sluggishness in carrying out an important and urgent directive from the
Government.

Then and later the civilians, politicians and officials alike, failed to
grasp that logistics defined the capability of the Army, and evolved
their policies without giving due weight to the possibility of counter-
action from the other side. To the officials in the Ministry of External
Affairs, the Cabinet secretariat and the Defence Ministry the problem
of the territory which they held China to have illegally occupied in the
western sector was essentially political, and the Chinese were to be
ousted by political manoeuvre. The forward policy did not appear to
them—as it did to the soldiers—as a military challenge to a far stronger
power, but as the necessary physical extension of a subtle diplomatic
game. By peaceful, even non-violent methods, seeding the disputed
territory with Indian flag posts and criss-crossing it with patrols,
Aksai Chin was to be won back for India, probably without the
firing of a shot except in random skirmishes. The civilians' impatience
with the tardiness of the soldiers, their incomprehension and annoyance

when Army H.Q. and lower formations complained that troops were being asked to perform tasks which difficulties of supply or access made impossible, reflected not only their conviction that China would not react forcefully, but their total ignorance of all things military. An Indian civil servant of distinction, himself a former Defence Secretary, once said: 'The ignorance of the civil servants in India about military matters is so complete . . . that we may accept it as a self-evident and incontrovertible fact.'[52] This reflected the fact that the Indian Government, politicians and civil servants alike, had had no experience of the military problems and technologies that became part of the civilian British and American cultures from the First World War on. When added to the alienation from, and distrust of the soldiery which Congress politicians had inherited from the period before independence, this inexperience goes far to explain the failure to relate political decisions to military factors which led both to the border war and to the Indian debacle.*

A more immediate consequence of the civilians' military ignorance was that the soldiers' demurrals or warnings were dismissed as tendentious or irrelevant, and even impugned as the expression of physical slackness or lack of fortitude. Early in 1961 Nehru was fending off criticism in Parliament with the claim that the military situation in the western sector had changed in India's favour. Reading this in the newspapers, the Corps Commander for the sector, General S. D. Verma, immediately wrote to his superior, General Thapar, pointing out that the Prime Minister's assurances bore no relation to the facts of the situation. These he had repeatedly set out in reports to Thapar; and Verma now asked that his letter be forwarded to Army H.Q. for the record, as he did not wish to be associated with the misleadingly optimistic view of the military situation which the Prime Minister was putting forward. Thapar asked him to withdraw this letter, saying that the Government fully appreciated the true position in the western sector, and that Nehru's remarks had been only for public consumption. Verma insisted.[53]

Shortly after this, Verma was superseded, when Lieutenant-General L. P. Sen was appointed G.O.C.-in-C. Eastern Command, and Lieutenant-General Daulet Singh G.O.C.-in-C. Western Command. Verma immediately resigned, as was the tradition when officers of his

---

* The Indians learned the lesson. Relations between the political leadership and the military during the short Indo-Pakistan war of 1965 were model.

seniority were superseded. There followed whispered charges against
him, leading to the formal inquiries already mentioned. Civilian
Intelligence investigators combed his record but found nothing in-
criminating; General Verma's pension was held up for a year, however,
and cleared only when he personally appealed to Nehru. Thus the
lesson was driven home: officers who spoke up got short shrift; those
who had kept quiet or said what they were expected to say were
preferred to those who balked or protested.

Officers responsive to civilian requirements, and ready to ignore the
basic precepts of the soldier's craft and override objections based upon
them, took over at Army H.Q. in mid-1961. Thereafter the Indian
Government could hurry on to disaster, insulated from the warnings
and protests, increasingly urgent, which continued to be voiced lower
down the military structure.

Whatever the demands and attitudes of the politicians and civil
servants in 1960-1, they came up against the hard rocks of fact—or
rather against the rocky, forbidding terrain of north-eastern Ladakh.
As against the five infantry battalions which Western Command had
said must be in the sector by late 1961, only one was actually inducted.
After this battalion (1/8 Gorkha Rifles) was deployed during the
summer of 1961, the Indian strength in the western sector was three
battalions (of which two were militia), without any supporting arms,
under a brigade headquarters now based at Leh. The posts and picquets
held by these troops were still on the same line as had been defined in
Army H.Q.'s orders in February 1960—well short of the Chinese
claim, except at Demchok. The Government's pressure for forward
moves had been resisted by the commands concerned, who were
unwilling to send troops where they could not be supplied or supported, and the only advances made while General S. D. Verma was in
command of XV Corps, the formation responsible for the area,
affected outposts around Demchok. After his resignation in the spring
of 1961 a post whose establishment he had resisted, at a point beneath
the Karakoram Pass named Daulet Beg Oldi, was set up; but this was
not in territory claimed by China. The forward policy remained an
intention.

If the Indians' strength in the western sector had by mid-1961 thus
been increased only slightly and with the greatest difficulty, their
position relative to the Chinese had changed drastically, and for the
worse. While the Indian road had not even reached Leh (the first,

experimental convoy got through only in October 1961; until then the troops were supplied by air or mule) the Chinese had pushed feeder roads up to their westernmost posts. The terrain they had to deal with was relatively easy, and they had plentiful labour and road-building equipment. In New Delhi this intensified Chinese activity on Aksai Chin was seen as a provocative and possibly menacing development. That the Chinese might be moving in reaction to the Indian diplomatic stance and to India's own military build-up, small and slow though that was, occurred to no one but some of the soldiers; one of these was later to point out to his Government that the Aksai Chin road was a vital strategic link for the Chinese, and to warn that they would react forcefully to Indian moves which threatened it, however distantly.*

At the end of 1960 Indian military intelligence reappraised the Chinese strength in the western sector, putting it now at a division, with some armour, and high mobility deriving from their road network and motor transport. Accordingly, Western Command informed Army H.Q. that a full Indian division was required in the sector if the Chinese threat were to be contained.

A division was needed; one regular and two militia battalions were all that the Indian Army had been able to deploy. The speed and weight with which the Chinese had outdistanced the laborious Indian build-up emphasized the military unreality of the forward policy—but not to the Indian Government, which continued to press for its implementation.

* * * * * * * * * * *

The Government was not being spurred to implement the forward policy by popular pressure. After the climax of the New Delhi summit meeting in April 1960 public interest in the boundary dispute had simmered down. The decade of the 1960s was to be a time of mounting troubles in India. With the brave optimism and sense of high national possibilities that had marked the first years of independence fading fast, the Government and the public had in 1960 many more pressing concerns than that posed by the presence of the Chinese in the inaccessible wastes of Aksai Chin. 'Fissiparous tendencies', as the Indians call

* See p. 254 below.

expressions of regional or communal particularism, were beginning to worry New Delhi: acceding to a long-sustained agitation the central Government bifurcated what it had hoped would continue as the bilingual state of Bombay, but was then standing fast against the Sikhs' demand for their own state;* in the north-east the Naga tribes were continuing their guerrilla war of secession; in south India there was agitation against Hindi as the country's official language; the Kashmir problem was dormant, but by no means dead. The third five-year plan was just beginning, but the confidence that had accompanied introduction of the first two plans was strained by now, and noticeable more in the planners' targets than in any expectations that they would or could be reached.

In foreign affairs, the signing of the Indus Waters Treaty with Pakistan in September 1960 appeared to suggest that even the most intractable disputes could at last be resolved, given patience, disinterested mediation and good will on both sides; but the talks between Nehru and President Ayub which followed signing of the treaty showed that Kashmir remained the nub, and that there the most that India was prepared to concede continued unbridgably distant from the least that Pakistan would accept. That meeting with Nehru convinced Ayub that his hopes of persuading India to some acceptable compromise on Kashmir were unreal, and from it began the long decline in relations between India and Pakistan which culminated in the war of September 1965.

Until this time, Pakistan and her Western friends had been making hopeful play with the idea of joint defence of the sub-continent. This idea dated back to the time of partition, when consideration was given to a permanent joint defence council,[54] and in 1948 Nehru told the Constituent Assembly that 'the question of joint defence is important from the point of view of both India and Pakistan, and Government will gladly consider this when the time is ripe for it.'[55] But when President Ayub mooted a proposal for joint defence in 1959, the context had so changed that Nehru dismissed it out of hand, with the question: 'Joint defence—against whom?'[56]

The unstated context of Ayub's suggestion was that India and Pakistan could bury their own quarrel and consort their defence policies *if India would only compromise on Kashmir* (which meant, at the very least, giving up the valley of Kashmir to Pakistan); and this was

* Conceded at the end of 1966.

enough to make the idea nonsensical to India. Beyond that, Pakistan was a member of CENTO and SEATO; and, as Nehru saw it, any move towards joint defence would entail connections with the Western bloc and thus impair the basic Indian stand in foreign relations. From Pakistan's point of view, too, the idea was inherently unreal; the only country by which the Pakistanis felt threatened was India, just as India felt threatened only by Pakistan. 'Joint defence' as suggested by President Ayub was never more than a Pakistani ploy, angled at those Westerners, particularly Americans, who liked to visualize linked defence pacts making strong, containing chains along China's boundaries. It was meant to make the point that India in her intransigence over Kashmir was leaving the sub-continent open to Communist attack—a contingency which in fact, and in spite of her treaty memberships, Pakistan like India believed to be so remote as to be unreal.

The Sino-Indian borders were at first quiet in 1960, after the New Delhi summit, disturbed only by isolated and in themselves trivial incidents. These were nevertheless the occasions for formal protests from both sides, with each complaining that the other was infringing the Prime Ministers' agreement that friction would be avoided.[57] Both sides complained, too, about trespassing overflights. Peking explained that high-altitude flights over north-eastern India were made not by Chinese, but by American spy-planes operating from Bangkok,*[58] and complained in turn about Indian flights over Aksai Chin. New Delhi rejected this complaint, rather than denying it; for the Indian Government, its aircraft making reconnaissance flights over Chinese-occupied territory in Aksai Chin could not be said to be intruding into China's airspace.

Nationals of the two countries residing in the border areas of the other suffered the ill-effects of the dispute. Indian traders and money-lenders in Tibet found increasing difficulties put in their way; India complained that Kashmiri Muslims, who were claimed as Indian nationals, were being harassed and terrorized. China replied that these people would be regarded as Chinese unless they opted for Indian nationality, and denied that any had been ill-treated—except for those who had been involved in the recent uprising. The Chinese complained that some Chinese nationals living in Calcutta and Kalimpong were

* In mid-1961 such a plane, operating though from Formosa, was brought down in Burma.[59]

being expelled; India replied that those expelled, a handful of the Chinese living in India, had been acting in ways prejudicial to India's national interest. Guards were placed on the Chinese trade agency in Kalimpong; the Indian trade agencies in Tibet and Indian officials touring under the terms of the 1954 agreement experienced increasing difficulty. In August the Indian Government expelled the correspondent of the New China News Agency and closed down its bureau in New Delhi, explaining that his dispatches had presented a one-sided picture of India by 'selecting critical comments and highlighting adverse opinions . . . from newspapers which are either not of any standing or are opposed to the Government'.* India protested at the confiscation of herbalist drugs from an Indian pilgrim by Chinese authorities; China replied that the drugs were highly poisonous. China complained that an Indian sentry had aimed his rifle at a bean-curd seller plying his lawful trade with the Chinese trade agents at Kalimpong; India replied that he had been let in anyway.

The meetings of officials to codify the disagreements on the boundaries —which had been the sole fruit of the April 1960 summit meeting— began in Peking in mid-June, continued in September in New Delhi and concluded after another session in Rangoon in November– December. As Nehru had foreseen, they produced two contradictory reports and, although voluminous, neither did more than elaborate or sometimes embroider the arguments which had already been deployed in the diplomatic correspondence. During these talks the Chinese submitted for the first time a map showing their idea of the alignment of the traditional and customary boundaries; this map was not identical with the 1956 map which Chou En-lai had said correctly depicted the traditional boundary in the western sector,[60] and the Indians protested that the new map claimed even more of their territory. The discrepancy was labelled 'creeping cartographic aggression' and much was made thereafter in diplomatic argument by New Delhi and in Indian propaganda of the difference between China's '1956 claim' and her '1960 claim'.

The 1956 map showed the whole of China, on a small scale and with the boundary marked by a line so thick that it would itself cover

---

* This was the first occasion on which the Indian Government had expelled a resident foreign correspondent, and it remained an isolated incident for many years. New Delhi continued one of the freest capitals for foreign correspondents; but the attitudes which produced this atmosphere had sharply changed by 1970, and the expulsion of the B.B.C. correspondent in that year suggested that the old tolerance might be replaced by its opposite.

a zone of nearly ten miles in width. This map★ showed the western sector of the Sino-Indian boundary running south-east from the Karakoram Pass (rather than roughly north-east as the Indians have it). The map which the Chinese submitted during the 1960 officials' talks confirmed this alignment in that it showed the boundary continuing from the Karakoram Pass south-east along the main chain of the Karakorams, rather than switching to loop over the Kuen Lun range to the north as it does in the Indian claim. But if the two maps are superimposed slight differences of alignment appear between their boundary markings in this sector. As they are different maps, on different scales, such divergences are to be expected; they are of the kind that can be explained by differences in survey between them—for example, a line connecting the same two features on both maps might run at slightly different compass bearings on each. Even the 1960 Chinese map was on a small scale, showing the whole stretch of the Sino-Indian boundary; the Chinese position was that since they were depicting only a 'traditional and customary boundary line', not a delimited boundary, to indicate anything but an approximate alignment would be unrealistic. The Indians, holding that the boundary as they claimed it was absolute and definitive, indicated their claim lines categorically and in detail, and pointed to these differences in approach to suggest that the Chinese were being vague or covert, in order perhaps to make more advanced claims later.

The earlier (1956) Chinese map did not, and by its nature could not, show a precise boundary alignment, and the only definitive cartographic statement of the Chinese version of what they called 'the traditional and customary boundary' is in the 1960 map. The Indian charge, based on literal comparison of those two maps, that China progressively claimed more and more territory is ill-founded, if not tendentious.

Both sides at the 1960 officials' talks were able to produce numerous maps supporting their own claims. Western cartographers, whose maps had—and have—world-wide influence, have based their depiction of the Indian boundaries on Survey of India maps directly, or

★ The 1956 Chinese map is published as Map 38 in *Atlas of the Northern Frontiers of India* (New Delhi, 1960). The 1960 Chinese map is in the *Officials' Report*, opposite p. 264. It might be noted that even after governments have agreed on their boundaries their maps, when overlaid, may show marked divergences. The maps attached by China and Pakistan to their boundary agreement were an example of this. It is only after a boundary has been jointly surveyed that identity between maps can be expected.

indirectly through such atlases of recognized authority as those of *The Times* or the Oxford University Press. Consequently the Johnson/ Ardagh claim to a trans-Karakoram boundary for India, which, as has been seen, was given wide currency in later nineteenth-century British maps, is to be found in maps published in many parts of the world through this century—and continues to appear on maps published to this day. Other cartographers have adopted the post-1954 Indian version of the western sector of the Sino-Indian boundary. So far as the eastern sector is concerned, the British delay in putting the McMahon Line on to their maps was increased in general cartographic practice. As has been seen, this led to the use in Nehru's book, *The Discovery of India* (1946), of maps which showed the north-eastern boundary beneath the foot-hills, and gave no indication of the McMahon Line; the Chinese, understandably, made a good deal of this in their argument and propaganda.

Most published maps are of weak evidential value in the considera-tion of boundary disputes, however; they are as likely to reflect a cartographer's—or a government's—idea of where a boundary *should* lie as any objective data about its actual alignment. The currency at present enjoyed by maps showing only the Indian version of the boundaries seems likely to reflect the Indian Government's practice of prohibiting import of any book which does not show its own version of such alignments—for many books the Indian market is not one to be sneezed at.

The argument on the merits of the dispute dried up, too, in 1960, after the summit meeting, to be renewed in a sharp rally of notes at the end of the year over the boundary treaty signed in October between China and Burma. This was the first boundary settlement made by China (understanding with Nepal was then only at the stage of formal agreement) and as such deserves examination.* It had implications, furthermore, for the Sino-Indian dispute.

The British, who had ruled Burma as a province of India from 1886 to 1937 and thereafter until independence as a separate colony, had been more successful in reaching agreement with China over the frontiers there than they had been on the other marches of the sub-continent. Treaties in the 1880s and notes exchanged between Britain

---

* For analyses of the Sino-Burmese settlement see Dorothy Woodman in *The Making of Burma* (Cresset, London 1962); Daphne E. Whittam in *Pacific Affairs*, Vol. 34, p. 178, and N. M. Ghatate in *India Quarterly*, Jan-March 1968.

and China in 1941 had defined most of the central and southern sectors of the boundaries; but that left the northern sector, from about the twenty-fifth parallel to the trijunction with India, undelimited. McMahon's line extended along part of the northern sector; but had no more been accepted by China there than had the main extent of that line, to the west. In 1948, the Chinese Nationalist Government informed the newly independent Burma that the boundary as shown on Burmese maps was unacceptable (it did the same with India). In 1950 Burma proposed to the new Government in Peking that the boundary question should be taken up. The Chinese put the matter off; but it became urgent when, in 1955, Burmese troops operating in the frontier region of the Wa state against retreating Chinese Nationalists clashed with units of the People's Liberation Army on the same mission. The Wa state was claimed by China on her maps, as was a large area north of the twenty-fifth parallel which Burma counted as her own territory. In all, about 70,000 square miles were in dispute, and when Burma asked China to withdraw her troops from the Wa state and across the boundary that the British had proposed in 1941, the Chinese replied that they did not recognize that line—although the Nationalist Government had agreed to it.

Burma and China thus reached the position that India and China were to come to four years later. Chinese maps claimed a large area which Burma considered her own (indeed, relative to Burma's size it was enormous, more than a quarter of her territory), while Peking repudiated Britain's attempts to establish boundaries and maintained that these would have to be re-negotiated. The clash of 1955, on a much larger scale than the skirmishes at Longju and Kongka Pass were to be, showed the dangers. But rather than accuse China of aggression and nail Burma's colours to the boundaries claimed by Britain with a refusal to negotiate them, as India was to do, U Nu, the Burmese Prime Minister, went to Peking in 1956 to seek a settlement. He found that having emphatically repudiated all past boundary agreements with the British, the Chinese were in fact prepared to open negotiations on the basis of the very boundary lines that the British had proposed; it was the origin of those boundaries in 'unequal treaties' imposed by Britain that was unacceptable to China, *not the alignments the British had proposed*. These were not what Peking would have preferred; indeed, China had historically resisted them (to the extent of referring the dispute to the League of Nations in 1935); but the British claims had been inherited by independent Burma, whose Government was friendly to China, and now Peking was prepared to make them the basis of a settlement.

Offering what U Nu described as a package deal for the whole Sino-Burmese boundary, China proposed that it should run in the north where McMahon had drawn it (although, of course, that invidious parentage was not mentioned); then down the Salween-Irrawaddy watershed to the boundaries already defined by treaty with Britain. China claimed a group of three villages, the Hpimaw tract, on the Burmese side of the line that the British had proposed, and said that the arrangement by which Burma, carrying on from Britain, was holding an area called the Namwan assigned tract under 'perpetual lease' should be abrogated because it was anachronistic. The Chinese intimated that the new arrangement which they had in mind for the Namwan tract would leave Burma in possession, noting that an important road linking two provinces of Burma ran through it. For her part Burma recognized, as Britain had done, that China's long-standing claim to the Hpimaw villages was reasonable. U Nu sponsored the Chinese package in the Burmese parliament as an equitable and practicable proposal.

Differences in interpretation of the package emerged in diplomatic exchanges, however. China sought an equivalent area elsewhere in return for ceding the Namwan tract, and maintained that the Hpimaw village area comprised about 150 square miles, while the Burmese put it at 56. Political opinion in Burma had by now become alive to the boundary dispute, limiting U Nu's room for manœuvre, and the matter had advanced no further when General Ne Win seized power in 1958. He took it up again, maintaining his predecessor's stand in all respects except that he agreed to exchange an equivalent area for the Namwan tract; and he proposed to go to Peking himself to clinch an agreement. After five days of negotiations in Peking, Ne Win signed a boundary agreement on January 28th, 1960, confirming for his country the boundary alignment it had sought since it became independent; and, with trivial divergences, the boundaries were those that Britain had claimed.* Ne Win congratulated the Chinese and

---

* China confirmed the 1894, 1897 and 1941 agreements with Britain and accepted the McMahon alignment in the far north. She ceded the Namwan assigned tract and relinquished rights, deriving from the 1941 agreement, to operate some mines on the Burmese side of the boundary. In return Burma ceded 59 square miles in the Hpimaw tract and an area on her side of the 1941 line, contiguous with China, thus, according to the Chinese, 'adjusting the unreasonable division of the [Panhung and Panlao] tribes into Chinese and Burmese parts by the 1941 line'. This area was equal in size to the Namwan tract, about

himself on the statesmanship with which they had settled a problem that had 'defied solution for close to one hundred years'[61] and later U Nu (who became Prime Minister again shortly after this) paid tribute to the Chinese leaders for the 'goodwill and understanding' they had shown throughout the negotiations.[62] Chou En-lai was to say later that the Sino-Burmese boundaries made a much more complicated problem than those between China and India.[63]

The Chinese were quick to point out the lessons the agreement contained for 'Asian countries seeking reasonable settlement of their boundary disputes'; and the Peking *People's Daily* went on to ask: 'Why can't things which have happened between China and Burma also take place between China and other Asian countries?'[64] But while General Ne Win was in Peking signing an agreement in which China accepted the McMahon alignment, Nehru had still been refusing to meet Chou En-lai to discuss the Sino-Indian boundaries.

India ignored the positive implications of Burma's agreement with China for her own boundary dispute, and made no comment until the agreement was converted into a treaty in October 1960.* Since Burma and India adjoin, the western extremity of the Sino-Burmese boundary had to be the eastern extremity of the Sino-Indian boundary; and as the latter was in dispute that set a drafting problem for the Burmese and the Chinese.† They got round it when wording their treaty by referring only to 'the western extremity' of their common boundary and leaving its location undefined. But the treaty included a map and on that the problem was insoluble; every line except a circle must have an end, after all. The treaty map showed the Sino-Burmese boundary ending at the Diphu Pass, in accordance with the McMahon Line,‡ thus, it would seem, giving India a strong new argument for maintaining that the McMahon Line must be the Sino-Indian boundary too. But instead of seizing solely on that point, India proceeded to argue

---

65 square miles. Discrepancies in the definition of the areas involved were to be resolved by the joint boundary committee, which was to be set up to survey and demarcate the boundary and draft the boundary treaty proper.[65]

* Surveying and demarcation of the Sino-Burmese boundary was completed with great dispatch—although the terrain made it a very difficult task — so that the treaty was ready for signing when U Nu visited Peking again for China's national day celebrations on October 1st, 1960.

† An identical problem arose when China and Pakistan settled their boundary. This had to meet the Pakistan–Afghanistan boundary, the Durand Line, which the Afghans disputed.

‡ The Diphu Pass is clearly marked on the map, of a scale of 1 inch to 8 miles, which the British and Tibetan representatives signed in Delhi on March 24th, 1914, and McMahon drew his line right through it.

that the trijunction lay not at the Diphu Pass but five miles to the
north of it!* Beside the fact that China had accepted the McMahon
alignment in her agreement with Burma, this was a quibble; but still
India complained that the Sino-Burmese treaty map showed the trijunction erroneously, 'with an adverse implication on the territorial
integrity of India'.[66] Peking replied that the location of the trijunction
could not be determined until all three parties were prepared to co-
operate, in other words until India agreed 'to seek a reasonable settlement of the boundary question' in friendly negotiations.

The exchange of notes about the Sino-Burmese boundary settlement
did nothing but bring out more sharply the deadlock which India and
China had reached. India reiterated that her boundaries with China
could not be a matter for negotiation, claiming that they stood defined
'without the necessity of further or formal delimitation'.[67] China
replied that 'this attitude . . . of refusing to negotiate and trying to
impose a unilaterally claimed alignment on China is in actuality
refusal to settle the boundary question'; and she warned that while
India maintained that position and kept up her 'unreasonable tangling',
China would 'absolutely not retreat an inch' from her own stand.[68]

That China was equably and equitably settling her boundaries with
her other neighbours tended to throw an adverse light on India's
position. Peking prodded at that sore point:

> Since the Burmese and Nepalese Governments can settle their
> boundary questions with China in a friendly way through negotia-
> tions and since the Government of Pakistan has also agreed . . . to
> negotiate a boundary settlement, why is it that the Indian Govern-
> ment cannot negotiate and settle its boundary question with
> [China]? Such a commonsense query is indeed rather embarrassing
> —but it is useless to get furious with China.[69]

Since those other boundary settlements redounded to China's credit,
it was argued at the time, and is suggested still, that China concluded
them for no other purpose than to embarrass India; the interpretation
is impossible to refute because it derives from the belief that China can

---

* The discrepancy resulted from British second thoughts. McMahon had drawn his line
through the Diphu Pass but later surveys had shown that, from the British point of view,
the Talu Pass, five miles to the north, made a better boundary feature. British maps therefore began to show the boundary as running through the Talu Pass.

Burma accepted this in 1957, according to Nehru,[70] but the Chinese maintained that,
while they were prepared to treat the McMahon Line as the *de facto* boundary, this had to
be the Line as McMahon drew it—not as the British or the Indians may have amended it.

never do anything that is practical and reasonable simply because it is such, but always for an ulterior and malignant motive.

Indian resentment was at its strongest when China opened boundary negotiations with Pakistan; not only did that again put the Indian approach to boundary questions in an invidious light, but it also militated against her stand in the Kashmir dispute. China had been wary in responding to Pakistan's proposal that their boundary should be delimited. This was made in November 1959 after Mr Z. A. Bhutto had returned from leading the Pakistani delegation to the United Nations convinced by his Burmese contacts there that Peking was prepared to reach reasonable boundary settlements with any of her neighbours who sought them. But more than two years passed before China responded to Pakistan's proposal.

Pakistan's border tract with China (between Afghanistan and the Karakoram Pass, where the Sino-Indian boundary begins) was at one time under the nominal suzerainty of the Maharajah of Jammu and Kashmir, and so since 1947, when that ruler acceded to India, has been claimed by India. This claim is juridical rather than political: some of the areas concerned were never part of Kashmir proper and that they could ever become in fact part of the Indian Union is inconceivable. But, even so, China and, for her own reasons, Pakistan* were punctilious when they announced simultaneously in May 1962 that to ensure tranquillity on the border and develop good-neighbourly relations they proposed to delimit their boundary. The boundary was described as being between Sinkiang and 'the contiguous areas the defence of which is under the actual control of Pakistan'; and it was stated that the agreement reached would be provisional, to be re-negotiated if necessary after India and Pakistan settled the Kashmir dispute. Thus the signatories avoided committing themselves on the question of sovereignty in Kashmir. But the Indian position is that all of the former Maharajah of Kashmir's dominions are part of India, and that there is no Kashmir dispute; and those who would please the Indian Government must subscribe to that view. India's reaction on this occasion was the sharper because it had until then been believed in New Delhi that China leaned to the Indian side in the Kashmir dispute.

* Pakistan's position is that Jammu and Kashmir is a territory in dispute between herself and India, and that the question remains to be decided in accordance with the wishes of the people of the area, to be expressed in a plebiscite under U.N. auspices. Therefore Pakistan would not claim that the territory she now holds adjoining China is yet legally part of Pakistan—though in fact, of course, she treats it as such.

India protested to China that 'there is no common border between Pakistan and the People's Republic of China', and charged that the proposal to delimit 'a non-existent common border' over territory that was legally Indian was 'a step in furtherance of the aggressive aims that China has been pursuing towards India in recent years'. (By this time, midsummer 1962, the language in the diplomatic exchanges between New Delhi and Peking had become heated.) Furthermore, the Indians went on, 'there is no boundary dispute in this sector . . .' and they declared that they would repudiate any Sino-Pakistani boundary agreement.[71]*

In an irate reply Peking asked whether India, 'after creating the Sino-Indian boundary dispute, wishe[d] to see a similar dispute arise between India and Pakistan'. The short answer to that, in fact, would have been 'yes'. Since 1960 the Indian Government had been trying to tutor Pakistan in the attitude proper towards China over the northern frontier, with the object of getting Pakistan to adopt India's approach. As Nehru put it, 'we treated the Pakistan Government in a friendly way in this matter because we thought that any action which they might take should be in line with the action we were taking in regard to this border, and should not conflict.'[72] The Indian position was that the boundary between Afghanistan and the Karakoram Pass had already been delimited by custom, tradition and treaty, and that therefore, like the Sino-Indian boundary proper, it could not be the subject of negotiations. India wanted Pakistan to follow her lead and deny the existence of a boundary dispute—that is, insist that China accept Pakistan's version of the boundary.

Instead, Pakistan agreed with China that the boundary which con-

* Earlier Pakistan had made the mirror point, warning the Security Council that 'no positions taken or adjustments made in the territories of the disputed state [of Jammu and Kashmir] by either India or China shall be valid'.[73] The President of Azad (Pakistan-held) Kashmir, K. H. Khursheed, said that if China came to any agreement with India 'over the head of the people of Jammu and Kashmir it would be tantamount to extending moral support to India's expansionist policy'[74] while, on the other side, Bakshi Ghulam Moham-med, Prime Minister of the Indian part of the state, was warning the Indian Government that 'Kashmiris and Ladakhis would not accept any cession of Ladakh territory.'[75]

   This overlay of the two disputes, the one on the Sino-Indian boundary, the other over Kashmir between India and Pakistan, would further complicate a Sino-Indian boundary settlement. China could now be expected to insist that any agreement made with India about the western sector of their boundaries be provisional, pending settlement of the question of sovereignty in Kashmir; for not to do so would be tacitly to accept the Indian case on Kashmir, at the cost of China's friendly relationship with Pakistan. On the other hand, for India to sign such a provisional agreement would be to reverse her long-standing position that the legal status of Kashmir was settled once and for all when the ruler of the state acceded to India in 1947.

cerned them had never been delimited, and on October 13th, 1962, negotiations began in Peking. (On the same day, not incidentally, China signed a boundary agreement with another neighbour, Mongolia.) After what Pakistani participants described as tough but reasonable negotiating, the two Governments jointly announced on December 26th, 1962, that 'complete agreement in principle had been reached', and procedures were established and set in motion for concluding a boundary treaty.*

The treaty signed in the following March delimited a boundary between Pakistan and China which followed for the great part of its length the line that the British had proposed to China in 1899. The most marked divergence from that line was in favour of Pakistan, giving her a trans-Karakoram boundary in one sector, between the Shimshal Pass and the Muztagh River; that area, one of those on which Hunza had grazing rights, had been under Chinese administration, and Peking's concession to Pakistan here involved evacuation, as well as departure from the watershed principle which otherwise guided the boundary makers. Thus, while Pakistan gave up only map claims, China actually ceded some 750 square miles of territory.

Like Burma, Pakistan had found that in boundary negotiations China insisted only that the departure point be that the boundary was undelimited (and in the instance of the Sino-Pakistan sector, even India could not cite a treaty foundation for her version of the boundary); and after that was prepared to compromise with her neighbour to achieve a mutually acceptable line.

* * * * * * * * * * *

These accounts of China's boundary settlements with Burma and Pakistan† have broken the sequence of the narrative, which has now to

* This announcement coincided with the arrival in Rawalpindi of an Indian [delegation which was opening a round of talks with Pakistan on Kashmir, and it was widely deduced that China by this timing had tried to throw a spanner in the delicate diplomatic works of those negotiations. In fact, Peking seems to have been persuaded to make the announcement on December 26th by Pakistan, whose Foreign Minister, Mr Z. A. Bhutto, hoped that this reminder of cordial rapprochement between his country and China would lead the U.S.A. to increase pressure on India to compromise on Kashmir.[76] No amount of American pressure could have achieved that end, however, and the tactic, like the talks, failed.

† China has concluded boundary agreements with Afghanistan, Nepal and Mongolia too. On China's other main outstanding problem in boundary settlement, with the U.S.S.R., Chou En-lai said in 1960: 'There is a very small discrepancy on maps, and it is very easy to settle'—an optimistic view which was soon to be belied.[77]

be taken back to the spring of 1961. The Indian officials' report, which
to a quick or unquestioning reader does seem a massive documentation
of the Indian case, had so strongly reinforced Nehru's conviction that
he believed it might have made the Chinese see the error of their ways.
'I cannot conceive of their having read this and not having felt that
their position was a weak one,' he told the Lok Sabha in August.[78]
To see whether there was any change in the Chinese stand, the Secretary General of the Ministry of External Affairs, R. K. Nehru (a cousin
of the Prime Minister), was sent to Peking in July on his way back from
Mongolia, and there met Chou En-lai. He found the Chinese position
unchanged. They were still ready, indeed eager, to negotiate a boundary
settlement with India, and it was intimated again that in such negotiations China would agree to the McMahon alignment. But the Chinese
were not prepared to accept the Indian claim line in the western sector,
and since that was for India open neither to compromise nor negotiation the way to a settlement was still barred.[79]

The news that the Secretary General had been to Peking to discuss
the boundary question aroused in India all the old suspicion that Nehru
was for peace at any price; that in his hankering for a settlement he
would appease China with gifts of what was regarded as sovereign
Indian soil. The Prime Minister had to bring out his familiar defence,
telling the Lok Sabha again that 'talking does not mean negotiating
anything',[80] and he even suggested that the Secretary General had been
in Peking only because that lay on the most convenient route back
from Mongolia.

The meeting between Nehru and Chou En-lai had left the follow-up
to the officials' reports indeterminate; and, apart from the exchanges of
diplomatic protests, complaints and accusations, the political stalemate
continued. It was paralleled on the ground.

The forward policy was still not being implemented, the Army
continuing to resist the Government's pressure for forward moves into
Chinese-claimed territory. In March 1961 Army H.Q. explained that
the limitations of air transport had made it impossible to induct the
proposed brigade into Ladakh, and that consequently for the time
being the small force in the sector could do no more than prevent the
Chinese from advancing across their own claim line (which they
showed no signs of intending), and defend Leh.[81] In April this was
followed up by a warning that the supply position in Ladakh was so
acutely difficult that even the defence of the sector was beyond the

Army's capabilities; in a letter to the Defence Ministry the officiating Chief of General Staff, who was by then General Kaul (Thimayya was still Army Chief) said: 'As things stand today, it has to be accepted that, should the Chinese wish to carry out strong incursions into our territory at selected points, we are not in a position to prevent them from doing so.'[82] In June the General Staff noted that unless the Air Force could treble the quantity of stores and supplies that it proposed to drop in Ladakh that month, several of the Army's recently established posts would have to be evacuated.[83]

In the summer of 1961, then, the Indian Army was maintaining with the greatest difficulty a line of posts and picquets that for almost its entire length was well short of the Chinese claim line in the western sector. The exception was at its southern extremity, where the Indians had established a post at Demchok (inside the Chinese claim line— Peking calls it Parigas) and in 1961 had sent out some picquets from there. Peking complained in August about these moves and some Indian patrolling just over the Chinese claim line near Spangur Lake, accusing India of having 'wilfully carried out armed provocations and expanded its illegally occupied areas in the Chinese border region'.[84] New Delhi retorted that the areas about which China complained were Indian; 'the allegation that Indian troops are intruding when they go to a part of Indian territory is manifestly absurd,' the note said, and the measures India adopted for defence within her own territory were no concern of China's.

That month, Nehru had told the Lok Sabha that there had been 'no further [Chinese] aggression anywhere';[85] but when replying, belatedly, in October, to the Chinese protest, India accused China of numerous 'recent intrusions'. Only two of eleven instances given were less than a year old, and some were trivial (one referred to an intrusion of eighty yards), while the description of others was vague.[86] China described these complaints as an attempt to create pretexts for India's own forward movement.[87] But the Indian note went on to list three new posts which it asserted that China had set up on Indian territory, 'making conclusive proof of further Chinese aggression'; and when news of this accusation came out in India there was an upsurge of angry criticism of the Government for what was seen as its failure to block a threatening and insolent Chinese advance. Taking their cue from the Government's distinction between the 1956 and 1960 Chinese claims, the Opposition and press blamed it for allowing China to fill out to its second and more advanced claim. Drawing lines on their maps to connect the posts that China was said to have newly established, they accused the Government of having lost to China the area thus enclosed, calculating this at 2,000 square miles. 'That is ridiculous,' Nehru argued; 'that is not true'; where the Chinese occupied a new point they exercised 'some influence round about it' but not over such wide areas. His critics were not convinced. 'They have advanced ten miles,' said a Jan Sangh M.P., 'it means ten by one hundred equals one thousand square miles of border.'[88]

Two of the allegedly new Chinese posts were to the north of the ruined Khurnak Fort and according to Nehru were 'actually on the international frontier'[89]—i.e. on the Indian claim line.* He conceded, when challenged about the new posts in Parliament in November, that the Government was 'not quite certain whether they are a mile or two on this side or that side, because it is rather difficult in these high mountain ranges to be precise about the actual line'. This admission drew the interjection from the Opposition benches: 'Then they must be on our side. If there is doubt then they are obviously on this side.'[90] The reasoning is not clear, but Nehru accepted it. Even if the posts were actually on the international frontier they would be 'a sign of aggressive mentality . . . and aggressive activities', he said. The implication of this remark seems to be that for India to set up posts right on what she held to be the international frontier was quite in order; but that for China to put up posts even on the *Indian* claim line was 'aggressive'.

But Nehru was in a quandary of the Government's own creating. India had accused China of 'renewed incursions', and now Parliament demanded an explanation of why the Chinese had been allowed to extend their grip. To defend himself from charges of laxity, Nehru belittled the extent of the Chinese advance, pointing out that in two years only three new Chinese posts had been established, fractionally, if at all, more advanced than the previous positions, and drew attention to India's counter measures: 'We have set up more than half a dozen new posts, important posts, in Ladakh.'[91] But such assertions invited charges of complacency and allowed Nehru's critics to suggest that he was belittling China's crime; so he had to tack again, saying that even

---

* The Indian claim line at this point runs through Khurnak Fort, following no physical features. Even those maps which show the broad scope of the Indian claim put Khurnak Fort well inside Chinese territory—e.g. NI 44-9, Series V 502 of the U.S. Army Map Service, based on a 1938 Survey of India map.

if the new Chinese advance was very small, even if in one area they were not clearly on the wrong side of the international boundary, still the Chinese were being aggressive. Characteristically, Nehru thus accommodated his words to the objections of his critics, and as a result his own formulations became progressively more extreme—probably more extreme than he originally intended.

The third of the Chinese posts about which India complained was in the Chip Chap valley, and this figured in a crucial meeting held in the Prime Minister's office on November 2nd, 1961. Present in addition to Nehru were Krishna Menon; the new Foreign Secretary, M. J. Desai, the new Chief of Army Staff, General Thapar; Kaul; the director of the Intelligence Bureau, B. N. Malik; and other officials. From this meeting emerged a new directive for implementation of the forward policy.

The External Affairs officials and Malik concluded from the existence of the new Chinese post in the Chip Chap valley that China was purposefully moving forward to fill out occupation to her claim line. The Army Chief, Thapar, said that although the post had first been seen by his troops in September, it was not possible to say when it had been set up; but Malik maintained that it was established after 1959–60. He argued that the Chinese intended to come right up to their claim line, but that they would keep away where Indian troops were present, even if it were only a dozen men. Therefore he proposed that the Army should quickly move forward to fill the vacuum, as otherwise the Chinese were bound to do so within a few months. In Malik's opinion, endorsed by the External Affairs officials, the Chinese were not likely to react to the establishment of Indian posts over their claim line except in diplomatic protests—certainly not with force.

These were the operative paragraphs of the directive that emerged from the November 2nd meeting:

(a) So far as Ladakh is concerned, we are to patrol as far forward as possible from our present positions towards the international border. This will be done with a view to establishing our posts which should prevent the Chinese from advancing any further and also dominating from any posts which they may have already established in our territory. This must be done without getting involved in a clash with the Chinese, unless this becomes necessary in self-defence.

(*b*) As regards U.P. [Uttar Pradesh, i.e. the middle sector] and other northern areas there are not the same difficulties as in Ladakh. We should, therefore, as far as practicable, go forward and be in effective occupation of the whole frontier. Where there are any gaps they must be covered either by patrolling or by posts.
(*c*) In view of the numerous operational and administrative difficulties, efforts should be made to position major concentrations of forces along our borders in places conveniently situated behind the forward posts from where they could be maintained logistically and from where they can restore a border situation at short notice.

The phrasing and priority of paragraphs reflect the balance of argument at the meeting, and show that the differences were not really resolved. The choice was between two opposite courses of action: an immediate move forward without preparation; or a build-up, necessarily slow, from which a substantial forward move could ultimately be launched. Both are reflected in the directive, but the adventurist course of immediate action more strongly: 'So far as Ladakh is concerned, we are to patrol as far forward as possible. . . .' Then comes a bow towards the 'numerous operational and administrative difficulties' adduced by the soldiers; and the concessional '. . . efforts should be made to position major concentrations of forces along our borders. . . .'

On the sound principle that first things come first, a cautious commander could justifiably have inverted the priority followed in the directive's paragraphing and left the patrolling and posts in Ladakh until he had built up the major concentrations from which to support such forward moves. General Daulat Singh of Western Command had shown by his reaction to earlier forward policy requirements that he was just such a cautious commander; but he was given no chance to opt for the sounder course. *All reference to building-up was omitted from the orders sent out to the two regional commanders concerned.* A letter of 5th December from General Thapar to Western and Eastern Commands stated that the Government had recently reviewed its policy on patrolling and establishing posts on the border, and then gave its decisions:

[In Ladakh] we are to patrol as far forward as possible from our present positions towards the International Border as recognized by us. This will be done with a view to establishing additional

posts located to prevent the Chinese from advancing further and
also *to dominate any Chinese posts already established in our territory.*

Comparison of the sentence here italicized with the original directive,
paragraph (*a*), shows that an ambiguity in the original has been
removed, toughening up the concept further. Thapar's letter continued: 'This "Forward Policy" shall be carried out without getting
involved in a clash with the Chinese unless it becomes necessary in
self-defence.' The next paragraph, referring to the middle and eastern
sectors, duplicated paragraph (*b*) of the Government's directive, but
the letter concluded with:

> I realize that the application of this new policy in Ladakh and on
> our other borders will entail considerable movements of troops
> with attendant logistical problems. I would like you to make a fresh
> appraisal of your task in view of the new directive from Govern-
> ment, especially with regard to the additional logistical effort
> involved. Your recommendations in this respect are required by
> me by 30 December, 1961. Meanwhile, wherever possible, action
> should be taken as indicated above.*

The forward policy had thus become the subject of a categorical order
from Army H.Q., for immediate implementation.

An explanation for this deliberate emendation of a Government
directive of the highest importance must be inferred; on the face of it,
it is most unlikely that any recorded explanation will ever be found
in the files. The first clue that can be noted is that in Nehru's concept
of the forward policy the build-up to support it was integral to the
whole design; as he described it in the Lok Sabha at the end of
November, 'it is a question of strong armed groups, relatively small
groups, going and either taking possession of a place or removing
somebody from some place . . . with strong bases behind to support
them'.[92] Again, at the beginning of December, resisting in Parliament
demands for what he described as adventurist action, he defined that
as 'taking some action without having a base to support [it]', and went
on: 'That is not fair to our men. They are brave and fine men, but it
is not fair to put them in that position and not fair to the nation to
take some action which cannot be supported and therefore which ends

---

* Neither the Government's original directive nor Thapar's letter passing that on to the
Commands has been published, but they were made available to the writer. From this
point the narrative draws heavily on unpublished material. See preface.

abruptly.'[93] It seems certain, then, that the change in the forward policy directive was not made at Nehru's behest, and likely that it was made without his knowledge.

There had by this time been a complete change in Army H.Q. Kaul had been officiating as C.G.S. since March but it was only in mid-summer that Thapar took over as C.O.A.S. and that the other changes in General staff posts, which gave Kaul a hand-picked group to work with, could be made. A later Army review of the General Staff work through this period found that systematic planning and co-ordination, which were the responsibility of the General Staff and the 'pre-requisites of proper military functioning, posture and balance', were progressively neglected; instead, there was 'acting on whims and sup-positions and then plugging holes, rather than deliberate military thought followed by planned actions'. As the General Staff, while neglecting its proper functions, interfered more and more with the conduct of operations at unit level its approach had repercussions throughout the military structure. This change in the direction and quality of the work of the General Staff from the middle of 1961 seems to be explicable only by the appointment of its new chief, Kaul, and the officers he selected.

That Kaul also favoured an aggressive posture towards the Chinese is shown in a minute he put up to the Defence Ministry while still officiating as C.G.S., some time before the forward policy directive was drawn up. This proposed that 'one of the most effective methods of stemming the Chinese policy of gradually creeping westwards across our borders in Ladakh would be to give them an occasional knock. . . . For instance, if we found one of their patrols in a setting tactically favourable to us, it would be worth our while to engage them in a short offensive action aimed at inflicting casualties and/or taking prisoners.' This proposal was not adopted; but Kaul's aggressive think-ing seems the likeliest reason for the deletion of the build-up phase from the forward policy directive.

Krishna Menon was at this time (October–November 1961) also urging the Army to take a more positive line in confronting the Chinese. By now the foreglow of the approaching general elections was heating up the Indian political scene, giving greater sharpness and resonance to the Opposition's charges and complaints and making the Government more sensitive. These factors added urgency to the side of the civilians in the silent and secret struggle that had been going on for a year and half between them and the Army. The civilians were confident that the Chinese would give way before the forward probes of Indian troops, no matter how few and lightly armed those were; they were therefore able to dismiss the tactical objections raised by the soldiers. The Army's own intelligence appreciation was that the Chinese would react vigorously to any moves challenging their possession of the disputed western territory, and beyond that it is a fundamental principle of war—and of common sense—that military plans cannot be founded on the assumption that an enemy will not react. While Thimayya was Army Chief the resistance of the soldiers could not be overruled; if he was pressed too far, there was always the possibility that he would go to the Prime Minister, or even resign. But from mid-1961 the civilians were dealing with soldiers at Army H.Q. who shared, or were ready to go along with, the assumption that political factors would prevent a strong Chinese reaction. Thapar himself did not hold that view, but his warnings that Chinese retaliation could not be ruled out were merely registered, never pressed, and Kaul was the man who counted. What had happened, then, in mid-1961 was that the straight contest over policy between the civilians and the soldiers was ended, in favour of the forward policy, by the appointment of key officers who shared the civilian assumptions and attitudes. It was replaced by another contest between Army H.Q. and formations below it, but discipline made that a contest that could be won only by H.Q.

★ ★ ★ ★ ★ ★ ★ ★ ★ ★ ★

The same day that the Indian Government drafted its forward policy directive China protested about forward moves which were already being made from Demchok. 'The Chinese Government has been following with great anxiety the Indian troops' steady pressing forward on China's borders and cannot but regard such action of the Indian side as an attempt to create new troubles and to carry out its expansion by force in the . . . border areas,' the note said.[94] If Chinese border guards had not been under orders to avoid conflict, the Indian movements, 'gross violations of China's territory and sovereignty', would have had very serious consequences. 'The Chinese Government deems it necessary to point out that it would be very erroneous and dangerous should the Indian Government take China's attitude of restraint and tolerance

8

as an expression of weakness.' In reply, New Delhi asserted that the Indian patrols were moving into their own territory and rejected the protest as unwarranted interference in India's internal affairs.[95]

In another note, Peking pointed out the implications of the argument that all territory claimed by India was *ipso facto* Indian territory and that China had no right to complain about what Indian troops did there. The logic was 'untenable and also most dangerous', the Chinese argued. If it were applied to the eastern sector of the boundary, where China held that the McMahon Line was illegal and that the true boundary lay beneath the foot-hills, 'the Chinese Government would have every reason to send troops to cross the so-called McMahon Line and enter the vast area between the crest of the Himalayas and their southern foot'.[96] Objectively, it was a fair point. The whole extent of the Sino-Indian boundary was disputed; and if India, rejecting China's repeated proposal that both sides should maintain the *status quo*, progressively moved forward into Chinese-occupied territory in one disputed sector, she would have no equitable grounds for complaint if China similarly began to patrol and set up posts on Indian-occupied territory in another.

But to the Indians, long past objectivity on the border question, Peking's was not a logical argument but a threat to add aggression to aggression. In the Indian view, none of the boundaries was in dispute. 'According to our thinking our trouble at the border is not a dispute at all,' Nehru had explained in Parliament a few months before. 'It is a question of words, perhaps; it is a dispute, of course, when we argue about something it is a dispute. But my point is it is not a dispute because we have no doubt about our own position in the matter. So far as we are concerned, we are clear that it is not a normal dispute but is just a claim on our territory—which is ours, and we are convinced that it is ours.'[97] From this it followed that the Chinese view of the logic of the situation could be ignored, and the Chinese warnings dismissed as the threats of an aggressor—the dismissal being all the easier because the Indians were convinced that such warnings were bluff. The Indian Government's fundamental border policy of *no negotiations* had locked India on to a collision course with China in the early 1950s and with the implementation of the forward policy the point of impact would be reached. But India was still confident that in this titanic game of chicken it would be China that swerved away.

The forward policy directive at the end of 1961 was not the only expression at the time of India's readiness to take unilateral and forceful action in territorial questions. There was also the case of Goa. The British left the sub-continent in 1947; the French handed over their little colony of Pondicherry in 1954; but the Portuguese stayed on in Goa and its enclaves, the territories on the west coast which had been theirs since the beginning of the sixteenth century. Indian diplomatic pressure had not persuaded Portugal to cede Goa—and of course the thought of giving the Goans independence never occurred to the Portuguese. In 1955 India attempted to force the issue by the methods that had often worked with the British, and *satyagrahis*, non-violent demonstrators, marched across the frontier into Goa; but when the Portuguese found that there were too many to arrest their police opened fire, killing several and wounding many. India severed diplomatic relations with Portugal, but the Portuguese stayed on in Goa. The public outrage that welled up in India over the shooting in 1955 died down, and by 1961 the Portuguese presence in Goa was a subject of rankling resentment, but not of pressing concern. The Government was committed to making Goa part of India but seemed also committed not to use force in order to do so, and it was under no strong political pressure in that regard.

In the pre-election autumn of 1961, however, the Government, chafed by charges that it had been truckling to China, was in a mood to give its resolve military demonstration. The foward policy could not be expected to yield dramatic results (not in the way India expected, anyway) and various factors pointed to Goa as a more fruitful theatre for action. In October an Afro-Asian seminar on Portuguese colonialism was held in New Delhi, and delegates made it sharply clear to Indian participants that so long as Portugal was allowed to rule Goa they would judge India's commitment to the cause of anti-colonialism to be shallow. Indian assertions that non-violence was a higher cause drew the rejoinder that in Portuguese colonies non-violence only met with repression and massacre—which the Indians, remembering how the *satyagrahis* had been shot down, could hardly deny. This seminar, Nehru said later, 'left us in a receptive mood, searching for something to do' about Goa,[98] and immediately after the seminar broke up he told a public meeting in Bombay that 'the time has come for us to consider afresh what method should be adopted to free Goa from Portuguese rule.'

Events then followed a familiar pattern. While Nehru declared

India's patience to be exhausted, the Government used the Indian press, uncritically responsive in this regard, to develop a propaganda campaign to the effect that Goan freedom-fighters were being slaughtered by the Portuguese; that there was a big build-up of NATO-supplied weapons in Goa which presented a serious threat to Indian security; that the Portuguese intended a 'tie-up with Pakistan which made the problem more urgent than the border dispute with China'.[99] Then border incidents began, trivial but seized upon in India as intolerable provocations. At the beginning of December troops were moved to the Goa frontier in such numbers and with such haste that the railway services in northern and western India were dislocated. With about a division of troops disposed for assault around Goa, more serious border incidents began, until to avoid them the Portuguese authorities pulled their border posts back.

Nehru had not made up his mind to order an invasion of Goa, it seems; certainly he had not yet given such an order. Deeply torn, caught again in the velleity that was so marked in his character, he let others more decisive and purposeful push events until they picked up their own momentum and could not be stopped. Thus he made his own role look worse than it need have. While political and military preparations for invasion were intensifying, Nehru was still affirming his and India's commitment to negotiations as the only way to settle international disputes, abjuring the use of force, and saying 'my whole soul reacts against the thought of war'.[100] By December there was a real and clamorous demand in political India for an invasion of Goa, and the propaganda on conditions in the colony was shrill and fanciful; foreign correspondents enjoyed their drinks in Panjim's peaceful pavement cafés while they listened to All-India Radio reporting that the city was under curfew, the Portuguese Governor in flight, and 'Goa commandos' from India fighting in the streets. Nehru's hesitation continued into the twenty-fifth hour. On the night of December 17th, the American Ambassador, Professor Galbraith, who had for days been trying to head Nehru off from an invasion, made his points with such effect that the Prime Minister was deterred. When Galbraith left, Nehru told Krishna Menon that the orders for the troops to advance into Goa, which he had approved for that midnight, should be suspended again—'D Day' had already been twice postponed.[101] Menon replied that it was too late; the troops, he said, had already begun their advance—although in fact they had not.[102]

Kaul, as C.G.S. and what amounted to personal military adviser to the Prime Minister, played a key role in planning the Goa operation and, it appears, in helping Nehru over his qualms. In his autobiography he recounts that Nehru, worried by adverse comment abroad, summoned him at the last moment to ask what the repercussions would be in India if the operation were called off. Kaul replied that it would be destructive for both military and civilian morale, and suggested that they should ignore foreign advice. Nehru, he says, 'reluctantly agreed'. Kaul's comment is apt: 'He was perhaps finally swayed to take this action because he realized his people expected him to liberate Goa. He thought that if he failed to act . . . both the people and the armed services might lose faith in him.'[103] Krishna Menon, for all his loyal affection, later gave a more destructive explanation of Nehru's vacillation over the Goa operation: 'You see,' he said, 'Nehru had a complicated temperament; he didn't like the vulgarity and the cruelty of it, but at the same time he wanted the results.'[104] A more charitable judgment of Nehru's role, and perhaps the fairest, was this: that Nehru, 'ill, old and tired, let himself be edged bit by bit into a situation from which escape was very difficult. He can be acquitted of hypocrisy, but not of failure.'[105]

The Indian seizure of Goa was quite in the way of the world, and few, if any, governments could denounce it without inviting reminders of the skeletons in their own closets. As President Kennedy wrote to Nehru: 'All countries, including the U.S.A., have a great capacity for convincing themselves of the full righteousness of their particular cause.'[106] But what made Goa more of a scandal and an irritant, of course, was the fact that India, and especially Nehru, had been such persistent advocates of the doctrine that the use of force was never justified as a means of settling international disputes. Now Indians insisted that the seizure of Goa was in no way a breach of their prescriptions for international conduct. Very few indeed criticized their Government's action; the press and the mass of political opinion enthusiastically supported it: 'Why is it that something that thrills our people should be condemned in the strongest language?' Nehru plaintively asked J. F. Kennedy.[107]

The Goa action had implications, both political and military, for the Indian Government's handling of its dispute with China. It showed how Nehru could drift into courses of action that allowed no retreat, and how amenable he could be to an excited political opinion, even when its urgings were contrary to his own instincts. It showed how amorphous and subjective were the decision-making processes of the Government; the seizure of Goa, like the forward policy, was not decided upon in Cabinet. It demonstrated the duality of India's attitude towards the use of force—reprehensible in the abstract and in the service of others, but justifiable both politically and morally when employed by India in disputes over what she regarded as her own territory. The Indian view of the seizure of Goa, as summed up in a political journal, was that 'no aggression has been committed, because we have regarded Goa ever since 1947 as our rightful territory. . . . To drive out an intruder who is in illegal occupation of part of our territory is not aggression.'[108]

This approach had obvious application to the boundary dispute with China, and Nehru was asked at his press conference after the Goa operation whether India now proposed to use force against the Chinese. He replied: 'The use of force is, of course, open to us and should be used by us according to suitability and opportunity.'[109] Lal Bahadur Shastri, the Home Minister, made the parallel explicit. 'If the Chinese will not vacate the areas occupied by her, India will have to repeat what she did in Goa,' he told an election meeting. 'She will certainly drive out the Chinese forces.'[110] Some politicians were so intoxicated by Goa that they began to talk of driving Pakistan out of Azad Kashmir as well as forcing China out of Aksai Chin. Sanjiva Reddy, then president of the Congress Party, said that India was 'determined to get Pakistani and Chinese aggression on its soil vacated before long'. The ceasefire in Kashmir could not be a permanent solution, he said; Pakistan-occupied Kashmir must be 'liberated'.[111]

On the military side the operation, which involved rather more than a division of troops with naval and air support, showed up the deficiencies in the Army's equipment; since the Portuguese put up no organized resistance against the overwhelmingly superior Indian forces, the operation did not test the capabilities of the troops or their commanders. The Indian units were in some cases short of their complement of rifles and sub-machine-guns, as well as of wireless sets or the batteries to run them and other communications equipment. The Army was experiencing a chronic shortage of boots, and in one battalion about half the men went through the operation in canvas gym shoes. Little of that came out in India—though it was the subject of wide discussion in the Army—and the Goa operation was hailed as a proud feat of arms. The widely circulated weekly *Blitz* called it 'Our Finest Hour'.

If the wish to take some of the heat out of the political public's demand for immediate military action against China was a factor in turning the Government's attention to Goa, that part of the calculation backfired. The easy victory over the Portuguese naturally encouraged the hope of a similarly signal success against the Chinese. The Indian journalist who compared the seizure of Goa with 'stamping on a mouse in the kitchen when there is a tiger at the door'[112] was not complaining about the mouse's fate but blaming his Government for not bagging the tiger too. The supposition that the speed with which the Goa operation was completed reflected the fine fighting fettle of the Indian troops (rather than the fact that the Portuguese put up no resistance) confirmed the Government's assurances that the Indian Army was in good shape.

The condition of the Army and other services had become an election issue, brought into sharp focus in Bombay where Acharya Kripalani had come to contest Krishna Menon's constituency. Campaigning for Krishna Menon there in January 1962, Nehru declared: 'I say that after Mr Menon became the Defence Minister our defence forces have become for the first time a very strong and efficient fighting force. I say it with a challenge and with intimate knowledge. . . . It is for the first time that our defence forces have a new spirit and modern weapons.'[113] Nehru spoke often in this vein, repeatedly assuring Parliament and public that the Army and other services were stronger than they had been since independence and were ready to meet any foreseeable challenge to the integrity or honour of India; were capable, indeed, even of dealing with a concerted attack from Pakistan and China. When critics painted the Government's border policy in terms of appeasement and weakness, Nehru depicted it as patience based on strength, resolve tempered with a humane concern about the catastrophic consequences for mankind if the two giants of Asia came to war. The critics in Parliament might dismiss his version of the situation in debate, but at bottom they accepted it. Illogically but proudly, the strongest critics of the Government's defence policies believed that, in spite of the weaknesses about which they complained, the Indian Army would quickly teach the Chinese a lesson if only it were unleashed. For the critics, it can be said that they had no concept of the real extent

of the Army's deficiencies,* as the soldiers were scrupulous in keeping
the details of their complaints and anxieties between themselves and
the Government. How Nehru could retain his confidence that in a local
affray Indian troops would get the better of the Chinese—as he did, to
the last—is less easy to explain; but Kaul, certainly, and perhaps other
senior officers fed that assumption.

Goa was a sideshow, deeply gratifying to aroused Indian national
passions but not for a moment deflecting them from their central preoccupation—the boundary dispute with China. That, said Nehru, was
more important to India than a hundred Goas.[114]

* * * * * * * * * * *

Orders began to go out from Army H.Q. for forward patrols even
before the forward policy directive had been issued as orders to the two
commands (there was a curious five-week delay between the drafting
of the political directive on November 2nd and its emended embodiment in Army H.Q.'s signal on December 5th). Those orders were
detailed and specific, stating which troops should move and when;
giving the routes to be followed and the areas in which posts were to
be established—decisions which would normally have been left to the
discretion of lower formations. The patrols and siting of posts were
directed by Kaul and his officers of the General Staff, in consultation
with Malik of the Intelligence Bureau and his deputy, Hooja, and
frequently with M. J. Desai, the Foreign Secretary. From the beginning
it was stated that the posts to be established were to be so sited as to
dominate the Chinese posts.

Acting on these orders, small parties of Indian troops moved out
eastward from all their main positions in the western sector through
the winter of 1961–2. The towering, naked ridges kept the troops to
the valleys, a necessity confirmed by the need to have flat dropping
zones (D.Z.s) on to which the Air Force could parachute their supplies.
The general altitude was in the region of 14,000 feet, and passes took
the patrols up as high as 16,000 feet. The temperatures were arctic, and

---

* The army was short of 60,000 rifles, 700 anti-tank guns, 200 two-inch mortars. Supply
of artillery ammunition was critically low; 5,000 field radio sets were needed, thousands
of miles of field cable, 36,000 wireless batteries. If vehicles of pre-1948 vintage were considered obsolete (and most were below operational requirements) the army was short of
10,000 one-ton trucks and 10,000 three-ton trucks. Two regiments of tanks were un-
operational because they lacked spare parts.

the troops' winter clothing was inadequate and in short supply. The
rarefied air meant that the troops could carry only small loads themselves; mules were not much use at those altitudes and there were, in
any event, few of these, and no yaks, the only reliable pack animal in
such conditions. All supplies, often including water, had to be air-
dropped.

When the forward policy began to be put into effect the Leh-based
114 Brigade had still only three battalions in command—one regular,
two militia. These troops were between them responsible for a front
of more than two hundred miles, stretching from the Karakoram Pass
to a few miles beyond Demchok. Under orders to patrol forward as
far as they could, the limit of their responsibilities was in theory the
Indian claim line on the Kuen Lun mountains more than a hundred
miles to the east, on the far side of the empty, freezing wasteland of the
Aksai Chin plateau—empty, that is, except for the Chinese.

The winter of 1961–2 was a relatively quiet one for diplomatic
exchanges, and Peking's next protest against the forward policy did
not come until March 1st, when a note described the forward patrolling
and establishment of posts as 'deliberate attempts to realize by force the
territorial claims put forward by the Indian government'.[115] This
opened a rally of diplomatic notes in which each side restated its
position. Essentially these were unchanged but the tone and emphasis
were in places new, and the notes can usefully be summarized here for
recapitulation.

As Peking saw the situation, China had from the beginning sought a
boundary settlement through friendly negotiations and urged that,
pending such a consummation, the two sides should jointly maintain
the *status quo*. Although India rejected the proposal for a joint twenty-
kilometre withdrawal, China had unilaterally stopped patrolling within
twenty kilometres of the boundary on her side. India, on the other
hand, had refused to open negotiations and steadily pushed forward,
first in the middle and eastern sectors and now in the west, while
loudly accusing China of aggression because of China's presence in an
area which had long been under Chinese control, and which since 1950
had been a vital land link between Sinkiang and Tibet. China maintained that the McMahon Line did not constitute a legal boundary, but
was nevertheless observing it and making no demands that India should
withdraw from the area between the McMahon Line and the foot-
hills, where China declared the traditional and customary boundary

8*

to lie. India had said that she desired a peaceful settlement, but 'what the Indian Government termed peaceful settlement is for China to withdraw from her own territory, which is in fact tantamount to summary rejection of peaceful settlement'. Similarly, India said that she desired maintenance of the *status quo*; but was in fact rejecting maintenance of the *status quo* and again demanding that China withdraw. 'Anyone who is sensible and reasonable can see that such a rigid and threatening attitude will certainly lead to no solution. . . . To refuse to maintain the *status quo* and to reject negotiations is to reject a peaceful settlement.' India's line of action 'is most dangerous and may lead to grave consequences'; but 'so far as the Chinese side is concerned the door for negotiations is always open.'[116]

In New Delhi's perception, the Sino-Indian boundary had long been settled and had the sanction of tradition and custom as well as the confirmation, for almost its entire length, of valid treaties and agreements. In recent years China had committed systematic and continuous aggression and 'sought to justify unlawful occupation by unwarranted territorial claims'. India wished to 'maintain the *status quo*' but that could only be done if the *status quo* were first restored by Chinese withdrawal from Indian territory. ('*Status quo*' was thus used to mean '*status quo ante*'.) Such withdrawal was a prerequisite for negotiations, which even then could only be on 'minor mutual adjustments in a few areas of the border'. As for the forward movement, 'it is the legitimate right, indeed the duty, of the Government of India to take all necessary measures to safeguard the territorial integrity of India.' India was 'dedicated to the use of peaceful methods for the settlement of international disputes' and peaceful withdrawal of Chinese forces from 'Indian territory' would go a long way towards restoring friendship between India and China.[117]

India had thus reiterated that she would not negotiate a boundary settlement. It had also been made explicit that Chinese withdrawal from the territory India claimed was a pre-condition for the discussion of even the minor adjustments in the Indian claim line which was all in the way of negotiations that India would agree to.

In the first half of 1962 another exchange of diplomatic notes buried the Panch Sheel agreement—on trade and intercourse in Tibet—which had been intended to cement the friendship of India and China, and set an example for Asia and the world. A note from China on December 3rd, 1961, reminded India that the 1954 agreement was due to expire in six months and proposed negotiations on an agreement to replace it.[118] Peking made no mention of the boundary dispute, holding that the two subjects were distinct and hoping that a new agreement on Tibet would ease relations with India and open the way to settling other questions.[119] This was an approach that India followed and prescribed in other contexts. For example, she has always advised Pakistan to leave the Kashmir dispute aside and amicably settle other issues, thus improving the general climate. But in this case New Delhi declined to negotiate a new agreement until China had withdrawn from the territory India claimed—'outrageous preconditions', Peking said, 'which demand China's subjugation'.[120] The trade which the 1954 agreement had been meant to protect was anyway almost dead by now, strangled—each side said, by the other—in the tightening of regulations and military dispositions on both sides, and the agreement lapsed on June 3rd, 1962. India withdrew trade agencies from Yatung, Gartok and Gyantse in Tibet, China withdrew hers from Kalimpong and Calcutta.

The forward policy was meanwhile beginning to bite in its toothless way. Small Indian posts were being established overlooking Chinese positions and sometimes astride the tracks or roads behind them; the General Staff theory was that the Chinese lines of communication would thus be cut, forcing the ultimate withdrawal of their posts. At the beginning of the year the Indian press and foreign correspondents in New Delhi, reflecting what they were being told by officials and staff officers, began to prophesy early steps by the Army to force the Chinese out of Aksai Chin.[121] China's warnings of 'grave consequences' if the Indians persisted in their forward movement became emphatic, but Nehru dismissed them. He explained to Parliament that the Chinese had become 'rather annoyed' because Indian posts had been set up behind their own, and reassured any members who might have thought the Chinese tone dangerous. 'There is nothing to be alarmed at, although the [Chinese] note threatens all kinds of steps they might take,' he said. 'If they do take those steps we shall be ready for them.'[122] In June Nehru again assured Parliament that the position in the western sector was 'more advantageous to India than it was previously'.[123]

By this time another infantry battalion (5 Jat) had been inducted into Ladakh and deployed into the forward movement. Like the other three battalions, this was broken down into small post-garrisons and patrols; by mid-summer there were about sixty Indian posts in the sector. Facing these was a full Chinese division. This meant that the Indians were over all outnumbered by more than five to one; but the effective disparity between their strength and that of the Chinese was far greater. It was not only that the Chinese were concentrated where the Indians were scattered, or that they were able to move in trucks where the Indians had to trek on foot; the Chinese had all regular supporting arms for their troops, while the Indian 114 Brigade had nothing beyond one platoon of medium machine-guns. The Chinese could be seen ranging their heavy mortars and recoilless guns on the Indian posts, and their infantry was equipped with automatic rifles. The Indians had nothing heavier than three-inch mortars and most of their posts lacked even those; the troops were equipped with the .303 Lee-Enfield rifle which had seen action before the First World War.* The posts which the Indians set up were no more than platoon or sometimes section positions, linked weapon pits scraped out in ground that was frozen to within a few inches of the surface even in summer. The troops lived in tents or makeshift shelters of crates or parachutes, and they were dependent upon air supply for all maintenance.

The Chinese began to react vigorously on the ground early in 1962; where the Indians set up a post overlooking a Chinese position, the Chinese would promptly take up more positions around it. In April Peking informed India that border patrols, which China had suspended in 1959, were being resumed in the western sector from the Karakoram to the Kongka Pass; and warned that if the Indians persisted in their forward movement, patrolling would be resumed everywhere along the frontier. This note described how the Indian troops in the Chip Chap valley axis had taken up positions on two sides of the Chinese post there, and were 'pressing on the Chinese post and carrying out provocation'. (The Indian Army evidently had no reason to complain about lack of spirit on the part of the troops carrying out the forward policy.) Peking said that if such provocations continued, the Chinese troops

---

* Development of an indigenously manufactured automatic rifle had been begun in India in 1953, and by 1956 a few models had been made for trials. The rifle satisfied the Army's requirements, and it was decided in the Quartermaster-General's department that it was ready for production. In March 1958 a paper agreed jointly by the service chiefs of staff was sent to the Production Board, a panel under the chairmanship of Krishna Menon. This paper set out a programme for fully equipping the Army with the Indian automatic rifle in four years. No action was taken on the proposal, and it was not until the final stages of the border war of 1962 that Indian troops were issued with automatic rifles; then it was only a few dozen, and they were the gift of the U.S.A. and Britain.

would be compelled to defend themselves, and India would be responsible for the consequences.[124]

The Indian Government dismissed such warnings as bluff and threatening Chinese moves on the ground as bluster. Early in May Chinese troops advanced on one of the new Indian posts in the Chip Chap valley in assault formation, giving every indication that they meant to wipe it out. Western Command asked permission to withdraw the post, and the request was passed up to Nehru. He believed that the Chinese were making a show of force to test India's resolution and said that the post should stand fast and be reinforced. When the Chinese did not follow up their threatening moves, it was concluded in the Government and at Army H.Q. that the Prime Minister's judgment and nerve had been triumphantly vindicated, and that the basic premise of the forward policy had been confirmed. Further confirmation was drawn from the Galwan incident.

The Galwan valley appeared on Army H.Q.'s maps as one of the best routes along which troops could move into Chinese-held territory. The track through the valley was in fact extremely difficult, and the Chinese had had a post at the head of the valley, Samzungling, since at least 1959; nevertheless a patrol up the Galwan, with a view to establishing a post that would dominate Samzungling, was among the first forward moves ordered by Kaul in November 1961. The attempt to follow the valley up-river in the winter failed, the terrain being too difficult; and in April Army H.Q. ordered that another route be tried, this time over the hills from the south. Lieutenant-General Daulat Singh of Western Command demurred, warning that any move to threaten the well established Chinese post at Samzungling would almost certainly evoke a violent reaction. He pointed out that as the Chinese had given notice that they were resuming patrolling in this sector, a threat appeared to be building up to the Indian posts already established, and therefore everything should be done to consolidate these rather than try to set up more. He concluded that, in the circumstances, no Indian post could be established at Samzungling. Kaul overruled him. The Galwan River was an axis 'along which the Chinese can make a substantial advance', he replied, and therefore they must be forestalled.

Accordingly, a platoon of Gorkhas set out from Hot Springs, trekking over the forbidding ridges, and after more than a month emerged on the upper reaches of the Galwan River, taking up positions there on

July 5th. In so doing, they not only cut off a Chinese outpost that had been established farther downstream, but were able to hold up a small Chinese supply party. The first Chinese reaction was diplomatic, a note of 'strongest protest' on July 8th asking for immediate withdrawal of the Indian troops and warning that China 'will never yield before an ever-deeper armed advance by India, nor . . . give up its right to self-defence when unwarrantedly attacked'.[125] India replied that her forces 'have regularly been patrolling the Galwan valley and have never encountered any Chinese infiltrators' there, and also lodged 'an emphatic protest' against the Chinese reaction on the ground, describing it as 'unwarranted aggressive activity'. Warning that Peking would be entirely responsible for any untoward incident, the Indian note said that 'China should stop the incessant intrusions deeper inside Indian territory and ceaseless provocative activities against Indian border guards'.[126]

The Chinese reacted on the ground on July 10th, advancing on the Indian post with a company in assault formation and quickly building this up to battalion strength. Through loudspeakers the Chinese, with interpreters, tried to play on the Gorkhas' national feelings, proclaiming that China was a better friend to Nepal than was India, and berating them for folly in serving India's expansionist ambitions.* The Gorkhas, cocking their guns rather than their ears, lay low. Seeing this as the most serious confrontation yet, the Indian Government called the Chinese Ambassador to the External Affairs Ministry and warned that if the Chinese troops pressed any closer to the Galwan post the garrison would open fire. Furthermore, if the post were attacked, India would take retaliatory action against Chinese positions.[127] In a few days the Chinese did pull back a little from the Galwan post (they had been within a hundred yards of it); but they continued to surround it in relatively great strength, cutting it off from ground supply. Western Command signalled New Delhi that any attempt to reach the post by land would provoke a clash, and asked for air supply; the reply came back the same day, that the post was to be supplied by the land route. In the reading taken in New Delhi, an eyeball to eyeball

---

* India, like Britain, has Gorkhas in her army under an agreement with Nepal, and some disquiet was expressed in Nepal at this time about the use of these troops in Aksai Chin. Nepal wished to retain cordial relations with Peking and was not happy to see Gorkhas bayonet to bayonet with Chinese troops. Under the agreement India has an obligation to inform Nepal when Gorkhas are being sent on active service, but whether the forward policy would amount to active service would, of course, be a matter of interpretation.

confrontation had been relaxed when China blinked—by not attacking the Galwan post—and so the moral initiative must be maintained by challenging the besiegers with a land relief party. Another small force was therefore dispatched to the Galwan. It turned back in August, under Chinese guns, when the Chinese said that they would fire if it advanced any farther. The use of force was not practicable, Western Command reported—it was beyond the Indians' present capacity and might touch off open hostilities. The Galwan post was supplied by air until the morning of October 20th, when it was wiped out.

News of the Chinese investment of the Galwan post was published in India on July 11th in reports that presented this as a new and provocative Chinese advance into Indian territory. When later it was appreciated that the Chinese had not carried out their physical and diplomatic threats to attack the post, a wave of triumph swept the press and the politicians. A Congress M.P. said that the incident had raised the morale of the whole nation.[128] The Chinese withdrawal 'in the face of the determined stand of the small Indian garrison', as the *Hindu* put it, was taken to confirm the basic logic of the forward policy, that if the Indian troops were resolute, the Chinese would do no more than huff and puff; that in the arena of Aksai Chin, as on the level of governments, the Chinese would swerve away before impact. The orders which had been given to the Galwan garrison were extended to all Indian troops in the western sector. From 'fire only if fired upon' the orders were changed to 'fire if the Chinese press dangerously close to your positions'.

Nehru described the Indian actions at this time as a dual policy, with the military moves on the ground complemented by steady diplomatic pressure. In keeping with this concept, India in May revived and slightly modified the proposal that Nehru had put forward in November 1959 for joint withdrawals behind each other's claim line. This proposal, as Nehru now assured the Indian Parliament again,[129] meant a very large withdrawal for the Chinese and a very small withdrawal for the Indians. China had rejected this before, and New Delhi now sweetened the pill a little by embodying in the official proposal the suggestion, which Nehru had previously made only in a press conference, that pending settlement of the boundary question, India would 'permit . . . continued use of the Aksai Chin road for Chinese civilian traffic'.[130] It was hoped in New Delhi at this time that, with the establishment of Indian posts in Chinese-claimed territory, Peking would now be more ready to take what the Indians considered to be the best way of saving China's face. After again asserting India's readiness to risk war with China, Nehru said in the Lok Sabha, on the day that the withdrawal proposal was renewed to Peking: 'If one is prepared to recover [the areas occupied by China] and one is strong enough, other things also help in the process and it is possible that those things plus our preparation for any action may result in some kind of agreement for these areas to be liberated.'[131] This, read in the context of the note delivered to Peking on the same day, suggests that Nehru believed that India's resolute advance into Chinese-occupied territory would ultimately make China accept the necessity of complete withdrawal, and that he hoped that the few Indian posts already established might already have brought the Chinese to that position.

If Peking had accepted the proposal, it is most likely that Nehru would—as far as his extreme pliability to domestic pressures allowed—have taken a very distant interest in the nature of the traffic on the Chinese road. But in the Chinese perception of the situation, the proposal was as unreal, and as much of an affront, as it would have been to India if Peking had proposed that India withdraw all personnel, civilian and military, from the area south of the McMahon Line, subject to China's allowing India to use roads in NEFA for civilian traffic. 'Why should China need to ask India's permission for using its own road on its own territory?' Peking expostulated in reply. 'What an absurdity!'[132] If the Indian Government wished its proposal to be considered seriously, the Chinese suggested, it would have been prepared to apply the same principle to the eastern sector; but Nehru had of course ruled that out, assuring the Lok Sabha that 'we are not going to withdraw in the east.'[133] In the note reviving the proposal for joint withdrawal India had gone very close to threatening China with war, by quoting a remark that Nehru had made in the Lok Sabha on May 2nd: 'India does not want, and dislikes very much, a war with China. But that is not within India's control.'[134] In rejecting the proposal as 'unilaterally imposed submissive terms', Peking pointed out that China was not a defeated country, and declared that she would never submit before any threat of force.

New Delhi's conclusion from this exchange appears to have been that the forward policy had simply not yet brought enough pressure to bear, and must therefore be pursued until China accepted the need for withdrawal.

The Indian troops in the western sector were pressing hard, setting up their puny posts within near range of the Chinese, acting as if they were the vanguard of a powerful army rather than the stake in a wild political gamble. But the forward policy was by no means bold enough for the Government's domestic critics, who continued to demand stronger and quicker action against China. Defending itself, the Government began to play the same numbers game that Nehru had decried when his critics used it. Official spokesmen drew lines on maps to connect the new forward Indian posts, calculated the area thus enclosed, and claimed that more than a quarter of the area 'overrun' by the Chinese had been recovered.[135] An Indian journalist who enjoyed ready access to the Prime Minister and reciprocated with fulsome praise reported that the troops in the western sector had made 'a general advance over a wide front of 2,500 square miles' and complimented Nehru on 'a unique triumph for audacious Napoleonic planning'.[136] The real situation did not go entirely unreported; one political columnist with good military contacts wrote in August that the Chinese enjoyed a ten-to-one superiority in the western sector and had all the advantages of terrain and communications.[137] But this was an isolated report; other journalists were writing that the Indians were in superior strength and better equipped than the Chinese, and suggesting that the latter were garrison troops of poor fighting quality. Like most people, Indians have better hearing for what confirms their own wishes, and the optimistic version of the situation in the western sector was given wider credence.

That did not, however, satisfy the Government's critics or diminish the clamour in Parliament for yet stronger measures to expel the Chinese. If, as the Government said, the situation in the western sector had now changed in India's favour, why, the Opposition wanted to know, was the Army not being launched in a massive and immediate offensive to sweep the intruders back out of Indian soil? 'The bogey of Chinese superiority . . . should not worry our military experts,' an Opposition M.P. told the Lok Sabha in August; not only were Chinese lines of communication very long, but their army was distracted, too, by the threat of 'revolt of a dejected and frustrated population'.[138] The atmosphere was conducive to jingoism, and some members were carried away. 'Two hundred Indian soldiers are equal to two thousand of the Chinese,' another M.P. declared in the Lok Sabha's debate on the border situation in August. 'Why should we be afraid of them? Why are we not able to hurl them back?' The same member said that if only the Government would give the call, in six months 'a well-trained army of four million Hindus will march to the Himalayas and throw back the whole Chinese force'.[139] When the truth did make itself heard it was ignored. Earlier in the summer the Indian Ambassador in Washington, B. K. Nehru (another cousin of the Prime Minister's), said flatly in the course of a television interview that the Indian defence forces were so badly equipped that they could not ensure the security of the country. Questions were raised in Parliament about his statement; but although M.P.s pointed out how the Ambassador had contradicted the Prime Minister's repeated assurances that the Army was fully capable of defending the frontiers, they were more concerned to suggest that B. K. Nehru be disciplined for an indiscretion than to find out which of the two statements was true.

New Delhi's charge that it was the Chinese who were advancing in the western sector, not the Indians, boomeranged. It was as if three people were arguing on a party line. The Government accused China of further aggressive intrusions; thereupon its domestic critics attacked it for supinely allowing the Chinese to get away with new advances; Nehru would then back away from the Government's accusations, telling Parliament that it was 'hardly correct' to say that the Chinese had made 'a fresh intrusion', since all that had happened was that, in apprehensive reaction to Indian moves, the Chinese had set up outposts; then Peking would break in, saying that Nehru had 'unwittingly let out the truth'.[140]

For the critics, the confusion did not obscure the fact that the Chinese were still in occupation of Indian territory. 'How Long, How Long in Shame' cried the editor of the *Hindustan Times* in his column, would the country have to wait before the Government gave China visible evidence that it was 'determined to fight for its honour'?[141]

There were saner voices. In the Lok Sabha, a member argued that in the western sector what amounted to a ceasefire line had emerged, and that neither China nor India could violate it with impunity. He suggested that India should give China the same pledge as she had given Pakistan with respect to the Pakistani-held and Indian-claimed part of Kashmir: 'that we would not resort to force to liberate the occupied areas.' In Calcutta *Yugantar*, a daily newspaper which generally followed the Congress line, warned that 'if India is to build her social life anew, if the five-year plans are to be fulfilled, there must be a stop to our having to spend tens of millions of rupees to maintain the posture of military strength along two thousand miles of our Himalayan boundaries', and it urged the Government to negotiate.[142]

But anxiety that the Government would negotiate and insistence that it should not were overwhelmingly the dominant attitudes in Parliament. The perennial misgivings that Nehru would seek a settlement by appeasement were revived by an ambiguous-sounding note that India sent to China on July 26th, 1962. The first clash since the Kongka Pass incident had occurred in the Chip Chap valley on July 21st, with two Indian soldiers wounded. The Chinese protest about this incident, lodged the same day, was minatory. 'China is not willing to fight with India, and the Sino-Indian boundary question can be settled only through routine negotiations,' it said; but while China had exercised self-restraint, it could not sit idle 'while its frontier guards are being encircled and annihilated by aggressors. At this critical moment the Chinese Government demands that the Indian Government immediately order the Indian troops to stop attacking the [Chip Chap] post and withdraw from the area. . . . If India should ignore the warning . . . and persist in its own way India must bear full responsibility for all the consequences.'[143]

The Indian reply, dispatched on July 26th, was notably placatory, and put what appeared to be a new kind of emphasis on the distinction which India had been drawing between the '1956 Chinese claim' and the '1960 Chinese claim'. Until now this distinction, and the charge that China had moved into the area between the two lines, had been made only to suggest that the Chinese were continuing to advance their claims and their positions; but this Indian note merely chided. 'It is true that the Government of India contest the validity of the 1956 Chinese map claim, but the Chinese local forces should not go beyond their own claim line confirmed by Mr Chou En-lai.' The note went on immediately to remind Peking that under certain conditions India was prepared to 'enter into further discussions' on the boundary question.[144]

The presence of Mikoyan, first deputy Prime Minister of the U.S.S.R., in New Delhi that week seems the likeliest explanation for the positive tone of the note. The Indian Government attached great importance to the Russian sympathy for the Indian position in the dispute and the Russians were urging negotiations. Another factor, quickly noted in India, might have been that Krishna Menon had just returned from the Laos conference in Geneva where he had had discussions with Marshal Chen Yi. But whatever induced the change in tone, there was another uproar as soon as the text of the July 26th note was released. It was read as a covert offer that if China would withdraw marginally in the western sector, to positions behind their '1956 claim line', India would begin negotiations on the boundaries.

In Parliament the note was described as disgraceful, 'a most shocking and surprising document';[145] but that does not adequately suggest the outrage it aroused. The *Hindustan Times* headed its comment THE ROAD TO DISHONOUR:

> The Government of India in its infinite wisdom has deemed the time opportune for a complete reversal of its China policy. It has all but sanctified the illegal gains of Chinese aggression in Ladakh as the price for the opening of a new round of negotiations with the overlords of Peking. In so doing it has broken faith with the people of India—the people and its Parliament.[146]

Answering such attacks, Nehru rebuked those who had had 'the temerity to suggest that we are going to take some action which would bring dishonour to India', rather than which he would prefer to be 'reduced to dust and ashes'. He then explained that there had been 'some misunderstanding and misinterpretation' of the Government's position, and he restated that.[147]

The Indian note of July 26th reintroduced the subject of discussions; and for the next ten weeks, while on the frontiers war drew steadily closer, the two sides were exchanging notes on possible further meetings between their representatives. This was the last chance for a peaceful resolution of the dispute or even for leaving it where it stood without resolution or conflict, and it must be followed in detail. As before, the basic Indian position and the modulations that this exchange produced were shrouded in intricate semantic formulations, a kind of cipher that can be understood only if the key is constantly in mind.

The nub of the July 26th note was the statement that India would be prepared to resume discussions on the basis of the 1960 officials' report, 'as soon as the current tensions have been eased and the appropriate climate is created'. It was from this and the apparent emphasis on a limited Chinese withdrawal to their '1956 claim line' that Indian critics concluded that their Government was seeking to reverse its whole policy. But when read in the context of the preceding diplomatic correspondence—as, of course, Peking would have been expected to do—it can be seen that the note did not change India's consistent position. New Delhi was prepared to talk 'as soon . . . as the appropriate climate is created'; but it had repeatedly been stated that the only way for China to create such a climate would be for her to withdraw from the territory which India claimed in the west. In the Indian phrasing, this was called 'creating a favourable climate for negotiations regarding the boundary' by 'a restoration of the *status quo* through the withdrawal of Chinese forces from Indian territory'.*

The Indian position was solid. Before there could be any talks or negotiations on the boundary question China must withdraw all personnel from the territory which India claimed. When that evacuation was completed, India would meet China at the conference table—*but only to discuss minor modifications of the boundary India claimed*. The Peking *People's Daily* saw the point: 'If the Chinese side should accept such conditions for negotiation, the Indian side would realise its territorial claims on China without any negotiations. In that case, would not negotiation itself become unnecessary?'[148]

Nehru reaffirmed that position in Parliament on August 13th, to meet the attacks that were being made on the Government on account of the July 26th note. He read a prepared statement (unusual for him): 'It is clear to us that any discussion on the basis of the report of the officials cannot start unless present tensions are removed and the *status quo* of the boundary which existed before and which has since been altered by force is restored.' That meant no meeting with China until the Chinese withdrew from the territory India claimed in the western sector. The statement then went on to declare India's readiness to embark on a *different kind of discussion*; but that was to counter a Chinese diplomatic move.

In replying to the July 26th note, Peking had reciprocated the reasonable and positive tone set by the Indians, while continuing to reject the Indian proposal for what to China was 'a one-sided withdrawal from large tracts of its own territory'. Peking thus rejected *the condition* that India had put upon the resumption of discussions, but at the same time accepted the proposal for discussions:

* For example, in a note of March 13th, 1962: 'The Government of India hope that the Government of China . . . will withdraw from this territory [which has always been the territory of India] and restore the *status quo*. Such a restoration of the *status quo* through the withdrawal of Chinese from Indian territory, into which they have intruded since 1957, is an essential step for the creation of a favourable climate for any negotiations between the two Governments regarding the boundary.'[149]

The Chinese Government approves of the suggestion put forth by
the Indian Government for further discussions on the Sino-Indian
boundary question on the basis of the report of the officials of the
two countries. There need not and should not be any pre-conditions for such discussions. As a matter of fact, if only the Indian
side stop advancing into Chinese territory, a relaxation of the
border situation will be affected at once. Since neither the Chinese
nor the Indian Government wants war, and since both Governments wish to settle the boundary question peacefully through
negotiations, further discussions on the Sino-Indian boundary
question on the basis of the report of the officials should not be put
off any longer. The Chinese Government proposes that such
discussions be held as soon as possible, and that the level, date,
place and other procedural matters for these discussions be immediately decided upon by consultations through diplomatic
channels.[150]

India was thus left like an angler whose hook has been taken by a fish
he does not in the least wish to land.

From New Delhi's point of view, it was plain that discussions with
the Chinese would serve no purpose. The only way to a settlement
acceptable to India was for China to agree to the Nehru proposal for
mutual withdrawal behind the other's claim line in the western sector;
and that China had repeatedly and explicitly rejected as 'one-sided
withdrawal from large tracts of its own territory'. Furthermore, to
enter into discussions with China in the absence of her agreement to
withdraw would have been to bring down on Nehru and the Government opprobrious charges of appeasement and breach of faith from an
aroused and resentful political opinion in India. Domestic considerations thus ruled out the resumption of a dialogue with China on the
basis of the officials' report (i.e. on the merits of the boundary dispute),
which the context showed would anyway be fruitless. But other
considerations, less immediate but still weighty, suggested that India
should not appear as curtly refusing to talk to China at all.

In the arena of world opinion India had all the advantages, so to
speak, of playing on the home field. The stands were packed with
supporters while India, wearing the democratic colours, played skil-
fully and resolutely against the brawnier team. The press and governments of the Western world cheered India on, as they saw her pluckily

standing her ground against what they believed to be the expansionist drive of China. Western opinion had long ago placed these two as the finalists in the Asian political league; and now the contest had been brought on, it seemed, by China's sudden seizure of Indian territory. The historical and documentary arguments about the boundaries were too obscure for any but specialists to follow, and even to them the archives that might show which side of the argument was nearer the truth were closed. It was a matter of taking the Indians or the Chinese at their word, and in the West generally there was no hesitation. Although the invasion of Goa had injured India's reputation, the consequent new scepticism about Indian attitudes and actions did not extend to her version of the rights and wrongs of the quarrel with China. Felix Greene explained the American reaction:

> So solidly built into our consciousness is the concept that China is conducting a rapacious and belligerent foreign policy that whenever a dispute arises in which China is involved, she is instantly assumed to have provoked it. All commentaries, 'news reports', and scholarly interpretations are written on the basis of this assumption. The cumulative effect of this only further reinforces the original hypothesis so that it is used again next time with even greater effect.[151]

The Americans were especially conditioned to the view that India and China were racing for the economic and political leadership of Asia. Calling for increased support for India's five-year plans in 1959 the then Senator J. F. Kennedy said: 'We want India to win that race with China . . . if China succeeds and India fails the economic-development balance of power will shift against us.'[152] President Kennedy's personal estimation of Nehru had been sharply lowered by the Prime Minister's visit to Washington in November 1961; the President later said it was 'the worst head-of-state visit' he had had, and described his conversations with Nehru as 'like trying to grab something in your hand only to have it turn out to be just fog'.[153] But if that meeting, according to Arthur Schlesinger in his chronicle of the Kennedy administration, left the President disappointed in his hopes that India would in the next few years be 'a great affirmative force in the world or even in south Asia', it of course remained American policy to help Indian development and back her in her quarrel with China. India's mounting antagonism towards China after 1959 did perhaps as much as the

changed American attitude to non-alignment to ease and augment the
flow of American economic assistance. Senator Sparkman, then
acting chairman of the Foreign Relations Committee, said in June
1962: 'We know right now that India is pressing very hard against
Communist China upon her north-eastern frontier,' and argued that
it would be unwise to discourage India by reducing aid 'at the very
time that she is moving in the direction that we have been wanting
her to move for a long time'.[154]

The British Government's support for India seemed as solid as that
of the United States, but it appears to have covered a division of
opinion in Whitehall. Some officials, notably in the Foreign Office,
pointed out that India's account of the historical argument for the
boundaries which she claimed was inflated; after all, the McMahon
Line and the attempts to get China to accept a boundary line in the
north-west had once been the Foreign Office's concern, and its archives
held the records. They therefore recommended somewhat less than
categorical British support for the Indian claims. The Commonwealth
Office, on the other hand—and strongly, it must be assumed, the High
Commission in India—was urging that whatever the ancient history
of the boundaries might be, the here and now of Britain's interest lay
in wholehearted and unqualified support of India. Inevitably, that
expedient course was followed.

But, if India could rely on the committed support of the Western
world, there were grounds for misgivings in New Delhi over the
attitude of the Afro-Asian countries. 'Our neighbours, our friends are
non-aligned even on the question of aggression by China against
India . . . they are leaning on the side of China,' Ashok Mehta complained,[155] and newspaper editorials declared that India was isolated,
with 'almost no friend in Asia'.[156] Afro-Asian governments, some of
them resentful anyway about what they took to be India's assumption
of leadership of the non-aligned world, were not as ready as the West
to take India's case at face value. Prepared to listen to China's explanation and arguments with open minds, they found in them ground for
questioning whether the general picture of reasonable, wronged India
and aggressive, intransigent China was an undistorted reflection of
reality. Finding themselves in the deep waters of the diplomatic-
historical argument between New Delhi and Peking, some of the
Afro-Asian governments clung to the one solid piece of ground they
could see, the question of negotiations; and there it seemed that China

wanted India to negotiate a settlement, while India was refusing. India proclaimed that in fact it was the other way round; but the realization that there were some who questioned the Indian version must have made New Delhi aware of the risk of too bluntly refusing to take up the thread of discussions with Peking.

To navigate between the international Scylla and domestic Charybdis in 1960 Nehru and his advisers had drawn the distinction between 'talks' and 'negotiations', so that he could receive Chou En-lai in New Delhi without appearing to go back on the basic position that the boundaries were not negotiable. Now, with China pressing for resumption of talks and domestic opinion angrily insisting that there should be none, New Delhi produced another subtle formulation. The statement which Nehru read in Parliament on August 13th, after reaffirming that there could be no discussion on the merits of the dispute (i.e. on the basis of the officials' report) until China had withdrawn, went on to state:

> The Government of India is prepared to discuss what measures should be taken to remove the tensions that exist in this [western] region and to create the appropriate climate for further discussions. This would be preliminary to any further discussions on the basis of the report of the officials with a view to resolving the differences between the two Governments on the boundary question.[157]

This meant that India was prepared to talk to China—*but not about the alignment of the boundaries*. Instead, India would discuss with Peking the steps by which Chinese withdrawal from the territory which India claimed could be effected. In other words, surrender still had to be unconditional, but the Chinese were welcome to make a preliminary visit to New Delhi in order to discuss the details of the surrender ceremony proper.

In the same speech Nehru accused China of setting conditions that made talks impossible. After the Geneva conference on Laos a fortnight before, Chen Yi had given an interview to a European broadcasting agency in which, when asked about the Indian proposal for mutual withdrawal, he said: 'To wish that Chinese troops would withdraw from their own territory is impossible. That would be against the will of six hundred and fifty million Chinese. No force in the world could oblige us to do anything of this kind.'[158] Quoting that statement, Nehru said that it 'means laying down pre-conditions which make it impossible for us to carry on discussions and negotiations'.[159] The point was made again in a note embodying the Indian counter-proposal for talks, dispatched on August 22nd. Chen Yi's remark and Peking's refusal to consider the Nehru proposal for mutual with-drawal were described as 'pre-conditions which contradict the repeated Chinese statements that they want to settle the boundary question peacefully through further discussions. And the note concluded: 'It is obvious that it is the Chinese who are laying down impossible pre-conditions and asking for acceptance of the Chinese claim regarding the boundary in this [western] region before further discussions start.'[160]

The Indian argument was that to start discussions before the Chinese withdrawal from the Indian-claimed territory would be 'pre-judging or acceptance of the Chinese claim'. Chinese withdrawal before discus-sions would, of course, have have been 'pre-judging or acceptance of the Indian claim'; but as in New Delhi's eyes the Indian claim line was in fact the international boundary that was as things should be. New Delhi's line of argument reflected the conviction that the disputed territory was wholly and absolutely Indian, and the corollary that China's presence there was a standing act of aggression. That made all protestations from Peking about China's desire for peace and willing-ness to settle the boundaries by mutual consent sound like blatant hypocrisy. On the other side, the Chinese belief that Aksai Chin had never been Indian and their conviction that the offer to waive their claims to territory south of the McMahon Line was reasonable, and indeed magnanimous, made Indian protestations seem just as hypo-critical; while the forward movements of Indian troops made Nehru's reassurances about peaceful methods sound like the crassest deceit. Nehru himself once glimpsed that contradiction of perception: 'If you start thinking as the Chinese do,' he said in May 1962, ' . . . thinking on the assumption that the territory in Ladakh, especially in the Aksai Chin area, is theirs and has been theirs, well, everything we do is an offence to them. But if we start on the basis of thinking that the territory is ours, as it is, then everything the Chinese do is an offence. It depends on with what assumption you have started.'[161] But that moment of insight was not allowed to inform New Delhi's handling of the dispute, which continued unwaveringly on its collision course.

The nuance of the Government's position—that it had agreed to discussions but not to the discussions which the Chinese wanted—was not appreciated by its critics at home, and attacks continued on Nehru for having agreed to sit down with an aggressor who was still in possession of Indian territory. But that was just the sort of bowling that the Prime Minister liked, and the batting conditions suited him perfectly. He laid about him. 'This is a childish and infantile attitude,' he told the Opposition in Parliament.

> First of all, there is a world of difference between negotiations and talks, a world of difference. One should always talk, whatever happens, whatever the position and whatever the chances. If I have the chance to talk I will talk to [the Chinese]. It is quite absurd not to talk . . . talking must be encouraged whenever possible. Negotiation is a very formal thing: it requires a very suitable background; it should not be taken up unless a suitable background comes. . . . Talking is an entirely different thing.

Nehru had been irritated by complaints about his having had the departing Chinese Ambassador to lunch and by attacks on Krishna Menon for having been photographed having a drink in Geneva with Chen Yi; he twitted his opponents with their ignorance of the ways of diplomacy in the modern world. 'They seem to think we must bring about untouchability in our [international] relations,' he said.[162]

In discussions in Parliament on the boundary situation Nehru was not defending only his Government's policy towards China. This issue acted as a prism, focusing a diverse range of complaints about and disapproval of the Government, as was shown in a motion put forward in the Lok Sabha's debate on the border situation in mid-August. This called for

> (a) 'Immediate breaking off of diplomatic relations with China'. (By this time the two ambassadors had been withdrawn; India's had been recalled first, but Nehru was adamant then and even at the height of the border war that diplomatic relations should be maintained, to keep open a channel of communication.)
> (b) 'Calling of a conference of free countries of South-East Asia to discuss common security measures'. (Two criticisms of Government policy were implied here: first, a failure to make India's case in the dispute understood in South-East Asia; secondly, its reluctance to take the lead in forming a defensive alliance against China with the smaller countries of the region.)
> (c) 'To arrange for military aid from other countries to gear up

our defence'. (It was fundamental to the policy of non-alignment, as Nehru had applied it up to this time, that India would not accept military assistance from anyone. Nehru argued that to accept military assistance would be tantamount to joining one of the cold-war blocks, and that the only way to reinforce the country's defences without jeopardizing its independence was to develop domestic industrial and ordinance capacity. He saw the reiterated demand that India should seek military aid as the expression of the basic dissatisfaction on the Right with the posture of non-alignment. He said that it was a sign of moral weakness to seek help from abroad, to think of enlisting in 'some military bloc to save us'. He would not let India 'rely on a foreign army to save its territory', he said, 'even if disaster comes to us on the frontier'.)[163]

(d) 'To improve our relations with Nepal'. (Since King Mahendra had aborted the democratic experiment in Nepal with a palace coup two years before, New Delhi had been outspokenly critical of his regime. Nepali émigrés had been allowed to operate freely across the Indo-Nepal border, making terrorist raids and seeking to arouse resistance to the King. By this time, August 1962, the Indian Government was trying to mend its fences with Nepal, however, and cracking down on the émigrés.)

(e) 'The Prime Minister himself should take over the Defence portfolio.' (The main focus of the misgivings in Parliament about India's defence preparedness—which in no way muffled demands for military action against China—was on Krishna Menon. Many on the Congress benches, as well as in the parties of the Right Opposition, believed him to be at the very least a crypto-Communist, and he was suspected of influencing Nehru in the direction of appeasement. The general respect and affection for Nehru, on the other hand, was still high and even some of his strongest critics used to suggest that he was being guided amiss rather than wrong-headed. He had held the Defence portfolio twice before.)

(f) 'The Prime Minister should come out with a categorical statement that there will be no negotiations with China unless and until they withdraw from Indian territory.' (As has been seen, this was the basic and unchanging Indian position; but categorical statements on any subject, even this, were alien to Nehru's style, and the nearest he would go to stating the position squarely was to say: 'I think the present situation in the frontier is such that we cannot have any serious talks with the Chinese.')[164]

* * * * * * * * * * *

In the remote wastes of the western sector, meanwhile, what Nehru had as early as November 1961 called a criss-cross of military posts[165] had become in places just that. In the Chip Chap valley the posts and picquets of the Indians and Chinese were numerous—between twenty and thirty—and closely interlaid; sometimes the Indian Air Force on its supply missions dropped loads on Chinese positions by mistake, and Peking irritably protested at these unwanted gifts of 'stuffed gunnies and wooden cases'.[166] On other occasions, the Indian troops would have to recover their air-dropped supplies from under the muzzles of Chinese guns. Firing from both sides had become almost commonplace. For the most part it was still harassing or ranging fire; but at the beginning of September, in the Chip Chap valley, the Indians put into effect the orders that they had been under since the Galwan valley confrontation began five weeks earlier. The Chinese advanced menacingly close to one of the Indian posts, disregarding orders to halt and back off, and the garrison opened fire at point-blank range. Several Chinese were killed, their bodies being left just outside the Indian perimeter. The Chinese chargé d'affaires was called to the Ministry in New Delhi, informed of the incident and asked to arrange for collection of the Chinese dead.*

Farther south, the area of greatest activity was in the Spangur gap; the Gurkhas had set up positions between the Pangong and Spangur Lakes, on which they patrolled in motor-boats which had been dropped to them in components. By the end of August the Indians had placed nearly forty posts in Chinese-claimed territory. Many of these were section picquets, manned by ten or a dozen men; others were platoon posts of between thirty and fifty. Outnumbered and out-gunned by an adversary with immense advantages of mobility and tactical situation, the Indian troops were more than vulnerable, they

---

* The Indian Government did not publicize this incident, preferring to let it pass in silence unless Peking wanted to let it out, but it was reported in *The Times* and the *Baltimore Sun* of September 12th, 1962, and the *Hindustan Times* of September 15th. The incident is not mentioned in the exchanges published in the Indian White Papers, but the *People's Daily*, writing of the final phase of the forward policy, later said that 'many of our soldiers were killed or wounded'.[167]

were helpless; the only questions, if they were attacked, were how long
they could resist, and how many Chinese they could kill before being
wiped out themselves. They were hostages to the conviction of Nehru
and his associates in New Delhi, civilian and military, that China would
never attack. After a tour of the western sector in June, Kaul reported:

> 'It is better for us to establish as many posts as we can in Ladakh,
> even though in penny packets, rather than wait for a substantial
> build-up, as I am convinced that the Chinese will not attack any
> of our positions even if they are relatively weaker than theirs.'[168]

Earlier, Nehru, rebuking his critics for urging the Government on
to more drastic measures, had rejected the thought of what he called
adventurist action, saying that it would not be fair to the Indian troops,
'brave and fine men';[169] but by the end of the summer there had been
a marked change in his attitude. 'We built a kind of rampart on this
part of Ladakh and put up numerous military posts, small ones and
big ones,' he said in Parliament in August. 'It is true that these posts
are in constant danger of attack with larger numbers. Well, it does not
matter. We have taken the risk and we have moved forward, and we
have effectively stopped their further forward march. . . . If [the
Chinese] want to they can overwhelm some of our military posts.
That does not mean we are defeated. We shall face them with much
greater problems and face them much more stoutly.'[170] Thus, it cannot
be said that Nehru was ignorant of the situation in the western sector or
that he failed to appreciate the risk to which the Indian troops were
exposed.

General Daulat Singh of Western Command was, on the other hand,
still by no means reconciled to the sacrifice of his troops in a gamble
that he saw as irrational and hopeless. In mid-August he wrote to
Army H.Q. pointing out the enormous superiority of the Chinese in
the western sector and the helplessness of the Indian posts which,
anchored as they were to the valley floors by the need for proximity
to their dropping zones, were dominated by the Chinese from higher
ground. 'Militarily we are in no position to defend what we possess,
leave alone force a showdown,' he wrote; and therefore it was vital
that no clash should be provoked. He deduced from the experience of
the past three years that 'China does not wish war with India on the
border issue provided we do not disturb the *status quo*'. But he argued
that as the Aksai Chin road was a vital strategic link for the Chinese,

they would react forcefully to Indian moves which threatened it, however distantly. He proposed therefore that, until Indian strength in the western sector was compatible to that of the Chinese (and for that he said a division of four brigades with all supporting arms was needed), the forward policy should be suspended. Some political solution should be found for extricating the beleaguered Galwan valley garrison; and he noted that the Chinese had made plain that, far from interfering with the Indians' withdrawal from the post, they would welcome it. Daulat Singh concluded with a lesson for his civilian masters:

> It is imperative that political direction is based on military means. If the two are not coordinated there is a danger of creating a situation where we may lose both in the material and moral sense much more than we already have. Thus, there is no short cut to military preparedness to enable us to pursue objectively our present policy aimed at refuting the illegal Chinese claim over our territory.

Daulat Singh had to wait nearly three weeks for a reply from the General Staff. When it came, it declared that events had justified the forward policy, and that its continuance was vital 'to stake our claim, as unless this is done [the Chinese] have a habit of pouring into any vacuum'. There was no mention of the reinforcements which Daulat Singh had said were essential even to allow him to maintain his present positions (four infantry battalions, a mountain artillery regiment and medium machine-guns); and the reply concluded that if a 'showdown is forced upon us we must do the best we can under the circumstances'.

At about this time a senior officer of the General Staff, on a visit to the eastern sector, was reported to have reassured officers there who thought the Chinese too strong to be tackled that experience in Ladakh had shown that 'a few rounds fired at them would make them run away'.

As August passed into September, the Chinese protests became more threatening. 'Shooting and shelling are no child's play and he who plays with fire will eventually be consumed by fire,' Peking wrote in mid-September. 'If the Indian side should insist on threatening by armed force the Chinese border defence forces . . . and thereby rouse their resistance, it must bear the responsibility for all the consequences arising therefrom.'[171]

Part III

THE VIEW FROM PEKING

Nehru is a rebel against the movement for national independence, a blackguard who undermines the progress of the people's liberation movement, a loyal slave of imperialism.

1949: *World Culture*, Shanghai.[1]

Nehru is a friend to China and an opponent of the imperialist policy of war and aggression.

1959: The *People's Daily*, Peking.[2]

It is Nehru who has refused negotiations. It is Nehru who has given the order to fight. He is bellicose to the bone.

1962: The *People's Daily*, Peking.[3]

There have been two strains in China's attitude towards India: first, the Marxist-Leninist perception, placing India in historical and dialectical context; secondly, the relationship with the Indian Government as a neighbour and fellow Asian power. To begin with, these were distinct and divergent; but events — and especially the boundary dispute — made them converge, so that India's actions became in China's view the demonstration of her political nature, taking her ineluctably into collision with China.

When in the late 1940s the Chinese Communists looked away from the turbulence in China itself, from which their own triumph was by then speedily emerging, they had no difficulty in identifying India's stage of political development. Nehru, who had long been in a relationship of mutual admiration with Chiang Kai-shek,[4] could have been the prototype of the national bourgeois leader, and the Congress Party a paradigm of the Kuomintang at an earlier stage of its development. To point the parallel, the Indian Government between 1948 and 1951 was using the army to put down a Communist-led uprising in the Telengana district of Hyderabad, where peasants had seized land and set up their own administration. It seemed that the Indian revolution might have begun. On receiving congratulations from the Indian Communists, Mao Tse-tung replied: 'I firmly believe that relying on the brave Communist Party of India and the unity and struggle of all Indian patriots, India will certainly not remain long under the yoke of imperialism and its collaborators. Like free China, a free India will one day emerge in the Socialist and People's Democratic family.'[5]

In her shaping international relations, too, India seemed to be setting out on the anti-revolutionary path. The United States, which had supported Chiang Kai-shek to what seemed — prematurely — the bitter end, was now preparing to support Nehru. 'It is on India that America has pinned her real hope,' a Chinese Communist journal noted in 1950. 'That is why the United States is giving priority to India in its Point Four and other schemes of assistance. Here it is a matter of

Nehru weighing his desire for U.S. assistance against his need to assume the hypocritical role of a progressive in order to deceive the Indian people.'[6]

India's apparent pursuance of Britain's Himalayan policy, to the extent of encouraging Tibetan separatism, went to confirm the Chinese Communists' judgment of the political character of the Nehru Government.* 'Nehru and company are openly engineering a cleavage between the different peoples in China . . . undermining their unity and interfering in China's internal affairs by declaring in the name of a foreign country that Tibet has never recognized Chinese suzerainty,' the *People's Daily* wrote in September 1949.[7] In the same month a Shanghai journal accused Nehru and India of serving 'the Anglo-American imperialist designs for the annexation of Tibet', and of themselves nourishing imperialist intentions. The imperialists, it concluded, had already made Nehru their substitute for Chiang Kai-shek.[8]

China's suspicions about India's intentions towards Tibet must have been confirmed by the Indian *démarche* over the Chinese Army's move into Tibet in 1950. But the diplomatic exchanges over that incident in fact, as has been seen,† marked a turning-point in India's policy, and the barometer for Sino-Indian relations was now to mark fair weather. On the broader diplomatic stage, China was finding that the new Indian Government was being helpful.

India had recognized the People's Republic in December 1949, the second country to do so,‡ and from that time she had been active in urging the case for making the new Government in Peking the representative of China in the United Nations. From the outbreak of war in Korea in June 1950, India exerted herself diplomatically to end it, and to head off the war between China and the U.S.A. which the deployment of the 7th Fleet in defence of Formosa seemed to make likely. These efforts in the cause of peace were welcomed in Peking. At the beginning of October China tried to use India as a hot line to Washington. Panikkar, the Indian Ambassador, was told by Chou En-lai that if

---

* The Chinese were not the only ones to notice the continuity of the new India's Himalayan policies. Writing in New Delhi in 1953, an American student of international affairs noted 'striking similarities between [India's] Tibetan policy and the one pursued by Britain when she was mistress of India'.[9]

† See p. 71 above.

‡ Burma was the first. India would have recognized Peking sooner, according to Krishna Menon, but out of diplomatic courtesy was waiting to let Britain do so first. Finally the Indians lost patience with Ernest Bevin's shilly-shallying.[10]

American forces crossed the Thirty-eighth Parallel, China would be forced to intervene in Korea.[11] It was not India's fault that that attempt failed; the Americans would heed no warnings. India played an important role in the negotiations to achieve a ceasefire in Korea, and evolved the formula on prisoner-of-war repatriation which at last broke the deadlock. China criticized India's role in those negotiations, but continued to approve the general line of her foreign policy.

The middle 1950s were the years of *Hindee Chinee bhai-bhai*. At the Bandung Conference of 1955, however, there was a muted but, on the Chinese side, much resented crossing of lines. Nehru quite openly tried to take Chou En-lai under his wing, disregarding, perhaps naïvely, the implication of superiority that this apparent kindliness must carry. Indians have often recalled this as one more incident meriting Chinese gratitude, but to the Chinese it must have appeared as the height of presumption, and the recollection of the incident could still irritate Chou ten years later. He recalled the incident to Pakistani journalists in China in 1965, commenting on Nehru's 'arrogance',[12] and at about the same time told some visiting Ceylonese politicians: 'I have never met a more arrogant man than Nehru.'[13] There was more to this than personal friction, of course. Panikkar had quickly understood, when he took up his post as Indian Ambassador to China, that his hosts looked at his country very much *de haut en bas*. The attitude towards India, he recalled, while genuinely friendly, was inclined to be a little patronizing. 'It was the attitude of a brother who was considerably older, and well-established in the world, prepared to give his advice to a younger brother struggling to make his way. [The] independence of India was welcome, but of course it was understood that China, as the recognized Great Power in Asia after the war, expected India to know her place.'[14] Panikkar described this as 'the Kuomintang attitude', but it appears to have been one of the things that did not change when the Communists took power.

In the Indian perception, however, India and China were more like twins in standing; and if there was seniority, then it was certainly on India's side. Nehru, after all, had been renowned in the world, his books read, his fortunes followed, when Chou En-lai was still no more than one of Mao Tse-tung's guerrilla commanders, unknown outside China, a Che Guevara of the 1930s.* By the time of the Bandung

* Edgar Snow recalled: 'Chou had been the first Communist leader I encountered when I crossed the Red Lines in 1936. He was in command of an East Front Red Army in a tiny

Conference, Nehru was at the peak of his influence and esteem in the international community; and for him personally the Asian-African conference seemed the triumph of a cause he had striven for since the Congress of Oppressed Peoples in Brussels, nearly thirty years before, where the idea of an Afro-Asian group of nations co-operating with each other had been born.[15] The Communist leaders of China, on the other hand, were still rather an unknown quantity, and Bandung (if the Geneva Conference on Indo-China of 1954 is counted a primarily European performance) was their debut on the Asian international scene. In the Indian view, and that of Western observers too, it had been largely through India's efforts that 'Communist China acquired a measure of respectability throughout Asia'.[16] Small wonder, then, that at Bandung it was Nehru who comported himself as 'the elder brother who was considerably older and well established in the world, prepared to give his advice to a younger brother struggling to make his way'. To Chou En-lai and his colleagues it must have seemed grotesque, however, that the Indian and national-bourgeois Nehru should aspire to be their sponsor.

Irritation at Nehru's and India's assumption of a right to leadership in Asia did not, however, affect the Chinese Government's policy; most probably their own confidence in the power of the revolution, and of China, kept their reaction more often amused than piqued. The Chinese gave Nehru full marks for his foreign policy. He was keeping a wary distance from the imperialists' bloc and denying it bases in India; he was quick to denounce their aggressions, as he did in the Suez war of 1956 and then the Anglo-American intervention in the Middle East of 1958; he was constant in his support of Peking's right to the China seat in the U.N. Nehru, as the *People's Daily* summed it up, was 'a friend to China and an opponent to the imperialist policy of war and aggression'.[17] Nor was this unexpected. Nehru's policies and attitudes were wholly in keeping with the Leninist reading of his character and role as leader of a nationalist bourgeois Government. 'In modern times, the national bourgeoisie of the colonial and semi-colonial countries, because of their contradictions with imperialism and the feudal forces, can take part in the revolutionary anti-imperialist

---

cave village north of Yenan. I had just entered camp when a slender figure in an old cotton uniform came out to greet me, brought his cloth-soled shoes together and touched his faded red-starred cap in a smart salute. . . . That was Chou En-lai, the Red bandit for whose head Chiang Kai-shek was then offering eighty thousand dollars.'[18]

and anti-feudal struggle during certain historical periods and to a certain extent, and therefore play a progressive role in history.'[19]

In this stage of their development, which in the Leninist scheme is labelled progressive nationalism, national bourgeois governments can not only play a constructive role; they also have a claim to Communist support. They reflect a temporary but valid alliance between the bourgeoisie and a part of the exploited classes, in the first stage of the struggle against imperialism.

But governments and leaders of this stamp are essentially of dual character, and the progressive Jekyll can quickly become the reactionary Hyde:

> The bourgeoisie of the colonial and semi-colonial countries, because of their class status, are inclined to compromise with imperialism and feudalism and are liable to waver in the anti-imperialist and anti-feudal revolution. One section, the big bourgeoisie, whose interests are closely connected with those of imperialism and domestic feudalism, are the reactionaries among the bourgeoisie. Under certain circumstances they may join in the national-independence movement but, when the broad masses of the people have really stood up, when class struggle becomes acute, and when bribed by the imperialists, then they will betray the revolution, suppressing the people, the Communist Party and the progressive forces at home and selling out to imperialism and opposing the socialist countries abroad.[20]

In the Chinese view, Nehru began his Jekyll–Hyde metamorphosis early in 1959, with the rebellion in Tibet.

The news in March 1959 that the revolt of the Khamba tribes of eastern Tibet had spread to the west, that there had been fighting in Lhasa and that the Dalai Lama was fleeing towards India, had aroused again all the Indian suspicion and resentment of the Chinese presence in Tibet. Nehru was caught once more in the dilemma that strong political pressures, as well as his own reactions, called for some words at least of sympathy and support for the Tibetan rebels; while considerations of diplomatic propriety pointed to keeping silent on a matter which India had recognized as China's business. He expressed the predicament in Parliament:

> 'We have no desire whatever to interfere in Tibet; we have every

desire to maintain the friendship between India and China; but at
the same time we have every sympathy for the people of Tibet, and
we are greatly distressed at their helpless plight. We hope still that
the authorities of China, in their wisdom, will not use their great
strength against the Tibetans, but will win them to friendly co-
operation in accordance with the assurances they have themselves
given about the autonomy of the Tibet region. Above all, we
hope that the present fighting and killing will cease.'[21]

With a more-in-sorrow-than-in-anger analysis, the *People's Daily*
rebutted Nehru's argument;* but the Chinese showed more concern
at India's actions than at Nehru's words. They had no objection, as
Chou En-lai said, to India's granting the Dalai Lama sanctuary, that
was normal international practice;[22] but they complained that 'the
impressive welcome extended to the Dalai Lama by the Indian Government' and the visit Nehru paid to him as soon as he arrived at Mus-
soorie (the Indian hill station where he made his first headquarters)
were an unfitting reception for a government to give the leader of a
rebellion in a friendly neighbouring state.[23] In fact the Dalai Lama's
'impressive welcome' when he reached Tezpur in north-east India was
partly an inevitable reflection of the presence there of two or three
hundred journalists, and the need for some formalization of his contacts with the press; but it was true that the Indian Government did
not keep the assurances which it had given Peking that the Dalai Lama
would not be allowed to engage in political activity against China
while he was in India. The Chinese also complained again about
activities of Tibetan émigrés in Kalimpong, charging that Kuomintang
and American agents were active there too, channelling anti-Chinese
propaganda, weapons and agents into Tibet across what was still a very
open border.

   In their analysis of Nehru's statements on the developments in
Tibet, the Chinese argued that he had misunderstood the situation
when he traced the rebellion to the clash between 'a dynamic, rapidly
moving society' and a 'static, unchanging society fearful of what
might be done to it in the name of reform'. The rebellion in Tibet
had been counter-revolution and nothing else, an attempt to sustain
the 'dark, cruel and barbarous serf system' by the classes which bene-

---

* It was rumoured in Peking when this article appeared that Mao Tse-tung himself had
written it.[24]

fited from it. There was nothing surprising in the outcry of sympathy for the rebels from 'the U.S. State Department, British colonialists, Syngman Rhee' and suchlike; 'but what surprises us,' the *People's Daily* went on, was that Nehru, who opposed such people and understood their plots and tricks, should have been 'pushed by that alliance into an important role in their so-called sympathy with Tibet movement'. It then quoted a passage from Nehru's autobiography, reflecting the Marxist theorizing in which he often indulged, without letting it affect his Fabian practice. 'The attempt to convert a governing and privileged class into forsaking power and giving up its unjust privileges has . . . always so far failed, and there seems to be no reason whatever to hold that it will succeed in the future.'

True, the Chinese observed; but 'now he blames us for not having been able to convert the privileged ruling class in Tibet into forsaking power and giving up its privileges.'

As for the feelings of sympathy and kinship which Nehru said underlay the expressions in India of outrage against Chinese actions in Tibet, kinship worked both ways. How would India like it if China were to set up a people's committee to support a rebellion in Assam or Uttar Pradesh? 'If the Indian Government can demand certain assurances from the Chinese Government on the grounds of deep sympathy and ancient links with the Tibetan people', why could not the Chinese Government make demands for assurances about India's internal affairs, 'also on the grounds of deep sympathy and ancient links'? (It is significant that the *People's Daily* did not make the allusion to the Naga rebellion that in the context would have been far more telling. The Nagas had been in rebellion as long as the Tibetans, and like the Tibetans they claimed separate national identity and demanded sovereign status to express and protect it. Like China in Tibet, India had been using troops in Nagaland to suppress what she regarded as a secessionist rebellion. That Peking did not refer to the Nagas suggests that the Chinese at this stage did not wish to provide occasion for their arguments to be taken as threats, and therefore advanced hypothetical instances from Assam and Uttar Pradesh.)

The *People's Daily* concluded mildly that Nehru 'disagrees somewhat with us on the Tibet question,' but recalled that 'in general he advocates Sino-Indian friendship,' and regretted that it had been necessary to argue with 'the respected Prime Minister of our friendly neighbour'.[25] If Peking could help it, the Indian reaction to the Tibetan

revolt was plainly not by itself going to be allowed to distort the cordiality which had through the 1950s informed Sino-Indian relations at
government level. But the Chinese did not lose sight of the Indian 'big
bourgeoisie', looking over Nehru's shoulder, as it were, and urging
him always to the Right. This class, in the Chinese view, maintained
'manifold links with imperialism and is, to a certain extent, dependent
on foreign capital. Moreover, by its class nature, the big bourgeoisie
has a certain urge for outward expansion', and therefore, while opposing imperialist intervention on the world scene, it reflected certain
influences of imperialist policy itself.[26] By Leninist diagnosis, then, the
Indian Government was prone to sudden swings to the Right, and there
were powerful forces, domestic and international, always trying to
change India's course in that direction. That such a change was in the
making began to appear to the Chinese in 1959, as the United States
and India moved closer together.

In Chinese eyes, the suspicion of neutralists in general and of Nehru
in particular that was so often expressed in Washington in the heyday
of the Eisenhower administration was the best recommendation that
the Indians could have. Conversely, the change in American attitude
which became apparent in 1959 was ominous; it suggested not only
that the United States was developing designs on India's non-aligned
virtue, but also that in Washington's appreciation New Delhi was ripe
to respond to such overtures. Peking would have begun to watch
Indian attitudes and policy for signs that New Delhi was being drawn
into the imperialists' camp.

The emergence of the Indian approach to the boundary question,
articulated in Nehru's letters at the end of 1958 and the beginning of
1959, was seen in Peking as such a sign. Until that time, the Chinese
had no reason to expect that settlement of the boundaries with India
would be any more difficult than with their other Asian neighbours.
Since 1954 Indian maps had shown a claim to the Aksai Chin territory
across which a length of the recently completed Sinkiang–Tibet road
lay; but Chinese maps indicated similar cartographic claims to territory
below the McMahon Line which, as Chou En-lai had told Nehru,
China did not intend to press when the time came for negotiating a
general boundary settlement. India had made it quite clear that she
would not consider any change in the McMahon alignment of her
north-eastern boundary, and that had been the *de facto* boundary since
1951. Unless China wished to pick an irresoluble quarrel with India,

there was no alternative to accepting the McMahon Line. On the other hand, there had been no indication that India would treat her map claim to Aksai Chin as more binding or absolute than Peking meant to make her own map claim to most of NEFA. Nehru had made it a point to state and restate his Government's position on the McMahon Line, in Parliament as well as other public forums in India; but there had been nothing to suggest that he would be equally adamant in claiming the boundary in the west that Indian maps had begun to show only five years before, and which had no more relation to actuality, to the *status quo* of control, than had China's map claim to NEFA.

Peking's negotiations with Burma had shown the Chinese, if they needed showing, that, once boundary questions became a political issue in a country under a national bourgeois government, that government came under domestic pressure to take an extreme and unyielding approach. So, from the beginning of the dispute, the Chinese pointed out that there was no pressing need for a boundary settlement; that if for internal reasons Nehru found it difficult to open negotiations, the whole subject could be left for quieter days. The *status quo* answered the requirements of both countries, and provided that neither disturbed it, there was no urgent need for its ratification by treaty. But the Longju and Kongka Pass incidents in the autumn of 1959 suggested that India did not mean to leave the *status quo* undisturbed. Those clashes were no less ominous to the Chinese than, on the other side, they were to the Indians.[27]

India's unilateral and unannounced modification of the McMahon Line in her own favour, with the establishment of posts at Longju, Khinzemane and Tamaden,* was serious from China's point of view only in that it demonstrated disregard for the basic principle that boundary changes had to be matters of agreement. The posts themselves had no military significance and apart from protesting to New Delhi, the Chinese left them alone. In Peking's account, the Indians fired first at Longju; but that the clash there was at least accidental finds circumstantial confirmation in the fact that China made no attempt to force out the Indian posts at Khinzemane and Tamaden once they were established. The Kongka Pass incident was even more ominous from China's point of view. Whoever fired first, the clash arose out of an

---

* See pp. 107–8 above. India's offer to discuss the alignment at these points came only *after* she had set up the posts; and then the offer was conditional upon China's accepting not only the McMahon Line, but also the Indian version of the boundary in the western sector.

attempt by a large Indian patrol to move into Chinese-occupied territory and set up a post there. This was a matter not of a few square
miles, as in the marginal Indian moves across the McMahon Line, but,
if India meant to implement her map claim, of an area of thousands of
square miles that, because of the road which crossed it, was of high
strategic importance to China.

In Nehru's letters and his Government's communications to Peking
at the end of 1959, India made her approach to the boundary dispute
quite clear. She would not negotiate a general boundary settlement,
but only minor adjustments of a mile here or there in the Indian claim
lines—and that only after China had withdrawn from Aksai Chin.
Moreover, the Longju and especially the Kongka Pass incident suggested that India was not only refusing to negotiate a settlement, but that
she also intended to try to assert her claims on the ground. To refuse
to negotiate and at the same time refuse to respect the *status quo* was
tantamount to rejecting a peaceful settlement of the boundary question.

India was insisting that China accept the unilateral Indian definition
of the boundary, and in so doing was not only clinging to the boundary
in the east which had originated in Britain's secret agreement with the
Tibetans in 1914, but in the west was advancing a claim that 'British
imperialism had fabricated covertly but never dared to put forward.'*28
And it was not as if any material Indian interest were involved in the
claim to Aksai Chin; 'India's ... demand ... that China get out of her
only traffic route to Western Tibet, a road India has no use for, was ...
seeking injury to China without benefit to India.'29

In the Chinese reaction to their reading of India's statements and
actions there was a strong strain of injured pride. Boundaries unilaterally imposed by stronger countries; rough disdain for Chinese
national sensibilities: there was nothing new to China in this, her history was replete with such manifestations of foreign arrogance and
power. But now, 'the days when the Chinese people could be bossed
around are gone for ever';30 'The liberated China can in no circumstances allow itself to be plunged back to the position of the injured old
China.'31 More mildly, Chen Yi said in Peking in September 1959
that, in attempting to impose the McMahon Line on China, India had
not 'given the slightest consideration to the sense of national pride and
self-respect of the Chinese people'.32

* It will be remembered that the British had never communicated the Johnson/Ardagh
alignment (from which the Indian claim derived) as a boundary proposal to China.

Starting, as Nehru once perceived, from the assumption that the disputed territory in the western sector was Chinese and always had been Chinese,[33] China felt that her own approach to the boundary question was fair and practical:

The Chinese Government has consistently held that an overall settlement of the boundary question should be sought by both sides, taking into account the historical background and existing actualities and adhering to the five principles of peaceful coexistence, through friendly negotiations conducted in a well-prepared way, step by step. Pending this, as a provisional measure, the two sides should maintain the long-existing *status quo* of the border, and not seek to change it by unilateral action, even less by force: as to some of the disputes, provisional agreements concerning individual places could be reached through negotiations to ensure the tranquillity of the border areas and uphold the friendship of the two countries. This stand is as fair as it is clear.[34]

That, in spite of China's reasonable approach, India was following a course that could lead nowhere but to an intractable dispute; had 'raised a wild clamour and created tension in relations'[35] with China; and was deliberately engineering provocations along the frontier:[36] all this showed that the real reasons for Indian actions must be sought beyond the factors of the boundary question. Submitted by the Chinese to the prisms of Marxist-Leninist analysis, the motives and causes of Indian boundary policy emerged clearly.

As the Chinese came to see it, the root cause of the boundary dispute lay in the 'ever-sharpening class contradictions and social contradictions and the deepening political crisis facing the Nehru Government'.[37] By the beginning of the 1960s, the Indian Government had substituted reactionary nationalism for anti-imperialist and anti-feudal revolution, and was tying itself more and more closely to the imperialist and feudal forces. But Peking continued for some time to see Nehru himself as a captive of the forces of reaction, who might yet free himself and become again a progressive influence on Indian policy. 'Under the leadership of Prime Minister Nehru the Indian Government has also done things beneficial to Sino-Indian friendship and the spirit of the five principles of peaceful coexistence,' the *People's Daily* wrote in September 1959. Nehru was 'respected in China', and it was a matter for regret that, 'instead of maintaining the wise attitude one expects of him', he had 'let himself be drawn into the whirlpool of anti-Chinese agitation in India.' Slanders from right-wing politicians and members of Parliament, and even certain officials, had necessitated a detailed refutation; 'but even under these circumstances we still regret that we had to touch upon Prime Minister Nehru in our dispute'.[38] In the last months of 1959, Nehru was still resisting the aroused domestic demands for an extreme and absolute approach to the border question, and his attempts to moderate the terms of the dispute within India seemed aimed at keeping the way open to negotiated settlement, even though the Indian Government was ruling that out in its diplomatic communications.

The Chinese attitude to Nehru began to change after 1960, and the New Delhi summit talks of April 1960 appear to have been the watershed. Communist diplomats in New Delhi were told by members of the Chinese delegation that Chou En-lai had been shocked by Nehru's intransigence, and he was later reported to have described Nehru as impossible to negotiate with, 'being both unreliable and impenetrable'.[39] Chou's resentment at Nehru's ambivalence showed in his comments in Katmandu after the New Delhi summit. 'How did Prime Minister Nehru treat us?' he asked, after recalling that the Chinese side had kept their public statements studiously friendly; 'he did not say it face to face, but as soon as we had left he attacked the Chinese Government as aggressors.'[40]

The Chinese did not openly denounce Nehru until late in 1962, but it seems reasonable to infer that they came to regard him as 'the loyal representative of the big bourgeoisie and big landlords of India', and the stooge of China's international enemies, from 1960.

Following what was seen as an increasingly reactionary policy at home,* after 1959 the Nehru Government also fulfilled China's ideological expectations abroad by continuing to move closer to the United States. Eisenhower's visit to New Delhi in 1959 was returned by Nehru in 1961, but of course the increasing flow of American economic assistance to India was in the Chinese view more telling. The level of American aid was seen as a barometer to Indian attitudes. American assistance to India in the twelve years from 1947 to 1959 had totalled less than two thousand million dollars; but from 1959 to 1962 more than twice as much was given or promised. To the Chinese, the conclusion was

---

* In 1959 New Delhi dismissed the Communist Government in the state of Kerala, an action that was, of course, noted in Peking.

obvious: 'The more anti-Chinese India is, the greater is the increase in U.S. aid';[41] this had increased 'in direct proportion to the extent to which the Nehru Government has served United States imperialism and opposed China'.[42] The Chinese traced the effect of India's mounting dependence upon the United States in the positions taken by New Delhi in the United Nations, the Congo, and South-East Asia, as well as in its 'chauvinist and expansionist policy' along the frontier. The same shift in Indian policies was discerned in Washington, the same conclusion expressed – although, of course, in very different words – and Peking noted that too. In mid-1961 *U.S. News & World Report*, an authoritative right-wing weekly, noted in Indian policy towards the world's trouble spots the same 'shifts from past leanings' that Peking had seen, and asked whether Nehru was 'changing his spots'.

> In April, twenty-four hours after attacking U.S. intervention in Cuba, Nehru reversed himself, calling President Kennedy 'dynamic' and suggesting that there might be two sides to the Cuban story. This reversal, it is noted, came on the eve of U.S. proposals to step up economic aid to India. Nehru's own economists have warned him that he cannot hope to solve India's immense economic and social problems at home without massive aid from the U.S.A. Accordingly, it is felt by some American officials that Nehru is more than eager for closer ties with America.

Nehru, the article concluded, was 'turning out to be a top favourite of the Kennedy Administration among statesmen of the world'.[43]

In their analyses of India's politico-economic policies, the Chinese argued that, in spite of having achieved political independence, India continued as a colonial economy, with its foreign investment increasing 150 per cent by 1960 – the British share doubling in that time; the American multiplying sevenfold.[44] Meanwhile, India had also become more and more dependent upon foreign aid, which had financed 9·6 per cent of the first Indian five-year plan, 20·6 per cent of the second, and 30 per cent of the third. A conservative Indian journal, *Capital*, pointed out in 1960 that 'almost the entire third plan depends on [foreign aid]: if the foreign aid does not come, the plan will have to be scrapped, since India's own foreign exchange reserves are already below the minimum considered necessary.'[45] So pervasive and profound had the dependence of the Indian economy become by 1962, the independent journal *United Asia* concluded, that 'any drastic cuts in, or cessation of, foreign aid would immediately engender a major economic crisis in India, accompanied by the closing down of large numbers of companies, reduced productions, unemployment and uncontrollable inflation.' (This prognosis was to be fulfilled to the letter when American aid was interrupted after the India-Pakistan war in 1965.) 'Wherever imperialist "aid" appears, genuine economic sovereignty and economic independence vanish for all practical purposes,' the Chinese noted later.[46]

As for the 'socialistic pattern of society' to the construction of which the Nehru Government was committed, the Chinese dismissed that as a farce.* 'The comprador† state monopoly capital which the Nehru Government has built up by means of so-called planning and foreign aid is not of a socialist character as is claimed by the modern revisionists, nor is it a force capable of promoting independent economic development of the nation as is asserted by certain economists. . . .' On the contrary, 'it reduces the Indian economy to an appendage of foreign monopoly capital.'[47]

Lenin had foreseen it all.

> Under conditions where private ownership of the means of production is preserved, all . . . steps to bigger monopolies and increased nationalization of production are inevitably accompanied by intensified exploitation of the labouring masses, intensified oppression, greater difficulties in repulsing the attacks of the exploiters, the strengthening of reaction and military despotism, and at the same time lead inevitably to incredible increases in the profits of the big capitalists at the expense of all the other strata of the population, to the saddling of the labouring masses for many decades with tribute to the capitalists in the form of payment of thousands of millions in the interests on loans.[48]

Again, the Chinese found confirmation of their interpretation in the comments of Indians. They quoted G. D. Birla, a 'big bourgeois' if ever there was one, and the head of a commercial and industrial empire

---

* 'The establishment of a socialistic pattern of society' became the stated goal of the Congress Party at its Sixtieth annual session, held in Avadi, on the outskirts of Madras, in 1955. At this session the inherent duality of the party, socialist and egalitarian in rhetoric, conservative and orthodox in its political support, found expression in that '-ic'. 'We want to have a socialistic pattern and not socialism,' as a key Congress speaker put it.[49]
† 'Comprador . . . 1. Formerly, a native house-steward. . . . 2. Now, in China, a native servant employed as head of the native staff, and as agent, by European houses.' (*Shorter Oxford English Dictionary*).

which enormously expanded in India through the 1960s, as reassuring a gathering of American businessmen that 'the public sector [in India] is going to act as a generator of private enterprises'.[50]

The first years of the 1960s saw the beginning of that intensification in public violence and political disaffection which was to be a dominant feature of Indian political development in the decade; and the Chinese heard in the mounting roll of political agitations across India the first rumbles of revolution as 'the impoverishment of the working people intensified, thus sharpening class contradictions'.[51] At the same time, they saw Nehru's Government having to make more frequent use of the armoury of repressive measures it had inherited from the British. They found another passage from Nehru's own Marxist phase to describe what they believed to be happening in India: 'So long as capitalism can use the machinery of democratic institutions to hold down and keep down labour, democracy is allowed to flourish, but when this is not possible than capitalism discards democracy and adopts the open fascist methods of violence and terror.'[52]

Drifting ever more to the Right in internal politics, in foreign affairs Nehru had, in the Chinese view, 'practically thrown away the banner of opposition to imperialism and colonialism . . . [and] suited himself to the needs of U.S. imperialism'. To 'stir up reactionary nationalist sentiment, divert the attention of their people and strike at progressive forces . . . and meet the demands of United States imperialism', the Indian Government had made itself 'the pawn of the international anti-China campaign.' That, Peking concluded, 'is the root cause and background of the Sino-Indian boundary dispute'.[53]

Thus China explained in Marxist-Leninist terms what was happening in India, and traced the motives for what the Chinese believed was a deliberate defection into the American camp, with the boundary dispute created as a pretext for domestic and international propaganda. But none of that analysis was advanced as explanation or justification of China's policy or actions towards India. This remained, from beginning to end, reactive – determined by India's actions towards China, not by the dialectical interpretation of the class character of the Nehru Government. Communist China's record in foreign relations is clear in this regard. Policy towards other governments springs from how they act towards China, not from their political character. Peking's motto might be taken to be, 'It's not what you are, it's the way that you act.' The Chinese attitude towards Pakistan illustrates the point.

In China's view, Pakistan had pursued an unfriendly policy towards herself through the 1950s: following the American lead in the United Nations by voting against discussion of the question of China's representation; and, although she had established diplomatic relations with Peking in 1951, maintaining unofficial but offensive contacts with the Chiang Kai-shek rump on Formosa; Pakistan was a member of SEATO and CENTO; and the Chinese had seen the Ayub Government's policy as one of increasing dependence upon the United States, with President Ayub's joint defence offer 'sowing discord in the relations between China and India'.[54] The 'Pakistani ruling clique has been playing a vicious role and adopting an extremely unfriendly attitude towards China' a commentator in the *People's Daily* wrote in mid-1959. 'The Pakistani Government should pull up the horse before the precipice, reverse its hostile stand towards the Chinese people and return to the road laid down by the Bandung resolutions and the road of Sino-Pakistani friendship.'[55] As has been seen, Pakistan for her own reasons did change course at the end of 1959, and, with an overture towards the settlement of the Sino-Pakistani boundary, took the road that led to cordial and civil relations with China, and ultimately to what was not far short of a tacit alliance against India.

By the Marxist-Leninist scale of political development, President Ayub marked at the beginning of the 1960s a stage further in capitalist decline than that reached by the Nehru Government. If in New Delhi the national bourgeoisie was falling more and more under the dominance of the big bourgeoisie, the feudal elements and the imperialists, the Ayub Government represented the next phase, with the quasi-democratic institutions of the immediate post-independence phase replaced by army rule. The displacement of the Communist Government in Kerala showed that the Communist Party of India operated on a very short leash, and as the Sino-Indian dispute sharpened, so the Indian Government bore down more heavily on the Communists—but in Pakistan the Communist Party had been banned for years. By any ideological considerations, then, China and Pakistan should have continued in a relationship of mutual distrust and antipathy. But even in the sourest moment of China's disapproval (Pakistan had been fêting a pilgrim party of Chinese Muslims from Formosa, en route to Mecca), it had still been noted in Peking that 'the Chinese people have always attached importance to Sino-Pakistani friendship and waited patiently for a change of attitude by the Pakistani Government'.[56] And when

Pakistan did 'pull up the horse before the precipice' and reverse its hostile stand, Peking responded. From the boundary settlement to other agreements of mutual benefit, such as Pakistan International Airways' landing rights in China, then to economic aid and substantial military assistance after the Indo-Pakistan war of 1965, the course of Sino-Pakistani friendship has been smooth.

China's full ideological denunciation of Nehru and his Government was not made public until very late in the development of the Sino-Indian dispute. In the middle of 1959 the *People's Daily*, very much more in sorrow than in anger and indeed almost apologetically, published its analysis of 'Nehru's philosophy in the light of the revolt in Tibet'.[57] But it was not until after fighting broke out on the border in October 1962 that another instalment, 'More on Nehru's Philosophy in the Light of the Sino-Indian Boundary Question', appeared. This anathematized Nehru; but between these statements China's communications with India were punctuated with appeals to Sino-Indian friendship, reminders that China would never close the door to a negotiated settlement, warnings at the last to Nehru to 'rein in on the brink of the precipice'. Peking reiterated repeatedly that 'there is no conflict of fundamental interests between China and India',[58] and maintained that the boundary question was essentially one of small and temporary importance. There is no reason to believe that if at any time before mid-October 1962 India had changed her policy towards China, either by agreeing to negotiate a general boundary agreement or even by simply suspending the forward policy, China would not have responded and encouraged Sino-Indian relations to simmer down.

Paradoxically, China's ideological salvoes against Nehru were not fired primarily to injure him or India; they were exchanges in another battle, with India in the line of fire. Almost from its inception, the Sino-Indian boundary dispute became enmeshed with the great falling out of China and Russia, and the two quarrels interacted and exacerbated each other. As the Chinese were to say, later, 'one of the important differences of principle between the Soviet leaders and ourselves turns on the Sino-Indian boundary question,'[59] and they traced the development of Russian policy from 'feigning neutrality while actually favouring India' to openly supporting her, in alignment with the United States.

The Russian desire to win friends and influence people in India was clamantly demonstrated in the ebullient Bulganin and Krushchev tour of India in 1955, and a programme of Russian economic aid had its small beginnings in that year. This was of a part with the Soviet Government's new policy of winning support wherever it could among the newly independent countries, regardless of whether, by Leninist criteria, those countries were being governed by their national bourgeoisie or even 'lackeys of imperialism'. China was to follow much the same policy in the 1960s, and the later Chinese criticism of Krushchev's support to anti-Communist regimes in the newly independent world appears to have been the doctrinal and retrospective expression of state enmity. But when, in the Chinese reading, the Soviet Union began to side with Nehru in his quarrel with China, and continued to assist India, adding military equipment to economic aid in spite of the mounting Sino-Indian hostility, ideological and state considerations fused.

The boundary question came into the open as a dispute pregnant with possibilities of violence, even of war, with the Longju incident at the end of August 1959. Much was made of it not only in India, where, since it was presented as the result of unprovoked aggression by the Chinese, there was a natural outburst of anger, but also in the Western world. There, India's expressed friendship and support for China had long been seen as purblind or perverse, and there was now a certain amount of *Schadenfreude* as it seemed that Nehru had received a nasty nip on the hand with which he had been patting the Chinese. From the Soviet point of view, the timing could not have been worse. Krushchev was about to set off on his momentous visit to the United States, putting into practice the changed view of the world and its political possibilities that he had expressed at the recent Soviet party congresses. In that fundamental reversal of Leninist orthodoxy, Krushchev had argued that war could be eliminated as a means of settling international issues, and that socialism could triumph in the world, without war. Through the summer of 1959 Krushchev had been working purposefully towards a *détente* with the U.S.A., and the announcement in August that he was going to Washington to meet Eisenhower appeared to crown that attempt with success.

In that context, the Longju incident had destructive implications for Soviet diplomacy. Inevitably, it was reported, without question, in the Indian version, as an instance of deliberate and unprovoked aggression by China. The Chinese account of the clash was ignored; the implication of Nehru's admission, shortly afterwards, that the boundary at this point had been 'varied' by India 'because it was not considered a good line', was completely missed.[60] Convinced already that China was a bellicose and bullying power, Western observers interpreted the Longju clash accordingly, and thus confirmed their own pre-conception. Those in the West who opposed *détente* between the U.S.A. and the U.S.S.R. were able to argue that by suddenly attacking India, China had only bared the true face of international Communism — unreliable and predatory. The small spark in the Himalayas was treated as if it were a flare, irradiating the risks of attempting coexistence with Communist powers, and thus putting Krushchev's protestations about the peaceful settlements of disputes in what, to the Russians, was a false light.

The Chinese appear to have realized the implications the Longju incident would have for the Soviet Union. On September 6th the Soviet chargé d'affaires in Peking was told the background of the incident as the Chinese saw it: that it had occurred on the Chinese side of the McMahon Line, with, according to the report of the Chinese frontier guards, the Indians firing first. It seems that these explanations carried no conviction with the Russians. Three days later the Soviet chargé d'affaires handed the Chinese Foreign Ministry a copy of an official comment on the Longju incident that was to be released by the Russian Government. The Chinese urged that the statement should not be published, and gave the chargé d'affaires the text of Chou En-lai's September 8th letter to Nehru, a sharply worded statement of the Chinese position which pointed to 'trespassing and provocations by Indian troops' as the cause of the armed clash at Longju.[61] Again on September 9th the Chinese urged Russia not to release the statement, but that night Tass circulated it.[62]

On the surface the statement was innocuous. 'Leading circles' in the Soviet Union regretted the incident, it said, and deplored the use that had been made of it (by implication, in the Western press) to drive a wedge between the two largest Asian states and to discredit the idea of peaceful coexistence. Soviet leaders were confident, however, that 'both Governments will settle the misunderstanding that has arisen'.

That the statement was significant, for all the triteness of its sentiments, was generally appreciated, not least in India; Nehru told the Lok Sabha that it showed that the Soviet Government was taking 'a more or less dispassionate view of the situation'.[63] The reaction in Peking, though contained at the time, appears to have been violent.

The Chinese said later that Moscow by 'assuming a façade of neutrality' and 'making no distinction between right and wrong', in merely expressing regret over the Longju clash had, by implication, favoured India and condemned China. Thus the Russians had advertised the internal differences in the Communist world; and they had done all this in defiance of Peking's advice, 'turning a deaf ear to China's repeated explanations of the true situation', in order to create 'the so-called Camp David Spirit and make a ceremonial gift to the United States imperialists'. Here, said the *People's Daily*, was 'the first instance in history in which a socialist country, instead of condemning the armed provocation of the reactionaries of a capitalist country, condemned another fraternal socialist country when it was confronted by armed provocation'.[64]

When Krushchev, glowing from Camp David, came on to Peking in October, the Chinese leaders tried to explain the Longju incident to him, pointing out that the place was north of the *de facto* boundary, and explaining that the provocation had come from the Indian side. Krushchev, however, they said, 'did not wish to know the true situation and the identity of the party committing the provocation, but insisted that anyway it was wrong to shoot people dead'.[65]

The Chinese were here experiencing a double difficulty that was to beset and damage them throughout their quarrel with India. First, there was their credibility gap, using that phrase here not as a euphemism for mendacity but to describe the almost universal tendency of people, when confronted with an outright contradiction between the Chinese and the Indians, to accept the Indian version as the truth. (This did not apply only to the Western world; the majority of the world's Communist Parties followed the Russians in accepting India's version of the dispute: a Polish delegation in Peking at the same time as Krushchev, for example, came away suggesting that China had deliberately 'stirred up trouble with India' in the two border incidents out of resentment at being left out of the super-powers' negotiations.)[66] And, secondly, there was the general readiness to draw the conclusion that, because the Indians got the worst of a skirmish or a battle, they could not possibly have provoked it.

War, its inevitability or avoidability; whether it could still serve the socialist cause or must, because of its nuclear dangers, always be avoided: this was at the heart of the doctrinal differences between China and Russia, so the implications of the Longju clash served both sides in their contest of scriptural allusions. Krushchev in Peking came out flatly against war as an instrument of policy; 'force, he said, must absolutely not be used against the capitalist world, no matter how strong the Communists might be'.[67] And the Chinese saw that they were again implicitly being chided for their part in the Longju clash.[68] In his report to the Supreme Soviet on his return from Peking, Krushchev maintained his neutral attitude towards the Sino-Indian dispute.[69] That he should do so after having heard Peking's explanations and having been left in no doubt of how bitterly the Chinese resented Russian neutrality on this question, must have seemed to China a calculated challenge and affront.

So far as the Communist movement itself was concerned, the Sino-Soviet split came into the open at the Rumanian Party congress in Bucharest in June 1960: and Krushchev put China's handling of her dispute with India at the heart of his denunciation of the 'Left revisionists' in Peking.

Krushchev rejected the Chinese complaint that the Soviet Union had let them down by refusing to take their side against India. In fact, he said, it had been the Chinese who had let down the cause of socialism. By quarrelling with India, they had not only failed to co-operate with the Soviet Union in encouraging India to move towards socialism; they had worked against it. Of course Nehru was a capitalist. But China's dispute with him had nothing to do with ideology; it was a purely nationalist quarrel, and it had done the socialist cause untold harm, quite apart from such details as losing Kerala to Communism.* The Chinese had no right to complain of lack of Russian support in such circumstances, especially as it was impossible to get at the rights and wrongs of the dispute. He taunted China with wanting the support of the Soviet Union in this matter, when the Chinese boasted of their colossal population, and Russia's population was less than that of India. The Chinese should take to heart Lenin's denunciation of great-nation chauvinism, he suggested, and remember that Lenin had been prepared to surrender territory for tactical reasons while Trotsky opposed it. The consequence of China's actions was that Nehru had become a national hero in India, which was just what the imperialists wanted. The Soviet Union, too, had her frontier problems, but she approached

---

* Krushchev was guilty of anachronism there. The Communist Government in Kerala had been turned out of office before the boundary dispute had really crystallized and before it had become a matter of political concern.

them in a responsible way; if she had acted like China, war would have been declared on Iran more than once. There had been plenty of clashes on the Russian-Iranian frontier, with casualties; but the Soviet Union would not allow such incidents to precipitate war, since that would contradict the true spirit of revolution.[70]

Krushchev there expressed the gravamen of the Russian attitude to China's position in the boundary dispute, which was to be constant through every turn of its development, except for one moment in the middle of the border war which climaxed it—which was also in the middle of the Cuba confrontation.* Ironically, the Russian position as they stated it, was precisely the same as China's. As *Pravda* put it:

> We have always believed, and continue to believe, that there were no reasons for the border conflict between India and China . . . and all the less for turning it into an armed clash. . . . There is no doubt that had the two sides sat down at a conference table and discussed their mutual charges calmly, soberly and without bias, the conflict would have been settled long ago. . . . The most difficult talks are better than wars, and disputed questions must be solved by peaceful means, at a conference table, and not by military methods.[71]

This, as has been seen, was the very argument which Peking had again and again urged on the Indians in the attempt to convince them that the boundaries must be settled by negotiation; that an equitable and mutually acceptable settlement could readily be achieved; and that for either side to attempt to implement its claims unilaterally must lead to a dangerous and possibly disastrous collision.

That the Soviet Union could thus preach the virtues of negotiation to the party which was most strongly converted to them suggests that the Russians, like Western observers, simply disbelieved what the Chinese were saying in, and about, their dispute with India. They appear to have concluded that the Chinese were lying in their accounts of what was happening on the borders, and being hypocritical in their proposals of negotiation. They were put off objective inquiry by the intricacies of the argument between Peking and New Delhi (Krushchev said 'it was impossible to get at the rights and wrongs of the dispute'); they seem to have taken at face value Nehru's protestations that he was

* See pp. 365–6 below.

eager to negotiate; and they could not believe that any country as weak as India would actually challenge China on the ground.*

In the complexities of Nehru's attitudes to the Soviet Union and to the dispute with China, it is possible that if Moscow's influence had been exerted to persuade Nehru to compromise, or to dissuade him from the forward policy, this would have been telling. The Soviet Union's demonstrative neutrality was an encouragement to India to persist in her approach to the boundary question, however, and Russian aircraft enabled the Indians to implement the forward policy. India's friends helped her on the way to disaster.

Good relations with India were central to Moscow's policy towards the developing countries, and no doubt the Russians' mounting rivalry and antipathy towards China inclined them to India's side. Another important element in the Russian attitude plainly lay in the parallels between the Sino-Indian and the Sino-Russian boundary questions. Krushchev made the point implicitly in his Bucharest speech: 'The Soviet Union, too, had her own frontier problems, but she approached them in a responsible way.' Krushchev referred only to the Iranian boundary, but he knew that there was a far bigger boundary question to be resolved with China. Chou En-lai had sought to take it up with him three years before.[72]

The Sino-Russian borders were the product of Imperial Russia's drive for territory, and China's weakness during the nineteenth century. Renewing the expansionist drive to the east that had begun two hundred years before, the Russians in the middle of the nineteenth century annexed all of China's territory north of the Amur River and east of its tributary the Ussuri, pushing the Chinese empire back and cutting her off from the Sea of Japan. At the same time, Russia was grinding into China in central Asia, pushing back the frontier of Chinese Turkestan (Sinkiang). China acquiesced in the loss of these huge areas in the Treaties of Aigun (1858) and Peking (1860). After the establishment of the Republic of China in 1911, however, Chinese nationalists began to demand the abrogation of the 'unequal treaties' which had been forced on China in her time of trouble, and the restoration of her former frontiers.

In the first fine careless rapture of revolutionary purity in Moscow, the impulse of the Bolsheviks was to purge themselves of their ill-gotten Tsarist gains. In 1917 L.M.Karakhan, acting Commissar for

* See p. 289 below.

Foreign Affairs, declared that the Soviet Government repudiated all unequal treaties concluded between the Tsarist Government and China; and this declaration was confirmed in the Karakhan manifesto of 1920.

> The Government of the Russian Socialist Federated Soviet Republics declares as void all the treaties concluded by the former Government of Russia with China, renounces all the annexations of Chinese territory, all the concessions in China and returns to China free of charge and forever all that was ravenously taken from her by the Tsar's Government and by the Russian bourgeoisie.[73]

But even then, there were Russians who saw their eastern possessions in a somewhat different light. 'Vladivostok is far away,' said Lenin, 'but this town is ours.'[74] The Soviet Government very soon came to the view that, unequal treaties or not, the Sino-Russian boundaries should stay where they were. The Karakhan manifesto they later glossed as merely a fundamental programme to be used as a basis for negotiation, and not a precise list of concrete steps to be taken by the Soviet Government.[75]

Chinese nationalists (and Nationalists) continued to take the Karakhan manifesto as meaning what it said, and when it came into existence in 1949 the People's Republic of China inherited an old dispute and long-standing irredentist claims. The Chinese Communists, however, took the same approach to the question of their boundaries with the Soviet Union as they did to the Sino-Indian question. Bitterly as they, like other Chinese, might resent the injustice of the 'unequal treaties' and the national humiliation that they symbolized, they were prepared to accept the boundaries thus established as a fact of life, and to regard the lost territories as gone for good. Again, every consideration of practical politics pointed to this course. To have sustained the irredentist claim to the territories lost a century before would have committed the new Communist China to an irresoluble and in all probability hopeless dispute with the Soviet Union; it was plainly never to be expected that the Russians would surrender territory they had held so long and had developed with cities like Vladivostok and Khabarovsk.

The Chinese made their approach clear to the Russians: 'Although the old treaties relating to the Sino-Russian boundary are unequal treaties, the Chinese Government is nevertheless willing to respect them and take them as the basis for a reasonable settlement of the Sino-Soviet boundary question.'[76] In 1960 the Chinese proposed to Moscow that negotiations should be held to settle the boundaries,[77] and at that time, it appears, they did not expect the process to be difficult. When he was asked about the problem of the Sino-Soviet boundaries at this time, Chou En-lai said: 'There is a very small discrepancy on maps, and it is very easy to settle.'[78] This was certainly an exaggeration: the boundaries stretched for thousands of miles and their original treaty definition had often been very vague, and based on sketchy surveys, if any. But, given a common approach and shared desire for settlement, agreement could no doubt have been reached.

When negotiations did begin in 1964, however, they broke down almost immediately. The Soviet Union adopted exactly the same approach to the boundary question as had India. As they put it later, the Russians maintained that 'throughout its length this frontier is clearly and precisely determined by treaties, protocols and maps',[79] and refused to enter into comprehensive negotiations. The most they were prepared to do was 'discuss the question of specifying the frontier line over individual stretches. . . .'*

To the Chinese, this meant that Moscow 'insisted that China recognize as belonging to the Soviet Union all the territory which it had occupied or attempted to occupy in violation of the treaties',[80] in addition to the territory to which they were entitled under the treaties. The Russian approach to negotiations amounted to saying: 'There is nothing to discuss except what we agree to discuss,' and was as unacceptable to the Chinese as was the Indian approach.

There were also significant differences between the positions taken in the two disputes, however. The Chinese were never as formal and explicit in their assurances to India that they were prepared to accept the McMahon alignment, as they were in assuring Moscow that they would respect the unequal treaties. The reasons for this are clear. Unequal or not, the treaties, delimiting the Sino-Russian boundaries were formal and legal compacts to which the Chinese Government of the time had subscribed. But so far as the Sino-Indian borders were

---

* The wording used by the Indians was strikingly similar: 'The Sino-Indian boundary, based on custom and tradition, follows natural features, and for the major part of this customary and traditional boundary is also confirmed by treaty and agreement. . . . [India] is prepared to discuss specific disputes in regard to the location of the boundary, and to make minor frontier rectifications by agreement, where they are considered necessary.'[81]

concerned, there was no such treaty basis. China had not been a party to McMahon's agreement with the Tibetans, and had repudiated it from the beginning; and as for the western part of the Sino-Indian borders, there had never been a boundary delimitation.

But such subtleties, in Russian eyes, might have been seen as no more than Mandarin casuistry, designed to pave the way for the introduction of sweeping territorial claims. Chou En-lai's letter to Nehru of September 8th, 1959 — the text of which was given to the Russians next day — said that 'the so-called McMahon Line was a product of the British policy of aggression against the Tibet region of China and has never been recognized by any Chinese Central Government and is therefore decidedly illegal . . . how could China agree to accept under coercion such an illegal line which would have it relinquish its rights and disgrace itself by selling out its territory. . . ?' Krushchev and his advisers, already mistrustful of China, would not have appreciated that she might be quite prepared to accept among equals at the conference table what the Chinese said that they would never 'accept under coercion'. To them, as to the Indians, China's arguments against the legality of the McMahon Line must have appeared to be claims to the territory south of it. Encouraged in such a claim against India, China might go on to raise demands for territory lost to the Tsars — first Tawang, then Vladivostok. There, from the Russian point of view, was sufficient reason to endorse and support India's position.

The similarity of the Indian and Russian approaches increased as the territorial question became an element of the Sino-Russian dispute in the 1960s. The Soviet Union, like India, declined to submit her boundaries with China to general re-negotiation. Like Nehru, the Russians reiterated their willingness, indeed their eagerness, to settle with China on minor boundary rectifications, but refused to enter into general boundary negotiations. 'No one disagrees,' *Pravda* wrote in 1964; 'the Tsarist Government carried out a predatory policy, just as the Chinese emperors carried one out themselves to the extent of their abilities . . . [but] the present border was fixed by life itself and treaties regarding the border cannot be disregarded.'[82] The Chinese, of course, had said explicitly that they were prepared to respect the old treaties, but the Russians were as deaf to Chinese assurances as were the Indians. China came to believe that Krushchev and his successors had engineered border disputes between China and the U.S.S.R. to serve ulterior purposes — as they believed Nehru had done. As the scale and intensity of such incidents grew in the late 1960s, China and the U.S.S.R. were to reach the same position as China and India had done in the early years of the decade; but now it would be the Russians who, as the militarily more powerful side, were tempted to strike a devastating punitive blow to pacify the borders and put down the challenge of what they saw as a threatening neighbour.

Of China's neighbours only the two big powers, the Soviet Union and India, refused to negotiate their boundaries. This might suggest that the smaller countries were bullied into settlements; but the circumstances and the terms of China's settlements with her smaller neighbours belie that. It seems more probable that the Russian and Indian perception of themselves in relation to China made Peking's insistence on equality, affirmed at the negotiating table, appear as a challenge to them.

As the Sino-Soviet quarrel intensified through 1960, Moscow's support of India became a key charge in China's ideological denunciation of Krushchev's 'revisionism'. In Peking's analysis, the revolt in Tibet marked the point of Nehru's swerve to the Right; and now that the national bourgeois Government in India had entered its second phase, with workers, peasants and intellectuals beginning their struggle against the bourgeoisie, Nehru, to postpone the day of reckoning, had manufactured a frontier dispute with China. In these circumstances, the path was clear for true Communists. They must oppose the Indian Government and support the oppressed classes of India in their struggle against it. But Krushchev, abandoning class positions, continued to support the Indian bourgeoisie and even sided with them against China. This showed that his analysis of the situation was distorted or corrupt, the Chinese argued.[83]

Unshaken, Moscow continued its support of India. The relatively small but quite significant contributions of economic aid were to amount to five billion rupees by 1963, in Peking's calculation.[84] But the Russians opened a new and, to the Chinese, a deeply provocative chapter in the autumn of 1960, with the small beginnings of what was to become a very big programme of military assistance to India. An Indian Defence Ministry mission to Moscow ordered Antonov-12 heavy transport aircraft and then 'Hound' helicopters, both turbine-engined and suitable for operation at the altitudes of 16–17,000 feet encountered in Ladakh. The heavy transports, ferrying military supplies to Leh, and the helicopters, carrying a dozen armed soldiers or an equivalent freight load, were vital tools for the Indian Government in the implementation of the forward policy. At first Russian airmen flew both the transports and the helicopters in Ladakh, training Indian co-pilots; but there were complaints at this in the Indian Parliament, from those who feared that the Russians would report to China on Indian military preparations.

In 1960 it was also reported that India was negotiating with the Soviet Union for the purchase of MiG jet fighters. These negotiations were prolonged—the deal was delayed by the vigorous protests of the British and American Governments—but it was confirmed in the summer of 1962 that India was to get MiGs.

In Peking's view, the Soviet Union thus moved beyond the ideological error of giving the Nehru Government moral support to the treachery of supplying it with the very military equipment needed to strengthen the Indian frontier moves against China. As the Chinese were to say of Krushchev, 'he backed the reactionaries in India in their armed attacks on Socialist China and, together with the United States, incited and helped them to perpetrate armed provocations against China by giving them military aid.'[85]

When in the autumn of 1961, the Chinese recognized the increased Indian military activity in the western sector as purposeful and co-ordinated—'an attempt to realize [India's] territorial claims unilaterally and by force'[86]—it seemed that the Indian Government was deliberately ending the lull that had fallen on the frontier after the Kongka Pass clash nearly two years before. With the support of the Russians now as well as of the imperialist block, Nehru and his Government appeared to be throwing down a challenge to China. 'India is clearly pursuing a policy of gradual encroachment on Chinese territory, nibbling it away bit by bit in a deliberate attempt to assert its territorial claims by armed force,' the *People's Daily* wrote in the middle of 1962.[87] In notes to New Delhi, the Chinese Government warned that it would be 'very erroneous and dangerous should the Indian Government take China's attitude of restraint and tolerance as an expression of weakness',[88] and a commentator in the *People's Daily* made the same point. 'The Indian authorities have been betting on the basis of a wrong assessment of the situation; they take the attitude of the Chinese Government in setting great store by Sino-Indian friendship and trying its utmost to avoid a border clash to be a sign of weakness and think it possible to bring China to her knees by the use of force.'[89] Later the

Chinese were more explicit; the Indians, they said, 'mistook China's long forbearance as a sign that China was weak and could be bullied. They thought that with the backing of the imperialists and the support of the Soviet leaders they had nothing to fear, and that as soon as they took action China would be forced to retreat and their territorial claims would be realized.'[90]

As India continued to refuse negotiations or any arrangement for avoiding clashes (except full Chinese withdrawal from Indian-claimed territory in the west), and as the Indian troops in the western sector pressed harder on the forward Chinese positions, chivvying and challenging them, the alternatives became clearer. China could either agree to withdraw from the territory that India claimed and try to negotiate a boundary settlement on India's terms, thus surrendering to India's diplomatic and military pressure at the cost of her own pride and prestige, as well as her strategic position in the Tibet-Sinkiang region; or China could take up the Indian challenge and fight.

Until the Indian forward policy began to make itself felt, the Chinese consistently pooh-poohed the thought of war: 'It is impossible to entertain the absurd idea that our two great friendly neighbours with a combined population of more than one thousand million might start a war over such temporary and local disputes,' Peking had written to New Delhi at the end of 1959.[91] But in their great debate with the Soviet Union, the Chinese had been maintaining that sometimes wars were unavoidable, and must not be shirked because Communists (i.e. Russian Communists) were fearful of nuclear war. Like the Russians, the Chinese wished to avoid major — and especially nuclear — wars; but they argued that they could not for that reason truckle to the imperialists or the lackeys of the imperialists. It was a matter of judgment; of slighting the enemy strategically and taking full advantage of him tactically, as Mao Tse-tung had put it. The enemy, 'U.S. imperialism and the Chiang Kai-shek clique', must not be overestimated; they were 'rotten to the core and had no future', and could therefore be slighted — in the strategic context. 'But in regard to any particular situation or specific struggle . . . we must never slight the enemy: on the contrary, we can win victory only when we take full account of him and devote all our energies to the fight.'[92]

After the border war began, Peking was to recall, with approval, an incident from the Sino-Soviet past. In 1929, after a dispute over the Chinese Eastern Railway, the Kuomintang Government of China.

rejecting Russian proposals for discussions, 'stirred up an armed conflict' by attacking the Russian border. Then the Soviet Union, 'compelled to act in self-defence', invaded Manchuria, destroyed a Kuomintang army, and withdrew to its own territory. That was the perfectly right thing to do, the Chinese now said. The resolute Russian counter-blow not only defended the interests of the Soviet Union, but also 'accorded with the interests of the Chinese people and of the revolutionary people of the world'.[93]

Such, then, was the thinking that lay behind the Chinese warning as the Indians determinedly pressed forward in the western sector of the Sino-Indian border in September, 1962: 'If the Indian side should insist on threatening by armed force the Chinese defence forces who are duty-bound to defend their territory, and thereby arouse their resistance, it must bear the responsibility for all the consequences arising therefrom.'[94]

Part IV

THE BORDER WAR

One cannot possibly seriously think that such a state as India, which is militarily and economically weaker than China, would really launch a military attack on China.

Central Committee of the Communist
Party of the Soviet Union, February 6th, 1960.[1]

Again and again, military men have seen themselves hurled into war by the ambitions, passions and blunders of civilian governments, almost wholly uninformed as to the limits of their military potential and almost recklessly indifferent to the military requirement of the war they let loose.

Alfred Vagts, *The History of Militarism*.[2]

(i) The Ridge and the River

During the summer of 1962 public attention in India was focused on the western sector of the borders. The Government's version of events, reversing the actuality, had propagated the belief that it was the Chinese who were purposefully pushing forward there, seeking to enlarge the area under their control. This, while successfully obscuring the facts of the situation so far as the outside world was concerned, left the Government exposed to domestic complaints that it was still not meeting the Chinese challenge with boldness and determination. While, in fact, pursuing a policy of the utmost recklessness, it was being blamed for excessive, even craven, forbearance. This meant that Nehru had deprived himself of all options. To take off the pressure in the western sector by suspending the forward policy would have been construed as surrender and betrayal of the national cause. Furthermore, any Chinese move on the ground which could be interpreted as a fresh provocation would have to be met with demonstrative and vigorous counter-measures, whatever the circumstances; since he had misled his public into the belief that the Indian Army had the strength to handle the Chinese, Nehru would have no choice but to make the Indian counter-action one of military force.

Thus the application of the forward policy in the western sector, where its objective was to push the Chinese out of territory India claimed, loaded the guns. But it was in the eastern sector, where China was observing the McMahon Line as the *de facto* boundary and was nowhere in occupation of territory claimed by India, that a marginal Indian move forward triggered the border war.

The eastern sector had been quiet for three years, since the Longju incident of August 1959. Shortly after that, Nehru and Chou En-lai agreed to a joint suspension of patrolling along the eastern boundary,[3] and the Indian Army was ordered not to patrol within two miles of the McMahon Line. The forward policy directive reversed those orders, and made the McMahon Line a live border again. Under the directive sent out by Army H.Q. in December 1961, Eastern Command was ordered to move posts forward as close as practicable to the McMahon Line; to set up new posts so as to establish effective occupation of the whole frontier; and to cover gaps between posts by patrolling. These orders confronted the troops concerned with tasks as difficult as those their colleagues in the west were facing. To reach the McMahon Line took sometimes weeks of trekking, but the acute problem lay in supplying the troops once they had set up the required posts. As in the western sector, all their needs had to be air-dropped; but whereas in the west good dropping zones were readily found on the valley floors, the precipitous, thickly jungled ridges of the North-East Frontier Agency made suitable dropping zones very rare, and the weather often made dropping missions impossible for weeks on end. In such circumstances, the more remote garrisons were placed in real danger of starvation.

As their colleagues in the western sector were doing, the senior officers responsible for the McMahon Line sector pointed out the impracticability of posting troops where they could not be supplied; as in the western sector, their representations were brushed aside. In February 1962 General Kaul went to Assam to deal personally with the protests of the Corps Commander there, Lieutenant-General Umrao Singh—as one of the soldiers concerned put it later, 'to browbeat and bully the doubtful generals who had misgivings about the whole idea of setting up forward posts'.[4] Kaul, assisted by Malik of Intelligence and the latter's deputy,[5] specified from the maps in Army H.Q. where the new posts were to be established, and the troops or Assam Riflemen were sent out accordingly. In the first half of 1962 some twenty-four new posts were set up along the McMahon Line.

Severe as were the difficulties for the troops implementing the forward policy in the eastern sector, these were not compounded by counter-actions of the Chinese. The latter did not react so long as the Indians kept to their own side of the McMahon Line. The flashpoints lay in those places, such as Longju, where the exact alignment was disputed. The Indians did not attempt to reoccupy Longju in 1962 (the Chinese had withdrawn from that hamlet some time in 1960); but they struck the spark that set off the border war when they established a new post in a sliver of disputed territory at the western extremity of the McMahon Line.

On the map which the British and the Tibetans signed in Delhi on March 24th, 1914, the McMahon Line terminated on the boundary with Bhutan at the latitude of 27° 44' 30" N. In this region there was no watershed to be followed, and McMahon drew his line along what his maps showed as outstanding ridge features. But when the Indians explored this north-western corner of NEFA in the 1950s, it was seen that if the McMahon Line were transposed from its map co-ordinates to the ground it would not lie along the highest ridge in the vicinity. The highest feature near the western extremity of the border was Thag La ridge, three to four miles north of where McMahon had drawn his line. There is evidence that the Indians had decided to treat Thag La ridge as the boundary at least from the beginning of 1959,* but they did nothing about it physically until August of that year. They then set up a post north of the McMahon Line as it was shown on their and all other maps, at a place called Khinzemane. India thus laid claim to, and moved into, a right-angled triangle of territory north of the map-marked McMahon Line, measuring roughly twelve miles on its southern base and four miles on its western side, an area of about twenty-five square miles.

The Chinese reacted instantly, appearing in strength of about two hundred, as Nehru told the Lok Sabha later in the month, and 'physically pushing back' the ten or twelve men of the Assam Rifles to a point a couple of miles in the direction from which they had come.[6] The Chinese then withdrew, and two days later the Indians returned to Khinzemane. The Chinese attempted to push them back again, but the latter apparently made plain that they would resist this time, and the Chinese acquiesced in their remaining at Khinzemane. New Delhi protested about the incident in a note to Peking on August 11th, claiming that Khinzemane was in Indian territory and that the boundary ran along the Thag La ridge 'traditionally as well as by treaty map'. By 'tradition' India referred to the practice of herdsmen from a village to the south, who used the area for seasonal grazing; but villagers from the north used it too. The claim that the treaty map showed the boundary on Thag La ridge, and Khinzemane itself in Indian territory, was false. Neither Thag La ridge nor Khinzemane is identified on the map, which shows the boundary as running due east–west here at the latitude of 27° 44' 30" N., while in this same protest note the Indian Government said Khinzemane was at 27° 46" N.[7]

China lodged her own protest about the incident, claiming that Khinzemane was 'undoubtedly part of Chinese territory'; complaining

* See p. 105 n above.

that the Indian actions constituted 'serious encroachments upon China's sovereignty and territorial integrity'; and warning that New Delhi would be responsible for the serious consequences if the Indian post was not withdrawn from Khinzemane.[8] In a mollifying reply, India proposed discussions about the precise alignment of the boundary at Khinzemane and other disputed points,* and requested China to leave the *status quo* at Khinzemane undisturbed by keeping her personnel to the north of Thag La ridge. India meanwhile would undertake not to change the position in the area herself, 'pending further discussions'.[9] China did not follow up her implicit threat of 'serious consequences' if the Indians did not withdraw, and the Indian post continued at Khinzemane unmolested for the next three years. The Chinese did not cross Thag La ridge—until after India had broken her own implicit undertaking by setting up another post in the area.

At the officials' meetings in 1960 the Indian side, both in the maps they submitted and verbally, claimed Thag La ridge as the boundary feature, putting the India-China-Bhutan trijunction at 27° 48′ N.[10] But while the Indian Government was thus clear and consistent in its own mind about the location of the boundary in the north-west corner of NEFA, either the Army was not informed about the cartographic anomalies of that area or Army H.Q. did not pass on the information. When the Khinzemane post was established, the Assam Rifles were under the control of the civilian arm, through the governor of Assam, and so the fact that the boundary at its western extremity did not follow their maps was not brought to the attention of the Army—or at least not of formations below Army H.Q. in New Delhi. The Army was, however, put under orders not to patrol the McMahon Line west of Khinzemane.

Since the narrative must now deal with Army formations and units and their commanders in some detail, the chain of command in the summer of 1962 had best be set out here. Army H.Q. was, of course, in New Delhi, with General P. N. Thapar as Chief of Army Staff and Lieutenant-General Kaul as his Chief of the General Staff with his hand-picked staff officers—of whom the most important were his deputy, Major-General J. S. Dhillon, and the Director of Military Operations, Brigadier Palit. Eastern Command H.Q. was at Lucknow, responsible for a vast arc of border from Uttar Pradesh through the McMahon Line, to the borders with Burma and East Pakistan, and for

* See p. 267 n above.

the campaign against the Naga rebels as well. Its G.O.C.-in-C. was Lieutenant-General L. P. Sen, the previous Chief of General Staff. Next came XXXIII Corps, with its headquarters at Shillong (six hundred miles from Lucknow), responsible for the whole Eastern Command area, and under Lieutenant-General Umrao Singh. Then came 4 Division, its headquarters at Tezpur (two hundred miles from Shillong), commanded by Major-General Niranjan Prasad; and its two infantry brigades, 7 Brigade—headquarters at Tawang with one battalion, another at Dirang Dzong, the third at Bomdi La—under Brigadier John Dalvi; and 5 Brigade, with its headquarters at North Lakhimpur and its three battalions scattered through the rest of NEFA. The third brigade of 4 Division (11 Brigade) was detached and on service in Nagaland.

Of the twenty-four new posts which Army H.Q. ordered to be set up on the McMahon Line in implementation of the forward policy in the first six months of 1962, none was in the Khinzemane area, and it is probable that this reflected knowledge at headquarters that the Government had undertaken not to disturb the *status quo* in that area if China did not. But if that was the case, no intimation of the special situation in the Khinzemane/trijunction area had been passed down to XXXIII Corps. So in May 1962, the ban on patrolling to the west of Khinzemane having just been lifted, Corps included among several posts that, apparently on its own authority, it was ordering to be set up, one at the trijunction of India, China and Bhutan. (At the same time a post was decreed at the India-China-Burma trijunction at the opposite end of the McMahon Line, but the terrain was so difficult that the patrol could not get near it.)

When the platoon patrol of Assam Rifles heading for the western trijunction reached the area in June they too disregarded the McMahon Line as it was marked on their maps, and treated the Thag La ridge, three to four miles to the north, as the boundary. Accordingly on June 4th a post was set up, not at the trijunction, which, because of its altitude and inaccessibility, was an impracticable site, but on the floor of the valley to the north of the map-marked boundary. The actual site of the post was a place called Che Dong, on the southern bank of a small river called the Namka Chu; but the patrol commander, presumably because he had misgivings about its position, named it Dhola, after a pass two or three miles south of the map-marked McMahon Line—thus making for the first of a complex of confusions.

The patrol saw no sign of the Chinese, although a reconnaissance party was sent up to Thag La, the pass itself, which overlooks the sizable Tibetan village of Le. This appears to confirm that the Chinese were, as they claimed,[11] still at this time observing in the eastern sector the 1959 agreement not to patrol the actual boundary. It might also explain why they took so long to react to the establishment of Dhola Post—although it seems unlikely that they did not learn of the new post soon after it was set up.

The patrol commander, an Army captain, left the new post under command of a junior commissioned officer and returned to Tezpur to make his report direct to the G.O.C. of the division, General Prasad, who happened to be his uncle. Brigadier Dalvi, in whose sector Dhola Post lay, had previously queried the wisdom of setting up a post which seemed certain to arouse a Chinese reaction, but had been told to 'lay off' as the new post was a matter of national policy[12]—it was the Galwan story over again. Now General Prasad queried the siting of Dhola Post in view of the anomalous nature of the boundary in the trijunction area. He proposed that, if Thag La ridge was going to be treated as the boundary, the post should be moved to Thag La (pass) itself. Corps passed that report and recommendation up, and it eventually reached the Ministry of External Affairs. That Ministry, of course, had known all about the western extremity of the McMahon Line since at least 1959 and had been claiming Thag La ridge as the boundary feature. Now, in spite of India's undertaking to Peking in 1959 not to change the position in this area, it replied that the Army, if it had not already done so, could assert Indian jurisdiction right up to the crest of Thag La ridge.

If, because of the undertaking to China, it had not been intended to set up another post in the Khinzemane area, the Ministry's *ex post facto* approval of Dhola Post marked the point of no return. If the officials' recommendation had been that because India had undertaken not to alter the *status quo* beneath Thag La ridge, the new post should be withdrawn, that might have been done then quietly and without difficulty. The Army certainly would have raised no objection; Dhola Post was tactically a liability, and could have been better sited a few miles to the south. As China had not by then reacted to the establishment of the post, it could have been moved without fear that the Government would be accused of buckling under to Chinese pressure. Perhaps the Ministry had simply forgotten about its earlier undertaking

to China;* but it seems more likely that the officials saw Dhola Post
as part of the policy of asserting full Indian rights on all territory
claimed by India. The soldiers in New Delhi had also, it later trans-
pired, given the civilians the impression that in NEFA the Army was in a
strong position to give the Chinese a nasty knock if an opportunity
offered itself. A local victory on the McMahon Line would, in that
view, show the Chinese that India really meant business and so ease the
way for the forward move in the west.

At all events, the establishment of Dhola Post was approved. No
reply went back to 4 Division, however, either to clarify the position
about the boundary or to approve the recommendation that the post
be moved to the main pass on Thag La ridge itself. But at 4 Division
H.Q. it was from the beginning appreciated that Dhola Post could well
lead to trouble with the Chinese. Apart from the fact that it was
situated in territory that the Army's own maps showed as Chinese, in
May a wooden board inscribed in Chinese had been found in the
vicinity and, when it was translated (in Tezpur in July) it was found to
proclaim: THIS IS OUR RIVER AND OUR MOUNTAIN. As a precaution, an infantry company was ordered from Tawang to Lumpu,
a place to the south of Dhola Post, then believed to be a day's march
from it.

China did not move against Dhola Post until three months after it
had been set up. During that time, the forward policy in the western
sector had brought the situation there to a point of high tension, with
firing frequent and casualties on both sides. The eastern sector remained
quiet until the morning of September 8th—when the Chinese subjected Dhola Post to the same treatment as they had used on the
forward posts set up by India in the west. A Chinese force advanced
suddenly down Thag La ridge and pressed close to the post. The post
commander had been apprehensive for several days, because a party
of his men had met Chinese troops and been told to leave the area or
they would be thrown out. He believed at first that the force approaching his post had come to make good that threat, and later he admitted
that in his reports to headquarters he had exaggerated the Chinese

---

* The suggestion that the Ministry could simply forget a matter of such importance is not
far-fetched. In 1965 the Government vigorously denied that there was any dispute about
the India–Pakistan boundary in the Rann of Kutch; the Ministry had quite forgotten
that about eight years before it had explicitly recognized the existence of such a dispute,
in an agreement with Pakistan. The Government was reminded of the earlier agreement
by a journalist.

numbers.[13] Apparently the first Chinese party numbered about sixty: the post commander reported their number at about six hundred, calculating that if he kept to the more realistic figure he would be told to handle the situation with his own small force, whereas the report that he was threatened by several hundred Chinese troops would be sure to bring the Army to his assistance.[14]

Dhola Post was not surrounded, and the Chinese gave no indication that they intended to attack it. But they settled into positions near and dominating the post, thus repeating in detail the tactics with which they had been countering the Indian forward moves in the western sector.

On September 16th Peking followed up the movement on the ground with a diplomatic protest. Recalling that the Indians had intruded into Khinzemane 'north of the so-called McMahon Line in 1959 and since hung on there', Peking complained that now they had further intruded into Che Dong. 'These systematic nibbling activities fully reveal how ambitious the Indian side's aggressive designs are . . . [and] also show that the Indian side is actively extending the tension to the entire Sino-Indian boundary.' The note concluded with the by now familiar warning that India would be responsible for all the consequences if she persisted.[15]

China's attitude to the marginal adjustments of the McMahon Line which India sought to make unilaterally was consistent. While China would observe the McMahon Line as the *de facto* boundary, that had to be the line as McMahon drew it, not as the Indians tried to modify it. The line had not been jointly surveyed (and could not be until India agreed to open general boundary negotiations); there was no verbal description of the boundary in the Anglo-Tibetan agreement of March 24th, 1914; and so the location of the line at any point could be determined only by reading off the longitude and latitude from the original treaty maps, of which both sides had copies, and transposing those to the ground.[16] By that approach, Dhola Post and Thag La ridge, like Khinzemane, were plainly north of the McMahon Line and in Chinese territory. Definitive transposition of the McMahon Line to the ground, with corrections where necessary to accord with the topography, could be made only in conjunction with a new survey made jointly by the two sides; until that was done the co-ordinates of the original map line must be observed by both sides. If either side were permitted to change the boundary at will, 'what boundary will there be between India and China?' Peking asked.[17]

This approach seems to be sound both practically and legally. Adjustments of the McMahon Line made unilaterally by either side to conform with terrain and convenience would inevitably be conceived to suit the side making them; and, indeed, all of the adjustments made by India pushed the line to the north, adding territory to Indian jurisdiction or claims. For political reasons alone, the Government could not have brought the boundary to the south and thus opened itself to charges of having ceded Indian territory. For parallel reasons, if the Chinese had begun to make unilateral adjustments to correct the McMahon Line from their point of view, the effect could only have been to push the boundary southward.

The Indian Government insisted, however, that, since it was known that McMahon's intention had been to run his boundary along the line of high ridges, and as Thag La ridge was a dominant feature just to the north of the map-marked line, the boundary must lie along Thag La ridge. The Government's determination that the McMahon Line and only the McMahon Line must be India's north-east boundary had by this time been joined by the resolve that the precise location of the line was a matter for India alone to determine. Three years before, Nehru had proposed discussions with China to decide marginal questions of the north-east boundary's alignment. As the confrontation at Dhola Post developed, the Chinese on the spot proposed that an Indian representative should meet their political officer to agree on limits to each side's local control. The proposal went all the way from the Dhola Post area to Nehru, then in London; he turned it down flat.*

In Indian eyes, Thag La ridge had become a definitive and absolute boundary, and Dhola Post was as indisputably Indian as New Delhi itself. The same could be said in theory of the Galwan River post or any other of the forward positions that India had by then set up in Chinese-occupied but Indian-claimed territory in the western sector. But, for political and psychological reasons, the Indian Government's reaction to the Chinese investment of Dhola Post was wholly different from its reaction to the identical Chinese moves against Indian positions in the west. There, posts invested or threatened by the Chinese had been ordered just to hold on; the problems were those only of fortitude and supply. But in the case of Dhola Post, the Government decided that not only must it be relieved forthwith, but the Chinese must be forced back to the northern side of Thag La ridge.

* See p. 308 below.

The anomalous—or unilateral—nature of the boundary as it ran along Thag La ridge was ignored in New Delhi. That, in sending troops across it, China had *reacted*—belatedly—to an Indian move, was forgotten. The Chinese were seen to have crossed the McMahon Line, that was all. They had done so openly, deliberately and (New Delhi believed) in considerable strength; to the Indian Government this could only mean that Peking had begun to implement the long-standing warning that if the Indians persisted in their attempts to realize their western claims by force, China might by the same logic move across the McMahon Line and into NEFA.[18] If the Chinese move across Thag La ridge was the first foray of China's own 'forward policy', to let it pass unchallenged must invite further incursions along the McMahon Line, with Chinese posts being established in NEFA just as Indian posts were being set up in the western sector. The length of the eastern boundary and the already stretched resources of the Indian Army would make it impossible to prevent such piecemeal incursions once they began in earnest. The answer was obvious. The challenge at Thag La ridge must be taken up, and the Chinese dealt such a blow there that not only would they recoil back across the ridge, but also give up the idea of any further incursions across the McMahon Line.

In the Indian measure of the situation, the logic of this was clear enough—but it carried the forward policy one explosive stage further. At first the thinking had been that Indian patrols would simply infiltrate into Chinese-occupied territory in the west, and that China would not retaliate; then it had become that Indian posts would cut off Chinese posts to compel their withdrawal, and that China would not retaliate; now it was that India would attack and force the Chinese back from a position they had taken up, and that China would not retaliate.

Even if political, official and military thinking in New Delhi had been different, the fact that the Chinese move across Thag La ridge was reported in the Indian press—as an incursion across the McMahon Line—two days after it occurred meant that anything but an immediate and forceful reaction would have brought upon the Government a new outburst of political and public criticism. Parliament was not in session; but what the Opposition and Congress back-benches would make of it if the Chinese were allowed to stay south of the McMahon Line could easily be imagined. Ever since the Government came under attack for dereliction in permitting China to move into Aksai Chin, its spokesmen had cited their alertness along the McMahon Line in partial self-exoneration. If China dared to encroach in that sector, they suggested, India would be found as vigilant and resolute as the Government's hottest critics could wish. The Government had maintained that the McMahon Line was absolute, clear and infrangible, and built up public confidence and expectation that even marginal incursions by the Chinese would not be tolerated. Furthermore, while official spokesmen had naturally made much of the great physical and logistical difficulties that the Army faced in dealing with the Chinese in the western sector, they had counterpointed these excuses with suggestions that along the McMahon Line the position was reversed. There, they said, the disadvantages were all on China's side, and the Indian Army correspondingly well placed to defend the border.

That was the reverse of the truth. Movement and road construction on the high Tibetan plateau were relatively easy, and the Chinese had laid lateral roads in the Tsangpo valley with feeders to the south which in some cases reached to within a few miles of the McMahon Line. These were all-weather roads—snowfall on the Tibetan side of the mountains is light—capable of taking the biggest military vehicles. Acclimatization was not a problem for the Chinese Army. Large forces had been stationed in Tibet for years, a good proportion of them on active service against the Khampa rebels; the troops were physically attuned to living and fighting at high altitude, and were suitably clothed and equipped. The situation on the Indian side of the crest line was cruelly different. The terrain between the Brahmaputra valley and the McMahon Line is broken and mountainous, and thickly jungled. Precipitation is very heavy, with the monsoon downpours followed by thick winter snows. The predominant lie of the valleys is north–south, making lateral movement extremely difficult, and even to trek up the valleys is slow and arduous. For a good part of the year the rivers, monsoon- or snow-fed and falling steeply, are unfordable; in places, as on the Lohit and Tawang rivers, they have cut sheer canyons as deep as three hundred feet. If these gulfs were bridged at all in 1962 it was only by narrow, cantilevered logs or rope-and-bamboo suspension bridges; mules could not cross the latter at all, and the wooden bridges only with risk and reluctance. To cut roads through such terrain takes huge labour, and even when laid they are exposed to constant landslides and wash-outs during the monsoon.

Conditions were thus disadvantageous to the Indians throughout

NEFA—but it is unlikely that the disadvantage was greater anywhere than at the very place where the Government decided on a direct military challenge to China. A Chinese road led to a point three hours' march behind Thag La ridge, and could carry seven-ton vehicles, but the area was six days' march from the Indian roadhead at Tawang. To Tawang from the foot-hills was five days if the condition of the road and the resilience of the vehicle allowed. Running across the grain of the ridges, the road snaked and twisted in an alternation of steep ascents and descents. Completed—in the sense that it reached Tawang—only in the previous year, the road lacked any of the staging equipment and organization required for the prompt movement of large bodies of troops. Landslides and deep snow on the high passes made the road frequently impassable, and then troops, fresh from the plains, had to march at altitudes of more than thirteen thousand feet carrying all the equipment they could manage. They reached Tawang exhausted and often sick with pulmonary oedema,* from sudden exertion at high and unaccustomed altitudes.

How was it, then, that until the very last Nehru and his officials in the Ministry of External Affairs believed that the advantages in NEFA lay with their Army, and that with these the Chinese could be given a salutary beating? Kaul and the Army Chief, General Thapar, had been to Tawang by road in the previous November and so should themselves have appreciated the enormous logistic difficulties that would face them if it came to operations on the McMahon Line. But as late as October 1962 Nehru was still telling journalists that in NEFA the advantage lay with India.[19] Plainly, there was deception somewhere; if Nehru was not deliberately misleading the public, then he had been deliberately misled by his senior military advisers. Krishna Menon too must either have been woefully misled or wilfully misleading. But wherever the deception originated, by September 1962 it had become an accepted truth in India. It made the public expectation of prompt and decisive action to throw the Chinese back from Thag La ridge keen and unshakable.

The Government did not have to be pushed into action by public or political pressure, however. The decision to hit the Chinese below Thag La ridge was taken even before the news of their having crossed it was published. At a meeting in the Defence Ministry in New Delhi

---

* A condition, often mistaken for pneumonia, which can quickly be fatal unless the patient is treated and taken to a lower altitude.

on the morning of September 9th it was decided that the Chinese must be evicted immediately and forcefully. But was this 'the Government' deciding? What exactly was 'the Government of India'?

The meeting was conducted by Krishna Menon. General Thapar attended, with General Sen of Eastern Command; Kaul was away in Kashmir on leave. S. S. Khera, the Cabinet Secretary, and S. C. Sarin, a joint secretary in the Defence Ministry, were there, and one or two other officials probably including Malik. Nehru had left for a Commonwealth Prime Ministers' conference in London on September 8th. As was his practice when he left the country, Nehru had been careful to give no indication of who should effectively head the Government in his absence. To do so would, in the context of the time, have been taken to indicate his preference in answers to the old question 'After Nehru, who?'; and Nehru, to the very last, was reluctant to give any such indication. Usually if the Cabinet met in his absence Morarji Desai, the Finance Minister, would take the chair; but on this occasion Desai was in London with the Prime Minister. Lal Bahadur Shastri, now Home Minister, was the senior remaining member of the Cabinet Defence Committee. But Krishna Menon did not attempt to convene that committee, or to consult Shastri; he took the momentous decision, to use force if necessary to evict the Chinese, on his own.

This was a natural effect of Nehru's style. He was accustomed to taking major decisions without consulting the Cabinet; other ministers sometimes followed suit in matters that pertained to their own portfolios. Krishna Menon, who was closest to the Prime Minister, would have assumed in this instance that the necessity of forceful Indian reaction was so evident that there was no reason to consult even Nehru— and that the assumption was correct was shown by the fact that Nehru, who was immediately informed of developments, made the eviction decision his own. Initially Krishna Menon had not favoured the forward policy, it seems (Kaul told the writer and others in 1962 that he had conceived that policy and 'sold' it to Nehru over Menon's head), and had leaned towards a negotiated settlement with China. But he had not been able to influence Nehru on those issues, and had gone along with the forward policy and, gradually, become one of its strongest proponents. Now he was to take a strong and public line on the necessity of ejecting the Chinese from Thag La ridge.

The officers present at Krishna Menon's meeting on September 9th raised the issue of the siting of Dhola Post relative to the McMahon

Line, pointing out that their own maps indicated that it was in Chinese territory (no reply to the inquiry initiated by 4 Division having been sent to Army H.Q.); they were told to disregard their maps and treat the crest of Thag La ridge as the boundary. General Thapar accepted the eviction order, apparently without demur, and a signal was passed down to XXXIII Corps: 9 Punjab (the battalion nearest to Dhola Post, which already had a company at Lumpu) was to move to Dhola Post immediately, with the rest of 7 Brigade to follow within forty-eight hours; all troops should go prepared for battle; 'no weakness will be shown'; if possible the Chinese troops investing Dhola Post should be encircled. The eviction operation was code-named LEGHORN.*

This order, the first of many such, was typical of the approach that Army H.Q. was to take throughout. It responded dutifully to the political requirements of the Government, but disregarded elementary military considerations—by ordering a brigade into extremely difficult and little-known country without reconnaissance or consideration of how the troops were to be supplied. It expressed the suspicion, characteristic perhaps of the worst staff officers in any army, that if commanders and men in the field are not sternly chivvied from above, they will 'show weakness' and not fight. And, without any reliable information about the strength of the Chinese near Dhola Post, it ordered aggressive action by the Indian troops as soon as they got there. This first order gave forewarning, to be amply fulfilled, that in these operations the political were always to override the military factors. There was no one in the decision-making circle at New Delhi to expound the real military considerations—or, at least, no one in a position to make himself heard and with the resolution to make sure that the military factors were taken into consideration. Of the role at the time of General Thapar it was said later by one who worked with him on the civilian side: 'He just seemed to swim with the tide, transferring his interests elsewhere, and as often as not letting his subordinate officers, especially those he thought might be able to soften Krishna Menon's temper, act as buffers between himself and the Defence Minister.'[20] As for the General Staff, although General Kaul was not in the picture at this time, being on leave, they throughout took the same unprofessional, over-optimistic and at bottom irrational view

---

* Perhaps one of the staff officers who had served in Europe in the Second World War found associations in Leghorn (Livorno), the Italian port. It seems unlikely that the operation was named after the breed of white chicken.

of the military possibilities as did the civilian leadership. General Sen, G.O.C.-in-C. Eastern Command, accepted and passed on orders without demurral; dismissed and overrode the representations of his subordinates; and was to make himself New Delhi's hatchet man in dealing with those officers in the field who were thought to be sluggish in carrying out orders.

Inevitably, a rift developed in the command chain, with the break appearing between Eastern Command and XXXIII Corps. The officers above had their eyes and ears on the civilian leadership and its political requirements, and accepted the civilians' assurances that no violent Chinese reaction need be expected; those below gave fuller weight to the logistical and tactical factors, to the capability of the Chinese, and to the fate of Indian troops. The military differences were embittered by long-standing personal animosity between General Sen and General Umrao Singh, of XXXIII Corps.

The sharp differences in approach were made plain in an appreciation of the situation submitted by Umrao Singh on September 12th. He assured his superior officers that he was determined to take prompt action, but suggested that the nature of that action must be based on the capabilities of his forces. He pointed out that the Chinese, who could build up quickly to divisional strength north of Tawang, could steadily outbid any reinforcements that the Indians could put into the Thag La area. All Indian supply to troops around Dhola Post would have to be by air-drop, while the Chinese roadhead was only a few miles behind Thag La ridge. His troops would be operating at altitudes of between 13,000 and 16,000 feet; winter was closing in, and therefore they would need heavy clothing and tents. In conclusion, Umrao Singh suggested that Dhola Post should simply be withdrawn to the map-marked boundary about three miles to the south (as India had withdrawn the post at Tamaden in 1959*); but if that were ruled out for political reasons, the Army's commitment should be limited to two battalions which should be deployed south of Dhola Post, and *south of the map-marked McMahon Line*, to meet any further advance by the Chinese.

On September 12th General Sen went to Tezpur and personally repeated the orders to Umrao Singh, General Prasad (G.O.C. 4 Division) and other officers. The Chinese must be thrown back over Thag La ridge, as the Government would allow no intrusions over the McMahon Line. All doubts about the alignment of the boundary in the

* See p. 110 above.

Thag La area must be put out of mind, and the evidence of the Army's own maps disregarded—the boundary ran along Thag La ridge. Troops could fire, at their discretion, on armed Chinese in Indian territory. Umrao Singh repeated for the record his view, and that of his divisional and brigade commanders, that the task of eviction was beyond them, and pointed out that the attempt could be made only at the cost of uncovering Tawang. The order was reaffirmed.

Meanwhile 9 Punjab had concentrated at Lumpu, and marched out for Dhola Post in the small hours of September 14th. This battalion was the only unit in a position to respond promptly to the orders given in New Delhi on September 8th—and it was at half strength, with about four hundred rifles against its full complement of eight hundred. The Punjabis had been inducted to Tawang in the previous winter, and, although they had been through hard times on short supplies, they were acclimatized. The second battalion of the brigade, 1 Sikhs, was at Dirang Dzong, on the eastern side of Se La (pass), because it could not be maintained at Tawang; and the third battalion was at Misamari, on the plains, preparing to entrain for a peace station in Punjab. This battalion, the 1/9 Gorkha Rifles, was a crack unit with vivid battle honours; but they had spent three hard years in NEFA and were tired and looking forward to their well-earned spell in a cantonment. Instead, they were turned round and ordered to the Thag La area.

So 7 Brigade, at the time it was ordered to move within forty-eight hours to Dhola Post, consisted in effect of only one battalion, and that at half strength. If Thapar and Sen were not informed of this fact either they or the General Staff, or both, were not doing their jobs.

By the time the Punjabis began the trek from Lumpu to Dhola Post on September 14th Army H.Q. had been informed that the number of Chinese below Thag La ridge was much less than first estimated, and was in fact fifty or sixty. The size at which the first Chinese move was put by the Dhola Post commander—six hundred—had been a key factor in determining the Indian reaction; if the number had been put more realistically at about sixty it is most unlikely that the reaction would have been so drastic. But even now that the Chinese numbers were reported so reduced there was no inclination in New Delhi to call off the move to evict the Chinese; on the contrary, Army H.Q. issued an order direct to the Punjabis that they were to capture Thag La and take up positions at two 16,000-foot passes on the ridge by September 19th![21] This order did not reach the Punjabis until September 19th itself, by which time they were spread out over a front of several miles on the Namka Chu, the fast-flowing and deep mountain stream by which Dhola Post had been established. They could see that the Chinese troops on the river were supported in strength from the ridge behind, and that the order was wholly beyond their capabilities: to have a chance of success, troops attacking prepared positions should have an advantage in numbers of at least three to one, as well, of course, as ample ammunition and some support fire. The Punjabis did not outnumber the Chinese they could *see*—it was obvious that the main Chinese strength was behind the ridge—and had only the ammunition in their pouches, about fifty rounds per man. Brigadier Dalvi, who had just reached the Dhola Post area, said later that he 'flatly refused to obey this order and informed Divisional H.Q. accordingly. G.O.C. agreed with [him] and protested to XXXIII Corps, who in turn asked Eastern Command to have the order countermanded'.[22]

The Punjabis had reached the Namka Chu early on September 15th. There were two routes from Lumpu to the Namka Chu; one, the shorter, crossed Hathung La (pass) at 13,500 feet, and involved steep climbs (ropes had to be rigged in places to help porters) and dangerous descents over stretches of slippery, lichen-covered boulders.* The Punjabis, moving on hard scale rations and pouch ammunition and leaving their heavy weapons, mortar ammunition and digging tools in Lumpu, had covered the distance in a forced march of just over twenty-four hours. For unacclimatized troops it would take two full days to the river and another to Dhola Post; for laden porters, the best part of three days. (The sun sets early in NEFA's deep valleys, and at this time of the year it was dark soon after four p.m.) The disadvantage of the Hathung La route was that troops moving up the Namku Chu did so under point-blank observation by the Chinese. But another route, which approached Dhola Post from the rear, crossed the much higher and more difficult pass named Karpo La I, which was at 16,000 feet and demanded a dangerous climb rather than a march. On neither route, of course, was there any cover. The troops bivouacked in the open. The Punjabis had winter uniform—though not made for snow and zero temperatures—but other battalions marched

---

* A curse to the troops negotiating such ground was that not only were boots in short supply, so were the hobnails and metal plates to give the soles purchase. For men carrying loads, heavy and repeated falls were almost unavoidable.

across the passes in October in cotton uniforms, with only thin sweaters against the wind. They carried one blanket per man.

The Namku Chu, unfordable at this time because of the monsoon rains and between twenty and fifty feet wide, runs like most of the streams in these mountains in a deep bed, with sheer banks twenty to thirty feet high. It was bridged at several points by logs, two or at the most three roped together, and the Indians numbered these from east to west as they moved up-river. The Punjabis encountered the Chinese in company strength on both sides of the river at Bridge II on September 15th.

> The Chinese were accompanied by a Chinese civilian official. They shouted in Hindi that the Indians should withdraw from the Namka Chu (Kechilang according to them) area as it was Chinese territory. They said that the Indian and Chinese peoples had an unbreakable friendship and this friendship should not be marred by petty border incidents. They asked . . . why [the Indians] had moved regular troops and claimed that they were only Chinese Frontier Guards and not soldiers of the People's Liberation Army. Finally they asked [the Indians] to send [their] local civil officers to discuss the exact location of the border, with a view to an amicable settlement and to prevent firing and bloodshed.[23]

In response to the last request, the Indian political officer for the area moved forward and was at Lumpu, on the way to meet his Chinese opposite number, when he was ordered to have no discussions with the Chinese. This was the proposal referred to Nehru.

The Punjabis had reached the river under orders to relieve Dhola Post, reopen the supply route to the post if it were closed, and prevent further Chinese incursions. Accordingly the commanding officer had spread the battalion out along the Namka Chu—two companies at the lower bridges, a third near Dhola Post itself, which was near Bridge III. He had sent a platoon to Tsangdhar, a commanding 14,500-foot feature with a flat area suitable for guns or heavy mortars—if such could ever be brought to the area. The Punjabis' positions were not mutually supporting, and were indeed stretched out over nearly seven miles, a two days' trek. They had been taken up, not with a view to defence, even less to attack; they were to prevent trespass.

Brigadier Dalvi had been ordered from his headquarters in Tawang to the Namka Chu on the evening of September 13th, General

Prasad, over the telephone from Tezpur, sharply rebuking hi ⸲ɯ foot having 'gone forward', and ordering him to move 'at onceDalvi ⹁ turned a Nelsonian ear to that part of the order—it being dark already —telling his G.O.C. that static made his order unintelligible.[24] It later emerged that Prasad had been told by General Sen to give Dalvi a 'rocket' and order him forward. This obsession with getting senior officers forward marked the whole build-up to the Thag La ridge operation—Prasad was later to suffer the same humiliation as Dalvi; the process reached its greatest absurdity when a senior staff officer at corps level whose duties were concerned with ceremonials, pay, pensions, welfare and discipline reported to 7 Brigade on the eve of their battle. Dalvi's comment on the order to go to the Namka Chu is apt: 'What was I to do "forward"? Brigade Commanders are not appointed merely to rush to the "scene of the occurrence"; they are expected to command and administer their brigades at a distance or they will only lose themselves in the confusion of combat and get a distorted picture of the tactical situation. They must, of course, visit the battlefield frequently to acquaint themselves with the ground and the battle situation and take personal charge when necessary. The decision is entirely theirs and not that of their superiors.'[23] He had made a personal reconnaissance of the Khinzemane-Namka Chu area only a few months before.

Dalvi had been in command of 7 Brigade since the beginning of the year. A graduate of the Indian Military Academy, then aged forty-two, he had served with infantry in Burma in the Second World War and been mentioned in dispatches. After the war his experience had been wide and his promotions regular; he had had first-hand experience of the logistical difficulties of the forward policy in the western sector, as a staff officer with Corps H.Q. there, and had volunteered for the command of 7 Brigade from that post.

While the Indians were thus laboriously building up the force on the Namka Chu, on the other side of the little river the Chinese were effortlessly keeping pace with them. There appeared to be two Chinese infantry companies between the river and the ridge when the Punjabis joined up on September 15th with the Assam Rifles platoon that had until then garrisoned Dhola Post; but next day a third company came down from Thag La. Intelligence reports put another Chinese battalion at Le, just behind Thag La, and by September 20th it was reported that the Chinese had two regiments (equivalent to Indian brigades) in the area, with divisional artillery and the rest of a division at Tsona Dzong, only some twenty miles back and linked almost to Thag La by road. There were also seen to be concentrations at Bum La, the pass leading to the old trade route direct to Tawang. These intelligence reports were received at Army H.Q. in New Delhi but reached the field formations only after a time-lag of from ten days to a fortnight, too late to be of any use in planning or operations. The intelligence received by the field formations was haphazard and inadequately assessed, as well as late; the Army's own intelligence system had atrophied, while the civilian Intelligence Bureau was ineffective.

The decline of military intelligence (M.I.) in India could be traced back to the last days of the British. There had been no Indians in M.I., so after 1947 all its personnel were new to the work. Furthermore, its role was diminished in favour of the civilian Intelligence Bureau (I.B.), staffed by police officers. This I.B. grew in influence and importance, while M.I. languished, its senior staff posts tending to become sinecures or stepping-stones. Under its director at this time, B. N. Malik, the Intelligence Bureau had, as has been seen, become an important voice in the innermost counsels of the Government; at bottom this influence derived from Malik's standing with Nehru. Access to and the confidence of the Prime Minister were the prerequisite of influence in the Government in those days, and Malik enjoyed them to the full. A former police officer, Malik was articulate and astute; his stewardship of dossiers on many of Nehru's colleagues and opponents and the importance of intelligence in domestic Indian politics would also have brought him close to the Prime Minister.

Reliance upon Malik's advice in some areas of domestic politics had grown by the 1960s into a willingness to accept almost as fact his predictions about Chinese behaviour. As has been seen, his appreciation —or rather divination—that the Chinese would not interfere with Indian posts once they were established had been the rock of faith upon which the forward policy was built; now his opinion that China would not unleash any massive retaliation if India used force against the Chinese below Thag La ridge similarly shored up the determination of the civilian leadership and the New Delhi soldiers to push on with Operation Leghorn. Curiously, the confidence that no strong Chinese reaction need be feared overrode even the Intelligence Bureau's own reports of mounting concentrations of Chinese troops at points just behind the McMahon Line; and certainly helped to close the ears of

Nehru and his official advisers to the explicit and repeated warnings in diplomatic notes from Peking that China *would* react, and most forcefully. Malik plainly relied on extra-sensory perceptions rather than on the regular disciplines of intelligence collection and assessment, and no doubt part of the explanation for the inordinate and indeed irrational trust placed in his predictions is that he was telling Nehru and his colleagues exactly what they wanted to hear.

Just how much Nehru and his colleagues wished to believe that the Chinese could without much trouble be forced back over Thag La ridge may be gauged by the strength of the political reaction to the news that the McMahon Line had been crossed. The report was circulated from Tezpur by a news agency on September 10th, and the Government at first tried to persuade the agency to withdraw it; officials told journalists in New Delhi who tried to confirm the report there that it was unfounded. The news agency stood by its reporter, however; the original story was followed up by others from north-eastern India which substantiated it; and on September 13th an official spokesman confirmed that 'some Chinese forces have appeared in the area of the Bhutan trijunction. . . .' Even then, and for some days after, the spokesman at the Ministry of External Affairs' regular evening briefings fenced with reporters to avoid saying squarely that Chinese troops had deliberately crossed the McMahon Line. 'A Chinese group appears to be on our side,' he said on September 14th.

The Government's attempt to cover up or at least muffle the news of the crossing of Thag La ridge was understandable. Whatever had to be done, the Government would be able to deal with the situation more comfortably if it did not have an aroused political opinion at its heels. But of course the attempt was bound to fail. It was not only the freedom of the press, and the skill of the Indian political correspondents in the capital; the Government leaked news like a sieve. At any time, sooner rather than later, journalists in the capital were usually able to find out what was going on; but at this time, as will be seen, the speed with which the Government's most secret decisions found their way into the press was extraordinary.

The official attempts to play down the story of Thag La ridge were thus like a fire extinguisher on a bush fire. The attitude of the Government's critics was that even if only one Chinese had crossed the McMahon Line, the Government would be betraying its obligations to the nation if he were not instantly expelled—and so much more drastic should the action be if the Chinese were across the line in force. Soon the Swatantra party was calling for Nehru's resignation on the grounds of his 'utter failure to protect India's borders',[26] and the Jan Sangh was demanding that the Government issue an ultimatum to China.[27] Parliament was not in session, but even without that sounding-board it was plain that a political storm was blowing up, and that it could be more violent than anything the Government had weathered before. The Opposition in Parliament was all bark and no bite, of course; but, dangerously, Congress opinion was just as outraged at what was universally believed to be a new Chinese aggression, unprovoked and insolent, and was growing just as impatient with the Government's counter-measures.

Government spokesmen and officials speaking privately to journalists thereafter laid a trap for themselves. For background, they let it be known that in the Government's view India could not allow China's challenge to pass, because if the Chinese were allowed to dig in and stay below Thag La ridge, it would open the way to a series of such probings and infiltrations all along the McMahon Line.[28] Having thus implicitly committed the Government to action, the spokesman and officials speaking to journalists for background began to make matters more difficult for themselves by suggesting that the situation below Thag La ridge was well in hand. Thus they encouraged the political demand for drastic action, and whetted the expectation that it would come soon.

The civilian officials, however, were only reflecting the assurances of the senior generals, notably those of General Sen of Eastern Command. The estimates he gave of the time needed for 7 Brigade to concentrate beneath Thag La ridge were throughout wildly optimistic. This may have arisen partly from his own ignorance, and that of some staff officers, of the conditions in NEFA; distances of a few miles on the maps, which officers accustomed to the plains of Punjab would expect troops to cover in hours, in fact might take days of exhausting trekking for troops in the mountains. Whatever the explanation, Sen first told the civilians that there would be a full brigade of troops on the Namka Chu, ready to move against the Chinese, by September 21st. In fact it was not until the beginning of October that any more troops reached the river to reinforce the half-strength battalion of Punjabis, and then it was only *one company*.

Backing up his subordinates, General Umrao Singh at XXXIII

Corps was certainly dragging his feet: or, to put it another way, was refusing to be hustled by Army H.Q. and Eastern Command into putting his troops where he could not supply them, to launch an operation that he and his subordinate commanders knew to be impossible.

While General Thapar did not accept the field commanders' appreciations that it was militarily impossible to clear the Chinese from below Thag La ridge with the forces that could be deployed in the area, he was uneasy about the Chinese reaction to the Indian assault. At a meeting in the Defence Ministry on September 22nd, Thapar said he thought it likely that China would retaliate against the Indian forward posts in the western sector, perhaps overrunning all of them east of the Chinese claim line. Such misgivings had been expressed before, and there was a stock civilian reassurance for them: the emphatic statement that China would *not* launch any general attack. The calculation in the Ministries of Defence and External Affairs was that a hard and demonstrative blow at the Chinese beneath Thag La ridge would not only see them retreating there, but thereafter taking a much more acquiescent line in face of Indian moves elsewhere. For reasons of prestige, the Chinese might feel impelled to compensate for their defeat below Thag La with some small, local actions in the western sector, it was thought. One or two Indian posts, probably including that on the Galwan, might be lost; but that was judged a price well worth paying to clear the Chinese back over the McMahon Line. This appreciation derived from the reading of the mood and character of the Chinese Government taken in the Ministry of External Affairs; it was confirmed by Malik's estimations, and it matched the confidence, widely felt in New Delhi, that no one would risk the odium of publicly assaulting a country as identified as was India with the cause of peace. Least of all would China do such a thing, so beholden was Peking to India for support in the United Nations and elsewhere.

Accordingly, Thapar's warning that the Chinese might retaliate in the western sector if the Indians persisted in the eviction operation in the east was rejected at the Defence Ministry meeting of September 22nd; and the order for the Army to evict the Chinese from the southern side of Thag La ridge was confirmed. Thapar then requested that the order be put in writing.

In the context, that may have been meant as a protest. Krishna

Menon had left to attend the General Assembly of the United Nations two days before, and so the Army Chief could press his misgivings without fear of a tongue-lashing. In fact, however, Thapar was doing no more than ask that normal practice be followed. Such a momentous order should have been in writing in the normal course of governmental practice. Furthermore, it should have been related to an appreciation by the General Staff, and included a statement of the national aim behind the operation; and it should have put the operation into a broader context so that the Army Chief would know what dispositions he could make from other areas. (The key question in that connection was what might be expected from Pakistan in the event of hostilities with China.) But not only had the eviction order never been put in writing; from the beginning of the crisis in New Delhi, pen had hardly been put to paper for confirming orders or recording minutes. From the first meeting to discuss the Chinese crossing of Thag La ridge, Krishna Menon had ruled that no minutes were to be kept—the better, he suggested, to preserve security. The measure did little good in that regard; but when the time came to try to tie down responsibility for decisions taken, it had made the trail very faint.

The soldiers were following suit. Orders from Army H.Q. to Eastern Command were often given by telephone, Thapar to Sen, usually with no confirmatory signal following; often, indeed, Sen was at the meetings in New Delhi, and so orders could be given directly, and again, of course, orally. At this time it was only at the level of Corps command and below that the normal procedures were being followed; later they were dropped even there, and officers, perhaps recognizing that the orders they were being made to pass on were improper or impossible to implement, did not commit themselves in writing. This cannot be justified as a streamlining of military bureaucracy to meet an emergency. When the pressure is on, and lives and national security depend upon the decisions taken by military commanders, the need for a written record is greater, not less. Bumph, as soldiers call it, that stream of military signals and reports, in duplicate or triplicate, with copies to lower and higher formations for information, is the best assurance a government and its troops can have that decisions will be taken with full thought, in the light of all known factors; and that those who make decisions will stand responsible for them.

So General Thapar's request on September 22nd that the eviction

order be put in writing came very late; the Army had, in fact, been
under that order for ten days. But still it put the civilians in momen-
tary difficulties. In Krishna Menon's absence in New York, the deputy
Defence Minister, K. Raguramaiah, was officiating for him. It appears
that he judged the confirmation of an order to take military action
against China beyond his normal competence (usually he was concerned with defence production, and keeping out of the Minister's
way); at all events, a telephone call was put through to Menon. Even
now, with the Chief of Army Staff raising questions about the wisdom
of the order for operations against the Chinese, with the Prime Minister
and the Defence Minister abroad, the Cabinet Defence Committee, or
what was left of it in New Delhi, was not consulted.

Thapar did not have to wait long for confirmation, however. It
came in a few hours, in these words:

> The decision throughout has been as discussed at previous meet-
> ings, that the Army should prepare and throw out the Chinese as
> soon as possible. The Chief of the Army Staff was accordingly
> directed to take action for the eviction of the Chinese in the
> Kameng Frontier Division of NEFA* as soon as he is ready.

The order was signed by S. C. Sarin, a relatively junior official in the
ministry.

For General Thapar, this was the moment of truth. His professional
judgment, that the eviction operation invited a Chinese reaction which
his forces would be quite incapable of handling, had been overruled.
His warning, based on a life-time's experience and training in the
soldier's craft, had been dismissed by his Minister, concerned for the
moment with the affairs of the General Assembly, half the world
away. There was nothing new in Thapar's predicament, it was as old
as war; and there was little doubt about his recourse. Napoleon had
set it out with precision:

> A commander-in-chief is not exonerated for his mistakes in war,
> committed by virtue of an order of his sovereign or of a minister,
> when he that gives it is far from the field of operations and knows
> little or nothing of the latest developments. Hence it follows that
> any commander-in-chief who undertakes to execute a plan which

* Kameng is the westernmost of NEFA's five divisions, and the Thag La area was considered part of it.

he considers bad is guilty. He should give his reasons, insist that
the plan be changed, and finally resign rather than become the
instrument of the ruin of the army.[29]

In the Indian context—or for Thapar, at least—the precedent was not
encouraging, however. Just three years before, his predecessor had
submitted his resignation because of a clash with Krishna Menon, and
as a result had been humiliated and humbled in the name of 'civil
supremacy'. Thapar was no Thimayya—and even Thimayya had not
had it in him to stand up to Nehru. Thapar accepted the order, and
passed it on to Eastern Command.

If Thimayya's aborted resignation in 1959 marked one point of no
return in the Indian Army's decline to crushing defeat at the hands of
the Chinese, Thapar's failure to offer his resignation at this point was
another. His judgment of the likely consequences of the eviction
operation having been offhandedly overruled by the civilian authority,
there was only one way in which he could resist further. Brigadier
Dalvi, who, much lower down the line of command, was to share
Thapar's predicament and finally submitted his resignation in protest,
later put it well: 'Resignation is the last constitutional resort of a service
chief in a democratic set-up, to focus national attention on a fundamental issue to give the nation an opportunity to debate the points of
disagreement between the civil and military authorities. In a democracy, this is the only safeguard against incompetent, unscrupulous or
ambitious politicians.'[30] But Thapar did not see it that way.

Having passed on the confirmed eviction order, Army H.Q. warned
Western Command that the impending operation might cause the
Chinese to attack some of the forward Indian posts. The troops should
therefore be alerted, the post defences strengthened if possible. If they
were attacked, they should fight it out.

While public attention and to a large extent the Government's was
focused on developments below Thag La ridge, the tension continued
to mount throughout September in the western sector too. As has been
seen, Army H.Q. was there, too, overriding all warnings and protests
from the area commander, who like General Umrao Singh at XXXIII
Corps believed that the Chinese would retaliate fiercely if pushed only
a little more; and knew that if that did happen, there were not the
military resources to meet the attack. The Chinese had recently begun
to occupy the dropping zones of the forward posts when these were

not within the post's defence perimeter, and on September 22nd an
order went from Army H.Q. to Western Command that henceforth
this was not to be tolerated. Chinese troops attempting to occupy
dropping zones or interposing themselves between the D.Z.s and the
posts were to be fired on. The civilians and New Delhi soldiers had
that summer convinced themselves that the Chinese would not stand
up to fire; that with a whiff of grapeshot, so to speak, their menaces at
the forward posts would be exposed as mere huffing and puffing.
What the order meant to the Indian troops concerned—often only in
platoon strength, sometimes no more than a section—can be imagined.
In every case they lived under the guns of far more strongly armed
Chinese troops, who outnumbered them by five or ten to one.

With the eviction order confirmed and passed down, demands for
implementation became more insistent. Sen now ordered General
Prasad forward from Tawang to get things moving, and as no helicopter was available the general had to trek to Lumpu; this was hard
going even for fit combat soldiers, and one who saw it said later that
Prasad's arrival at Lumpu 'was not a pretty sight'.[31] But, the physical
ordeal apart, ordering the G.O.C. of the division forward served no
purpose beyond that of satisfying the militarily uninformed that
everything possible was being done to get the eviction operation
launched as quickly as possible. Furthermore, it took him out of
contact with his command for three days, while he was trekking, and
away from his H.Q. for longer.

Brigadier Dalvi had meanwhile established a headquarters at Lumpu,
and General Prasad joined him there on September 25th. Sen had
ordered an outline plan for the operation to be prepared, Umrao Singh
had passed on the order to Prasad, and now Prasad told Dalvi to
prepare the plan. Prasad knew as well as Dalvi that the eviction of the
Chinese was militarily impossible, and that the very preparation of a
plan of operation might only strengthen the high command's delusions
on the score. But if it set out the tactical and maintenance problems
forcefully enough, it might educate Eastern Command and Army
H.Q.—and, anyway, preparation of the plan had been ordered.

The tactical problem facing the Indians was daunting enough, quite
apart from that of supply. The Namka Chu was still unfordable and
the narrow, slippery bridges which crossed it were all covered by
Chinese guns. The Thag La ridge ran downward from west to east,
so an advance from the east would have been steeply uphill. The

central approach, over the river and up the face of the ridge, was again very steep and dominated by the Chinese positions; troops advancing that way could have been wiped out under cross-fire. The only practicable approach to the objective, Thag La, was from the west, from a feature called Tsangle, to a knoll, Tseng-jong, from which an attack could be launched on the Chinese river positions from their rear and flank. Even this paper plan was wholly unreal, for it had to be based on the assumptions that the Chinese would not reinforce; and that they would take no counter-action to the Indian advance, but would wait where they were and at the last retreat without putting up a serious fight. Those were the assumptions in New Delhi, and Dalvi had to base his plan upon them, rather than upon what his own military training told him the Chinese reaction would be.

But from the point of view of Dalvi and Prasad, the obvious tactical weaknesses of the plan of attack were less important than the force and detail with which the prequisites for action were stated. This was where the high command was to be made to see the impossibility of Operation Leghorn.

Rations for thirty days for the whole brigade would have to be air-dropped and stocked before any more troops were inducted to the river; minimum artillery requirements for a brigade attack—a battery and a half of field guns and ammunition—would also have to be brought in; ample ammunition, for small arms, mortars and machine-guns, and the brigade's full complement of weapons—all of this, and more, would have to be stored on the Namka Chu before the operation could begin. It worked out at five hundred and eighty tons of material. The requirement was by no means unreasonable for a brigade attack against an enemy in battalion strength, strongly entrenched in commanding positions and heavily armed; but to meet it in the circumstances was utterly impossible. The land-route over Hathung La could not be used for anything but small loads, and anyway there were few porters. All supplies would have to be air-dropped on the only flat patch of ground in the area, at the place called Tsangdhar, south of the river and about two thousand feet above it. The dropping zone was so small that it could be effectively used only by Dakota aircraft, which could fly slowly enough to have a chance of hitting it with their loads; and it was too distant from the troops' main positions to be a good source of supply since all loads would have to be manhandled from there, by the troops themselves and over steep and difficult trails. As for artillery, the only guns that could possibly be dropped to the brigade were the light pieces of the paratroops, and they would be of little use because they were out-ranged even by the Chinese infantry mortars. There was, furthermore, a deadline to all this. Unless the requisite material was supplied by October 10th, the operation could not be launched for another six months. The snows would have begun by late October, and the operation would have to be completed well before that.

General Umrao Singh helicoptered to Lumpu on September 26th. He went over Dalvi's plan, advised that the requirements be raised further, and counselled greater prudence. He then accepted the revised plan—thereby making it his own—and took it to Sen at Eastern Command on September 29th.

By this time the politicians in New Delhi, those in the Government and Congress Party as well as the Opposition, were getting impatient. From the outset official comment and briefings had been confident, and no serious attempt was made to keep the eviction order secret. It was reported in *The Times* in a dispatch of September 23rd and confirmed a few days later by the *Times of India* in these words:

The Government of India took the political decision ten days ago to use force if necessary to throw the Chinese intruders out. The Army was accordingly instructed to take the steps necessary to clear the Chinese from Indian territory across Thag La ridge, if they did not withdraw on their own in reasonable time. The Army authorities have been given the freedom to choose the time and tactics best suited for an operation of this type, the object of which is not to capture or inflict casualties on the Chinese intruders but to force them to withdraw to their side of the border.[32]

Plainly, whoever gave that briefing hoped still that the Chinese could be shooed back over Thag La ridge. This optimism that India's objective would be achieved soon and without difficulty induced an expectant public excitement at first; but as time passed without action to follow up official reassurances and fulfil the leaked commitment to attack, the initial gratification at the Government's apparent resolve cooled into suspicion that it had been bluffing.

Impatience was sharpened by reports of skirmishes in the Thag La area. In the first part of September all had been quiet along the Namka

Chu, and in the early days of the confrontation there was even some wary fraternization across the river, with the Chinese offering cigarettes to the tobacco-less Indians and even handing over some para-chuted Indian supplies that had landed in their lines. With loud-speakers the Chinese assured the Indian troops that the two Govern-ments would soon open talks to resolve the boundary question, and asked for caution so that firing should not worsen the situation. Meanwhile the Chinese continued their defence preparations, digging bunkers and clearing lines of fire. 'Sometimes the Chinese would magnanimously inform us that they were about to fell a tree, and that we should not get unduly alarmed if we heard loud crashing sounds,' Brigadier Dalvi recalled.[33] But with opposing troops, tensed for possible combat and at the closest quarters, clashes were inevitable. The first shooting occurred on September 20th. The Chinese had from the beginning had a sentry post at the southern end of Bridge II, and it appears that the Indians had been attempting to chivvy them back. This is a Chinese account of an incident on September 17th:

> While two Chinese frontier guards were on sentry duty ... more than sixty Indian soldiers closed in on them from three directions. The two Chinese soldiers immediately shouted to the Indian soldiers to halt. But the Indian troops pressed forward even faster. Several of the Indian troops gathered round them at a distance of about ten metres and some came as close as three metres to one of the guards, aiming their British-made rifles and Canadian-made sub-machine-guns and howling out at the top of their voices in wanton provocation.[34]

This sentry post was involved in the incident of September 20th, it appears; each side accused the other of starting it, but the shooting left two Chinese dead, five wounded on the Indian side.[35]

Peking protested, and demanded that 'the Indian side immediately stop its attack and withdraw', warning that the Chinese would defend themselves and fire back if the Indians opened fire. 'The situation in the ... area is extremely serious,' the note said, 'and flames of war may break out there.'[36] The *People's Daily* wrote in the same vein: 'The situation is most critical and the consequences will be serious. Let the Indian authorities not say that warning has not been served in advance.'[37] The Indian replies and counter-protests used almost the same language as Peking, calling on China to 'cease aggressive activities on Indian territory' and withdraw to the north of Thag La ridge or 'be responsible for all the consequences'.³⁸ Both sides were sabre-rattling—but India's scabbard was empty.

Official Indian accounts of exchanges of fire below Thag La ridge, with the Chinese blamed for provoking them, made the questions from journalists and politicians more pressing—when was the Army going to complete the job it had been given? Members of the Government and officials began fending them off by suggesting that the field commanders were being sluggish or worse. In a background interview at the beginning of October Lal Bahadur Shastri, the Home Minister, told the writer that the Army, having been so long at peace, had lost its fighting spirit; but that this was being remedied by certain command changes, and the necessary action would soon begin. In other briefings, officials were more pointed; they put the blame explicitly on the field officers, and on General Umrao Singh.

Umrao Singh had gone from Lumpu to Eastern Command H.Q. at Lucknow on September 29th to submit his appreciation and operation plan to General Sen. Sen had refused to accept the requirements Umrao Singh had stipulated for the operation—which, as has been seen, were in fact plainly impossible to meet. Overruled, Umrao Singh put his protest in writing, pointing both to the impracticability of the action he was being ordered to launch and to the impropriety of Sen's handling of the situation. Eastern Command was ordering the movement of platoons and companies; would they please restrict themselves to their proper role of setting tasks, and leave the method to the men on the spot? he asked.

Umrao Singh's resistance left Sen and General Thapar in a trap of their own constructing. From the start they had been assuring the civilians that the eviction operation was feasible and could be accomplished soon and quickly. (Their misgivings had been about the repercussions *elsewhere* on the borders, and those had been met by the civilians' assurance that no general Chinese reaction was to be expected.) But three weeks had passed without action, and now Umrao Singh's appreciation, plan and stipulations made it plain that if it were left to him Operation Leghorn would not be launched at all. The dilemma seemed acute. But in fact the answer was, for Sen and Thapar, simple— sack Umrao Singh. Sen brought Umrao Singh's written protest to the attention of Army H.Q. as an example of tetchy uncooperativeness, and on October 2nd Thapar and Sen asked Krishna Menon for

II

permission to remove him from command of XXXIII Corps. Menon agreed. According to Sen,[39] he asked Menon to appoint Major-General Manekshaw instead—that same Sam Manekshaw who a year before had been arraigned on the charge that he had spoken disrespect-fully of the Defence Minister and his favourites. Menon, in Sen's account, 'hit the roof' and refused point-blank. Menon had seen to it that, although Manekshaw had been exonerated of the charges brought against him, his promotion to lieutenant-general had not come through; and plainly he was determined that his critic was not going to be rehabilitated just because he was needed for operations against the Chinese. Here was another turning-point. Had Menon forgotten his rancour, had Thapar or Sen insisted, on threat of resignation, on Manekshaw's appointment, there can be no doubt that Manekshaw would have taken precisely the same position as had Umrao Singh. Perhaps the expectation that this would be the case confirmed Menon's determination, and eased Sen's acquiescence.

The question of who would replace Umrao Singh was left open for the moment. It was decided, however, between Menon, Thapar and Sen, that Umrao Singh was not simply to be removed from command of XXXIII Corps; instead, another corps was to be formed to take over operations on the north-eastern border. No explanation for that decision is to be found on the record; but the reasons for it are plain enough. First, the look of things. If Umrao Singh were simply removed from his command, questions would inevitably be raised. If it emerged that he had been sacked because of differences with his superiors over the practicability of the promised operations against the Chinese, the cat would be out of the bag and there would be a public and political uproar with unpredictable consequences. He had to be displaced quietly, and the neatest way to do that would be to leave him as a corps commander but deprive him of responsibility for Operation Leghorn. The most practical way of doing that would have been to divide the responsibilities of XXXIII Corps; responsibility for the operations against the Nagas and for the border with East Pakistan would be shifted to a new corps, with Umrao Singh to command it and give continuity; XXXIII Corps would continue to be responsible for the NEFA border and Operation Leghorn, but under a new com-mander. But that approach raised a further difficulty—what about the staff officers at XXXIII Corps? It could be assumed that they, having processed the appreciations of the lower formations and made their own for Umrao Singh, would share his judgment on the impracticability of the eviction operation. To put a new commander on top of the old staff might be to get nowhere; he would have to be a very self-willed man to overrule the concerted advice of his staff, all very much more informed on the problem than he could be, the moment he took over.

It was decided, therefore, that a new corps should be formed, under a new commander, *and should be made responsible for the immediate launching of Operation Leghorn*. Thus, caught between the need to get rid of Umrao Singh without appearing to do so and the need to get the eviction operation started immediately, Menon, Thapar and Sen combined the worst elements of all courses open to them. If the change had been made in the course of administrative rationalization, several weeks, preferably one or two months, would have been allowed for the formation of the new corps and its induction to its responsibilities. For a corps to be formed from scratch, overnight, and from the moment of its inception take command of a major operation must be unique in military history. In reality, of course, that did not happen. The new corps, designated IV Corps, was initially a phantom formation, a public-relations and political device to enable Menon, Thapar and Sen to get the operation they had promised launched quickly. It was the only way in which they could achieve that end without further quibbling over such trivia as the relative strengths of attackers and defenders, or supplies of ammunition and food.

Having hit on the idea of a new corps, they needed to command it a man in the Light Brigade mould, who would see that it was his not to reason why. The man was at hand. General Kaul had been on leave in Kashmir since September 3rd. Krishna Menon had objected to the Chief of General Staff's taking leave when the situation on the borders was so tense; but Kaul, pointing out that Nehru, Morarji Desai and Krishna Menon himself all proposed to be away from India in September, retorted that the time could not be really critical, and insisted.[40] Even when the Army was ordered to evict the Chinese below Thag La, and although Thapar feared a drastic Chinese reaction, he did not recall his C.G.S. Kaul found no reason in the mounting crisis to cut short his leave, but Nehru's return from abroad on October 2nd appears to have persuaded him to punctuate his time in the hills with a couple of days in the capital. He returned to New Delhi on October 1st and Thapar roped him in next day to resume his duties as

C.G.S. On the late evening of October 3rd, however, it was decided that Kaul should take over the new IV Corps.

The posting of the C.G.S. to corps command at such a time was unusual. If major operations were in prospect, the role of the C.G.S., key man at Army H.Q., was as crucial as that of corps commander. Only if the C.G.S. had the record of a noted fighting commander would this move have made sense, and, as has been seen, this was certainly not the case with Kaul. But to him the chance to command the new corps must have looked like stepping down to glory. As the progenitor of the forward policy, Kaul shared to the full the faith that no massive Chinese reaction to Indian challenges need be feared. The briefing he received on returning to his duties, both from Sen and his own staff, must have presented Operation Leghorn as a pushover, unnecessarily delayed by the sluggishness and timidity of Umrao Singh and the field officers below him. That Kaul had never commanded troops in combat was a hole in his record; the paper pasted over it by his P.R. men could never deceive anyone in the Army, however successful it might be with the politicians and the public. Here was a chance to take over a vital but straightforward operation which could quickly and dramatically be pushed through, leaving Kaul, plumed with victory, to return to a grateful capital. This was Kaul's moment of hubris.*

To Nehru and Krishna Menon, Kaul must have looked like a saviour. With Kaul in command, they could look forward to having the eviction operation completed by the time that Parliament re-assembled, or very soon after; both were convinced that the operation was a straightforward one, since China would not hit back. Nehru and Menon on the one hand, Thapar and Sen on the other, were joined in a quartet of delusion. The generals were convinced that *if* the Chinese did not react, Operation Leghorn could speedily succeed; Nehru and Menon were convinced that the Chinese *would* not react. The two delusions fused in the belief that all would soon be well if only the right man was in command of the troops. Nehru had returned from his tour (taking in Ghana and Egypt on the way back from London) as convinced as ever that no heavy Chinese retaliation need be feared. When Thapar repeated to Nehru his misgivings about the

---

* In his own account of these events, Kaul states that he accepted command of IV Corps with misgivings, but as a dutiful soldier. Generals Thapar and Sen told the writer that Kaul volunteered; Krishna Menon, when asked by the writer why Kaul had been appointed, replied: 'He was the only volunteer.'

possibility of Chinese counterblows in the western sector Nehru, according to Kaul, replied that he had 'good reason to believe that the Chinese would not take any strong action against us'.[41]

Kaul went to see the Prime Minister the night he was appointed to command IV Corps, and gives this account of Nehru's thinking:

[He said] he agreed with some of his advisers in the External Affairs Ministry that we had tolerated the Chinese intrusions into our territories far too long and a stage had come when we must take—or appear to take—a strong stand irrespective of consequences. In his view, the Chinese were establishing their claim on NEFA by coming into Dhola which we must contest by whatever means we had at our disposal. He therefore hoped the Chinese would see reason and withdraw from Dhola but in case they did not, we would have no option but to expel them from our territory *or at least try to do so to the best of our ability*. If we failed to take such action, Nehru said, Government would forfeit public confidence completely.[42]

Kaul is an unreliable guide to these events, but this summary of Nehru's view rings true. Nehru was once again a prisoner of events. If those continued on the course they had been given they *might* lead to military disaster; but it was *certain* that if Nehru now tried to change that course, 'Government would forfeit public confidence'.

Kaul spent the night of October 3rd picking and rousing officers to staff his headquarters and in the morning left by air for Tezpur and his rendezvous with destiny. His companions later testified that while on the plane he had told them that the newspapers would headline his appointment next morning, and said that if he failed in his mission the Government might well fall.

* * * * * * * * * * *

While the climax was building up below Thag La ridge, India and China were playing out their last rally of diplomatic exchanges. Would they meet to talk again before the skirmishing on the borders broke into battle? And if so, what would be the frame of reference for their discussions? As before, China sought a meeting; as before, India refused.

In August the Indians had informed Peking that they would be glad to receive a Chinese representative in New Delhi to discuss joint with-drawal from the disputed territory in the western sector. This was the 1959 Indian proposal for the withdrawal of each side behind the claim line of the other; and as Nehru reassured Parliament now, 'obviously it involved [the Chinese] withdrawing over a large area and our with-drawing over a very small area.'[43] In the terminology of the Indian notes this proposal had become 'measures . . . to restore the *status quo* of the boundary in this region which has been altered by force during the last five years and to remove the current tensions in this area so as to create the appropriate climate for peaceful discussions'.[44]*

The Indian position was thus, that there should first be discussions on the modalities of joint withdrawal in the western sector, which would see that China withdrew from all of the territory India claimed, while India withdrew only the forward posts recently established there plus the post established earlier at Demchok. Once those withdrawals were accomplished, India would proceed to talks on the basis of the officials' report of 1960. Such talks, however, would not be concerned with a general boundary settlement; only with minor, vernier adjust-ments of 'the international boundaries'—i.e. the Indian claim lines.

Replying on September 13th, Peking accused India of seeking 'excuses for rejecting discussions'; and, pointing to the continuing Indian military moves in the western sector, said that the Indian approach, the dual approach as Nehru called it, amounted to 'sham negotiations and real fighting'. China would welcome negotiations, if seriously intended; but would 'resist, whenever attacked'. Peking then reiterated the proposal, first made by Chou En-lai in November 1959, that the armed forces of both sides should each withdraw twenty kilometres along the entire boundary, and urged that further discussions on the basis of the officials' report should be held quickly. '[China] formally proposes that the two Governments appoint representatives to start these discussions from October 15th first in Peking and then in Delhi, alternately. The details can be discussed and decided upon through diplomatic channels.'[45]

The two sides appeared to be drawing closer to a reopening of dis-cussions. But each was proposing different discussions, and the difference was crucial.

On September 19th New Delhi agreed to talks beginning in Peking on the date that China proposed—but to India's talks, not China's.

* See p. 250 above.

'The Government of India are prepared to hold further discussions at the appropriate level to define measures to restore the *status quo* in the Western Sector which has been altered by force in the last few years and to remove the current tensions in that area,' New Delhi replied. The October 15th talks could be arranged *when China had indicated acceptance of that Indian formulation*.[46] By this time the Punjabis were in position along the Namka Chu, but the Indian proposal concerned talks only on the western sector. India refused to discuss the eastern sector at all.

When China replied, on October 3rd, the situation along the Namka Chu had become as tense as that in the western sector. Peking dismissed the Indian demand—that 'China must withdraw from vast tracts of her own territory before discussions on the Sino-Indian boundary question can start'—as absolutely unacceptable. But the Chinese said they were against setting any pre-conditions to talks, and would not object to discussing any question that India might raise. They therefore proposed that the Indian representatives should come to Peking, as agreed, on October 15th, with each side committed only to discussing any aspect of the boundary question that the other wished to raise, and made it plain that China would raise the situation below Thag La ridge.[47] Thus the two distinct sets of talks would be combined if the Chinese proposal were accepted.

But in its reply, on October 6th, the Indian Government retracted even its former agreement to open discussions on joint withdrawals in the western sector, declaring that it would 'not enter into any talks and discussions under duress or continued threat of force'. India would talk only after the Chinese forces had been withdrawn over Thag La, *and* after Peking had explicitly acknowledged that the talks would concern only mutual withdrawals in the western sector.[48] This China described as 'finally categorically shut[ting] the door to negotiations'.[49]

In the Indian perception, China was seeking to utilize a new and deliberate intrusion across the eastern boundary to bring the McMahon Line within the scope of talks that would lead to general negotiations. At the heart of the Indian position was the resolve that the McMahon Line should never be opened to re-negotiation, and so the refusal to discuss the situation below Thag La ridge was axiomatic, even automatic. The mounting dissatisfaction in India at the Government's delay in fulfilling its past promises to hold the McMahon Line inviolate cemented the public opposition to the opening of any talks with the

Chinese, and made it certain that any renewed meetings, no matter how New Delhi described them, would be bitterly criticized as appeasement. Its retraction in the note of October 6th extricated the Government from the awkward dilemma into which it had been put when, in August, Peking ignored the Indian pre-conditions and took up New Delhi on the idea of discussions.*

India's refusal was categorical as well as explicit; but the note at the same time blamed China for preventing talks, and India persisted with the allegation that it was Peking which had refused to negotiate. Thus ten days after India retracted her provisional agreement to talk, she charged in another note that 'it is the Government of China who are not only refusing to undertake talks and discussions . . . but are creating further tension and conflict . . . in the Eastern sector', i.e. below Thag La ridge.[50] As usual, most onlookers accepted the Indian version, especially since Nehru to the last maintained that he was ready and willing to talk; on his return to India he said: 'I shall always be prepared for talks, whatever may happen, provided that the other side is decent, and it is self-respecting for us. I have never refused to talk to anyone.'[51]

* * * * * * * * * * *

The headlines the day after Kaul left New Delhi handsomely fulfilled the prophecy he had made on the plane.

SPECIAL TASK FORCE CREATED
TO OUST CHINESE
Gen. Kaul Leaves For NEFA
To Assume Command
INDIAN ARMY POISED FOR
ALL-OUT EFFORT

The reports in two newspapers[52] said that Kaul had been especially entrusted by the Government with the job of forcing the Chinese back over Thag La ridge. The *Times of India* described him as 'a soldier of extraordinary courage and drive', and the phrase 'task force' was common to both reports. Kaul himself, or members of his staff acting on his orders, had given briefings to the political correspondents of the two leading newspapers, ignoring the fact that Kaul's appointment and

* See pp. 245–6 above.

the formation of the new corps should have been matters of the highest military secrecy. Making the best of it, the Defence Ministry that evening confirmed the facts, but said that the new corps had been created as a normal administrative reorganization and that there was no question of any special task force having been formed. The situation on the McMahon Line was said to be well in hand, however, so naturally the Defence Ministry's gloss did nothing to diminish the optimistic expectation that the Army would soon drive the Chinese off Indian soil in NEFA.

Kaul and his hand-picked officers arrived in Tezpur late on the afternoon of October 4th. He was met at the airport by General Sen,[53] an inversion of service protocol which demonstrated the underlying reality. Formally, Sen was Kaul's superior; but in fact Kaul was the Supremo, charged by Nehru himself with a vital operation and reporting to New Delhi direct. From now on Sen and his Eastern Command were relegated to the wings, emerging only when Kaul momentarily left the stage, indisposed.

As soon as he arrived, Kaul formally notified Army H.Q. that he was taking command. Although at that time Kaul had only a skeleton staff, and IV Corps itself only a notional existence, he declined Umrao Singh's offer to lend him some of the XXXIII Corps staff officers who knew the problem. This confirms that to Kaul—and probably to Army H.Q. too—IV Corps was only a device to give him direct command of Operation Leghorn. Kaul's task was to command 7 Brigade in the operation and, that completed, return to his job in New Delhi—no new C.G.S. was appointed, Kaul's deputy continued to officiate pending his return. After Operation Leghorn had been completed, IV Corps could be wound up or properly constituted under a new commander.

The meeting of Kaul, Sen and Umrao Singh must have been a charged occasion. Sen and Umrao Singh had long been hostile, and that Sen had now had Umrao Singh displaced cannot have improved their relations. Umrao Singh and Kaul, on the other hand, had been friends since their earliest days in the Army. Umrao Singh now restated his view of the impossibility of putting Operation Leghorn into early effect; but Kaul can have had no ears for the appreciations of his predecessor.

The military dispositions in NEFA had changed somewhat in the preceding weeks. Another infantry brigade (62nd) had been inducted

11*

from central India but immediately broken up, its three battalions sent off in different directions and then further divided. Malik, the Intelligence Bureau director, had been pinpointing places of likely Chinese penetration, and troops were being sent to the places he picked out on Army H.Q.'s maps, with no thought for overall military planning. Two of the fresh battalions were thus used in plugging what Malik thought were holes; the third (4 Garhwal Rifles) had been sent to Tawang to reinforce 1 Sikh in defence there. (Tawang had by now been set up as a separate brigade area, under an *ad hoc* Brigade H.Q. commanded by an artilleryman). 62 Brigade H.Q. sat on the plains at Misamari, without troops, and soon its commander was changed.

Under Sen's direct orders, two battalions were moving towards the Thag La area. These were 1/9 Gorkha Rifles, the unit which had been bound for a peace station in Punjab after three years in NEFA, and 2 Rajput. The Rajputs had also just completed a three-year tour in NEFA, and were on the plains preparatory to moving to Uttar Pradesh. They had been operating at Walong, at the eastern extremity of the border, and if any thought had been given to the possibility of general operations in NEFA they should have been sent back there; but instead they were posted to 7 Brigade, and ordered to Lumpu. Trucks could not take them farther than Dirang Dzong since the road was impassable, so they had to march from there to Tawang, over Se La. They were not acclimatized to high altitude; they were wearing cotton summer uniform; and they marched through continuous rain, bivouacking in the open. With a day's rest at Tawang, the Rajputs reached Lumpu on September 24th, having been two weeks on the march. The Gorkhas marched in to Lumpu by about September 26th, bringing 7 Brigade's theoretical strength to three battalions. But the units were in bad shape after their long forced march; they were also both severely under strength, and had with them only their light weapons and the ammunition they could carry in their pouches. The day after the Rajputs reached Lumpu, Brigadier Dalvi sent one of their companies forward to the Namka Chu to reinforce the Punjabis.

The Indian dispositions when Kaul took over were, accordingly, the following:

On the Namka Chu—9 Punjab, plus one company of 2 Rajput; one platoon of medium machine-guns (two guns).

At Lumpu—H.Q. 7 Brigade; the other two companies of 2 Rajput; 1/9 Gorkha Rifles; a troop of heavy mortars and the remainder of the machine-gun company; and some engineers. Another infantry battalion, 4 Grenadiers, was on the way to Lumpu but did not reach there until October 9th.

At Tawang—Two infantry battalions (1 Sikh and 4 Garhwal Rifles) under 4 Artillery Brigade, which had been made responsible for the defence of Tawang when 7 Brigade moved out; some mountain guns and heavy mortars.

Rest of N.E.F.A.—Under 5 Infantry Brigade, five battalions, but these had been widely dispersed and were generally not in strength of more than two companies. One battalion was on the way to Walong.

Looking at the deployment of the troops on the Namka Chu in closer focus, the four infantry companies were spread out over a front of about seven miles along the river—three days' trek from one flank to the other. Sen at the beginning of October had ordered the occupation of Tsangle, the feature on the extreme west of Thag La ridge which opened the approaches to the main pass from the west, and which Dalvi and Umrao Singh had said should not be occupied until the eviction operation was to be launched; to occupy it prematurely, they argued, would be to forewarn the Chinese of the Indians' intentions. Sen overruled them, and a company of the Punjabis had been dispatched to Tsangle, two days' march from their other positions, on October 4th. Sen had also ordered that 7 Brigade was to aim at stocking only fifteen days supplies before launching the operation, rather than the thirty days Umrao Singh had stipulated. Umrao Singh's protest at that order, which he called militarily unsound, was almost his last signal before he was shunted off to the Naga and Pakistan fronts.

On October 4th, while Kaul, Sen and Umrao Singh were conferring at Tezpur, General Prasad, G.O.C. 4 Division, had gone to Lumpu again to see Dalvi. When asked by the latter what had happened to the appreciation and plan of operations that they had put up, together with Umrao Singh, Prasad, according to Dalvi, replied: 'Look here, old boy, no one is interested in your bloody appreciation. They are only interested in your D-Day for evicting the Chinese.' He then told Dalvi about Umrao Singh's replacement by Kaul; and ordered him to leave at once for the Namka Chu. Dalvi protested: 'I told him there was little dignity in senior officers scurrying away like thieves in the night—who were we afraid of, the Chinese or our own superior commanders?' But of course he went.[54]

Next day Kaul himself came to Lumpu. He had left Tezpur intending to meet Prasad—who had moved up towards the Namka Chu—and had told his staff that he would not return until Leghorn was completed. But after take-off he decided instead to go to Lumpu, where he arrived in the afternoon. The brigade major, in charge in Dalvi's absence en route to the Namka Chu, went with other officers to see who had come in the unexpected helicopter, and was the first to feel the rough side of Kaul's tongue. Kaul told him of the impression in New Delhi that the brigade was reluctant to get on with the job; said that officers who were slow in obeying orders would be sacked; and ordered the troops then at Lumpu to march out then and there for the Thag La area. He curtly overrode the brigade major's demurral that there were no supplies on the Namka Chu to support the brigade, saying that tons of supplies were being dropped at Tsangdhar (in fact, the dropping zone there had been closed by weather for five days). When the brigade major reminded him that of the supplies being dropped at Tsangdhar, only some thirty per cent could be retrieved, Kaul retorted: 'My orders are, retrieve or starve.' The only concession he would make was that the troops should move out at first light next morning rather than immediately—there being only an hour's daylight left. So on October 6th the Gorkhas and the Rajputs marched out—still in cotton uniforms, with one blanket per man; carrying fifty rounds per man and their light weapons, leaving other equipment at Lumpu or still farther behind where they had unloaded it in their forced march from the plains. They were sent over the more difficult of the two routes to the Namka Chu, the 16,000-foot Karpo La I Pass, and then down to Tsangdhar at 14,500 feet, there to await further orders. So bad were the conditions on the march, so weakened the troops by now that, according to Dalvi, some died on the pass or at Tsangdhar.[55]

Kaul then flew on to Serkhim, where a helipad had been constructed overnight to receive him, and there met Prasad. Next day, October 6th, Kaul sent a long message back to Army H.Q. Reflecting what he had learned from Prasad, and also perhaps the warning emphases given by Umrao Singh at Tezpur, this signal emphasized the difficulties facing him. He reported a heavy Chinese build-up below Thag La ridge, with artillery, heavy mortars and medium machine-guns in evidence, 'apart from the other dangerous* weapons they

* A revealing choice of adjective. For the combat soldier the only 'dangerous' weapons are those with faulty safety-catches.

possess such as recoilless guns and automatic rifles'. It now appeared that the Chinese battalion below Thag La ridge was supported by a regiment just behind—nevertheless Kaul said that he was accordingly accelerating the concentration of the Indian force, and committed himself to launching Operation Leghorn by October 10th. He was 'taking every possible step to outwit the enemy and capture our objective'; but he warned of the possibility that the Chinese might overrun the Indian forces. He proposed therefore that the Air Force should be alerted, so that offensive air support could quickly be deployed to retrieve the situation.

October 10th was the date given in Umrao Singh's appreciation as the day by which the operation would have to be started—*if* sufficient supplies had been concentrated by then. Now Kaul had taken that as the deadline for launching the operation, *without the stipulated supply base*. Committed to beginning the eviction operation within four days, Kaul had no time to lose. There was nowhere for helicopters to land near the Namka Chu—the only flat, clear areas were on the Chinese side—and so, when Kaul and his party set out for Dhola Post early on October 6th, they had to foot-slog over Hathung La. Kaul was in a greater hurry than his physical condition could sustain—he was no more accustomed to the altitude than his troops—and so he had him-self carried part of the way up to the pass, pick-a-back on a sturdy Tibetan porter. A good number of troops were toiling up the track too, and saw their corps commander thus riding by.

Kaul reached Dhola Post early in the afternoon of October 7th and spent the rest of the day studying the ground. It cannot have been an encouraging sight. The Namka Chu was still fast-flowing and deep. The valley was thickly timbered, movement was difficult except on the tracks, fields of fire limited. On the Indian side the ground rose gradually from the river bank for five hundred yards or so and then steeply to the Hathung La ridge, about four thousand feet higher than the valley floor; the dropping zone at Tsangdhar was at the crest of that ridge. On the northern, Chinese-held side, the shelf of gently rising ground was narrower, and the rise to the towering Thag La ridge steeper; indeed, in most places almost precipitous. There was one place, however, where the northern bank of the river led on to flat pasture ground for about a thousand yards before rising to a hill feature, Tseng-jong. This commanded and outflanked the Chinese positions directly opposite Dhola Post, and occupation of Tseng-jong had been the first-phase objective of Dalvi's initial plan of attack.

The Indian positions and their lines of communications were dominated by the Chinese, who, with plentiful labour in addition to their
infantry and equipment for digging and clearing timber, had prepared
strong bunkers with communicating trenches and forbidding fields of
fire. The Indians, on the other hand, with few entrenching tools or
axes, had not been able to dig in effectively—the Chinese had taunted
the Indian troops for trying to cut logs with entrenching tools and
shovels.[56]

On the evening of October 7th, having completed his own reconnaissance of the scene of operations, Kaul sent another message to New
Delhi. Kaul's signals were unusual in that they were sent direct to
Army H.Q., with copies to Eastern Command, thus short-circuiting
the usual channels—but not only for that reason. They were immensely
long; chatty, descriptive, even anecdotal, more like letters from the
front to a fond uncle at home than military signals. They were dictated
to his personal staff officer and, when his longhand flagged, to Brigadier
Dalvi—who later remarked that 'the role of amanuensis sits ill on a
harassed senior brigadier.'[57] The signals would then be sent by runner
back to Lumpu; thence telephoned to a wireless post; there enciphered
and transmitted via Tezpur to New Delhi. Their length was such that
they took up to eight hours to transmit, blocking the wireless channel
meanwhile to all other traffic. Even with topmost priority, the first of
Kaul's messages from the Namka Chu took three days to reach New
Delhi.[58]

In his signal of October 7th, Kaul described the difficulties confronting him: the strength of the Chinese, who, he now said, were building
up to a regiment below Thag La; the nearly desperate supply position,
which left the Indian troops still with little more than the ammunition
they had carried in their pouches (fifty rounds per man), and necessitated their being put on hard rations from that day; the lack of winter
clothing, with two of the three battalions in summer uniforms, with
one blanket per man—and bivouacking that night at 15,000 feet (Kaul
did not explain that this was the result of his own orders). Kaul was
doing no more than put into his own words the description of the
situation that had been coming back from the Namka Chu ever since
the Indian build-up commenced—although the situation had become
much more precarious since he ordered up the rest of 7 Brigade. But
his signal went on:

Despite all these difficulties I am taking every possible step to carry
out orders I have received from Government and you [i.e. General
Thapar]. I must point out however that despite our success in
initial stage of the forthcoming operation the Chinese are bound
to put in a strong counter-attack . . . to dislodge us from the
positions we capture. I have no resources with which to meet this
threat and therefore recommend in view of importance of operation in this area all military and air resources are marshalled now
for restoration of position in our favour.

He himself would stay with 7 Brigade until the operation was completed, Kaul said.

Kaul's faith that the Chinese would not fight back and that, therefore, the operation he had volunteered to command would be a pushover was clearly coming under great strain. He could no longer
dismiss reports of the strength of the Chinese positions, the power of
their weapons, and the ease with which they were reinforcing, as the
exaggerations of officers with no stomach for battle; he could see all
that he described with his own eyes, since the Chinese made no
attempt to hide their weapons or disguise their strength. But 'despite
all these difficulties' he was going ahead with Operation Leghorn, and
keeping to the date he had set for launching it, October 10th. He was
going to put 7 Brigade into an attack on an enemy who were at least
equal in numbers and could speedily be reinforced; who were far more
heavily armed; and who occupied defensive positions of great strength.
He was going to do this before his troops had any of the fire support,
ammunition or reserve supplies that a brigade attack in the circumstances required. It was to be David against Goliath, when David had
no sling; or it was to be the Charge of the Seventh Brigade. Disaster
was inevitable; and that Kaul had begun to sense this can be discerned
in his signals. Twice he had warned New Delhi that, while he would
vouch for the initial success of the operation, he had no reserves with
which to hold off counter-attacks, and had asked for 'military and air
resources to be marshalled' to restore the situation. (None knew better
than he, as C.G.S., that there were no military resources to be marshalled—or at least none near enough to make any difference to the
odds on the Namka Chu. He could see for himself that tactical air
support would make little difference in this sort of terrain.) If, now, the
Chinese did react—and Kaul still seems to have clung to the hope that

they would not—and overran or flung back the Indian troops after these had made their initial advance, he would be in a position to say that he had forewarned New Delhi of just that eventuality, and had specified what must be done to back him up. If they failed to follow his advice, the fault would lie with Army H.Q. and the Government, not with himself.

Also on October 7th Kaul received from Army H.Q. a report originating from the Indian Consul-General in Lhasa, whose informants had told him that heavy mortars and artillery in divisional strength had been seen concentrating on the Chinese side of the McMahon Line behind Thag La, and that the troops were talking of an attack on Tawang. That this information was passed on to Kaul at his headquarters on the Namka Chu without comment, with no indication of what importance was attached to it by the Intelligence Bureau, the General Staff or the Government, suggests that, if Kaul was beginning to hedge his bets in the record against the possibility of disaster, those in New Delhi were not behind him in that regard. If those guns and mortars were used in a drive on Tawang, Kaul would not anyway be able to complain that New Delhi had failed to warn him. The absence of comment on the Lhasa report may also suggest that those concerned in New Delhi were now in that paralysis of will and even of mind that comes on the gambler when he has staked his all.

Next day, October 8th, Kaul began his opening moves in Operation Leghorn. He ordered the Rajputs and the Gorkhas down from Tsangdhar to join the other troops along the river line. Tsangdhar was a good defensive position, and the dropping zone was there; so at least the bulk of 7 Brigade could be supplied while it was there without the long carry down to the river. The Namka Chu was, as Kaul later described it, 'a dangerous low-lying trap' for the Indians;[59] but still he brought more troops into the trap. On October 9th the two battalions reached the river line (Tsangdhar was a full day's march away, even when the march was downhill) and took up positions around Bridges III and IV.

On October 9th Kaul disclosed his intentions. He told Prasad, Dalvi and the other officers that in spite of the difficulties which he could now see for himself, he had no option but to make some move on October 10th, whatever the cost, as this was the last date acceptable to the Cabinet.[60] He then ordered the Rajputs to move next day to Yumtso La, a 16,000-foot pass, a mile or so to the west of Thag La and higher;

there they were to take up positions behind and dominating the Chinese.

This move would have put the Indians on to the crest of Thag La ridge; from there a strong and well supported force could have made the Chinese positions on the southern face of the ridge untenable. As it was, the Rajputs could have been wiped out on the way, as their route was well covered by the Chinese; or if they did reach their objective, they would certainly have starved or frozen to death there, as there was no possible way of supplying them. For the officers who heard the order, it was unbelievable. Kaul now knew as well as they did the condition of the Indian troops, and could see as well as they could the great strength of the Chinese positions; yet he was proposing to commit a battalion in a move to which the Chinese were bound to respond violently—they had repeatedly warned that they would not allow any Indians across the river. 'A variety of astonished gazes greeted Kaul's announcement,' Dalvi recalled; '. . . General Kaul at first had the smug look of a conjuror holding the rabbit by the ears, later he had a look of defiance as if daring anyone to question his orders.'[61]

Kaul brushed aside the demurrals raised by Dalvi and Prasad, who pointed out that the troops could not survive at 16,000 feet without winter clothing, and could not be supplied; that unless the Indians could lay some covering artillery fire the Rajputs could be slaughtered on the way. He agreed, however, that a patrol should be sent out before the whole battalion was committed; that should leave immediately, find the best place to cross the river, and cover the move of the Rajputs at first light next morning. The patrol's objective would be Tseng-jong.[62]

A patrol of the Punjabis, some fifty strong, accordingly crossed the river about noon on October 9th, and reached Tseng-jong just before dusk. The patrol commander sent a section with a Bren gun up on to the ridge to give cover from the flank. The Chinese made no move to interfere with the Punjabis on their way to Tseng-jong, or to attack them that night. Kaul, who that day had received a signal from Thapar affirming the Government's full faith in him, was cock-a-hoop; those who had warned that Chinese reaction was certain felt, as Prasad put it later, 'bloody fools'.[63] That night Kaul dictated another of his long signals, in which he said that by 'bold and speedy tactics', taking the enemy by surprise, he had been able to compensate for the manifold disadvantages under which his force suffered, and had made a good start to the task of clearing Thag La ridge of the enemy. He reported that his troops were in fact already in occupation of the crest—a reference to the section that had been sent out from Tseng-jong. Forebodings were entirely absent from this signal. Kaul described the scene; told how clearly he could see the enemy; recounted how, while he and his subordinate commanders were in conference, two automatic-rifle shots had been fired from a Chinese position just across the river: perhaps they were meant to provoke, perhaps just to cause confusion, perhaps they were fired accidentally, he mused. But, anyway, his tale went on, a Sikh from the Indian positions nearest to the place from which the shots had been fired stood up, Bren gun on hip, and, bushing out his beard, challenged the Chinese to shoot him if they dared. Kaul reported that he had had the officers collected during the day to give them a pep talk; had found them all in good heart, and assured them that he would stay with them until the operation was completed.

Next morning, the Rajputs grouped and began to move towards the bridges on the way to Yumtso La; it was October 10th, and Kaul was keeping to his deadline. But then at last the Chinese reacted, and shattered not only his plan to evict them but also the premise upon which India had constructed the forward policy and her whole handling of the border dispute. Kaul sets the scene: 'The day dawns in this part of the world very early. It was about 04.30 hours when I was getting ready and my batman was boiling water for tea. I had hung my mirror on the branch of a tree near my bunker just above Bridge IV and had started shaving when I heard considerable fire from across the river.'[64] A full battalion of Chinese had emerged from their positions and, contemptuously ignoring the Indians along the river, moved quickly down the ridge, to form up for an attack on Tseng-jong. At the same time, the Indian position there came under fire from heavy mortars.

If there was something of Walter Mitty in Kaul, this must have been the moment when the secret dream turned into nightmare reality. The dream was of commanding troops in victorious battle: the reality was the little Indian force on a hillock barely a mile away; the Chinese troops, plainly visible and outnumbering the Indians by nearly twenty to one; the smashing mortar barrage. Dalvi has him exclaiming: 'Oh my God, you're right, they mean business.'[65] Kaul later wrote of this moment: 'Frankly speaking, I had now fully understood all the implications of our predicament. . . . I thought we should reconsider the whole of our position in this theatre.'[66]

Kaul handed control of the battle to Dalvi. Conferring with him and Prasad, he decided that he must personally apprise Nehru of the situation and, insisting that Prasad accompany him, set off down the Namka Chu for New Delhi. He had agreed with Prasad and Dalvi that eviction of the Chinese was a chimera, and that the brigade should be withdrawn from the Namka Chu to positions which it could hold, and where it could be supplied; but he would not authorize his subordinate to put these tactical moves into effect, extricating the bulk of the troops and leaving only a screen around Indian flag-posts. Instead, he ordered that while, pending a decision in New Delhi, the eviction operation should be suspended, the brigade should meanwhile hold its positions along the Namka Chu and at Tsangle.

The first Chinese assault on the Indians at Tseng-jong had meanwhile been beaten off. The Chinese, apparently unaware of the section covering the Tseng-jong position from the flank, came under enfilade fire as they bunched for their attack and suffered heavy casualties; if they had been in any doubt on this score, the Chinese must quickly have realized that, ragged and under-armed as the Indians might be, they were still skilled and determined soldiers. The commander of the Punjabis at Tseng-jong asked for covering fire from the mortars and machine-guns on the river line so that he could extricate his troops from a hopeless position; Dalvi refused. His predicament was painful. The machine-gun officer on the river was pressing for permission to open up on the Chinese; the Punjabis needed covering fire for their withdrawal to the river line. But if the main force had been engaged in the little battle for Tseng-jong the Chinese could have wiped it out; Dalvi could not risk the whole force to help the small detachment on Tseng-jong.

As the Chinese pressed their attack Dalvi ordered the Punjabis to disengage and retreat to the river. The Chinese let them go, and held their fire as the survivors crossed the bridge to the south bank. Indian casualties in this action were seven killed, seven missing, eleven wounded; the Chinese put theirs at thirty-three killed and wounded.[67] The Chinese buried the Indian dead with full military honours, in plain view of their comrades on the river line.[68]

On his way back, Kaul signalled New Delhi that a grave situation had developed and requested permission to return to give a first-hand account of the 'new and sudden development'. It was vital, he said, that he see Nehru before the latter's departure for Ceylon, set for October 12th.

The implications of the little battle of Tseng-jong were grave indeed. For the first time the Chinese had forcefully resisted an Indian forward move; they had attacked an established Indian position, and they had done so with massive force and determination. The attack on Tseng-jong had belied the conviction that was at the heart of the forward policy, and that was the rationale for the presence of the Indian troops on the Namka Chu, as in all the isolated, advanced posts in the western sector—the conviction that the Chinese would never deliberately and determinedly attack Indians, but would rather themselves retire when their bluff was called.

Kaul spent a restless night below Hathung La. Like so many of the troops, he was now suffering from a pulmonary disorder consequent on his exertions at altitudes to which he was unaccustomed. Again he had to be carried over the pass.[69] A helicopter was waiting for him at the nearest helipad to lift him to Tezpur, and he reached New Delhi about eight o'clock that night, October 11th—just in time for a meeting at the Prime Minister's house.

This meeting appears to have been the fullest conference on the border crisis held in New Delhi up to this time. Nehru was in the chair; Krishna Menon, the Secretaries of the Cabinet, External Affairs and Defence, were there on the civil side, with other officials; on the Army side, there were Thapar, Sen, Kaul and General Staff officers. The Air Force chief was there too. India now plainly faced a dangerous crisis—but still Nehru did not bring the Cabinet or even the Cabinet Defence Committee into consultation.

The meeting was opened with a report on the Tseng-jong battle by Kaul, by all accounts graphic and subjective. What followed his opening statement is not clear; there are nearly as many versions as there were participants, and to reconstruct even partially what passed at this crucial conference it is necessary to put together the common elements in varying accounts. When, after describing the situation on the Namka Chu, Kaul was asked for his recommendation, he did not urge the withdrawal of 7 Brigade; he proposed instead that India should seek speedy and copious military assistance from the United States. That was dismissed, apparently with some irritation, by Nehru, and Kaul went on to suggest that the eviction operation must be postponed. By his own accounts, Kaul did then suggest that 7 Brigade be pulled back from the Namka Chu to better tactical positions, but other participants contradict him. For example S. S. Khera, then Cabinet

Secretary, states that Kaul's recommendation was to 'hold the line of the Namka Chu and hold on to Tsangle', and that Kaul added, 'If a chance occurs for us to go across and do something, I will report.'[70] A consensus that the eviction operation would have to be postponed appears to have emerged, but no clear instructions were issued even on that score. Certainly there was no formal revocation of the order. Discussion then focused on whether 7 Brigade should stay on the Namka Chu or pull back for the winter. The soldiers appear to have been of divided opinion. Thapar and Sen advocated that the troops should stay where they were. Kaul says he put forward three alternatives: continue to build up and launch an attack despite Chinese superiority; cancel the attack order but keep the brigade on the river line; or retire to a more advantageous position.[71] This in fact would have made it almost inevitable that the second alternative would be preferred, leaving the troops on the river; too many reputations were committed by now to Operation Leghorn, on the civilian as well as the service side, to allow it to be demonstratively abandoned by withdrawal of the main body of troops. According to a number of accounts, Nehru told the soldiers that such decisions must be theirs, and asked them to concert their views and then advise the Government what should be done; Thapar and Sen next morning told Krishna Menon that the Brigade should stay where it was. That version finds confirmation in the words of Nehru himself, who after the debacle told Parliament that the vital military decisions had been 'taken by Government in full consultation with the Chief of [Army] Staff and other senior army officers concerned and in the light of their expert advice. This applies particularly to the decision that the Army should not withdraw in October–November 1962 from its forward position in NEFA.'[72] Another reference of the Prime Minister's suggests that he was told that the field commanders *wished* to keep the brigade on the Namka Chu. The civilian authorities had not ordered the soldiers to 'stick it out where the conditions were not very favourable', Nehru told Parliament; 'but our soldiers themselves have a reluctance to go back, and they stuck on at considerable cost to them.'[73]

So far as the military side of India's handling of the border dispute was concerned, Nehru, it seems, was throughout punctilious in leaving decisions to the soldiers—at least, he must have believed he was leaving the decisions to them. But having by his own long-sustained and open favouritism to Kaul assisted in the demoralization of the Army high command, by 1962 he was no longer dealing with professionals, but with courtiers. So, when he sought professional decisions, he heard only what his military advisers believed he wished to hear—and with his assurances that China would not 'do anything big' he gave them the political guidance they hoped for. This process of mutual delusion produced at the October 11th meeting the decision that 7 Brigade should stay where it was.

The next morning Nehru left for a three-day visit to Ceylon—it was business as usual, care was being taken not to suggest that anything very dramatic or critical was developing on the borders. Always accessible to the press, he stopped at the airport for a few words with reporters that turned, of course, into an impromptu press conference. By then a month had passed since the Government confirmed that Chinese troops were across the McMahon Line, and more than a fortnight since the press reported that the Army was under orders to force them out. There had been continuing reports in the newspapers about skirmishes below Thag La ridge, always suggesting that Indian troops were beating off Chinese attacks. The previous day the Tseng-jong battle had been reported as severe fighting, with Chinese troops attacking an Indian position. Doubts were growing about whether the Government had really ordered the Army to take the offensive. The first question put to Nehru at the airport was, therefore, what orders had been given to the troops in NEFA.

'Our instructions are to free our territory,' Nehru replied. The reporter followed up: 'When?' Nehru said: 'I cannot fix a date, that is entirely for the Army.' He then 'pointed out that wintry conditions had set in already in the [Thag La] region, and the Chinese were strongly positioned because they were in large numbers and were situated on higher ground. Moreover, the main Chinese base on their side of the border was quite near.'[74] Then the correspondents turned to the other major question of public interest, seeking assurance that the Government had no intention of beginning talks with China. Nehru said: 'As long as this particular aggression [i.e. the Chinese presence on the southern slope of Thag La ridge] lasts, there appears to be no chance of talks.'[75]

After the debacle Nehru was criticized for this public confirmation of the eviction order, and accused of having deliberately misled the country. Certainly his words left a misleading impression, and no doubt Nehru knew it. An answer on oath would have had him replying that the eviction order had been suspended because the operation was beyond the capability of the Indian troops, and saying that it might be a very long time before that situation could be changed. But to have admitted as much would have belied everything Nehru had ever said about the military aspects of the border problem. Furthermore, there is reason to believe that the previous night Kaul had encouraged Nehru to tell the public that the eviction would in due course be carried out; a participant at the conference claims to have heard this, and later Nehru, defending his airport statement, said it was not his decision alone; 'it was the viewpoint of the military people too, they wanted to do it, otherwise I would not have dared to say anything like that.'[76] Nehru did, too, try to lend a sobering balance to his answer by giving a fairly strong intimation of the disadvantages which the troops below Thag La ridge were facing, with his reference to wintry conditions and the Chinese advantages of terrain and supply.

If it was Nehru's intention to emphasize the negative and warn the public of the difficulties that the troops had to meet below Thag La, the public was not listening. Official spokesmen had for so long been giving assurances that everything in NEFA was under control that Nehru's cautionary words carried no weight now. That very morning in the press the meeting of the previous night was described as the Prime Minister's 'reassuring consultations' with his civil and military advisers. That Nehru himself was not really convinced of the difficulties was shown by his return, when briefing Indian correspondents in Colombo only a few hours later, to the nostrum that in NEFA the physical advantages were all on India's side.[77]

Little wonder, then, that the Indian public heard in Nehru's words at the airport only what it wanted to hear—a call to battle. The press was enthusiastic. 'Mr Nehru . . . has told the country, clearly and firmly, what it has been waiting to hear,' said the *Statesman* next day; 'that the armed forces have been ordered to throw the Chinese aggressors out of NEFA and that until Indian territory in that area is cleared of them there can be no talks with China.' Down in the south, the *Hindu* thought exactly the same: 'The whole country will welcome Mr Nehru's statement. . . .' And there were many other similar expressions of approval.*

* Nehru's political career—and therefore modern Indian history—is marked by instances when statements made by him, apparently without due thought, have had momentous and sometimes calamitous consequences. Perhaps the best-known incident is that of July 1946, when at a press conference Nehru torpedoed the delicate agreement achieved be-

So complete was the public confidence in the prowess of the Indian Army that it seems to have occurred to no Indian to wonder whether the troops below Thag La ridge were able to carry out the orders that Nehru had confirmed. In dispatches to *The Times*, the writer referred to the tendency in India—encouraged by the Goa operation—to ascribe invincibility to the Army, and reported that it was resisting the political demand for hasty and unprepared action.[78] Disapproving of those reports, a New Delhi editor with good official contacts passed on the corrective tip that the Chinese below Thag La ridge were known to be 'third-rate garrison troops', who would present no problem to the Indians once the attack began. That information, which presumably originated in Malik's crystal ball in the Intelligence Bureau, was also sent up to 7 Brigade—who could check it for themselves. Dalvi said of his first close contact with the Chinese: 'I must admit I was impressed with the Chinese soldiers. These were no scruffy Frontier Guards; they appeared to be healthy, well-clad, well-armed and determined troops.'[79]

The universal impression in India, however, was that the Indian troops on the Namka Chu were a strong, properly equipped and confident task force, held back from surging over an inferior Chinese force only by the excessive forbearance or timidity of their Government. Nehru's airport statement was taken as the announcement that the leash had at last been slipped, and India began to await news that her soldiers had won back Thag La.

Nehru's words were read as a positive statement of martial intent in other countries, too. The *New York Herald Tribune* headed its editorial NEHRU DECLARES WAR ON CHINA; the *Guardian* described the statement as an ultimatum.[80] Similar conclusions were drawn in China. The *People's Daily* said: 'In his capacity as Prime Minister Nehru has openly and formally authorised the Indian military to attack China's Tibet region at any time.' The editorial concluded: 'A massive invasion of Chinese territory by Indian troops in the eastern sector of the Chinese boundary seems imminent,' and, addressing 'all comrade commanders and fighters of the People's Liberation Army guarding the Sino-Indian border', warned them to increase their vigilance a hundred-

---

tween Congress and the Muslim League over the Cabinet Mission's plan for a united, independent India. A comment made on the 1946 occasion fits Nehru's 1962 airport statement as well: 'It was a moment in history when circumspection should have been the order of the day. There was much to be gained by silence. The fortunes of India were in the balance, and one false move could upset them.'[81]

fold because 'the Indian troops may carry out at any time Nehru's instructions to get rid of you.' The Chinese had some advice for Nehru too: 'Pull back from the brink of the precipice, and don't use the lives of Indian troops as stakes in your gamble.'[82]

★ ★ ★ ★ ★ ★ ★ ★ ★ ★

Comfortable in their thick, padded uniforms and confident in their numbers and weapons, the Chinese looking down from strong bunkers on Thag La ridge at the unfortunate Indian troops on the river line, hungry, cold, and as exposed to the elements as to their enemies, must have judged Peking's warning to them superfluous. Plainly China had no grounds whatever for *fearing* an Indian attack; but she had every reason to expect it. No secret had been made of the Indian Government's intention; the Chinese Embassy in New Delhi no doubt read the newspaper accounts of the preparations for the eviction operation as closely as did Indians. On the Namka Chu itself, the only explanation for the tactical deployment of the Indian troops was that they were holding the bridges in order to cross the river, and seeking to take up commanding positions on the northern bank to cover their eventual assault. Had their purpose been defensive, the main Indian positions would have been on the ridge behind them, from where good fields of fire could interdict a river crossing by the Chinese— and they would have demolished the bridges, as the Chinese had demolished some. Chinese Intelligence seems to have got wind of the October 10th timing of Operation Leghorn, and on October 8th the Soviet chargé d'affaires was called in to the Foreign Ministry in Peking and told that India was on the point of launching a major attack. According to the Chinese, Krushchev told the Chinese Ambassador in Moscow a few days later that his Government had similar information, and said that if China were attacked it would be natural for her to fight back. The Chinese remarked that India's use of Russian helicopters and transport aircraft to prepare her offensive had not helped Sino-Russian goodwill among the Chinese frontier guards.[83]

The Indian note of October 6th had, in Peking's view, 'finally categorically shut the door to negotiations' by insisting that before there could be any meeting, Chinese troops must pull back over Thag La ridge; and that even then discussions could only concern the modalities of Chinese withdrawal from the territory which India claimed in the western sector. For months the Chinese Government had been warning India, as strongly and clearly as possible, that if India persisted in the forward policy China would retaliate; but the warnings had been ignored—or thrown back—and Indian troops had continued to press forward. As early as July Peking had concluded that the Indian Government was taking as a sign of weakness the fact that there had been no forceful Chinese reaction to the forward policy;[84] and, as has been seen, this diagnosis was correct. In New Delhi the fact that China, for all her diplomatic protests and movement of troops, did not attack the forward posts in the western sector was taken to confirm the basic premise of the forward policy and encouraged the Government to persist with it.

While ignoring all China's warnings to desist from probing forward in the western sector, India had in June, with the establishment of Dhola Post, begun to apply what appeared to be exactly the same tactics to take over territory she claimed north of the McMahon Line. Now the Indian Army was preparing to attack the Chinese where they had reacted to the establishment of Dhola Post. The first Indian attempt, at Tseng-jong on October 10th, had been beaten back easily enough, but with heavy Chinese casualties. That the Indians had learned no lesson from that repulse but intended to mount further attacks as soon as they were ready, Nehru himself had publicly confirmed; and that the troops along the Namka Chu were still deployed for assault, indeed were being reinforced, showed that his words were not bluff.

What was the Chinese Government to do?* China could persist with the policy that she had followed hitherto, preventing Indian forward moves by the threat of force when she could and, when that failed, reacting vigorously in local actions. There was no doubt that, in the western sector, any fire-fights between Indian posts or patrols and the Chinese troops would see the Indians wiped out or captured; and in the Thag La area the Chinese positions were so strong and so easily supported that any Indian attack in foreseeable circumstances could be broken and thrown back. While thus holding the line against Indian military pressure, China could continue trying to persuade India that the only way to a boundary settlement was through negotiation, and

---

* The writer has had no access to information about Chinese thinking or policy formulation other than published statements. Those, and the development of the Sino-Indian quarrel to this point, provide a basis for inference; but the section that follows is deductive.

to convince other governments that the Chinese position was reasonable; that if there was conflict on the boundaries, it was the result of India's behaviour. But by now Peking had reason to doubt whether this policy was worth while. A reversal of the Indian approach certainly seemed out of the question. At the beginning of the dispute, Peking had believed that 'the misunderstanding about China of those who harbour no ill-will [cannot] continue for long. Because, if China were really committing aggression against and posing threat to India or any other country, ten thousand denials would not alter the fact; if it is otherwise, although ten thousand propaganda machines tell the world about China's "aggression" and "threat" they will only discredit the propagandists themselves.'[85] But that expectation had been belied. The Western countries were, of course, solidly with India; but the Soviet Union was also in sympathy with her, as were most of the fraternal parties, and many Afro-Asian countries seemed to be leaning to India's side. India's credibility had proved higher than China's, and therefore continued skirmishing along the Sino-Indian boundaries, with India all the time accusing China of provoking clashes and committing aggression, could only further damage China's standing in the world. India was already making great play with charges that China was using brute force; it might be healthy to show what could happen when China really did so, when the odium, if any, might be mixed with respect.

Militarily, too, indefinite prolongation of the situation on the boundaries would be injurious to China. Easy as the Indian pressure was to ward off when it came to the issue, it still kept the whole great sweep of the Sino-Indian boundaries alive, requiring troops to be kept in battle-readiness, creating a heavy logistical demand and complicating the problem of pacifying Tibet. For the army to be put and kept in a defensive posture, only to react to challenges launched at times and places of India's choosing, would make no sense to any strategists—and would certainly flout Mao Tse-tung's military teaching.* Finally, while the Indian Army was for the present a ramshackle force, it might not remain such. The Americans had weapons to spare. Washington had long been wooing India, and the Indians had already begun to respond.

* Even the account of the border dispute most strongly critical of China concedes that 'rather than be forced into a defensive position to protect its posts from piecemeal Indian Army operations launched on India's terms, it made military sense for the Chinese Army to mount a general offensive on its own terms along the entire border.'[86]

By October 1962, then, the arguments against China's allowing the present situation to drag on were telling. What alternatives were there? Settlement on India's terms must have been as unthinkable then as always. The total unacceptability of the Indian terms apart, it would have meant abject surrender to pressure, something which, having 'stood up' in the revolution, China meant to have done with for ever—'the liberated China can in no circumstances be plunged back to the position of the injured old China.'[87] The alternative, then, was to meet the Indian challenge with a counterblow so powerful and resolute as to end it.

The political objective of the military action would be to bring India to the negotiating table, by showing once and for all that the Indian attempt to achieve a settlement on her own terms, by moving into Chinese-held territory, was futile. But failing that, it would suffice if India were made to accept that the *status quo* had to be left alone until she was prepared to embark on general boundary negotiations.

The balance of such considerations was enough, it seems, to swing the decision-makers in Peking to decisive action. But there were other factors which, though probably secondary, might have been taken to confirm the rightness and indeed unavoidability of the decision. That China thought of herself as going to 'humble India and so seize the leadership of Asia', or to 'put a brake on India's development by forcing her to build up militarily'—western formulations especially popular in the U.S.A.—seems uncharacteristic and unlikely. As Chinese, those in the Government in Peking would presumably never for a moment have supposed that any country but China could ever aspire to the leadership of Asia; as Communists, they certainly never supposed that India, with its capitalist system and national bourgeois government, could challenge China in a race to development. Even in 1962, when the Great Leap Forward had failed and China's economy was in difficulties, such a thought must have seemed absurd to Peking's Communist purists. But the Indians—Nehru particularly, with his suggestions that war between India and China would shake the world, and that neither was able to 'knock the other flat'[88]—had evidently come to think of their country as the equal of China, or even her superior; perhaps it occurred to the Chinese that it would do nothing but good to demonstrate to India and to the world the fallacy of such assumptions.

And there was the other dimension in which the Chinese would, it seems, have found bonuses for their decision to hit back at India on the borders. The Sino-Indian dispute had become a factor in China's great falling-out with the Soviet Union. A blow at India might bring what the Chinese saw as Nehru's covert alliance with the Americans against themselves into the open and so expose the ideological error of Moscow's support for India. It could not fail to damage the Nehru Government domestically, and so help the oppressed classes in India and the forces of revolution there. Both results would demonstrate the correctness of Peking's stand against Moscow. There was, furthermore, the question of war itself. Moscow was arguing that even local wars must be avoided, lest they escalate into nuclear confrontations of great powers. The Sino-Indian dispute would be an ideal test case; the American commitment to India's side was plain, and by striking the protégé China would be flouting the patron. Drastic military action against India, conducted with surgical precision in the service of consistent political objectives, would show not only that war was still a necessary instrument of policy, but also that imperialists and their stooges could, as Mao Tse-tung had said, be slighted—provided only that full account was taken of their tactical strength and weaknesses, and 'all our energies devoted to the fight'. An effective military blow against India would, thus, be checkmate in two distinct games.

To be effective, however, such a blow would have to be on a grand scale. For China merely to wipe out the forty or so small posts the Indians had established in the west under their forward policy might achieve nothing; it could not be expected to change the Indian Government's attitude to negotiations, and would leave the western sector to be disturbed again as soon as the Indians felt able to start moving forward once more. The real provocation for China lay in the west; but politically as well as militarily the opportunity for demonstrative and destructive retaliation lay only in the east, in a strong move into the disputed territory beneath the McMahon Line. The Indians' actions below Thag La ridge thus served China's needs admirably, in that they provoked retaliation where that had to be deployed if it were to be effective. This raises the question: was the Chinese investment of Dhola Post on September 8th a trap, conceived to lead the Indians into exactly the course they followed?

From the Chinese point of view, their action at Dhola Post was no different from what they had been doing to Indian posts established in what they regarded as their own territory in the western sector. They confronted Dhola Post with an outnumbering force—though of only about sixty men, not five or six hundred, as believed in India—and urged its little garrison to withdraw, meanwhile warning New Delhi of the serious consequences its 'fresh incursions' would entail.[89] Dhola Post was indubitably *north* of the McMahon Line: had the Chinese brought about such a confrontation to the south of the line, that would clearly have been a trap; but at this time even the Indians had not accused China of crossing the line proper,[90] and the clashes in the eastern sector had resulted from India's unilateral, northward modifications of the line. When Indian posts had thus been beleaguered in the western sector there had been no violent reaction from India; on what grounds could the Chinese have expected their pressure on Dhola Post to bring about a big local concentration of Indian troops for offensive action? This Indian reaction was irrational, and therefore, it seems, cannot have been predictable.

The likeliest conclusion is that the Chinese investment of Dhola Post was not conceived as a trap. A doubt lingers, however, from the curious ten-week delay between the establishment of the post and the Chinese reaction to it. That the Chinese did not learn of the new post as soon as it was set up is possible, but most improbable; was there then calculation in the delay in reaction, and therefore in the move against Dhola Post in September? The question must be left open.

At all events, as the Indians escalated the confrontation at Dhola Post into a trial of will and strength, Peking must have seen the opportunities this opened. India's own actions were now extending the tension to the eastern sector, until then dormant; they thus provided the occasion for Chinese military action across the McMahon Line.

Just when the final decision to attack was taken in Peking cannot be discerned. The Chinese Army was concentrating at least from the beginning of October, judging by the report of the Indian Consul-General in Lhasa. But this need not indicate that the attack order had already been given in Peking. The likeliest date of decision would seem to lie in mid-October: between October 6th, when New Delhi shut off the exchange of notes about a meeting to discuss the border situation, and October 17th, when the Chinese troops on Thag La ridge were seen to begin active preparations for their actual assault.

* * * * * * * * * * *

The indecisiveness of the meeting in Nehru's house on October 11th was reflected in subsequent confusion and contradictions about what was to be done next. Should preparations continue for an immediate resumption of Operation Leghorn? Or could the bulk of 7 Brigade be pulled back from the Namka Chu, to winter in positions where the troops could be supplied? Kaul returned to his headquarters at Tezpur on October 13th and informed his subordinates that he had failed to convince the Government about the facts of the situation on the Namka Chu; that the eviction order stood and must be carried out. General Thapar, on the other hand, appears to have understood that Leghorn was to be postponed, since a few days later he told Eastern Command to estimate what troops and supplies would be needed to launch an eviction operation the following spring.

For the next nine days there was argument and uncertainty. The record becomes so confused, in fact, as to suggest that by now deliberate attempts were being made to obscure it, in order that blame could be deflected if disaster befell. Krishna Menon, Kaul and the General Staff still hoped that the Chinese could somehow be thrown back, and were determined, above all, that there should be no withdrawal from the Namka Chu. Since the initial Chinese investment of Dhola Post, Menon had been insistently demanding quick action to force them back across the ridge. Much of the real drive for the eviction operation had come, throughout, from him and the officials, to be transmitted without enthusiasm by Thapar, more zealously by Sen, and picked up and boosted by Kaul. Now Menon's public commitment to early, determined action to evict the Chinese was even clearer than Nehru's: on October 14th he declared that it was 'the policy of the Government of India to eject the Chinese from NEFA, whether it takes one day, a hundred days or a thousand days', and to fight it out in Ladakh 'to the last man, the last gun'.[91] To permit the withdrawal of the bulk of the troops from the Namka Chu would be to demonstrate the hollowness of such vaunts, and the public disappointment would inevitably be taken out first on Menon, when Parliament reassembled. Kaul was committed to keeping the troops on the river line for the same reasons. With fanfare and panache he had assumed command of the operation to throw back the Chinese; if now, instead of the awaited bang of victory from Thag La ridge, the politicians, press and public heard only the whimper of retreat, there would be a renewed and intensified outcry for his head, too. As for the General Staff, Kaul was their Chief and they continued to work with him. All concerned knew, of course, that a withdrawal from the Namka Chu would instantly become public knowledge. If Peking did not proclaim it first, the news would leak out in New Delhi.

While those behind were thus crying 'Forward!', those before were crying 'Back!' Brigadier Dalvi and General Prasad knew that it was logistically impossible to maintain 7 Brigade on the Namka Chu through the winter. Nevertheless, the brigade was reinforced, thus compounding the problems of maintenance. Another battalion (4 Grenadiers) reached the river between October 12th and 14th; they had been sent from Delhi and were, accordingly, unacclimatized and exhausted, and were no better equipped than the other battalions. In the next few days about four hundred and fifty porters arrived—more mouths to feed and backs to clothe as they brought no rations or winter clothing with them. By now there were in all about 3,000 men on the Indian side, 2,500 of them troops. There were winter clothing and tents for only two or three hundred; the rest still wore their cotton summer uniforms, and, lacking axes or digging tools, made the best shelters they could out of branches or parachute material. The first snow fell on the valley floor on October 17th. A few more mortars were carried over the passes, and four of the paratroops' field pieces were dropped by parachute; but only two were recovered in usable condition. The gunners, brought direct from the Parachute Brigade's base at Agra, marched over the 16,000-foot Karpola I route and suffered fatal casualties on the way from the unaccustomed altitude and cold.[92]

The troops had been on hard rations since October 9th, but even so the ration reserve was down to two days. There was no sugar, salt or matches. More and bigger aircraft had been put to supplying the force but that did not materially improve the supply situation. The bigger aircraft, Fairchild Packets, could not fly low and slow enough to have a reasonable chance of hitting the tiny dropping zone at Tsangdhar. The hours in which they could try were limited; from first light until about half-past nine, when cloud covered the D.Z. A good number of drops were lost or smashed because the parachutes failed to open: to conserve foreign exchange, the Army had for years been returning used parachutes for repair and repacking in India. Only thirty per cent of the loads dropped were being retrieved. The problem for 7 Brigade did not end with retrieval of the air-drops, of course; the supplies had to be carried in man-loads down the steep 3,000-foot descent from the D.Z. to the troops along the river— and their positions by now stretched seven days' march from end to end. Civilian porters were deserting and the Army's own Pioneers refusing to carry loads unless they were given food and winter clothing.

To pit troops in such circumstances against an enemy superior in every detail of military strength would be absurd or criminal; to leave them where they were through a winter of heavy snow and temperatures below freezing-point would be to condemn them to steady and severe attrition from exposure and illness and, before long, starvation. In war soldiers have endured as much, and fought; but this was not war it was a political ploy.

On October 12th 7 Brigade received a signal from Kaul confirming that the troops were to stay where they were; the same day they heard on a radio news-broadcast Nehru's confirmation that they were still under orders to clear the Chinese off Thag La ridge; and, according to Dalvi, on October 16th he was told that the Defence Minister had given the Army November 1st as the last date acceptable to the Cabinet for completion of the operation.[93]*

The field officers had emphatic support from the key staff officer at IV Corps for their contention that the bulk of the brigade must be pulled back. Brigadier K. K. Singh, the Brigadier General Staff (B.G.S.), was pointing out in forceful, written appreciations the impossibility of keeping the brigade on the river. He urged that, instead, the force on the Namka Chu should be thinned out to one battalion and concentrated in positions tactically supporting Dhola Post. The other three battalions should be pulled back to winter and re-equip in Lumpu. This was almost exactly what General Umrao Singh had recommended six weeks before.

Within the overriding question of whether the brigade should be kept on the Namka Chu or withdrawn was the question of Tsangle. This was a position, marked by a herdsman's hut, at the source of the Namka Chu in a small lake. On the only detailed map of the area

---

* There is no mention of this new deadline in the Army's report on these events. But the board of inquiry did not take evidence from Dalvi, and 7 Brigade's records were destroyed, or lost in the debacle. As orders were being passed orally, with no written confirmation, the absence of a record of this instruction is not surprising. Comparison of Dalvi's account in his book, *Himalayan Blunder*, with that assembled in the Army's report shows that he is a careful and accurate chronicler.

Army H.Q. had, based on an out-of-scale sketch, Tsangle was represented as two or three miles from Dhola Post; in fact it was more than
two days' march away. Survey maps of the area placed it inside Bhutan,
but the Indian Army was ordered to disregard that boundary, as it had
disregarded the map-marked McMahon Line. (A representative of the
ruler of Bhutan called at IV Corps H.Q. in due course to complain that
Indian troops had crossed the boundary.*) Tsangle was of tactical
significance because through it lay a possible flank approach to the
Chinese position beneath Thag La, and Dalvi's provisional plan for a
partial eviction operation had laid down that the advance should be
through Tsangle to Tseng-jong. He, backed up by Umrao Singh,
had urged that no move should be made to Tsangle before the operation actually began, so that the advantage of surprise should not be
lost; but, overruling his subordinates, General Sen had ordered the
position occupied by a company at the beginning of October. The
Chinese promptly dispatched troops to cover that approach.

When Kaul left the Namka Chu to make his report to Nehru, he
ordered that the Tsangle position must be held unless the Chinese put
pressure on it, in which case General Prasad could withdraw it at his
discretion. But a few days later Kaul changed this, and ordered that
Tsangle be held at all costs. Dalvi, Brigadier K. K. Singh at IV Corps,
and Prasad all urged that Tsangle should be evacuated; its maintenance
added a severe additional burden to the general supply problem. Dalvi
describes the difficulty of supplying Tsangle:

> There was no direct route from Bridge IV, due to impassable
> bluffs. This forced us to adopt the circuitous route via Tsangdhar.
> By mid-October the turn-around time had increased to five days,
> over icy paths and slippery gradients. It was impossible to carry a
> worthwhile payload on this route, as the carriers themselves had to
> be self-contained for ten days. . . . Most porters began dumping
> their loads *en route* and the more stout-hearted were delivering
> quantities that were not worth the effort of sending them there.
> . . . Snow clothing had to be provided to all porters commuting
> between Tsangdhar and Tsangle due to the extreme cold and the
> altitude of Tsangle, 15,500 ft. Both the troops and the porters had

* Bhutan is a sovereign country, and the King has repeatedly declined India's offer to
station troops there for defence purposes. There is no defence treaty between Bhutan and
India. The treaty governing their relations stipulates only that Bhutan shall be guided by
India in the conduct of her foreign relations.

to be protected against the bitter cold or else they would have perished. The only solution lay in undressing the defenders of the Namka Chu and providing the minimal requirements for the defenders of Tsangle. This was a most unhappy solution.[94]

But Kaul was adamant. Menon, the officials and Army H.Q. had all, it appears, come to attach high political and strategic importance to holding the Tsangle position. At a conference in Tezpur on October 17th, attended by Krishna Menon, Sen and Kaul, the need to hold Tsangle was reaffirmed; and Dalvi was ordered to send another company to reinforce the company already there. The retention of Tsangle and the build-up of the garrison there were the final straw for 7 Brigade, stretching their supply effort to breaking point, and so depleting the force on the river line as to make it hopelessly vulnerable.

Thus the predicament of 7 Brigade steadily worsened. Meanwhile, the pulmonary trouble that Kaul had developed on the Namka Chu had not cleared up and by October 17th he had a fever, with difficulty in breathing and general discomfort. The medical officer at IV Corps H.Q. diagnosed a bronchial allergy exacerbated by a respiratory infection, stress and exertion. That night, as Kaul's condition seemed to be worsening, Army H.Q. was informed; the chief medical adviser of the Government of India was forthwith dispatched to Tezpur from New Delhi to treat him. This officer, arriving early on the 18th, judged that Kaul's condition was more serious—so serious, in fact, that although there was a well equipped military hospital at Tezpur the patient should immediately be flown to New Delhi for treatment. Kaul himself telephoned General Thapar and obtained his consent to returning again to the capital; Kaul says that he also obtained General Sen's permission to leave the theatre of operations,[95] but Sen maintains that the first he knew of his corps commander's illness and absence was when he learned that he was in New Delhi—by no means the only flat contradiction between these two.

Kaul was not put into hospital when he reached New Delhi on October 18th, but went straight to his own house.[96] That his illness was not serious is confirmed by the fact that he did not relinquish command of IV Corps. Instead, with maps strewn over his bed and telephones handy, he continued to issue detailed orders for the movement of troops on the Namka Chu. He sent them both direct to

IV Corps in Tezpur by long-distance telephone and by signal through Army H.Q.'s channels.

On the night of October 18th Kaul ordered two more companies to strengthen Tsangle; one to be deployed at Bridge V, and the other put to patrolling between Bridge V and Tsangle. By the time this order was passed on (orally) by General Prasad to Dalvi, it was evident that an all-out Chinese attack on the brigade positions was imminent, and Dalvi angrily protested. Prasad had already tried that, however, his protest being relayed to Kaul in his bedroom at 5 York Road, New Delhi; the reply had been that the build-up at Tsangle must be carried out, and it was coupled with the threat that officers who defaulted in executing the order would be removed. Prasad passed this warning on to Dalvi, saying that he and his battalion commanding officers would be court-martialled if they raised any more objections or arguments against the Tsangle moves.[97]

On October 18th Chinese activity on the southern face of Thag La ridge had been seen to intensify. The build-up of stores had been increasing for days, with hundreds of ponies engaged, as well as labour battalions. Troop movements began on the 19th, a force of two thousand being counted at Tseng-jong. The Indians could see Chinese marking parties at work, preparing for a night advance—the Chinese made no attempt to conceal their intentions. Dalvi reported these unmistakable preparations for attack to Prasad, who was at the Tactical H.Q. of 4 Division at Zimithang; Dalvi said that the brigade would not be able to hold off a Chinese assault if caught in its present deployment, and asked permission to pull in the Tsangle force and the troops supporting it. That would relieve about a battalion's strength of troops to re-deploy on a much shortened front and, by giving some depth to the defences, significantly strengthen them. But the orders Prasad had received from Kaul were categorical; Tsangle must be held at all costs. Prasad refused to take responsibility for disobeying the order, and refused Dalvi's urgent requests. Speaking from his headquarters near Dhola Post, in the presence of his brigade major and other officers, Dalvi then told Prasad that 'rather than stand by and see the troops massacred' he would put in his resignation; 'it was time someone took a firm stand'. Dalvi's words were noted and Prasad passed them up to IV Corps H.Q. in Tezpur; but the officer in charge there, Brigadier K. K. Singh, could not take the responsibility for reversing the clear orders of the corps commander, and promised to contact Kaul in New

Delhi. Nothing more was heard at 7 Brigade on this score, and before dawn next morning the remaining companies of the Gorkhas prepared to move off towards Tsangle.

On the night of October 19th–20th, the Chinese troops deployed for their assault; they lit fires to keep themselves warm while they waited, so confident were they that the Indians would not open fire. By this time the water level had dropped, and the Namka Chu was fordable—all the thought the High Command had given to holding the bridges was wasted, those logs had become irrelevant. During the night the Chinese crossed the river to the west of Bridge IV—the Indian positions were so far separated, sometimes by gaps which took hours to cover, that such infiltration was impossible to prevent once the river became fordable. Some of these troops struck straight up the ridge to Tsangdhar; the remainder grouped for a dawn attack, from the flank, on the Indian positions on the river. At 05.00 on October 20th, the Chinese fired two Very lights; on the signal, Chinese heavy mortars and artillery, drawn up without cover on the forward slope of Thag La ridge, opened a heavy barrage on the central Indian positions. 'As the first salvoes crashed overhead there were a few minutes of petrifying shock,' Dalvi recalled. 'The contrast with the tranquillity that had obtained hitherto made it doubly impressive. The proximity of the two forces made it seem like an act of treachery.'[98]

The weight of the Chinese attack was thrown against the Indian positions in the centre of the river line; the Gorkhas and the Rajputs bore the brunt of the assault. Their positions had been infiltrated; some of the Gorkhas were caught on the move to Tsangle when the Chinese artillery opened up; the Rajputs were attacked simultaneously from two sides. The Indian units fought back fiercely against the overwhelming odds, but one after another their positions were overrun—the Indians met the final Chinese assaults with the bayonet. By 09.00 the Gorkhas and Rajputs on the river line were finished. The Chinese had by then brought Tsangdhar under attack. By then this vital position was defended only by a weak company of Gorkhas—which had been preparing to march out to Tsangle—and the two paratroop guns. Firing over open sights, these fought on until the crews were wiped out.

The brigade quickly lost cohesion as a fighting force. The telephone wires from headquarter to the battalions were cut by the barrage. The signallers of the Rajputs and Gorkhas had to close down their radios to take up rifles. On the point of being outflanked on two sides, Dalvi, whose headquarters was in the valley with his troops, asked Prasad for permission to withdraw; he had remained in contact with 4 Division, finding Prasad still anxious that Tsangle be reinforced, even if only by a platoon, as this move had been ordered 'at the highest level'![99] Permission to withdraw was granted, and Brigade H.Q. headed for Tsangdhar in the hope of re-forming with the Gorkhas.

The obvious Chinese plan was to break through in the centre and seize Tsangdhar and Hathung La; with those in their hands the remaining Indian troops on the river line would be cut off from escape and supply alike, and could be dealt with at leisure or broken up as they approached the passes. The plan worked perfectly—as it should have done, considering the enormous Chinese advantage in firepower and numbers. The Punjabis and Grenadiers on the right flank of the Indian position were not assaulted, but were engaged heavily by the Chinese across the river; Prasad ordered them to withdraw via Hathung La, but the Chinese got there first and caught the Indian troops coming up towards them. The remnants of the brigade struck west and, suffering great privations, trekked through Bhutan back to India. Trying to make his way with a small party across country to join up with the rest of 4 Division, Brigadier Dalvi was taken prisoner on October 22nd. General Prasad and his Tactical H.Q., threatened by another Chinese prong which had developed from an initial attack on Khinzemane, trekked back to Tawang, reaching there on the evening of October 22nd. 7 Brigade had ceased to exist.

And Tsangle, that position of high political and strategic importance, the holding of which had facilitated the destruction of the brigade— the Chinese ignored it. Tsangle had tactical significance only in the context of Operation Leghorn, and anyway the Chinese maps, like India's, probably showed it in Bhutan.

* * * * * * * * * * *

The Chinese attacked simultaneously in the western sector, assaulting Indian posts in the Chip Chap River valley, on the Galwan, and in the Pangong Lake area. The main Galwan post, which had been invested since August, was not heard from again after reporting that the Chinese had begun to shell it. The posts fought as best they could but were soon overwhelmed, the little garrisons being either killed or captured. Under orders from Western Command, some of the smallest and most isolated posts in these areas, which did not come under attack on the first day, were withdrawn. The forward policy, like Operation Leghorn, had met with the fate which from the beginning the real soldiers had foreseen.

(ii) *Between Two Passes*

On the night of October 18th, when the Chinese had begun their final preparations for assault, there was a riot outside the Prime Minister's resident in New Delhi—demonstrators attempted to break through the police cordon to take their complaints to Nehru. The result was injury to about twenty people, including women and police. This demonstration had nothing to do with the hostilities looming on the northern borders: it was a protest against what its organizers called the Government's 'apathy towards the grievances and demands of the poor'.[100] Because this narrative has concentrated on the boundary dispute it may have left the impression that this had become the exclusive or overriding concern of political India, but such was not the case. Even as late as October 1962 the mounting tension on the borders was not the subject of continuous reporting in the Indian press; sometimes border developments would be front-page news, sometimes they would be carried inside the papers, but often there would be no mention of the borders. Such silence was more frequent with the provincial and smaller journals, but even the English-language papers with national circulations were sometimes dropping the border story. A headline in the *Hindu* in mid-October, UNPROVOKED ATTACK ON INDIA, referred not to anything happening on the borders but to an incident in Nepal in which Nehru had been burned in effigy. The agitation against the English language; the fall of the Government in the state of Kerala; shooting on the border with Pakistan; a new twist in Sikh politics in Punjab—the range of domestic political interest was as wide as ever.

So far as the borders were concerned, there were no forebodings or apprehensions whatever. Until the very last, the political public in India was being led to expect a victorious Indian attack on Thag La. In an interview published on October 19th Krishna Menon reaffirmed the Government's determination to 'throw the Chinese back until Indian territory is cleared of all aggression', and gave an account of what was happening on the Namka Chu. There, he admitted, the

Chinese outnumbered the Indians, and their supply base was closer than India's; nevertheless, he said, attempts they had made to develop a bridgehead on the south side of the river had been beaten back again and again.[101] The same day, the *Statesman* carried the headline, UNCONFIRMED REPORT OF BIG INDIAN PUSH, referring to a leak from the Defence Ministry according to which the Indians below Thag La had advanced two miles on a fifteen-mile front. Next day the newspapers carried an official denial of that story. A few hours after those editions appeared, news of the disaster on the Namka Chu began to reach New Delhi.

A shaken Krishna Menon, asked by journalists where he thought the advancing Chinese could be stopped, said: 'The way they are going there is not any limit to where they will go.'[102] All the past assurances about the physical advantages that India enjoyed in NEFA were reversed, to become the excuses for defeat. At a public meeting that night, Menon explained that India 'had not conditioned her reserves for war purposes'. Her soldiers were fighting at great heights and had to be supplied from the air, whereas the Chinese bases could be supplied from the Tibetan tableland. 'I am not whining about it,' he went on, 'but I want you to understand there are some difficulties in this matter.'[103]

The Prime Minister was for once inaccessible to the press, and Parliament was not in session; but next day he received two Opposition M.P.s, who reported him calm, reassuring, and, if anything, inclined to play down the Chinese attack. One of the newspapers that morning had proclaimed INDIA IS AT WAR;[104] but Nehru told the M.P.s that the Government was not proposing to sever diplomatic relations with Peking, and had no intention of seeking military aid. They asked whether 'arms aid offered by friendly countries without strings might now be accepted', and were told that India was able to get the arms needed within the present framework of her policy, which was opposed to military aid.[105] In the first shock, there was no tendency to blame Nehru for what was happening on the northern frontier; rather, there was an instinctive swing of sympathy and trust towards him as the embodiment of an injured and resolute India. Not for the first time, Krishna Menon served as a surrogate target, and a determined move to bring him down took shape three days after the Chinese attack.

The complaint from some thirty Congress M.P.s who met in New

12*

Delhi on October 23rd was not that Parliament and the country had been misled by the Government, but that Nehru, Parliament and the country had been misled by Krishna Menon. 'Parliament had been told time and again that conditions were not altogether favourable in Ladakh to check the Chinese advance [but] an air of confidence had been created in the country about the position in NEFA',[106] as a newspaper put it, and for that the M.P.s blamed Menon. They took their complaint and charge to Nehru but at first he deflected them, saying that it was not the time for post-mortems. Kripalani and other Opposition M.P.s joined the attack, calling on Nehru to take over the Defence portfolio himself; but the main thrust of the attack on Menon came, as it had to, from the Congress Party. As more and more M.P.s reached New Delhi so the numbers behind the move to oust Menon grew, and the Chief Ministers of the states (who then were all Congressmen) tilted the balance. The President, Dr Radhakrishnan, played a part in concerting the Chief Ministers' demand for Menon's ouster, and that made the attack strong enough to dislodge him—but at first only from the Defence portfolio, and only formally.

On October 31st it was announced that Nehru was taking over the Defence portfolio but that Menon was continuing in the Cabinet as Minister for Defence Production, a new post. This was a change which had, in fact, been mooted some years before, and dismissed then by Menon as the machinations of 'vested interests opposing him';[107] but in the context of October 1962 it was a move typical of Nehru's political style. Conceding the principle that Menon must relinquish the Defence portfolio, Nehru still tried to flout Menon's critics (who were also his own) by retaining him in the Cabinet, and thus, predictably, he lost any political respite that might have accrued if his acquiescence in the demand for Menon's head had been full. Suspicions that Nehru's concession had amounted to nothing more than a change of titles were confirmed next day when Krishna Menon was quoted as saying: 'Nothing has changed,' and political correspondents reported that in fact there had been no change in the working of the Defence Ministry.[108] To quell such misgivings a formal notification was issued, showing Nehru responsible for the great bulk of the Defence Minister's work, and Menon with not much more than ordnance responsibilities; but since Menon was also declared to be responsible for 'any other matters that may be assigned by the Prime Minister from time to time', the suspicion was nourished that he would in practice continue to run the ministry. On November 7th, Nehru faced the Congress Parliamentary Party and played his last card in defence of Menon. The complaints against Menon should in fact be levelled at the Government as a whole, he suggested, and if resignations were wanted he might have to proffer his own. There are various versions of the retort from a leading Congressman, but the gist is constant: 'Yes, if you continue to follow Menon's policies we may have to live without you too.' Next day Menon's resignation from the Cabinet was announced. For the first time, Nehru had been openly defied by the Congress Party, and his threat of resignation, formally an ultimate deterrent, had been exposed as bluff. Menon's ouster had become a sacrifice necessary for his own survival.

There were several aspirants for the Defence portfolio, notably B. J. Patnaik, the Chief Minister of Orissa, who had come to the centre to cut out a role for himself in national politics, and to whom Defence would have given a flying start. But Nehru, although well disposed to Patnaik, declined to bring him into the Cabinet and left him instead with a secret mission—which later emerged as being the organization of guerrillas from among Tibetan, and particularly Khampa, refugees. The idea was that such irregulars, trained and armed in India, could be sent back across the border to harass Chinese lines of communication. A guerrilla training school was set up near Dehra Dun, but whether its graduates ever went into action against the Chinese is not known. There were raids across the border into Tibet after 1962, it seems; George Patterson, a writer with close Tibetan connections, claims to have participated.

Nehru chose Y. B. Chavan, the Chief Minister of Maharashtra, to replace Menon—Chavan accepting with great reluctance and arriving in the capital the day the border war ended.

Menon's ouster, and the manner of it, were the first expressions of the profound changes in the political balance in New Delhi that the defeats on the border were producing. Nehru's moral authority, which until then had been nearly absolute, was waning fast. The Congress Parliamentary Party had begun to assert itself; and behind that the Chief Ministers for the first time had played a decisive part in the politics of the centre.

The world outside, or at least the Indian view of it, was also undergoing some marked shifts. In the West, the Chinese attack was seen as an assault on the chief Asian bastion of democracy—'the first round of the struggle for the Asian mind between the Communist and non-Communist giants of the continent', as the *Daily Telegraph* put it. There were calls for U.N. intervention, as in Korea,[109] and *The Economist* said that 'the temptation to gloat over India's present predicament should be resisted'; succumbing, *The Times* printed as an editorial, without comment, an apologetic of Nehru's: 'We were getting out of touch with reality in the modern world and living in an artificial atmosphere of our own creation.' But the general reaction in the Western world was one of quick and unquestioning sympathy and support for India, led by the British and American Governments. Present Kennedy wrote to Nehru: 'Our sympathy in the situation is wholeheartedly with you. You have displayed an impressive degree of forbearance and patience in dealing with the Chinese. You have put into practice what all great religious leaders have urged, and so few of their followers have been able to do.' And he followed up that applause for the spirituality of India's policies with an offer of material assistance. Professor Galbraith, the American Ambassador, was naturally taking great satisfaction from the emotional swing of grateful Indian opinion towards the United States, and doing everything he could to encourage it. Accordingly, he issued a statement that his Government recognized the McMahon Line as the international border, 'sanctioned by modern usage'. Until then the Americans had been studiously non-committal on this score and even now Galbraith had to overcome the reluctance of the State Department before he was authorized to endorse the McMahon Line. He issued his statement immediately he received the Department's approval, lest there be second thoughts in Washington under pressure from Formosa — and no sooner had he got it out than a 'frantic protest' did come in from the Nationalists.[110] The British Government was as prompt and unqualified in its expressions of sympathy for India and condemnation of China, and in its offers of help.

But if the Western world was solidly with India, the reaction of the non-aligned governments whose leadership India had sometimes aspired to was by contrast reserved and wary — in a word, non-aligned. An Indian correspondent in the Middle East reported: 'Not a single expression of sympathy for India has come from any Arab Government, any political party or newspaper, or public personality even a week after the invasion'.[111] From Africa another reported that Kenyatta and other leaders were being non-committal[112] and Nkrumah of Ghana went farther than that by rebuking Britain for her prompt offers of military assistance to India. 'Whatever the rights and wrongs of the present struggle between India and China', he wrote to Macmillan, the British prime minister, 'I am sure that we can all serve the cause of peace best by refraining from any action that may aggravate the situation.'[113] Nkrumah's attitude was the more offensive to Indians because Nehru had just visited him in Ghana. Ethiopia and Cyprus were the only countries among those which had attended the 1961 Belgrade Conference of non-aligned governments to come out openly on India's side from the outset. Others showed themselves more interested in filling the role so often until then India's, of urging restraint and patience on both sides and volunteering to act as mediators. When Parliament reassembled Nehru expressed his resentment at those of India's friends abroad, 'well-intentioned countries', who were trying to bring about a ceasefire. 'People advise us to be good and peaceful as if we are inclined to war,' he said. 'In fact, if we are anything, as the House well knows, we do not possess the war-like mentality and that is why for the purposes of war there is weakness. . . . So, people talking to us to be good boys and make it up has no particular meaning, unless they come to grips with the issues involved.'[114] The 'so-called non-aligned countries' (unexpected phrasing, from Nehru) were confused, he said, and a little frightened of China, too, so 'it is no good our getting angry with them [because] they do not stand forthright in our defence, in support of our position.'[115]

The reaction in the non-aligned world was less damaging to India's interests than the pacificatory line at first taken by Moscow, which for once leant clearly to the side of China. The first intimation of this shift had been received in New Delhi on October 20th, a few hours after the Chinese attack, in the form of a letter to Nehru from Krushchev, expressing concern at reports that India intended to take up arms to settle her boundary dispute with China, and warning that this was 'a very dangerous path'.[116] (The Indians, of course, had made no secret of their intention to use force against the Chinese below Thag La; the Russian Ambassador had met Krishna Menon twice while Operation Leghorn was being prepared[117] and no doubt Menon told him all about it—he might have hoped that word that India meant business, passed to Peking from Moscow, would persuade the Chinese that discretion was in this case the better part of diplomacy.) Krushchev's letter urged that Nehru should accept the Chinese proposals for talks. Worse was to follow. On October 24th Peking renewed the proposal for disengagement and talks, and next day *Pravda* commended the Chinese move as sincere and constructive, providing an acceptable basis for the opening of talks. The editorial said:

> The question of the China–India frontier is a heritage from those days when British colonialists – who drew and re-drew the map of Asia at their own will – ruled on the territory of India. The notorious 'McMahon Line', which was never recognized by China, was foisted on the Chinese and Indian peoples. Imperialist circles have done everything in their power to provoke an armed clash by speculating on the border conflicts connected with this Line. The imperialists are dreaming day and night of setting these great powers at loggerheads, as well as undermining the Soviet Union's friendship with fraternal China and friendly India.

Pravda went on to note that 'reactionary circles inside India' were fanning the conflict, and warned that 'even some progressively-minded people' might yield to chauvinistic influences in the heat of the moment.

The critical implications and pro-Chinese undertone of the Russian position came as a blow to the Indian Government. As the political correspondent of the *Hindu* put it,

> It was thought that at best the Russians would continue to adopt a neutralist attitude. All these hopes were dashed to the ground when *Pravda* came out with an editorial wholeheartedly endorsing the Chinese stand. . . . Mr Krushchev's letter to Mr Nehru runs on exactly the same lines as the *Pravda* article.
>
> The reaction in the capital, not only in official and non-official circles but also among a section of the Indian Communists, is one of dismay, and the Soviet attitude is regarded not only as unkind but even as offensive.[118]

The Russians, to suggest that their change of attitude was more than one of words, intimated to the Indian Embassy in Moscow that they would not be able to fulfil their commitment to supply India with MiG fighters.[119] For the next couple of weeks Moscow havered on that question.

What had happened was that the Caribbean game of chicken had reached its crisis almost precisely at the same moment as the one in the Himalayas. The first evidence that Russian missiles were in Cuba was detected in Washington late on October 14th. The administration kept its discovery secret for a week, until it had decided how the situation was to be handled; on October 22nd President Kennedy announced the American intention of putting the island under a selective blockade, and next day the American Ambassador in India left a copy of his statement with the Indian Government. In his confrontation with the United States, it was plainly of high importance for Krushchev to do everything possible to repair the rift between Moscow and Peking – or rather to suggest to the world that it had been repaired – and therefore to come out on China's side in her quarrel with India.* (China later dismissed the temporary change in the Russian tone as 'a few seemingly fair words [spoken] out of considerations of expediency'.)[120]

Sharp as was the first disappointment with the Russian stand, Nehru quickly saw the point. Before the end of October he replied to an American television interviewer who asked him about the Russian attitude: 'I should imagine that developments [in] Cuba, et cetera, probably made it necessary for them not to fall out with China.' He said he hoped that now the missile problem was 'out of the way' (Krushchev having agreed on October 28th to withdraw the missiles) that the Soviet Union would return to its former position – which it soon did.[121]

* * * * * * * * * * *

The first and all-important decision for a retreating force to make is, where to make a stand? It is a question that can be answered only in terms of the military factors of time, terrain and logistics, and an error in the answer is enough to fate an army to a second defeat.

The first impulse of General Thapar and General Sen was to try to hold Tawang. Sen helicoptered to Tawang on October 22nd and gave orders to the troops there – two infantry battalions (1 Sikh and 4 Garhwal Rifles) and some artillery – that Tawang was to be held at all costs, saying that two more brigades would be inducted quickly to

---

* It was then, and afterwards, suggested that China timed her attack to coincide with the missile crisis. As Joseph Alsop put it in the *New York Herald Tribune* on November 12th, 1962, 'China could easily have been warned unofficially by their important Cuban contacts or perhaps by their sympathizers in the Soviet general staff. It was hard to believe, at any rate, that it was just pure chance.' It is impossible to be certain, but to the writer it appears that the timing of the October 20th attack is adequately explained by the development of the Sino-Indian dispute and such local factors as the water level in the Namka Chu. It is easier to believe this, at any rate, than that Chinese Intelligence and prescience (about the extent of the American reaction to the presence of missiles in Cuba) was sufficient to enable them to time their attack so exactly.

reinforce them. He had to spend the night in Tawang, his helicopter having returned to Tezpur without him, and next morning met General Prasad, just in from Zimithang with his Tactical H.Q. staff. Each of these officers in his account of that meeting implied that the other had lost his nerve — Sen, being the senior, was of course in a position to have his version accepted — and there is dispute about what orders Sen left when he flew back to Tezpur on October 23rd. But both in Army H.Q. and at IV Corps in Tezpur, heads that were probably cooler than either were arguing strongly that it would be disastrous to try to hold Tawang.

The Chinese had developed a three-pronged attack. The force which had overwhelmed 7 Brigade, thought to be about three regiments, had turned south-east, come through Shakti, and was at Lumla, less than ten miles from Tawang, on October 23rd; that force had joined up with the second prong which had come through Khinzemane and down the Nyamjang Chu; on the 23rd a third line of advance was opened through Bum La and straight down the old trade route to Tawang, which was thus threatened from north and south. Tawang had no natural defences; plainly any troops that attempted a stand there would be overcome as easily as had been those on the Namka Chu. In New Delhi, the Director of Military Operations (D.M.O.), Brigadier Palit, was strongly urging on Thapar that Tawang must be evacuated; Thapar consulted Nehru, who said that where and how they would fight must now be a matter for the military themselves to decide. In Tezpur the Brigadier General Staff (B.G.S.) of IV Corps, Brigadier K. K. Singh, was similarly urging Sen. Kaul was out of the picture again, having been persuaded to hang up his telephones and relinquish command of IV Corps on the morning that the Chinese attacked.

Consequently, on October 23rd orders went out from IV Corps to the force at Tawang that they were to withdraw *to Bomdi La*, some sixty miles back on the road to the plains: that, in the calculations of IV Corps, was *the farthest point to the north where the Indians could build up more quickly than the Chinese*. All formations concerned were informed that the build-up was to be at Bomdi La.

But at Army H.Q. the D.M.O., Brigadier Palit, was urging just as strongly that the troops should be ordered to hold *at Se La*, a high pass only about fifteen miles behind Tawang. Palit, before Kaul picked him for D.M.O., had commanded 7 Brigade in NEFA, and formed the view that Se La was an impregnable natural position which had to be held if an invader were to be denied access to the plains. That view, urged by the forceful and articulate Palit, must have been welcome to Krishna Menon and perhaps to Thapar; for all the Prime Minister's injunction that the decision must be taken purely on military grounds, they cannot have overlooked the fact that the more territory was yielded to the Chinese, the worse the reverse on the Namka Chu must look. At all events, later on October 23rd Sen countermanded the order to pull back to Bomdi La and ordered that Se La must be held. Brigadier K. K. Singh urged that New Delhi be told that it would be logistically impossible to build up sufficient defences at Se La; but Sen replied that the Cabinet had decided that Se La should be held and the Government's orders must be implemented.

That decision was crucial—and disastrous. Se La was tempting. The pass itself was 14,600 feet high, and it was flanked by peaks a thousand feet higher. The 5,000-foot climb from the Tawang valley was very steep, and the road was dominated from the pass and its flanks. The road to the plains ran through Se La, and only tracks by-passed it. It was a strong defensive position—but it was a trap for the Indians. Se La was too far from the plains for it to be quickly built up as the main defence position; the road at best could take only one-ton vehicles and it was a long, gruelling trip of several days from the foot-hills to Se La. There were good dropping zones near the pass; but still the terrain made air supply wasteful and precarious, while the weather made it wholly unreliable. Furthermore, Se La was too high: its defence would require troops to operate at altitudes between 14,000 and 16,000 feet, while the garrison would have to be made up of units brought straight from the plains, without acclimatization. Finally, Se La was too near Tawang; the Chinese could mount their assault against it with the minimum regrouping, and without having to move their bases forward.

The decision to hold Se La entailed the defence of Bomdi La and the road between as well. The Chinese could outflank Se La on any of several tracks, and sufficient forces would have to be kept in reserve to keep the road free of Chinese blocks. The decision to hold Se La committed the Indians to holding a very deep area, from Se La to Bomdi La, separated by some sixty miles of difficult and unreliable road through high, broken country.

Air support of this position would be limited to supply missions. The

Government had decided that tactical air support with bombers or ground-attack aircraft must be ruled out for fear of Chinese retaliation against Indian cities, especially Calcutta. The memory of the huge panic that swept Calcutta during the Second World War when some random Japanese bombs fell there, with repercussions far beyond the city, was enough to make the Government resolve that it must not be risked again. Considering the terrain in NEFA and the limitations of the Indian Air Force, it is doubtful whether its intervention in a tactical role could have had much effect; but those were not the considerations that made the Government rule it out.

Tawang was evacuated on October 23rd, some hundreds of civilians, including lamas from the monastery, going with the troops. The Chinese occupied Tawang, unopposed, on the 25th. The Indians took up positions on and behind the Jang River, with the more or less intact battalions from Tawang reinforced with stragglers who had got through from the Namka Chu debacle, and with non-combatant personnel. On the night of October 24th one battalion, 4 Garhwal, panicked, broke and began to trickle back; but these troops were intercepted and braced, to be put back in the line. Later this battalion cleared its record by beating off repeated Chinese assaults from its positions flanking Se La.

The Chinese paused after they occupied Tawang. After October 20th they had attacked Indian posts elsewhere along the McMahon Line, and these had fallen back under varying degrees of pressure. At the eastern end of NEFA they came down on October 24th-25th to Walong and made some probing attacks; but thereafter NEFA fell into a lull.

Meanwhile in the western sector, the Chinese had followed up their first attacks by moving south and concentrating on other Indian forward posts. On October 21st they overran the posts on the north side of Pangong Lake after severe fighting, the Gorkha garrisons fighting almost to the last man. On the 27th they attacked the posts around Demchok with similar results. Some posts, including Daulet Beg Oldi, were evacuated on orders of Western Command, before the Chinese attacked—and Daulet Beg Oldi was not occupied by the Chinese; it was outside their claim line. General Daulet Singh of Western Command was methodically and rapidly building up strength on his threatened Chinese front by pulling troops out of Kashmir. All the command's transport reserves were pooled and deployed to the job

of reinforcing the Ladakh front, and the Indian strength there grew
quickly. By the first week of November a Divisional H.Q. was established at Leh, with an additional brigade of four infantry battalions; by
November 17th another brigade had been inducted to Leh.

On the eastern front, however, there was no such decisiveness or
dispatch. IV Corps got a new commander on October 24th, Lieutenant-
General Harbaksh Singh, who had been stationed in Simla. Sen removed General Prasad from the command of 4 Division, replacing
him with Major-General A. S. Pathania — a soldier with a good combat
record in the past, but who was now catapulted from heading the
National Cadet Corps in New Delhi, an armchair job of the most
relaxed kind, to commanding a division in action. Much of Eastern
Command's energies were occupied with command changes like
these. The commanding officer of 62 Brigade was changed, the brigadier who had trained and commanded the formation being replaced
by a newcomer, Brigadier Hoshiar Singh; 65 Brigade was kept kicking
its heels in Bomdi La, without any orders, until the new divisional
commander's request for a replacement of its brigadier was granted;
the commander of 5 Brigade, responsible for the Walong sector, was
also changed. Almost keeping pace with the dropping and changing of
commanders, units were posted and cross-posted until no brigade in
NEFA had its original battalions under command.

It seemed that IV Corps might, on the other hand, be settling down.
General Harbaksh Singh, taking over command on October 24th,
began energetically to make reconnaissances and appreciations of his
sector and task.

* * * * * * * * * * *

This time it was Peking who used a verbal smoke-screen to obscure the
reality of what was happening on the ground. On October 20th the
Chinese Defence Ministry issued a statement which said that at 07.00
hours that morning the Indian troops had launched large-scale attacks,
not only on the Namka Chu but also from their posts in the Chip Chap
and Galwan valleys in the western sector. 'In self-defence, the Chinese
frontier guards were compelled to strike back resolutely, and cleared
away some aggressive strong points set up by the Indian troops in
China's territory,' the statement went on. There the Chinese took over
the tactic of 'turning truth on its head' of which they had often — and

not without reason—accused India. The troops on the Namka Chu put in no attack on October 20th; they were in the process of reinforcing Tsangle, which was certainly an aggressive move, but to say that 'under cover of fierce artillery fire [they] launched massive attacks against the Chinese frontier guards all along the [Namka Chu] and in the Khinzemane area' was simply to fabricate.[122] To say that the Indian troops in the western sector 'launched a general attack' from their isolated and puny posts was grotesque.

In thus sacrificing truth to what was apparently considered propaganda advantage, the Chinese played into New Delhi's hands by obscuring what had actually happened. That the Indians had intended to attack the Chinese below Thag La ridge was by then known everywhere; Nehru's airport confirmation of October 12th had told any interested government which had not already got wind of Operation Leghorn what was afoot. If Peking had simply said that, rather than waiting for the Indians to deliver the attack they had so loudly heralded, the Chinese Army had got its blow in first, it would have been hard for New Delhi to cry 'aggression' with any credibility: the doctrine of the pre-emptive strike is too widely accepted nowadays for any successful practitioner to be generally condemned. As it was, however, the Chinese charge that the Indians had 'launched massive attacks' rebounded from the general scepticism about India having the strength to attack China; and was almost immediately belied by Peking's own announcement that the defensive actions of the Chinese 'frontier guards' were carrying them over successive Indian positions.

It may be significant that Chou En-lai did not at first subscribe his name to the false statement that the Indians had attacked on October 20th. Writing to Nehru on November 4th, he said only that the Indian troops on the Namka Chu had 'made active dispositions for a massive military attack',[123] and that was precisely true: a brigade attack with four battalions could certainly be described as massive in the scale of skirmishing along the borders up to that time. In a letter to the Afro-Asian governments ten days later, however, Chou also wrote that India had 'launched massive attacks all along the line'.[124]

The conjunction of military and diplomatic measures was at the heart of the operation on which China was now embarked, and her next diplomatic move was adroit in both timing and content. A statement released in Peking on October 24th concisely recapitulated the course of the dispute with India, concluding with a reminder that three times in the past three months India had rejected China's proposals for talks without pre-conditions, and that Nehru had then publicly ordered the Indian Army to 'free Indian territory'. The statement then pointed to the impossibility of settling the boundary question by force, and the need to reopen peaceful negotiations; and set forth three proposals to that end:

(1) That both sides affirm that the dispute must be settled peacefully; agree to respect the line of actual control [as of November 1959]; and withdraw their armed forces twenty kilometres from that line.

(2) If India agreed to that, Chinese forces would be withdrawn to the north of the McMahon Line.

(3) The Prime Ministers should meet again, in Peking or New Delhi, to seek a friendly settlement.*

Chou En-lai included these proposals in a letter to Nehru the same day, the first communication between the Prime Ministers since they parted in New Delhi in April 1960. He urged that 'we should look ahead [and] take measures to turn the tide' rather than argue over the origin of the conflict, and appealed to Nehru to respond positively.[125]

The Chinese proposal was not new in any detail; it was the same as Chou put forward originally in his letter to Nehru of November 7th, 1959, altered somewhat to take account of the fact that Chinese troops were now south of the McMahon Line. (On October 21st Peking had announced that Chinese troops had been told they could disregard the McMahon Line in their operations on the eastern sector – and that day the troops moved south of Hathung La, the boundary feature according to China.) In effect, the Chinese proposals would have created a

---

* Textually: (1) Both parties affirm that the Sino-Indian boundary question must be settled peacefully through negotiations. Pending a peaceful settlement, the Chinese Government hopes that the Indian Government will agree that both parties respect the line of actual control between the two sides along the entire Sino-Indian border, and the armed forces of each side withdraw twenty kilometres from this line and disengage.

(2) Provided that the Indian Government agrees to the above proposal, the Chinese Government is willing, through consultations between the two parties, to withdraw its frontier guards in the eastern sector of the border to the north of the line of actual control; at the same time, both China and India undertake not to cross the line of actual control, i.e. the traditional customary line, in the middle and western sectors of the border.

(3) The Chinese Government considers that, in order to seek a friendly settlement of the Sino-Indian boundary question, talks should be held once again by the Prime Ministers of China and India. At a time considered to be appropriate by both parties, the Chinese Government would welcome the Indian Prime Minister to Peking; if this should be inconvenient to the Indian Government, the Chinese Premier would be ready to go to Delhi for talks.[126]

ceasefire line along the 'line of actual control', the term which Peking
had from the first used to describe the situation when the dispute came
to a head in 1959. The Chinese would have pulled back over the
McMahon Line, and Indian troops in the remaining forward posts in
the western sector would have withdrawn to the line that the Indian
Army had held before the forward policy was put into effect in 1961.
Then, to create a demilitarized zone along that line, the armed forces
of each side would each pull back another twenty kilometres—civil
personnel would not be involved in those withdrawals. There was no
ambiguity in these proposals, although they were not stated in precise
locational detail. Thag La ridge was not mentioned, for example, nor
for that matter was the McMahon Line; but the phrase 'the line of
actual control' had throughout been used by Peking to describe the
situation in November 1959, when the Chinese were nowhere south
of the McMahon Line, or even south of Thag La ridge—though when
the Indians *were* established at Khinzemane. The only territorial change
that acceptance of the proposals would have entailed for India was
that the posts set up in the western sector, over the Chinese claim line,
in pursuance of the forward policy, would be withdrawn—where they
had not already been wiped out—and that Dhola Post could not have
been re-established.

The Chinese described their proposals as equal, mutually accom-
modatory and based on mutual respect—'not arbitrary and arrogant'[127]
—and, seen objectively, they merit the description; but, of course, India
could not see them objectively. To the Indians, the Chinese had simply
added a new and more violent aggression to the long-standing aggression involved in the Chinese presence in territory India claimed in the
western sector; and they were now seeking to confirm their criminal
gains through diplomacy.

New Delhi rejected the Chinese proposals instantly—indeed without
waiting to receive them officially, but going by the news agencies'
account of their contents. In its reply, released in New Delhi as a
statement on October 24th, the Indian Government first claimed that
it was 'wedded to peace and peaceful methods [and had] always sought
to resolve differences by talks and discussions . . . with China'; but, it
went on, 'India cannot and will not accept a position under which
Chinese forces continue to commit aggression into Indian territory,
occupy substantial Indian territories and use these as a bargaining
counter to force a settlement on their own terms.'

The statement proceeded to confuse the Chinese proposal, before advancing a counter-proposal.

> There is no sense or meaning in the Chinese offer to withdraw twenty kilometres from what they call 'line of actual control'. What is this 'line of actual control'? Is this the line they have created by aggression since the beginning of September? Advancing forty or sixty kilometres by blatant military aggression and offering to withdraw twenty kilometres provided both sides do this is a deceptive device which can fool nobody.

That the officials in the External Affairs Ministry in New Delhi were really uncertain about the meaning of the Chinese proposals is most improbable; 'the line of actual control' had a clear and consistent meaning in Peking's usage. But the Chinese had left an opening by not going into more detail, and the Indians exploited it – to ask for clarification is a classic diplomatic way of playing for time. The counter-proposal followed:

> If the Chinese professions of peace and peaceful settlement of differences are really genuine, let them go back at least to the position where they were all along the boundary prior to 8th September, 1962. India will then be prepared to undertake talks and discussions, at any level mutually agreed, to arrive at agreed measures which should be taken for the easing of tension and correction of the situation created by unilateral forcible alteration of the *status quo* along the India–China boundary.[128]

If China accepted that proposal, India would be prepared to welcome Chou En-lai to New Delhi, the statement concluded.

If China was being consistent, so was India. This counter-proposal was in fact precisely the proposal that New Delhi had put forward on October 6th when retracting the earlier agreement to begin talks.* It would have had the Chinese drawing back over Thag La ridge (the date September 8th referred to the initial Chinese investment of Dhola Post) and relinquishing the posts they had captured in the western sector; so that the Indians could return to them and to their positions at Dhola Post, elsewhere on the Namka Chu, and at Khinzemane. Once China had accepted and implemented that, India would be prepared to talk – but only about Chinese withdrawal from Aksai

* See page 327 above.

Chin. Nehru sent the Indian statement, with its proposal, to Chou
En-lai on October 27th, in a letter remarkable for its mildness con-
sidering the context of what Nehru called 'a Chinese invasion of
India'.[129]

Nehru was criticized in India for the civil tone of this letter to Chou
and the weakness of its counter-proposal. After the Chinese attacks the
mood in India equated any agreement to negotiate with surrender—
one M.P. saying that the mere suggestion that India should agree to
talks must be treated as high treason.[130] Thus it was inevitable that
China's proposals would be rejected, and the requested clarifications
when they came could make no difference.

In another letter, dated November 4th, Chou En-lai crossed the t's
and dotted the i's of his Government's proposals. The 'line of actual
control' they referred to was basically the same line as he had proposed
as the starting-point for mutual withdrawal in November 1959, he
explained. 'The fact that the Chinese Government's proposal has taken
as its basis the 1959 line of actual control and not the present *line of
actual contact* between the armed forces of the two sides is full proof
that the Chinese side has not tried to force any unilateral demand on
the Indian side on account of the advances gained in the recent counter-
attack in self-defence.' (Italics added.) The Indian counter-proposal,
with its provision for the return of Indian troops to their dispositions
for attack on the Namka Chu and to the forward posts in the western
sector, he likened to 'such as [is] forced on a vanquished party'. 'How
can the Chinese Government agree to revert to such a position?' Chou
asked, and appealed to Nehru to reconsider the Chinese proposals.[131]

Nehru's next letter is striking in its change of tone.[132] The first letter
he wrote after the Chinese attack had been muted and carefully civil;
now he hit out, describing the Chinese attacks as 'cold-blood[ed] . . .
massive aggression' and declaring that for India to accept the Chinese
proposals 'would mean mere existence at the mercy of an aggressive,
arrogant and expansionist neighbour'. He reiterated that the Indian
troops must go back to the positions they had occupied all along the
boundaries on September 8th, and suggested that China could demonstrate her *bona fides* by withdrawing her forces to the positions they
held in November 1959. The effect of that would have been to see the
Indians re-established in all their forward posts, while the Chinese
stayed well back from the positions they had set up to counter India's
forward policy.

At the heart of the Indian position was the insistence that the Chinese withdraw over Thag La ridge, and that Indian forces return both to the area beneath Thag La (Dhola Post and Khinzemane) and to the posts, most of them by now overrun, set up in the western sector under the forward policy. That is what was implied in the insistence on return to the positions of September 8th.

The diplomatic exchanges during the lull that followed the Chinese occupation of Tawang showed that New Delhi's approach to the boundary dispute had changed only to harden. The Indians were as adamant as ever that they would not negotiate a boundary settlement, and their insistence on return to their forward posts in the western sector, as well as to the Namka Chu, showed that the designs and assumptions which underlay the forward policy were unchanged. By smashing the puny threat that India had built up to the Chinese positions below Thag La, and by wiping out half the forward Indian posts in the western sector, Peking had gained nothing. The Indians, feeling that they had lost a battle but not yet begun to wage a war, were more confident than ever, and the political mood in India had now become almost unanimously bellicose. For China to keep her troops where they were would be to invite a long campaign of attrition, with the Sino-Indian boundaries becoming a running sore while the Indians steadily built up the scale and determination of their attacks. To draw back over the McMahon Line, on the other hand, would be to invite the jeering interpretation that the Chinese Army had made discretion the better part of valour; that, unless fortified by surprise and over-whelming numbers, the Chinese were chary of trading blows with India. It would, moreover, leave the boundary dispute unresolved. If this had been all Peking had planned, the attempt to mesh military action with diplomatic manœuvre so as to resolve the dispute with India once and for all, could have been written off as a fiasco.

But the Chinese conception had by no means been fully implemented, indeed it had only just begun to be put into effect. Before the October 20th attacks, a senior minister in Peking had been heard to say that China was going to have to advance well to the south of the points in local dispute, and then withdraw.[133] The first attacks had been like the jab of a boxer which seemingly only jolts his opponent, but in fact sets him up for the knockout.

If the military side of China's operation was working out as planned, so was the political side. The defeat on the Namka Chu and his belief that India was at the beginning of a long, though undeclared, war with China had swept away Nehru's resistance to accepting military aid. Only a few weeks before, he had again roundly rejected the suggestion that India might seek arms aid, saying it meant becoming 'somebody else's dependent'; identifying the acceptance of military aid with 'joining some military bloc', he had declared he would never agree to this, 'even if disaster comes to us on the frontier'.[134] But on October 29th, when the American Ambassador called on Nehru offering any military equipment India might need, the offer was instantly accepted. That night, the writer reported to *The Times*: 'The decision to accept American military assistance, reversing policies that India had cherished since she became a nation, was taken formally at a Cabinet meeting today; but Mr Nehru had been convinced already by his service advisers that only with equipment in the quantity and quality that the United States could provide would the Indian Army be able to defeat the Chinese.' Lists of India's military needs had already been prepared and were handed to the Americans; the embassy in New Delhi expressed dismay not only at the scope of the Indian requests, but also at the disorganization which the confusion of the indents displayed. The Pentagon, using its new, computerized stock-keeping methods, was quickly able to get the first supplies on the way, however; flown from West Germany in jet freighters, they began landing in India five days later.

Chou En-lai drew this to the attention of heads of the Afro-Asian governments: 'The Indian Government has openly begged military aid from the United States,' he said.[135] The *People's Daily* described India's acceptance of American military aid, in addition to the economic aid she had long been receiving from the U.S.A., as 'a development of historic significance':

> It points to the fact that the Nehru Government has finally shed its cloak of non-alignment policy. . . . The more Nehru depends on U.S. imperialism, the greater the need is there for him to meet the needs of U.S. imperialism and persist in opposing China. And the more he persists in opposing China, the greater the need for him to depend on U.S. imperialism. Thus he is caught in a vicious circle. His gradual shedding of his policy of 'non-alignment' is precisely the inevitable result of his sell-out to U.S. imperialism.[136]

If this development served to confirm Peking's analysis of the

nature of the Nehru Government—making a key point in the argument with Moscow—it must also have underlined to Peking the importance of not letting the fighting drag on. A Western correspondent
in Peking early in November reported a Chinese official 'disgustedly'
saying to him: 'As long as the Indians go on attacking us they will get
anything they want out of the United States. They're making millions
of dollars out of these skirmishes, they'll probably go on for ever.'[137]

What to the Indians appeared as an ungrateful chariness among the
Afro-Asian governments who were declining to come out clearly on
the Indian side, may to the Chinese have indicated that India's version
of events was now at last being met with some scepticism: in mid-
November Chou En-lai addressed a letter to the heads of Asian and
African governments explaining China's stand, thanking them for
their 'fair-minded endeavours to promote direct negotiations between
China and India', and affirming that China wanted only a peaceful
settlement of the dispute with India.[138]

Moscow's sudden objectivity about the dispute had died, meanwhile, with the relaxing of the Cuba crisis; as Nehru expected, the
Russians had quickly reverted to what was, to the Chinese, neutrality-
on-one-side. Early in November Moscow began calling on both sides
to bring about a ceasefire and negotiations, ignoring the fact that India
had just refused negotiations once more.[139] In Peking's view, the Cuba
confrontation had been brought on by Krushchev's 'adventurism', in
deploying Russian missiles in Cuba in the first place; then com-
pounded by his 'capitulationism' in backing down under American
pressure, and removing them. The completion of the Chinese operation
against India would show the world that the threats and vaunts of the
imperialists and their creatures could be ignored with impunity and
defied with benefit, thus underlining the pusillanimity and incom-
petence of Khrushchev and his 'revisionist clique'.

* * * * * * * * * * *

The first defeats ushered in India's phoney war. Shock wore off into
resolution, that grew into optimism, and war came to be seen and enjoyed as India's hour of greatness, of which the fruits could only be
national unity and ultimate triumph.

The initial reaction to the Chinese attack was one of unfeigned
astonishment and outrage. It was almost forgotten that the Indian

Army had been about to take offensive action; ignored, that the Government had refused to meet the Chinese for talks. If the Chinese 'had any claim they could have discussed it and talked about it and adopted various means of peaceful settlement', Nehru now complained.[140] 'Why, in the face of our patience, goodwill and obvious anxiety for settlement, have the Chinese persisted in this aggression?' Asok Mehta asked later,[141] and the Lok Sabha put it formally in a resolution in which it affirmed the 'resolve of the Indian people to drive out the aggressor from the sacred soil of India': 'This House notes with deep regret that in spite of the uniform gestures of goodwill and fellowship by India towards China . . . China has betrayed that goodwill and friendship . . . and has committed aggression and initiated a massive invasion of India.' In the disapproval of China's use of force it was not entirely forgotten, however, that India had intended something of the same. 'We are perfectly justified in pushing them and attacking them,' Nehru pointed out.[142]

The reaction among the Indian political classes and, to some extent, among the urban masses was vigorous. Public meetings were held, every political party, including the Communists,* condemning the Chinese. There was a rush on army recruiting stations; less constructively, students burned effigies of Mao Tse-tung and Chou En-lai, and pledged their dedication to the national cause in signatures inked with their own blood; the shops of Chinese in New Delhi and Calcutta, shoemakers or curio dealers, were mobbed, and their owners beaten up. Japanese diplomats plastered their cars with 'rising sun' emblems and identifications in Hindi lest a hasty mob mistake them for Chinese. The Government introduced an ordinance which empowered it to treat even Indian citizens of Chinese descent as enemy aliens, and several thousand were interned in camps in Rajasthan—they were later expelled to China. The Government announced its intention of forming a home guard and a national rifle association, and of enlarging the national cadet corps so that every university student could be enrolled. Schoolgirls drilled and marched, members of Parliament were photographed taking aim with rifles—in Punjab the ministers of the state Government decided to appear in the legislature in military uniform.[143]

---

* By this time, however, the inherent division within the Communist Party of India had been turned into a barely disguised split by the strain of the border dispute. The party leadership's action in condemning China for the border fighting and pledging the party's unqualified support to Nehru can be seen in retrospect as making the final, open split into two parties unavoidable.

The great industrial and commercial house of Birla presented a minia-
ture rifle range to the nation, so that citizens in New Delhi could learn
to shoot with ·22 rifles. Slit trenches were dug in the capital's public
gardens and sandbags piled at the doorways of Government offices.
Morarji Desai, the Finance Minister, opened a national defence fund
which would accept money, gold or ornaments—'Ornaments for
armaments' became a popular slogan—and floated an issue of defence
bonds; he called for austerity and economy for all. It was announced
that ordinance factories would be working extra shifts.

Such manifestations of popular commitment to the struggle with
China were acclaimed as proof that the signs of disunity and 'fissi-
parousness', which had been so worrying in preceding years, were in
fact superficial; that beneath them lay an emotionally integrated
nation. The Lok Sabha praised 'the wonderful and spontaneous response of the people of India to the emergency . . . this mighty upsurge
amongst all sections of our people'.[144] More poetically, Nehru thanked
China for an action which, he said, had 'suddenly lifted a veil from the
face of India, [giving] a glimpse of the serene face of India, strong and
yet calm and determined, an ancient face which is ever young and
vibrant'.[145] This was matched from the Opposition front bench, where
a Socialist invoked 'the blood of our martyred jawans, [which] is becoming the seed of a new, virile nation that is being born in our
country'.[146]

Ignoring the obvious gusto of the response to what was felt to be
war, Nehru insisted still on the inherent and unshakable pacifism of
Indians. In contrast to the Chinese, who, he said, were conditioned to
war and seemed to 'think that war was a natural state of affairs', here
were the Indians, 'disliking it, excessively disliking the idea of war—
emotionally disliking it, apart from not liking its consequences'. In-
voking Gandhi, he reminded Parliament that 'basically we are a
gentle people', and expressed his fear that war would change all that.
'It alarms me that we should become, because of the exigencies of war,
brutalized, a brutal nation. I think that would mean the whole soul and
spirit of India being demoralized, and that is a terribly harmful thing.
Certainly I hope that all of us will remember this.'[147] Belief in the inherent and peculiar pacifism and gentleness of the Indian people was
central to Nehru's perceptions, and he had made much of it in the
course of the dispute with China; not only in his domestic utterances,
but also in his letters to Chou En-lai, and in the diplomatic notes to

Peking. Nehru's belief in this myth derived perhaps from his closeness to Gandhi; the truth must lie somewhere between Nehru's view of 'a gentle people,' and Nirad Chaudhuri's – that 'few human communities have been more warlike and fond of bloodshed [than the Indians]'.*148

At this time, however, Nehru's qualms about 'brutalization' were out of key. Intense gratification with the public response was to be heard in almost every comment, and was epitomized in a *Times of India* cartoon. Captioned WAR WITH CHINA, this showed Nehru and his Cabinet colleagues smugly surveying a wall of graphs, labelled EMOTIONAL INTEGRATION, INDUSTRIAL PEACE, PEOPLE'S FAITH IN GOVERNMENT, and the like; all the graphs were zooming up, and Nehru was commenting: 'We never had it so good.' In fact the Prime Minister made the point more elegantly: 'This challenge may be converted into opportunity for us to grow and to change the dark cloud that envelops our frontiers into the bright sun not only of freedom but of welfare in this country.'149

Although the popular reaction was much magnified by the enthusiasm of the Indians who gauged and valued it, there was certainly a wide response to what was presented as the challenge of war with China. It was by no means a 'mighty upsurge', but there was at least a ripple across the deep waters of the society. For the political classes, the reaction was spontaneous and much as it would have been in any other country that suddenly felt itself at war, without any of the pangs and pains usually associated with that process. War to such Indians was remote, romantic and therapeutic. For the urban masses it was a circus, an opportunity to join a parade, shout slogans. For the villages, it was remote but vaguely alarming, a threat to the village rather than to the nation – which is anyway a concept beyond the interest of the village mass in India. There was initially a good response to the appeals for contributions for the defence fund but this before long soured, with complaints that local officials were coercing villagers to contribute and that the poorest sections were being badgered.

In contrast to the excitement and commitment that was being encouraged in India, in China the fighting was consistently played down, the conflict minimized. A Western correspondent in Peking reported

---

* Chaudhuri argues that 'Hindu militarism is a genuine and powerful force, influencing Indian foreign policy.' Particularizing, he asserts that 'the conflict with China . . . was inspired almost wholly by Hindu jingoism, with the Hindu possessiveness as a second, underlying factor.'150
Gandhi himself once noted that the Indian people had 'always been warlike'.151

that 'newspaper coverage is more political than military and even Chinese successes have constantly been played down. There has been no attempt to make the reader keenly war-conscious. Rare and laconic situation reports are printed in the guarded words of the New China News Agency.'[152]

The Indian Government in its statements and rhetoric, on the other hand, treated the border fighting as an undeclared war. 'We may not be technically at war,' Nehru explained, 'but the fact is that we are at war, though we have not made any declaration to that effect—it is not necessary at the present moment to do so, I do not know about the future.'[153] Throughout, however, Nehru resisted strong pressure to break off diplomatic relations with Peking and in the United Nations, which happened to be considering the perennial question of China's representation just after the fighting broke out, India maintained her support for Peking, although no longer taking the lead in pressing the issue.

A state of emergency was declared, giving the central Government overriding powers and suspending civil liberties, and Parliament was called into session ten days early (Nehru had resisted demands for an immediate emergency session). By this time the shock of the Namka Chu debacle had worn off, to be replaced by something like euphoria— 'mafficking in defeat', it has been called.[154] 'There has been a palpable growth of confidence in New Delhi that, whatever the Chinese intentions, they can be held and in due course beaten', the writer reported to *The Times* at the end of October. The lull in NEFA was punctuated only by accounts of aggressive patrolling or artillery bombardments by Indian troops, the newspapers reporting 'heartening indications that after the initial reverses the Indian troops in NEFA were beginning to consolidate themselves into effective defensive positions, and were even initiating attempts to dislodge the Chinese from Indian territory'.[155] This renewed confidence, with Krishna Menon relegated from the front benches to the rear, took the edge off Parliament's disquiet and anger when it convened on November 8th. Nehru, of course, still had a lot of explaining to do, but he was confident, and not at all apologetic.

He gave as the basic reason for the Indian reverse the fact that the troops had been outnumbered. The only hint of the argument there had been about whether 7 Brigade should be pulled back from the Namka Chu lay in this passage: 'The only fault we made . . . if it is a fault, was even to stick [it] out where the military situation was not very favourable. It was not that we told them to stick it out—it is folly for any politician to say so. But our soldiers themselves have a reluctance to go back, and they stuck on at considerable cost to them.'[156] From such statements it might be inferred that Nehru was never informed about the urgent representations being made by the field commanders for the speedy withdrawal of the troops. Kaul, Sen and Thapar must have left him with the impression that the troops had 'a reluctance to go back'.

Rumours of the inadequate equipment and supplies of the troops below Thag La ridge were circulating in the capital by now, and to meet them Nehru repeated at length the arguments, long familiar to Parliament, for relying on domestic manufacture for armaments. Both Houses* heard him in attentive silence and with much of the old respect; indeed, his stature in Parliament was for many members and for the moment magnified by the feeling that he had become the country's war leader—one member who questioned his fitness for that role, Professor Ranga of the Swatantra party, found little support. Nehru for his part was confident enough to snub a member who interjected a question about arms, 'It is really extraordinary that many persons here who know nothing about arms talk about arms,' he snapped. He was as if rejuvenated by the shock of the Namka Chu battle, and by the exciting atmosphere of resolute preparation for war. Some spoke of Dunkirk and Churchill, and perhaps Nehru savoured the associations.[157] As was the case with Krishna Menon, the Prime Minister had on the question of armaments taken the heat out of the Opposition's assault by conceding the heart of their demand. Since 1954, when Pakistan began to receive American military aid, and especially since the first boundary clashes with China in 1959 the Government had been urged to follow suit and accept whatever assistance was available to strengthen the armed services, and Nehru's refusal to thus jettison the independence that was the core of non-alignment was bitterly criticized. In the previous session of Parliament he had said that 'taking military help is basically and fundamentally opposed to a non-alignment policy, [it] means practically becoming aligned to that country.'[158] But now American jet transports were landing in India at the rate of eight flights a day, each carrying about twenty tons of equipment—automatic rifles, heavy mortars, recoilless guns, et cetera. The British had been even quicker off the mark; their

* Under the Indian Constitution ministers can speak in both Houses of Parliament.

first loads of arms aid were landed in New Delhi the day Nehru accepted Kennedy's offer of help.

It was plain that only the United States had the means and the motive to provide the massive assistance India required, if decades of neglect of her military establishment were quickly to be made up. But, perhaps so that the turning to Washington would not be too conspicuous, the Indian Government made their appeal for military assistance general, and emphasized that the Soviet Union had been approached as well as the U.S.A. The Indian request was for military equipment to be supplied immediately and on nominal or very lenient financial terms. The British made their first contributions an outright gift, the Americans left terms to be negotiated later; the French, among others, saw no reason for waiving their usual commercial requirements, and earned a certain amount of ill-will in New Delhi as a result. In the moment of crisis, India even turned to Israel, a country with which she had refused to open diplomatic relations for fear of losing Arab support for her position about Kashmir. New Delhi asked, however, if the weapons Israel agreed to provide could be delivered in ships that did not fly the Israeli flag — thus India might avail herself of Israel's help without incurring Arab displeasure. But Ben Gurion is reported to have replied: 'No flag, no weapons,' and when a shipment of heavy mortars did arrive in Bombay it came in an Israeli ship.[159]

With American weapons being unloaded only a few miles away, the Indian M.P.s could no longer accuse the Government of letting its commitment to non-alignment jeopardize the country's security. Some instead found parallels in the lend-lease that had kept Britain going after 1940; India should point out to the west that she was fighting a world war on behalf of democracy, an Independent member suggested, and echo Churchill's words: 'Give us the tools and we will finish the job.'[160] Nehru maintained that because the supplies of armaments were 'unconditional and without any strings' they did not affect non-alignment.[161] That they did affect the independence of India's foreign policy he was soon to see, when Britain and the United States used their supply of armaments — with the implicit threat to cut it off — to lever Nehru into reopening negotiations with Pakistan over Kashmir.

Yet across six days of debate, in which one hundred and sixty-five members spoke, the Opposition, with some echoes from the Congress benches, managed still to mount a generalized critique of the Government's policies. Although New Delhi's explanations and persuasions

13

had by now succeeded in getting more countries to condemn China,* the feeling that India had been let down was still strong. 'How is it that so large a number of these countries [for whom] we did so much in the many spheres of world politics' were not sympathizing with and supporting India? the Swatantra party leader asked. Matching the resentment towards the non-aligned and Afro-Asian countries, which were felt to have failed to repay India's past generosity towards them, was a wave of enthusiasm for the United States and the Common-wealth—'a great fellowship of nations suddenly stirred to a sense of reponsibility for the security and freedom of one of its members', as it was described by the *Hindustan Times*. In a chaos of reconsiderations of fundamental foreign policy attitudes, New Delhi changed even its approach to the Nationalist Government on Formosa. As one news-paper put it: 'India should manœuvre to spring a second front on the Chinese. . . . This means that we must do everything to activate For-mosa's invasion threat on the south China coast . . . [and] to this end liaison with Taipeh and even more so with the Pentagon is called for.'[162] The Indian Government did make approaches towards the Formosa regime, and the following March a Nationalist representative came to New Delhi for talks with the Ministry of External Affairs.[163] The Chinese Nationalists were ready to join India, of course, in all ex-pressions of hostility towards the Peking Government; but they were careful to point out that when it came to the question of the boundary dispute there were no differences between themselves and the Chinese Communists. The Formosa Government released a formal statement at the end of October. 'The so-called McMahon Line is a line uni-laterally claimed by the British during their rule over India. The Government of the Republic of China has never accepted this line of demarcation, and is strongly opposed to the British claim.'[164]

Another marked vein in the criticisms voiced in Parliament was impatience at Nehru's harping on the special peaceableness of Indians, and the depth of the national commitment to non-violence. This was partly because Nehru was transparently using evocations of his party's

---

* On November 7th New Delhi counted thirty-nine: Ethiopia; Ecuador; Guatemala; Jordan; Luxembourg; Mexico; Dominican Republic; U.S.A.; U.K.; Bolivia; Nicaragua; France; Ceylon; Cyprus; New Zealand; Australia; Trinidad; West Germany; Holland; Switzerland; Venezuela; Costa Rica; Iran; Norway; Chile; Haiti; Japan; Greece; Libya; Congo (Léopoldville); Uganda; Panama; Canada; Philippines; Iceland; Nigeria; Argen-tina; Italy; Malaya.

An Indian cartoonist showed officials urgently conning globes and maps, and explain-ing: 'We've never heard of the latest country to support us.'

Gandhian past to ward off criticism of the Government's military un-
preparedness; but more deeply, perhaps, it expressed the feeling that,
now war had come, the memory of Subhas Chandra Bose, who had
taken up arms with the Japanese against Britain, was more meaningful
to Indians than that of Gandhi and his non-violence.[165]

From the end of October the general optimism that the worst was
over and that victories were at hand steadily grew, encouraged by
official accounts of what was happening in NEFA. INDIANS ATTACK
UNDER COVER OF ARTILLERY—HEARTENING FORWARD THRUSTS
IN NEFA, the press proclaimed.[166] A Congress M.P. who had been to
the front reported that the morale of the troops was exuberant; he
told the House that, disregarding all physical discomfort, 'they are
simply shouting our Mahatma Gandhi's name and the Prime Minister's
name to enthuse themselves'.[167] Lal Bahadur Shastri told a public
meeting on November 12th that 'India was now strong enough to
repulse the Chinese attackers and was building its military might to
drive the invaders from Indian soil.'[168] The Chinese in October and
the beginning of November continued their methodical elimination
of the Indian forward posts in the western sector, concentrating their
troops and then softening the Indian positions with intense barrages
before overrunning them with infantry—on one occasion, according
to wireless reports from the post, the Chinese used tanks. But these
continuing defeats in the western sector did not shadow the optimism
that in NEFA the story would be different. Attention was focused
especially on the Walong front, and expectation that a big Indian
victory was in the making there was sharpened with headlines on
November 16th—JAWANS SWING INTO ATTACK.[169]

* * * * * * * * * * *

The belief that the Chinese would not launch further attacks in NEFA,
that with the debacle on the Namka Chu the worst was over, was
shared in Army H.Q., too, and permeated down the line of command.
In several instances, orders given in the first shock for troops to move
at shortest notice to NEFA were countermanded when the Chinese
stopped their advance, and for three weeks after that there was little
urgency in the Indian build-up around Se La. Contingency planning
for the defence of NEFA had always been based on the assumption that
Pakistan would not take advantage of a Chinese attack; but in October

1962 intelligence reports of President Ayub's attitude to India's difficulties led to second thoughts in New Delhi, and reluctance to siphon
troops from the Punjab across India to the north-east. American representations to Pakistan and subsequent reassurances to the Indians relieved that anxiety, but the result of the delay in taking troops from
Punjab was that, of the three divisions that were finally moved from
there, only one brigade saw action against the Chinese. One of the
Punjab divisions was sent to Sikkim, the other two arrived in NEFA
well after the ceasefire. The division in Nagaland, close at hand, was at
first ordered to prepare for a move to NEFA, but when the lull descended
was stood down; and when, finally, the move did take place, it was
piecemeal, with the brigades and units scattered and broken up.

That the Chinese were being more single-minded and urgent in their
approach was soon shown in reports from the forward Indian troops in
their screen positions below Se La ridge. They could hear the blasting of
explosives as the Chinese rushed construction of a road from Bum La
on the McMahon Line down the old trade route to Tawang, working
twenty-four hours a day and steadily getting nearer. Early in November
aerial reconnaissance showed Chinese trucks moving in Tawang – the
road was through. The Chinese then began improvements on the Indian
road from Tawang towards Se La. Meanwhile they were patrolling
forward towards and around the Indian positions, and – although this
was not yet known to the Indians – penetrating into NEFA by passes
and trails to the north-east of Se La.

General Harbaksh Singh did not last long at IV Corps. After four
days familiarizing himself with the tactical problems before him and
visiting Walong and other forward areas, he issued an order of the day
to the troops, expressing his pride in them and calling them to battle,
'with abiding faith in our nation and our leaders and in the sacred cause
of our motherland. . . .' This message was dramatically overtaken,
however, by a news broadcast on All-India Radio that same night: it
had been officially announced in New Delhi that General Kaul, having
recovered from the 'chill and severe attack of bronchitis which he had
contracted in the front line', was resuming command of his corps.

Learning of this only from the broadcast, General Sen protested to
General Thapar against this second change in the command of the new
corps within four days; according to Sen, Thapar replied that Kaul
was returning at the Government's insistence because he had to be
rehabilitated.[170] Some wild rumours had circulated in New Delhi

when it got out that Kaul was back in the capital; one was that he had been put under house arrest for deserting his post. When Parliament reassembled, Nehru made an opportunity to do his bit towards the rehabilitation of his protégé. 'I want to mention his name especially because quite extraordinarily unjust things have seen said about him', Nehru said. He pointed out that Kaul had gone to NEFA within twenty-four hours of his appointment to the corps command, and went on:

'Some people say he had not had any experience of fighting. That is not correct. He had the experience of fighting in Burma. He was our military attaché in Washington when the trouble occurred in Kashmir, but he begged us to send him there. We sent him there, and he was there. I doubt, knowing a good many of our officers and others — many of them are good — in sheer courage and initiative and hard work, if we can find anybody to beat him.'[171]

Whatever Nehru believed about Kaul's military record, the truth was as General Thimayya had put it when he said: 'Every sepoy in the Army knows that Kaul has never been a combat soldier, you can't hide that sort of thing in the Army. The officers don't respect Kaul.'[172] Reactions among the troops in NEFA when they heard that Kaul was resuming command of the Corps were in tune with Thimayya's view. The officers at 4 Division H.Q. heard the announcement on the radio news and, according to one present, the expressed comment was: 'He's come back? Now God help us!'[173]

The writer called on General Kaul at his house on October 26th, just before he resumed command, and found him completely recovered, and not at all cast down by the debacle on the Namka Chu. He described the deficiencies and weaknesses of the Indian troops, and said that his tactics had been deliberately 'a policy of cheek'. The Tseng-jong battle had been the result of his move to feel out Chinese intentions. He was confident that the Chinese could be held at Se La, and in due course beaten back.[174]

Kaul's return to IV Corps was essential if his career was to be salvaged. If he returned to the General Staff, having relinquished the only combat command he had ever held, after only a few days and on what would be regarded as the hackneyed plea of ill-health, even such powerful political backing as he enjoyed would be unlikely to advance him further. The military reconsiderations, of course, were wholly against his reappointment; General Harbaksh Singh had worked himself into the situation, with which Kaul was by now unfamiliar — his brief sojourn in NEFA had been concerned exclusively with the Thag La area, now enemy territory. But it was not Kaul's reputation alone that stood to suffer if he was not rehabilitated; disgrace or failure for Kaul must add to the political difficulties of Menon and, at one remove, Nehru. Political and personal considerations alike would thus have pointed to Kaul's being given another chance. He resumed command of IV Corps on October 29th; Harbaksh Singh was shifted to XXXIII Corps, Umrao Singh being kicked upstairs to a staff job in New Delhi.

The Indian forces in NEFA were meanwhile being built up — but in a manner quite contrary to the Army's previous intentions. In October 1959 Eastern Command, then under General Thorat, had recommended a triple-tiered defence structure in the north-east. Under this scheme, the main lines of entry into NEFA from Tibet were to be watched by posts set up as near as practicable to the McMahon Line; these posts were to be no more than a trip wire, expected to fall back before a Chinese advance. Behind the forward line of posts, secondary strong points were to be established, strong enough to fight delaying actions and make the invader regroup and bring his logistical bases forward before advancing again. The third tier was the defence line upon which it was hoped that the invader, his lines of supply overstretched, could be broken. Bomdi La was to be one anchor of the defence line, its other bastions were to be no farther from the plains than could readily be supplied and built up. The virtue of this concept was that it turned the extreme difficulties of the NEFA terrain to the service of defence, leaving it to the Chinese to struggle with extended and tenuous supply lines while the Indian Army's main positions had short lines of communication to the plains. The disadvantages, from the Indian point of view, were political. The defence line strategy could be presented, and was, as the military expression of what after 1959 was seen as the Government's slackness in defending the boundaries. Accurately reflecting both the content and reasoning of the defence line plan, the Associated Press reported from New Delhi at the end of October 1959 that 'the Indian Army has abandoned any hope of defending large areas of India's Himalayan frontier against Communist China. . . . India's military strategy would be to concede large areas virtually without a fight. The Indians would be prepared to resist only at points deep within their own territory'.[175]

The defence line concept was nevertheless accepted, and became the basis for the Army's planning in NEFA. Originally the requirement of troops for the scheme was put at a division of four brigades; but in 1961 General Sen assessed a minimal requirement of two divisions (six brigades). As has been seen, when the Chinese did cross the McMahon Line there were only two Indian brigades in NEFA. Thereafter, the defence line concept was thrown overboard. As troops were inducted to NEFA they were distributed widely, not in the light of an overall defence plan but according to the Intelligence Bureau's estimates of where the Chinese were likely to move. In battalion or company strength, or even less, troops were sent trekking into the hills with what weapons and ammunition they could carry, to take up positions picked out on maps at headquarters in New Delhi, and to be supplied by an air arm already greatly strained. These deployments had nothing to do with military considerations, but were made out of the felt political need to engage the Chinese on the McMahon Line itself, and they were rationalized with the belief that no strong Chinese attack was to be expected. Nehru made those points in Parliament in November, in explaining why the Army had tried to fight below Thag La ridge, 'under very disadvantageous circumstances from a military point of view', when previously the intention had been to make the main line of defence farther south. This had been done, Nehru said, 'partly because to the last moment we did not expect this invasion in overwhelming numbers, partly from the fact that we disliked . . . the idea of walking back in our own territory'.[176] Speaking five years after the border war, Krishna Menon conceded that it would have made better strategic sense 'to let [the Chinese] come into Indian territory in depth before giving them a fight'. But, he said, 'this is a kind of thing which we were unable to persuade our public opinion to accept then.'[177] Menon thus admitted, without apparent qualms, that he and his Prime Minister had consciously gone against the dictates of strategic advantage to mollify an uninformed and shallow 'public opinion'.

Under the defence line plan, the Army would not have gone in strength into the hills at the eastern end of NEFA, but would have waited around Teju, in the Brahmaputra valley, and Hayuliang, in the foot-hills, for the Chinese to make their way down through immensely difficult country. An old trade route this way, always arduous, had been made impassable by an earthquake in 1950, and it would not be possible for anything more than light raiding parties to reach the plains by this route. But when it came to the point in 1962 – the Intelligence

Bureau having pointed to the Lohit valley as a likely line of march for the Chinese—the Indians built up at Walong, about a hundred miles from the roadhead at Teju—two weeks' march, so difficult is the terrain. There was an airstrip at Walong, but it was so small that the only I.A.F. aircraft which could use it were the little Canadian Otters, capable of carrying no more than six armed soldiers at a time. Two infantry battalions and some Assam Rifles were deployed at Walong and at the forward post of Kibithoo, two days' march away, when the Chinese attacked there on October 21st. Kibithoo could not be supplied and the troops were withdrawn to Walong after three days. The Chinese followed up, but their first attacks on the Indian positions at Walong were beaten off with heavy losses, and both sides settled down to patrolling and building up, with the lull punctuated by Chinese probing attacks.

The problems of the Indian build-up were multiplied by organizational chopping and changing. Initially the Walong sector was the responsibility of 5 Infantry Brigade, part of 4 Division; but after the fall of Tawang it was decided to create a new divisional headquarters. This was to command the whole of NEFA, less the Se La–Bomdi La sector, which was under 4 Division. The new formation, designated 2 Division, was put under Major-General M. S. Pathania (a cousin and namesake of the new G.O.C. 4 Division, A. S. Pathania) and was allotted 181 Brigade for the Walong sector; but that did not suit M. S. Pathania and he insisted that 181 Brigade be moved out of his command entire. His request was conceded, and accordingly 11 Brigade finally took over the Walong sector on October 31st. The battalions at Walong had thus been commanded by three different brigadiers and staffs within ten days. The same sort of thing was happening with 4 Division, where the other Pathania was similarly demanding changes in his brigade commanders, and it seems to be explicable only in terms of personal relationships between the officers concerned.

Confusion arising from these command changes directly affected the rate and effectiveness of the Indian build-up. A brigade was kept kicking its heels at Bomdi La for nearly a week, without orders, because A. S. Pathania would give it none until he got the brigadier he wanted. A Gorkha battalion was moved to Walong, then back to the plains, and up to Walong again.

By the beginning of November 2 Division had settled down. The G.O.C., M. S. Pathania, had the brigadier he wanted, with three infantry battalions and some Assam Rifles platoons at Walong. He was convinced, and in turn convinced Kaul, that if he could add one more battalion to the Walong force, he could drive the Chinese back to the McMahon Line in that sector. The staff at IV Corps thought differently; they put the Chinese strength at Rima, just over the McMahon Line, at a division, and passed that appreciation to M. S. Pathania on November 11th. But the appreciation was not passed down to the brigade which would have to do the fighting, and preparations for an Indian attack went on. The opening attack was planned for November 13th, and the operation was to be completed on November 14th.

The additional battalion began to arrive in Otter-loads only on November 13th, but 11 Brigade did not delay its attack to await the reinforcements. Kaul and M. S. Pathania had come up to Walong and were there to watch the operation, but this is not enough to explain the determined adherence to the established timetable for attack. The dates had no military significance; there was no question of synchronization with operations in other sectors. But November 14th was an important date for those planning the Walong attack: it was Nehru's birthday. What would be a better present for the Prime Minister, turning seventy-three, than what in a signal to New Delhi from Walong Kaul hoped would be 'our first major success against the enemy'?

On November 14th, two companies of the 6th Kumaon battalion, supported by heavy mortars and some field guns that had been para-dropped to support the attack, moved into an assault on a commanding hill held by the Chinese, in what was believed to be company strength. The Kumaonis, stocky hillmen from the foot-hills of the western Himalayas, had held the Chinese in a fierce action at Kibithoo; had had to retreat for two days to get back to Walong; had been put into another local attack about ten days before and had been in patrol action almost constantly—but they were used again for the birthday attack. They fought for six hours, under heavy fire from Chinese bunkers, but were still fifty yards from the crest when they stopped, spent. That night a Chinese counter-attack cleared the surviving Kumaonis off the hill, less than half of the attackers returning to their base. This was the action hailed by Indian newspapers on November 16th under the headline JAWANS SWING INTO ATTACK.

The Chinese followed up the retreating Kumaonis and penetrated the main Indian defence positions, which the effort of the attack had

13*

weakened. Having fired off all the shells with the batteries in support of the Kumaonis, the Indian artillery could not engage the main Chinese assault when it came at first light on the 16th. The Indians fought grimly: after the ceasefire, returning Indian parties found some positions with every man dead at his post. But, with key defences overrun, the brigade position become untenable and at about 10.00 hours Kaul authorized the brigadier to order withdrawal. Some troops did not receive the order and fought on until their ammunition ran out or they were killed. Kaul and M. S. Pathania left Walong in the 'last but one Otter'.[178] In a long and frantically worded signal from Teju, Kaul reported the defeat at Walong and concluded:

> It is now my duty to urge that the enemy thrust is now so great and his overall strength is so superior that you should ask the highest authorities to get such foreign armed forces to come to our aid as are willing to do so without which, as I have said before and which I reiterate, it seems beyond the capacity of our armed forces to stem the tide of the superior Chinese forces which he has and will continue to concentrate against us to out disadvantage. This is not a counsel of fear, but facing stark realities.

The idea of getting allied expeditionary armies into India had apparently been in Kaul's mind for some days. The Cabinet Secretary had called on him when he was laid up in New Delhi, and, according to that official, Kaul 'produced from beneath his pillow a paper of recommendations. India should seek help of some foreign powers; Chiang Kai-shek and the South Koreans should be induced to invade China with American help. "Some foreign armies should be invited to come and assist the Indian Army to mount a major offensive over the Himalayas." Ten new divisions must be raised and put into action within the next twelve months. Military and economic efforts should be put under a new command, with a G.O.C.-in-C. as a sort of supreme commander — with H.Q. at Delhi or perhaps at Agra.'[179] Kaul did not say who he thought this Moghul Supremo should be.

The remnants of the Walong brigade, control lost, made their way down the Lohit valley towards the plains in broken units and small parties. Their positions at Walong had been divided by the 300-foot-deep gorge of the unfordable Lohit River, spanned only by a single rope bridge (the Chinese brought rubber boats to cross it), and the surviving troops on the east bank suffered heavy losses in their retreat, from privation as well as Chinese ambushes. 11 Brigade had gone the way of 7 Brigade; unbalanced for a hopeless attack and broken up by a determined and well-planned Chinese assault. The Chinese did not pursue the retreating remnants.

Kaul did not return to his Corps H.Q. at Tezpur, although his chief staff officer there urged him to do so, but next day, November 17th, he went in a helicopter to look for the remnants of 11 Brigade. Spotting the brigadier, he had the helicopter landed; Kaul in his book wrote: 'I then rushed up to where he was as fast as I could and heaved a sigh of relief seeing [the brigadier] and his party safe. I offered to take him and some selected officers back with me to Hayuliang for refreshments after which they could come back to their men. Quite rightly, however, he said he would rather remain with his men.'[180] Kaul returned to Hayuliang and there received a message that General Thapar, the Chief of Army Staff, and General Sen of Eastern Command, were on their way to his headquarters at Tezpur. Kaul went straight back, but they got there before him. The curtain had gone up on the climax in the crucial Se La–Bomdi La sector; but, before tracing that turbulent last act, the narrative must report what was happening in the western sector.

There, Western Command, acting on its own initiative, had continued an urgent and heavy build-up, withdrawing troops from the ceasefire line in Kashmir and, by pooling all available transport, bringing them into Ladakh. The road from Leh to Chushul had been completed in the first week of October and by mid-November Chusul was a brigade position. The village itself and the airstrip were outside the Chinese claim line, but some of the Indian defences to the east were across that line, and by this time were, in fact, the only remaining Indian positions in Chinese-claimed territory in the western sector. All the other posts had either been wiped out or withdrawn. Western Command, unlike Eastern Command and IV Corps at the other extremity of the borders, showed more concern for the survival of the troops than for ordering isolated units to 'fight it out' in useless and sacrificial gestures. When there was a tactical reason for ground to be held, the troops did fight it out, to the last round or the last man; but they were not, as so often in the eastern sector, left to hold tactically insignificant and indefensible positions until overrun.

Western Command had made Chushul vital ground, foreseeing that if the Chinese intended to take Leh, then the Spangur gap between the mountains, in which Chushul lies, made their obvious route,

Positions had accordingly been taken up on the hills to the east—just across the Chinese claim line. Some of these positions were more than 16,000 feet high (Chushul itself is nearly 14,000) and these altitudes, in winter, made grimly arduous conditions for troops. Frozen ground could not be dug and had to be blasted; the rarity of the air restricted even acclimatized troops to short bursts of physical activity; there was no wood for fuel or building bunkers, everything had to be carried up by the troops from the valley, and in small loads; mules were no good at these altitudes and although there were a few yaks in Chushul the troops could not manage them. Nevertheless, positions of some strength had been built up by November 17th.

Until then the only sign of Chinese had been of reconnaissance patrols, which had carried out close and open observation of some of the Indian positions—themselves still under orders not to fire unless attacked or menaced. But infantry in strength were seen moving up on November 17th; artillery bombardment of the Indian outposts, airfield and brigade positions in the valley began in the small hours of the 18th, and at first light infantry assaulted the Indians in their hill positions. Heavy mortars, recoilless guns and rockets softened the shallow Indian entrenchments; beaten off in frontal attacks, the Chinese moved to envelop the Indian positions, taking them from the flank or rear after savage hand-to-hand fighting. Of one company of another Kumaoni battalion (13 Kumaon), which had dug in on a ridge called Rezang La, three wounded reached Battalion H.Q. in the valley, five were taken prisoner; the rest of the company were still in their positions when an Indian party climbed to Rezang La three months later—frozen as they died, weapons in hand. Only the Chinese dead had been removed, and the evidence of battle showed that of those there had been many.

Five hours after the Chinese launched their assault the hill positions had all been overrun or evacuated as they became untenable, and the Indians concentrated on high ground around Brigade H.Q. in the valley. But the Chinese did not follow up. They stopped at their claim line and no attack was made on Chushul itself.

In the Se La–Bomdi La sector of NEFA, meanwhile, relatively sluggish as the pace of the Indian build-up had been, 4 Division had by November 17th a full complement of infantry, ten battalions all together, and a modicum of supporting arms: field artillery, heavy mortars, even a dozen light tanks. But that force, which if concentrated in defence could have been formidable, was spread out over three main locations, separated by sixty miles of narrow, difficult and unreliable mountain road. The main defences were around Se La, where 62 Brigade, under its new commander, Brigadier Hoshiar Singh, had five battalions under command; at Bomdi La was 48 Brigade, with three battalions; and roughly halfway between them, at Dirang Dzong,* was the headquarters of the division, with 65 Brigade and two infantry battalions. From Misamari on the plains to Se La was one hundred and forty miles, a round trip of six days for trucks that had no trouble on the way. Air drops and road supplies were supplying the troops at Se La, but they needed almost all they got for daily maintenance, and their reserves of ammunition were, accordingly, still low, and their defence *matériel*, such as barbed wire, digging equipment, mines, still short. Se La had been given priority, and the supply position at Bomdi La was consequently worse.

The great spread from Se La to Bomdi La was a grave inherent weakness in the division's posture, and Se La, the key to the defences, had proved under reconnaissance to be not as impregnable as it looked at first sight. The actual pass was a strong defensive position, but tracks flanked it to north and south. Bomdi La provided a very strong position of three commanding hill features and, given enough troops, could have made an extremely difficult task for attackers; Dirang Dzong, lying in the valley, had few defence advantages, and 4 Division had made no attempt to fortify the area; headquarters staff were living in huts and tents, almost no earthworks had been dug. The divisional posture was designed to meet a Chinese thrust down the main road, and if the Chinese had come only that way, fighting up to Se La and doggedly down the road axis, the Indians could have taken a heavy toll of the attackers. But there was a side door to the whole position — the Bailey Trail.

When Captain F. M. Bailey made his great exploratory trek into Tibet in 1913 to obtain the geographical intelligence which would enable McMahon to draw his boundary line, he cut back from the Tsangpo River into what became NEFA along a fairly straightforward north–south route. Crossing the main crest line at the Tulung Pass, he and his companion, Captain Morshead, the surveyor, made their way

---

* A Dzong is a Tibetan administrative and religious centre, part fortress, part monastery. When this tract was under Tibetan administration the Tawang Dzong was the main centre, and Dirang a secondary centre.

over the Tse La* at 15,600 feet, then through Poshing La at about
14,000 feet and down to Tembang, a village on a spur overlooking the
main valley between Se La and Bomdi La, and by 1962, commanding
the road. That the Chinese could follow Bailey's footsteps and come
out on the road between Dirang Dzong and Bomdi La was foreseen in
General A. S. Pathania's initial appreciation of his task; but he believed
that it would not be possible for them to come that way in any strength,
and in that assumption he was backed up by Army H.Q. in New Delhi
and by the Intelligence Bureau. Bailey had described parts of the road
as very bad[181] and what had been difficult for a party of half a dozen
or so in 1913 could be impassable for large bodies of troops fifty years
later. So, perhaps, the appreciation went. If a Chinese raiding party did
come that way to block the road, it could be cleared by troops from
Bomdi La or from Dirang Dzong—or so it was thought.

The task given Pathania and 4 Division was to hold Se La, and thus
block entry through NEFA to the plains. But initially there was a proviso in Pathania's orders from IV Corps authorizing him to pull back
from Se La and make Bomdi La his main defence position, if the
Chinese struck at Se La before he had been able to build up there in
strength sufficient to hold them. No date or force level was given at
which this proviso would lapse; and so, from the beginning, a possibility was left open for 4 Division to pull back to Bomdi La. There was
no clear concept at any level of how the battle would shape if it began.
If the Chinese did cut the road behind Se La it might be held as a 'box',
the strategy that the British armies had successfully developed in the
latter Burma campaign during the Second World War. But to hold a
position with the enemy all around demanded not only high morale
from the troops, but also absolute reliability in air supply; by November 17th the Se La garrison had supplies for only one week of combat.
And if Se La was intended to be made a box, with Bomdi La another
strong point to the rear, what were 4 Division H.Q. and 65 Brigade
doing camping in their huts and tents at Dirang Dzong? If the Chinese
outflanked Se La in any strength they could quickly wipe out Divisional
H.Q. The disposition of 4 Division reflected, it seems, the underlying
and resilient Indian faith that the Chinese would not attack.

Increasing the difficulties inherent in the deep spread of his division,
Pathania from the beginning of November had been dispatching small
bodies of troops to block what he saw as likely routes for Chinese out-

* Quite distinct, and about twenty miles on the map from Se La.

flanking moves. A company was sent to Phutang, south of Dirang Dzong, in case the Chinese cut through Bhutan and outflanked Se La that way; a platoon was sent up the Bailey Trail to reinforce an Assam Rifles post at Poshing La, about half way to the McMahon Line. These troops were taken from the Bomdi La garrison.

As November advanced, the Bailey Trail was paid progressively more attention by Pathania and 4 Division H.Q. On November 12th another platoon was ordered out from Bomdi La to reinforce the first at Poshing La, and next day two more platoons. Thus a company (from 5 Guards) had been detached from the Bomdi La garrison and sent towards Poshing La, in dribs and drabs. Confirmation that the Chinese were coming down the Bailey Trail was received late on November 15th, in a wireless signal reporting that the advance elements of the Indian troops had encountered the enemy in battalion strength and been wiped out. This report was passed to Divisional H.Q., but Pathania pooh-poohed the estimate that the Chinese numbered about a battalion. Intelligence had assured him that no movement in such large numbers could take place on that route until next summer. He ordered another *company* to be sent up the Bailey Trail to restore the situation. Next day, however, the rest of 5 Guards were sent from Bomdi La to move up the Bailey Trail and clear it of Chinese. In case the enemy diverged towards Divisional H.Q., another company was sent from Dirang Dzong north to block a possible route; to replace it a company was brought to Dirang Dzong from Bomdi La.

On the night of November 16th the Bomdi La garrison had thus been reduced from three battalions (twelve companies) to six companies, about a third of the strength that the position required for adequate defence.

The Guards meanwhile were marching through the night towards Tembang, at the bottom of the Bailey Trail. Reaching there early on November 17th, they dug in, and were attacked soon after midday. The Chinese strength was put at about fifteen hundred. The Indians held them for about three hours, inflicting heavy casualties, but then began to run out of ammunition, and with permission from 48 Brigade tried to withdraw to Bomdi La. With darkness falling, and in extremely thick jungle, control was lost, and the Guards broke up. None got back to Bomdi La; weeks later stragglers appeared on the plains. Again Indian troops, off balance, with no logistical support, and ammunition limited to what they could carry in a forced march, had been pitted against Chinese in superior numbers, and paid the price. With the disintegration of the Guards the Chinese had cut the road between Bomdi La and Dirang Dzong.

While the Guards were fighting their losing battle at Tembang, another Indian battalion was beating back repeated Chinese assaults. The Guards had been pulled out of the positions that they had prepared at Bomdi La to meet the enemy half way, but the defence of Se La was proceeding according to plan. At first light on the 17th, the Chinese attacked a battalion deployed several miles north of Se La as a screen force, and between dawn and mid-afternoon five attempts to reduce the defences were beaten back; this resolute action was fought by 4 Garhwal Rifles, the unit which had panicked and broken behind Tawang three weeks before.

According to plan, Brigadier Hoshiar Singh, commander of 62 Brigade, then ordered the Garhwalis and other screening troops to pull back to the main defences around the pass itself. With five battalions in mutually supporting positions and sufficient artillery, these were very strong—strong enough to hold out as long as their supplies did. But, as the outline and weight of the two-pronged Chinese attack on the divisional position became clear, Pathania began to plan and prepare for withdrawal. In the early afternoon of the 17th, he asked IV Corps at Tezpur (to which he was connected by telephone) for permission to pull his headquarters out of Dirang Dzong and move it southward. Kaul was still helicoptering around the rear of the lost battle in Walong, and the staff officer in charge at IV Corps refused to approve Pathania's request.

With the emergence of the Chinese in strength at Tembang, cutting the road back to Bomdi La, Pathania began to press for permission to pull 62 Brigade off Se La. As Pathania now saw the position, the fact that the Chinese had cut the road meant that Se La would be wholly dependent upon air supply; and that if the enemy kept up the pressure for a week they could roll up the Se La defences as their supplies ran out, and wipe out the garrison. Meanwhile Dirang Dzong, which was not prepared for defence at all and had a large proportion of non-combatant troops in the two formation H.Q.s there, could easily be overrun by the Chinese. From steadily underestimating the danger of Chinese movement down the Bailey Trail, Pathania had now probably swung to exaggerating the strength of the enemy force behind him. What he now proposed was sound, *if the timing were ignored.* If 62

Brigade withdrew from Se La, joined up with the Dirang Dzong force and then, clearing the Chinese roadblock, concentrated as a force of nearly three brigades at Bomdi La, the Indians would be in a far stronger position. This was, of course, what the staff officers at IV Corps had strongly urged at the beginning—that the stand should be made at Bomdi La where a strong force could be built up and supported from the plains. Provision for such a redeployment had also been in his original instructions, and, as the Chinese attack built up through November 17th, Pathania began to urge that it be put into effect. But what, under the pressure of approaching battle, Pathania failed to see was that the option of consolidation was no longer open to his division. What would have been a sound move before the Chinese began their attack had become a sure course to disaster from the moment that attack developed. By then, there were only two alternatives open to 4 Division: a fighting stand in the positions prepared, in the hope of staving off defeat until the failure of supplies made it inevitable; or a belated scramble back to Bomdi La, with all the risks of rout attendant upon hurried retreat down a mountain road already open to harassment by the enemy.

On the evening of the 17th Pathania telephoned IV Corps again, seeking permission to pull the troops off Se La. Kaul had still not returned, but Thapar and Sen had arrived at the Tezpur headquarters and he spoke to both of them. Those officers, of course, were Kaul's superiors and both had been closely engaged with the planning of resistance to the Chinese attack, so that they could plead neither lack of authority nor ignorance. But they declined to give Pathania any orders; he would have to wait for Kaul's return. The subsequent hour or so in the quiet corps headquarters at Tezpur, with the Chief of Army Staff and the G.O.C.-in-C. Eastern Command refusing to take responsibility for an urgent operational decision when there was no one else to take it, was the real nadir for the Indian Army, not the impending debacle among the steep ridges of NEFA.

Pathania meanwhile had also been speaking to Brigadier Hoshiar Singh. What passed between them now and later that night is disputed; Hoshiar Singh was killed a few days later, and Pathania's version does not match the reports of the surviving headquarters officers and battalion commanders of 62 Brigade, on which this account draws. When Pathania proposed withdrawal from Se La, Hoshiar Singh protested that his troops could hold out; moreover, the Garhwalis and other screen troops were still on their way back to the main defences, and there could be no question of pulling the brigade out before they got back. If ordered to do so, Hoshiar Singh would begin the withdrawal the following night, but he said it would be disastrous to attempt it that night. Pathania appears to have accepted that appreciation, since the only immediate action that he ordered was for two companies from Se La to be sent back to Dirang Dzong so as to augment the defences there. IV Corps was not informed of this, or of similar transfusions that Pathania made from Bomdi La to Dirang Dzong.

Kaul got back to his headquarters at about half-past seven that night (17th), and soon afterwards spoke to Pathania. By then, word had reached 4 Division H.Q. that Chinese troops were moving around Se La and threatening to cut the road again, this time between Se La and Dirang Dzong. Thus, if 62 Brigade did not withdraw immediately, they might not be able to get back at all. Pathania's request for permission to pull the brigade back was urgent. Kaul made the case for sticking it out that night at least, but gave no final order on the telephone. There was then a discussion between Kaul, Thapar, Sen and Brigadier Palit, the D.M.O. who had come to Tezpur with Thapar— *all IV Corps staff officers were ordered out of the room*. After about half an hour, Kaul emerged with a signal which he handed to Brigadier K. K. Singh, the B.G.S. IV Corps, for immediate transmission to Pathania; that signal was an order to pull back from Se La and Dirang Dzong to Bomdi La.

It happened that just then direct communication with 4 Division had been lost, and so K. K. Singh had the message passed up to 48 Brigade at Bomdi La, for relaying to Dirang Dzong. But, within a few minutes, Kaul called him to say that the signal must be stopped. It had not been relayed from Bomdi La and was caught there and cancelled.

What had happened, it appears, was that Brigadier Palit was urging that the division must be told to stand fast at Se La. He had been overruled at first, but he persisted, warning Thapar and Kaul that 'the Army could never face the nation if twelve thousand troops ran away without giving battle', or words to that effect; and this admonition convinced his superior officers that they had been hasty in ordering a withdrawal to Bomdi La. Kaul, with Thapar and Sen, then drafted another signal to 4 Division, and this was dispatched:

1. You will hold on to your present positions to the best of your

ability. When any position becomes untenable I delegate the
authority to you to withdraw to any alternative position you can
hold.

2. Approximately 400 enemy have already cut the road Bomdi
La–Dirang Dzong. I have ordered Commander 48 Brigade to
attack this enemy force tonight speedily and resolutely and keep
this road clear at all costs. You may be cut off by the enemy at
Senge Dzong [behind Se La], Dirang and Bomdi La. Your only
course is to fight it out as best you can.

3. 67 Infantry Brigade less one battalion will reach Bomdi La by
morning 18th November. Use your tanks and other arms to the
fullest extent to clear lines of communication.

Read out of its context, this signal was a masterpiece of military buck-
passing. It could be read two ways. If Pathania decided that the battle
must be fought out at Se La, the authority to do so lay in the signal:
'You will hold on to your present positions to the best of your ability.
. . . Your only course is to fight it out as best you can.' If however, he
decided withdrawal was necessary because the Se La position had become untenable, the signal authorized him to pull back. But since Kaul
knew when he sent the signal that Pathania already judged Se La
untenable and was urging immediate withdrawal, it was in fact
not an order to hold, but permission to withdraw. It amounted to a
repetition of the signal which had been stopped, but it was phrased
to shift responsibility for the decision – any decision – back to
Pathania.*

Kaul's order to the commander of 48 Brigade at Bomdi La to use
tanks and infantry to attack the Chinese road block 'speedily and resolutely' had been given over the telephone to Brigadier Gurbax Singh,
the commander. Gurbax Singh protested. He pointed out that he was
left with only six rifle companies to defend Bomdi La; that the Chinese
were already moving up around his remaining positions; that to send a
force out at night along a narrow, winding road already commanded
by the enemy was to throw it away. At night, dust from the unsealed
road would mingle with the heavy ground mist and make a blinding
fog; the tanks, whose usefulness in this terrain was anyway minimal,
would be wholly useless. Kaul agreed to suspend his order until next

---

* In his book Kaul quotes this signal and blames Pathania for the debacle, saying that the
latter's orders to withdraw from Se La were 'against the spirit of my instructions'.

morning, when two battalions of reinforcements were expected to reach Bomdi La.

Kaul's ambiguous signal to Pathania did not in fact reach 4 Division until the early hours of the next morning, and Pathania was left with what Kaul had said on the telephone: that 62 Brigade could *prepare* for withdrawal but that final orders would be given only in the morning. Ambiguity again: prepare might mean 'plan for' or it might mean 'make preliminary moves for'.

Earlier, Hoshiar Singh had confirmed to his battalion commanders that there was no question of withdrawal that night, and the Brigade was making contingency plans for withdrawal the following night. The troops in their dug-in positions around the pass waited for the Chinese, whose movements through the night sometimes showed clearly as they lit their hurried way along trails with burning torches, and sometimes could be picked out by the sudden barking of dogs from the few tribal villages, now deserted by their inhabitants. But before midnight there was another telephone conversation between Hoshiar Singh and Pathania, and as a result of this one of the battalions, in a key position at Se La, was ordered to withdraw immediately to a point beneath and behind the pass. Pathania was to maintain that this move was Hoshiar Singh's idea, and that it amounted to redeployment on Se La, not the beginning of withdrawal from it; but Hoshiar Singh is reported to have told his protesting battalion commander that he was himself under categorical orders to pull these troops back immediately. Whoever initiated this move (and the context was certainly that Pathania wanted withdrawal as soon as possible, while Hoshiar Singh was trying to delay it) it unlocked the Se La defences for the Chinese.

Soon after midnight, the troops concerned were ordered out of the positions in which they were braced to meet a dawn attack—the Chinese had not yet fired a shot—and came back to the pass through the positions of two other battalions. This wholly unexpected movement, carried out without notice in darkness, might have had an unnerving effect on troops of the highest morale, and the morale of these troops was already strained. Whatever confidence they had left in their commanders might have been dissipated by the vacillation that showed in the sudden reversal of their orders to stand and fight. As for the enemy, wherever Indian troops had met him they had been overwhelmed. Only a few days before, a strong fighting patrol of about two hundred men sent out from Se La had been ambushed and wiped out. It is small wonder, then, that the unexpected withdrawal left some of the other troops, now in forward positions, ready to break.

The Chinese, still without firing, followed up the withdrawing Indians closely and occupied the positions which these had prepared. When the Chinese opened fire troops of one battalion began to break and move back. With the brigade position thus beginning to dissolve, and the Chinese already inside it, Hoshiar Singh must have decided that he now had no option but to order the general withdrawal, planned for the following night, to be put into effect forthwith.

It seems probable that the original Chinese intention had been to strike simultaneously at the remaining Indian positions in both sectors of the boundary on November 18th. At dawn of the 18th they assaulted the last Indian troops in territory claimed by Peking in the western sector, rolling up the hill positions east of Chushul. At the Walong end of NEFA, the birthday attack may have opened up an opportunity too good to be missed and so brought on the main assault by two days; and dawn on the 18th found the Indian defences on Se La emptying, the troops who had prepared them making their way down the road to the rear, their heavier weapons, artillery and stores left where they stood. Among these were American automatic rifles, still in crates. The Chinese were moving into the deserted positions around the pass and opening fire on the retreating Indians beneath them.

At Dirang Dzong, in spite of the alarm felt and expressed by Pathania the previous night, dawn found quite a different scene. Two tank officers who came to Divisional H.Q. for orders at about five in the morning found all quiet there, the officers sleeping in their huts, men rolled in their blankets on the verandahs, no sentries posted and — as they later described it — 'a complete absence of war-like atmosphere'. Telephone communications were still through both to Se La (where 62 Brigade H.Q. was behind the actual pass) and Bomdi La, and Pathania learned soon after the tank men visited his headquarters that the Se La troops were retreating towards Dirang Dzong. But he also learned that the Chinese had appeared on the road behind Se La, where they threatened to cut off the retreat. At about this time, the C.O. of a company Pathania had dispatched earlier to cover one of the approaches to Dirang Dzong turned up, badly shaken, to report that his troops had been heavily attacked; he had left them in the middle of the action. Almost simultaneously, Chinese opened light small-arms fire on

Divisional H.Q. from a range of about a thousand yards. It was the last straw.

Pathania ordered 65 Brigade, with him at Dirang Dzong, to withdraw to the plains; he left his headquarters and gave hurried oral orders to the cavalrymen, laagered not far away, to try to fight through to Bomdi La, and if they could not do so, to abandon their tanks and head for the plains. Pathania, with fellow officers and a few troops, then left Dirang Dzong—heading, he later explained, for Phutang to pick up the company of Indian troops he had stationed there and move the long way round to Bomdi La; but at Phutang he learned that Bomdi La had fallen, and made for the plains.

No one took command at Dirang Dzong in Pathania's place. The force there—about two battalions of infantry, a squadron of light tanks, a battery of field guns, and hundreds of personnel from Divisional and Brigade H.Q.s—was left soon after seven in the morning of November 18th to a *sauve qui peut*. There were attempts by officers of the rank of major and below to rally troops into a scratch force around the tanks and fight to Bomdi La, but this sputtered out against Chinese resistance just down the road. One of the battalions reached the plains as a unit, the rest straggled through in small parties. Chinese ambushes took a toll, so did the wild country and the winter. Divisional H.Q. did not inform anyone that it was quitting the field; the commands at Se La and Bomdi La were left quite in the dark, as was IV Corps in Tezpur.

Some degree of control was maintained for a while over the troops withdrawing from Se La, and the first Chinese found enfilading the road to the rear were cleared. But then the head of the solid, moving column came under heavy fire from machine-guns. Some attempts to knock out the guns, organized by Hoshiar Singh, failed; with the road impassable the retreating troops bunched in confusion, the Chinese fire taking heavy casualties, and then the brigade disintegrated into small parties, making for the plains individually. Many of the parties were ambushed and killed or captured in the following days, Brigadier Hoshiar Singh being shot dead at Phutang on November 27th.

By mid-morning on November 18th, then, 48 Brigade at Bomdi La was the only organized Indian formation left in NEFA. The brigade had six rifle companies stretched round a perimeter originally taken up by twice as many, and consequently there were many gaps; but the troops were awaiting the Chinese attack in prepared positions and were supported by field guns, heavy mortars and the guns of four light tanks. The advance party from one of two reinforcing battalions had arrived and promptly been deployed to fill one of the gaps in the defences; the rest of the reinforcements were some hours down the road. That the Chinese could take Bomdi La was certain — but it looked as if they were going to have to fight for it. Then, at about 11.00 a.m. Kaul came through on the telephone from Tezpur and ordered 48 Brigade to send out a mobile column to relieve Dirang Dzong (not knowing of course that by then it was empty, except for a few sick lying in the divisional hospital). Brigadier Gurbax Singh protested again: his position had not changed, no reinforcements exceps fifty men of the advance party had arrived, to pull troops out of his defences would be to open Bomdi La to the Chinese. Kaul angrily and categorically ordered him to get the mobile column on the road within half an hour, whatever the consequences to Bomdi La.

Two more infantry companies were thereupon pulled out of the defences, and with two tanks and two mountain guns formed into a column to fight down the more than twenty miles of winding mountain road towards Dirang Dzong. Sappers, cooks and clerks were organized into makeshift platoons to fill gaps in the perimeter — and took the first shock of the Chinese assault about ten minutes after the column had moved off. The first attack was beaten off but the infantry from the column, ordered back to their original positions, found them occupied by the Chinese and were caught in the open when the next — major — Chinese attack came. The position held by the makeshift platoon was overrun, and the Chinese brought fire on to Brigade H.Q. and the administrative area. Indian counter-attacks failed. The field guns, firing over open sights, and the tanks held the Chinese back; but by four p.m. Gurbax Singh ordered a withdrawal to Rupa, a point about eight miles south. He expected to find the reinforcing battalions there; but one of them was well short of Rupa and the other, coming up a different route, moved into Bomdi La after the brigade had evacuated. The Chinese did not fire, and after dark Gurbax Singh went back to Bomdi La and extricated it.

The brigade began to organize a defence around Rupa on the night of the 18th, but then received orders from IV Corps to pull right back to Foothills, a village just above the plains. Troops were moving accordingly, when orders were received from Kaul to make a stand at Rupa! Kaul, again, was not at his headquarters but at Foothills, and from there he had sent a messenger to the brigade. Orders to the troops were changed accordingly, and they turned back to Rupa—coming under fire as they did so from the Chinese, who had already taken up dominating positions in the hills around. That made defence at Rupa impossible, and the brigade, still being fought as a unit, was ordered by Corps H.Q. to retire on Chaku, the next place of possible resistance down the road. The Chinese followed on the hills for a while, harassing the Indian troops on the road, but then broke contact. The brigade—which was now no more than the remnants of three battalions, making about one battalion in strength—marched back through November 19th, reaching Chaku just after dark. An advance party had made a reconnaissance of the area, allotting positions so that units could take them up on arrival; the retreat was still controlled. But the Chinese struck at Chaku from three sides soon after midnight, ambushing a column that was bringing up supplies and ammunition. Burning vehicles illuminated the defences, and the Chinese soon penetrated them. Now at last the brigade broke, control was lost, and the sur-viving troops made for the plains in small parties.

With the disintegration of 48 Brigade at about three o clock in the morning of November 20th, no organized Indian military force was left in NEFA or in the territory claimed by China in the western sector. Militarily the Chinese victory was complete, the Indian defeat absolute.

The retreat had not stopped, however. Kaul returned to Corps H.Q. in Tezpur late on the night of November 19th, convinced that the Chinese would thrust on to the plains. Next morning, after conferring with General Sen and in the latter's presence, Kaul gave orders for Corps H.Q. to move immediately to Gauhati, nearly a hundred miles to the west and on the other side of the Brahmaputra. Brigadier K.K. Singh and some other staff officers urged that their duties required them to stay in Tezpur; after argument Kaul stayed, too. The rest of Corps H.Q., apart from immovable elements such as the hospital and its patients, were on the road to Gauhati by that afternoon. Next day Kaul helicoptered over some of the trails on which the survivors of 4 Division were straggling towards the plains and gave A. S. Pathania and some wounded men a lift to Tezpur.

* * * * * * * * * * *

News of the fall of Walong was released in New Delhi only on November 18th, after preliminary accounts of fierce fighting there, and came as a greater shock than the debacle at Thag La ridge. There, the Indian troops were believed to have been taken by surprise; in the public eye the Chinese attack had appeared as an infantry Pearl Harbour. But in Walong, which was believed to be a vital stronghold barring an easy path to the valley of the Brahmaputra, the Indian Army had had three weeks to prepare itself—in fact was on the offensive—and was now reeling back again. At the same time, in the evening briefing to the press, it was announced that the Chinese had attacked Se La and that fighting was going on there. Next day at noon, after a nervous and distracted Lok Sabha had sat through question hour, Nehru stood up to give the latest information.

A week-end had supervened since the House had last met, in a glow of optimism, expecting news of an Indian victory at Walong. Now the Prime Minister not only confirmed the fall of Walong—which had been reported in the morning newspapers—but said that Se La had fallen, too. The House heard Nehru's short statement in dead silence, but when he sat down angry questioning and expostulation broke out from the Opposition benches. It grew into uproar, with the Speaker's calls for order being shouted down or ignored. This was the sort of moment that until then had always brought the Prime Minister to his feet, his dry and sarcastic voice cutting through the din, reining the House in more effectively than could the Speaker, because he carried greater authority. But on this occasion of national crisis, which plainly called for calm and self-control in Parliament, Nehru sat silent. His old dominance of the House was gone for good, and he must have felt it.

That night Nehru made a broadcast to the nation which did not help restore his position. The Churchillian flourishes which had touched his rhetoric during the three weeks of the phoney war were missing, his voice now was old and tired, and his words were dispirited and dispiriting. He had the fall of Bomdi La to add to the growing chronicle of disaster, and addressed himself particularly to the people of Assam: 'Now what has happened is very serious and very saddening to us and I can well understand what our friends in Assam must be feeling, because all this is happening on their doorstep, as one might say. I want to tell them that we feel very much for them and we shall help them to the utmost of our ability.' The reaction to this speech in Assam was bitter; it was felt there that Nehru had been bidding a sad farewell to the people of the state in the expectation that they would soon be under Chinese occupation, and in tacit recognition that the Government could do nothing about it. Nehru went on: 'We shall not be content till the invader goes out of India or is pushed out. We shall not accept any terms that he may offer because he may think that we are a little frightened by some setbacks. . . .'

Of this day, November 20th, the American Ambassador noted in his diary: 'It was the day of ultimate panic in Delhi, the first time I have ever witnessed the disintegration of public morale.' Fear was now in the air, and rumours: that the Chinese were about to take Tezpur, even land paratroops in the capital, that General Kaul had been taken prisoner. Of this latter report President Radhakrishnan observed: 'It is, unfortunately, untrue.'[182]

Late that night Nehru made an urgent, open appeal for the intervention of the United States with bomber and fighter squadrons to go into action against the Chinese. His idea was that American aircraft would undertake strikes against Chinese troops on Indian territory if they continued to advance, and would also provide cover for Indian cities in case the Chinese air force tried to raid them. The appeal was detailed, even specifying the number of squadrons required – fifteen.[183] This suggests that Nehru had taken some service advice but he neither consulted nor informed his Cabinet colleagues. The only copy of this appeal was kept in the Prime Minister's secretariat, instead of being sent to the Ministry of External Affairs in the usual way.*

* Nothing was known of all this in India for more than two years. Then in March 1965 the late Sudhir Ghosh, a Congress M.P. to whom President Kennedy had told the story of Nehru's desperate appeal soon after it was made, referred to it in a speech in the Lok Sabha. The reaction was violent, and curious: Ghosh was arraigned for desecrating the memory of the father of non-alignment, and with a falsehood. Lal Bahadur Shastri, by then Prime Minister, called for Ghosh and said that he knew nothing about any such appeal, and moreover there was no record of anything like it in the files of the ministry. Ghosh asked him to check with the Americans and said he would retract and apologize if they denied that the appeal had been made. But the American Embassy, when asked, confirmed that the appeal had indeed been made, and offered to show the Indians the original (a further search turned up a copy in the Prime Minister's secretariat files). Galbraith's *Journal* describes the original appeal.

The rest was rather shoddy. Shastri made a carefully worded statement in Parliament, literally true but misleading in effect. Ghosh had mentioned an American aircraft carrier being ordered to the Bay of Bengal; Shastri now denied that Nehru had *asked for an American carrier*, and stated that none had come to the Bay of Bengal. Ghosh, behaving with more loyalty and dignity than Shastri deserved, kept silent although his probity had been impugned, because many Indians did not want to know that Nehru, in a moment of panic, had forgotten all about non-alignment. Ghosh told the story in his autobiography, however.[184]

Even in 1965 Krishna Menon could not bring himself to believe that Nehru had made this appeal. 'Panditji did not make this request,' he said; '. . . there was one thing about Panditji, whatever the cost to himself, he would not do a thing of that kind.'[185]

In response, an American aircraft carrier was dispatched from the Pacific towards Indian waters; but the crisis passed twenty-four hours after Nehru made this appeal, and the aircraft carrier turned back before it reached the Bay of Bengal. Nehru had also asked for transport aircraft, and that part of his appeal was immediately granted with the dispatch to Indian of a squadron of C–130s, big turbo-jets.

That appeal was not the only step, taken in the shock of the debacle, to be quickly repented. Nehru from the beginning of the hostilities had been at pains to emphasize that India was not fighting Communism because she was fighting China; the distinction was necessary not only to the posture of non-alignment, but to cushion India's relations with the U.S.S.R. But on November 20th orders went out from New Delhi to the state capitals for the arrest of several hundred leading members of the Communist Party. The intention was to arrest only those who belonged to the left wing of the now practically sundered party, putting behind bars those who had not identified themselves with the leadership's commitment to support of the Government. But, thanks to a muddle in the Home Ministry, the lists of names for immediate arrest, drawn from the files of the Intelligence Bureau, were sent to the state capitals without being vetted. The result was that many of the party's centrists as well as some of its pro-Moscow wing were gaoled. It was realized immediately that a mistake had been made; Nehru complained about it to Shastri, the Home Minister, and said it would give India a bad name in the Communist countries. But since simply to open the gaol doors and let them all out again would be to compound the embarrassment, it was decided to release those mistakenly imprisoned one by one, so that it did not look like a confession of error.[186]

While the Home Ministry was thus looking to the country's security, some politicians were worrying about its political stability. A group of Congress M.P.s from both Opposition and Congress approached President Radhakrishnan with the suggestion that he should step in with some kind of President's rule, suspending Parliament and making the Cabinet an advisory committee to the President, with Nehru as chief adviser. There was no constitutional provision for such a step; the proposal was woolly and impracticable, short of a coup. It expressed mistrust in Nehru as a war leader and the belief that a non-political figure like Radhakrishnan, in no way associated with the policies that had led to disaster, was the man for the hour. The President gave the M.P.s who approached him no encouragement; but because the idea was bruited about the capital by some politicians known to be close to him (notably T. T. Krishnamachari) the suspicion arose in the Prime Minister's house that Radhakrishnan had not been wholly averse to it.*

In Tezpur, meanwhile, apprehension that the Chinese were launched on a full invasion of India naturally found sharper expression, and it was feared that the invaders would reach the town in a few hours. On the morning of November 18th, Kaul had telephoned the District Commissioner to give him the latest news of the military situation, and painted such an alarming picture that the official departed for Calcutta with his family shortly afterwards. (He was, in fact, on the point of handing over his responsibilities in the course of normal transfer, and found in Kaul's account of irresistible Chinese armies rolling towards Tezpur no reason to delay his departure in order to await the arrival of his successor.) The new District Commissioner arrived to find that the civil administration had ceased to function, the townspeople having been warned through loudspeakers that the authorities could no longer be responsible for their safety. Some local politicians had stepped into the breach in their own way and mustered a little crowd for an address.

'Fired in the sun of their own emotions, [they] described Tezpur as the bastion of the defence of India and advised people to stay in their own homes and die under enemy bombs rather than evacuate. Then, after a good deal more of this kind of stuff, the politicians left, and the citizens of Tezpur prudently began to do the same.'[187] Great crowds, including released convicts and inmates of the local asylum, gathered at the ferry point to be carried across the Brahmaputra River in the stern-wheel paddle steamers that ply there, carrying up to a thousand people a trip rather than their safe load of three or four hundred. At the State Bank, some who stayed raked through the hot ashes of a fire, started in an attempt to burn some £300,000-worth of currency, including coin; the bank officials had tried to get rid of the coin by throwing it in a lake but gave that up when people began diving for it.[188] The town, filling with bewildered tribespeople from NEFA at one end while its regular inhabitants poured out at the other, could soon have become the scene of riot and looting; but the new District Com-

---

* After these events a marked coolness developed in Nehru's attitude to Radhakrishnan, with whom previously he had been friendly, and perhaps this suspicion was one factor. Another might have been the President's role in concerting the pressure of the state Chief Ministers against Krishna Menon; while his widely quoted statement that the debacle was the consequence of 'our credulity and negligence' must have stung Nehru.

missioner got some food shops opened and began to build up order
again. Army engineers, acting on their own authority, took over the
power house and other vital services. It was fortunate that there were
not many engineer troops available; the central Government had sent
the Director of Civil Defence to Assam to put a 'scorched earth' policy
into operation, and this official was making plans to blow up anything
capable of demolition in Assam, from the Tezpur airport to the oil-
fields at Digboi. There was talk of burning the tea gardens, too; and of
course all power houses, waterworks and the like would have gone up
—if personnel had been available to do the job.

The disorganization at Tezpur was later blamed on the state Government and local administration, but at least part of the responsibility can
be traced to instructions of the Home Ministry in New Delhi which
looked to selective evacuation of the town and destruction of currency,
files, petrol pumps and power house. Young people were to be given
priority in evacuation lest they be indoctrinated by the occupying
Chinese; families of Government servants were also to be among the
first to be sent out. An urgent message to New Delhi from the Assam
Government strongly recommended that ministers be added to the list
of essential personnel for evacuation because if they fell into enemy
hands it would be a slur to the nation and a blow to public morale.[189]

Kaul, again, had personally briefed two ministers of the state Government at his headquarters on the morning of the 20th, telling them that
the Chinese were coming—a paratroop landing at Misamari was
possible, he said, an air raid on Tezpur likely—and that therefore Corps
H.Q., 'on the orders of higher authority', was going. Their departure
in a big convoy of Army vehicles added to the congestion on the roads
out of Tezpur, and to the fear in the town.

But the demoralization of the Indian Army was at last about to be
treated, and in the only way it could be—by surgery, from the top
down. General Thapar had returned to New Delhi from Tezpur late
on November 19th and submitted his resignation to the Prime Minister.
Even now Nehru's first thought was that Kaul should succeed Thapar
as Chief of Army Staff.[190]* He discussed it with Radhakrishnan (there
was still no Defence Minister) and the President, dismissing the idea of
appointing Kaul as absurd, suggested Lieutenant-General J. N.

* Two years later Krishna Menon could still say: 'The Indian Army is poorer without
Kaul. He was not an armchair commander, and he functioned with great courage and
daring on those precipitous heights—some day the country will recognize it.'[191]

Chaudhuri, the G.O.C.-in-C. Southern Command, as the new Army Chief. Nehru concurred. Next morning he announced in the Lok Sabha that Thapar had been granted long leave on grounds of health, and that General Chaudhuri was to officiate as Chief of Army Staff. The House cheered.

Chaudhuri's first order was that troops retreating in the north-east should take up positions where they believed they could make a stand, and then retreat no more. Then he removed Kaul from command of IV Corps, replacing him with General Sam Manekshaw — the man whose career Kaul had tried to break by having him charged with disloyalty, and whom Krishna Menon had refused to appoint to command the new corps at the beginning of October. Corps H.Q. was ordered back to Tezpur, just twenty-four hours after it had been ordered out.

The reaction in Assam to the Prime Minister's speech, and reports of the breakdown of the administration in Tezpur, led to Lal Bahadur Shastri's being sent there to brace the civil authorities and report on the situation to Nehru. At about six o'clock on the morning of November 21st the Home Minister's party gathered at New Delhi airport to take the single daily flight to Assam. Noticing a crowd and an air of excitement around the news-stand, one of the party went to buy a paper and saw a headlined announcement that China was going unilaterally to stop the fighting and then withdraw from NEFA. Shastri and his companions drove immediately to the Prime Minister's residence, and found him just up and still dressing. He gave Shastri the impression that he had not heard of the Chinese announcement, although the news had reached the newspapers several hours before.[192] Thus the Government learned that China had been engaged not on an invasion of India, but on a giant punitive expedition.

Part V

CEASEFIRE

We never went into Chinese territory. And even if it was 'disputed' territory in Chinese eyes, did that justify them starting a war? For us, it was not disputed territory. It was ours.

Krishna Menon[1]

Make wiping out the enemy's effective strength our main objective; do not make holding or seizing a city or place our main objective. . . . In every battle, concentrate an absolutely superior force . . . encircle the enemy forces completely and strive to wipe them out thoroughly. . . . Fight no battle unprepared, fight no battle you are not sure of winning.

Mao Tse-tung[2]

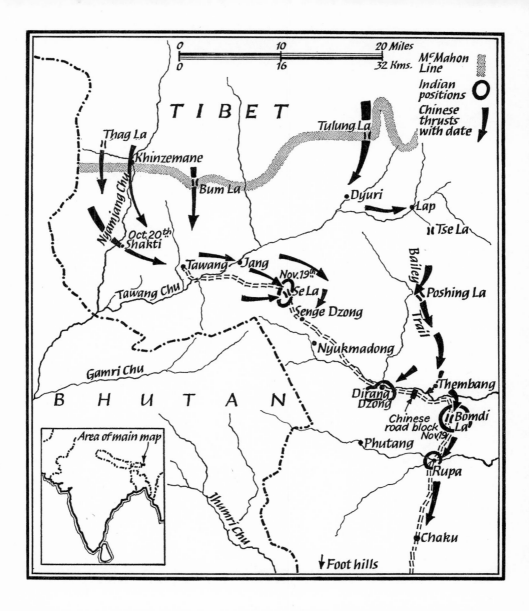

The world learned on November 21st, 1962, that the fighting in the Himalayas between its two biggest countries was to be ended by China's unilateral ceasefire and withdrawal. *The Times* expressed the nearly universal reaction: 'Astonishment almost blots out relief at the sudden Chinese decision.' Just before midnight on November 20th the Chinese Government announced that in another twenty-four hours its forces would cease fire, and in another nine days they would begin to withdraw. The previous night, Chou En-lai had called the Indian chargé d'affaires to his residence and told him in detail of China's intentions:[3]* now these were proclaimed:

(1) Beginning from . . . 00.00 on November 21st, 1962, the Chinese frontier guards will cease fire along the entire Sino-Indian border.
(2) Beginning from December 1st, 1962, the Chinese frontier guards will withdraw to positions 20 kilometres behind the line of actual control which existed between China and India on November 7th, 1959.

That was clear enough, but the statement spelled it out:

In the eastern sector, although the Chinese frontier guards have so far been fighting on Chinese territory north of the traditional customary line,† they are prepared to withdraw from their present positions to the north of the line of actual control, that is, north of the illegal McMahon Line, and to withdraw twenty kilometres back from that line.
In the middle and western sectors, the Chinese frontier guards will withdraw twenty kilometres from the line of actual control.

---

* Mysteriously, New Delhi appears not to have received a report of this meeting from the *chargé* until after Peking's announcement. Officials later explained this in terms of delays in transmission and deciphering, but it is hard to see how that could account for twenty-four hours.
† That is, the line along the foot of the hills, the pre-McMahon Line boundary.

The Indians would be expected to keep their armed forces twenty kilometres away from the line of actual control, too, and China 'reserved the right to strike back' if they did not do so. Both Governments could establish civilian police posts on their side of the line, however; and Peking proposed that officials meet on the border to discuss the siting of such posts, implementation of the joint withdrawals, and return of prisoners. Then the two Prime Ministers should meet again to seek an amicable settlement: Nehru would be welcome in Peking, but if that were inconvenient for him, Chou En-lai would be prepared to go to New Delhi again. China hoped that India would 'make a positive response'. But, 'even if the Indian Government fail[ed] to make such a response in good time', China would put her stated intentions into effect.[4]

This was the proposal that Chou En-lai had first made to Nehru in his letter of November 7th, 1959, (hence the allusion to that date to define 'the line of actual control'), and reiterated after the Namka Chu battle. Again and again in the course of the dispute China had urged it on India as the only possible way to de-fuse the borders and clear the way for settlement; as consistently, India had rejected it—most recently and brusquely on October 24th, after the first Chinese attack. Now, at the point of a smoking gun, a victorious China imposed not a victor's terms but what she had proposed all along. The difference was that it had now ceased to be a *proposal*. China intended to put it into effect, and warned of grave consequences if India did not reciprocate on her side by keeping troops twenty kilometres back from the line. But that warning was watered down by another. If the Indians attempted to resume the forward policy in the western sector, or to move troops back into the Thag La triangle, 'China reserves the right to strike back'. There was the real trigger clause in Peking's declaration of intent.

Later the Chinese explained their plan. They had advanced into the territory south of the McMahon Line 'in order thoroughly to rout the Indian reactionaries and to shatter their plan of altering the border *status quo* by armed force, and to create conditions for a negotiated settlement'. There was nothing incomprehensible about these measures, the Chinese said, and cited as proof of their effectiveness that the Indians had 'begun to have a little more sense, and the border tension has basically eased'.[5] The Chinese move came as a surprise only because the Indian version of what was happening was so widely accepted.

Even those who did not credit that China had embarked on an invasion of India thought that 'negotiation from the strength of total occupation of all Chinese territorial claims was the logic of their military advance'.[6] But that would not only have belied the approach China was taking to all boundary questions, it would also have kept the Sino-Indian sector a running sore. If the Chinese remained in NEFA the Indian Army would inevitably start probing up from the plains when it had recovered, and Peking would then have an unending campaign on its hands. Looking back at the border war in 1966 Lord Caccia, former Permanent Under-Secretary at the Foreign Office, said that as far as he knew 'the Chinese withdrawal to their original lines after a victory in the field [was] the first time in recorded history that a great power has not exploited military success by demanding something more'.[7] But it was not territory that China sought, it was a settled boundary, and the military operation had been directed to that end. Withdrawal was integral to the concept, the final move required to bring a calculated military and political manœuvre to a triumphant checkmate.

No military action that stopped short on the borders could force the Indian Government to negotiate; therefore the Chinese operation could not be sure of achieving the underlying aim of formal delimitation of the Sino-Indian boundary. But that could wait, as Peking had suggested to the Indians in 1960; and the Chinese Army had now made sure that in the meantime — or at least for several years — the *status quo* would be left undisturbed, with no more deliberate encroachments or provocative sallies from the Indian side.

So far as the Indian Army was concerned, there was no doubt about what the response to the ceasefire must be. The new Chief of Army Staff, General Chaudhuri, reported that his forces were in no condition to do anything but reciprocate the Chinese move, and ordered that after midnight the troops should not fire unless fired upon. For the politicians, as usual, it was a different story. In the lobbies of Parliament that morning and on the broad pillared balcony where the press correspondents gathered before the sitting began, the most frequent word in the excited talk was 'humiliation'. However relieved the soldiers felt, for the civilians the unilateral Chinese ceasefire rubbed salt in the wounds. Opinion was nearly unanimous that Peking's 'offer' must be rejected out of hand — some Congress M.P.s from Assam who advocated acceptance were shouted down. Caught again between intractable military realities and the urgings of an aroused political opinion, Nehru played for time. After first introducing the new Defence Minister, Chavan, to the House, Nehru simply said that no official message about a ceasefire had been received from Peking, and that until one came he would express no opinion about the Chinese proposals. As for negotiations, 'our position . . . continues to be . . . that the position as it existed prior to September 8th, 1962, shall be restored'.[8] This measured, cautious reaction was in sharp contrast to the instant and categorical rejection with which the Indian Government had met China's previous diplomatic move, and it seems to have been the result of some strenuous persuasion by Galbraith. Fearing demonstrative and out-of-hand rejection and seeing that it would only make the Indian position worse, he had urged the Government to be non-committal.*

The moment the Prime Minister sat down Opposition members were on their feet, denouncing what Frank Anthony called 'a typical piece of calculated Chinese trickery' and demanding assurances that the Government would ignore the ceasefire and continue to refuse negotiations. 'Decency, dignity and self-respect require that we negotiate only after the barbarians are driven out,' another member cried. Asoka Mehta said that the Chinese move was 'fraudulent', others saw it as an ultimatum. As usual the massed benches of the Congress Party were relatively restrained, but opinion was solid there, too, that the Chinese proposals must be rejected. Later that day all the Opposition Parties except the Communists issued a joint statement: 'The Chinese offer of a unilateral ceasefire is only another of their notorious manœuvres, calculated to cause confusion and disruption in our national front, gain time for consolidation and build up for another infamous offensive and prevent us from mobilizing resources from inside and outside and create doubts in the minds of our friends in world democracy.' The Prime Minister must not allow himself to be taken in, the statement continued, and the Government should reassure the nation that it would stand firmly by the policy of determined resistance and no negotiations.[9]

That night it was announced that the text of China's declaration had been received, but the spokesman would not comment beyond saying:

---

* The American Ambassador had by now become in effect a privy councillor to the Indian Government, a role Galbraith played with zest and tact. His *Ambassador's Journal* (Hamish Hamilton, London, 1969) is revealing about these events.

'Let us wait and see.' Neither then nor later would officials confirm that the troops had been ordered to observe the ceasefire. That would have been taken as admission that India had surrendered. The Government strove to give the impression that, on the contrary, India had just started to fight. The day the ceasefire came into effect Nehru, who was very fond of the young, reassured a gathering of schoolchildren that 'the war with China will be a long-drawn-out affair, it may take years—it may take so long that some of you will be fit and ready to fight it.'[10]

In the diplomatic exchanges with Peking the Indian Government played for time, too, using again the technique of feigned incomprehension. The day New Delhi learned of Peking's ceasefire declaration, a member of the Chinese mission was called to the Ministry of External Affairs and asked for clarifications. What precisely was meant by the 'line of actual control'? What exactly did the Chinese mean by the position prior to September 8th?[11] Two days later the Chinese chargé d'affaires was called and more questions put to him. Did the proposed Chinese withdrawal twenty kilometres behind the line of actual control refer only to the western sector? If the Chinese withdrew twenty kilometres from the McMahon Line, 'where will that be?' Will China set up checkposts south of the McMahon Line?[12] The questions were quibbles when they were not, as Peking described them, meaningless,[13] and in every case the answers were to be found in Peking's original ceasefire statement. These were restated by the Chinese diplomats in New Delhi, but the Indian Government complained to Peking that the clarifications offered were still vague, and would require further elaboration 'before the Chinese ceasefire proposals can be fully considered'.[14]

What China intended, of course, fell short of what the Indian Government desired. The Indian demand, as advanced after their initial defeats, was that before there could be any discussions the Chinese must withdraw to the positions they had held prior to September 8th—the date on which they invested Dhola Post. Such a withdrawal would have had the Chinese pulling back over Thag La ridge and, in the western sector, evacuating all the Indian posts set up under the forward policy and overrun in the fighting. The Indians would then have been able to resume the positions they had held inside the Chinese claim line in the west, and north of the map-marked McMahon Line in the Thag La area. As Peking had pointed out in the ceasefire declaration, the withdrawal of Chinese troops for twenty kilometres all along the 1959 line of actual control would in fact place them well behind their positions of September 8th, 1962. But in New Delhi's view it was not enough for the Chinese to withdraw their *troops*; the Indians wanted all Chinese personnel to withdraw; and they wanted to return to their forward policy positions themselves, in the wake of the Chinese withdrawal.

A week after the ceasefire, Chou En-lai wrote again to Nehru, appealing for Indian reciprocation of the Chinese measures. He urged that the Chinese proposals had given 'full consideration to the decency, dignity and self-respect of both sides', and argued that their implementation would not involve gain or loss of territory for either side. But he warned that Chinese withdrawal could not by itself be expected to prevent clashes, and that Indian refusal to co-operate would jeopardize the ceasefire.[15] If the Chinese had expected that the brutal surgery of their military operation would change the disputatious Indian approach, Nehru's reply must have disabused them. He touched on all the old Indian arguments, implying that they were proven and accepted by China, and assumed that Chou accepted the Indian version of the origins of the fighting. 'As you know, the earlier minor clashes occurred because your forces attacked the small Indian patrols of posts guarding against surreptitious aggressive intrusions in Indian territory . . .' and so on. He reiterated that 'positive clarifications' were required on the 'rather confusing and complicated' Chinese proposal, and urged again 'the clear and straightforward [Indian] proposal' for restoration of the situation that obtained before September 8th.[16]

A sharply worded Chinese note of December 8th accused India of 'deliberate haggling and evading an answer'. Peking put three blunt questions: 'Does the Indian Government agree, or does it not agree, to a ceasefire? . . . Does the Indian Government agree, or does it not agree, that the armed forces of the two sides should disengage and withdraw each twenty kilometres from the November 7th, 1959, line of actual control? . . . Does the Indian Government agree, or does it not agree, that officials of the two sides should meet. . . ?' But the Indian position was such now that the only possible public answer to the questions was: 'Yes and no.' For domestic and international effect Nehru and his colleagues were saying that the struggle with China would continue, that the deceitful Chinese proposals must be rejected, the Chinese warning, that India must not send troops right up to the

McMahon Line, defied. But in fact the Indian Army was under orders to preserve the ceasefire and avoid giving any provocation to the Chinese. It had no intention of moving right up to the McMahon Line again; and through Mrs Bandaranaike, Prime Minister of Ceylon, Nehru even gave an indirect and secret assurance to Chou En-lai on that score.[17] The forward policy was dead, with the two or three thousand Indian soldiers lost in the fighting; but the fundamental position of the Indian Government had only been confirmed by the defeat on the borders. *No negotiations* remained the basic Indian stand. If that was ever to be changed it could only be long after the bitter humiliation of the border war had faded, and after Nehru and his colleagues had left the scene. But, as from the beginning, that unyielding and unchanging refusal to negotiate had to be cloaked, the onus for preventing settlement shifted to Peking.

As always, this was not difficult for the Indians to achieve, so high was their reputation for a pacific approach, so low the general opinion of China. The border war, almost universally reported as an unprovoked Chinese invasion of India, had only confirmed the general impression that Peking pursued a reckless, chauvinistic and belligerent foreign policy. Explanations for the unilateral Chinese ceasefire and withdrawal were sought outside the Sino-Indian context. There was speculation that a Russian ultimatum might have brought it about;[18] or that the Chinese called off their invasion because the United States had cleared its hands of the Cuba confrontation and would have intervened to help India. Others were ready to accept the popular Indian explanation, which was that the Chinese had had to stop and then withdraw because they had overstretched their lines of communication and were vulnerable to Indian counter-attack; that, in fact, the Chinese withdrawal had been 'basically inspired by fear', as an Indian M.P. put it.[19] In time it almost came to be believed that the Chinese had turned tail rather than face 'the unexpected anger of the Indian people when aroused,' as Nehru put it.[20]

★ ★ ★ ★ ★ ★ ★ ★ ★ ★ ★

So far as the NEFA front was concerned, the ceasefire that came into effect at midnight on November 21st was a formality. Organized fighting there had effectively ended nearly forty-eight hours before, when the remnants of 48 Brigade had finally been broken up at Chaku. After that, the two sides ceased to be in contact anywhere in the eastern sector. The Chinese had not followed up the Indian troops retreating down the Lohit valley from Walong, nor did they press on after those making for the plains from Chaku. Although the Chinese seem to have made no attempt to round up the thousands of Indian troops out-flanked and left behind by their advance, skirmishes continued in NEFA for a week after the ceasefire. Some parties of Indians were ambushed on their trek to the plains, sometimes suffering heavy casualties in these actions. Most of the retreating Indians had no knowledge of the cease-fire, and it appears that in some instances Chinese troops disregarded it.

In the western sector, the ceasefire was more definitive. There the Chinese had not advanced on Chushul after overrunning the forward Indian positions, around the heights at Rezing La, but they had been shelling the Indians around Chushul itself and the airstrip; that firing ceased at the given time. The Indian Army in the western sector had suffered from none of the confusion and indecision that had com-pounded the rout in the east, and was still in a fighting posture at the ceasefire, ready to give battle if the Chinese advanced further. Heavy reinforcement of the Chushul force continued, and within a few days of the ceasefire the Indians were sending out patrols again to develop contact with their enemy and test his intentions.

On the plains below NEFA the Indians were more cautious. A new brigade there was ordered not to move across the Chinese claim line, i.e. to keep back from the hills themselves; and Army H.Q. instructed IV Corps to make no provocations and avoid patrol clashes. As the survivors from the debacle trickled on to the plains they were collected into unit groups, preparatory to the long task of reorganizing them and repairing their broken morale. Survivors continued to emerge from the foot-hills for several weeks, so arduous was their trek back, and many Indian troops died from exposure or starvation on the way.

It was a long time before any count of Indian losses could be made. In 1965 the Defence Ministry released these figures:

Killed	.	.	1,383
Missing	.	.	1,696
Captured	.	.	3,968

Twenty-six of the Indians died of wounds in captivity, the remainder were repatriated; the sick and wounded within a few weeks after the ceasefire, the remainder after six months. About ninety per cent of the Indian casualties were suffered in NEFA.

The Indian Army later estimated that the Chinese had used three divisions in the NEFA fighting; one normal and one light division for the main thrust through Tawang, Se La and Bomdi La to the foot-hills; and another division—or possibly a regimental group—for the Walong action. The Indian force in NEFA numbered at its maximum about twenty-five infantry battalions, equivalent to just under three normal infantry divisions; so probably the Chinese, overall, had only a narrow numerical superiority. But the Indian forces were so scattered that in most of the actions the Chinese would have had no difficulty in putting into effect Mao's teaching: 'in every battle, concentrate an absolutely superior force.' Where that was not done—as, probably, at Se La—the Chinese were saved hard fighting by the dissolution of the Indian position before it was struck.

Where the Indians stood and fought the Chinese appear to have suffered heavy casualties. At Thembang, for example, where the Guards made their stand on November 17th, Indian intelligence later concluded that the Chinese had suffered between three and four hundred killed. Evidence of substantial Chinese casualties was found when the Indians returned to the Walong battlefield and to Rezang La in the western sector. Not one Chinese prisoner was taken by the Indians.

The Chinese followed through to the foot-hills below Chaku only in strong patrols, and the Indian Army used the ceasefire to begin reconstruction of its forces in the north-east. Chaudhuri, the new Chief of Army Staff,* proposed to transfer the displaced Kaul to a training command in Punjab, but the latter put in his resignation. Nehru, in Kaul's account, attempted to dissuade him and then wrote him a letter of condolence:

My dear Biji,
    I am sorry that you are retiring. I tried to induce you not to do so but as you were determined on it, I could not do anything about it. The events which have led to your retirement are sad and have distressed many of us. I am sure, however, that you were not specially to blame for them. A large number of people and perhaps just the circumstances were responsible for them.

    * His appointment was confirmed after Thapar's period of leave expired.

14*

I am sure that a man like you, full of energy and patriotism, should not merely rest without doing anything useful for the country. Perhaps a little later you can find this useful work. . . .

Yours affectionately,

JAWAHARLAL NEHRU[21]

According to Kaul, Nehru later amplified that closing hint, telling him that he might be appointed lieutenant-governor of Himachal Pradesh. Feelers were apparently put out in New Delhi to test the likely political reaction. Perhaps the Prime Minister concluded that it would be too strongly adverse to Kaul's appointment, even to such a sinecure; at all events the idea was dropped. But at Nehru's behest Kaul was later employed by a Dr Teja, a financier who had persuaded the Prime Minister to provide huge sums of Government money to finance a ship-building industry. Kaul resigned before long, and Teja was indicted for fraud.

General Thapar was more fortunate. He was made Indian Ambassador to Afghanistan, his appointment being one of the last papers signed by Nehru before his death in 1964. General Sen continued as G.O.C.-in-C. Eastern Command until he resigned from the Army, some time after these events. General Prasad, whom Sen had removed from command of 4 Division after the Namka Chu debacle, was reinstated when he appealed personally to the President, and given another division, this time in Western Command. During the 1965 India-Pakistan war he allowed his personal papers to fall into enemy hands, and these were found to include a protest against his supersession, with numerous bitter criticisms of his superiors and the Government, with which Pakistani propaganda made great play. Prasad left the Army immediately. General A. S. Pathania, who had commanded 4 Division in its Se La–Bomdi La debacle, resigned soon after the ceasefire. Brigadier Dalvi was repatriated in May 1963. He had been held separate from the other captured Indian officers, indeed in solitary confinement, but was brought together with his compatriots of the rank of major and above for repatriation. The Chinese, explaining that they thought the route back through NEFA taken by other Indian prisoners would be too arduous for the officers, took them by road and air to Kunming, where they were picked up by an Indian Air Force plane.

Dalvi was thereafter given two substantive promotions, and commanded a brigade in action in the 1965 war with Pakistan. He ap-

peared to be on his way to high rank, but in 1966 was superseded in promotion to the rank of major-general and accordingly resigned. The Indian Army thus lost an outstanding officer, but there may be wider compensation in the account Dalvi later wrote of the Namka Chu operation and its background, under the apt title *Himalayan Blunder*.*
This may come to be regarded as a classic of military literature, epitomizing the predicament of the officer under orders which he knows must lead to the destruction of his command.

General Manekshaw rose from command of IV Corps to be G.O.C.-in-C. Eastern Command, and in 1969 was appointed Chief of Army Staff. Krishna Menon stayed on the Congress back benches until the general elections of 1967, when the party organization in his Bombay constituency denied him the Congress nomination: he stood as an independent and was defeated. His opponent having died almost on the morrow of the election, Menon tried again, and was again defeated. In 1969 he stood as an independent for a by-election in West Bengal, with the support of the United Front Government there, and this time was returned to the Lok Sabha.

* * * * * * * * * * *

In India, and to some extent abroad, there was scepticism that China would fulfil her proclaimed intention to withdraw behind the McMahon Line. But on November 30th the Defence Ministry in Peking confirmed that the Chinese forces were about to begin their withdrawal, and punctually on December 1st they began to pull back. The withdrawal was slow. On December 5th the Chinese handed over some wounded Indian prisoners at Bomdi La, and it was not until about a week later that they began to pull out from there. The Chinese had a lot of tidying up to do, and went about the task with meticulous, even fussy, care. They made it a matter of principle, or pride, that all the equipment left behind by the retreating Indians should be handed back to them in as good condition as possible. Accordingly it was collected, stacked, piled or parked; cleaned, polished, and carefully inventoried — small arms, mortars, artillery, trucks, shells and ammunition, clothing, and all the other impedimenta of a defeated army. Among the equipment returned were a few American automatic rifles, the first instalment of American military assistance, captured at Se La

* Especially resonant in Indian ears as this was a familiar coinage of Gandhi's.

before they could be uncrated and issued to the troops; and a Russian helicopter, in serviceable condition.

Peking asked New Delhi to arrange for the *matériel* to be received, and Indian civilian parties were sent to take control of it, the Chinese checking off the items and taking receipts. China did not publicize this extraordinary transaction, and said later that there was no intention to do so; it was simply a gesture 'to further demonstrate . . . sincerity for a peaceful settlement'.[22] But although they co-operated by formally receiving the returned *matériel*, the Indians bitterly resented what they felt as an added humiliation, and denounced the Chinese gesture as a propaganda manœuvre – thereby drawing attention to it.

The Indian Army did not return to NEFA on the heels of the withdrawing Chinese. Administration was taken over by civilians, who reached Tawang on January 21st, 1963; and it was many months before the first Indian troops moved back into NEFA. The ceasefire remained informal, Indian observation of it tacit, though careful. New Delhi ignored the Chinese demand that Indian troops be withdrawn twenty kilometres from the line of actual control in the western and middle sectors, and Peking did not press that point. But in the eastern sector the Indians kept out of the territory between Thag La ridge and the map-marked McMahon Line, and patrolling up to the McMahon Line was left to the Assam Rifles The Army, its own tactical interests coinciding with the Chinese demand, now kept well back.

* * * * * * * * * * *

In the aftermath of the ceasefire, the Indian Government found that among the Afro-Asian countries there was a marked inclination to give Peking credit for a genuine attempt to return the dispute to the negotiating table. New Delhi felt itself under pressure to accept the Chinese ceasefire proposals, and resented it. 'Those who do not understand the full significance of the deceptive Chinese proposals naturally ask why we cannot accept [them],' the official spokesman in New Delhi explained at the end of November; and Nehru noted with some exasperation that the non-aligned countries were failing to grasp things that were obvious to India.[23]

President Nasser of the United Arab Republic was giving the Indian Government no grounds for complaint at this time, however. The Indians found him 'one hundred per cent' behind them, and prepared to act as their stalking horse by putting forward as the proposals of the U.A.R. suggestions in fact made by the Indian Government.[24] The U.A.R., with Indian encouragement, mooted the idea of convening a conference of Afro-Asian Governments to discuss the ceasefire and possible bases of bilateral negotiation. Mrs Bandaranaike, Prime Minister of Ceylon, agreed to convene the conference in Colombo, and six delegations met there on December 10th; Ceylon, the U.A.R., Cambodia, Ghana, Indonesia and Burma were represented. The Governments concerned had previously been carefully briefed by special ministerial missions from New Delhi as to the minimal Indian requirements. In essence, this remained the restoration of the positions that obtained on September 8th: in other words, that the Indians should be permitted to return to the posts set up in the western sector under the forward policy, and to Dhola Post in the east.

Accordingly, the U.A.R. delegation in Colombo pressed for full restoration of the September 8th position; but as that would plainly be unacceptable to China, and was therefore resisted by the other conferees, a compromise was evolved. So far as the eastern sector was concerned, the Colombo powers proposed that the line of actual control (i.e. the McMahon Line) could serve as the ceasefire line. This ignored China's stipulation that both sides should keep their armed forces twenty kilometres back from the line, but left the question of specific areas in dispute, such as that below Thag La ridge, for future bilateral discussion.

The nub of the Colombo proposals, as of the whole dispute, lay in the western sector, however. There, the Colombo powers proposed that China should carry out the twenty-kilometre withdrawal which she had proposed in the ceasefire announcement; but that there should be no reciprocation on the Indian side, the Indians staying where they were. Then, 'pending a final solution of the border dispute, the area vacated by the Chinese military withdrawals will be a demilitarized zone to be administered by civilian posts of both sides to be agreed upon, without prejudice to the rights of the previous presence of both India and China in that area.'[25] This passage of the Colombo proposals pointed to the return of the Indians to the area they had infiltrated under the forward policy, and was thus the crucial concession from New Delhi's point of view. But, perhaps deliberately, and presumably in spite of the Egyptians' representations, the proposals were ambiguous at this point, and could be read to imply that the presence of

Indian civilian posts across the line of actual control (i.e. the Chinese claim line) in the western sector had 'to be agreed upon' by China.

When Mrs Bandaranaike came to New Delhi in January to submit the Colombo proposals, the Indians persuaded her to allow them to remove that ambiguity. The Indian Ministry of External Affairs drafted, and Mrs Bandaranaike released, 'clarifications' of the original proposal.* This was the key passage: 'The demilitarized zone of twenty kilometres created by the Chinese military withdrawals [in the western sector] will be administered by civilian posts of both sides. This is a substantive part of the Colombo Conference proposals. It is as to their location, the number of posts and their composition that there has to be an agreement between the two Governments of India and China.'[26] Nehru then informed Mrs Bandaranaike that India accepted the Colombo proposals, as thus clarified, in principle.[27] At the same time Chou En-lai informed Mrs Bandaranaike that China accepted the proposals in principle,[28] and it seemed that the two sides were for once in agreement.

But Chou stated what he called 'two points of interpretation' which were in fact reservations. As 'clarified' by the Indian Government, the proposals looked to China's fulfilling most of the provisions of her ceasefire declaration, but exempted India from any obligation of reciprocity. Chou now suggested that in the east, as in the west, the Indians' military forces should stay where they were. But the crux, from the Chinese point of view, appears to have lain in his second 'point of interpretation'. He argued that the Indians should not be allowed back into the strip in the west into which they had infiltrated under the forward policy, either with troops or civilian personnel. To allow this, Peking maintained, would be 'tantamount to recognizing as legitimate the Indian armed invasion of this area and its setting up of forty-three strongpoints there between 1959 and 1962'.[29] Instead, Chou volunteered that China would pull all her posts out of that area, civilian as well as military. Chou suggested that neither his 'points of interpretation' nor reservations on the Indian side should delay the opening of talks. Such differences could be resolved in the talks themselves.

But the Indian Government was as resistant as ever to any kind of direct exchanges with the Chinese. 'We cannot have any kind of talks,

---

* Mrs Bandaranaike admitted that the New Delhi 'clarifications' were drafted by the Indian Government in her March letter to Chou En-lai. The document, she wrote, was 'prepared by the Government of India . . . [and] is expressed in the language of the Indian Government'.[30]

even preliminary talks, unless we are satisfied that the condition we had laid down—about the 8th September position being restored—is met,' Nehru told the Lok Sabha.[31]

The situation was as confused and apparently contradictory as ever. China was again urging the early opening of negotiations; India was refusing, and setting conditions even for limited official 'talks'. But the Opposition in Parliament was pressing Nehru for ever clearer undertakings that he would not talk to the Chinese until they had vacated every inch of Indian soil; while he was seemingly flouting those demands with reiterations of his old pledge to talk to anyone, at any time—'even to an enemy in the midst of war'.[32] Beneath the rhetoric, however, the Indian approach was unchanged; they were seeking a way to avoid meeting the Chinese without seeming to rebuff the attempts of the Colombo powers. Peking's reservations to the Colombo proposals gave the answer. On learning of these, the Indian Government promptly declared that it accepted the Colombo proposals, as clarified by themselves, '*in toto*', and declared that there could be no further step towards talks or discussions until Peking had also accepted the proposals together with the Indian clarifications *in toto*. Once again, skilful Indian diplomacy had avoided negotiations by making physical concessions by China a precondition. And once again the onus for obstructing a meeting seemed to be left on China.

The general impression that it was India who was anxious to explore every avenue for peaceful settlement and China who was balking was strengthened by a reference Nehru made at this time to the possibility of referring the boundary dispute to the International Court at The Hague. Previously Nehru had categorically ruled out any adjudication or arbitration on the main boundary dispute,* but now he seemed to reverse that stand. He told the Lok Sabha: 'I am prepared when the time comes, provided there is approval of Parliament, even to refer the basic dispute of the claims on the frontier to an international body like the International Court of Justice at The Hague.'[33] This was reported in the foreign press as a substantive Indian concession, while Nehru's gloss on his remark, a little later, went unnoted. The reference to the International Court was ill-received in the House, members objecting to the suggestion that a part of the motherland could be made the object of adjudication, and Nehru immediately backed away. It had

* While offering to submit minor variations of the Indian claim to arbitration or adjudication. See p. 118 above.

been a casual remark, he explained. 'What I said was that if and when the time came for it, if the House agrees, if Parliament agrees, we might perhaps think of it.'[34] In spite of the qualifications with which he had watered down his first reference to the International Court, Nehru later quoted it to Chou En-lai, citing this as proof of his sincere desire for a peaceful settlement.[35] The gambit was safe, there was no possibility of Peking's accepting it and submitting a question concerning China's sovereignty to adjudication—especially by a body on which China was represented by the K.M.T.

By this time it was plain that the Indian Government's determination not to negotiate a settlement had only been confirmed by the defeat on the borders. Writing to Nehru in April 1963, Chou En-lai accused him of taking a dishonest approach, and of having no intention whatever of holding negotiations. India, he said, had exploited ambiguities in the Colombo proposals to interpret those as conforming with the Indian demand for restoration of the September 8th positions, and was now trying to convert them into an adjudication and force them on China. As for the reference to the International Court, that was 'plainly an attempt to cover up the fact that the Indian Government refuses to negotiate'. Chou reiterated China's readiness to open negotiations immediately on the basis of the Colombo proposals, which both sides had accepted in principle. But, he went on, 'if the Indian Government, owing to its internal and external political requirements, is not prepared to hold negotiations for the time being, [China] is willing to wait with patience.'[36]

A year later Nehru said in Parliament that he would be willing to consider opening talks if the Chinese completely evacuated the twenty-kilometre strip on their side of the line in the western sector (implying that India would waive her insistence on the re-establishment of Indian posts in that zone).[37] Chou En-lai had previously proposed exactly that compromise, and when the idea was put to the Chinese Government by two emissaries of Bertrand Russell, who had discussed it with Nehru, the Chinese did not rule it out; but they said that the proposal, if seriously meant, should come from the Indian Government itself. New Delhi, however, instantly denied that the Russell emissaries had been entrusted with any message from Nehru, and said only that if the Chinese evacuated the western strip 'the new situation . . . might merit consideration'.[38] But by this time the Chinese Government had decided that it would be useless to open discussions on the borders with

India unless there was evidence of a radical change of Indian approach. There was every reason to believe, Peking said,

> that the Indian Government will not be prepared to negotiate the boundary question in earnest and bring about a settlement even if all its pre-conditions are fulfilled. It has always been the attitude of the Indian Government that it completely denies the existence of a boundary question between China and India. It arbitrarily holds that the alignment it claims is the fixed boundary between China and India; and at most it admits the existence of some minor 'differences'. Hence it holds in effect that Indian-occupied Chinese territory is not negotiable, that the question of Indian-craved Chinese territory is not negotiable either, and that negotiations, if any, must be confined to China's withdrawal or India's entrance. . . . In these circumstances, it can be foreseen that no results will be obtained even though boundary negotiations are held.[39]

The diplomatic exchanges, which New Delhi continued to publish, went on for years. The laurels for debating skill rested with the Indians, who continued to present themselves as the aggrieved party, and the Chinese as aggressive and recalcitrant. On the ground the position was reversed. There the boundaries had in fact already been settled by China's crushing victory.

★ ★ ★ ★ ★ ★ ★ ★ ★ ★

As the dust of battle subsided, most of the internationally conscious class of Indians had to come to terms with a sad new world. The abiding truths of yesterday had been falsified. Those who had been regarded as supporters and friends had failed in the first role and consequently been dropped from the second. By giving more thought to stopping the fighting than to the causes and merits of the dispute the non-aligned countries, in the Indian view, had been guilty of betrayal; that Indian herself had preached just that approach to the world's brawls was forgotten. There was strong resentment at what were called 'these amoral neutralists who have refused to give India the unreserved sympathy and support she has asked for'.[40] The Soviet Union also came in for a share of this displeasure. The United States, Britain, and other Western powers, on the other hand, had been seen to step forward staunchly in the hour of India's need, denouncing China, offering India weapons and other assistance.

The emotional climate in which non-alignment, and especially Indian attitudinizing about it, had flourished was profoundly changed. In the wider international environment, too, the circumstances which had made India's non-alignment meaningful and, recently, welcome had also changed. The cold war was over, giving way to a period of wary *détente* between the United States and the Soviet Union. America's most active efforts were increasingly to be in Asia, against China. It was too early for it to be discerned that the Soviet Union too was moving in that direction; but it could be seen that there were the beginnings of a serious split between Moscow and Peking. India's falling-out with China fitted in with the emerging new pattern of big-power relationships, allowing her to move towards what was in effect bi-alignment—with Washington and Moscow, against Peking. The Russians were not put off by the substantial American military assistance to India (Nehru had informed Moscow of his appeal to the U.S.A. for help, the Russians had replied that they understood both the request and the need for it):[41] on the contrary, the Soviet Union steadily built up its own contributions of economic and military assistance to India. After 1965, when American military aid was cut off, Moscow became India's biggest source of defence equipment.

In the immediate aftermath of the border war, however, it appeared that India was simply moving closer to the United States. Nehru maintained that non-alignment was alive and unimpaired; but in January 1963, according to Galbraith, the Indian Foreign Secretary expressed his Government's willingness 'to work with the United States both politically and militarily in the rest of Asia' for the containment of China.[42] Nothing came of this offer—the State Department appears from Galbraith's account to have been chary—and perhaps it represented the extreme Indian swing away from the pre-1962 attitudes. But open confirmation of the distance India had travelled under the shock of the border war was to be seen in the presence in New Delhi of an American military mission and the squadron of C-130 transports, ferrying American supplies to Ladakh. On receipt of Nehru's call for help President Kennedy had dispatched Averell Harriman to India with a team of high-level State Department and Pentagon advisers and General Paul Adams, commander of the mobile strike force which the United States kept ready for emergency ground action. The Chinese announced their ceasefire before Harriman and the others left Washington but, unlike the aircraft carrier detailed for the Bay of Bengal, this mission did not turn back. Arriving on the evening of November 22nd, after an eighteen-hour flight in a converted jet tanker, the Americans were taken almost immediately to meet the Prime Minister. Harriman was well known to, and liked by Nehru and they met as friends; but there seems to have been some constraint in Nehru's attitude. 'His letters to Kennedy asking for help had painted a desperate picture, but face to face Nehru seemed to want to avoid talking about it all,' Roger Hilsman, a member of the mission, wrote later, observing that 'it must have been difficult [for him] to greet Americans over the ruins of his long-pursued policy of neutralism.'[43]

The Harriman mission, which was paired with one from Britain led by Duncan Sandys, laid the groundwork for substantial military assistance for India over the next three years, under an agreement reached soon after this between Kennedy and Harold Macmillan, the British Prime Minister, at Nassau.* The Americans' first task was to discipline the Indians, whose requests were exuberant: 'The United States wanted to help, but India would have to be realistic about the cost and complexity of modern defences,' Harriman told them.

Later in 1963 a joint Anglo-American air exercise was held in India, with long-range fighter aircraft flying in to operate from Indian Air Force bases. At the time it was not known that Nehru had called for just this sort of intervention in November 1962, and the Government were hard put to it to explain this rehearsal for the speedy erection of an 'air umbrella'. They did so by suggesting that it was just to train Indian technicians and by denying 'any commitment by the [British and American] Governments to assist India . . . should it be attacked'.[45] They emphasized too that the Soviet Union was also helping India to build up her defences.

Nehru had always explained his earlier resistance to acceptance of military aid by pointing out that to incur such dependence upon other governments would inevitably entail a reduction in India's independence, and the truth of that must have been brought home to him at his first meeting with Harriman. 'With exquisite delicacy' (according to

---

* The Nassau agreement was for one hundred to one hundred and twenty million dollars' worth of small arms, ordnance machinery and ammunition, the cost being shared equally between the U.S.A. and Great Britain.

one of his associates), Harriman 'hinted at the need for a settlement of the Kashmir dispute and for taking measures for joint defence with Pakistan'.[46] The delicacy soon disappeared, and Harriman and Sandys launched an all-out effort to use the promise of arms aid to lever India into settlement with Pakistan. That meant compromise by India, involving at least the surrender of a good part of the valley of Kashmir, and there was never a chance that India would agree to that. The British and the Americans had been misled by a mirage effect of India's mood of 'nothing matters but repelling the Chinese'. Indians at all levels were saying that the time had come to settle with Pakistan — but they meant, settle on the *status quo* in Kashmir. To the Pakistanis, that was no settlement, but rather a refusal to reach one. Nevertheless, Harriman and Sandys pressed on (the latter pushing harder), and a week after their arrival it was announced that Nehru and President Ayub of Pakistan were to meet in an attempt to resolve the Kashmir dispute. The very next day, to the chagrin of Sandys, Nehru reassured an alarmed Parliament that he would not consider anything that involved 'an upset of the present arrangement in Kashmir'. What he had in mind for his meeting with Ayub, plainly, was not 'negotiations' but 'talks'. The Indo-Pakistan exchanges broke down after a series of fruitless preliminary meetings at ministerial level, when it became unmistakable that the most India was prepared to concede towards a settlement — modification of the ceasefire line in Kashmir — fell unbridgeably short of the least Pakistan would accept.

American arms aid continued, however, over strenuous and alarmed protests from Pakistan, until Pakistan's attempt to shake Kashmir out of India's grip by force set off their three-week war in 1965. Then American arms aid was cut off, and India thereafter turned to the Soviet Union for military assistance. At the same time Pakistan, who, beginning with her own boundary settlement, had progressively moved into more cordial relations with Peking, began to receive military equipment from China.

The Indian role in international affairs after the border war was never what it had been before. Largely this no doubt reflected the impact of that debacle: an India whose weakness had been so brutally exposed, and who, for all her protestations to the contrary, seemed to be in tacit alliance with the United States against China, could no longer claim the role of leader of the non-aligned countries. But beyond that, the 1960s were to be for India the beginning of a period of mounting domestic difficulties. The border war and its consequences perhaps accelerated these but they were, it seems, inherent in the country's political and economic development, and India's international role was bound to be diminished as her economic straits and internal political weakness intensified.

* * * * * * * * * * *

India emerged from the border war feeling that the fruits of defeat might not, after all, be so bitter. The country appeared to be united as never before, and the Government was so confident that this was no passing phenomenon that it suspended the committee it had set up to promote national integration, arguing that the war had done its work for it.[47] As for the defeat itself, the myth-makers were soon at work. A week after the ceasefire a journalist wrote from Tezpur: 'If Dunkirk has gone down in history as the best example of British courage and determination in the face of the greatest odds, the planned withdrawal of several thousand Indian jawans [soldiers] and officers from the besieged 14,000-ft Se La region in NEFA will surely be regarded by future historians as a great page in military history.'[48] By and large the official explanations for the debacle were accepted, the blame put on the Chinese rather than on the Indian Government or on the military leadership. It was suggested that the Chinese had won because they fought in overwhelming numbers, without regard for casualties, and took the defenders often by surprise. Much was made of the climatic and logistical difficulties that faced the Indian troops, few asking why, unprepared, they had been made to engage the Chinese in circumstances so adverse. The Army was instructed to conduct an inquiry into the reverses in NEFA, but the inquiring officers, Major-General Henderson Brooks and Brigadier P. S. Bhagat, V.C., were ordered not to concern themselves with individual responsibilities for the debacle; as Chavan, the Defence Minister, later put it in Parliament, they were 'not in any way [to] undertake a witch-hunt into the culpabilities of those who were concerned with or took part in these operations'.[49] Furthermore, they were not allowed to question officers in the General Staff or in other sections of Army H.Q., nor given access to Army H.Q's records. General Thapar declined to give a statement to the board of inquiry, but offered to record his own comments on the report when it was completed – a procedure which his successor ruled out as entirely improper. Kaul submitted two long statements. Some officers in Army H.Q., notably Brigadier Palit, the D.M.O., submitted reports to the new Chief of Army Staff, Chaudhuri, but these were not passed on to Henderson Brooks. Neither was the report Brigadier Dalvi submitted on his repatriation from China in May 1963 — and in fact by then the inquiry was almost closed.

Thus Henderson Brooks and his colleague did not have access to the full picture, and were cut off from inquiry into the crucial exchanges between the civilian leadership and Army H.Q. Decisions made there could, however, be followed in their impact on lower formations, and the Henderson Brooks report traces the roots of disaster to the 'higher direction of war', and the failure of the senior soldiers, after mid-1961, to resist policies that they knew — or should have known — to be militarily impractical. The report followed the NEFA fighting in detail and the responsibility of Kaul, Sen and Thapar for the debacle was made clear although the blame was left tacit. By the nature of the events it described, however, the report could not have been but most damaging to Nehru and the Government, and therefore it was classified, and kept, top secret. Explaining that 'we should never . . . say or do things which could only give heart to the enemy and demoralize our own men', Chavan merely made a statement to Parliament about it.[50] This mildly noted that there had been some interference from higher Army levels with tactical matters that should have been left to those in the field, and that 'shortcomings' had been apparent among some commanders above brigade level. Chavan explained the 'series of reverses' from the Namka Chu to Bomdi La, by the fact that 'these battles were fought on our remotest borders and were at heights not known to the Army and at places which geographically had all the disadvantages for our troops and many advantages for the enemy.' He offered as consolation the thought that 'such initial reverses are a part of the tide of war and what matters most is who wins the last battle.' The Henderson Brooks report was by no means a whitewash, but, thus diluted by the Government, it was used as such and there was little the Opposition could do about it. It was known too, of course, that whatever errors of commission and omission had led to the debacle in NEFA the Defence Ministry and the Army were now under new leadership, and that a massive reorganization, enlargement and re-equipment of the Army were under way. The Congress Party was therefore ready to let bygones be bygones; and it is likely that the Henderson Brooks report will not be published until after the first non-Congress Government takes office in New Delhi.

Nehru made no gesture towards resignation, and he and his Government thus survived, apparently not much the worse, a disaster which would surely have overturned any other democratic Cabinet. On the surface, even Nehru's personal standing did not seem to have been greatly reduced; the general feeling that the country continued at war tended to muffle criticism of the leader.* But in fact Nehru's old moral and political domination in Parliament and the Congress Party was gone, not to be recovered in the eighteen months of life that remained to him. The executive of the Congress Parliamentary Party had come into its own as an independent political force when it challenged Nehru over Krishna Menon and forced the latter's resignation, brushing aside Nehru's hint that he might go too. After this the old relationship, in which the Congress Party could be brought to panic by the mere suggestion that Nehru wished to step down for a while, could not be re-established.

These shifts in the inner balance of power in New Delhi were natural and even overdue, but while Nehru continued as Prime Minister they made for uncertainty and indecision. Under the state of emergency proclaimed in November the central Government had overriding powers over the states as well as over individuals, and there were hopes that with strong governance to direct the patriotic surge generated by the border war, India might now make great strides. But these hopes were belied; without a war, the war effort soon petered out. Before the border fighting, when Nehru was in his prime, it might have been said that India had a dictator who would not establish a dictatorship; under the state of emergency, she had a dictatorship, but no dictator.

One area in which the Indian Government did show decisiveness and determination was that of defence. Stinted for years, the armed services, and especially of course the Army, were now given almost a blank cheque. In the next two years India's defence expenditure more than doubled.† The Army formed six new infantry divisions, organized

---

* The Congress Party tried to use the emergency to stifle such criticism. The party issued a circular which noted that the Opposition parties were 'taking advantage of the emergency for throwing mud against Congress', and that 'even the Prime Minister is attacked'. It called for vigorous counter-measures, and proposed that 'it should be emphasized that those who criticize [Nehru] are traitors'.[51]

† India's defence expenditure, in millions of rupees: 1960–61, 2,809; 1961–2, 3,125; 1962–3, 4,739; 1963–4, 8,161. The price rise in this period was about 8 per cent. (Figures from annual budgets.)

and armed for combat in mountainous country, and was able to replace its obsolete equipment and stores with the latest available American and British supplies. Although a good deal of the expense was covered by military assistance, the suddenly increased outlay on defence inevitably had a distorting effect on the third Five Year Plan, which had begun in 1961. The Indian development effort had begun to labour in the late 1950s but in the succeeding decade flagged and failed. The burden of rearmament and of developing and maintaining a strong defensive posture along the northern borders was undoubtedly at least one of the main factors in this failure.

The political position of the Army in India had been charply changed, almost reversed, by the debacle. There would be no more interference by the civilians in internal Army matters, in future it would be the chastened politicians who would know their place, rather than cavalierly keep the soldiers in theirs. The politicians' perennial fear of an Army coup was sharpened. In a letter to Bertrand Russell in December, Nehru referred to 'the danger of the military mentality spreading in India, and the power of the Army increasing'.[52] The Government made plans to anticipate any attempt by the military to seize power. B. J. Patnaik, in addition to his responsibilities in recruiting and training Tibetan refugees for guerrilla action in their homeland, was put in charge of the Government's counter-coup planning, and Malik of the Intelligence Bureau seconded to work with him. Senior officers were watched, their conversations 'bugged', even those of the visiting Chief of the Imperial General Staff, General Sir Richard Hull, according to one of those most closely concerned with this operation. Special battalions of the Central Reserve Police were posted near the capital, plans made to whisk Nehru away to safety in a hiding-place in the old city before the Army could get him. These fears were unfounded, the soldiers were quite content to get on with their own jobs, the happier for the huge task of re-equipment and expansion which they now faced. But that the fears were real and persistent was to be shown the day Nehru died, May 27th, 1964. General Chaudhuri, the Army Chief, ordered several thousand extra troops into the capital to police the route of the cortège and the cremation ground: this was enough to make Malik suspect that the coup was at last in the making, and the Government intensified its watch. Chaudhuri went down with heat-stroke after the funeral, and this no doubt helped reassure the civilians: later he was asked to explain by

Chavan, the Defence Minister, and with indignation pointed out that from his experience of Gandhi's funeral he had good reason to believe the extra troops might be needed to control the crowds. Again, the alarm was silly as well as false, and there may be something in the suggestion that it had something to do with Malik's personal resentment against Chaudhuri on account of the latter's criticism of the Intelligence Bureau's role in the 1962 debacle.[53]

In broader political terms, something like a marked shift to the Right appeared as a consequence of the border war. More accurately, perhaps, the intrinsic shallowness and weakness of the Indian Left as a national political force had become apparent. The boundary dispute had accentuated the old division in the Communist Party of India, and the border war widened it into an open split. The right-wing Communists then in control of the party's machinery proclaimed their unconditional support of the war effort and called for 'monolithic support' for Nehru, 'to strengthen his hands and carry out his behests'.[54] The Government's impulsive arrests of Communists at the height of the crisis, followed by selective release of the Rightists, underlined the division in the party, which thereafter moved steadily towards a formal split, with the emerging schism between Peking and Moscow providing the ideological alignment. The split in the Communist delegation made their influence in Parliament even less than it had been. The party, under Left leadership, retained its strength in Kerala and West Bengal, however, and subsequent elections showed that their avowed sympathy for Peking, and their refusal to denounce China for aggression, lost the Left Communists no popularity.

The supposed weakening of the non-Communist Left was traced primarily to Krishna Menon's relegation, which left the Rightists in the Government with only a failing Nehru and their own past socialist commitments to contend with. But, again, the Congress Left had always sounded more important than it was. Over the years since independence many of the Socialists had left the party—splitting again on the Opposition benches—and while Nehru was able to put the imprint of egalitarian commitments on Congress policy formulations, the Right, especially powerful at the state level, had no difficulty in seeing that such policies were not effectively implemented. Now the disaster to which Nehru's handling of foreign policy had led the country exposed the whole range of policies associated with his leadership to more open attack by his opponents within Congress, as well as from the Opposition.

On the Right, the Jan Sangh probably reaped some benefit from the nationalist emotions aroused by the border war, and from the sense of national humiliation, more lasting, that followed it. But the influence of the Sino-Indian dispute on the political balance within India was far from radical, and probably it did no more than accelerate trends already in progress.

The decline of Nehru, in personal bearing as well as political stature, was one of the most marked and perhaps saddest consequences of the border war. 'I think he collapsed,' Krishna Menon said later of Nehru after 1962: 'it demoralized him completely because everything he had built up in his life was going.'[55] The remaining youthfulness was stricken from his shoulders, and he was left stooped and unsteady, cherishing a bitter sense of injury against the Chinese, who he felt had betrayed him and all he had striven for. Criticism began to be open; the old question 'After Nehru, who?' came to be asked with lively interest and even anticipation, the approaching change seen now as something to be welcomed.

* * * * * * * * * * *

After the border war, much less was heard in India about forcing the Chinese 'to vacate their aggression'—although in 1970 the opposition Congress tried to commit the Government to doing just that. The forward policy was not revived. The Army built up its strength in Ladakh and opened roads to its forward positions; but these remained outside the Chinese claim line—and the dispositions were defensive. The soldiers appreciated that the tactical advantages in the western sector were so overwhelmingly with the Chinese that it would never be possible to develop and sustain a major offensive against them there. If the Chinese were ever to be driven off the Aksai Chin plateau, it could only be after they had been defeated militarily elsewhere. But the overall superiority in numbers of the Chinese Army and their advantages in movement on the Tibetan plateau make it likely that the Indians can never hope to mount a successful offensive action anywhere on the northern borders—so long as China's central power is unbroken.

While the borders thus settled down into an armed truce, diplomatic relations between China and India were also frozen in a sort of limbo.

Diplomatic relations with Peking had not been broken off, for all the pressure on Nehru to do so. He did, however, close the Chinese consulate in Bombay, a concession to domestic opinion which cost India her consulate in Lhasa—a loss which must have made Lord Curzon turn in his grave. It was years before anyone in India was bold enough to suggest that one day relations with China would have to be mended, and when Mrs Indira Gandhi, then Prime Minister, did put out feelers to that effect in 1969 she was criticized in Parliament. The Chinese, for their part, showed no interest in improving relations with India. Chinese maps continue to ignore the McMahon Line and show the eastern boundary with India running along the edge of the Brahmaputra valley, just as India's maintain the claim to Aksai Chin; presumably, however, Peking's long-standing offer to negotiate a boundary settlement on the basis of the *status quo* when India is ready to do so still stands. But thus to go back to the beginning would mean India's tacit admission of error, and recantation of the deeply cherished belief that in 1962 she was the innocent victim of unprovoked Chinese aggression. That will never be easy.

Notes

ABBREVIATIONS

The following abbreviations are used in the notes. For full titles of the works referred to, see the bibliography.

Atlas	*Atlas of the Northern Frontier of India*
Brecher 1959	*Nehru: A Political Biography.*
Brecher 1968	*India and World Politics.*
Lamb 1960	*Britain and Chinese Central Asia.*
Lamb 1964	*The China–India Border.*
Lamb 1966	*The McMahon Line.*
P.M.S.I.R.	*Prime Minister on Sino-Indian Relations.*
qu.	Quoted in . . .
Report	*Report of the Officials . . . on the Boundary Question.*
S.I.B.Q.	*The Sino-Indian Boundary Question.*
W.P.	*Memoranda and letters . . . between . . . India and China; White Papers.*

HISTORICAL INTRODUCTION: THE LIMITS OF EMPIRE

1 Prince Gortchakoff, summarized by Alexis Krausse, qu. Michael Edwardes, *Asia in the European Age* (Thames & Hudson, London, 1961), p. 180.

2 W. K. Fraser-Tytler, *Afghanistan* (O.U.P., London, 1953), p. 189.

3 Lord Curzon, *Frontiers*, Romanes Lecture of 1907 (O.U.P., London), p. 49.

4 Sir James Outram, qu. Fraser-Tytler, op. cit., p. 130.

5 Qu. Gunnar Myrdal, *Asian Drama* (Pantheon, New York, 1968), p. 179.

6 Secretary of State to the Viceroy, May 21st, 1880, qu. Fraser-Tytler, op. cit., p. 153.

7 Fraser-Tytler, op. cit., p. 188.

8 G. J. Alder, *British India's Northern Frontier, 1865–95* (Longmans, London, 1963), p. 100.

9 Lord Hardinge, qu. Khushwant Singh, *A History of the Sikhs* (O.U.P., London, 1966), vol. 2, p. 57 n.

10 Curzon, op. cit., p. 39

11 *Journal of the Royal Society of Arts*, vol. 84 (1935), p. 2.

12 Zahiruddin Ahmad, *Tibet and Ladakh: A History* in *Far Eastern Affairs* No. 3 (Chatto & Windus, London, 1963), p. 45

13 A. P. Rubin, 'The Sino-Indian Border Disputes' in *International Comparative Law Quarterly*, Jan. 1960, p. 102.

14 Khushwant Singh, op. cit., p. 22.

15 K. M. Panikkar, *The Founding of the Kashmir State* (Allen & Unwin, London, 1953), p. 80.

16 Khushwant Singh, op. cit., p. 23.

17 Ahmad, op. cit., p. 53.

18 Clerk to Government of India, September 4th, 1841, qu. Alastair Lamb, *Britain and Chinese Central Asia: The*

Road to Lhasa (Routledge & Kegan Paul, London, 1960), p. 67.

19 Cunningham, qu. Alastair Lamb, *The China–India Border: The Origins of the Disputed Boundaries* (Chatham House Essay: O.U.P., London, 1964), p. 64.

20 Strachey, qu. Lamb 1964, p. 65.

21 Op. cit., pp. 69–70; p. 65.

22 Qu. Margaret W. Fisher, Leo E. Rose, Robert A. Huttenback, *Himalayan Battleground: Sino–Indian Rivalry in Ladakh* (Pall Mall Press, London, 1963), p. 62.

23 Op. cit., p. 63.

24 H. Lawrence to Vans Agnew, July 1846, qu. Lamb 1964, p. 66.

25 Report by Dr Thomson, Oct. 1849, op. cit., p. 68.

26 Op. cit., pp. 83–4.

27 Shaw, op. cit., p. 85.

28 Hayward, ibid.

29 Lawrence, qu. Alder, op. cit., p. 28.

30 Op. cit., p. 34.

31 Lamb, 1964, p. 86.

32 Y.W. Wyllie, qu. Alder, op. cit., p. 97.

33 Forsyth, qu. Alder, op. cit., p. 278.

34 Op. cit., p. 223.

35 Salisbury to Lytton, op. cit., p. 309.

36 Qu. W. F. Van Eekelen, *Indian Foreign Policy and the Border Dispute with China* (Martinus Nijhoff, The Hague, 1964), p. 161.

37 Alder, op. cit., p. 287.

38 Op. cit., p. 222.

39 Alastair Lamb, 'The Aksai Chin', an unpublished paper.

40 Dane to Ritchie, July 4th, 1907, qu. Lamb 1964, p. 101.

41 *Report of the Officials of the Governments of India and the People's Republic of China on the Boundary Question* (Government of India, New Delhi, 1961), p. CR–81.

42 Ibid.

43 Lamb, 'The Aksai Chin'.

44 Lamb 1964, p. 102.

45 Fisher, Rose & Huttenback, op. cit., p. 69.

46 Ibid.

47 North–west Frontier Intelligence Report, Dec. 1896, qu. Lamb (The Aksai Chin).

48 Lamb 1964, p. 83.

49 Text of the Ardagh memorandum in Dorothy Woodman, *Himalayan Frontiers* (Barrie & Rockliff, London, 1969), pp. 360–3.

50 Elgin to Hamilton, Dec. 23rd 1897. Text in Woodman, op. cit., pp. 364–5.

51 Elgin to Hamilton, Sept. 25th, 1895, qu. Lamb 1964, p. 99.

52 Satow to Lansdowne, Nov. 3rd, 1903, qu. Lamb 1964, p. 104.

53 Text in Lamb 1964, pp. 180–2.

54 Ampthill to Curzon, qu. Lamb 1960, p. 307.

55 Hardinge to Crewe, Sept. 1912, qu. Lamb 1964, p. 109.

56 *The Sino–Pakistan 'Agreement'* (Government of India, New Delhi, 1963), p. 2.

57 *Report*, pp. CR–81–2.

58 Lamb 1960, p. 177.

59 Op. cit., p. 155.

60 Op. cit., p. 39.

61 Op. cit., p. 240.

62 Rubin, op. cit., p. 120.

63 Op. cit., p. 117; W.P.I, pp. 1–21.

64 Curzon, op. cit., p. 140.

65 Lamb 1964, p. 125.

66 Alastair Lamb, *The McMahon Line: A Study in the Relations Between India, China & Tibet, 1904 to 1914* (Routledge & Kegan Paul, London, 1966), pp. 315–17.

67 Ibid.

68 Mackenzie, qu. Lamb 1966, p. 318.

69 Jenkins, qu. Lamb 1966, p. 299.

70 Op. cit., p. 301.

71 Brodrick, Secretary of State for India, qu. Lamb 1966, pp. 13–14.

72 Text in Lamb 1966, pp. 251–7.

73 Issue of October 28th, 1910; see op. cit., p. 195.

74 Sir Robert Reid, *History of the Frontier Areas Bordering on Assam* (Government of Assam Press, Shillong, 1942), p. 217.

75 Lamb 1966, p. 340.

76 Reid, op. cit., p. 222.

77 *Report on Chinese Activity on the Mishmi Border, Sept. 9, 1912* (Political & Secret Dept., India Office), qu. Woodman, op. cit., p. 131.

78 Reid, op. cit., p. 222.

79 Qu. Lamb 1966, pp. 337–8.

80 Op. cit., p. 361.

81 e.g. F. M. Bailey, *No Passport to Tibet* (Hart–Davis, London, 1957), pp. 40–1.

82 Government of India to Secretary of State, June 29th, 1911, qu. Reid, op. cit., p. 224.

83 Hardinge to Crewe, op. cit., p. 227.

84 Op. cit., p. 228.

85 See note 77 above.
86 Government of India to Secretary of State, September 21st, 1911, Reid, op. cit., p. 226.
87 Text in Woodman, op. cit., pp. 370–81.
88 Note of C.G.S. June 1st, 1912, qu. Reid, op. cit., p. 281.
89 Lamb 1966, p. 362.
90 Foreign Office memorandum August 1912, qu. Woodman, op. cit., p. 149.
91 Morley in House of Lords, July 28th, 1913, qu. Lamb 1966, p. 468.
92 H.M.G. to Bell, qu. Woodman, p. 186.
93 Curzon, op cit.
94 Lord Curzon, Frontiers (O.U.P., London, 1907), p.53.
95 Qu. Woodman, op. cit., pp. 166–7.
96 Qu. Lamb 1966, p. 505.
97 Woodman, op. cit., pp. 176–7.
98 F.O. 535/18 Indian to Bell: Simla, September 3rd, 1915, qu. Woodman, p. 186.
99 Texts in Lamb 1966; pp. 247–57.
100 Op. cit., pp. 535–6.
101 Sir Charles Bell, qu. Woodman, pp. 194–5.
102 Bailey, op. cit., p. 277.
103 Published reduced in scale in Atlas of the Northern Frontier of India (Govt. of India, New Delhi, 1960) and The Sino–Indian Boundary Question, Enlarged Edition (Foreign Languages Press, Peking, 1962).
104 Texts in Lamb 1966, p. 618, and Woodman op. cit., pp. 384–5.
105 Qu. Lamb 1966, p. 548.
106 Ibid.
107 Reid, op. cit., p. 296.
108 Captain Nevill, qu. Reid, op. cit., p. 292.
109 Reid, op. cit., p. 298.
110 Journal of the Royal Society of Arts, vol. 84 (1935), p. 2.
111 Langley to Jordan, qu. Woodman, op. cit., p. 183.
112 H. E. Richardson, Tibet and its History (O.U.P., London, 1962), pp. 122–3.
113 Op. cit., p. 124.
114 Lamb 1966, p. 553.
115 American Journal of International Law, Vol. 61 (1967), p. 827.

116 Qu. John Addis, 'The India–China Border Question' (unpublished paper for the Center for International Affairs, Harvard, 1963), p. 27, from the edition of Aitchison in the Harvard Library.
117 Foreign Secretary to Government of India, 22nd May, 1928; 1916, p. 3939, Part 1, No. D.53 (a) – A.T.27.
118 PZ 2785/36 April 9th, 1936, Caroe to Walton, qu. Woodman, op. cit., p. 200.
119 Assam Chief Secretary, Sept. 1936, qu. Reid, op. cit., p. 295.
120 Foreign Secretary to India Office, July 8th, 1936, qu. Woodman, op. cit., p. 200.
121 Political (External) Dept., Collection No. 36, File 23 : R. 2222/38.
122 Ibid.
123 Report, p. 136.
124 Op. cit., p. CR–9.
125 Assam Government to Political Officer, Balipura Tract, qu. Reid, op. cit., p. 295.
126 Ibid.
127 Op. cit., p. 296.
128 Ibid.
129 Ibid.
130 Ibid.
131 Ibid.
132 PZ 2947/1939, 4th May 1939 : Political (External) Dept., Collection No. 36, File No. 23.
133 Reid, op. cit., p. 296.
134 C. von Furer–Haimendorf, Himalayan Barbary (London, 1955), pp. xi–xii.
135 Royal Central Asian Journal (1950), pp. 152 ff.
136 Op. cit. (1950), pp. 152 ff.
137 Op. cit. (1944), p. 165.
138 Report, p. CR–105.
139 Op. cit., p. CR–106.
140 Lamb 1966, p. 548.
141 Report, p. CR–211.
142 J. P. Mills, Royal Central Asian Journal (1950), p. 161.
143 Foreign Relations of the United States, 1943; China (Washington, D.C. 1957), qu. Edgar Snow, The Other Side of the River (Gollancz, London, 1963), p. 589.
144 See note 24 above.

PART I: COLLISION COURSE

1 Parliamentary Debates, Lok Sabha, 20th November, 1950; Vol. V, No. 4 cols. 155–6.

2 Arnold Toynbee, Between Oxus and Jumna, (O.U.P., London, 1961), p. 190.

3 Myrdal, *Asian Drama*, p. 185.
4 Owen Lattimore, *Inner Asian Frontiers of China* (Beacon Press, Boston, 1951), p. 236.
5 Qu. Myrdal, op. cit., p. 181.
6 Richardson, *Tibet and its History*, p. 173.
7 Tieh Tseng-li, *Tibet—Today and Yesterday* (Bookman Associates, New York, 1960), p. 199.
8 Richardson, op. cit., p. 176.
9 Op. cit., p. 178.
10 *World Culture* (Shanghai) qu. Girilal Jain, *Panchsheela and After: Sino–Indian Relations in the Context of the Tibetan Insurrection* (Asia Publishing House, Bombay, 1960), p. 8.
11 *Report*, p. CR–8; Richardson, op. cit., p. 176.
12 Richardson, op. cit., p. 174; Nehru to Chou En–lai, 26.9.59, W. P. II, p. 39.
13 Lamb 1960, pp. 88 ff.
14 Texts in *Indian Press Digests*, No. 1 (University of California Press, Berkeley, Feb. 1956), pp. i–ix.
15 Qu. Jain, op. cit., p. 18.
16 M. D. Wainwright, in *The Partition of India: Policies and Perspectives 1935–1947*, C. H. Philips and M. D. Wainwright, editors (Allen & Unwin, London, 1970).
17 K. M. Panikkar, *In Two Chinas: Memoirs of a Diplomat* (Allen & Unwin, London, 1955), p. 113.
18 *Report*, p. CR–101.
19 Lt. Gen. B. M. Kaul, *The Untold Story* (Allied Publishers, Bombay, 1967), pp. 161–163.
20 See, for example, Patel's 1950 letter to Nehru, p. 72 and n.
21 Myrdal, op. cit., p. 185.
22 See note 1 above.
23 *Prime Minister on Sino–Indian Relations* (Government of India, New Delhi, 1961), Vol. I, part i, pp. 184–185.
24 Ibid.
25 Unpublished official papers.
26 Richardson, op. cit., p. 176.
27 Chinese note of 26.12.59, in *Notes, Memoranda and Letters Exchanged Between the Governments of India and China* (Government of India, New Delhi), White Paper III, pp. 62–3.
28 Indian note of 12.2.60, W.P. III, p. 91.
29 Ibid.
30 Stuart Schram, *Mao Tse-tung* (Penguin Books, London, 1966), p. 249.

31 Van Eekelen, *Indian Foreign Policy*, p. 40.
32 Transcription from the original memorandum by D. R. Mankekar. The passage, in indirect quotation, appears in his book, *Guilty Men of 1962* (Tulsi Shah Enterprises, Bombay, 1968), p. 138.
33 A. P. Rubin, *American Journal of International Law*, Vol. 59, No. 3, July, 1965.
34 Chou En–lai to Nehru, 17.2.59, W.P. III, p. 55.
35 *Documents on International Affairs, 1955* (O.U.P., London, 1958), p. 423.
36 See Political Map of India, 1st Edition, 1950. This is reproduced in S.I.B.Q.
37 *Sino–Pakistan 'Agreement'*, p. 2.
38 *Report*, p. 143.
39 Mankekar, op. cit., p. 140; and Indian note 4.11.59, W.P.II, p. 22.
40 Mankekar, op. cit., p. 139.
41 Nehru in Lok Sabha, 24.2.61; *P.M.S.I.R.* I i, p. 386.
42 Note of 17.7.54, W.P. I, p. 1.
43 Richardson, op. cit., p. 228.
44 Note of 24.9.56, W.P. I, p. 19.
45 Rajya Sabha, 20.2.61; *P.M.S.I.R.* I i, p. 386.
46 Note of 24.9.56, W.P. I, p. 19.
47 Chinese note of 26.12.59, W.P. III, p. 67.
48 *Report*, p. CR–83.
49 Nehru to Chou, 14.12.58, W.P. I, p. 49.
50 W.P. II, p. 52.
51 Qu. Van Eekelen, op. cit., p. 204.
52 C. D. Deshmukh, qu. Michael Brecher, *Nehru: A Political Biography* (O.U.P., London, 1959), p. 458.
53 H. M. Patel in *Studies in Indian Democracy*, S. P. Aiyar and R. Srinivasan (eds.) (Allied Publishers, Bombay, 1965), p. 206.
54 Ibid.
55 Walter Crocker, *Nehru: A Contemporary's Estimate* (Allen & Unwin, London, 1966), p. 87.
56 Krishna Hutheesingh, *Nehru's Letters to His Sister* (Faber & Faber, London, 1963), p. 95.
57 Brecher, 1959, p. 256.
58 Op. cit., p. 530.
59 S. S. Khera, *India's Defence Problems* (Orient Longman's, Bombay, 1968), p. 187.
60 Nehru to Chou, 14.12.58; W.P. I, p. 48.

61 Nehru in Rajya Sabha 10.9.59; *P.M.S.I.R.* I i, p. 137.
62 Nehru in Rajya Sabha, 10.9.59; *P.M.S.I.R.* I i, p. 137.
63 See W. P. I, p. 49; and Nehru in *P.M.S.I.R.* I i, p. 137.
64 Chou to Nehru, 8.9.59, W.P. I, p. 27.
65 W.P. I, p. 26.
66 W.P. I, p. 28.
67 Parliamentary Debates, Vol. V, No. 4, cols. 155–6.
68 Note of 21.8.58, W.P. I, p. 46.
69 W.P. I, p. 47.
70 W.P. I, p. 51.
71 W.P. I, p. 53.
72 *The Times*, 8.9.59.
73 Nehru, Rajya Sabha 10.9.59; *P.M.S.I.R.* I i, p. 138.
74 W.P. I, pp. 55–7.
75 W.P. I, p. 67.
76 W.P. I, p. 70.
77 Lok Sabha, 17.9.53, qu. Karunakar Gupta, *India in World Politics: A Period of Transition; Suez Crisis 1956 — Paris Summit 1960* (Scientific Book Agency, Calcutta, 1969), p. 86 n.
78 Nehru, qu, Gupta op. cit., p. 74.
79 W.P. I, pp. 60–2.
80 W.P. I, pp. 63–5.
81 George Patterson, *Tibet in Revolt* (Faber & Faber, London, 1961), pp. 152–3.
82 *Asian Recorder* 1959, pp. 2624–5.
83 Patterson, op. cit.
84 W.P. I, p. 69.
85 Press conference, New Delhi, *Peking Review*, 3.5.60, p. 22.
86 Qu. in Indian note of 26.4.59, W.P. I, p. 68.
87 W.P. I, pp. 73–6.
88 Text of the Dalai Lama's statement in *The Question of Tibet* (Foreign Languages Press, Peking, 1959), pp. 67 ff.
89 W.P. I, p. 76
90 W.P. I, p. 78.
91 Lok Sabha 12.9.59; *P.M.S.I.R.* I i, p. 149.
92 W.P. II, p. 44.
93 Note of 10.9.59, W.P. II, p. 9.
94 Note of 27.8.59, W.P. I, p. 43.
95 Op. cit., p. 44.
96 Bowett, *Self–Defence in International Law*, qu. A. O. Cukwarah, *The Settlement of Boundary Disputes in International Law* (Manchester University Press, London, 1967), p. 7.

97 e.g. Chou to Nehru, 8.9.59, W.P. II, p. 32.
98 W.P. II, p. 3.
99 Nehru to Chou, 26.9.59, W.P. II, p. 45.
100 *Times of India*, 30.8.59.
101 *Times of India*, 31.8.59.
102 B. G. Verghese in *Times of India*, 4.11.59.
103 W.P. II, p. 6.
104 Mankekar, op. cit., p. 140; Nehru in Rajya Sabha 28.11.61; *P.M.S.I.R.* I i, p. 27.
105 *Times of India*, 24.10.59.
106 Nirad Chaudhuri, *The Continent of Circe* (Chatto & Windus, London, 1965), p. 109.
107 Myrdal, op. cit., p. 289.
108 Ibid.
109 *Statesman* (New Delhi), 30.8.59.
110 *P.M.S.I.R.* I i, p. 68.
111 Op. cit., p. 55.
112 Op. cit., p. 66.
113 Op. cit., p. 91.
114 Op. cit., pp. 118–19.
115 Lok Sabha 4.9.59; *P.M.S.I.R.* I i, p. 120.
116 Op. cit., p. 134.
117 Strachey to Lawrence, qu. Lamb 1964, pp. 69–70.
118 Lok Sabha 12.9.59; *P.M.S.I.R.* I i, p. 148–9.
119 Op. cit., p. 99.
120 W.P. II, p. 42.
121 Gopal's role emerged in conversations with the writer at the time and subsequently. Cited with permission.
122 See previous note.
123 Rajya Sabha 4.9.59; *P.M.S.I.R.* I i, 116.
124 Op. cit., p. 117.
125 Lok Sabha 12.9.59; *P.M.S.I.R.* I i, p. 147.
126 Lok Sabha 10.9.59; *P.M.S.I.R.* I i, p. 135.
127 Qu. Gupta op. cit., p. 163.
128 Lok Sabha 12.9.59; *P.M.S.I.R.* I i, p. 150.
129 Ibid.
130 Lok Sabha 10.9.59; *P.M.S.I.R.* I i, p.131.
131 W.P. II, p. 29.
132 Op. cit., pp. 27–33.
133 Lok Sabha 12.9.59; *P.M.S.I.R.* I i, p. 150.
134 W.P. II, p. 40.
135 Lok Sabha 27.11.59; *P.M.S.I.R.* I i; p. 210.

15

136 W.P. I, p. 61.
137 *Asian Recorder*, 1959; pp. 2758–90.
138 W.P. I, p. 38.
139 Lok Sabha 12.9.59; *P.M.S.I.R.* I i, p. 153.
140 To a Parliamentary committee, qu. *Times of India*, 20. 11. 59.
141 Nehru to Chou, 26.9.59, W.P. II, p. 38.
142 Op. cit., p. 40.
143 Op. cit., p. 125.
144 Ibid.
145 *Report*, p. CR–65.
146 Note of 30.3.61, W.P. V, p. 24.
147 Lok Sabha 5.12.61; *P.M.S.I.R.* I ii, p. 45.
148 Unpublished paper for the Pacific Coast Regional Conference of the Association for Asian Studies, Los Angeles, June 15th, 1967.
149 Curzon, *Frontiers*, p. 54.
150 W.P. II, p. 45.
151 *Times of India*, 8.10.59.
152 e.g. W.P. II, p. 56.
153 W.P. II, pp. 19–24.
154 *Times of India*, 26.10.59.
155 Qu. *The Times*, 30.10.59.
156 Qu. *Times of India*, 26.10.59.
157 Lok Sabha 25.11.59; *P.M.S.I.R.*, I i, p. 189.
158 B. G. Verghese, *Times of India*, 25.11.59.
159 Qu. *Times of India*, 2.11.59.
160 Qu. Gupta, op. cit., p. 164.
161 Rajya Sabha 10.9.59; *P.M.S.I.R.* I i, p. 135.
162 Lok Sabha 12.9.59; *P.M.S.I.R.* I i, p. 155.
163 Walter Lippmann, *The Public Philosophy* (Little, Brown & Co., Boston, 1955), p. 55.
164 Crocker, op. cit., p. 105.
165 W.P. III, pp. 45–6.
166 *Peking Review*, 3.11.59.
167 W.P. II, p. 45.
168 Ibid.
169 W.P. III, pp. 47–51.
170 *The Times*, 21.11.59.
171 *Times of India*, 2.11.59.
172 Lok Sabha Debates, Nov. 1959. No. 8 cols. 1711–12.
173 *The Times*, 23.11.59.
174 e.g. B. G. Verghese, *Times of India*, 25.11.59.
175 *Hindustan Times* (overseas edition), 3.9.59.
176 *Times of India*, 6.10.59.
177 *Times of India* 10.10.59.

178 Lok Sabha Debates, Vol. XXXV, No. 8, col. 1712.
179 Lok Sabha Debates, Vol. XXXVII, No. 26, col. 6271.
180 Ibid.
181 From official transcript.
182 Lok Sabha 14.8.62; *P.M.S.I.R.* I ii, pp. 115–16.
183 W.P. III, pp. 52–7.
184 W.P. III, pp. 58–9.
185 *Times of India*, 14.9.59.
186 *Times of India*, 9.10.59.
187 Report of the Official Languages Commission (Govt of India, 1956), p. 48.
188 *P.M.S.I.R.* I i, pp. 246–7.
189 *The Times*, 11.12.59.
190 Qu. Z. A. Bhutto, *The Myth of Independence* (O.U.P., London, 1968), p. 49.
191 TASS, 9.9.59; text in John Gittings *Survey of the Sino–Soviet Dispute* (O.U.P., London, 1968) p. 327.
192 Lok Sabha 12.9.59; *P.M.S.I.R.* I i, p. 156.
193 *People's Daily* (Peking), 27.2.63.
194 W.P. III, pp. 60–82.
195 Nehru to Chou, 5.2.60, W.P. III, p. 83.
196 Rajya Sabha 12.2.60; *P.M.S.I.R.* I i, p. 296.
197 Lok Sabha 22.2.60; *P.M.S.I.R.* I i, p. 303.
198 *The Times*, 13.2.60.
199 W.P. III, pp. 83–4.
200 *Times of India*, 23.2.60.
201 Lok Sabha 22.2.60; *P.M.S.I.R.* I i, pp. 307–11.
202 Lok Sabha Debates, Vol. XXXVII, No. 7, col. 1184.
203 Indian officials to the writer at the time.
204 *Times of India*, 6.4.60.
205 Qu. *The Times*, 18.4.60.
206 *Evening Star* (Washington), 19.4.60.
207 Supreme Court Reports, 1960; Vol. III, pp. 250 ff.
208 W.P. III, pp. 85–98.
209 W.P. IV, pp. 8–16.
210 Indian officials to the writer at the time.
211 *Indian Express* (New Delhi), 21.4.60.
212 *Times of India*, 21.4.60.
213 W.P. III, pp. 60–82.
214 *Peking Review*, 3.5.60, p. 20.
215 *Hindu* (Madras.) 27.4.60.
216 *P.M.S.I.R.* I i, p. 334.
217 Pandit Sunder Lal to the writer at the time.

218 *Times of India*, 5.1.60.
219 Recounted to the writer at the time by one of those present.
220 *Times of India*, 24.4.60.
221 Chou to Nehru, 17.12.59, W.P. III, p. 53.
222 Nehru to Chou, 16.11.59, W.P. III, p. 49.
223 See Point VI, Chou's statement at New Delhi press conference 25.4.60, *Peking Review* 3.5.60.
224 Lok Sabha 26.4.60; *P.M.S.I.R.* I i, p. 338.
225 *Peking Review* 3.5.60, p. 18.
226 *P.M.S.I.R.*, p. 339.
227 Indian officials to the writer at the time.
228 *Peking Review* 3.5.60.

229 Text of press conference ibid.
230 *Hindu*, 27.4.60.
231 *P.M.S.I.R.* I i, pp. 332–3.
232 *Peking Review* 3.5.60, p. 14.
233 W. P. III, p. 50.
234 *P.M.S.I.R.* I i, pp. 330–2.
235 Lok Sabha Debates, Vol. XLIII, No. 57, col. 13612.
236 *Times of India*, 27.4.60.
237 Lok Sabha 26.4.60; *P.M.S.I.R.* I i, p. 334.
238 Chou at Katmandu press conference, *Peking Review*, 3.5.60.
239 Lok Sabha Debates, Vol. XLIII, No. 57, col 13798.
240 e.g. note of 26.12.59, W.P. III, p. 80.
241 *Peking Review*, 3.5.60, p. 14.

PART II: THE FORWARD POLICY

1 Qu. *New York Times*, 11.11.62.
2 Unpublished paper.
3 Lok Sabha 29.4.60; *P.M.S.I.R.* I i, p. 356.
4 *Times of India*, 11.10.59.
5 Kaul, *Untold Story*, p. 280.
6 Conversations with the writer.
7 Note of 26.12.59, W.P. III, pp. 77–8.
8 e.g. Lok Sabha 5.12.61; *P.M.S.I.R.* I ii, p. 37.
9 *P.M.S.I.R.* I ii, p. 36.
10 Lok Sabha 25.11.59.
11 Maharajah of Bikaner, Lok Sabha Debates, Vol. XXXVII, No. 26, col. 6678.
12 Op. cit., col. 6667.
13 Lok Sabha 26.11.59.
14 Lok Sabha 27.11.59; *P.M.S.I.R.* I i, p. 202.
15 6.12.61; *P.M.S.I.R.* I ii, p. 62.
16 *Times of India*, 4.12.61.
17 Rajya Sabha 8.12.59; *P.M.S.I.R.* I i, p. 233.
18 Lok Sabha Debates, Vol. XXV, No. 8, col. 1697.
19 Lorne J. Kavics, *India's Quest for Security; Defence Policies, 1947–1965* (University of California Press, Berkeley, 1967), p. 19.
20 Op. cit., p. 13.
21 Op. cit., p. 23.
22 *Chronology of Pakistan, 1947–1957* (Government of Pakistan, Karachi), 1958, p. 73.
23 Liaquat Ali Khan, press conference, 15.7.51 (official text).
24 Brig. J. P. Dalvi, *Himalayan Blunder*

(Thacker & Co., Bombay, 1969), p. 36.
25 Kavics, op. cit, p.95.
26 Dalvi, op. cit., p. 36.
27 Kavics, op. cit., p. 84.
28 G. S. Bhargava, *The Battle of N.E.F.A.: The Undeclared War* (Allied Publishers, Bombay, 1964), p. 104.
29 Welles Hangen, *After Nehru, Who?* (Hart–Davis, London, 1963), p. 56.
30 Kaul paraphrases this letter in his book, p. 329. This extract is from another source (see preface).
31 Kaul, op. cit., pp. 320–1.
32 Kavics, op. cit., p. 146.
33 Kaul, op. cit., *passim*.
34 Op. cit., p. 70.
35 Op. cit., p. 74.
36 Brecher 1959, p. 307.
37 Dalvi, op. cit., p. 93.
38 Khera, *India's Defence Problems*, pp. 220–1.
39 Kaul, op. cit., p. 191.
40 Qu. Khera, op. cit., p. 222.
41 Dalvi, op. cit., p. 94.
42 Frank Anthony, M.P. to the writer.
43 Lok Sabha Debates, Vol. LIV, No. 41, col. 10577.
44 Khera, op. cit., p. 74
45 Kaul, op. cit., p. 41.
46 Op. cit., p. 317–18.
47 Hangen, op. cit., p. 272.
48 Op. cit., p. 245.
49 Kaul, op. cit., p. 321.
50 Mankekar, *Guilty Men*, p. 143.
51 Ibid.

52 H. M. Patel, *The Journal of the United Service Institute of India.* Vol. LXXXIV, No. 356 (July 1954), p. 249.
53 Dalvi, op. cit., p. 86.
54 *Times of India*, 7.7.47, qu. Kavics, op. cit., p. 35 n.
55 Constituent Assembly Debates, Vol. IV, p. 2722, qu. ibid.
56 Rajya Sabha 4.5.59; *P.M.S.I.R.* I i, p. 42.
57 See W.P. IV, *passim.*
58 W.P. IV, pp. 34–5.
59 *P.M.S.I.R.* I ii, p. 80.
60 Chou to Nehru, 17.12.59, W.P. III, p. 53.
61 *Peking Review*, 2.2.60, p. 12.
62 *Peking Review*, 3.5.60, p. 15.
63 S.I.B.Q., p. 7.
64 *Peking Review*, 2.2.60.
65 Ibid.
66 W.P. V, p. 20.
67 W.P. V, p. 24.
68 W.P. V, p. 26.
69 W.P. VI, p. 101.
70 Lok Sabha 15.2.61; *P.M.S.I.R.* I i, pp. 376–8.
71 W.P. VI, pp. 96–105.
72 Lok Sabha 7.5.62; *P.M.S.I.R.* I ii, p. 91.
73 *Hindu*, 17.4.60.
74 *Dawn* (Karachi), 20.4.60.
75 *The Times*, 20.4.60.
76 Pakistani officials to the writer.
77 *Peking Review*, 3.5.60, p. 13.
78 Rajya Sabha 22.8.61; *P.M.S.I.R.* I ii, p. 7.
79 Ministry officials to the writer, Sept. 1961.
80 Lok Sabha 16.8.61; *P.M.S.I.R.* I ii, p. 1.
81 Mankekar, op. cit., p. 145.
82 Op. cit., p. 146.
83 Ibid.
84 W.P. V, p. 49.
85 *P.M.S.I.R.* I ii, p. 2.
86 Note of 31.10.61: W.P. V, pp. 51–4.
87 W.P. VI, p. 7.
88 *P.M.S.I.R.* I ii, p. 14–23.
89 *P.M.S.I.R.* I ii, p. 15.
90 Ibid.
91 *P.M.S.I.R.* I ii, p. 20.
92 Lok Sabha Debates, Vol. 49 (1961) col. 1857.
93 Lok Sabha 5.12.61; *P.M.S.I.R.*, pp. 46–7
94 Note of 2.11.61, W.P. VI, p. 1.
95 W.P. VI, p. 8.
96 Note of 30.11.61, W.P. VI, p. 4.
97 Rajya Sabha 20.2.61; *P.M.S.I.R.*, I i, p. 380.
98 Press conference, New Delhi, 27.12.61; from official text.
99 Qu. Crocker, op. cit., p. 120.
100 *The Times*, 5.12.61.
101 Kaul op. cit., p. 74.
102 Michael Brecher, *India and World Politics: Krishna Menon's View of the World* (O.U.P., London, 1968), p. 131.
103 Kaul op. cit., pp. 300–1.
104 Brecher, 1968, p. 131.
105 Crocker, op. cit., p. 127.
106 Arthur M. Schlesinger, Jnr, *A Thousand Days: John F. Kennedy in the White House* (André Deutsch, London, 1965), p. 460.
107 Op. cit., p. 458.
108 *Link* (New Delhi), 24.12.61, p. 5.
109 Press conference, New Delhi, 28.12.61 from official text.
110 *Hindu*, 6.2.62.
111 Bhutto, *Myth of Independence*, p. 62.
112 Frank Moraes, qu. Schlesinger, op. cit., p. 460.
113 A. G. Noorani, *Our Credulity and Negligence* (Ramday Bhatkal, Bombay, 1963), p. 73.
114 Lok Sabha 7.12.61; *P.M.S.I.R.* I ii, p. 65.
115 W.P. VI, p. 14.
116 Chinese notes of 1.3.62 and 22.3.62, W.P. VI, p. 14, p. 21.
117 Indian notes 13.3.62 and 30.4.62, W.P. VI, p. 17, p. 32.
118 W.P. VI, p. 188.
119 Note of 11.5.62, W.P. IV, p. 200.
120 Ibid.
121 e.g. *Daily Telegraph* (London), 11.1.62, 25.3.62; Associated Press in *Dawn*, 22.1.62.
122 Rajya Sabha 3.5.62; *P.M.S.I.R.* I ii, pp. 86–7.
123 Lok Sabha 20.6.62; qu. Addis, 'Border Question'.
124 30.4.62, W.P. VI, p. 39.
125 W.P. VI, p. 78.
126 Note of 10.7.62,W.P. VI, p. 82.
127 W.P. VI, pp. 81–2. The latter part of the warning was delivered only orally: ministry officials to the writer at the time.
128 Lok Sabha Debates, Vol. 49, No. 6, col. 1616.
129 Lok Sabha 14.5.62; *P.M.S.I.R.* I ii, p. 94.

130 W.P. VI, p. 43.
131 14.5.62; *P.M.S.I.R.* I ii, p. 94.
132 W.P. VI, p. 56.
133 *P.M.S.I.R.* I ii, p. 94.
134 14.5.62; *P.M.S.I.R.* I ii, p. 94.
135 e.g. *The Times*, 28.7.62, *Blitz* (Bombay), 7.7.62.
136 *Blitz*, 7.7.62.
137 Romesh Thapar, *Economic Weekly* (Bombay), 11.8.62.
138 Lok Sabha Debates (3rd Series), Vol. 6, No. 6, col. 1505.
139 Op. cit., col. 1530.
140 W.P. VI, p. 80.
141 *Hindustan Times* (New Delhi), 18.7.62.
142 *Yugantar*, 8.8.62.
143 W.P. VII, p. 1.
144 Op. cit., pp. 3–4.
145 Lok Sabha Debates, Vol. 6, No. 6, col. 1496.
146 *Hindustan Times*, 10.8.62.
147 Lok Sabha 13.8.62; *P.M.S.I.R.* I ii, p. 101.
148 *People's Daily*, 7.9.62.
149 W.P. VI, p. 18.
150 W.P. VII, p. 18.
151 Felix Greene, *A Curtain of Ignorance* (Cape, London, 1965), p. 223.
152 Qu. Schlesinger, op. cit., p. 454.

153 Op. cit., p. 457.
154 *New York Times*, 10.6.62.
155 Lok Sabha Debates, Vol. 9, col. 2959.
156 e.g. *Ananda Bazar Patrika*, 14.9.62.
157 Lok Sabha 13.8.62; *P.M.S.I.R.* I ii, p. 102; and W.P. VII, p. 37.
158 *Hindu*, 4.8.62.
159 *P.M.S.I.R.* I ii, p. 102.
160 W.P. VII, p. 36.
161 Lok Sabha 2.5.62; *P.M.S.I.R.* I ii, p. 84.
162 Lok Sabha 14.8.62; *P.M.S.I.R.* I ii, pp. 115–16.
163 Op. cit., p. 119.
164 Op. cit., p. 121.
165 Op. cit., p. 26.
166 W.P. VI, p. 114.
167 *Peking Review*, 2.11.62.
168 Qu. Mankekar, op. cit., p. 41.
169 Lok Sabha 5.12.61; *P.M.S.I.R.* I ii, p. 46–7.
170 Lok Sabha 14.8.62; *P.M.S.I.R.* I ii, pp. 113–14.
171 W.P. VII, p. 68.
172 Guy Wint, *Observer* (London), 27.5.62.
173 Elie Abel, *The Missiles of October* (MacGibbon & Kee, London, 1966), pp. 42–3.

PART III: THE VIEW FROM PEKING

1 Qu. Girilal Jain, *Panchsheela and After* (Asia Publishing House, Bombay, 1960), pp. 8–9.
2 *Peking Review*, 12.5.59.
3 *Peking Review*, 25.10.62.
4 Brecher 1959, p. 276.
5 Qu. Van Eekelen, *Indian Foreign Policy*, p. 28.
6 *Observer* (Shanghai), 11.4.50, qu. Jain, op. cit., p. 15.
7 Op. cit., p. 18.
8 *World Culture* (Shanghai), qu. Jain, op. cit., p. 8.
9 Mark Feer, *India Quarterly*, Oct.–Dec. 1953, p. 367.
10 Brecher 1968, p. 136.
11 K. M. Panikkar, *In Two Chinas*, p. 110.
12 Reported to the writer by the journalists.
13 Wilson, *A Quarter of Mankind* (Weidenfeld & Nicolson, London, 1966), p. 266.
14 Panikkar, op. cit., pp. 26–7.
15 Brecher 1959, p. 109.
16 Op. cit., p. 588.

17 *Peking Review* 12.5.59.
18 Snow, *The Other Side of the River*, p. 74.
19 *Peking Review*, 2.11.62.
20 Ibid.
21 *P.M.S.I.R.* I i, p. 37.
22 Press onference, New Delhi; *Peking Review*, 3.5.60, p. 22.
23 *Peking Review*, 12.5.59.
24 Tibor Mende, *China and her Shadow* (Thames & Hudson, London, 1961), p. 114.
25 *Peking Review* 12.5.59.
26 Ibid.
27 Chou En-lai, qu. *S.I.B.Q.*, p. 6.
28 Foreign Ministry spokesman, qu. *Peking Review* 20.4.62, p. 11.
29 Anna Louise Strong in *China Reconstructs* (March 1960) qu. Jain, op. cit., p. 224.
30 *Peking Review* 15.9.59.
31 Chinese note, 11.5.62, W.P. VI, p. 200.
32 *Peking Review*, 15.9.59.
33 Lok Sabha 2.5.62; *P.M.S.I.R.* I ii, p. 84.
34 *Peking Review*, 15.9.59.

35 Chou to People's Congress, *Peking Review*, 15.9.59.
36 Teng Hsaio–ping at Moscow conference, 1960, qu Edward Crankshaw, *The New Cold War: Moscow v. Pekin* (Penguin Books, London, 1963), p. 126–7.
37 *Peking Review*, 2.11.62.
38 *Peking Review* 22.9.59.
39 Qu. Crocker, *Nehru*, p. 107.
40 *Peking Review*, 3.5.60, p. 14.
41 *Peking Review*, 17.8.62.
42 *Peking Review*, 2.11.62.
43 *U.S. News & World Report*, 29.5.61.
44 *Peking Review*, 2.11.62, quoting official Indian statistics.
45 Qu. *Peking Review*, 12.4.63.
46 Ibid.
47 *Peking Review*, 26.4.63.
48 Ibid.
49 *Indian Press Digests* No. 2 (University of California Press, Berkeley, July 1956).
50 *Peking Review*, 26.4.63.
51 Ibid.
52 Nehru in *Glimpses of World History*, qu. *Peking Review*, 2.11.62.
53 *Peking Review*, 2.11.62.
54 *People's Daily*, 23.7.59.
55 Ibid.
56 Ibid.
57 *Peking Review*, 12.5.59.
58 e.g. note of 22.3.62, W.P. VI, p. 24.
59 *Peking Review*, 8.11.63.
60 Lok Sabha 12.9.59; *P.M.S.I.R.* I i, p. 149.
61 W.P. II, p. 32.
62 *People's Daily*, 2.11.63. See n. 191, Part I.
63 Lok Sabha, 12.9.59. *P.M.S.I.R.* I i, p. 156.
64 *People's Daily*, 27.2.63; *Peking Review*, 8.11.63.
65 *People's Daily*, qu. *Peking Review*, 8.11.63.
66 *New York Times*, qu. Donald S. Zagoria, *The Sino–Soviet Conflict, 1956–61* (Princeton University Press, Princeton, 1961), p. 280.
67 Crankshaw, op. cit., p. 88.
68 *Peking Review*, No. 45, 1963, p. 19.
69 Zagoria, op. cit., p. 283.
70 This account of Krushchev's speech at Bucharest is taken almost verbatim from Crankshaw, op. cit., p. 108.
71 *Pravda*, 19.9.63.
72 Chou, qu. Dennis J. Doolin, *Territorial Claims in the Sino–Soviet Conflict* (The Hoover Institution, Stanford, 1965), p. 71.
73 Op. cit., p. 14.
74 Op. cit., p. 52.
75 Op. cit., p. 14.
76 Letter from Chinese Communist Party to Moscow party, 29.2.64, qu. Doolin, op. cit., p. 38.
77 Statement of Govt of China, 24.5.69 (from official text).
78 At Katmandu press conference, *Peking Review*, 3.5.60, p. 13.
79 Statement of Govt of U.S.S.R., 13.6.69.
80 Statement of Govt of China, 26.5.69.
81 Note of 12.2.60, W.P. III, pp. 85–6.
82 Doolin, op. cit., p. 51.
83 Teng Hsaio–ping at Moscow, 1960, qu. Crankshaw, op. cit., pp. 126–7.
84 *Peking Review*, 8.11.63.
85 *Red Flag*, 21.11.64, qu. Doolin, op. cit., p. 23.
86 W.P. VI, p. 3.
87 *Peking Review*, 20.7.62.
88 W.P. VI, p. 1.
89 *Peking Review*, 27.7.62.
90 *Peking Review*, 8.11.63.
91 W.P. III, p. 80.
92 Mao Tse–tung, qu. *Peking Review*, 14.10.60.
93 *People's Daily*, 27.10.62; see M. Mackintosh, *Juggernaut* (Secker & Warburg, London, 1962) for this incident.
94 W.P. VII, p. 68.

PART IV: THE BORDER WAR

1 Qu. *Peking Review*, 8.11.63.
2 Alfred Vagts, *The History of Militarism* (Allen & Unwin, London, 1938), p. 33.
3 W.P. III, p. 45, p. 53.
4 Dalvi, *Himalayan Blunder*, p. 71.
5 Kaul, *Untold Story*, p. 318.
6 Lok Sabha, 28.8.59; *P.M.S.I.R.* I i, p. 87.
7 Note of 11.8.59, W.P. I, p. 41.
8 Note of 1.9.59, W.P. II, pp. 1–2.
9 Note of 10.9.59, W.P. II, pp. 9–10.
10 *Report*, pp. 12–13.
11 e.g. W.P. VIII, p. 41.
12 Dalvi, op. cit., p. 134.
13 Op. cit., p. 217.
14 Ibid.
15 W.P. VII, p. 74.

16 W.P. VII, p. 34, p. 41; *People's Daily*, 20.10.62.
17 Note of 6.10.62, W.P. VII, p. 104.
18 Notes of 2.11.61, W.P. VI, p. 4; 16.10.62, W.P. VII, p. 119.
19 See n. 77, below.
20 Khera, *India's Defence Problems*, p. 204.
21 Dalvi, op. cit., p. 211.
22 Op. cit., p. 214.
23 Op. cit. p. 208.
24 Op. cit., p. 193.
25 Op. cit., p. 196.
26 *New York Times*, 16.9.62.
27 *Hindu*, 25.9.62.
28 *The Times*, 17.9.62.
29 Qu. in an unpublished Indian Army report on these events.
30 Dalvi, op. cit., p. 51.
31 Op. cit., p. 232.
32 *Times of India*, 27.9.62.
33 Dalvi, op. cit., p. 222.
34 Peking Radio broadcast of 9.11.62, qu. *India Quarterly* (New Delhi), April–June 1967, p. 102; also W.P. VII, p. 80.
35 W.P. VII, pp. 83–4; Dalvi, op. cit, p. 219.
36 W.P. VII, pp. 83–4.
37 *People's Daily*, 22.9.62.
38 Note of 25.9.62, W.P. VII, pp. 86–7.
39 To the writer, Calcutta, May 1967.
40 Kaul, op. cit., p. 353.
41 Op. cit., p. 365; confirmed to the writer by General Thapar, Kabul, 1967.
42 Ibid. (Kaul's italics).
43 Rajya Sabha, 22.8.62; *P.M.S.I.R.* I ii, p. 124.
44 W.P. VII, p. 37.
45 W.P. VII, pp. 71–3.
46 W.P. VII, pp. 77–8.
47 W.P. VII, pp. 96–8.
48 Note of 6.10.62, W.P. VII, pp. 100–2.
49 Note of 6.11.62, W.P. VIII, p. 63.
50 Note of 16.10.62, W.P. VII, p. 119.
51 *Hindu*, 2.10.62.
52 *Times of India*, *Statesman*.
53 Kaul, op. cit., p. 370.
54 Dalvi, op. cit., p. 261.
55 Op. cit., p. 271.
56 Op. cit., p. 308.
57 Op. cit., p. 284.
58 Ibid.
59 Kaul, op. cit., p. 376.
60 Dalvi, op. cit., p. 285.
61 Op. cit., p. 288.
62 Op. cit., p. 88.
63 To the writer, May 1967
64 Kaul, op. cit., pp. 380–1.
65 Dalvi, op. cit., p. 292.
66 Kaul, op. cit., p. 383–4.
67 W.P. VII, p. 108.
68 Dalvi, op. cit., p. 301.
69 Kaul, op. cit., p. 385.
70 Khera, op. cit. p. 225.
71 Kaul, op. cit., p. 386.
72 Lok Sabha Debates 1962, Vol. 13, col. 1331;qu. Kavics, op. cit., p. 185.
73 Lok Sabha, 8.11.62.
74 *Statesman*, 13.10.62.
75 *The Times*, 13.10.62.
76 Lok Sabha Debates, Vol. 19, col. 2213, qu. Kavics, op. cit., p. 185.
77 Bhargava, *Battle of NEFA*, p. 83.
78 *The Times*, 8.10.62.
79 Dalvi, op. cit., p. 210.
80 Felix Greene, *A Curtain of Ignorance*, p. 233.
81 Leonard Mosley, *The Last Days of the British Raj* (Weidenfeld & Nicolson, London, 1961), p. 27.
82 *People's Daily*, 14.10.62, qu. *Peking Review*, 19.10.62.
83 *People's Daily*, 2.11.63.
84 W.P. VI, p. 91.
85 Note of 26.12.59, W.P. III, p. 80.
86 J. Rowland, *A History of Sino–Indian Relations* (Van Nostrand Inc., Princeton, 1967), pp. 183–4.
87 Note of 11.5.62, WP. VI, p. 200.
88 Lok Sabha, 7.12.61; *P.M.S.I.R.* I ii, p. 72.
89 W.P. VII, p. 74.
90 See Nehru Rajya Sabha, 9.11.62, *P.M.S.I.R.* I ii, p. 164.
91 *Times of India*, 15.10.62.
92 Dalvi, op. cit., p. 315.
93 Op. cit., p. 330.
94 Op. cit., p. 326.
95 Kaul, op. cit., p. 390.
96 Ibid.
97 Dalvi, op. cit., p. 327.
98 Op. cit., p. 264.
99 Op. cit., p. 366.
100 Reuter, main file, 19.10.62.
101 *Blitz*, 19.10.62.
102 *The Times*, 21.10.62.
103 *Statesman*, 21.10.62
104 *Hindustan Times*.
105 *Statesman*, 22.10.62.
106 *Statesman*, 25.10.62.
107 *Times of India*, 4.4.60.
108 *Hindu*, 2.11.62.
109 Lord Altringham, in the *Guardian* (London).
110 John Kenneth Galbraith, *Ambassador's*

Journal: A Personal Account of the Kennedy Years (Hamish Hamilton, London, 1969), p. 440.

111 *Statesman*, 29.10.62.
112 *Hindu*, 4.11.62.
113 *Observer* Foreign News Service (London), 11.11.62.
114 Lok Sabha, 8.11.62; *P.M.S.I.R.* I ii, p. 150.
115 Rajya Sabha, 9.11.62; *P.M.S.I.R.* I ii, p. 167.
116 Kuldip Nayar, *Between the Lines* (Allied Publishers, Bombay, 1969), p. 152.
117 Nehru to Krushchev, qu. op. cit., p. 151.
118 *Hindu*, 29.10.62.
119 Nayar, op. cit., p. 180; Galbraith, op. cit. p. 448.
120 *Peking Review*, 8.11.63.
121 *Hindu*, 1.11.62.
122 Note 20.10.62, W.P. VII, p. 123.
123 W.P. VII, p. 9.
124 *S.I.B.Q.*, p. 26.
125 W.P. VIII, pp. 3–4.
126 W.P. VIII, p. 1.
127 *Peking Review*, 2.11.62, p. 10.
128 W.P. VIII, p. 6.
129 W.P. VIII, pp. 4–5.
130 *Statesman*, 29.10.62.
131 W.P. VIII, pp. 7–10.
132 W.P. VII, pp. 10–13.
133 Qu. Dennis Bloodworth, *Observer*, 2.12.62.
134 *P.M.S.I.R.* I ii, pp. 118–19.
135 *S.I.B.Q.*, p. 34.
136 *People's Daily*, 11.11.62.
137 J. Marcuse, *Sunday Times* (London), 4.11.62.
138 *S.I.B.Q.*, pp. 35–6
139 *Pravda*, 5.11.62.
140 Lok Sabha, 8.11.62; *P.M.S.I.R.* I ii, p. 144.
141 *Current* (London), Dec. 1962.
142 Lok Sabha, 8.11.62; *P.M.S.I.R.* I ii, p. 149.
143 Nirad Chaudhuri, *Continent of Circe*, p. 110.
144 Resolution of 8.11.62.
145 Lok Sabha Debates, Vol. IX, No. 6, col. 1645.
146 Lok Sabha Debates, Vol. IX, No. 2, col. 386.
147 Rajya Sabha, 9.11.62; *P.M.S.I.R.* I ii, pp. 167–8.
148 Chaudhuri, op. cit., p. 98.
149 Lok Sabha, 8.11.62; *P.M.S.I.R.* I ii, p. 152.

150 Op. cit., p. 107.
151 Robert Payne, *The Life and Death of Mahatma Gandhi* (Bodley Head, London, 1969), p. 328.
152 J. Marcuse, in *Sunday Times*, 6.11.62.
153 *Hindu*, 31.10.62.
154 Chaudhuri, op. cit., p. 144.
155 *Statesman*, 31.10.62.
156 Lok Sabha, 8.11.62.
157 Lok Sabha, 8.11.62; *P.M.S.I.R.* I ii, p. 146.
158 Rajya Sabha, 22.8.62; *P.M.S.I.R.* I ii, p. 129.
159 *Le Monde* (Paris), 6.4.68.
160 Frank Anthony in Lok Sabha, 8.11.62.
161 Lok Sabha, 8.11.62; *P.M.S.I.R.* I ii, p. 151.
162 *Indian Express* (New Delhi), 7.11.62.
163 *Washington Post*, 30.3.63.
164 *Current* (London), Dec. 1962.
165 Lok Sabha Debates, Vol. IX, No. 2, col. 395.
166 *Statesman*, 30.10.62.
167 P. S. Ehring (private secretary to the Prime Minister), in Lok Sabha.
168 *Statesman*, 13.11.62.
169 Ibid.
170 To the writer, Calcutta, June 1967; and in *Hindustan Standard* (Calcutta), 18.1.67, in pseudonymous article, 'Who Was to Blame?'
171 Lok Sabha, 8.11.62; *P.M.S.I.R.* I ii, pp. 148–9.
172 Hangen, *After Nehru, Who*, p. 261.
173 Major–General A. S. Pathania to the writer, June 1967.
174 From contemporary notes.
175 *New York Times*, 31.10.59.
176 Lok Sabha Debates (14.11.62), No. 6, col. 1651.
177 *Statesman* supplement, 'Black November', November 1967.
178 Kaul, op. cit., p. 408.
179 Khera, op. cit., p. 231.
180 Kaul, op. cit., p. 408.
181 Bailey, *No Passport to Tibet*, p. 231.
182 Galbraith, op. cit., p. 487.
183 *The Times* (Washington report), 5.12.64.
184 Sudhir Ghosh, *Gandhi's Emissary* (Rupa & Cox, Calcutta, 1967), chapter 12.
185 Brecher 1968, pp. 172–3.
186 Nayar, op. cit., p. 179.
187 Rawle Knox, in the *Observer*, 25.10.62.
188 Ibid.
189 Nayar, op. cit., p. 191.

190 Sources close to the President, to the writer at the time.

191 Brecher 1968, p. 177.
192 Nayar, op. cit., p. 172.

PART V: CEASEFIRE

1 Brecher 1968, p. 168.
2 *Quotations* (Peking 1968), pp. 95–6.
3 Chou to Nehru, W.P. VII, p. 24; also Khera, *India's Defence Problems*, p. 185.
4 W.P. VIII, pp. 17–21.
5 *Peking Review*, 8.11.63, p. 21.
6 *The Times*, leading article, 22.11.62.
7 *Sunday Times*, 12.6.66.
8 *P.M.S.I.R.* I ii, p. 196.
9 *The Times*, 22.11.62.
10 *Hindu*, 23.11.62.
11 W.P. VIII, pp. 23–4.
12 Op. cit., pp. 21–3.
13 Op. cit., p. 31.
14 Op. cit., p. 26.
15 Op. cit., pp. 24–6.
16 Op. cit., pp. 28–31.
17 Letter from Mrs Bandaranaike, Prime Minister of Ceylon, to Chou En–lai, 7.3.63. The text of this letter was released by M. R. Masani, the Swatantra M.P., at the beginning of 1964. Extracts from it were carried in Indian newspapers but it appears that the full text is available only in the Bombay newsletter *Opinion* of 11.2.64.
18 Victor Zorza in the *Guardian*.
19 Frank Anthony in Lok Sabha, 10.12.62: L.S.D., Vol. XI, No. 25, col. 5171.
20 Galbraith, *Ambassador's Journal*, pp. 490–1.
21 Kaul, *Untold Story*, p. 452.
22 *Peking Review*, 25.1.63, p. 11.
23 Noorani, *Our Credulity and Negligence*, p. 111.
24 Nayar, *Between the Lines*, p. 185.
25 W.P. IX, p. 185.
26 Op. cit., p. 186.
27 Ibid.

28 *Peking Review*, 1.2.63, p. 10.
29 *People's Daily*, 28.1.63; qu. *Peking Review*, 1.2.63, p. 12.
30 Mrs Bandaranaike to Chou En–lai, 7.3.63. See note 17 above.
31 Lok Sabha Debates, Vol. XII, No. 29, col. 5996.
32 *The Times*, 8.12.62.
33 Lok Sabha Debates (10.12.62), Vol. XI, col. 5092.
34 Op. cit., col. 5215.
35 W.P. IX, p. 6.
36 W.P. IX, pp. 10–13.
37 *The Times*, 13.4.64.
38 W.P. X, pp. 3–6.
39 Note of 9.10.63, W.P. X, p. 10.
40 Qu. *The Times*, 31.12.62.
41 Roger Hilsman, *To Move a Nation: The Politics of Foreign Policy in the Administration of John F. Kennedy* (Doubleday, New York, 1967), p. 331.
42 Galbraith, op. cit., pp. 525–6.
43 Hilsman, op. cit., p. 331.
44 Ibid.
45 *The Times*, 23.7.63.
46 Hilsman, op. cit., p. 331.
47 J. P. Narayan, *Statesman Weekly*, 22.6.68.
48 *Statesman*, 28.11.62.
49 Statement in Lok Sabha, 29.9.63.
50 Ibid.
51 Qu. *Studies in Indian Democracy*, S. P. Aiyar and R. Srinivasan, p. xxxix.
52 Qu. Bertrand Russell, *Autobiography*, Vol. III (Allen & Unwin, London, 1969), p. 152.
53 Brecher 1968, p. 87.
54 *People's Daily*, 9.3.63.
55 Brecher 1968, p. 7.

Selected Bibliography

This bibliography is restricted to books quoted in the course of the work.

OFFICIAL PUBLICATIONS

Atlas of the Northern Frontier of India (Govt. of India, New Delhi, 1960).

Chronology of Pakistan, 1947–57 (Govt. of Pakistan, Karachi, 1958).

Notes, Memoranda and Letters Exchanged and Agreements Signed Between the Governments of India and China; White Paper (Ministry of External Affairs, Govt. of India, New Delhi, 1959–63). (Cited as W.P.)

Prime Minister on Sino-Indian Relations (Govt. of India, New Delhi, 1961, 1963. (Cited as *P.M.S.I.R.*)

The Question of Tibet (Foreign Languages Press, Peking, 1959).

Report of the Officials of the Governments of India and the People's Republic of China on the Boundary Question (Govt. of India, New Delhi, 1961). (Cited as *Report*)

The Sino-Indian Boundary Question. Enlarged edition (Foreign Languages Press, Peking, 1962. (Cited as *S.I.B.Q.*)

GENERAL WORKS

Abel, Elie, *The Missiles of October* (MacGibbon & Kee, London, 1966).

Alder, G. J., *British India's Northern Frontier, 1865–95* (Longmans, London, 1963).

Aiyer, S. P. and S. Srinivasan, eds., *Studies in Indian Democracy* (Allied Publishers, Bombay, 1965).

Bailey, F. M., *No Passport to Tibet* (Hart-Davis, London, 1957).

Bhargava, G. S., *The Battle of NEFA: The Undeclared War* (Allied Publishers, Bombay, 1964).

Bhutto, Z. A., *The Myth of Independence* (O.U.P., London, 1968).

Brecher, Michael, *Nehru: A Political Biography* (O.U P., London, 1959). (Cited as Brecher 1959)

Brecher, Michael, *India and World Politics: Krishna Menon's View of the World* (O.U P., London, 1968). (Cited as Brecher 1968)

Chaudhuri, Nirad, *The Continent of Circe* (Chatto & Windus, London, 1965).

Crankshaw, Edward, *The New Cold War: Moscow v. Pekin* (Penguin Books, London, 1963).

Crocker, Walter, *Nehru: A Contemporary's Estimate* (Allen & Unwin, London, 1966).

Cukwarah, A. O., *The Settlement of Boundary Disputes in International Affairs* (Manchester University Press, London, 1967).

Curzon, Lord, *Frontiers* (O.U.P., Oxford, 1908).

Dalvi, Brigadier J. S., *Himalayan Blunder: The Curtain-Raiser to the Sino-Indian War of 1962* (Thacker & Co., Bombay, 1969).

Doolin, Dennis J., *Territorial Claims in the Sino-Soviet Conflict: Documents and Analysis* (The Hoover Institution on War, Revolution and Peace, Stanford University, 1965).

Edwardes, Michael, *Asia in the European Age* (Thames & Hudson, London, 1961).

Fisher, Margaret, Leo Rose, Robert A. Huttenback, *Himalayan Battleground: Sino-Indian Rivalry in Ladakh* (Pall Mall Press, London, 1963).

Fraser-Tytler, W. K., *Afghanistan: A Study of Political Developments in Central and Southern Asia* (O.U.P., London, 1953).

Galbraith, John Kenneth, *Ambassador's Journal: A Personal Account of the Kennedy Years* (Hamish Hamilton, London, 1969).

Ghosh, Sudhir, *Gandhi's Emissary* (Rupa & Co., Calcutta, 1967).

Gittings, John, *Survey of the Sino-Soviet Dispute 1963–1967* (O.U.P., London, 1968).

Greene, Felix, *A Curtain of Ignorance* (Cape, London, 1965).

Gupta, Karunakar, *India in World Politics: A Period of Transition: Suez Crisis 1956 – Paris Summit 1960* (Scientific Book Agency, Calcutta, 1969.)

Hangen, Welles, *After Nehru, Who?* (Hart-Davis, London, 1963).

Hilsman, Roger, *To Move a Nation: The Politics of Foreign Policy in the Administration of John F. Kennedy* (Doubleday, New York, 1967).

Hutheesingh, Krishna, *Nehru's Letters to his Sister* (Faber & Faber, London, 1963).

Jain, Girilal, *Panchsheela and After: Sino-Indian Relations in the Context of the Tibetan Insurrection* (Asia Publishing House, Bombay, 1960).

Kaul, Lt.-Gen. B. M., *The Untold Story* (Allied Publishers, Bombay, 1967).

Kavics, Lorne J., *India's Quest for Security: Defence Policies 1957–1965* (University of California Press, Berkeley, 1967).

Khera, S. S., *India's Defence Problems* (Orient Longmans, Bombay, 1968).

Khushwant Singh, *A History of the Sikhs*, Volume 2 (O.U P., London, 1966).

Lamb, Alastair, *Britain and Chinese Central Asia: The Road to Lhasa, 1767–1905* (Routledge & Kegan Paul, London, 1960). (Cited as Lamb 1960)

Lamb, Alastair, *The China–India Border: The Origins of the Disputed Boundaries* (Chatham House Essay: O.U P., London, 1964). (Cited as Lamb 1964)

Lamb, Alastair, *The McMahon Line: A Study in the Relations Between India, China and Tibet 1904 to 1914* (Routledge & Kegan Paul, London, 1966). (Cited as Lamb 1966)

Lattimore, Owen, *Inner Asian Frontiers of China* (Beacon Press, Boston, 1951).

Mackintosh, M., *Juggernaut* (Secker & Warburg, London, 1962).

Mankekar, D. R., *The Guilty Men of 1962* (Tulsi Shah Enterprises, Bombay, 1968).

Mende, Tibor, *China and Her Shadow* (Thames & Hudson, London, 1961).

Mosley, Leonard, *The Last Days of the British Raj* (Weidenfeld & Nicolson, London, 1961).

Myrdal, Gunnar, *Asian Drama: An Enquiry into the Poverty of Nations* (Panetheon, New York, 1968).

Nayar, Kuldip, *Between the Lines* (Allied Publishers, Bombay, 1969).

Noorani, A. G., *Our Credulity and Negligence* (Ramday Bhatkal, Bombay, 1963).

Panikkar, K. M., *The Founding of the Kashmir State* (Allen & Unwin, London, 1953).

Panikkar, K. M., *In Two Chinas: Memoirs of a Diplomat* (Allen & Unwin, London, 1955).

Patterson, George, *Tibet in Revolt* (Faber & Faber, London, 1961).

Payne, Robert, *The Life and Death of Mahatma Gandhi* (Bodley Head London, 1969).

Philips, C. H. and M. D. Wainwright, eds., *The Partition of India: Policies and Perspectives* (Allen & Unwin, London, 1970).

Reid, Sir Robert, *History of the Frontier Areas Bordering on Assam* (Govt. of Assam Press, Shillong, 1942).

Richardson, H. E., *Tibet and its History* (O.U P., London, 1962).

Rowland, J., *A History of Sino-Indian Relations* (Van Nostrand Inc., Princeton, 1967).

Russell, Bertrand, *Autobiography*, Vol. 3 (Allen & Unwin, London, 1969).

Schlesinger, Arthur M. Jr., *A Thousand Days: John F. Kennedy in the White House* (André Deutsch, London, 1965).

Schram, Stuart, *Mao Tse-tung* (Penguin Books, London, 1966).

Tieh Tsing-li, *Tibet — Today and Yesterday* (Bookman Associates, New York, 1960).

Vagts, Alfred, *A History of Militarism* (Allen & Unwin, London, 1938).

Van Eekelen, W. F., *Indian Foreign Policy and the Border Dispute with China* (Martinus Nijhoff, The Hague, 1964).

Von Furer-Haimendorf, C., *Himalayan Barbary* (Murray, London, 1955)

Wilson, Dick, *A Quarter of Mankind: An Anatomy of China Today* (Weidenfeld & Nicolson, London, 1966).

Woodman, Dorothy, *Himalayan Frontiers* (Barrie & Rockliff, London, 1969).

Zagoria, Donald S. *The Sino-Soviet Conflict, 1956–61* (Princeton University Press, Princeton, 1961).

UNPUBLISHED PAPERS

Addis, John, 'The India–China Border Dispute', a paper for the Center for International Affairs, Harvard, 1964.

Field, A. R., 'The Historical Basis for the Indian Boundary Claims, paper for the Pacific Coast Regional Conference of the Association for Asian Studies, June 1967.

Lamb, Alastair, 'The Aksai Chin'.

PERIODICALS

India Quarterly.
International Comparative Law Quarterly.
Journal of the Royal Society of Arts.
Journal of the United Service Institute of India.
Royal Central Asian Journal.

Index

474INDEX

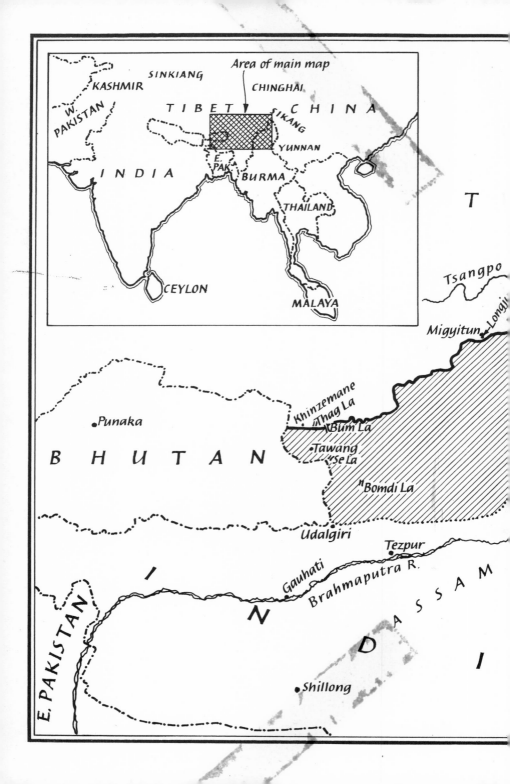